Lionheart and Lackland

Lionheart and Lackland

KING RICHARD, KING JOHN AND THE
WARS OF CONQUEST

Frank McLynn

JONATHAN CAPE
LONDON

Published by Jonathan Cape 2006

2 4 6 8 10 9 7 5 3 1

Copyright © Frank McLynn 2006

First published in Great Britain in 2006 by Jonathan Cape
Random House, 20 Vauxhall Bridge Road, London SW1V 2SA

Random House Australia (Pty) Limited
20 Alfred Street, Milsons Point, Sydney,
New South Wales 2061, Australia

Random House New Zealand Limited
18 Poland Road, Glenfield, Auckland 10, New Zealand

Random House South Africa (Pty) Limited
Isle of Houghton, Corner of Boundary Road & Carse O'Gowrie,
Houghton 2198, South Africa

Random House Publishers India Private Limited
301 World Trade Tower, Hotel Intercontinental Grand Complex,
Barakhamba Lane, New Delhi 110 001, India

The Random House Group Limited Reg. No. 954009
www.randomhouse.co.uk

A CIP catalogue record for this book is available from the British Library

ISBN 0224062441
ISBN 9780224 062442 (from January 2007)

Typeset by Palimpsest Book Production Limited, Grangemouth, Stirlingshire
Printed and bound by William Clowes Ltd, Beccles, Suffolk

For Pauline

Illustrations

MAPS

Introduction

I have always been fascinated by the personalities of Richard I and King John but, Shakespeare aside, knew little of them apart from the various filmic representations over the years. That Richard was a born-again warrior I realised from many celluloid extravaganzas and I still remember with amusement Virginia Mayo's characterisation in *King Richard and the Crusaders:* 'Fight, fight, fight. That's all you think of, Dick Plantagenet!' Although one critic described the sound effects for that movie as the sound of Sir Walter Scott turning in his grave, Scott himself had historians turning in their graves and has attracted two hundred years of academic contempt for his notions of Saxons and Normans still at each other's throats in the 1190s – which did not stop Michael Curtiz and his producers annexing the idea for the famous *The Adventures of Robin Hood* in 1938. Since all these screen depictions showed Richard as the good guy and John as a creature of the night, I assumed this was a stereotype that could quickly be dispatched after some serious historical research. Imagine, then, my surprise, when my own sleuthing in ancient documents turned up what is in effect a reinforcement of the stereotype. But the honest historian must perforce go where the evidence leads him. If it has led me into areas which will not please the champions of King John, so be it. John's defenders, it seems to me, work mainly by denying the reliability of the most famous chroniclers and questioning their good faith. In some quarters a rather curious bifurcation has arisen: charters, letters patent and pipe rolls good; Roger of Howden, Matthew Paris and Roger of Wendover bad. Like most types of revisionism, this ascetic approach generates as many absurdities as the previous and allegedly gullible vantage point. To those who say that chronicles are a poor source for medieval history, I reply that charters are an inadequate guide to human personality, and it is that with which I am principally concerned in this would-be dual biography. I hope my debt to all the fine scholars who have worked in this field is clear and is sufficiently acknowledged in the notes. But declaring an interest, I have to confess that the academic who has most influenced me is the great John Gillingham, a man whose wit, humour and humanity are as obvious as his erudition and scholarship. Needless to say, I am not attempting to co-opt him or anyone else into responsibility for any errors that have crept into the text. I also acknowledge the sterling assistance given me by Will Sulkin and Tony Whittome at Random House and my wife Pauline at home.

Farnham, Surrey, 2006

1

I F WE JUDGE ONLY by reputation and mythology, Richard I was the greatest king of England in the Middle Ages and his brother John the very worst. The good brother/bad brother dichotomy is a staple of most myths, as old as Cain and Abel. And it is surely significant that Shakespeare saw dramatic potential in the flawed John Lackland, whereas Richard, a creature of epics, did not serve his purpose.[1] Richard was supposed to be a second King Arthur, although the Dean of St Paul's, Ralph Diceto, who chronicled his reign, established to his own satisfaction that the Saxon Cerdic (traditionally one of the historical Arthur's enemies) was his ancestor. Shakespeare too never dealt with the greatest of all English stories – King Arthur and the Round Table – for its saga-like dimensions could not be accommodated in five acts. Richard and Arthur, it seems, were both too stubborn and irreducible even for Shakespeare. Richard I, Coeur de Lion, has always had a magnetic hold on the imagination for he seemed to be Arthur redivivus: the once and future king really had returned and, as foretold, had carried the Cross to Jerusalem.[2] Yet even if we discount myth and legend, the historical Richard still has the power to astonish. He did, after all, start his life with certain gifts. He was lucky, for third sons born to royal dynasties rarely attained the purple. And he probably had the most impressive parentage of all English monarchs. Despite the voluntarists and the existentialists, it remains a fact that every human being is far more determined by parentage than we usually allow ourselves to admit. But this is a necessary explanation for Richard and not a sufficient one. John had the same parents but was a totally different individual. Here we almost confront a nature/nurture paradigm, for John's education, socialisation and general formation were entirely different from his brother's. Apart from the obvious factors of differential innate individual human psychology, we must look to environment, milieu and culture. In this respect Richard's relationship with his mother and his upbringing in Aquitaine are the factors that most clearly differentiate him from John.

The man known to history and legend as Richard the Lionheart became king of England in 1189, just over one hundred years after the death of William the Conqueror. At the same time he assumed the titles of Duke of Normandy and Count of Anjou. To understand the implications of this tripartite title, we have to go back in time, to 1100, the year William the Conqueror's son William Rufus was mysteriously killed in the New Forest. Henry, the youngest and only English-born son of the Conqueror then seized the royal treasure and was elected king in the only manner accepted as legitimate in Anglo-Saxon times: by the Witan. Henry I next quickly moved to defeat his brother Robert Curthose, duke of Normandy, but his easy victory (Robert was kept in jail for twenty-eight years after the battle of Tinchebrai in 1106) brought him into collision with King Louis VI of France, and almost constant warfare marked the next twenty years. When Henry's only legitimate son William was drowned at sea in 1120 in the White Ship disaster, Henry named his widowed daughter Matilda (previously married to Emperor Henry V of Germany) as his successor. In 1128 she was married to Geoffrey Plantagenet, son of the count of Anjou. From this union came Henry, later to be the second English king of that name, and Richard's father.[3]

Henry I's death in 1135 plunged England into civil war. Stephen, son of Henry I's sister Adela, seized the throne despite a previous oath of fealty to Matilda. Six years of anarchy and devastation followed, though some scholars think that the chaos and disruption were exaggerated in early propagandist accounts. Stephen seemed conclusively defeated in 1141, but the triumphant Matilda alienated London with her harsh taxation and personal greed. The so-called 'Lady of the English' was never crowned, for a rebellion overthrew her and placed Stephen back in the saddle. On her return to France, in 1148 Matilda renounced her own ambitions, made over her claims to her son and threw all her energies into securing the throne for the young Henry. In 1150 the 17-year-old became Duke of Normandy and the following year, when his father died, he added Count of Anjou to his titles. In January 1153 he landed in England to claim the throne. When Stephen's son Eustace died, the 57-year-old Stephen, an old man by the standards of the time, gave up the struggle and acknowledged Henry as his successor, dying soon afterwards.[4] Crowned king in 1154, Henry II founded the Plantagenet or Angevin dynasty of English kings and ruled a domain that stretched from the Scottish borders to the Pyrenees – the inaptly named Angevin empire.

Much of what we know about the personality and character of Henry II comes from Walter Map, a clerk at Henry's court, also Canon of St Paul's Cathedral; from Peter of Blois, his secretary; and from Gerald of Wales, for many years a member of his court. Although Map is not always impeccable as a historical source – his taste for levity makes him accept any old scurrilous or apocryphal story as gospel – there is no reason to think that his physical portrait of Henry is inaccurate. A redhead who wore his hair short, Henry appeared more leonine than his famous lionhearted son. Of medium height, with ruddy, freckled complexion, Henry had a large head and grey, implacable eyes which were said to glow red or become bloodshot when he was angry. Stocky, broadchested, with strong and massively developed arms, Henry was a charismatic personality, whose magnetism seemed concentrated in the ferocious-looking face and eyes; Map said there was something about the man that made you want to stare at him over and over again.[5] His voice was harsh and guttural, liable to crack and produce falsetto notes. In modern terms he would be called a 'fitness freak', for he was obsessed with keeping his weight down by constant exercise and even fasting; observers said that this was a wise precaution since he had a natural tendency to obesity. In a hard-drinking and gourmandising age Henry was notable for his abstemious attitude to food and drink.[6]

Henry was not a believer in the king as star, dressed in sumptuous raiment, with a dazzling entourage of flunkies and hangers-on. He culti-vated a more popular persona, wearing functional, hunting or casual clothes, albeit of the finest material; he was often seen with needle and thread, mending a torn tunic. He refused to wear gloves, except when hawking, so that his calloused and horny hands suggested a son of toil rather than a monarch. As a hunter he was a perfect Nimrod, particularly delighting in the exploits of birds of prey and in riding down stags with hounds.[7] Primarily a man of action, he was also intelligent, articulate and literate – unusual traits in twelfth-century rulers; he had been tutored by the top scholars of his day both in England and France. With a reten-tive memory, genuine academic curiosity and a thirst for learning, Henry possessed what passed in his day for encyclopedic knowledge, and this made him self-confident, intellectually audacious and combative in debate. Something of an intellectual by the standards of his day, he liked to retire to his private apartments with a book and was well read for a layman. 'With the king of England,' said Peter of Blois, his one-time secretary, 'it is school every day, constant conversation with the best scholars and discussion of intellectual problems.'[8] His memory was not

just attuned to learning and linguistic attainments – his Latin was reputedly excellent and he had a smattering of other tongues – but was used
to manipulate men and events, for he could recall names and faces at a
moment's notice. Superficially he was a model of courtesy, charm and
politeness, affable, sober, modest, generous and stoical. Hardworking,
energetic and indefatigable, he rose before dawn and spent his days
campaigning or hunting. It was not unusual for him to ride five times
the distance of his courtiers or to go for long walks on his quick-striding
muscular, bowed legs, sometimes trekking so far that his feet were
cracked, sore and blistered. At court he seldom sat but bounded around,
and paced about, wearing his followers out by his refusal to sit down.
Disdaining regular hours, he was a notorious 'night owl' who liked to
keep his courtiers awake into the small hours of the morning. He liked
to conduct political business while doing something else, polishing a
spear, perhaps, or adjusting a bow. Almost unbelievably impatient, he
bolted his food, and could never be still for an instant. At Mass he
fidgeted, pulled at his courtiers' sleeves, whispered jokes and scribbled
notes or doodled as if he were a naughty boy. The single word that sums
up Henry is restlessness. As Walter Map put it: 'He was impatient of
repose and did not hesitate to disturb almost half Christendom.' Peter
of Blois expressed it another way after vainly following his master's tracks
through Normandy and Aquitaine: 'Solomon says that there are three
things difficult to be found, and a fourth hardly to be discovered: the
way of an eagle in the air; the way of a ship in the sea; the way of a
serpent on the ground; and the way of a man in his youth. I can add a
fifth: the way of a king in England.'[9] Modern observers might diagnose
a form of depression or even attention deficit syndrome.

Henry's extreme restlessness is well conveyed by Peter of Blois. 'If
the king has promised to remain in a place for a day – and particularly
if he has announced his intention publicly by the mouth of a herald –
he is sure to upset all the arrangements by departing early in the morning.
As a result you see men dashing around as if they were mad, beating
their packhorses, running their carts into one another – in short giving a
lively imitation of Hell. If, on the other hand, the king orders an early
start, he is certain to change his mind, and you can take it for granted
that he will sleep till midday. Then you will see the packhorses loaded
and waiting, the carts prepared, the courtiers dozing, traders fretting,
and everyone grumbling. People go to ask the maids and the doorkeepers
what the king's plans are, for they are the only people likely to know the
secrets of the court. Many a time when the king was sleeping a message

would be passed from his chamber about the city or town he planned to go to, and though there was nothing certain about it, it would rouse us all up. After hanging about aimlessly for so long we would be comforted by the prospect of good lodgings. This would produce such a clatter of horse and foot that all Hell seemed let loose. But when our courtiers had gone ahead almost the whole day's ride, the king would turn aside to some other place where he had, it might be, just a single house with accommodation for himself and no one else. I hardly dare say it, but I believe that in truth he took a delight in seeing what a fix he put us in. After wandering some three or four miles in an unknown wood, and often in the dark, we thought ourselves lucky if we stumbled upon some filthy little hovel. There was often a sharp and bitter argument about a mere hut, and swords were drawn for possession of lodging that pigs would have shunned.'[10]

Henry liked to appear generous in public and hospitable to strangers, tipping his servants lavishly, giving alms expansively, relieving the plight of the poor from his private granaries and even making good the losses of shipwrecked crews. He had a particular feeling for those in peril from the sea, and ordained heavy penalties for wreckers or plunderers of shipwrecks. When in the spotlight, he came across as courteous, polite, patient, stoical and solomonic. Such apparent charm and saintliness is often a defence mechanism, a mask under which very dark forces are hidden. The real Henry was wilful, secretive, manipulative, volatile, crafty, slippery, vindictive, brooding, unforgiving, treacherous, cynical, mendacious, perjurious and maybe even nihilistic. 'He was always ready to break his word', said Gerald of Wales, while Thomas Becket, his former friend and later mortal enemy said that in slipperiness he surpassed Proteus.[11] Only a small circle of intimates saw the real Henry. He was too intelligent to prize waging war as a thing in itself, as William the Conqueror had, but, in anticipation of Clausewitz, saw it pragmatically as the pursuit of political ends by other means. The one thing he could not abide was any opposition to his will, and any such occurrence elicited a volcanic outburst. He was spectacular when angry, when the usual persona was dropped and a furious, near madman was observed. Such were his carpet-chewing rages that he would often roll around on the floor, screaming and yelling or grind his teeth audibly. On one occasion he fell out of bed in a rage, tore the stuffing from his mattress and began masticating it.[12] His taste for women bordered on satyriasis, and in this area he was ruthless and unscrupulous, taking women for one-night stands or longer affairs entirely as the fancy took him. His habitual infidelity and the many bastard children he produced would cause much trouble during his reign. Some said his libido was such that he had to hunt all day to avoid spending it in bed, though Henry himself always adduced the weight-loss argument. He also knew how to assuage the rage of jealous husbands and fathers. With a deep, though cynical, understanding of human nature, he knew when to employ the carrot and when the stick and when to meld them.[13] Walter Map maintained that his mother, the Empress Matilda, had inculcated this lesson. 'I have heard that his mother's teaching was to this effect, that he should spin out the affairs of everyone, hold long in his own hands all posts that fell in, take the revenues of them, and keep the aspirants to them hanging on in hope; and she supported this advice by an unkind analogy: the untamed hawk, when raw meat is frequently offered to it and then snatched away or hidden from it, becomes keener and more prone to obey and attend.'[14]

Such was Richard's father. Yet Richard inherited more than just his father's genetic legacy, since there was a wider Angevin culture involved in his paternity. Emerging from the mists of history in the ninth century, the rulers of Anjou came to the fore in the succeeding century, acquiring the title of count, and consolidating their power base in the Loire valley partly through conquest and partly by astute intermarriage with the ruling families of adjacent domains such as Amboise, Vendôme and Maine. The Angevins later became famous for their stone castles – at Montbazon, Saumur, Touraine, Langeais, Chinon and Loches – and the wealth of the two main cities, at Angers and Tours.[15] Anjou was thought to have the perfect climate – Mediterranean heat tempered by breezes from the Atlantic – and was known as the Garden of France. It was a land of vineyards and heterogeneous flowers and trees representing its median position in the French-speaking world: on the one hand oaks, broom and camellias, on the other cedars, palms and fig. The Angevins had the reputation for being warlike, ferocious, ambitious and expansionist, with the ruling classes notably tall, good-looking and often with a distinctive red-gold hair 'à la Titian'. Notably anticlerical (with the exception of the saintly Fulk II the Good in the tenth century), the Angevin male noble was a byword for debauchery, womanising and feuding. The Normans, who detested the Angevins, routinely described them as barbarians who lived like animals, gnawed joints of meat like savage beasts, looted like pirates, desecrated churches and executed priests and monks for sport.[16]

The animosity between Angevins and Normans must have abated by the beginning of the twelfth century, for Fulk, count of Anjou, the fifth of that ilk, pulled off a great coup by arranging a brilliant marriage for his son Geoffrey with Matilda, daughter and heiress of Henry I of England; Fulk departed on crusade in the Holy Land and handed over Anjou to Geoffrey as a wedding present. But the marriage was not a success, largely because Matilda was such a domineering personality; this was the very quality that lost her England when she had Stephen on the ropes in 1141. Headstrong, overbearing, tactless, haughty, arrogant and abusive, Matilda alienated everyone she came in contact with, even her own kinsmen. The general consensus was that Matilda was an over-masculine woman; her lack of the traditionally feminine qualities appalled contemporaries who thought her a freak of nature. Since Geoffrey was cold, shallow, sly and selfish, the love of power and the cunning so observable in Henry II would appear to have come from mother and father respectively, rather than the other way round, as in conventional expectations. And since Matilda acted like a virago and indicated to her husband that, as a king's daughter, she had married beneath her, it was not long before he ignored her and consoled himself with a harem of mistresses. Nonetheless, the duty of founding a new dynasty had to be performed, so it was into this loveless union that Henry II was born on 5 March 1133 at Le Mans.[17]

Henry II would continue the Angevin pattern of contracting unhappy marriages and, even more so, conformed to the tradition of family feuding that everyone agreed was the Achilles heel of the Angevins.[18] What the young Richard thought of this dubious legacy we can only guess, but we know for certain that he relished yet another aspect of the Angevin tradition, which was that the family was, quite literally, the devil's brood. The Angevins had annexed the legendary story of Melusine as their own. A woman of stunning beauty married one of the counts of Anjou and bore him four children. She seemed the perfect wife in all respects but one: she refused to attend Mass or, if forced to go, always found an excuse to leave before the Consecration of the Host. Gradually suspicions arose and the count's courtiers warned him that his wife's behaviour was causing a scandal. The count decided to put her to the test. He insisted she attend Mass then, as the moment for the Consecration approached, hemmed her in with four armed men so that she could not leave the church. As the retainers went to lay hands on her, she slipped from their grasp, seized two of her children and began to ascend into the air before the horrified gaze of the churchgoers. Like a wraith she floated out through a window; neither she nor the two abducted children were ever seen again. The conclusion was that the countess was the devil's own daughter, who could not look upon the body of Christ.[19] What the fate was of the two children she left behind was not recorded, but presumably they were held to have grown up and reproduced the devil's spawn.

Henry II was a towering personality but his wife, the mother of Richard and John, was scarcely less so. Born in 1124, Eleanor, countess of Poitou and duchess of Aquitaine was a notable beauty who first became a queen in 1137 when the ailing king of France, Louis the Fat, married his seventeen-year-old son to her; he succeeded to the throne of France as Louis VII a month later when his father, worn out with gout and gluttony-induced obesity, died – but scarcely in the legendary position in the saddle, since for the last ten years of his life he had been too corpulent to mount a horse. Eleanor of Aquitaine had a dark complexion, black eyes, black hair and was curvaceous with a superb figure that never ran to fat even in old age. She was also at the time the western world's richest and most prestigious heiress. From her father Duke William X, ruler of a dynasty originally established in Poitiers in the ninth century – and thus in many ways very like the Angevins – she had inherited vast territories.[20] The exact feudal relationship of the dukes of Aquitaine to the Capetian kings of France is a disputed academic subject, but it is clear that Aquitaine in the twelfth century was a virtually autonomous and decentralised principality, with only the most tenuous relationship with the kings of France. The dynastic marriage in 1137, and Duke William X's death in the same year, undoubtedly moved Aquitaine into the orbit of France though, by transferring nominal power to Paris, it simply increased the anarchy and warlordism in the south. Not only did the rulers of Aquitaine make merely a nod in the direction of the kings of France but their own power was severely circumscribed: their vassals paid them lip-service only and the dukes' writ really ran only in and around the immediate environs of Bordeaux and Poitou.[21]

From the earliest days Eleanor's marriage was controversial: many said it was invalid by canon law as being within the prohibited degrees of consanguinity. Childless until the age of 23, when she finally bore a daughter, Eleanor was a disappointment to her husband in every respect but her undoubted physical charms. A year later, in 1146, according to the chronicler Gerald of Wales and Walter Map, she had an affair with Count Geoffrey of Anjou (Henry II's father), although many modern historians discount the story.[22] An emancipated woman by the standards of the time, she accompanied King Louis on the disastrous Second Crusade (1147–49), where she was said to have led her own troops and dressed like an Amazon. More stories of infidelity followed her on the crusade: she was alleged to have had an affair in Antioch with Count Raymond of Poitiers, the city's ruler. The entire saga of promiscuity, infidelity, seduction and rape in the Middle Ages is a thorny subject on which scholars disagree vehemently: some see medieval royal households as a hotbed of casual rape and forced concubinage, while others accuse chroniclers like Map and Gerald of Cambridge of anti-Angevin propaganda, misogyny or both.[23] Whether Eleanor really was unfaithful as charged, or simply the victim of hostile, educated contemporaries, it seems clear that by the end of the Second Crusade, King Louis, whatever his initial besotment, was estranged from his wife. When Eleanor spoke of an annulment and stressed the fourth and fifth degrees of kinship by which she and Louis were consanguineous, the king arrested her and placed her in humiliating purdah. Following a perilous return from Jerusalem, the warring royal pair sought the intercession of the Pope in an interview in Rome, but Eugenius III sided with Louis and refused to grant an annulment.[24]

Marital relations must have been resumed, for Eleanor gave birth to another daughter in 1150. But in 1151 the 18-year-old Henry of Anjou, Geoffrey's son, came to Paris to pay homage to King Louis for his guarantee of Normandy, part of a 'definitive' peace patched up that year between Louis and Geoffrey of Anjou. Once again the historical record is cloudy: Eleanor romancers claim that at this meeting Henry saw the 29-year-old Eleanor and, so far from being put off by the eleven-year gap in their ages, fell madly in love with her. It is even alleged that the pair became lovers at this point, and that the entire courtship and marriage was a matter of impulse, disturbed hormones and unfettered emotions. Some say Eleanor had tired of Louis's effeminacy and generally lacklustre calibre as a lover and wanted a husband who could dominate her; alternatively, the 'power devil' theorists claim she aimed to dominate her husband.[25] Furthermore, it is alleged, Henry's desire was fanned when his father warned him against Eleanor's wiles and cautioned his son that he had already 'known' her. It is more likely that hardheaded calculation carried the day: both could see the material advantages of marriage to the other should the opportunity present. In Henry's case the chief consideration is likely to have been that Aquitaine was an even more important power base than Normandy at this juncture, when he had still not secured a firm promise of succession to the English throne from Stephen. The chance came in 1152 when Louis, frustrated by the lack of a male heir after fifteen years of marriage, finally agreed to an annulment. The marriage between Louis and Eleanor had effectively been on the rocks since 1147–48, there were persistent rumours about the queen's infidelity and her alleged infertility or at least inability to conceive a son, and by now personal incompatibility between the couple had hardened into mutual antipathy.[26] We may infer that Eleanor and Henry had laid contingency plans and the fortuitous death of Henry's father Geoffrey (he developed a fever after swimming in the Loire) removed another obstacle. When a synod of bishops formally annulled Eleanor's marriage in March 1152, she acted quickly, but she had to. Once she was no longer married, she was a potential prey for land-hungry suitors and if she did not marry Henry rapidly she ran the risk of being abducted, raped and dragooned into a forced marriage. In fact, as she travelled to meet Henry, both Count Theobald of Blois and Geoffrey of Anjou (Henry's brother) tried to seize her.[27]

All turned out successfully and on Whit Sunday, 18 May 1152, Henry and Eleanor were married in Poitiers. At a stroke Henry doubled his continental possessions and gained massively in wealth, power and status; indeed he was richer in lands and economic and military resources, more powerful, in a word, than Louis, supposedly his feudal superior. The marriage caused a sensation. Louis declared himself shocked and angered by the marriage, feeling both that Eleanor had duped him into an annulment when she had already planned her next step and that Henry had broken feudal law by taking her as his wife. Anti-Eleanor historians have always suspected her of cold-blooded revenge and humbug, in that she married her ex-husband's greatest political rival, who was himself within the degrees of consanguinity that provided the ground for her annulment.[28] But many scholars feel that Louis's complaints had little substance: there was no need for Henry to seek Louis's permission before marrying Eleanor, nor was he debarred from using the ducal title until he had paid a feudal 'relief' to Louis, as the king alleged. Louis was not the only one, both then and later, to believe that Eleanor had manipulated him through a diabolical lust for power, but the plain fact is that Louis needed the annulment more than she did, as he was desperate to beget a male heir. As for the unseemly haste in which Henry and Eleanor supposedly celebrated their wedding, Louis's third marriage followed after an even shorter gap than that between the annulment and Eleanor's union with Henry.[29]

But in human affairs perception is all, and reality nothing. Whatever the merits and demerits of the case, Louis felt that he had been double-crossed. Perhaps his courtiers hinted, as many later historians have, that in letting Eleanor go he had behaved with egregious stupidity. He summoned the allegedly errant pair to explain and, when they ignored him, he declared war and put together a formidable coalition of Henry's enemies who hated him for one reason or another. Among those he enlisted were Eustace of Boulogne, Geoffrey of Anjou, Henry of Blois, count of Champagne and his brother Théobald, count of Blois – some disappointed suitors of Eleanor, others political rivals or personal foes. Yet in a six-week campaign Henry smashed his enemies then turned north and began preparing an invasion of England.[30] The great risk Henry had taken was that Eleanor would be unable to provide him with an heir but in 1153 she confirmed his best hopes by giving birth to a son, William. The same year saw Henry's triumphant landing in England, the fortuitous death of Stephen's son Eustace and Stephen's reluctant acceptance of Henry as the next king of England. The run of good fortune continued: in August 1154 Eleanor announced that she was pregnant again, in October Stephen died, and in December Henry and Eleanor were crowned king and queen of England in Westminster Abbey. Henry's family was soon expanding. In 1155 Eleanor gave birth to another boy, Henry and in the same year Henry acknowledged a bastard son, Geoffrey, as part of his household. But the next year brought mixed fortunes. The three-year-old heir William died, and to balance this loss Eleanor could produce 'only' another girl, Matilda. Nonetheless, many historians feel that during her childbearing years Eleanor had, if not quite the perfect love match, then at least the kind of relationship she wanted.[31]

At first the union of Henry and Eleanor, and the 'empire' of England and western France thus formed, seemed like a fairy-tale arrangement. Both partners were dynamic, energetic, intelligent, cultured; both were strong personalities and highly-sexed; both were ambitious, proud, stubborn and worshippers of power. The cross for Eleanor to bear was that she was obliged to condone her husband's habitual infidelities while remaining faithful herself. And it cannot have escaped her, though it may have done in the first flush of euphoria when freeing herself from Louis, that the time would come when she was past childbearing age and Henry would still be a lusty priapist in his thirties.[32] Henry showed no restraint and virtually flaunted his womanising, spawning a raft of bastards as he ploughed his way through the females of England. In compensation Eleanor meddled in statecraft and was an accomplished politician, winning the disapproval of contemporary chroniclers who regarded her as a 'power devil'. Additionally, they felt that many of her political decisions, some of momentous import, were taken purely out of pique and sexual jealousy at Henry's mistresses. Eleanor of Aquitaine is a controversial figure, in her private life, her cultural influence and her political status. Some say she affronted contemporaries by her lust for power, others that she did merely what was expected in the Middle Ages of a woman with power, and that we have underrated both how many resources a medieval female oligarch had and the degree of tolerance given them; on this view the hostile chroniclers were merely weaving black propaganda. Certainly there was something about Eleanor that could provoke people to hatred. Some described her as a latter-day Messalina while others said that the legend of Melusine was actually a foretelling of her reign and that a shrieking flight through church windows could be expected.[33]

If Eleanor was, as her champions allege, a woman who lived primarily for love, she must have been disappointed from an early stage with the marriage to Henry. The king, it seemed, was at her side just long enough to make her pregnant before departing on some other hunting escapade or 'urgent' business of state; some sceptics, indeed, have even described him as a 'burnt out case' dissipating his energies on the chase and neglecting politics until some sudden crisis forced him to rush off to a new theatre of war.[34] Others defend his restlessness on the grounds that medieval monarchs had perforce always to be on the move, since, given the knife edge on which medieval economies operated, the pressure on food resources and even sanitation would become intolerable if, with their huge households and retinues, they stayed in any one place for very long. Certainly one can trace the later wanderlust in Richard – what Sellars and Yeatman famously described as 'Richard Gare de Lyon' – to his father's example. Henry's womanising did not cease as he roamed about his empire, and the very year after his coronation he acknowledged a bastard son, Geoffrey, as a true prince. How Eleanor reacted to the philandering is uncertain. Some of her biographers claim that she was insanely jealous and even that she hit back with an affair with the troubadour Bernard de Ventadour in 1153–54 while Henry was in England. But this seems implausible, not only because Eleanor was almost permanently pregnant at this time but because of the 'treasonable' quality of extramarital intercourse by a queen. Most probably Eleanor allowed herself flirtations, even of the heavy kind. More solidly based is the idea that because of her preoccupation with political intrigue and meddling in affairs of state Eleanor neglected her maternal role and inflicted psychological damage on her children, not only through obvious failure to be a 'hands on' parent but by the anxiety she may have transmitted because of her power-seeking.[35]

It is a nice question whether Henry's infidelities or his cavalier way with his wife's possessions were more upsetting to the queen. Eleanor regarded Aquitaine as a power in its own right and was obsessed with its rights and privileges. As one of her most perceptive critics has remarked, 'the needs of the territories which she had inherited south of the Loire were always uppermost in her thoughts'.[36] What particularly seems to have nettled her was the settlement Henry made with Louis of France in 1156. The Capetian king soon allowed himself to be convinced by Abbot Suger – one of the first in the long line of clerical 'powers behind the throne' in French history – that his initial hostility towards Henry II had been an impulsive mistake, that the long-term interests of the French crown were best served by accepting the nominal submission of vassals he could not force into submission – such as the militarily superior Henry of England. Henry for his part saw the virtues of diplomacy at a difficult stage in his reign and made secret overtures to Louis. On 5 February 1156 he met the French king on the borders of Normandy and formally did homage to him for Normandy, Anjou and Aquitaine. It seems clear that this obeisance particularly angered Eleanor, who felt that the interests of Aquitaine were being swept aside and that her beloved South was being ruthlessly absorbed into the larger Angevin empire; the fact that her ex-husband was the titular beneficiary can scarcely have helped.[37] But as yet she was but a woman in a man's world. If she was to make inroads on Henry's arrogance, it would have to be through her sons. It must have been with particular joy that she gave birth to her third son, Richard on 8 September 1157, little more than a year after the birth of Matilda. Richard was the fourth child she had borne Henry in five years (though the first-born, William had died aged three in 1156).

Eleanor's unusually long sojourn in France from August 1156 to February 1157, during which period she spent months at Saumur, Aquitaine, Limoges and Bordeaux, was probably the longest single sustained time she spent with her husband and it was then that the future Lionheart was conceived. Eleanor crossed the Channel in February 1157 (Henry did not join her until April) but had to remain in London when the restless Henry headed west for a campaign against the Prince of North Wales. Unsuccessful in this, he summoned his nobles to meet him in Chester, but was back in Oxford in early September just in time for the birth of his third son. Eleanor's confinement, which, in the meticulous way of Henry's administration, had to have the sum of twenty shillings recorded in the Pipe Rolls by way of expenses, was in Beaumont

Palace and there, in what was then the appropriately named King's House, the future mighty warrior first saw the light of day. But his mother would not have suckled him, as noblewomen avoided breast-feeding. Following the custom of the day, the infant Richard was placed in the care of a wet nurse named Hodierna, who became the salient immediate influence on his young life. A native of St Albans, she gave birth to a famous man in her own right, for her son (the same age as Richard and, according to legend, born the same night) was the eminent schoolman Alexander of Nequam, later scientist, theologian and alchemist. Richard was hugely attached to Hodierna, and, when he became king, showered her with largesse; soon a wealthy woman, Hodierna won fame as probably the only wet nurse in history to have a village named after her – for the old name for West Knoyle in Wiltshire was Knoyle Hodierne.[38] How much day-to-day interest Eleanor took in her son is not recorded, but she is alleged to have been influenced by a traditional prophecy of Merlin, which in turn was alleged to refer to the reign of Henry II: 'The eagle of the broken covenant shall rejoice in the third nesting.' This typically obscure and sibylline utterance was interpreted as follows: Eleanor was the eagle, the broken covenant was the failed marriage with Louis VII, and the third nesting was the birth of the third son, Richard.[39] The fact that, strictly speaking, Richard was not Eleanor's third nesting, for she had also given birth to daughters, presumably worried no one, for once one accepts the premise of Nostradamus-style prophecies, almost any meaning can always be extracted from them. What is factual is that Henry took no interest in any of his children, for in 1160, when Richard was three, Archbishop Theobald of Canterbury explicitly asked the king to return to England from France, on the grounds (among others) that he was neglecting his children.[40]

Needless to say, Henry ignored the request. According to his own lights he had no option but to pursue the itinerant life. To a lesser extent this was also true of Queen Eleanor. Travelling either on horseback or in unsprung cylindrical wagons, gaudily painted and with leather roofs so that the royal procession sometimes looked like a mountebank's parade or a meretricious procession of strolling players housed in coloured pumpkins, Eleanor and her ladies carted documents, money, clothes and jewellery around much of western France and England. More than two hundred members of the king's household – stewards, chamberlains, treasurers, keepers of seals, bodyguards – made up the royal entourage, and this vast number would be supplemented whenever Eleanor accompanied Henry, for she too brought a bevy of officials, servants and functionaries, all with clothes and impedimenta. It sometimes almost passes belief that a relatively primitive society like that of twelfth-century England could have boasted so many occupations: secretaries, account-ants, constables, archers, attorneys, clerks, bailiffs, knights, esquires, chamberlains, chaplains, painters, ushers, huntsmen, heralds, dog-handlers, laundresses – even barbers, gamblers, jesters, fortune-tellers, whores and pimps. Some contemporaries likened the itinerant court to a travelling brothel, and some reprobates even excused their sexual excesses as being a form of 'compensation' for the poor food and wine they had to consume on the road. Winchester, Westminster, Windsor, Woodstock, Nottingham, Gloucester, Marlborough, Oxford and Clarendon (near Salisbury) were just some of Henry's favourite haunts, and here we speak of his English travels alone. The ordeal of travel was not helped by Henry's unpredictability, his frequent and rapid changes of mind, his refusal to be tied down to a rational schedule, his restlessness and impulsiveness, and his indifference to food and luxury. Even though young Richard was Eleanor's favourite son and she was far more directly influential on him than Henry was, the child saw little enough of his mother.[41]

The only truly omnipresent and pervasive influence on the young Richard was Aquitaine itself, and its culture and ethos. Formerly a Roman province of Gaul, an independent duchy under the Merovingian kings of France and even, for about a hundred years in the ninth century an autonomous kingdom, it was by Henry II's time once more a duchy with complex feudal allegiances. It was always more Roman than the lands to the north, having been conquered from Rome by the Visigoths, not the Franks. Aquitaine, literally 'the land of waters' from the rivers that stri-ated it (the Garonne, Charente, Creuse, Vienne, Dordogne and Vézère), stretched from Poitou in central France to Gascony in the south, taking in the counties of Saintonge, Angoulême and Limousin. Eleanor of Aquitaine, the richest heiress in the world, possessed Poitou and Gascony as well as Aquitaine, but it was the Romano-Basque people of Aquitaine who were closest to the queen's heart. Her mother tongue was the *langue d'oc*, a Provençal dialect of French, whereas in Poitou it was the *langue d'oeil* that was spoken.[42] Cynics said that Aquitaine combined all the vices of Poitou to the north (warlike, turbulent, quarrelsome, moneyminded) with all the faults of the Gascons to the south (cynical, promiscuous, braggart and hedonistic), but the Aquitanians regarded themselves as a cut above everyone else, elegant, chic, stylish and cultured, neither frivolous like the Gascons nor humourless like the Poitevins. They despised northerners and had a favourite saying: 'No good ever came from a king who lives north of the Loire.' Ralph of Diceto conceded that it was as close to earthly paradise as the medieval world could get: 'Aquitaine overflows with riches of many kinds, excelling other parts of the western world to such an extent that historians consider it to be one of the most fortunate and flourishing of the provinces of Gaul. Its fields are fertile, its vineyards productive and its forests teem with wild life. From the Pyrenees northwards the entire country is irrigated by the River Garonne and other streams; indeed it is from these life-giving waters (*aquae*) that the province takes its name.'[43]

Four aspects of Aquitaine were especially salient. First, its thriving economy rested on salt and wine. Salt was produced along the entire Atlantic coast, but especially at Bayonne, the bay of Bourgneuf, and at Brouage (between the isles of Oléron and Rhe). The wines of Aunis, Saintonge and Bordeaux were especially famous, but vinous connoisseurs had a penchant for the fine white wine of La Rochelle, famous enough to be exported and a key element in the twelfth-century prosperity of that Atlantic port. La Rochelle's success is said to have killed off wine-growing in England – not such a difficult task as English wine was widely held to be no better than vinegar. But La Rochelle's flourishing export trade, and the customs and duties the duke of Aquitaine could levy on it, made it the key to the duchy's wealth. The surplus thus extracted enabled the ruling classes of Aquitaine to indulge in conspicuous consumption of a distinguished, artistic kind. This was the second feature of Aquitaine that contemporaries noted. The new polyphonic music of the abbey of St Martial in Limoges was famous throughout Europe. Limoges was noted for the visual arts, especially enamelling. The cathedral at Angoulême and the Church of Notre Dame la Grande in Poitiers displayed high-class sculpture, but some thought that the carving in the Romanesque churches of the Saintonge area were even more magnificent.[44] Thirdly, Aquitaine lay on the pilgrim road to the shrine of St James at Santiago de Compostela, a destination rapidly growing in popularity for pilgrims from England and the north. The cult of St James, slayer of Moors, was something of a medieval fetish, and a journey to Spain also enabled the pious traveller to check out the scenes where Roland, hero of the most famous *chanson de geste*, died while fighting the Muslim invaders (actually the historical Roland was killed in an ambush by Basques). A popular twelfth-century guide to pilgrims played up all the regional stereotypes already mentioned and worked on a fairly crude north–south, civilisation–barbarism typology. Thus the Poitevins are tough, warlike, brave, handsome, cultured, generous, hospitable but in Aquitaine people grow their hair long and shave their faces – clearly an obvious sign of effeminacy – and the people are soft, idle and do not keep their women on a tight enough leash. By the time one reaches Gascony, one is truly beyond the pale, for the locals are licentious drunkards who take no trouble about their appearance. Gascons, says the guide, live promiscuously like animals, with everyone sleeping under the same roof regardless of sex or class, gorging their ravening appetites from a communal cooking pot, disdaining to sit at table and then fornicating at will like animals.[45]

Yet the fourth aspect of Aquitaine was historically by far the most important, and also the most significant in the life of the young Richard, for the land was the centre of the troubadour cult. Whereas the *chansons de geste* celebrated martial exploits and military qualities, the troubadours popularised the notion of romantic love. The idea of courtly love, which drew on sources as various as Plato, the Arabic classics and the cult of the Virgin Mary, placed women on a pedestal and was supposed to embody the 'completion' of the code of chivalry; its images, values and ideals were so at variance with the sordid reality of everyday life in the twelfth century that they acted as a kind of other-worldly compensation or escapism. Lyric poetry, written in the honeyed *langue d'oc* vernacular, to the sensuous and often lascivious accompaniment of medieval instruments (pipe, tabor, viol, fidel, rebec), deified women at the expense of the merely martial male sex. The influence of the notions thus inculcated and disseminated – of courtesy, chivalry, honour and courtship – cannot be overstated, and it survived the formal suppression of the troubadours when their malign 'heresies' were thought somehow bound up with the quite separate gnosticism of the Cathars and Albigensians of the early thirteenth century. One has only to think of the romantic notion of the beautiful woman once glimpsed and never seen again, which survives in Thomas Hardy and even Orson Welles's *Citizen Kane*, or the Robert Graves view of Woman as superior to Man, to see that the troubadour view is with us still.[46]

The old view of Eleanor of Aquitaine was that she was a kind of neurotic Emma Bovary of her time, that she tried to turn Aquitaine – and particularly her seat at Tours – into a female Camelot, that she convened 'courts of love' to debate such issues as whether sexual partners should make a pretence of wishing for new lovers and fresh embraces so as to measure the passion, loyalty, constancy and commitment of the other. An entire set of biographers of Eleanor interpreted

her purely in terms of the *toujours l'amour* formula.[47] The modern genera-
tion of scholars tends to find that this view of Eleanor is a total fiction,
a conceit based on the uncritical reading of Andreas Capallanus
(Andrew the Chaplin)'s *On Love*, a kind of updating of Ovid in which
Eleanor and her daughter Marie de Champagne figure largely, and that
the alleged chronology of 1174–96 when 'courtly love' was supposed
to be at its apogee is the intrusion of a wholly imaginary space-time.
Revisionism in turn breeds counterrevisionism, so that some scholars
feel that Eleanor as Queen of Love has some validity, though not necessarily naturalistic. The counterrevisionists are fond of pointing out that
sceptical professional historians may simply be incompetent to de-
cipher or interpret vernacular writing of the 'courtly love' variety.[48] The
one thing that can be stated with certainty is that the troubadours as
a class were thriving in Aquitaine during Richard's minority and some
of their names are well known: Bernard de Ventadour, Jauffre Rudel,
Cercamon, Marcabru.[49] After all, Eleanor's grandfather has some claims
to be considered the first troubadour and the so-called 'second troubadour', Ebles of Ventadour, came from the Limousin. Duke William
IX (1071–1126) was a famously handsome crusader, who transcended
the limitations of a purely warrior code by being a jokester in the Abe
Lincoln mould; the historian William of Malmesbury said that he took
nothing seriously and 'turned everything into a joke and made his
listeners laugh uncontrollably'. But the truth is that William believed
that the way not to take life seriously was to take his work seriously
and to be the ultimate professional as a poet.[50] His influence was considerable, and Aquitaine under Eleanor was a troubadours' paradise. The
story of an affair between Eleanor and Bernard de Ventadour is almost
certainly apocryphal, but Bernard did seek her patronage (as well as
that of Henry II) and probably addressed her directly in a song as
follows:

> *Can la freid' aura venta*
> *deves vostre pais,*
> *veyaire m'es qu'eu senta*
> *un ven de paradis*
> *per amor de la genta*

(When the cold wind blows from the direction of your country, it seems
to me that I felt a breeze from paradise for love of the lady)[51]
    We know for certain that the young Richard was deeply influenced

by troubadour culture, and he was always generous to poets. It is known that he was profoundly interested in music and probably aspired to the skill attributed to the perfect prince in the Anglo-Norman *Romance of Horn*. This prince, unlike Machiavelli's later version, is a master not of statecraft and double-dealing but of musical instruments – 'there was no musical instrument known to mortal man in which the princely Horn did not surpass everyone'. His talent was especially marked when he plucked the harp: 'anyone who watched how he touched the strings and made them vibrate, sometimes causing them to sing and at other times to join in harmonies, would have been reminded of the harmony of heaven'.[52] Richard may not have been the virtuoso performer thus alluded to, but his popularity among the troubadours attests to his skill as a songwriter and his mastery of the art of political satire in song and vernacular form; there is a well-authenticated story that the adult Richard capped a political *chanson* from the duke of Burgundy with one of his own, full of sardonic humour. The jongleur Ambroise thought Richard a highly talented songwriter and librettist. The Cistercian monk Ralph of Coggleshall was an eyewitness when Richard 'conducted' the clerks of his royal chapel when singing in the choir, urging them with hand gestures, facial expressions and body language to greater polyphonic efforts, much as a modern maestro might do.[53]

Richard saw almost nothing of his father during the first ten years of his life. When he was two years old, in 1159, he may have glimpsed him when Henry came south for an ill-fated campaign against Toulouse. Henry considered that Toulouse was rightfully part of the duchy of Aquitaine, as it had once been a major city in the Carolingian kingdom of Aquitania. But in the eleventh century the counts of Poitiers had established themselves as dukes of Gascony and, as part of the knock-on effect, the counts of Toulouse had tried to reconstruct the old Roman province of Septimana by building political alliances with Narbonne and Carcassonne, extending their links with Provence (then part of the German empire) and even with Barcelona and Spain. The city of Toulouse lay at the nodal point of communications and trade routes west–east between the Atlantic and the Mediterranean and north–south between the Massif Central and the Pyrenees. Without control of Toulouse, the Poitevin control of Aquitaine was both weakened and incomplete. In 1159 Henry asserted his right to the city as part of the 'dowry' consequent on his marriage to Eleanor. King Louis of France also coveted Toulouse, and had even campaigned to acquire it while still married to Eleanor, so he could not allow his great rival to gain possession of so important a prize. He began by diplomatic stalling, hoping to bog Henry down, but the restless English king soon decided to force the issue by arms. He assembled a huge army and marched south. Louis then hoodwinked him by going to Toulouse and offering it his protection. Henry next faced the ticklish problem of having to press the siege and take his nominal feudal overlord (Louis) prisoner. While he procrastinated, autumn came on and his army began to be ravaged by sickness. Diversionary attacks by Louis on Normandy soon had Henry marching north again, leaving his Toulouse campaign as an embarrassing failure. Many historians feel that the debacle outside Toulouse marked the end of Thomas Becket's influence on Henry. Becket had been a 'hawk' over the campaign and had raised 700 knights himself. His advice was that Henry should not hesitate to assault Toulouse and take Louis prisoner, for the French king had forfeited his status as feudal overlord by fighting against Henry in breach of existing treaties. Henry was persuaded by other courtiers that Becket's advice was unsound and, in the aftermath of the fiasco, began to reinterpret his old friend as a man of seriously flawed judgement. Becket, for his part, may have seethed inwardly that he was no longer the king's right-hand man and, consciously or unconsciously, may have decided to assert himself against Henry once he became archbishop of Canterbury.[54]

Between 1159 and 1167 Henry visited Aquitaine just once, in 1161 when he laid siege to, and captured, the castle of Castillon-sur-Agen on a flying visit.[55] For the most part, Henry's overriding interests lay in the north. Aquitaine was notorious as a province where the local lords guarded their autonomy fiercely and resented encroachments from feudal overlords. Henry aimed at the typical Anglo-Norman centralism and chafed at the 'anarchy' of Aquitaine. Eleanor was quite happy with the old system and with the military guardianship of her maternal uncle Ralph de Faye, seneschal of Poitou, whom she regarded as her strong right arm. Henry, though, mistrusted de Faye and appointed his own men to many important military and ecclesiastical posts.[56] The extent of disaffection, feuding and anarchy in Poitou has been much debated by academic specialists, but Henry himself was in no doubt that it constituted a threat to his authority and that Eleanor was too soft on recreant local lords. The barons of Aquitaine responded to his cracking of the whip by withdrawing their collaboration from Henry and speaking openly of his 'tyranny'. In 1167 Henry decided that he would have to make another visit to Aquitaine. His particular aim was to curb the power of two aristocratic families, the Lusignans and the Taillefers, counts of Angoulême, whose castles controlled all the land routes between Poitiers, Saintes, La Rochelle and Bordeaux. Unable to make common cause, the Taillefers and Lusignans took a terrible mauling from Henry, with estates laid waste and the great castle of Lusignan razed to the ground. It was only the fact that Henry was once again called north by the threat from King Louis of France that saved the Lusignans and Taillefers from utter destruction and enabled them to rebuild their fortunes.[57] Leaving Earl Patrick of Salisbury as his military satrap in Aquitaine, Henry sped north. Heartened by his departure, the Lusignans returned to the ruins of their castle and set about rebuilding it. When he heard this, Henry turned in his tracks, putting off a summit conference with the French king. Unfortunately, Louis construed the postponement as an insult and was soon intriguing with the Lusignan and Taillefer rebels. The next important development was the death of Earl Patrick after an ambush by the Lusignans. The unsavoury episode left Henry with the feeling that the Poitevins were unregenerate traitors.[58]

Whether Richard actually met his father on these occasions we have no means of knowing, but both the major campaigns in the south were relevant to Richard quite apart from the paternal incursion into the maternal domains. On the 1159 campaign Henry met Count Raymond Berengar of Barcelona, an important ally in the war against Toulouse, made a treaty of alliance and sealed it with the betrothal of the two-year-old Richard to one of the count's daughters. But, as with so many of the slippery Henry's solemn promises, this 'betrothal' simply answered his political requirements of the moment. Nothing came of it, and the shadowy daughter of the count of Barcelona vanished into the historical obscurity that is ever the lot of most of mankind (some say she died in infancy).[59] By the time Louis's pressure on Normandy forced him north from Aquitaine in 1168, Henry was once more ready to use Richard as a political bargaining counter. At a peace conference in Montmirail in January 1169, called when both sides had wearied of the interminable war between them, Henry stated that it was his intention to take the Cross and crusade in the Holy Land. Since he wanted the future of his domains settled, he proposed making his son Henry his clearly nominated heir in Normandy, Anjou and Maine, with Richard as the plainly accredited future duke of Aquitaine. Both sons would do formal homage to Louis for their domains and, to seal the compact, Richard would be betrothed to Louis's daughter Alice (Alys).[60] Much of the conference at Montmirail was taken up with Louis's attempts to mediate between

Henry and his erstwhile friend and now exiled Archbishop of Canterbury, Thomas Becket. The archbishop managed the rare feat of alienating both sides by his intransigence but he proved a shrewd prophet. He told Louis the reason he would not give the categorical assurances of submission Henry required was because Henry was not to be trusted; he was an inveterate oath-breaker and perjurer.[61] Louis soon learned to his cost that Becket was right. Henry took the peace treaty hammered out at Montmirail as a green light enabling him to deal mercilessly with the rebels of Aquitaine, who were even then rebuilding the castles he had destroyed. So far from going on crusade, Henry made it clear that his concerns would always centre on the extended Angevin 'empire'. In a further campaign in the spring and early summer of 1169 he dealt harshly with the unruly barons of Poitou: the count of Angoulême was forced to submit and a well-known local resistance leader Robert de Seilhac died in unsavoury circumstances in one of Henry's prisons.[62] But Henry could never devote all his energies to Aquitaine. Not only was he at war with the kings of France for most of his reign, but he also had military operations in Britanny, Normandy, Wales, Scotland and even Ireland to dissipate his attention and resources. And 1170 was a critical year for Henry for other reasons. In August that year he was seriously ill and for a while thought likely to die. But throughout the year he had a renewed confrontation with the rambunctious Thomas Becket to deal with – a crisis that ended only when four of his knights took literally an 'if only' angry aside from the king ('will no one rid me of this turbulent priest?' were the alleged words, though scholars claim there is no evidence he ever spoke so explicitly) and murdered him in Canterbury Cathedral on 29 December.[63]

For much of his early life Richard exists for us only in occasional glimpses. We find him more and more in the company of his mother, as when he and Eleanor laid foundation stones for the monastery of St Augustine in Limoges in 1171, yet usually the record is shadowy. But in 1172 he finally emerged into the clear daylight of documented history. Aged fourteen and rising fifteen, on Trinity Sunday 10 June of that year in the abbey church of St Hilary in Poitiers he was formally invested as duke of Aquitaine. This dark thick-walled cathedral church positively pullulated with history. Here Charles Martel had prayed before his great victory over the Moors at Tours in 732 by which legend, if not history, credited him with having saved Europe from Islamic serfdom. Here too King Henry's faithful servant Earl Patrick of Salisbury was buried. Sensuousness ruled that Sunday, for the air inside the Church was thick with incense, while sumptuary laws seem to have been waived, allowing a riot of colour within the hallowed walls, as even serfs donned motley and bright raiment. On the altar steps the immensely tall youth Prince Richard stood proud, alongside his mother, at fifty by all accounts still a beauty. Eleanor was bedecked in gorgeous fashion: with her greying locks hidden under a silk kerchief, she displayed on her head the gleaming, gilded coronet of Aquitaine, her grandpaternal bequest; while, to show she was also queen of the Angevin empire she wore a scarlet cloak on which were picked out three golden leopards of Anjou. In either hand she held a sceptre: in the right was the golden staff of Aquitaine and in the left the golden rod she had carried at her coronation as Henry's queen eighteen years before. She was every inch the regal presence, graceful and impassive during the long liturgical service, her gaze fixed on the altar in the solemn way she had learned since childhood. Richard seemed truly the golden warrior, his long shoulder-length blond hair and fair skin melting into an aureate haze with gold trappings that adorned yet another leopard-spotted mantle.[64]

The bishop descended to the choir and conducted the royal couple to the foot of the altar. As Eleanor and her son knelt there, the bishop removed the coronet from her head and placed it on Richard's momentarily before returning it to her; one of his deacons at once stepped forward with a plain silver-girt crown that Richard would wear until the true coronet came to him permanently on his mother's death. The symbolism was clear to everyone. The bishop then motioned to the abbot's chair, where Richard took his seat to receive honours in his own right. A deacon in embroidered dalmatic approached bearing a wide scroll of scarlet silk, handed it to the bishop and withdrew as his superior unfurled it. Then all heads in the Church were lowered as the sacred lance of St Hilary was produced; lance and banner were the true signs of ducal authority and both were now blessed. Since a lance could not be proffered to a woman, the bishop ignored Eleanor and presented the lance to Richard. Laying his hands on the insignia of office, Richard then swore a solemn oath as duke of Aquitaine. When the cheering from the congregation died down, the banner of St Hilary was produced and another oath taken on this precious relic. Richard faced his vassals and swore that he would follow the banner wherever it took him on behalf of Holy Mother Church and God's Right; the implication was that when adult he would crusade in the Holy Land. So finally ended the *Ordo and Benedicendum Ducem Aquitaniae.* Both participants and congregation had fasted overnight to witness the sacred event, so that when the doors of the Church were flung open both noble and commoner rushed out to gorge themselves at festivities. But Richard was not yet done with sacred ceremonies. A few days later, in Limoges, he was once more proclaimed duke in the Church of St Martial. The climax of this ceremony came when the ring of St Valerie was slipped on Richard's finger. The martyred St Valerie was the patron saint of Aquitaine and her allegedly thousand-year-old body was still preserved at Limoges – proving to its citizens that Limoges was more important than Poitiers. This time Richard did not hand back the relics to the priestly caste after touching them but retained the ring and wore it during the feast that followed, returning it to its sanctuary at the high altar only late at night. The ulterior significance of the two ceremonies at Poitiers and Limoges was not just that Richard had come of age and entered man's estate; he had also asserted his right to the dukedom of Aquitaine independently of any feudal duties he might owe his father Henry or King Louis of France. In symbolic terms the saints Hilary and Valerie, protectors of Aquitaine, had allowed him to 'take seizin' of their relics; it followed, then, that only those saints could deprive him of his rights, regardless of what Louis and Henry said or did. Eleanor, always wildly possessive about Aquitaine, had used particular artifice to make sure her favourite son would inherit her duchy.[65]

The early 1170s saw Richard complete the transition to manhood. There is remarkable unanimity about certain key features of his character and personality. His appearance was often commented on. He was very tall – though the hyperbolic estimate of 6ft 5ins, a similar height to that ascribed to Harald Hardrada of Norway, evinces merely the medieval cavalier way with numbers and statistics – and had his father's penetrating blue eyes. The hagiographic chronicler Richard de Templo described him at the time of his coronation: 'He was tall, of elegant build; the colour of his hair was between red and gold; his limbs were supple and straight. He had quite long arms which were particularly suited to drawing a sword and wielding it to great effect. His long legs matched the rest of his body.'[66] Although we know nothing of the details of his military education, his later career makes it clear he must have been an apt pupil with sword and lance. His education in arms, and his prowess with them, made him a believer in military solutions and in violence as a means to an end. The contrast with his more hedonistic elder brother Henry was marked; as Gerald of Wales commented: 'Henry was a shield but Richard was a hammer.' Where some men, his brother Henry among them, prized tournaments as things-in-themselves, Richard valued them only as an aid to martial training and seems to have taken part in only a few jousts, reserving his formidable skills as horseman and swordsman for the battlefield. He was also uninterested in the traditional ducal and regal pursuits of hunting and hawking, indulging in them only when killing time or held up by contrary winds when trying to set sail. Richard despised dilettantism and admired professionalism and ruthlessness. He even affected to be pleased about his family's reputation as the devil's brood and gloried in the apophthegm about his family attributed to St Bernard: 'From the Devil they came and to the Devil they will return.'[67]

But Richard was not just a rough-hewn warrior. As a talented musician and songwriter, he had a command of Latin sufficient to discomfit a less erudite archbishop of Canterbury, and could parry and thrust with words as deftly as with the sword. There is simply too much evidence of his eloquence, verbal sharpness and skill in debate to be discounted as merely the flattery of sycophantic courtiers. His conversational style was described as bantering, half joking, half serious; he never made the classic mistake of the half-intelligent, which is to mistake earnestness for profundity.[68] Like his father, he believed in putting the over-mighty clergy in their place from time to time. Much later in Richard's career the great preacher of the day, Fulk of Neuilly, ventured to chide him for having three daughters, Superbia, Luxuria and Cupiditas (pride, avarice and sensuality) and suggested that he would never receive the Grace of God as long as they remained at his side. Richard thought a moment, then replied: 'I have already given these daughters away in marriage. Pride I gave to the Templars, Avarice to the Cistercians and Sensuality to the Benedictines.'[69] Turning the tables on him, the troubadour Bertran de Born called Richard 'Nay and Yea'. This was an enigmatic accolade, which some have construed to mean that Richard was fickle and volatile, saying first one thing and then its opposite or that he said one thing and meant another. But, bearing in mind Bertran de Born's close association with Eleanor and Richard rather than Henry II, the most likely interpretation is that the troubadour was paying a genuine compliment, stressing a capacity for self-confidence, quick decision and terse delivery – Richard Black and White, as it were.[70]

Yet above all Richard was a product of the South and a lover of Aquitaine which was why, in later life, to the consternation of Anglocentric historians he neglected England and Normandy. More than once Richard dabbled in the affairs of Spain, and it is surely not too far fetched to regard this interest as the seedbed of the later crusader, for Spain was famous most of all for its struggle against Islam and the Moorish invaders. Although the author of the famous pilgrim's guidebook inveighed against the Gascons for their drunkenness, lechery and poor table manners – they squatted around a fire instead of sitting at table, they shared the same cups and the same bedrooms and presumably therefore possessed women in common – he came close to apoplexy when he described the Basques and the people of Navarre. Among the crimes set down to *their* account were the following: they all ate out of a single cooking-pot like pigs at a trough; their speech was most akin to dogs barking; they had no shame about exposing their genitals especially when warming themselves at a fire; they treated women like beasts of the field and sometimes literally so as they practised bestialism with mules and horses and even attached chastity belts to these animals to prevent interlopers enjoying their ruminant favours.[71] But to Richard this sort of propaganda was arrant nonsense; he preferred the freedom, hedonism and sybaritism of the warm south to the straitjacket of the priest-ridden north. Unquestionably the major influence in this as in so many other aspects of his young life was his mother, who idolised him and called him 'the great one'. Richard's status as his mother's favourite son is well conveyed in state documents, where Eleanor habitually refers to him as her 'dearest son' (*carissimum*), while John is merely her 'dear son' (*dilectum*). The warmth of the relationship between mother and son was now about to have explosive and potentially catastrophic consequences.

2

—◦—

E VEN WHILE SHE CHERISHED her beloved Richard, Eleanor of
Aquitaine continued her amazing career as queen and woman.
Apart from her other qualities, she was a childbearing machine
of superb efficiency. In September 1158 she gave birth to her fourth
son Geoffrey, her seventh child, and the fifth with Henry. Geoffrey as
an adult turned out to be short of stature, but fair and handsome, looking
more Norman than Poitevin. The most charming of the Devil's Brood,
he would also prove the most untrustworthy. Shrewd, cunning, a humbug
and hypocrite with a compulsive tendency to deceit, Geoffrey had one
saving grace: charm. With his mother's vivacity, he was a plausible, persuasive rogue, and with his 'gift of the gab' he could talk his way out of
anything, and into a multiplicity of intrigues, usually directed at his father.
Gerald of Wales described Geoffrey as 'overflowing with words, soft as
oil, possessed, by his syrupy and persuasive eloquence, of the power of
dissolving the seemingly indissoluble, able to corrupt two kingdoms with
his tongue; of tireless endeavour, a hypocrite and a dissembler'. Roger
of Howden's assessment was along the same lines but pithier: 'Geoffrey,
that son of perdition'.[1] In 1161 Eleanor bore her second daughter, also
called Eleanor and in 1165 her third, Joan (or Joanna). John, born on
Christmas Eve 1166, and named for the saint's day, was her last child,
the product of a rare marital coupling when Henry held one of his itinerant courts at Angers. Twenty-nine years separated the birth of Eleanor's
first child, Mary, from the last-born, and the age gap between John's
mother and father now loomed alarmingly: Eleanor was 42 but Henry
still only 34. The adult John always struck observers as being the most
purely Poitevin of Henry's sons, being short and dark, a true child of
the south. In time he would rival Geoffrey for treachery. He saw little
of his mother during his childhood, as in 1169 she dropped him off at
the abbey of Fontevraud in Anjou, in the care of the Church, ostensibly to be trained as an oblate and, it seems, he remained there five

years. According to some sources, at the age of six he was moved to the
household of his brother Henry, the 'Young King' where he received
the rudiments of knightly training. His academic education was entrusted
to Ranulph Glanville, one of Henry's senior officials.[2] But modern
scholars tend to doubt this story, and instead emphasise the five-year
continuity at Fontevraud, the termination of which can be precisely dated
to July 1174, for on the eighth of that month Henry II took John with
him from Normandy to England.[3]

Much about John's early years is doubtful, but some aspects have
become clearer as a result of modern research. For a long time it was
thought that the story that he was born in Oxford was simply a corruption of the known fact that his brother Richard was born there; it now
appears that both brothers may have emerged from the womb there.[4] It
also seems likely that Eleanor of Aquitaine was born in 1124 (rather
than 1122, the traditional date), and that her childbearing record has been
obfuscated by Ralph of Diceto's clear statement that Henry II and
Eleanor had *six* sons, two of whom died in childhood. This means that
in addition to William (1153–56), somewhere along the line there was
another short-lived male baby.[5] Also a date of 1124 rather than 1122 for
Eleanor's birth means that she may have borne John not quite so dangerously near the menopause as has sometimes been thought – though all
such generalisations are difficult, for in the twelfth century fifty counted
as extreme old age. It always used to be thought that Eleanor slowed down
in her childbirth pattern, whether because of stillbirth or lowered fertility
with the onset of the menopause, and there may be truth in these asser-
tions, but a last child at 42 puts Eleanor more in the realm of naturalism
than mythology.[6] But why was John, unlike his brothers, placed in
Fontevraud from the age of three to seven-and-a-half? It is highly unlikely
that he was earmarked for a career in the Church, and the misleading
term 'oblate' probably means no more in this context than that he was
a 'boarder' at the abbey. John and Joan were the two youngest children,
both put into care at Fontevraud because of Eleanor's absence on the
business of Aquitaine. In some ways it was an odd choice for John, for
it was a 'double abbey', ruled by an abbess, where the women outranked,
and were served by, the men[7]; it was a questionable environment for a
prince, and an absurd one if John were really being trained as a prince
of the Church, where male hierarchy was the dominant ethos. Many
plausible reasons have been given for the choice of Fontevraud: it was
equidistant from Eleanor's domains in the south and Henry's in the north;
both children, and especially Joan, needed female attendants; the abbey

had close ties to both Henry's and Eleanor's families; the nuns were aristo-cratic ladies; and, possibly clinchingly, Henry's first cousin Matilda of Flanders was there as a nun in the years 1169–74.[8]

In later years John was notable for quasi-autistic tendencies, and he always seemed to have a grudge against the world. This has been plau-sibly linked to Eleanor of Aquitaine's neglect of him. Some cultural historians have alleged that John's infancy was not especially lonely and deprived, both by the general standards of royal childhood and the ethos and values obtaining in the twelfth century. Mothers, it is said, bore chil-dren but they did not nurture them, and it was servants, tutors and others who brought them up.[9] But this collides with the known fact that Eleanor was much more involved with her older children, and especially Richard, than most high-born ladies of the time *and* that, in addition, she signally neglected John.[10] John's upbringing was markedly different from that of his siblings in a number of ways. Because of the seven-year age gap between him and Geoffrey, he had no brother with whom he could bond. He saw far less of his mother than his brothers had.[11] He had very different relations with his sisters from those of his brothers; he did not know his eldest sister at all, and even Joan, his companion in Fontevraud, was sent off to be married when she was nine. With an absent mother, no grandmother and no sisters during his formative adolescent years, it would not have been surprising if John developed misogynistic tendencies, and there is much in his later career that points in that direction. John's upbringing lacked stability also. Because he was his father's favourite and constantly with him – which also meant constantly travelling and being on the move with the itinerant court – he lacked the security of a settled home environment, which Eleanor certainly provided, for three elder sons.[12] Given that Eleanor and Henry were far from model parents for a variety of reasons, some of them obvious in the narrative already provided, and the 'Devil's Brood' were never easy children at the best of times, John's problems as a child can be seen as overdetermined and exponential.

From the very first John showed himself to be a peevish, cross-grained individual. The chronicler Richard of Devizes once saw the youth virtually frothing at the mouth in a fury of frustration while he lambasted Chancellor Longchamp: 'His whole person became so changed as to be hardly recognisable. Rage contorted his brow, his burning eyes glittered, bluish spots discoloured the pink of his cheeks, and I know not what would have become of the chancellor if in that moment of frenzy he had fallen like an apple into his hands as they sawed the air.'[13] There were other such incidents. Fulk Fitzwarin was a playmate of John's at Henry's court and was often the recipient of the young prince's foul tempers. 'It happened one day that John and Fulk were alone in a chamber, playing chess. John took the chessboard and struck Fulk a great blow with it. Fulk, feeling hurt, kicked John hard in the stomach, so that he banged his head against the wall and became faint and dizzy. When John swooned, Fulk became frightened and thanked his stars that there was no one in the room but themselves. He rubbed John's ears and eventually brought him round. John then went wailing to his father the king. "Hold your tongue," said Henry, "you are always squabbling. If Fulk has done what you say, you probably deserved it." He then called for John's tutor and ordered him to be thrashed for having complained.'[14]

John was a thorn in his father's side before he could walk and talk, and the reason for this was the shambolic feudal system itself. Throughout his reign Henry was constantly looking over his shoulder at his nominal overlord, Louis of France. The French king loomed as a more formidable threat once he sired a son with his new wife Adela of Champagne. Contemporary eyewitnesses tell us that Paris was a riot both of colour and humanity in August 1165 when Louis was finally able to announce the birth of a male heir. Through a cacophony of church bells and tocsin calls the capital of France seemed to be on fire as the common people spontaneously lit hundreds of bonfires. A public proclamation established that the child's name was Philip and promised that he would make France great: 'By the Grace of God there is born to us this night a King who shall be a hammer to the English.'[15] Philip was brought up to hate the English and their kings, his hatred doubtless fuelled by the rueful and envious broodings of his father, who both detested Henry and Eleanor personally and resented their great power. Louis once told Walter Map: 'Your lord the king of England, who lacks nothing, has men, horses, gold, silk, jewels, fruit, game and everything else . . . We in France have nothing but bread and wine and gaiety.'[16] The significant thing from Richard's point of view is that within two years in the 1160s two men were born who were to prove his mortal and implacable enemies: Philip of France and his own brother John.

Yet even without the unwelcome news that Louis, the supposed monk, had proved himself lusty enough to sire a son, Henry faced myriad problems in securing solid successions for his sons while unwinding the Ariadne's thread through the labyrinth of medieval feudalism. In theory feudalism was a clearly constructed pyramid of hierarchical rights and duties; in practice it was arcane and confusing. Some writers have likened the power of the Capetian kings of France to the modern United Nations; to use Walter Bagehot's terms, the 'dignified' aspect of feudal overlordship was impressive but the 'efficient' reality was that those who were formally vassal-states and vassal-kings defied their superiors with impunity, just as superpowers do with the UN today. Just as, other things being equal, nation-states like to make a show of deference to the UN to ward off the spectre of international chaos, so in the eleventh century vassal rulers saw ceremonial, religious and hierarchical reasons for paying lip-service to notions of fealty. Most of the de facto independent states within the confines of modern-day France recognised the king of the royal territory in the Ile de France as their feudal superior and accepted their technical position as fiefdoms by swearing oaths of homage. Technically, homage was the acknowledgement of land tenure, while fealty implied oath-taking, though naturally the formal acceptance of overlordship was usually combined with an oath of fealty. These oaths were the most important form of legal obligation in medieval society but, as has been widely realised, the paradox was that by the time the oath was the most important foundation of legal titles, it was itself largely a legal fiction; some scholars have gone further and suggested that most of so-called feudalism is a fiction.[17] Men swore homage simply to get the feudal lord's seal on their title deeds, then broke their oaths shamelessly. In the twelfth century the role of the oath as the guarantor of the feudal pyramid – king, dukes, great counts, lesser counts, barons, knights, peasants – was still potent though of steadily diminishing importance. From 1066 to 1204 it made no sense for a king of France to give orders to his 'vassal' the duke of Normandy, and, if he did give them, they were sure to be disregarded or disobeyed. Nonetheless, the dukes of Normandy still went through the farce of doing homage for the duchy.

Feminist historians have gone to great lengths to try to work up the importance of women in the society of the Middle Ages, but there is really no need for any special pleading, as females were of overriding importance, if only because, biologically, they survived better than infant males. Nubile heiresses had to be found husbands and, by definition, in exogamy, a woman marrying 'out' handed her husband new fiefs if and when her brothers died. These new fiefs were the source of much of the conflict among medieval states. Female inheritance of land conceivably could – and often did – bring mortal enemies together as fellow-subjects under a common government.[18] Blood-feuds cut across the lines of feudal obligation and, in any case, female inheritance almost made nonsense of the supposed hierarchical pyramid by making the vassal more powerful than the lord. In the eleventh century every great man held a number of otherwise unconnected fiefs, each with its separate traditions and history, and held these fiefs from a number of lords. If the lords made war on each other, the vassal had to choose between them, so inevitably ended up being branded as traitor by one of them. To take the example of Henry II in France, he was count of Anjou and Maine and lord of Touraine by direct inheritance from his father, duke of Normandy through his mother, duke of Aquitaine through his wife, and in addition had shadowy claims to Auvergne, Toulouse and Britanny in the form of homage from local lords plus a claim to the hereditary Seneschalty of France. The office of Seneschal was in the gift of the king of France, and Louis had cunningly given it to Henry as it was the Seneschal's duty to suppress rebellious vassals. One of Louis's great rivals therefore had a duty to waste his substance and resources subduing men who in terms of *realpolitik* should have been his friends.

To an already complex structure Henry II added another layer when he sought a role for his sullen, jealous and rebellious brother Geoffrey, who had intrigued with King Louis against him. Originally possessor of the castles of Chinon, Loudon and Mirabel – and disappointed at these meagre morsels dispensed to him by Henry – Geoffrey lost even these as a result of allying himself with Louis and finding himself on the losing side. Henry, showing the complaisant attitude to treachery by kith and kin that was to be a marked feature of the Devil's Brood, found a niche for him as Count of Nantes or Lower Britanny. The duchy of Britanny proper had been stable until the death of Conan III in 1148, but thereafter the territory was rent by civil war. Worn down by the endless factional turmoil and weakened by Geoffrey's acquisition of Nantes, Duke Conan IV (or 'Conan the Little') gradually became tired of the struggle. When Geoffrey died at 24 in 1158 he tried to regain Nantes, but Henry claimed it was his as the inheritance of his brother.[19] Crushed and demoralised, Conan lingered on a few more years until, in 1166, he sought permission from Henry to retire to his fief at Richmond in Yorkshire. With no sons, and his sister Constance certain to be married to a foreign lord, he realised that the game was up anyway. Henry nominated Constance's husband as a cipher duke and forced him to do homage to him personally for Britanny. At the conference at Montmirail in 1169 which ended the war between Henry and King Louis, Conan IV accepted that his daughter should be betrothed to Henry's son Geoffrey.[20] Realising that Britanny was now a lost cause, he chose to do homage to Henry rather than Louis as overlord of the duchy. Since the Devil's Brood had all done hierarchical homage among themselves and Henry II had made the meaningless gesture of accepting Louis as his feudal lord, it followed that a Breton knight now owed fealty to the following, in ascending order: Duchess Constance, daughter of Conan; to Geoffrey, her betrothed; to the Young King Henry, to whom Geoffrey had done homage; to the Old King (Henry II); and finally to King Louis. Unless all these were in agreement, our putative Breton knight was bound to end up acting treacherously to someone.

The arrangements for Henry II's first born proved particularly troublesome, especially as the machiavellian king tied them up with devious political manoeuvrings of his own. Both King Louis of France and the dukes of Normandy claimed the border territory between their domains along the lower Seine as part of their sovereign territory. These marches were known as the Vexin, and the Vexin became a regular and predictable bone of contention between Henry and Louis; possession of the frontier fortress of Gisors was particularly sought after. In 1151 Henry had been forced to cede Gisors to Louis but he always hankered after its return.[21] Thinking like a chess player, the cunning Henry contrived a way to get it back without force of arms. The key was the new Pope. The year 1159 saw a protracted struggle for the Apostolic Succession in Rome between Victor IV, backed by the German emperor, and Alexander III, backed by Louis of France; it was another papal schism, another year of pope and anti-pope of the kind that would bedevil the Middle Ages. Alexander feared that Henry II would back Victor against him as an automatic reaction to Louis's backing of his own candidacy. But Henry had taken soundings in England, which convinced him Victor was so unpopular there that his own endorsement of Victor would carry significant political risks for himself. Determined, therefore, to back Alexander, he pretended to be agonising over the choice so as to wring a crucial concession from the new Pope. Two cardinals visited Normandy to canvass support for Alexander, so Henry told them his recognition of Alexander would depend on the Pope's recognition of an immediate marriage between his son Henry and Margaret of France.[22] The marriage of a six-year-old boy to a four-year-old girl seemed on the face of it more than a little peculiar, especially as the would-be bride was the daughter of the groom's mother's first husband, but there was no obstacle in canon law, since the annulment of the union of Eleanor and Louis meant that in the Church's eyes no marriage had ever existed. Now Henry played his masterstroke. Louis could hardly oppose the wishes of a pontiff he had played such a major part in electing, so Henry insisted that Louis's daughter Margaret be given the fortress of Gisors as a dowry. The fortress would not actually pass into the hands of the English king's son until the marriage was celebrated, and in the meantime Gisors would be occupied by the Knights Templar as stakeholders. It did not take great sapience to foresee that the limbo period of the Templars would be a very short one – and this is indeed what transpired.[23]

Louis was furiously angry once he realised how he had been duped. Henry called in the papal favour immediately by achieving the marriage of young Henry on 2 November 1160. Louis mustered his forces for war but thought better of it and instead patched up an uneasy truce with the slippery Henry. But the 1160s found Henry obsessed with securing an undisputed succession for his eldest son. It was unfortunate for him that this decade also saw him locked in conflict with Thomas Becket, who was consecrated Archbishop of Canterbury in 1162. As Henry's relations with Becket worsened, he found himself in a dilemma for which not even his devious mind could compass a solution. Pope Alexander, now secure in his papal office, felt he had already adequately discharged his debt to Henry over the election, angering his ally Louis of France in the process, but now here was Henry asking him for two further major favours, mutually incompatible. Henry wanted his eldest son crowned king in his lifetime, as the Capetians liked to do, and he also wanted Becket transferred to a titular see where he could not intervene in politics. A weary Alexander explained that he could grant one of the two boons but not both, since a true coronation had to be performed by the Archbishop of Canterbury, following papal permission. Unable to cut the Gordian knot, Henry eventually had his son crowned king of England on 24 May 1170, with Becket's bitter rival Archbishop Roger of York officiating.[24] Thereafter young Henry was always known as the Young King to distinguish him from the Old King, his father and namesake. This coronation was a fiasco in another sense, apart from its dubious legality, for Margaret was unable to cross from France for the ceremony (some say she arrived late, others that she was deliberately delayed at Caen), leading Louis to suspect that Henry was trying to cut her out of the succession.[25] Fearing papal sanctions in the form of an interdict or excommunication, Henry came up with yet another ingenious plan. He offered Becket a peaceful return to England on a 'no fault' basis and the opportunity to recrown his son. Becket accepted at a meeting with the king in France on 22 July 1170.

Becket did not live to carry out a proper coronation, as he was murdered in Canterbury Cathedral on 29 December 1170. Henry came close to joining him in eternity the very same year. In August he lay seriously ill at Domfront in Normandy and thought likely to die. In a will drawn up at the time he confirmed the arrangements made with Louis at Montmirail the year before and codified some of the arrangements made then and since.[26] The young Henry's situation was regularised both by the dubious coronation and by the fact that he had already done homage to Louis's son Philip in his capacity as Louis's Seneschal. Geoffrey's position, too, was clearer, since in May 1169 the 10-year-old had crossed from England to Britanny and accepted the homage of the Bretons at Rennes; he received another bonus two years later when Conan the Little died, handing him the territory of Richmond in Yorkshire as well. But Richard, who had almost certainly not been present at Montmirail, received fresh confirmation as the heir of Gascony and Poitou. His position in the south had been further cemented with his betrothal at Montmirail to Lady Alice (Alys), second daughter of Louis of France by his second wife, Blanche of Castile.[27] The arrangement was that Alice was to be brought up in the land of her betrothed but, instead of sending her to Aquitaine, the devious Henry kept her with him at his own court, which spent most of the time travelling between England and Normandy. Henry's thinking in making the decisive tripartite division between his three eldest sons was that his 'empire' was actually too fractious and unruly to be governed from the centre, and this was particularly so in the south, which was so turbulent that it could not be managed from England or Normandy but only from Poitiers or Bordeaux. Henry was well aware of the Poitevins' taste for rebellion: it was commonly said that they had the hairy shins of wolves since they behaved like wolves to their neighbours. To keep the feudal pyramid coherent, Richard did homage for his holdings to Henry the Young King. So within a year Henry had done homage to Louis, Louis had invested the Young King with the Duchy of Normandy and the counties of Maine and Angers, and both Geoffrey and Richard in turn had done homage to the Young King. When Henry II recovered from the near-fatal illness, he was almost immediately consumed by the crisis arising from the murder of Becket. A year of public sorrow and contrition led in 1172 to his formal submission to the Pope at Avranches and his public absolution, after he swore that he had neither commanded nor desired Becket's death. In August the same year Henry the Young King was crowned again, this time with his wife Margaret alongside him, in Winchester Cathedral.[28]

Immediately after the reconciliation with the Church at Avranches, Henry turned his attention to the problems of Richard and John, and this was to lead to the greatest crisis of his reign. Henry had not so far paid much attention to the South during his reign, but now he decided to cut off King Louis from Spain and in the process neutralise his old enemy Count Raymond of Toulouse, who had been intriguing with Emperor Frederick Barbarossa of Germany to become lord of Provence. An axis comprising Louis, Raymond and Frederick Barbarossa was an alarming idea, so Henry acted decisively to nip this inchoate development in the bud. He began by neutralising Louis and Raymond's endeavours south of the Pyrenees by betrothing his daughter Eleanor to King Alfonso II of Castile. Then he sought a marriage for his son John with the daughter of Count Humbert of Maurienne, whose domains stretched from the shores of Lake Geneva to Turin, including all the Alpine passes between. The count, aware of his strategic position but desperately short of cash, agreed to a dowry of 5,000 marks and the recognition of John as his heir. Alarmed by this encirclement through dynastic marriage, both the king of Aragon-Barcelona and his long-term enemy Raymond of Toulouse suddenly saw the dangers of being destroyed piecemeal by the Angevin empire. Consequently, when Henry met Count Humbert at Montferrat in the Auvergne to discuss the details of John's marriage (January 1173), both King Sancho VI of Aragon-Castile and Count Raymond thought it politic to attend. Henry secured one of his greatest diplomatic triumphs when the great lords accompanied him back to Limoges. There, in February 1173, in company with Alfonso of Castile and his rival Sancho of Navarre, he not only received Count Raymond's homage for Toulouse but acted as 'honest broker' in arranging a peace treaty between Raymond and the king of Aragon.[29] His brilliant diplomacy made Richard's inheritance in Aquitaine even more secure, but there remained the problem of John. Henry had often joked that his youngest son should be called 'Lackland' as he lacked the vast territories his brothers commanded[30], but the joke backfired on Henry. On the journey to Limoges, Count Humbert had time to reflect on the rather one-sided marriage arrangements and asked rather pointedly what John would be contributing to the marriage. Caught off guard and on the spur of the moment, Henry incautiously said that, why, of course, John would be inheriting the castles of Chinon, Loudun and Mirebeau; on the spot he signed a document assigning this trio of fortresses to John.[31]

It was at this point that the Young King came clearly into the historical picture in his own right, having so far played the dutiful son. The

18-year-old was the original fairy-tale prince: popular in his time he has been a favourite of romancers ever since and was the only one of the Devil's Brood not to attract harsh criticism. To begin with, he was tall, fair and good-looking: 'the most handsome prince in all the world, whether Saracen or Christian'.[32] Looking like a northerner but with the southerner's traditional taste for frivolity and dissipation, charismatic, affable, courteous, benign, charming, young Henry was a creature of romance in more senses than one. A devotee of tournaments, he filled his kingdoms with jousts and thus enhanced the status of knights. 'Henry the Young King made chivalry live again, for she was dead or nearly so. He was the door by which she entered. He was her standard bearer. In those days the great did nothing for young men. He set an example and kept men of worth by his side. And when men of high degree saw how he brought together all men of worth they were amazed at his wisdom and followed his lead.'[33] Yet against these undoubted advantages, the Young King had many grave faults. He was vain, shallow, irresponsible and impatient, a man who wanted the good things of life *now* and was unwilling to wait. A hedonist and wastrel, permanently in debt, he was prodigal, improvident, insouciant and foolish; the notion of paying his way or balancing budgets was unknown to him. Henry had tried to train him in court politics and administration, especially after the first coronation in 1170, but the young man proved an unwilling apprentice, lazy, incompetent and empty-headed. As with most charismatic figures, he was given the benefit of the doubt, and sagacious observers, bedazzled by his charm and magnetism, put their intellectual faculties on hold and indulged in a primitive form of sun worship. Henry was bored by everything that did not involve adventure, pleasure or high excitement of all kinds. Essentially a case of arrested development, the Young King always remained a child at heart, a hopeless politician, incapable of thinking things through or calculating several moves in advance like his father, unable to concentrate on anything serious. Like many weak men he took advice from the last person he had spoken to and then changed his mind as successive opinions were delivered.[34]

It is clear that, at least when his son was a youth, Henry II idolised the young man. His desire to decentralise his empire was sound but his understanding of human nature was poor for, by dividing his domains and setting up his sons as rivals to his power, even ordering his vassals to do homage to them, he was putting irresistible temptations in front of them; some writers have suggested that he committed the classic King Lear mistake. But the Young King did not lack malicious advisers who urged him to assert himself against his father. Shortly after the second coronation and before Henry II's great conference at Limoges, where he made the incautious promise to give John the three castles, Henry the Young King had a meeting with King Louis (November 1172), who mischievously urged him to assert himself as a king in fact as well as name now that he had been crowned.[35] Perhaps an even more salient influence on the Young King were the troubadours, the propagandists of chivalry itself. Throughout the Young King's life the troubadour Bertran de Born was never far away, fanning discontent between father and son for his own reasons. 'I would that the great men should always be quarrelling among themselves', he wrote, in a highly revealing statement.[36] Some have always seen Bertran de Born as the evil genius behind the Young King. The classic medieval statement is in Dante's vision of Hell, where the troubadour is found in the eighth circle, walking with his head in his hand, swinging it by the hair as if it were a lantern. Dante puts the following words into his mouth: 'I am Bertran de Born, he that gave to the Young King the ill encouragement. I made father and son rebellious to each other. Achithophel did not more with Absalom and David by his wicked goadings. Because I divided persons so united, I bear my brain, alas!, divided from its source which is in this trunk.'[37]

But the influence of the troubadours, real or alleged (and it probably was real), cannot alone explain the scope and extent of the Young King's discontents. Young Henry had about him in his own dissolute court his own version of the young Prince Henry V's Poins, Pistol, Bardolph, Peto and Falstaff; in this as in other ways the relationship of Henry II and his son uncannily pre-echoes that of Henry IV and Henry V, and all the evidence suggests that these 'irregular humorists' constantly stirred the pot about their master's political impotence. It angered the Young King that his father would give him no real power and that when he gave an order to his father's agents and officials in England, it was habitually disregarded. He was supposed to be the crowned king of England and had received the homages of Normandy and Anjou, yet his father had assigned no lands whose revenue would allow him and his queen to live in the proper state. His father chose the members of his household and had even had the 'impertinence' to dimiss one of them.[38] His explicit demand for his inheritance had been brushed aside as a poor joke on two occasions when he lobbied his father. Henry's answer presumably would have been that he had tried to give his son responsibility but he had shirked it; a true king needed to be administratively competent, not just a showpiece figurehead in glittering finery. Yet the putative answer is unconvincing: Henry should have taken the measure of his son's failings before promoting him so high so fast. Another grievance was that Henry would not allow him unlimited access to money to fund his lavish lifestyle. He had to borrow money from private sources, usually Jewish moneylenders who in this era were despised as much for the sin (so defined in canon law) of Usury as for being 'the killers of Christ'. To make matters worse, the moneylenders regarded Henry's son as a bad risk, since he had no real security in his lands and possessions.[39]

Then there was the fact that Henry and Pope Alexander had made all the decisions about the archbishopric of Canterbury without consulting him. Shortly after his first coronation Henry had met Becket at a famous conference at Freteval on the borders of Touraine in France and agreed to the terms of the exiled archbishop's return to England. Reasons of high politics and relations with the papacy were involved in Henry's decision to seek a compromise, but one of the terms accepted was that Becket would be able to discipline the archbishop of York and the bishops of London and Salisbury who had assisted at the first coronation of the Young King. Becket's heavy-handed excommunication of all three clerics (with the authority of a papal bull) just before he crossed the Channel was one of the precipitants towards his murder at the end of the same year, but what infuriated the Young King was that the divines who had officiated at his own coronation had now been branded ecclesiastical outlaws. Pointedly he refused to receive Becket at Windsor when the archbishop returned to England. The restoration of harmony with the Pope and the appointment of the new Archbishop of Canterbury in 1170–72 had likewise been carried out without any consultation with the Young King.[40] But most of all the Young King enviously compared his own career unfavourably with that of his father when a young man; at seventeen Henry II had been ruling fatherless in Normandy and now the Young King was already nearly two years older than when Geoffrey of Anjou had handed over the duchy of Normandy to his son. There was the added consideration that Henry II was still only forty. How long would the Young King have to wait? Now came the last straw: the demand for the castles of Chinon, Loudun and Mirebeau. This was a grotesque interference in the Young King's domain, and was anyway a transparent ruse whereby Henry wrested back control of three key fortresses from an eldest son who had angered him both by his peremptory demands and his intrigues with King Louis. The Young King would have none of it. Not only did he not give his consent, as Count of Anjou, to the handover but he used the occasion to demand, yet again, the real transfer of some part of the lands he had supposedly inherited: it did not matter which – it could be England, Normandy or Anjou.[41] And so the six-year-old John became the pretext for a mighty struggle between the two Henrys. As one historian has noted, the issue of the castles 'stirred up a trouble which was never again to be laid wholly to rest until the child who was its as yet innocent cause had broken his father's heart'.[42] The Young King, a poor politician, showed his hand by telling his father that King Louis and the barons of Normandy and England wanted the transfer of lands. The shrewd Henry II immediately realised that this was no sudden temper tantrum by his son but part of a long-planned and deeply-plotted manoeuvre. He therefore insisted that the Young King accompany him on his progress north to Normandy. As yet, he did not realise how far the tentacles of the plot reached, so left his wife with Geoffrey and Richard at Poitiers. This was despite a warning from the two-faced Raymond of Toulouse – who had been stirring the pot with Richard and Eleanor – that his entire family was ranged against him: 'I advise you, King, to beware of your wife and sons.' A conspiracy of such dimensions seemed incredible, so Henry concentrated on the Young King, virtually dragging him and his entourage with him as far as Chinon. There, on 5 March 1173, the Young King bribed the castle guards to lower the drawbridge, allowing him and his followers to decamp by night. There followed a long and breathless pursuit across what is now north-west France, across the Loire, towards Normandy, through Le Mans, Alençon and Argentan. But it was all in vain: on 8 March the Young King crossed the French border and headed for Paris. Henry II sent a deputation of bishops across the frontier to demand his son's return. In a famous scene, King Louis asked the envoys who had sent them on such a bizarre errand. They replied that it was the king of England who sent them. 'What nonsense,' Louis replied, 'the king of England is here. His father may still pose as king, but that will soon be over, for all the world knows he has resigned his kingdom to his son.'[43]

To his consternation and stupefaction Henry II now realised that his wife Eleanor, his sons Richard and Geoffrey and other great magnates were all in league with Louis. Geoffrey, almost fifteen, was already revealing his true serpentine nature; it seems he had ambitions for an independent Britanny. He also saw the chance to indulge his taste for plundering and looting, which was to be so marked a feature of his career. Some claim that Geoffrey was the most intelligent of the Devil's Brood but he was certainly the one without any redeeming features. He

accepted evil as an irreducible fact of life and even revelled in the knowledge. He seemed to have something of a grudge against the Church,
perhaps because it preached the triumph of good and the doctrine of
redemption, but it is certain that he took a particular relish in sacking
and despoiling churches, abbeys and shrines. Richard and his Poitevin
allies were meanwhile angry that at the great meeting with the southern
powers at Limoges on 21–28 February, when Henry II achieved his great
diplomatic triumph, Count Raymond had paid homage for Toulouse to
the king of England rather than to himself, the lord of Aquitaine, whose
right to Toulouse had already been recognised by King Louis. But all
three sons had, in their own minds at least, compelling motives for rising
up against their father. The spectre of anarchy and chaos, never far from
the surface in the Angevin empire, was once more abroad. It seemed
that yet another of those ancient prophecies of Merlin in which Roger
of Howden, convinced believer in miracles and the supernatural, so
delighted was about to be fulfilled: 'The cubs shall awake and shall roar
loud, and, leaving the woods, shall seek their prey within the walls of
the cities. Among those who shall be in their way they shall make great
carnage, and shall tear out the tongues of bulls. The necks of them as
they roar aloud they shall load with chains, and shall thus renew the
times of their forefathers.'[44]

Yet it was the defection of Eleanor of Aquitaine that most shocked
contemporaries. It was a seismic event that seemed to betoken the swal-
lowing up of the natural world by a realm of chaos, for such unwifely
behaviour seemed against the laws of Nature themselves. Ralph of
Diceto, dean of St Paul's, seeking for parallels for the events of 1173–74,
claimed to have found more than thirty examples of sons rebelling against
fathers but none of queens raising the standard of revolt against their
kings and husbands.[45] Peter of Blois, one of Henry II's political protégés
(he had whisked him from the Norman court in Sicily to serve as his
secretary), an erudite, witty, acidulous man and a noted literary stylist,
reminded Eleanor in a letter of all the famous biblical injunctions
requiring a wife to obey her husband and pointed out that many ecclesiastical sanctions, including, at the limit, excommunication could be exercised against her for this 'sin'. Invoking the chaos principle, he wrote:
'Unless you return to your husband you will be the cause of general
ruin.'[46] More patronising commentators, citing 'woman's weakness'
asserted that, although she was responsible for her sons' rebellion, she
was more sinned against than sinning. The usual story was that she had
been misled by her uncle and confidant Ralph de Faye, seneschal of

Poitou, who was well known to favour Aquitainian separatism and to be a major influence on her.[47] But Eleanor was her own woman and needed no *éminence grise* to seduce her down unwise byways. We know for certain that the decision to rebel was hers and hers alone; for one thing, her sons Richard and Geoffrey would have listened to their mother but would not have heeded mere counsellors, even ones as eminent as Ralph de Faye. Given that Eleanor was the guiding spirit of the conspiracy and that Richard, the classic mother's boy, would do all in all as she did, the only remaining question is, why did Eleanor act as she did?

A variety of explanations has been offered, and we have to work upwards or inwards towards the most plausible. The most far-fetched is the suggestion that Becket's murder was the trigger for Eleanor's rebellious actions. The idea is that Eleanor's apostasy was so sudden – she had spent most of 1170 supporting Henry's policies – that we must seek a key event between December 1170 and the revolt in 1173, and that event could only have been Becket's assassination.[48] Presumably, the thinking is that for the first time Eleanor saw Henry for the monster he was and noted how in the opinion of all Europe he was a moral pariah. Eleanor did not see Henry for two years until the Christmas court of 1172, and some dramatists have seized on this court as *the* decisive moment when the marriage unravelled in a dramatic way, perhaps following a row about the king's plans for her beloved Richard, when she might have taunted him for his tyranny and the murder of Becket. The trouble with this argument is that by 1172 Henry had won European opinion round by his abject obeisance to the Pope and his obvious contrition for the murder, which he never authorised.[49] Moreover, Eleanor and her sons were never particularly close to Becket, so the entire theory seems a *post hoc* contrivance. More promising is the idea that Eleanor deeply resented her position as a non-entity in the reign and government of Henry II, that she came to feel she had miscalculated by her marriage to the king, which brought her neither the power nor influence she assumed to be her due; maybe Henry's overpowering mother Empress Matilda, who did not die until 1167, was a factor in this.[50] The only snag with this idea is that it does not explain why Eleanor rose in revolt in 1173 rather than at some earlier time, and, if she was really vexed by Matilda, she would presumably have wished to wipe the smile off her face before her demise. In a word, chronology works against an argument from purely personal pique.

Similar considerations apply to one of the most popular of all motifs allegedly explaining the rebellion of 1173: the 'hell hath no fury' theme, according to which Eleanor could finally take no more of Henry's infidelities and particularly the serious long-standing liaison with Rosamund Clifford. The affair with 'Fair Rosamund' seems to have begun in 1165 and continued until her death in 1176.[51] Of Henry's passionate love for Rosamund there can be little doubt, as in 1191 we still hear of her tomb, covered in silk cloth, being devotedly attended by the nuns of Godstow Priory; Henry had made this a condition of a generous gift to the convent. The legend of Eleanor of Aquitaine makes her out to have been incandescent with fury over this liaison and to have murdered Rosamund. One story has her personally tearing the mistress's eyes out and another coldly offering the trapped paramour the choice between poison or the knife. What none of the myths explain is how Eleanor could have accomplished all this while she was Henry's close prisoner. Yet even if we discard all this nonsense and admit her powerlessness in the matter of Rosamund, it is still possible that Eleanor was that figure beloved of romance: the sexually jealous, vengeful woman. 'Eleanor did not take revenge by murdering Rosamond; she did it by raising Poitou,' is one modern verdict.[52] Another writer concurs: 'Henry had broken faith: he had prized lechery above creative sharing, and now the joy of courtly love was gone forever.'[53] But one does not have to be a feminist to find this view of Eleanor deeply patronising and insulting, and it is indeed absurd to imagine Eleanor motivated to revolt in this way.[54] She was a woman of the world and had made a hard-headed match with Henry right at the start, though doubtless sexual attraction played its part. And it is somewhat anachronistic to import the 'wronged woman' scenario into the snakepit of twelfth-century politics. Any intelligent queen – and no one has ever denied Eleanor that epithet – accepted that her husband would have mistresses; indeed, according to the troubadour code, true love between husband and wife was impossible anyway.

Perhaps this alerts us to the true motive for rebellion. Maybe the 1173 rebellion had nothing to do with the collision of personalities but instead represented a clash of cultures? According to this view, Aquitaine, home of the troubadours, represented hedonism, dalliance, the cult of open-handed largesse, the sentimentality expressed in the *aubades* when a lover departs from his lady in the dawn's early light, a milieu of music, dancing, tournaments, knight-errants and fair damsels in distress, while Henry's dominions to the north symbolised sobriety and joylessness, the world of the quotidian, of stubborn and irreducible facts, the boring domain of penny-pinching accountants, nit-picking lawyers and pedantic administrators, scouring the latest royal writs for loopholes and escape clauses. It was the cult of adultery against the institution of marriage, neo-paganism against the doctrines of the Church and, ultimately, the world of the female and feminine values against the male and masculine ideals.[55] Why else was the Young King permanently in debt, except that his open-handed generosity was in collision with the mean-mindedness of the North? But the myth of Aquitaine as a kind of Camelot *avant la lettre* and courtly love as a dominant ideology has been taken too seriously by some historians.[56] Moreover, the idea of an 'aesthetic' Eleanor ranged against a 'philistine' Henry falls foul of the obvious objection that Henry in fact commissioned more artists and poets than she did – he had more money – and even Bertrand de Ventadour wrote more for Henry than for Eleanor.[57]

When we have discarded all the fanciful scenarios for Eleanor's defection in 1173, there remains the overwhelming probability that she was motivated solely by her concern for Aquitaine and the fear that it was being absorbed anonymously in Henry's Angevin empire. Eleanor loved her southern domains, and many scholars think that in the twelfth century Aquitaine was the most important territory in what is now France, certainly wealthier than King Louis's 'France' and more important for a would-be empire builder than either Normandy or England.[58] In this context the homage sworn by Raymond of Toulouse may have been the real precipitant for her rebellion. It was true that at Limoges Raymond had done homage to Richard but he had also done homage to the Young King. Well aware of the Anglophobe feeling among Poitou nobles – a definite cause of the death of Earl Patrick of Salisbury – she knew that they, as well as she, resented any implication that there was a pyramid of power and influence that placed England and Normandy above Aquitaine. It may even be that her anger was more furiously concentrated by the ceremony at Limoges, for the dukes of Aquitaine had always claimed Toulouse and yet there was Count Raymond offering homage and so, by implication, reinforcing a de jure claim to Toulouse, repudiating her own claims. The fact that Henry was backsliding for Anglo-Norman and Angevin *raison d'état* may also have occurred to her; it was unlikely to have slipped her mind that the king had been prepared to fight for Toulouse in 1159 but no longer.[59] At any rate we know for certain that Eleanor was the guiding hand behind the conspiracy, for Richard and Geoffrey, at fifteen and fourteen respectively, would not have rallied to anyone else in defiance of their father.

The anti-Henry alliance that Eleanor had revised was formidable. There was no question here of some comic-opera palace revolution;

instead there was the most deadly threat that Henry II ever faced. The motives of the rebels were bewilderingly heterogeneous, mainly to do with strictly local ambitions and grievances. In Normandy and England there were particular discontents about the technicalities of knight-service, with Henry trying to change the rules so that the barons were forced to supply more men. He also ruffled feathers by trying to elimi-nate corruption in Normandy via a new form of Domesday Book. Ralph of Diceto says that most men joined the Young King 'not because they regarded him as the juster cause, but because the father . . . was tramp-ling upon the necks of the proud and haughty, was dismantling or appro-priating the castles of the country, and was requiring, even compelling those who occupied properties which should have contributed to his treasury, to be content with their patrimony.'[60] Of the southern lords, apart from Ralph de Faye, Count William of Angoulême, Geoffrey and Guy of Lusignan and Geoffrey de Taillebourg, lord of Parthenay, enlisted under the rebel banner. Farther north Count Théobald of Blois, Matthew, count of Boulogne and his elder brother Count Philip of Flanders pledged their support to the Young King. In England four magnates declared for him: the earls of Norfolk, Leicester, Chester and Derby. Ralph de Fougères raised Britanny in rebellion against Henry. But it was the support of the kings of France and Scotland that seemed most likely to portend success for the Young King. For the first time ever all parts of the Angevin empire were in simultaneous revolt, and Henry was aware that there were many ambivalent nobles who were sitting on the fence, waiting to see how events turned out. Particular suspicions were enter-tained about Richard de Clare, lord of Leinster, about the king's cousin Earl William of Gloucester, and also the bishops of Durham and Lisieux.[61] The chronicler Roger of Howden took the view that all who were not with Henry were against him and, on this basis, roundly declared: 'nearly all the earls and barons of England, Normandy, Aquitaine, Anjou and Britanny rose against the king of England the father'.[62] In Paris Louis summoned a great council of French barons to pledge support to the Young King, and in return Young Henry and his brothers swore never to make peace with their father unless King Louis and the French barons had consented.[63] Horsetrading, not to mention chicken-counting, was the order of the day at the council, as the great lords extracted their pound of flesh for their support, in the form of lands, estates and castles.

Never a man to panic, Henry II calmly stood on the defensive, waiting to see what his enemies would do. His situation would have been perilous indeed, if there had been a first-class military mind directing the coalition, as he simply did not have the manpower to cover all the potential theatres of war. It would have been easy to catch Henry between two fires, depriving him of any local military supremacy, and he would have been forced to act lest the fence-sitters concluded he was losing and started stampeding to join the Young King. On paper, then, he had few obvious cards to play. What he did have was vast financial resources and, as a consequence of this, a fearsome battle-hardened army of ruthless mercenaries of alien tongue – Basques, Brabançons, Navarrese, Germans. The role of mercenaries was crucial in medieval warfare. They were usually either crossbowmen or light horsemen, armoured in mail, unable to face charging knights. These 'routiers' were essential for siegework, as knights got bored with it and could not be disciplined; mercenaries on the other hand, once paid, had either to obey orders or be hanged. Routiers were regarded as low-lives, beyond the pale, condemned to eternal damnation by the Church, since in canon law a man who risked his life for wages was a kind of suicide. A mercenary was automatically excommunicate, whereas a vassal following his liege lord escaped theological anathema because he was merely fulfilling his feudal obligation to a superior. Only real thugs and gangsters served as mercenaries; when not employed they banded together as highwaymen or 'routiers' properly so-called, to loot, rape and plunder. They were largely recruited from the Low Countries, where there was surplus population. Such was Henry's secret weapon.[64]

Henry also took heart from the failure of large parts of faction-ridden Aquitaine to join his enemies – they used the civil war as a golden opportunity to pursue ancient feuds that Henry's rule had hitherto dampened down – and from his low opinion of King Louis's strategic skills. In this last judgement he was soon proved correct. Instead of coordinating simultaneous assaults on all parts of the Angevin empire, in May Louis and the Young King began operations with a less than inspired three-pronged probe into eastern Normandy, which gave Richard his first taste of battle; the idea was that all three armies would converge on Rouen while Earl Hugh of Chester led the Bretons in the west on a diversionary thrust. The Young King invested the castle of Gournay, Louis of France besieged Verneuil, while Philip of Flanders, commanding the northern operation, laid siege to Drincourt but lost heart after his brother Matthew of Boulogne was killed by a sniper's crossbow quarrel at the end of August, and ordered a retreat. Louis ordered all coalition forces to pull back, but this was a grave error. Sensing that his moment had come, Henry made one of his lightning counter-attacks, first routing King Louis's rearguard near Vernueil, then turning rapidly westwards to bottle up the Breton rebels at Dol, west of Avranches, in eastern Britanny. The Bretons had imagined themselves to be along for the easiest of rides but now, panic-stricken at Henry's forced marches, they lost their nerve and surrendered without a fight; Earl Hugh and Ralph de Fougeres became Henry's first prize captives of the campaign.[65]

The outcome was much as Henry had hoped and imagined. Louis, a man who liked easy victories, became despondent and put out peace feelers. A conference was held at Gisors, where Henry offered generous terms to his sons: four castles and half the revenues of Aquitaine to Richard, with similar proposals to Geoffrey and the Young King. He was even prepared to increase the revenues on the decision of an independent arbitrator but adamantly refused to waive his overall jurisdiction.[66] Louis advised the sons to reject the terms, for Earl Robert of Leicester had put fire in his belly and proposed a new stratagem. The earl crossed to Norfolk with a force of Flemings and joined the English rebels at Framlingham. The grand rendezvous point for all the Young King's English supporters was to be Leicester, but, as the East Anglian force under Earl Robert marched west, it was intercepted and defeated by a scratch force loyal to Henry II that was said to have been outnumbered four to one. Great slaughter ensued in the fens, and Earl Robert joined the lengthening roster of rebel captives. Freed from immediate anxieties in England, Henry campaigned in Touraine and on the Loire during November–January 1173–74, ignoring the usual 'winter quarters' break from fighting. After leading his Brabançons in a thrust south of Chinon, taking the castles of La Haye, Preuilly and Champigny and threatening the lands of Ralph de Faye, he had another of those amazing strokes of luck that always seemed to attend him. His wife Eleanor tried to escape from the war zone and join her sons, but on the road from Poitiers to Paris was captured while disguised as a man, betrayed, some said, by Henry's secret agents in Poitou; henceforth she would be Henry's prisoner and never see freedom again until his death. Meanwhile, a major French attack on the nodal town of Séez in southern Normandy was also beaten off by his forces. By the spring of 1174 the initiative seemed to lie with Henry, and Louis's defeatism was again pronounced.[67]

Henry could now afford to regroup, retrench and consolidate. Louis dithered over his next move right through spring and into summer. Finally, he opted for the strategy he should have employed from the very beginning. To draw Henry from his position in Normandy, the coalition would have to mount a major threat to England and this time the omens were propitious, for King William of Scotland was finally ready to make his move. In collusion with northern rebels under Roger de Mowbray and secretly advised by the bishop of Durham, William crossed the border, laid siege to Carlisle and proceeded to gobble up a string of lesser castles at Liddell, Burgh, Appleby, Harbottle and Warkworth. Yet the war in England soon bogged down in an inconclusive struggle in the Midlands, centring around the rebel stronghold of Leicester, with coalition forces maybe just having the edge for a while. But King William's campaign in the north-east was running out of steam, with Carlisle, held for Henry II, still defiant, and meanwhile King Henry's bastard son scored a crushing victory over Roger de Mowbray, who was trying to link up with the rebel core at Leicester.[68] And still Henry remained unperturbed in Normandy, refusing to cross the Channel and provide Louis with the opportunity he yearned for: another invasion of the northern Angevin empire. The coalition therefore braced itself for what it hoped would be the masterstroke: a substantial invasion of England to be led by Count Philip of Flanders and his Flemings. Finally alarmed by this, Henry sailed from Barfleur to England on 7 July. When the coalition learned of his arrival, they foolishly did not press on with the invasion plan and instead Philip of Flanders joined Louis for a large-scale assault on eastern Normandy and Rouen.[69]

Yet even while they drew up their forces outside Rouen, Henry enjoyed yet another slice of his almost supernatural good luck. On arrival in England, the king visited Becket's tomb at Canterbury and, barefoot and fasting, submitted to a public scourging, to show that the cause of the rebels had nothing to do with vindicating the cause of St Thomas. A few days later it seemed that God had given him the nod of approval. On 13 July King William of Scotland and his knights were surprised in the mist near Alnwick by a scratch force of loyalists; among the few who survived the resultant slaughter was William himself. The capture of the Scottish king tore the heart out of the rebels, who felt themselves accursed. Henry moved rapidly down to the Midlands, where the opposition collapsed like a house of cards.[70] So easy was his victory that the king was back in Barfleur on 8 August, just a month after he had departed. Thinking he had all the time in the world, Louis had gone about the siege of Rouen in a leisurely fashion, and now he was taken in the rear. So desperate was Louis to seize Rouen that he tried to take the city by trickery, breaking the sacred terms of a truce as part of the subterfuge, but just failing, again in the most aleatory circumstances. When Henry and his army arrived next day and began mauling the French troops, Louis once more lost heart and retreated. By the end of September he was suing for peace.[71] As King Henry's treasurer gloatingly remarked: 'So the mighty learned that to wrest the club from the hand of Hercules was no easy task.'[72]

Yet if Louis so signally bowed the head to a greater general, the 16-year-old Richard was made of sterner stuff. The capture of his mother seems to have enraged him so that the iron entered his soul. In the spring of 1174 he tried to capture the great mercantile centre of La Rochelle, using the trading rivalry of nearby Saintes against it. But the young Richard was no match for his father, who made another of his lightning swoops, westward, while Richard imagined he was celebrating Whitsun in Poitiers. Richard and a handful of followers made an undignified scramble to escape and fled downstream to the castle of Taillebourg, leaving behind most of his military stores and equipment, to say nothing of his best knights and archers captured in Saintes.[73] But the Scottish king's debacle and Louis's weakness soon left the young duke of Aquitaine out on a limb. The three-week truce between Louis and Henry on 8 September expressly excluded Richard, who now became king Henry's target. Not daring to face his father in battle, Richard steadily retreated, increasingly at a loss and angry as he realised the scale of his desertion by Louis and the Young King. Finally convinced that his cause was lost, on 23 September Richard threw himself on his father's mercy. Weeping, he prostrated himself before the king and begged forgiveness.[74] Henry raised him up and gave him the kiss of peace, but punished him by more stringent terms than those refused at Gisors. At the reconvened conference on 29 September at Montlouis (between Tours and Amboise), Richard accepted half the revenues of Aquitaine but only two non-castellated demesnes. The Young King did much better: two castles in Normandy and £15,000 annually. On the other hand, he was forced to accept the conditions that had originally propelled him into rebellion: he had to grant John the disputed castles and revenues in England, Normandy and Anjou.[75]

Henry II's indulgence to his rebellious sons, akin to Napoleon's notorious connivance at his brothers' faults and crimes, to say nothing of his leniency towards other rebel leaders, attracted astonished comment at the time, and not everyone approved his merciful approach. It was said that he should have followed up his advantage by smiting King Louis hip and thigh and, in particular, that he should have extirpated the troublesome Flemings. Yet Henry was as good as his word: he made peace on the basis of how things were before the war began, except that he insisted on demolishing a swathe of rebel castles. It was said that after 1174 ruined castles could be seen throughout the Angevin empire, visible testaments to Henry's determination that his supreme power could not be denied.[76] But there were no executions or forfeitures and the king did not levy ransoms for those captured in battle. By 1177 even those rebel lords who had been most uncompromising in their opposition to Henry were free once more: the earls of Chester and Leicester, Ralph de Fougeres. King William of Scotland paid the heaviest price for the events of 1173–74: he had to declare himself Henry's liegeman, to make a public submission at York and to surrender five castles in Scotland. Henry did, however, draw the line at declaring himself overlord of Scotland or intervening in Scottish affairs.[77] All this was misconstrued by those who habitually confuse restraint with weakness. Henry's motives for smoothing things over were simply that he did not want an endless cycle of war and civil disturbance, which a draconian reaction to the rebellion would certainly have engendered, and he was concerned that the barons who had taken no part in the rebellion on either side had converted themselves into local warlords, largely free of royal influence. He derived immediate satisfaction in other ways, tightening up central government, making tax evasion more difficult, taking a hard line on the forest laws. Above all, he made sure that men loyal to him occupied every castle in England.[78]

But he could not long allow the 'neutral' magnates to be virtual kings in their own domains, and this problem was particularly acute in Aquitaine, where most of the great barons had held aloof during the armed struggle of 1173–74. It soon became abundantly clear that they had not had the slightest interest in the cause of the Young King, but had simply used his revolt as an excuse to throw off the Old King's overlordship. It may be that Henry was particularly impressed by the cool-headed way the 17-year-old Richard had handled himself during the latter stages of the rebellion, for in January 1175 the king sent his second son to Aquitaine with a dual set of orders: he was to raze all castles occupied by the rebels during the rebellion and he was to bring to heel the neutral lords who now bade fair to turn their bailiwicks into independent principalities.[79] In effect Henry appointed Richard his Regent in the south, with full powers over all Angevin armed forces there and all revenues and officials. There was a prime irony here, in that Richard was turning against some of the very people he had urged to rebel against his father, but Henry had given him a bed of nails, since the 'independent' lords of Aquitaine were arrogant, contumacious and self-confident, not having tasted the horrors

visited on Normandy, Britanny and the north by the combination of
mercenaries and blitzkrieg. Richard at once proved his calibre and evinced
a genius at siegecraft by reducing the powerful castle of Agillon-sur-Agen,
even though his critics have always tried to belittle this feat, on the grounds
that the castellan, Arnold of Bouteville, was not a major baron.[80]

At first he was able to pick off his enemies one by one, but by the
beginning of 1176 they had made common cause, presenting a formidable coalition of southern barons: the count of Angoulême, Viscount
Aimar of Limoges, Viscount Raymond of Turenne and the lords of
Chabanais and Mastac. Even the dauntless Richard soon found the task
beyond him, and went to England in April 1176 to consult his father on
the next step. Henry made available large sums of money and fresh
cohorts of mercenaries, only to find that his opponents in turn had hired
a force of Brabançons, commanded by the count of Angoulême's eldest
son, Vulgrin Taillefer.[81] On his return to the continent, Richard hastened
to meet this force in Poitou and defeated it in May at Bouteville near
Angoulême.[82] Pressing on to Limoges, then a city in two parts, Richard
cunningly made use of the ancient rivalry between 'city' and 'citadel' (the
two different parts of the town) to force its capitulation after a couple
of days' siege. Early in July the Young King joined him at Poitiers. Young
Henry had petitioned his father for permission to make a pilgrimage to
Santiago de Compostela, but the Old King suspected this was just a ploy
to enable his eldest son to raise another rebellion. He therefore ordered
him to assist his brother in the Aquitaine campaign. The Young King,
however, flounced off once he had got a taste of Richard's martial
ability. He did not like campaigning, resented being under Richard's orders,
and was jealous of his military talents.[83] Undeterred, Richard took the
castles of Châteauneuf and Moulinef and then pressed on to Angoulême
for a final reckoning with Aimar, Angoulême, Chabanais and the others.
Bottled up in the citadel these grandees seemed to have nothing to lose by
fighting on, and desperate combat was expected in a last-ditch stand, but
the rebels surrendered tamely after just six days. Richard sent the great
lords prisoner to England for Henry to deal with; at Winchester on 21
September 1176 William of Angoulême and the other Aquitaine rebels
had to make the self-same obeisance on their knees that the humbled
Richard had endured two years earlier.[84] But Richard was already a military hero as a result of this campaign; truly he had won his spurs.

By 1176 the career of Henry II fully justified his treasurer's boast
that he was 'the greatest of the illustrious rulers of the world'.[85] He had
decisively relegated Louis of France to second place, and even the great

Frederick Barbarossa, Holy Roman Emperor, was no longer the colossus of yore after his defeat at Legnano by the Lombard League in this very same year. Henry's fame had spread to the point where in November 1176 his court at Westminster received envoys from Barbarossa, from Emperor Manuel Comnenus in Constantinople, the duke of Savoy and the count of Flanders. He was clearly recognised as a power broker in Spain, and the kings of Aragon and Castile asked him to act as arbiter in all their disputes, pledging themselves to abide faithfully by any decision. Even the king of Sicily was interested in Europe's new supremo, and asked for the hand of his daughter Joan in marriage.[86] For the first time in its history England was a major European power. Henry and his second son were both recognised as great warriors. But the 19-year-old Richard was already showing himself to be a very different proposition from his 46-year-old father. Henry waged war only when he had to.[87] Richard, on the other hand, loved war and everything about it, clearly placing himself on a line that runs through history from Alexander the Great to General George Patton. The shrewd Gerald of Wales put his finger on the fundamental flaw in Richard's personality, which was that he 'cared for no success that was not reached by a path cut by his own sword and stained with the blood of his adversaries'.[88] Even if Aquitaine had not been a notorious cockpit of anarchy, the omens for peaceful resolution of its problems were not favourable.

3

◁○▷

As Henry II approached the medieval equivalent of old age in his mid-forties, he tried as far as possible to take a back seat in the administration of his dominions, hoping that active involvement in the Angevin empire could be left to his sons. His basic plan was that the Young King would continue to be groomed for the succession, which made England his main sphere of influence; Geoffrey would act as the king's deputy in Normandy and Britanny and Richard would rule in Aquitaine. Roughly speaking, one might say that Henry aimed at a kind of Angevin federalism, where each province would be self-governing and even have its own coinage. But his federalism was always the strong federalism of an interventionist monarch, not the weak version of one who was tired of life or politics. He was prepared to cut a lot of slack for his restless sons, but would not tolerate the same latitude being given by the sons towards subject lords. And his own restlessness often worked against his basic project. In the late 1170s he was concerned to bring Aquitaine finally under effective central control and he also began to dabble in Spanish affairs. Given that Richard already faced a thornier problem than Geoffrey – for in Aquitaine there was simply Henry's nominal overlordship and a lot of internally independent vassals – Henry's expectations placed greater stresses on Richard's shoulders than on those of his brothers. It would be an exaggeration to call the situation in Aquitaine anarchy, but there were no strong central structures of law and politics there, as in England, Normandy or Anjou and, moreover, the south had not yet felt Henry's mailed fist, as this area had not been the cockpit of the struggle against King Louis of France.[1] In the years before Richard was formally recognised as duke of Aquitaine – in 1179 – all this began to change.

As a military leader Richard was improving all the time. Since Henry was keen to intervene in the affairs of Spain, he began by ordering Richard to make sure the road from Bordeaux south to the Pyrenees was as secure as roads at the height of the Roman or Mongol empires. Clearing the farrago of bandits, feudal levies and rebellious lords from the traditional pilgrim route meant sustained warfare. Basing himself at Bordeaux for the Christmas feast of 1176, Richard swept south early in the new year and laid siege to Dax and Bayonne while his armies of Brabançons trawled the entire territory from Bordeaux to Cize on the Spanish border. Having emulated his father with a stunning winter campaign, waged over the Christmas festivities when no one was ever supposed to be on the warpath, Richard prematurely announced that the pacification of Aquitaine was complete and discharged his mercenaries.[2] No longer on the payroll, the savage Brabançons began to pillage and plunder the countryside. The backlash was severe: an 'army of peace' organised by the disgruntled clergy and nobility caught the Brabançon marauders off guard near Brive and slaughtered them mercilessly.[3] Henry thought that Richard had his hands full in the far south, so sent the Young King on an auxiliary mission to bring to heel the rebellious territory of Berry in north-east Aquitaine. Here was yet another collision between Angevin centralising power and local folkways. Ralph de Deols, lord of Berry, died and left his daughter as sole heiress. In England an unmarried heiress was at the disposal of her overlord, who could marry her off to a husband of his choice, but this right was not recognised in Berry. When King Henry claimed wardship of the heiress, and her kin refused to give her up, warfare was the inevitable result. But Richard was irritated by the arrival of the Young King for two different reasons. In the first place his uninvited intervention clearly encroached on Richard's rights as duke of Aquitaine but, then, he proceeded to campaign so feebly that Richard concluded he must secretly be favouring the rebels.

Then the Old King heard disquieting rumours that Louis of France did not intend to stand idly by. Fearing possible intervention against the Young King in Berry, Henry sent an embassy to Paris, demanding a final resolution of the agreement to marry Margaret and Alice, Louis's daughters. In short, he asked that the Vexin be handed over as Margaret's dowry and Berry likewise be earmarked for Alice.[4] This was cool cheek on Henry's part, for everyone knew that it was Henry who had broken the terms of the previous agreement by hanging on to Alice far too long – she had been fifteen years at Henry's court and, it was widely whispered, was already his mistress. Indeed the situation had already reached the stage where Pope Alexander, primed by Louis, was threatening to place the entire Angevin empire under a papal interdict if the Alice marriage was not soon celebrated. For a year the nuncio at Henry's

court had been insisting that Alice either be married to Richard forthwith or returned to her father.[5] Always a master of stalling, Henry signed
a new fourfold agreement with Louis in September 1177 at the so-called
Colloquy of Ivry. He agreed to submit the Berry dispute, in which Louis
claimed an interest, to arbitration; he agreed that Richard would marry
Alice; and he proposed a non-aggression pact with Louis on condition
that the two of them went on crusade to save the beleaguered Christian
kingdom of Jerusalem. This last condition was crucial: Louis dearly
wanted to take the Cross but dared not leave for Palestine with France
and his young son Philip at the mercy of the Angevins.[6] But Henry had
no more intention of going on crusade than he had of returning princess
Alice. Moreover, in typical Henrician mode and again in defiance of this
agreement, he and Richard continued campaigning in Berry and solved
the issue there by military force, under the pretext that he (Henry) finally
had time to punish the rebels who had submitted to him at Winchester
in September 1176.[7] Henry continued to enrage and outwit Louis. In
November 1177 he and the French king held a fruitless conference at
Graçay about their competing claims in the Auvergne. Then, in a political coup that demonstrated how clearly money could speak, Henry
suddenly purchased the vast fief of La Marche from a despondent and
abdicating duke. Technically subject to Aquitaine, La Marche had always
enjoyed virtual independence, so here was another signal instance of
Henry's tightening power.[8]

   Henry's policies in the late 1170s have to be understood in light of
a threefold aim. He continued his long, bitter conflict with Louis and
France, opting for diplomacy until and unless Louis lost patience; meanwhile he was determined once and for all to break the local power of
Angoulême and its allies – the same who had caused him so much trouble
in 1175–76 – because Angoulême commanded the important trade routes
in the Charente valley and was potentially poised to dominate west-central
France; and finally he aspired to be *the* power in northern Spain.
Unfortunately the later ambition collided with an equal and opposite one
entertained by the young King Alfonso II of Aragon, count of Barcelona,
who had fantasies of being the 'emperor of the Pyrenees' and in 1178
allied himself with Castile as a prelude to gobbling up Navarre.[9] The
fact that Alfonso stood forth as a champion of troubadour culture at
the very moment Richard was finding himself at odds with the troubadours within Aquitaine added further ingredients to a very turgid political bouillabaise. It was mainly to counter the expansionism of Aragon
that Henry in 1178 again sent Richard to the far south. As Richard

advanced on Dax, he received some welcome tidings: Alfonso's ally the count of Bigorre had been seized by the townspeople who wanted to hand him over to Richard to avoid the rigours of a siege.[10] Alarmed by this development, Alfonso, who regarded Bigorre as his true friend, was forced to come in person before Richard to plead for his comrade and ally and to give surety for his behaviour. Triumphant on the Spanish border, Richard then turned back to deal with the opposition in Angoulême, now led by Count William's son Vulgrin. William himself, after the humiliation at Winchester, departed for a pilgrimage in the Holy Land and, as his son had not made the submission, technically he was within his rights to resist Richard. Vulgrin allied himself with the powerful baron Geoffrey de Rancon, an important figure in Poitou and the veteran of revolts in 1168 and 1173–74. De Rancon's castles at Pons and Taillebourg were so situated as to be able to cut communications between La Rochelle and Saintes in the north and Bordeaux in the south,[11] so it was to the investment of these strongholds that Richard applied his already formidable skills in siegecraft.

The siege of Pons began badly, as it became clear that Geoffrey de Rancon had laid in huge food supplies and would not crack easily. For Richard, on the other hand, his credibility as duke of Aquitaine hinged on being able to bring Geoffrey to heel.[12] To save face, he invested, forced to surrender and then demolished five easier targets, the castles at Richemont, Genzac, Marcillac, Grouville and Anville. Having thus restored his men's morale after the humiliation at Pons, he gambled every-thing on an attempt to reduce the supposedly impregnable fortress of Taillebourg – a task no one had even attempted before because of its supposed impossibility. The stronghold of Taillebourg was situated on an outcrop of rock on the right bank of the River Charente. Three sides were inaccessible on account of the sheer rock face and the fourth, approached over marshy ground, was protected by a triple ditch and a triple wall; additionally, the castle was well stocked with food and defended by well-armed men. On 1 May 1179 the dauntless Richard brought up siege engines and trebuchets and began bombarding this fourth side, pitching his tents alarmingly close to the walls. With his wonderful eye for ground, he saw that the one weak card in an other-wise unbeatable hand was that Taillebourg would have to open the town gates if the burghers wanted to make a sortie. He then unleashed his troops on a scorched-earth rampage around the nearby fields and vine-yards. Seeing the smoke of their ravaged property drifting skywards on a daily basis, the defenders finally took the bait and sallied out on 8 May.

The sortie was repelled with heavy losses and, as the defeated throng crowded back into the town that lay beneath the citadel itself, the pursuers followed them in before the gates could be closed. Richard's troops spent three days ostentatiously laying waste the town and taunting the garrison in the citadel with having seized most of their supplies. Finally the defenders in the citadel could take no more and surrendered.[13] Aghast at this 'impossible' exploit, Geoffrey de Rancon threw in the towel and surrendered Pons also. Outflanked by this surprise development, Vulgrin had no choice but to capitulate. Richard methodically razed Taillebourg and Pons then went on to demolish the walls of Angoulême and Montignac, controlling the River Charente, which he had demanded as the price of making peace with Vulgrin.

At the age of 21 Richard had crowned a five-year apprenticeship in the art of war with a stunning success. Having crushed all opposition he went to England to be greeted by his father with all the honours due a military hero. As a warrior Richard was a hard worker, a close observer and meticulous planner, not too proud to learn from his mistakes or take advice from followers like Theobald Chabot.[14] Siegecraft was almost more important than winning battles for a twelfth-century conqueror in western Europe for it meant victory without enormous loss of life and without tempting the fates; too many battles hinged on luck or accident or depended on circumstances one could not control. A master of sieges was therefore more highly esteemed than a battlefield commander. Sieges were seldom protracted, for in a long drawn-out affair, where a castellan stubbornly refused to surrender after a suitable period of time had elapsed in which to save face, there was the danger of a wholesale sack and massacre. Usually a commander would refuse to surrender and then do so some days later, unless the besiegers concluded that the mission was impossible and moved on elsewhere. It was normal practice to set a date for surrender, leaving the overlord or allies time to relieve the castle. If they failed to do so, once the castellan had delayed the enemy for long enough, it was in everybody's interest that sense, i.e. surrender, should prevail. The art was to work out how long a castle could hold out before a bloodless surrender occurred; if the castellan surrendered too soon, the element of enemy hampering was lost; if too late, the besiegers might assuage frayed tempers and casualties with atrocities. In the twelfth-century kaleidoscope of shifting alliances not to mention fratricidal warfare, where today's enemy was tomorrow's ally, it made no sense to shed blood needlessly. And it was usual for surrender terms to be observed punctiliously.[15] Certainly while he fought in Western Europe, Richard always obeyed these traditional rules.

After the triumph at Taillebourg, Richard's biography enters a black hole, for the sources unaccountably dry up for the year 1180. In part this was because Henry II was in France and the chroniclers naturally focused on his achievements and exploits. But it surely was in part because Aquitaine was unusually quiet. Led by old Count William of Angoulême, the vanquished of 1179 travelled *en masse* to the Holy Land, glad to be away from the scene of their humiliation by Richard.[16] Meanwhile Richard, as duke of Aquitaine, enjoyed powers over the province no ruler had ever managed to attain before. As far as the south was concerned, Henry's policy of devolving power to his sons while still retaining overlordship was proving itself. Henry always had autocratic and centralising tendencies and his 'federalism' was always pragmatic, but he worked within the art of the possible. Military dictatorship was not an option for the Angevin empire, as the necessary technology was lacking and, even with Henry's vast revenues, it was too expensive to try, for another situation like that of 1173–74 might arise, where all potential enemies suddenly became actual simultaneously. The use of force therefore had to be selective, focused on the most dangerous threats. In contrast to the Young King's lacklustre performance, Richard had proved a sensational success, though the very success was dangerous, since one day the son might think himself strong enough to defy the father. For Richard the problem was that he was now bitterly unpopular in Aquitaine. Although he was almost certainly not a harsh ruler, he did believe in the Latin motto *oderint dum metuant* (let them hate provided they fear), and certainly made the pips squeak all the way from La Rochelle to the Pyrenees.[17] Stripped of their traditional liberties and privileges, the dispossessed nobility brooded and bided their time, waiting for Richard to make a bad mistake. Their chance came in 1182.

The crisis in Angoulême that year was in many ways a rerun of the imbroglio at Berry four years earlier. Once again it involved a collision between Angevin overlordship and local mores and customs. Count Vulgrin of Angoulême died, leaving only an infant daughter, Matilda. This meant, according to Richard, that Matilda should inherit the county of Angoulême and he, as duke and overlord, should have wardship over her: in effect it was introducing the English law of primogeniture into an alien context. Naturally, this was not at all how the brothers of the dead Count Vulgrin, who stood to gain from the traditional divided inheritance, saw matters. In their eyes Richard's stance was a tyrannical breach of the ancient traditions of western France, which ultimately called in question the entire structure of fiefs and thus introduced uncertainty and chaos. Driven out by Richard when they contested his claim, Vulgrin's brothers Richard and Aldemar fled to their half-brother Aimar of Limoges, where they were joined by the count of Périgord and the viscounts of Ventadour, Comborn and Turenne. These men were united in what they saw as a sacred struggle against Richard's contempt for their inheritance customs.[18] Richard struck back hard at them, launching a surprise attack on the count of Périgord's fortress at Périgeux in April 1182, then cutting a swathe through the Limousin territory of his foes, burning and looting as he went. Although temporarily with a local inferiority in numbers, Richard had received assurances that his father was on the way to help him, and his confidence was not misplaced. At a conference at Grandmont in May, Henry summoned the rebels before him to hear their predictable complaints about Richard's tyranny, though the mere fact of the conference led some optimists to suppose that Henry was secretly displeased with Richard's actions. Such hopes were vain. Henry dismissed the charges as mere baronial contumacity and began a systematic campaign of reducing enemy strongholds in the Limousin. He and Richard, collaborating on a major military mission for the first time ever, took castle after castle: Excideuil, St Yrieix, Pierre-Buffière, Puy St-Front. Joined on 1 July by the Young King and his forces, the tripartite army swept all before it, forcing the rapid surrender of Aimar of Limoges and Elie of Périgord; Richard took particular delight in demolishing the walls of Périgord.[19]

It was quite clear that the combined forces of the Angevin empire were irresistible and no enemy could stand against them. The trick was to divide the Devil's Brood, and this was a task for which the troubadour Bertran de Born was particularly suited. He set himself at once to whip up discontent against Richard and to inveigle the Young King into fresh rebellion. Bertran de Born is himself an historical conundrum in more ways than one. A fine poet and a mighty warrior, he was a genuinely wicked human being. The source of his manifold discontents was that his father had bequeathed the family castle of Hautefort jointly to Bertran and his brother Constantine. Bertran found this intolerable and fought an almost continuous mini-civil war against Constantine, in which the castle constantly changed hands. This struggle was a microcosm of the father-son conflict in the wider kingdom, for Constantine sought and received support from Henry the Old King and Bertran from Henry the Young King. Within Aquitaine Bertran, who could put 1,000 men in the field was forever at daggers drawn with his neighbours the count of Périgord and the viscount of Limoges and above all Duke Richard, who

composed his own political satires or *sirventes* in response to Bertran's
and easily held his own in the ideological duel; indeed it has been
suggested that Bertran's low output of love songs was basically caused
by his concentration on the political battle with Richard. He liked to
insinuate to the Young King that Richard was becoming too powerful
and it was a grave mistake to help him quell the opposition within
Aquitaine. Bertran de Born was at root a cynic who tipped over into
nihilism and advocated political anarchy: 'I would that great men should
always be quarrelling among themselves' was his most famous dictum.[20]
A believer in 'the war of all against all' and 'permanent revolution' Bertran
was an obvious forerunner of both Thomas Hobbes and Leon Trotsky.
An avowed lover of war – 'peace gives me no comfort', he declared –
he reveals through his poems a malevolent ideology of 'chivalry' that
Dante found deeply shocking. Bertran loved war because it carried off
both the mighty and the lowly and he famously stated that the pleasures
of sleep, drink and food could not compare with the cry of 'charge',
the sight of riderless and disembowelled horses neighing in agony or the
sound of wounded men crying out for mercy.[21] At first blush his love
of war should have aligned him more naturally with Richard than with
the Young King, but Richard's love of war was always purposive rather
than mindless and he always despised de Born.

Some historians have affected to relegate Bertran de Born to the
briefest of footnotes, on the ground that he has been taken too much
at his own inflated estimate.[22] Yet his influence on the Young King seems
undeniable. And even if he were only a minor political gadfly, he represented something significant in the state of Aquitaine. The struggle
between the rebels of the south and the Angevin empire turns out to
have been more socio-economic than cultural. Bertran de Born and the
other troubadours were usually spokesmen and propagandists for the
minor nobility – *la petite noblesse* – constables of castles, holders of minor
fiefs, landless younger sons of knightly families. The aim of the troubadour ethos was a new, more broadly based nobility, with class distinctions more important than distinctions of wealth and power. Alongside
the promotion of courtly love, hunting and tournaments, they advocated
increasing the number of courtiers and forcing the great magnates to
share their wealth with lesser barons. The ethos of constant warfare was,
in the minds of more thoughtful troubadours, though not Bertran de
Born, a means of forcing the great barons to keep landless knights
permanently on their payroll and thus in time to accept a de facto
widening of the nobility. It can be seen why, for most of the troubadours,

Richard was public enemy number one. In their eyes he was a boorish pragmatist, uninterested in tournaments or courtly love. They portrayed him as a harsh lord and a despot because he refused the customary Aquitaine right of vassals to wage war on each other without leave of their common lord. From Richard's point of view, he was bringing civilisation to the south. He kept mercenaries and routiers but they were paid punctually and so did not rampage through the countryside. He believed in what later writers would call 'the monopoly of violence' for he expressly forbade his vassals to hire mercenaries; any routiers who came into Aquitaine other than in his service were hunted down ruthlessly, hanged, drowned or blinded. Peace, rigidly enforced laws, legal codes that emphasised primogeniture and swept away uncertainty and dispute, and a clearly stratified hierarchy of the kind the Angevins preferred sounded the death-knell for the ambitions of *la petite noblesse*.[23]

Bertran de Born did not abandon hope. Another ace in the hole for him was the new king of France. Philip Augustus had been a sickly child, to the point where Louis VII of France visited England in 1179 and got Henry II to accompany him to Becket's shrine at Canterbury. There he prayed for the intercession of the saint and martyr on behalf of the seriously ill Philip. His prayers were answered but he himself suffered a severe stroke almost immediately on returning to France. He died on 18 September 1180.[24] Unlike Henry, he was never unscrupulous, but was modest, God-fearing and chaste, living proof that a king could also be a model of chivalry. Although he could not match Henry in deeds and achievement, he left behind a far more glowing reputation, and his career did much for the prestige of the French monarchy. His successor, Philip Augustus, was only fifteen at the time, but was destined to become one of the great kings of France, second only to Louis XIV in power and magnificence according to some historians. Philip was another paradox, a physical coward who never mastered horsemanship or learned to ride properly – it was said that the one destrier he could master was kept in readiness to carry its rider away from any fighting at full tilt – but he became a master strategist and the hammer of the Plantagenets.[25] Where the ruthless Henry II had always been able to outwit the ingenuous Louis VII, the Devil's Brood were to find that they had in the new French king a man even more cunning and ruthless than their own father. From very early days he was convinced he had been marked down by destiny to carry the house of Capet to glory. When still no more than a child, he sat dreamily at a meeting of the King's Council, chewing a hazel twig. When asked what was on his mind, he replied that it was his ambition to make France as great as it had been in Charlemagne's day.[26] He began his reign as he meant to go on by intervening in the crisis over Vulgrin of Angoulême in Aquitaine and accepting the homage of Angoulême. Bertran de Born could scarcely believe his luck. 'Now we will know for sure', he wrote, 'whether king Philip takes after his father or follows in the footsteps of Charlemagne.'[27]

Things were starting to go de Born's way, but he had one final obstacle to remove before the Young King could be persuaded to break ranks with his father and brothers. At young Henry's side rode the original knight paladin *sans peur et sans reproche*, Sir William Marshal. Since 1170 the Young King's *mesnie* (military household) had been led by Marshal, who was already famous throughout Europe. He had led something of a charmed life, having narrowly escaped death as a child. In 1152 his father Geoffrey Marshal was besieged by King Stephen in Newbury Castle. In accordance with the usual custom, he agreed to surrender on a given date and sent out his son William as hostage; then he broke his word and, by the laws of the sword, the boy's life was forfeit. The ruthless Geoffrey shrugged the matter off: he said that as his wife was with him in the castle, he could spare a son, since he had both the hammer and the anvil with which to make others. Stephen reluctantly gave the order for the boy to be killed – he had to, or the whole business of hostage-taking would lose credibility. But when he emerged from his tent, he saw the child playing gleefully with the headman's sword; his heart ruled his head and he pardoned the boy.[28] When Henry II ascended the throne of England, young William Marshal was sent to Normandy to be brought up by his cousin the count of Tancarville. After receiving a thorough grounding in the use of arms, he proved himself a natural with lance and sword and soon made his mark in tournaments.

In 1168 he became famous for prowess in real battle also. He was in Earl Patrick of Salisbury's party when the earl was killed, sensationally – for great lords were not supposed to die in battle – during Eleanor of Aquitaine's campaign against the earls of Lusignan. This death was considered murder by medieval reckoning for, by the rules, if you caught an enemy out hunting when he was not wearing his chain mail, you had to take him prisoner, not kill him. William donned his hauberk but his horse was immediately killed under him. He landed on the ground unharmed and then took up station by a thick hedge which protected his back, where he defied the men of Lusignan to try their luck. When they charged, he killed six horses and held his own against their mailed riders, being overcome finally only when a Poitevin rider jumped his horse over the hedge and was able to work round behind him; William was taken prisoner with a speared thigh. As a prisoner he was treated harshly to make him keen to pay the suggested ransom, and lay with his wound untended until a kitchen-maid took pity on him and gave him a dishcloth to bind up his wounded leg. William's problem was that, as a landless younger son, he had no tenants to ransom him and might well have died in a Lusignan dungeon. It was Eleanor of Aquitaine, out of admiration for his gallantry in the Earl Patrick episode, who ransomed him from her private purse.[29]

William Marshal soon became the Lancelot of his time – the knight everyone wanted to beat but no one could – and was acknowledged as the king of tournaments. Early medieval tournaments, and certainly those in the twelfth century, are much misunderstood, since there is an almost inevitable 'feedback image' from the ideal-type of tournament familiar from Malory. In the eleventh century one-on-one combat would have been regarded as a curiosity, since tournaments featured companies of knights fighting each other all day long. Knightly combat in this era, whether in a tournament or on the battlefield, was not concerned with killing opponents but capturing them for ransom. The 'battleground' was seldom a special area surrounded by caparisoned horses and gaily-coloured tents but simply the high road, at the side of which were wicker-work pens or 'lists' where those who found the going too tough could rest and recuperate on 'safe' ground until they felt energetic enough to rejoin the combat; indeed almost the only rule of 'chivalry' in this period was the sanctity of the lists, and all kinds of dirty tricks were employed to gain the advantage. When William Marshal became the Young King's military counsel, he always advised him to hang back at the beginning of the day and make a limp showing, allowing the other side to exhaust itself during the heat of the day, then charge in the evening when the opponents were tired and prisoners could be picked up easily. Prisoner-taking was the name of the game; deaths in tournaments were rare except through falls from horses or being cut up by hooves. Ransom levels were set much lower than in real warfare, and usually the terms of captivity in these cases were not severe. The immediate advantage to the victor was that he took possession of the horse and chain mail, a considerable prize.[30] In this way William Marshal soon became not just famous but wealthy. One summer, while fighting on the side of a Flemish knight, Sir Roger de Gaugi, he took 103 knights prisoner with their horses and mail plus many more riderless horses. Immensely strong – he was able to carry a knight in his armour clean off the battlefield – generous, wildly popular, he was said to be tolerant of most things except lending money at interest. A famous story was told of him that an interlocutor tried to make him angry by reciting the details of various 'sins': William listened impassively to tales of adultery, theft and the breaking of clerical vows but became incensed only when usury was mentioned.[31]

On paper William was the perfect mentor and guardian for the Young King, who was obsessed with tournaments. But there were several problems. In the first place, even when coached by William and taught all his lore, Young Henry was not very good at jousting. Although tall, strong and handsome, he simply could not be bothered to put his back into knighthood as a real professional would: his attention span was too limited, he was too easily bored and in jousting, as in so many other ways, he was a dilettante. Gradually he became more and more irritated with William's success and fame. In tournaments opponents tried to unhorse William Marshal but ignored the Young King. Troubadours composed poems about the great Marshal, not about the great Henry. It did not help matters that William could be tactless and, in his cups, could rival d'Artagnan's Gascon boastfulness. The Young King liked to try to put him in his place by reminding him of his duties as a liegeman. But events always seemed to conspire to place him in a bad light and William in a favourable one. On one occasion the Young King found himself out of money in a Flemish town, unable to pay the (inevitably) huge bills run up by himself and his sycophantic entourage. The burghers simply refused to accept his word that he would pay, closed the gates against him and lined the walls to prevent him from leaving. Condemned to remain a virtual prisoner until money was fetched from his duchy in Normandy, the Young King was providentially delivered by William Marshal, who pledged on his word of honour as a knight that the debt would be paid.[32] Immediately the situation was transformed and the gates opened, for the solemn promise of the greatest knight in Christendom was an international currency. Unlike both Old and Young Kings William Marshal always kept his word.

Yet another problem was that Henry II banned all tournaments in his domains, as did Kings Louis and Philip in France proper (the Ile de France). Enforcement of this law was impossible in Aquitaine and intermittent in Normandy, but sometimes the Young King dared not defy his father openly and was forced to decamp to Flanders or Brabant, in terms of tournaments the Reno or Las Vegas of their day. Henry II's opposition to tournaments was twofold: they damaged crops and property and they were condemned by the Church, which Henry was anxious

to conciliate in the post-Becket years. According to canon law, tournaments stood in much the same light as mercenaries: they were anathematised as a form of suicide, and this was confirmed by Canon 14 of
the Second Lateran Council in 1139. In theory, to be granted absolution
after Confession for having taken part in a tournament, you had to give
back all ransom money, horses and armour gained through jousting, so
that not a groat of financial profit remained.[33] Since William Marshal
was honourable, he often nagged the Young King about holding tournaments in Normandy, thinking they should be held only in the godless
Low Countries. For all these reasons the Young King chafed under
Marshal's tutelage and looked for a way to take him down a peg. We may
suspect the direct or indirect influence of Bertran de Born in the final
parting of the ways. The Young King was notably uxorious and cherished his wife queen Margaret, who was popular, even though she
indulged her selfish and calculating brother Philip. Despite the reputedly
happy marriage, the royal couple were childless, as a son born to Margaret
died in infancy and there were no further pregnancies. Suddenly rumours
began to proliferate that the admiration Margaret expressed for William
Marshal and the easy relations they enjoyed betokened something more
than mere liking. After listening to troubadour-inspired tittle-tattle that
Marshal was now Lancelot in another sense, with Margaret as Guinevere,
the Young King angrily accused Marshal of being over-familiar with his
wife. Intemperate words were exchanged, and William Marshal stormed
from the meeting, leaving his service immediately after. The Young King
claimed he had dismissed Marshal for 'conduct unbecoming'.[34]

When the Young King suddenly quit the 1182 campaign with Richard
against the count of Angoulême and rushed back to a tournament in
the Low Countries, it was clear that Bertran de Born's poison had done
its work and he had removed the main moderating influence on Henry
II's eldest son. Time had not mellowed or improved the Young King:
instead of twelve years' experience since his coronation he had merely
one month's worth repeated more than a hundred times. Henry was
classically one of those personalities that relish freedom without
authority, rights without duties, power without responsibility. At the very
moment Henry was carrying out his administrative overhaul in England,
in the years 1176–79, the Young King chose to be absent on the continent, flitting into tournaments in the Low Countries whenever it was
suggested he did anything useful in Normandy. As Ralph of Diceto
tersely put it: 'Henry the son of the king of England, leaving the
kingdom, passed three years in French contests and lavish expenditure.'[35]

He spent money like water, indulging in the kind of mindless fripperies more redolent of the Sun King at Versailles five centuries later. Some of his *jeux d'esprits* recall the lunacies of Domitian or Elagabulus, the most decadent emperors of ancient Rome. On one occasion he held a banquet for a hundred knights, all of them called William. Whenever his father asked him to help Richard in Aquitaine, the Young King would take an unconscionable time about getting there, would then half-heartedly join in a siege, then become bored and depart without a word to anyone.[36]

Surrounded by toadies and sycophants, all young wastrels like himself, the Young King adored to spend money, but hated its reality. Groaning with debt which he yearned not to pay, or to write off by simple decree, he was rescued time and again by his father or William Marshal, which simply made him more resentful, since that meant, in his mind, that they were patronising him or 'giving him laws'. At the same time Bertran de Born and the other troubadours urged on him the credo that largesse was a ruler's most desirable quality – not surprisingly, since they would end up the major beneficiaries of a glad-handed prince. To encourage him in his mindlessness, his courtiers showered him with compliments, making him out to be the greatest knight in Christendom, the flower of chivalry. Pro-French propagandists joined in the encomia, especially after the Young King's death.[37] Gerald of Wales wrote: 'He was the honour of honour, worthy to be the ornament of the whole world; the splendour, glory, light and summit of chivalry; surpassing Julius Caesar in cunning, Hector in courage, Achilles in strength, Augustus in conduct, Paris in beauty . . . He was another Hector, the honour of his knights, the terror of his foes, the love of all; a thunderbolt of war, in every mind the chief hope or the chief fear; in peace mild, affable, kind and generous; in war terrible.'[38]

The Old King was visibly ageing and the Young King was both heir apparent and joint king. But he did not have the patience to wait until he could succeed to the throne naturally. By 1182 the temptations had once again become too great. He wanted the real powers Richard enjoyed in Aquitaine and he wanted them now. His visits to Aquitaine had persuaded him that there was wholesale opposition to Richard in the duchy and he could win a civil war against him there, but he was not certain what side his father would take in such a fratricidal dispute. In autumn 1182 he asked Henry to be given outright rule in Normandy, but the king refused. The Young King stormed off, declaring he would take the Cross, and went to Paris to see the young monarch Philip

Augustus, who realised that here could be the first instrument of his lifelong campaign to destroy the Angevins.[39] Philip liked the Young King personally and was grateful for the help he had given him in 1180–81 when some of the French nobles under the counts of Blois and Flanders had opposed his succession. Henry II soon cajoled his son back to his side by offering him an increased annual allowance (equivalent to £110 a day) and a year's pay for his troops plus the upkeep and subsistence of a hundred knights; in return the son swore an oath that he would remain faithful to the king and make no more demands. The Young King now had three choices: he could remain loyal to his father in accordance with his oath; he could go to Jerusalem on crusade; or he could make war on Richard. The last always seemed the most tempting prospect. Richard himself had crusading ambitions – indeed that was the rationale for his heavy taxation of Aquitaine – and the Young King had no wish to compete in Outremer with a proven warrior. Dozens of prominent would-be rebels were just waiting for the nod from the Young King before rising against Richard, and they had already opened secret channels to the young man, promising they would recognise him as duke of Aquitaine. From all sides the Young King heard the same story – that Richard 'oppressed his subjects with burdensome and unwarranted exactions and by an imperious despotism'.[40]

By the autumn of 1182, however, Bertran de Born was beginning to despair. He had no hopes of Philip Augustus, whom he now despised for his lack of martial talent. And the southern barons were genuinely afraid of Richard and wanted an almost cast-iron guarantee of success before they would rise against him. As de Born said: 'I am making a *sirvente* against the cowardly barons, and you will never hear me speak of them, for I have broken a thousand spurs on them without being able to make a single one of them run or trot.'[41] This was the point at which yet another angel of darkness came to his aid. The most evil of all the Angevins finally emerged from the shadows. Knighted by his father in 1178 at twenty, Geoffrey, lord of Britanny combined the qualities of the Young King with those of his younger brother John. On the one hand he was handsome, charming and debonair; on the other cruel, scheming, serpentine, mendacious and untrustworthy. In some ways he was by far the most natural ally for Bertran de Born since he believed in mindless violence – he would gut houses and lay waste towns on a whim – and was forever changing sides. He had no fixed beliefs and would fight with anyone against anyone. An indefatigable intriguer, he poisoned Richard's mind against the Young King when he performed so badly at Berry while simultaneously stoking resentment in the Young King against Richard.[42] Careful and methodical, he did not at first reveal his hand as duke of Britanny. Unlike Richard, he made no real attempt to impose his father's law and left the old traditions and folkways of Britanny alone and gave his easy-going minister Roland de Dinan a free hand. In 1181 Henry II allowed him to marry Constance, heiress of the late Conan IV of Britanny. Since the Old King habitually interfered in his sons' private lives and had humiliated Richard by not allowing him to marry Alice, this concession could be seen as a great favour. Henry indeed seemed very indulgent towards Geoffrey and there is even some evidence that he secretly encouraged him to meddle in his brothers' affairs in Normandy and Aquitaine on the 'divide and rule' principle. But Geoffrey secretly hated his father. In his mind Henry had toyed with him by allowing the marriage to Constance after a lifelong betrothal. Moreover, even when he became duke of Britanny by rights of succession through his marriage, Henry would still not let him rule there independently.[43] His resentment towards his father thus had the same cause as Richard's, but Richard did not harbour deep, abiding hatred the way Geoffrey did.

Geoffrey planned his strike against his father meticulously. First he established that the quid pro quo for non-interference in Breton folk-ways was that his writ should run in all corners of Britanny. He campaigned against the nominally independent Viscount Guiomar of Leon and crushed him in 1179. With growing confidence he then dismissed Roland of Dinan and replaced him with his own henchman Ralph de Fougeres – a known enemy of both Richard and Henry II.[44] A better judge of human beings than the Old King could have inferred a lot about Geoffrey's true filial feelings from that alone. While Guiomar, following the example of so many defeated magnates in this era, departed on crusade, Geoffrey allowed his eldest son to have nominal suzerainty over the north-west of the duchy but established his own hegemony by fortifying the port of Morlaix and occupying it with his own troops. Cunningly, Geoffrey established tight administrative and ecclesiastical control before his masterstroke in 1185, when his famous Assize estab-lished the principle of primogeniture in succeeding to fiefs.[45] In June 1182 he used the occasion of a visit to his father at Grandmont to intrigue with the anti-Richard barons of the Limousin. The chroniclers tended to impute Geoffrey's motives to simple moral depravity, to see him as Original Sin incarnate, but it may be that Geoffrey's devious mind was working towards the day when his father was dead. If a revolt removed Richard and the feeble Young King assumed the Crown, it would not be hard for Geoffrey to become the power behind the throne and the real decision-maker in the land. Everyone thought that, as a third son, he had done extremely well, but Geoffrey thought Britanny far too small a cockpit for his ambitions.[46]

By autumn 1182 rebellion was again breaking out in Aquitaine. The perfidious Taillefer brothers and their ally viscount Aimar once more broke their word, hired mercenaries and denounced the treaty to which they had put their names. This was the moment for the trio of plotters, Geoffrey, Bertran de Born and Philip Augustus, to find the *casus belli* that would justify waging war on Richard, and he fell into their trap by forti-fying and rebuilding Clairvaux Castle, a fortress nominally in Anjou, which he aimed to use against his next most likely opponent, viscount Chatellerault of Poitou.[47] Clairvaux was disputed territory, as under one interpretation of feudalism it belonged to Poitou and on another to Anjou. The Young King naturally claimed that Richard was fortifying strongholds in his (Henry's) domain but, unless he was simply being disputatious or trailing his coat, he should have submitted the dispute to the Old King.[48] Nonetheless, he was confident that in an armed chal-lenge to Richard he would have the support of his father. Some say the Old King was losing his touch in not acting decisively right at the begin-ning, but other authorities claim that the real problem was located in Henry II's erratic personality: 'Although extremely sensitive to what he took to be betrayal in others, Henry II showed a remarkable capacity for deceiving himself about his sons, and an astonishing indulgence even to their most patent duplicity.'[49] The upshot was that he prevaricated and, instead of issuing a judgement, summoned all his sons to a Christmas court at Caen: it was to be a magnificent occasion, and none of his sons or liegemen were allowed to hold any other court that Yuletide.

In the simulated ambience of peace and goodwill William Marshal thought he discerned a good chance to patch up his quarrel with the Young King. He offered to refute the calumny that he had been queen Margaret's lover by challenging any of his accusers to single combat. The peevish Young King said that Marshal was simply offering a contest he was sure to win, which was no proof at all. Marshal riposted that he would face any three champions on successive days and, if any of them beat him, he would admit his guilt whatever the truth. The Young King still did not fancy the odds so, in desperation, Marshal offered to have a finger cut from his right hand just before the joust, promising he would fight with the wound still bleeding. When the boorish Young Henry would not even accept this offer, Marshal asked for a written passport and set off on pilgrimage to the shrine of the Magi at Cologne.[50] This high drama aside, the Christmas court was notable mainly for backstairs intrigue. Among the thousand knights who assembled in the vast halls of the Caen palace was the inevitable Bertran de Born, who had already been doing his best to whip up opposition to Richard. His *sirvente* on the subject of Clairvaux was both arch and insinuating: 'Someone had dared to build a fair castle at Clairvaux in the midst of the plain. I should not wish the Young King to know about it or see it, for he would not find it to his liking; but I fear, so white is the stone, that he cannot fail to see it from Mateflon.'[51] Meanwhile at Caen de Born lobbied both the Old King and Richard for support against his brother Constantine who held the family castle at Hautefort. In a bizarre but not untypical melange of caddishness and chivalry de Born claimed that only the beauty of Henry II's daughter Matilda, now married to the exiled duke of Saxony, prevented him from dying of boredom during the tedious proceedings at Caen.[52]

Naturally his best chance to regain Hautefort was finally to tip the Young King over into rebellion, but the Old King's diplomacy at first made this a difficult aim to compass. Henry announced a conference at Mirebeau where the disaffected barons of Aquitaine could put their grievances to him. Then he persuaded an initially very reluctant Richard to hand over Clairvaux to him. Finally, he sought to bind up the wounds of the Angevin empire by a complex skein of renewed oath-taking. First his sons were to swear perpetual fidelity to him; this they did without demur. Then he sought to impose oaths of overlordship binding his younger sons to the Young King. Geoffrey accepted readily enough – it fitted well with his own designs – but Richard refused adamantly. He pointed out that royal brothers were supposed to be equal in status and so he should not have to swear an oath of submission on the Gospel; if the Young King had rights of primogeniture from his father, he, Richard, had a countervailing right of inheritance from his mother. In feudal terms Richard was right for, though Henry II had inherited portions of his empire from his mother and father, Aquitaine was his only by the right of marriage to Eleanor. Moreover, Richard's arguments about equality were validated by the existing system of homage: the Young King did homage to the king of France for Normandy, as did Richard for Aquitaine, so, feudally speaking, both brothers were on the same footing.[53] In other words, Richard's case was that, in trying to get him to swear an oath of subjection to the Young King, Henry II was trying to change the rules and make Aquitaine answerable to the rest of the Angevin federation rather than to France.

After much cajolery Richard finally agreed to pay the required homage *provided* the Young King made a solemn pronouncement that Richard and his heirs would possess Aquitaine forever. At this point the Young King drew back and upset all his father's careful diplomacy. He refused the proferred conditions because the new terms of homage conflicted with the secret assurances he had already given de Born and the Aquitaine rebels. On 1 January 1183 the Young King came clean and admitted as much: he told his father he had pledged himself to the rebels because of the Clairvaux affair. But Henry II trumped this ace by pointing out that Richard had already handed over Clairvaux to him. He insisted that the oaths of peace and the amended terms of homage be implemented and told the Young King that he intended to force the rebels to re-affirm the original treaty at Mirebeau. Finding themselves in a trap, Geoffrey and young Henry recast their plans. Geoffrey 'volunteered' to go south and bring the Limousin rebels to Mirebeau and the Young King, in collusion with him, then announced that he would follow Geoffrey to bring maximum pressure to bear. His true intention, of course, was to get the rebellious barons to sign up to him as duke of Aquitaine.[54] Even more deviously, he got his father to agree that at Mirebeau the rebels would not have to confirm the original treaty but could negotiate a new one instead. When Richard heard of this new instance of 'goalpost moving' he exploded. In an angry scene with his father he remonstrated vociferously: why had he and Henry campaigned together to crush the rebels in 1182 if a farcical surrender to their demands the next year was to be the net outcome? Tempers ran high at the father-son conclave. Finally losing patience with his father's approach, Richard told him bluntly that Aquitaine came from his mother, not the Angevins, and therefore it lay outside the king's jurisdiction. The meeting ended badly and Richard stormed out; he swept out of the court contemptuously, without royal permission, and rode south to fortify his castles in Poitou.[55]

The battle lines were now clearly drawn. The Young King and Geoffrey were fighting against Richard, and expected their father to join them after Richard's 'unreasonable' behaviour. The Young King secretly hoped that, with Richard defeated, he would then be able to dethrone his father and inherit the entire empire. Richard was determined this would not happen and, rather than accept such an outcome, was prepared to break away from the Angevin federation and declare Aquitaine an independent duchy. Much hinged on Henry II's actions: would he really go to war against Richard on behalf of rebels the two of them had just defeated? And what was the king of France's role in all this? Just to be on the safe side the Young King sent his beloved wife Margaret to Philip's court in Paris. He then rode south to join Geoffrey and the rebels at Limoges. At first everything went well for the insurgents. Aimar and his mercenaries browbeat the city of Limoges into joining the revolt, and every day news of the disarray in the Angevin family brought more recruits and waverers to the rebel banner. On paper Richard faced a daunting and almost impossible task, given the strength of the forces arrayed against him. But none of his enemies possessed his military genius. In no mood for peace or compromise, he first struck out at Geoffrey's forces in Britanny and scattered them. Then, on 12 February, after riding non-stop for forty-eight hours, he and his cavalry fell on Aimar's routiers at Gorre near Limoges, when the mercenaries confidently imagined he was still the other side of Poitiers. Richard himself slew the mercenary leader William Arnald and with the others used his draconian exemplary methods of drowning, blinding and hanging. Aimar and a handful of followers managed to get away only because Richard's horsemen were too exhausted to pursue them.[56]

The Old King now came south with a handful of followers to try to patch up a peace before his empire disintegrated. Already angered by reports that his son Geoffrey had persuaded the disaffected Aquitaine nobles not to meet him at Mirebeau, he was thrown into incredulous consternation as he approached Limoges. The garrison in the citadel of St Martial there – it was yet another city with a clear bifurcation between town and castle – panicked and attacked the tiny royal party; Henry narrowly escaped with his life. He then sought safety with Richard at Aixe, where the Young King visited him and tried to explain away the armed contretemps outside Limoges. Shocked and angry at such lèse-majesté, the Old King would not listen. The Young King returned to Limoges to tell the rebels that one moment of madness had placed the king on Richard's side; the dauntless Aimar made ready for a siege. There followed two weeks of pointless overtures and negotiations while Richard and his father assembled enough troops to deal decisively with the enemy. During one of these parleys the king was again shot at, and an arrow would have found its target if his horse had not suddenly reared its head and caught its death blow from the shaft.[57] Still shaken by the Young King's treachery and scarcely able to believe that his cosseted heir might actually wish him dead, Henry grimly built up his forces, gradually and remorselessly tipping the scales against the rebels. There is some evidence that the Young King himself thought he had gone too far and tried to save himself from the vortex of events, but Geoffrey and Aimar held him to his unfaithful course. Reduced to appealing to the Taillefer brothers to rise again and attack Richard's castles, the Young King found his fortunes momentarily enhanced when Philip Augustus finally made the first moves in what would be a thirty-year war against the Angevins. The arrival of his Brabançons for a time reduced Aquitaine to a chaos of plundering mercenaries, guerrillas and condottieri. Atrocities proliferated, especially at St Léonard de Noblat and Brantôme where the routiers left hardly a stone standing and massacred the inhabitants to the last infant.[58] With the entire south in a state of vicious civil war, the evil genius of the piece, Bertran de Born, managed to wrest Hautefort from his brother.

Like so many others caught up in the confusing welter of feudal loyalties, William Marshal, returning from Cologne, could not be sure where his primary loyalty lay, to King Henry or to the liege lord who had dismissed him. He decided to resolve the conflict by placing himself at the Young King's side and trying to steer him in the direction of peace. Always Henry had at his side the guardian angel William Marshal and the angel of darkness Bertran de Born. This time events worked in Marshal's favour, for it turned out that the Young King's seneschal, who had been the principal accuser against Marshal in the charge of adultery with Queen Margaret, had concluded that the Old King would prevail in the coming test of strength and had decamped from Young Henry's court. For the flaky Young King this fact, much more than Marshal's offer of trial by combat at Caen, was the clincher. He welcomed William Marshal back enthusiastically and asked him whether there was any way out of the current impasse. Marshal said that the face-saver for all knights who had made a disastrous mistake was to take the Cross. In a solemn ceremony in Limoges the Young King vowed he would go on crusade, provided only that all existing rights reverted to him on his return.[59] But all this soon seemed academic for at last, by the beginning of March, Richard and his father concluded they had sufficient forces to deal decisively with the enemy. Ignoring the bands of plundering routiers, they concentrated on the citadel of St Martial and dug in for an arduous siege. Now out of money, the Young King was reduced to becoming a routier himself, plundering and rampaging through the land, looking for money to pay his mercenaries, particularly targeting churches and monasteries. By the beginning of May his fortunes were rising again, for even Richard and Henry, the masters of siegecraft, had found St Martial a nut too hard to crack. Facing large-scale desertions from the demoralised besiegers, lashed by wind and rain in their tents while their foes in the citadel taunted them, Henry and Richard raised the siege. The pendulum of war seemed to be swinging decisively the Young King's way when other great magnates, following King Philip's example, began thronging into Aquitaine, principally Hugh, duke of Burgundy and Raymond, count of Toulouse. It was only with the sudden arrival of their ally King Alfonso II of Aragon that the Old King and Richard were able to hold their own. The Young King, elated by the turn of events, went over to the offensive at Limoges and captured Richard's old base at Aixe. Then fate intervened. Suddenly, on 26 May 1183 young Henry fell ill with a fever. The end came soon; he died on 11 June.[60]

On his death the rebellion collapsed like a house of cards; since the entire purpose of the revolt was to make the Young King duke of Aquitaine, there was no longer any point in the struggle. Hugh of Burgundy and Raymond of Toulouse returned home. Bertran de Born ruefully reflected that he had backed the wrong horse and now thought he should have raised up Geoffrey instead.[61] Heartened by yet another dramatic pendulum swing, Richard and Henry returned to Limoges to besiege St Martial. On 24 June Aimar surrendered and the citadel was razed to the ground. While Henry headed back to Anjou, Richard and Alfonso besieged Bertran de Born in his 'impregnable' castle of Hautefort; it fell after seven days and was returned to Constantine.[62] As Richard proceeded to lay waste the lands of the count of Périgord, one by one the rebels surrendered; either their castles were demolished or King Henry's troops occupied them. Geoffrey was punished by being deprived of all castles in Britanny. Bertran de Born was left with a life-long grudge against King Alfonso for the loss of Hautefort. Henry II rewarded the Spanish monarch lavishly for his help, but it is recorded that Alfonso took all this money home with him instead of ransoming his men, or at least so the bitter Bertran de Born claims.[63] Henry took the Young King's death very hard. 'He cost me much, but I wish he had lived to cost me more', was his magnanimous tribute. Perhaps at some level he resented the fact that Richard had now moved into pole position as heir apparent, or maybe his confidence was shaken in his (Richard's) hold on Aquitaine, for when the rebels laid down their arms Henry resumed direct control of some of the castles he had given Richard before the war.[64] Richard accepted the loss of face stoically, consoling himself with the thought that he would soon succeed the ailing Henry. Certainly his martial reputation, which had dipped in April–June during the abortive siege of St Martial, was even more widely acknowledged than before. Bertran de Born, his implacable enemy, paid tribute to

Richard's gifts of tenacity, resourcefulness, unswervingness, claiming that it was unlikely his side could have prevailed ultimately even if the Young King had not died and describing his foe as 'more dangerous than a wounded boar'.[65] And he also recognised, as Henry II never seemed to, that Richard's motivation was always the love of Aquitaine which he had inherited from his mother. It was for Aquitaine, de Born conceded, that Richard had 'gained and given and spent so much wealth, and dealt and received and withstood so many a blow, and endured so much hunger and thirst, and so much fatigue from Agen as far as Nontron'.[66] Always a poor judge of his sons, Henry was now about to precipitate a fresh crisis in his empire by his failure to understand this simple fact about Duke Richard of Aquitaine.

4

◦—⟡—◦

WHILE HIS THREE BROTHERS battled for supremacy in the great conflict of 1183, the 16-year-old John finally began to emerge from the obscurity of his childhood. Hitherto he had featured largely as a bargaining counter in Henry's dynastic ambitions. The proposal to marry him to Alice, the daughter of the count of Maurienne, had triggered the great war of 1173–74 but, undaunted by this experience, when the would-be bride died, Henry switched tack and announced in 1176 that John was to be a great lord in both Wales and Normandy. He would be made count of Mortain and would marry Isabella of Gloucester, heiress to that great earldom on the Welsh Marches.[1] It was typical of Henry that this scheme was almost immediately put into cold storage and another plan, to make John king of Ireland, was put in its place, though the idea of the earldom of Gloucester, to be held simultaneously, was kept on; there was nothing unusual about this as an idea in itself, since Geoffrey was the earl of Richmond in England as well as being duke of Britanny. Henry also announced that the earldom of Cornwall was being reserved for John.[2] So, by the time he was nine, John had already been betrothed to two different girls and been earmarked for four different great offices. Not surprisingly, people were confused: was it conceivable that John could one day be count of Mortain, earl of Cornwall, earl of Gloucester *and* king of Ireland. The one thing that was clear was that John was his father's favourite son, at least of the legitimate brood. Henry had a higher opinion of the Young King but the younger Henry had betrayed him too often. The Old King never warmed to Geoffrey but entertained no particular animus against him, but he gradually came to hate Richard, especially as Richard continued to defy him over Aquitaine. Here was a tangled family constellation indeed. On the one hand was a king with a queen who had rebelled against him and whom he kept in captivity; on the other was a collision of affections for their children. Eleanor adored Richard, liked the Young King, tolerated

Geoffrey and despised John. Henry II adored John, liked the Young King, tolerated Geoffrey and hated Richard.

Why were Richard and John mother's favourite and father's bête noire and vice versa? Something of the bonds between Eleanor and Richard has already been explained, but her distaste for John may have been because he was born as the result of a casual and 'one-off' coupling with the king when he had already virtually set her aside in favour of his many mistresses and especially the royal favourite Rosamund Clifford. Some historians even construe John's entry into Fontevrault at the age of six as a signal instance of maternal 'dumping'. Henry's partiality for John may have been because the traumatic events of 1173–74 left him bitter and unable ever again to trust his three eldest sons fully. But there was clearly something more, some mysterious alchemy that allowed Henry to look with indulgence on his youngest son's foibles and weaknesses: in a phrase, John was the classical 'spoiled brat'. John's defenders claim that Henry discerned in him from an early age a personality like his own, and an inchoate grasp of statecraft and administration that exceeded his brothers'. Henry's distaste for Richard was because he and his second son were fundamentally in competition for the same space; the pair suffered from the familiar lack of attraction in the case of people who are too alike. Both were hard men, and rather cold, both warriors whose rage could boil over in an instant, both worshippers of power and devotees of the strong, centralising state. They despised time-wasting, hedonism, frivolities and tournaments and were alike in their intelligence and cast of mind. Perhaps most significantly, both could take the long view and sacrifice short-term expediency for long-term gain. Richard was marginally less cunning and certainly less cynical than his father; their differential attitude to crusading is instructive. Yet, most of all, we are probably reduced to that baffling phenomenon: visceral dislike.

As a teenager, John never looked likely to rival Richard in any department. As an adult he never grew taller than 5ft 5ins. He had thick, dark-red curly hair and a powerful, barrel-chested body which in later life ran to fat. In terms of bookish learning John had been well educated, first at Fontevrault, then in the household of the Young King and finally with the justiciar Ranulf Glanville, the chief legal officer of England. Chroniclers noted a similarity between him and his brother Geoffrey. Gerald of Wales said that 'one was corn in the ear, the other corn in the blade'.[3] Observers had already tagged Geoffrey as the most gifted of the Devil's Brood, for he had some of Richard's talent as a warrior and greater abilities than the Young King in fighting tournaments, yet as a courtier he had a genius for silky intrigue, beguiling words, and manipulative flattery. Like most accomplished liars, he knew all the arts of deception, so that he was rarely taken in by the falsehoods of others.[4] John could not match Geoffrey in all these areas, but he was his equal in cunning, and some have rated him the most intelligent of Henry II's sons, surpassing even Geoffrey. On his day he could be genial, witty, generous and hospitable. Yet as a boy he seemed at first destined to go the way of the Young King: devoted to instant gratification, pleasure and luxury, he could not bear to be crossed in anything and preferred idleness and debauchery to the professional training of knighthood. Hunting, hawking, drinking, gambling (especially backgammon) were his favourite pastimes. He also liked music, though he had no time for troubadours and the kind of song-making that so entranced Richard and the Young King. He loved sumptuous clothing, finery and jewellery (particularly gold artefacts) and in another era he might almost have been considered a dandy or an aesthete. Lethargic, dilatory and insouciant, living purely for the moment, he was the epitome of selfishness and immaturity; his one saving grace was that he was excessively deferential to both parents.[5]

Two aspects of John's early formation are worthy of special attention. One is that his early contact with the Church at Fontevrault seems to have turned him violently against the Christian religion. He devoured recondite works of theology and even liked to take them on campaign with him later in life, but he read them so that he would have ammunition for mocking religion. Always something of a bookworm by the standards of medieval monarchs, he later acquired many patristic manuscripts from Reading Abbey as well as works by French historians and some of the ancient classics (Pliny the Younger was a particular favourite). He loved making esoteric anticlerical jokes in the later manner of Swift or Voltaire, but the wit depended on a close knowledge of Church theory and practice. He liked to make gratuitously ribald and blasphemous remarks – 'By God's teeth!', 'By God's feet!', etc. – and to shock churchmen by his heretical stance on items of Church doctrine; his favourite motif was the patent absurdity of the Resurrection. Once, when a buck was slaughtered at the end of a hunt, he remarked pointedly: 'You lucky beast, never forced to murmur prayers or be dragged to Holy Mass.'[6] John may well have been the first atheistic king in English history. The other facet of his early life, paradoxically in the light of the foregoing, was that he was taken under the wing of the other Geoffrey in Henry II's life: the illegitimate son he had sired on a famous courtesan named Ykenai shortly before his marriage to Eleanor. Born around 1151 and brought up initially in the same household as the legitimate sons, Geoffrey was trained for the priesthood but did not take his final vows and, some time in the 1160s, became Archdeacon of Lincoln. Later he was bishop of Lincoln and, after Henry II's death, archbishop of York. Always staunchly loyal to King Henry, the bastard Geoffrey was a great consolation to him during the dark days of 1173–74 when all his adult sons were against him. After the famous victory over King William of the Scots in 1174, the Old King famously said to the illegitimate Geoffrey: 'You alone have proved yourself my lawful and true son. My other sons are really the bastards.'[7]

When Henry II appointed this Geoffrey to be John's unofficial guardian, he was doing a number of odd things. In the first place, he was aiming at the solidarity between natural and legitimate progeny he had always hankered after but which his wife Eleanor, for obvious reasons, had opposed. Secondly, he was putting together in partnership the two offspring he most cared for, one from either side of the blanket. Thirdly, and unwittingly, he was increasing John's anticlericalism for, when it came to role models, it was his silver-tongued deceiver of a full-brother Geoffrey whom John preferred, rather than the episcopal half-brother. Yet for all his priestly exterior, the bastard Geoffrey was fully his legitimate namesake's equal when it came to worldly ambition. Although the chapter of Lincoln had elected him their bishop, and he enjoyed the considerable revenues of this diocese, Geoffrey still declined to take Holy Orders. He calculated that the dark days of 1173–74 might come again and that this time all the legitimate sons, including John, would rise against the father; in that case, it was not inconceivable that King Henry might disinherit the lot of them and nominate his beloved bastard as his successor. Geoffrey vacillated so long that at last the Pope made a new appointment to the see of Lincoln. Henry then named Geoffrey his chancellor until, much later, the offer of the archbishopric of York made him abandon his fastidious lay stance and he accepted priesthood and diocese together. Henry clearly ran the risk that this ambitious cleric might be another Becket; like him he had also been Chancellor. Although Geoffrey did not disappoint him, the fact that Henry had put John under his wing once again demonstrated that he was utterly hopeless as a judge of human nature when it came to his sons. The most John derived from Geoffrey's tutelage was more insight into machiavellianism and a greater contempt for churchmen.[8]

At Michaelmas 1183 King Henry dramatically evinced his hostility to

Richard and his partiality for John. He summoned both sons to Normandy and peremptorily ordered Richard to hand over Aquitaine in return for John's homage. Superficially the demand was reasonable, since everyone in the royal family was to move up a rung after the Young King's death, with Richard stepping into his dead brother's shoes and John into Richard's. But Richard had not toiled in the heat of battle in Aquitaine for eight years simply to give the duchy away on his father's haughty say-so; besides, he correctly reckoned that if he accepted his 'promotion', he would end up a cipher like the Young King. Even his bitter foe Bertran de Born saw the force of Richard's position: he opined that a prince who lived on the charity of another did not deserve to be a true monarch but only a king of fools.[9] Richard stalled convincingly and asked for three days' grace before he gave his final answer. At nightfall he rode away at full speed for Poitou; when he was far enough away he sent an envoy to tell his father he would *never* give up Aquitaine. Henry was reduced to impotent fury. His problem was that he had neglected the south and never built up a power base in Aquitaine: there was a 'Court' party of Richard and his followers and a 'Country' party of the rebels but no king's party.[10] To compound the Old King's problems, Philip Augustus of France weighed in with the demand that the marriage portion of the Young King's widow – Gisors and the castles of the Vexin – should be returned to France. At a conference at the traditional meeting place by the tree at Gisors on 6 December 1183 Philip agreed to let Henry keep the Vexin temporarily, on the strict understanding that he pay queen Margaret 2,700 livres and that the Vexin passed into the hands of whichever of his sons eventually married Alice, Louis VII's daughter. The suggestion here was clear and sinister: Henry was toying with the idea of cutting Richard out by marrying Alice to John. Henry then did homage to Philip for *all* his continental possessions, implying that the hierarchy worked Philip–Henry–Richard not simply Philip–Richard, as Richard claimed.[11]

Yet neither threats nor blandishment, feudal blackmail nor cajolery could force Richard to give up Aquitaine. Finally in anger and frustration the Old King told John that if he wanted the duchy he would have to take it by force. Richard was prepared for that obvious next step, and showed his defiance by binding lords to him by generous gifts at his Christmas court at Talmont, north of La Rochelle. And now for the first time we hear another famous name in Richard's biography, that of Mercadier, most famous commander of routiers and from this moment Richard's faithful comrade. Mercadier first made his mark in February 1184, when he sacked Excideuil as punishment to Aimar of Limoges, who was still trying to take advantage of disharmony within the Angevin family.[12] Less surprisingly, the figure of Richard's brother Geoffrey started to loom more and more in the saga. Although Richard and Geoffrey had been formally reconciled in the summer of 1183, Richard, rightly, did not trust him. Manipulating John with great ease, Geoffrey inveigled him into the invasion of Aquitane and together the brothers raided Poitou. Richard responded with his favourite stratagem when dealing with Geoffrey: a retaliatory raid into Britanny. The resulting anarchy was not at all what the Old King wanted. In autumn 1184 he summoned all three sons to England, and in December, at Westminster, they were once more publicly reconciled.[13] To set the seal on family amity Henry even released Eleanor of Aquitaine from house arrest for the occasion. But he was no nearer solving the problem of princess Alice, whom he still kept jealously at his court, combining adultery with *raison d'état*. One way out might have been to marry one of his sons to Frederick Barbarossa's daughter and the other to Alice. The emperor was willing and the project got some way off the ground, for in 1184 an imperial embassy led by the archbishop of Cologne actually went to England and arranged the betrothal of Richard to one of Barbarossa's daughters – not Agnes, as is so often stated. Unfortunately the girl died before a match could be arranged, yet another of the medieval millions who died in anonymity.[14] Henry prevaricated and kept both Richard and John in England over Christmas 1184. By sending Geoffrey to Normandy as 'governor', he was probably throwing out a very broad hint to Richard that, if his defiance continued, he might inherit nothing or, at least, if he so passionately wanted to hang on to Aquitaine, he would have to forgo the rest and see another brother installed as king. Richard said nothing, obtained his ticket of leave from England as soon as possible, and returned to his beloved province early in the new year.[15]

This was the juncture where Henry decided to make John king of Ireland and send him there with an expedition. But first he had to put Richard in his place. He declared him responsible for the continuing hostilities between him and Geoffrey and announced that there would be a definitive solution of the problem. When he crossed to Normandy in April 1185 to muster an army, it seemed that military force was to be the answer. Then suddenly, whether because of a sudden brainwave or because this was his intention all along and he simply wanted to make Richard sweat, he announced that Eleanor of Aquitaine would be restored to her suzerainty of the province and that henceforth the duchy would be ruled in a tripartite fashion by himself, Eleanor and Richard.

This cut the ground from under Richard, as he could scarcely deny the claims of his beloved mother, the source of his own legitimacy as ruler of the duchy.[16] But Henry's third part of the control in the south turned out to be a forlorn hope and, with Eleanor still virtually a prisoner, the reality was that Richard was in place in Aquitaine and there was little Henry could do about it unless he wished to campaign there in person. The cliché about possession and the law had never seemed so apt. In May 1186, at yet another of the endless parleys at Gisors, Henry finally agreed with Philip of France that Richard would definitely marry Alice, but once again the date of the wedding was left maddeningly vague and postponed into the future. The real loser from Gisors was Geoffrey. Realising that this agreement meant the end of his hopes of inheriting England and Normandy or of being king, he went down the same route as the Young King. Effectively he abandoned his father, threw in his lot with Philip, was rewarded by being appointed seneschal of France, and finally laid ostentatious claim to the territory of Anjou.[17]

Vexed by Richard and Geoffrey, Henry had to face the alarming fact that no role had yet been found for his beloved John, now eighteen and old enough to make a mark in the world. Early in 1185 the right opportunity seemed to have arrived, for the patriarch of Jerusalem arrived with an unusual proposition. Baldwin IV, the Christian king of the Holy Land, was dying from leprosy, and it occurred to the patriarch, to whom it fell to find a successor, that the house of Anjou was the answer. The royal house of Jerusalem was, after all, a cadet branch of the house of Anjou, and where better to look than in England, where there were three royal sons without a crown? The patriarch caused a minor sensation in England, as much for the keys of the Holy Sepulchre he brought with him as for his stirring oratory, which was said to have moved his aristocratic audience at the Reading court to tears. But Henry, the hard-headed pragmatist, had reports from his spies that made Jerusalem seem a bed of nails: it turned out that the so-called king was little more than a general of feudal armies with little civil authority, that he had no real powers beyond the charisma of whichever personality occupied the throne, and that the Holy Land was a snakepit of intrigue, backstabbing, factional strife and political uncertainty. The hapless patriarch, not knowing his man, came hopefully to an interview with Henry at Clerkenwell on 18 March 1185, only to find himself the principal player in a farce. Primed by Henry, each of the English barons trooped forward to say that his considered, unbiased opinion, given without any consultation with anyone else, was that

England was at present in crisis and no members of the royal family could be spared for Jerusalem. After much cant and humbug about his soul, Henry nearly found his elaborate charade scuttled by John, who begged on bended knee for permission to take up the patriarch's offer. By indignantly turning this down, Henry showed the patriarch that he had only ever been trifling with him.[18]

In 1185 Henry II sent his beloved John to Ireland to be king there. Henry's turbulent relations with Ireland went back at least as far as 1167 and possibly earlier. Ever since William Rufus allegedly saw the Irish coastline from Wales on a clear day, it had been at the back of the minds of the Norman kings of England that the island to the west would make easy pickings, but always the situation in France absorbed their attention. Some said that Henry II had set his sights on Ireland as early as the council of Winchester in 1155 but that his mother the empress had opposed an invasion scheme.[19] Modern historians tend to scout this idea and stress instead the interest of Pope Adrian IV (the only English pope, born Nicholas Breakspear) in modernising and reforming the Irish church, which was beyond the control of Rome. According to this view, Henry had no real interest in Ireland but was pointed in the direction of conquest by the papal bull *Laudabiliter* promulgated by Adrian in the mid-1150s, which explicitly named Henry as true king of Ireland and defender of the faith there. Adrian and his theologians played on Henry's fear of anarchy by portraying Ireland as a land of benighted, ravening savages, beset by heresies, religious deviancy, pagan-Christian syncretism and all manner of 'vice' placing immortal souls in peril.[20] What disturbed Normans and pontiffs alike was the essential 'otherness' of Ireland. There seemed to be no strong ruler whom one could threaten or cajole, for the so-called 'high king' was not a true monarch in the sense understood in the rest of Western Europe but part of a 'triarchy' of king, Church and *brehons* or traditional lawmakers. Irish rulers were far more constrained by the Church and traditional laws, which even in late Anglo-Saxon England had been largely a system of rubber stamps for the king. In sum, Ireland was not even like England in 1066 but like the same realm at a much earlier phase of development, as the shrewd observer William of Newburgh noted.[21]

For reasons not entirely clear, twelfth-century Ireland became a theatre of conflict between traditionalists and modernisers; the kings of Munster and Leinster were the modernisers while the king of Connacht was the conservative. In the ideological wars in Ireland in the 1150s and 1160s the conservatives seemed to be winning until, in 1167, king Dermot

MacMurrough of Leinster went to Europe to seek aid from Henry II. He met Henry in Aquitaine and got letters patent from him allowing the recruitment of freelances in England.[22] In 1170 the most famous of these went to Ireland – Richard, son of Gilbert de Clare, 1st earl of Pembroke, and better known to history as Strongbow, a 'busted' earl down on his luck, whose pedigree, said Gerald of Wales, was much longer than his purse.[23] Strongbow taught king Dermot new military techniques: building motte-and-bailey forts, using disciplined infantry, heavily armoured knights and skirmishing archers. Dermot soon gained the upper hand in Ireland and began to aspire to the high-kingship, but died in 1171, having first married his daughter to Strongbow. On the strength of this union, and in defiance of Irish law and custom, Strongbow claimed to be his heir in Leinster. Next Rory O'Connor, king of Connacht, besieged Strongbow in Dublin. Strongbow offered to be his vassal if he could keep Leinster but Rory refused, thinking he had the Norman interloper in a trap. To universal consternation, Strongbow sortied from Dublin and routed Rory's army; there now seemed little between Strongbow and the coveted high-kingship.[24]

This was the point where Henry II took a hand. Alarmed at the turn of events in Ireland, in October 1171 he landed with an army at Waterford and proclaimed himself overlord of Ireland. Gervase of Canterbury claimed that Strongbow had invited him to Ireland and Henry accepted purely because he wanted to get out of England until the sound and fury over the Becket murder died down. This makes little sense, and preferable is the version that Henry had always coveted Ireland and cunningly used Strongbow as a stalking horse, intervening at the right moment to 'part the combatants' in a way later politicians would emulate.[25] Yet this too is ultimately unconvincing, for the letters patent that Henry issued to king Dermot do not show him notably enthusiastic – which would explain why it took Strongbow three years (until 1170) to decide to chance his arm. What is certain is that Henry was angry when he heard that Strongbow was trying to make himself Dermot's heir in Leinster and ordered him home.[26] He went to Ireland to nip Strongbow's ambitions in the bud, for the adventurer's unexpected success – and especially the amazing victory over Rory O'Connor outside Dublin – opened up the possibility that Ireland would go the way of Sicily and become yet another breakaway Norman kingdom.[27] It may be asked why Henry did not simply expel the Norman invaders, but he was a realist who knew that this was a 'hydra's head' and that dozens more freelance adventurers and mercenaries would follow the trail that

Strongbow had blazed. Strongbow meanwhile manoeuvred cleverly, in full knowledge of how dangerous Henry could be: he offered to surrender all his Irish conquests if the king granted him Leinster as a fief. After a show of anger Henry agreed, provided Strongbow surrendered all castles and important ports.[28]

Henry's stay in Ireland turned into a six-month sojourn, as the worst storms recorded in the Irish Sea that century kept him in Dublin until Easter 1172. But he used the time well and achieved his main ambition – to show what would happen to anyone, Norman or Irish, who defied him. The supposedly modern doctrine of 'credibility' was alive and well in the twelfth century. Strongbow was confirmed as lord of Leinster, but without Dublin, Wexford and Waterford, which Henry garrisoned with his own men. He also gave the kingdom of Meath to Hugh de Lacy to counteract Strongbow's power; de Lacy was given the title of constable and the powers of a viceroy.[29] This was a first-class appointment, but the Old King did not have the courage of his convictions. De Lacy was shrewd and far-sighted, and cultivated a policy of peace and reconciliation which might have yielded spectacular long-term dividends. Unfortunately Henry suspected him of having Strongbow-like ambitions, particularly when he married Rory O'Connor's daughter in 1180, which made it seem like a rerun of the union between Strongbow and Dermot's daughter.[30] Having originally appointed de Lacy to stop Strongbow becoming too powerful, he then had to go into reverse and raise the so-called earl of Pembroke up again. This was why Hugh de Lacy served as viceroy only in 1172–73, being replaced by Strongbow in the years 1173–77. It was only on Strongbow's death in 1177 that Hugh regained the viceroyalty, which he held until 1184. After dealing with his Normans by divide and rule, Henry was content to accept an oath of fealty (personal loyalty) from the Irish kings; he did not insist on homage, which would have changed the terms on which they held their land. Rory O'Connor, after some peevish indecision, eventually became the king's man, which put him, like the other kings, under a personal, not feudal obligation.[31]

Henry's divide and rule policy in Ireland (Rory O'Connor, Strongbow, Hugh de Lacy) fell apart in 1177. The death of Strongbow coincided with the aftermath of serious rebellion, caused by the abuse of power by Henry's military commanders. At the same time Hugh de Lacy's power was increasing alarmingly, to the point where he was the true overlord in the land, and some even suspected him of aiming explicitly at a crown. Henry dealt with the crisis by dividing Ireland into fiefs, preempting any attempt by the local Norman warlords to carve up the country into their own private fiefs. More significantly, he appointed John king-designate of Ireland, although the nine-year-old clearly could not yet be sent across the sea to claim his realm.[32] An anxious seven years passed, with Henry's attention often elsewhere – on Richard, the Young King and Geoffrey principally – but at last the Old King thought his favourite son was ready for the task. In 1184 Henry announced that the 'total dominion' of Ireland would pass to John. He sent John Cumin, archbishop of Dublin, to prepare the way for John's arrival and recalled Hugh de Lacy; to prevent a power vacuum Philip of Worcester was sent as governor of Ireland pending John's takeover.[33] On the fourth Sunday of Lent, 1185, Henry knighted John and tried to confirm him as king of Ireland by getting the Vatican to confirm Adrian IV's original promise. The papacy itself was in a state of flux in these years, with Adrian being succeeded by Alexander III and then Alexander by Lucius III. Alexander had confirmed Adrian's 'donation' to Henry, but Lucius changed tack and proved unwilling to go along with Henry's ideas for an Irish crown for John. It was only when Urban III succeeded Lucius late in 1185 that the Vatican once again smiled on Henry and issued the necessary bull recognising John's kingship.[34]

With a large retinue and accompanied by the chronicler Gerald of Wales, specially chosen as historian of the expedition by Henry, John sailed to Waterford. The incursion on Irish soil was well prepared, and Henry had spent a vast amount of money making sure that his favourite son had all the dignity, trappings and resources of a real king.[35] The local Irish nobility thronged to meet him, but John struck a wrong, indeed an absurd, note right away. As one of the magnates approached him to make the kiss of peace, John pulled his beard. This was the signal for his entourage to behave like a pack of schoolboys: they made fun of the Irish barons and showed them marked discourtesy, astonishing their would-be hosts by their callow effrontery. The delegation left John's presence as soon as possible and made its way to the court of the king of Limerick. They told the king that their new supposed overlord was a mere stripling, newly hatched and wet behind the ears as it were, and his entourage was a bunch of similarly ill-endowed youths, matching their master in greenhorn ignorance, naivety and rudeness.[36] The king of Leinster had previously agreed with his colleagues in Connacht and Cork that, other things being equal, they would accept John as the new high king of Ireland and make formal submission to him. But the envoys' reports suggested that other things were not equal, that they had been sent a court jester as a ruler and that, if this was how John behaved when confronted by missionaries of peace, what egregious injustice might he not mete out if genuine complaints and grievances were brought before him. They decided to remain aloof, to pay no homage to John, and to wait and see what transpired. John had scarcely set foot in Ireland before he had persuaded a host of erstwhile enemies to make common cause against him.[37] As he moved north to Dublin, John found himself spurned and avoided instead of being hailed as a redeemer. Learning nothing from this, he and his riotous companions spent their time wenching and carousing by the banks of the Liffey, further alienating the locals by staggering around drunkenly in a variety of sumptuous raiment.

The new high king compounded his initial blunder by making land grants to his cronies, in Tipperary, Waterford and Wexford, and building castles to enforce his rule, in Waterford, Tipperary and Kilkenny. Not only did John's henchmen and acolytes start alienating the previous Norman settlers, but the new charters creating the estates made it clear to the native Irish that John envisaged no real place for them in the future scheme of things.[38] Old allies of Henry II from 1171, such as the king of Thomond, were soon converted into deadly enemies. Ireland became the cockpit of armed warfare, with skirmishes and battles galore instead of the peaceful transfer of power Henry II had hoped for. On one occasion a hundred severed heads were presented to John as proof of the punishment that all Irish 'rebels' would receive. But there was also severe fighting around the castles of Ardfinnan and Tibberaghny as well as in Meath, where one of the Irish kings was treacherously slain during a parley with the Normans.[39] The casualty rolls in John's army mounted alarmingly, and soon the man who would be king of Ireland found himself seriously short of money. John then made things worse by refusing to pay his troops their wages, leading them to desert in droves and begin plundering the countryside, thus giving an extra twist to the spiral of violence and alienating the local population still further. The idea of a partnership between Irish and Normans, which Hugh de Lacy had pushed and which to sceptics seemed a forlorn hope even in the days of Strongbow, was given its definitive *coup de grâce* by John.[40] Hugh de Lacy, the real power in Ireland, cooperated formally with John and even accompanied him on part of his itinerary, but distanced himself from the ill-advised new land grants John made to his cronies, hinting to the Irish that peace would be possible if they could deal with him alone. Indeed, the only significant military victories gained in 1185 were not won by John but by de Lacy and his lieutenant William Le Petit.[41]

John, who often managed to combine stupidity with cunning, left Ireland after eight months of fruitless activity, having achieved nothing. He complained to his father that de Lacy would not relinquish the reins of power and in particular prevented the Irish kings from paying him tribute or sending hostages. Whether Henry, who was well informed by Gerald of Wales and from other sources, took this excuse for John's incompetence seriously is doubtful, but any thought of curbing Hugh de Lacy was made otiose when he was assassinated the following year.[42]

John's political failure in Ireland was as clear-cut as anything could be, so it is astonishing that there have been attempts to rehabilitate his reputation in this area.[43] Even more obvious was his military failure. John signally failed to adapt normal Norman warfighting to Irish conditions. It soon turned out that heavily armoured knights were worse than useless in thickly wooded countryside, especially as the cavalry charge, relying as it did on a concentrated cloud of horsemen, could not be used in such circumstances. The heavy armour and the high curved saddles on the destriers made mounting, remounting and dismounting extraordinarily difficult and militated against speed – the essential factor when fighting what were virtually guerrillas. What was needed for the new warfare of skirmish and rapid disengagement was a body of light horsemen who could pursue the enemy into hills or rough terrain. To counter-attack the Irish shock weapon of mobile slingers, John should have deployed equally mobile and agile bowmen, who were available in Wales. Most of all, perhaps, the system that worked so well in England and France – building great castles from which armies sallied forth – had to be changed so that the fortresses became more akin to blockhouses, built right across Ireland in accordance with a clear, overarching strategy.[44] The clear impression is that John was too lazy to think all this through and too tight-fisted to lay out the sums of money for its implementation. His failure was particularly galling both to himself and his father, as his brother Richard had solved far more complex military problems in southern France. Richard, it seemed, was a real warrior; John was merely a dilettante wastrel.

At first the Old King's reaction to John's hangdog return to England in disgrace was to send him back to Ireland with another army, a determination strengthened by the arrival of the papal bull from Rome confirming the kingship together with a crown of peacock feathers embroidered with gold.[45] John was actually on his way back to Ireland in 1186 and had got as far as Chester when he was hurriedly recalled.[46] His father had received the sensational news that his other son, and

John's sometime ally against Richard, Geoffrey had been trampled to death at a tournament in Paris. The truth was more prosaic: he died on 19 August from a fever contracted after being badly cut up by horses' hooves, and it was this fact alone that saved him from dying excommunicate. Instead of being anathematised, he received a splendid funeral in Notre Dame Cathedral. Philip of France, his close friend, was said to have been so grief-stricken that he was with difficulty prevented from throwing himself into the grave alongside him.[47] Not only was this a crisis for the Angevin family, but Philip immediately claimed custody of Geoffrey's two daughters and threatened an invasion of Normandy if Henry II did not hand them over. Henry patched up a hurried truce with Philip, to last until January 1187, and the centre of political gravity again switched to the south of the Angevin empire. In 1185, while John was in Ireland, Richard had been engaged in yet another of the interminable wars with Raymond of Toulouse, probably in collusion with the perennial and seemingly irrepressible Angevin nemesis, viscount Aimar.[48] In 1186 Richard counter-attacked and in April played his trump card: a new treaty made with King Alfonso at Najac-de-Rouergue enabled him to launch Spanish troops against Raymond. The count of Toulouse buckled under the threat and sent frantic appeals to King Philip, pointing out that he could not face the host Richard had now assembled.[49] The year 1187 opened with both sides dazed by the rapid pace of events and therefore playing for time with new truces and ceasefires. In February Richard joined his father in Normandy, and together they parleyed with Philip at Gisors, extending the truce to midsummer. But peace did not come by a thousand truces; rather the two sides hardened in their attitude and determined to make their next armed encounter decisive.[50]

Meanwhile in Britanny, Geoffrey's death had created a complicated situation that would eventually have grave repercussions for John. Geoffrey's title as duke derived from his marriage to Constance, daughter of Conan, and it followed that the fief must pass to her children. When Geoffrey died Constance was pregnant, and Britanny waited to see if she would produce a son; otherwise the inheritance would go to Constance's infant daughter Eleanor. Sure enough, in March 1187, she gave birth to a boy. Eleanor of Aquitaine, who had gradually been released by Henry from the harsh, earlier terms of her imprisonment, was now sufficiently back in the saddle that she felt able to intervene in matters like the name of her grandchild. Constance, though, knowing of the latent antipathy of Bretons for the Angevin overlordship, thought it would be politic to humour her subjects with a homegrown name. Since

King Arthur and the knights of the Round Table were currently all the rage, she named her son Arthur. Eleanor of Aquitaine was irrationally enraged by Constance's 'defiance' and made it the work of what remained of her life to see that the Breton prince would never gain the throne of England – for as Geoffrey's son, he was second only to Richard and ahead of John in the succession. But the squabble over Arthur's name was as nothing to the dissension over the issue of wardship. Eleanor of Aquitaine at first claimed the right to educate her grandson, but Henry overruled her, thinking the guardianship of a possible successor should be his. But now arose the irony of ironies. Geoffrey had always been trouble while he was alive, but now his shadow seemed to loom over the realm from the grave. His famous Assize of 1185, possibly the only worthwhile achievement of his life, explicitly gave the feudal overlord the wardship of ophaned minors. Philip of France was quick to seize his opportunity. He sent envoys to Britanny to demand that Arthur be given up to him, in accordance with the explicitly stated laws of Britanny. Henry refused to surrender the boy, but he was angry about this latest development, as he always liked to cloak his machiavellianism in a tissue of feudal legal nit-picking and logic chopping; yet in this instance he was caught out in a barefaced 'might is right' posture.[51]

Pressing home his advantage, Philip again raised the issue of his sister Alice. The agreement of March 1186 had not made it clear whether the Angevins kept the Vexin if Alice remained unmarried. The disingenuous Henry II now explained his reluctance to marry Alice to any of his sons on the grounds that it would confuse the question of whether the Vexin belonged to Normandy by hereditary right.[52] But Philip had every justification for wanting to see a speedy resolution of Alice's future: she was now twenty-six and Henry's ludicrous insistence that Richard was too young to marry fooled nobody. Partisans of Henry have claimed that his motivation was political: he wanted to keep Alice as a pawn, to have her in his power so Philip could not marry her off to anyone else. It is astonishing how certain some modern historians are that Henry never seduced Alice, when general probability is massively on the side of this version of events. Henry had a long-standing reputation for seducing female wards and hostages, including the daughter of Eudo of Porhoet, one-time pretender to the dukedom of Britanny.[53] Demands for documentary evidence of illicit sexual liaisons are intrinsically absurd, but they allow the sceptics to shelter behind an absence of charters or pipe rolls. Yet the overwhelming likelihood is that in the case of Alice Henry was actuated by purely carnal motives. All the (admittedly circumstantial) evidence points to the fact that Alice was his mistress, and had been since 1180; moreover, he wanted to keep it that way. Richard, it seems, had refused to marry Alice because he was not prepared to take his father's leavings, but Henry dared not admit this to Philip. There is additional evidence that Alice bore Henry a son, who died in infancy.[54] Another theory is that Henry was planning to marry Alice and beget sons who might one day inherit both the kingdom of France and the Angevin empire. It was rational to expect that Eleanor of Aquitaine might die soon, for at sixty-four she was already very old in medieval terms. If he hastened her end by poison or some other form of murder while she was in his custody, that would certainly mean war to the knife with Richard at the very time Philip Augustus was flexing his muscles. Whichever interpretation we adopt, it is clear that the entire issue was a running sore. Any time Philip wanted a *casus belli*, he had only to resurrect this grievance and have international opinion on his side.

The winter of 1186–87 saw a period of 'phoney war', with both sides marking time but the initiative lying with France. Finally in June 1187 Philip made his move and invaded Berry. Richard and John held Châteauroux long enough for Henry to come up with the main army and force Philip to raise the siege. It would have been normal practice at this stage for Philip to retire prudently, but the flame of anti-Angevin anger burned brightly within him and he felt that his prestige and credibility were at stake. He therefore went for the option few monarchs in Western Europe ever risked in this era: pitched battle. It is worth mentioning that neither the warrior-prince Richard nor Henry II himself had ever fought a real battle hitherto – most of their engagements were either skirmishes or surprise attacks where one side was massacred. Fortunately, perhaps, at this very juncture a legate arrived from Pope Urban III to admonish both sides that Christian troops should not be wasted in this way, as they were needed in the Holy Land. Nobles on both sides tried to work out a solid peace treaty and, when this proved impossible, settled for a two-year truce. In the course of these negotiations, something happened to sour Richard considerably. The best guess is that Philip, alarmed by the combined power of the Angevins, tried to suborn Richard and told him of Henry's offer to marry Alice to John, with Aquitaine as John's wedding present.[55] In a fury, when the conference broke up he did not go with his father but accompanied Philip to Paris.

In the French capital Philip continued to drip poison into Richard's ear, revealing Henry's full duplicity on the subject of Alice and John and his ultimate scheme to disinherit him (Richard). He also found Richard personally to his liking, probably not as much as he had relished the more charming Geoffrey but enough so that Roger of Howden reported: 'Philip so honoured him that every day they ate from the same dish, and at night the bed did not separate them. Between the two of them there grew up so great an affection that King Henry was much alarmed and, afraid of what the future might hold in store, he decided to postpone his return to England until he knew what lay behind this sudden friendship.'[56] The closeness between the two men has seduced the unwary into imagining that a homosexual affair is indicated, but this is a hopelessly anachronistic reading. Two men sharing a bed would have a clear sexual meaning in the twentieth century but, taken on its own, it meant little in the twelfth century; to take the example nearest at hand, Henry II and William Marshal also did likewise, and the heterosexual credentials of Henry are unimpeachable. Even kisses were more commonly used in this epoch as signs of peace or friendship rather than of Eros.[57] Other evidence of a 'homoerotic' Richard is also vulnerable to the anachronistic fallacy. Incautious observers have sometimes tried to turn his later coronation ceremony, from which women were excluded, as an example of 'misogynism' but women were regularly excluded from such bachelor parties; medieval warriors, like the Achaeans in the *Iliad*, liked their women to dine separately.[58]

Nevertheless, the persistent canard that Richard was homosexual will not go away and is not so easy to dispose of on other grounds.[59] There is the mysterious incident when a hermit rebuked him in 1195 in the following words: 'Remember the judgement of Sodom and abstain from illicit acts, for if you do not, God will punish you in a fitting manner.' But it is quite possible, as the great Lionheart scholar John Gillingham has argued, that 'Sodom' could denote general sinfulness rather than homosexuality.[60] In general, twentieth-century writers on Richard have been too inclined to take the *a priori* method pioneered by the explorer and *Arabian Nights* translator Sir Richard Burton in the nineteenth century, whereby any notable historical figure not producing an heir must be assumed to be homosexual – but it should be emphasised that this is not a purely modern fault.[61] Medieval chroniclers regarded homosexuality as 'unnatural' and were keen to pounce on anyone they suspected of being guilty of this 'ungodly' vice. Richard's case seems to be that of the 'dog that barked in the night', in that if there had been a bark one of the chroniclers would have recorded it. Yet his failure to produce an heir does seem puzzling. Was he infertile? Was his wife barren? Was he asexual or sexually neuter? Or was he lowly-sexed or uninterested in marriage?

Perhaps, as some have suggested, he was eventually bullied into marriage by Eleanor of Aquitaine? Overall, the consensus of opinion is fixing on the idea that his wife Berengaria was barren, but because she did not remarry after his death this thesis is unverifiable.[62]

Besides, in the Middle Ages there were simply too many stories about Richard's alleged extramarital exploits current for the idea of a homosexual Richard to make sense. The evidence varies in levels of credibility. When Richard's subjects in Aquitaine were groaning under his strict rule, they alleged about him that 'he was evil to all men, to his own men worse, and to himself worst of all; he carried off the wives, daughters and kinswomen of his freemen by force and made them his concubines; and when he had sated his lust on them he handed them over to his knights for whoring.'[63] This is standard atrocity propaganda of the kind routinely produced against real or imaginary oppressors; given that Richard employed mercenaries in his wars against the Aquitaine rebels, we can well believe there were high levels of rape, but to make Richard personally responsible for them and in the forefront of promiscuous lechery strains belief. But he certainly had one acknowledged bastard, named Philip, born in the pre-1189 period who is said to have become lord of Cognac in later life. There are also rumours of another son called Fulk, allegedly born to a woman called Jeanne de St Pol, and indeed one of these illegimate sons features in Shakespeare's *King John*.[64] A thirteenth-century tale relates that Richard was consumed with lust for a nun of Fontevraud, and threatened to burn the abbey down if he could not have her. According to the Dominican friar Stephen of Bourbon, who told the story, the nun in question, hearing that it was her eyes that had so bedazzled Richard, cut them out and said: 'Send the king what he so much desires.'[65] Such lore would never have accumulated around a known homosexual. And the widowed Berengaria would not have exhibited such grief that she seemed, according to Bishop Hugh of Lincoln, close to total nervous and mental collapse, if she had been lamenting a sham marriage to a sodomite.[66]

The likelihood is that Richard, as ever, occupied a middle position on the spectrum of the Devil's Brood. Neither as uxorious as the Young King nor as prone to womanising as his father, he nonetheless contrasted strongly with John, who really was a priapic satyr. 'Not a woman was spared if he was seized by the desire to defile her in the heat of his lust', was one contemporary judgement.[67] John cared not if he was dealing with noblewomen or even the wives of his own friends and comrades. When young he lusted after the wife of Sir Eustace de Vesci and made it a mafia-like point of 'honour' that he be allowed to have her. Eustace cunningly pretended to agree to be cuckolded but substituted a whore for his wife; when the foolish John boasted next day about the wife's prowess in bed, Eustace could not resist telling him the truth.[68] Angered by this further slur on his 'honour', John made powerful threats against de Vesci, who promptly fled from court with his wife. He lived to be a powerful enemy, one John later regretted having crossed. Even more promiscuous than his father, John sired at least seven bastards as against his father's known three, though for obvious reasons an exact tally in such cases is impossible. Nonetheless, even John could not match the twenty-one bastards notched up by his great-grandfather Henry I, which allows some historians to claim that he was not beyond the bounds of the normal for a medieval prince.[69] We certainly know more about both his mistresses and his illegitimate offspring than we do in the case of Richard. The wife of Henry Pinel, Clementia, Suzanne, Hawise, countess of Aumale, and a fair unknown to whom he sent a chaplet of roses from his justiciar's garden in 1212, give him a more clear-cut sexual profile than his brother's, and in many ways we know more about John's private life than Richard's, including the names of six of his bastards: Geoffrey, Richard, Oliver, Richard, Osbert and Joan.[70]

Although he lacked his brother's military genius he had wider interests. He had more administrative ability, a greater sense of the art of the possible, was more cunning and devious. In time he also turned himself into an above average general. Infinitely more complex than Richard, who often seems one-dimensional in his obsession with martial prowess, John was in many ways a psychological oddity. The alternating bursts of frenetic energy and lethargy suggest a manic-depressive tendency towards 'bipolar affective disorder' or cyclothymia.[71] Yet one should not exaggerate John's unique qualities. Although he was well known to imitate his father by biting and gnawing his fingers in rage, or even set fire to the houses of men who had offended him, this was a general, shared Angevin characteristic. Even Richard had a reputation for violent, uncontrolled fits of temper, and there was the later, probably apocryphal story, that he had killed the brother of the duke of Austria with a chessboard after a trivial quarrel when they were both being brought up in Louis VII's court.[72] It may be that even his father towards the end sometimes lost patience with John in this regard. Such at least is the import of Gerald of Wales's story that in Winchester Castle Henry had a chamber hung with paintings but left one space blank until one day he filled it with a design of his own imagining. 'There was an eagle painted, and the four young ones of the eagle perched upon it, one on each wing and a third upon its back tearing at the parent with talons and beaks, and the fourth, no smaller than the others, sitting upon its neck and awaiting the moment to peck out its parent's eyes. When some of the king's close friends asked him the meaning of the picture, he said. "The four young ones of the eagle are my four sons, who will not cease persecuting me even unto death. And the youngest, whom I now embrace with such tender affection, will someday afflict me more grievously and perilously than all the others.'"[73]

Yet in the critical years of 1187–89, when Henry contended both with Philip Augustus and Richard, John scarcely appears in the official record, except as a pawn in Henry's elaborate guess-the-successor game. In the summer of 1187 Henry sent a swathe of envoys to Paris to ask Richard to return to him, but persuading him was an uphill task. At first Richard showed his contempt by pretending to comply and then suddenly swooping down on the castle of Chinon and carrying off the large amount of silver coin in the treasury there, for use in a rearmament programme in Aquitaine. When Henry continued to importune him, to the point where there was virtually a messenger a day arriving at Philip's court, Richard at last sensed he had played this particular game long enough, so went to Angers and swore yet another of the 'eternal' oaths of homage and fealty to his father – this was at least the sixth time he had so sworn.[74] Yet if Henry thought he had solved the problem of his eldest son, events soon conspired to disabuse him. On 4 July 1187 in the Holy Land the new Muslim conqueror Saladin utterly defeated the new king of Jerusalem and occupied the Holy City. The Christian kingdom of 'Outremer' – the land beyond the sea – was in imminent danger of extinction. That autumn, at Tours, not long after the reconciliation at Angers, Richard took the Cross without informing his father or his new friend Philip – he was the first western ruler to do so.[75] Bertran de Born saw distinct possibilities for his war of all against all project in the Third Crusade now being proclaimed throughout Europe and said of Richard: 'He who is count and duke and will be king has stepped forward, and by that his worth is doubled.'[76] But both Henry and Philip were stunned. Henry shut himself away for days and would see no one, while Philip angrily reflected that if Richard departed for the Holy Land, the entire contretemps over Alice would continue; how could his sister be brought to marry a man who was away on crusade?[77] The whole Franco-Angevin vendetta was now to acquire a totally different colouring as the cause of Christianity versus the infidel absorbed universal attention in Western Europe.

5

━━━━━━━━━━━━━━━━━━━━━━<◦>━━━━━━━━━━━━━━━━━━━━━━

F ULLY TO MAKE SENSE of the era 1187–93 in Richard's life, and
especially the years after 1189, we have to turn aside from the
running conflict between France and the Angevin empire to
examine the labyrinthine complexity of Middle Eastern politics in the
same epoch. The most militarily successful of all the Crusades, the first,
saw Christian and Norman princelings established in what later became
known as Outremer – the Christian lands beyond the sea. The great
Prince Bohemond established himself in Antioch, and Godfrey of
Bouillon stormed Jerusalem in 1098 and massacred thousands of Muslim
defenders. To achieve security, the new princelings had to conquer all
the coastal cities of Palestine, to ensure seaborne communications with
Europe, and then to conquer Galilee to safeguard the frontier with the
Muslim state of Syria, based on Damascus.[1] From the mid-twelfth century
onwards, the 'Franks', as the Christians were habitually termed by their
Muslim enemies, also expanded into southern Palestine and established
famous fortresses like Krak. The conquest of Tyre in 1124 was particularly important, as it deprived the Egyptian fleet (the Egyptians were the
natural enemies of Outremer) of watering facilities north of Ascalon.[2]
By 1131 the Crusader kingdom comprised most of Palestine and the
coast of Syria, both the inland cities of Jerusalem, Tiberias, Antioch and
Edessa and the coastal cities of Latakia, Tortisa, Tripoli, Beirut, Tyre,
Acre, Caesarea, Haifa, Jaffa and Ascalon. The largest cities were Jerusalem
and Acre, with a population of about 25,000 each out of a total for the
entire kingdom of Jerusalem of some 250,000. Two points are salient.
By and large the crusader kingdoms and provinces were ruled by the
younger sons of minor European aristocratic households, for the motivation to go on crusade was remarkably similar to the motives for the
conquistadores four hundred years later as described by Bernal Diaz: 'to
serve God and to become rich'. Yet the crusaders could never have
enjoyed the success of the First Crusade or the halcyon period of

colonisation thereafter but for the weakness of the Fatimid regime and the general paralysis in the Muslim world caused by the doctrinal and ideological warfare between Sunni and Shia factions.[3]

The crusader states benefited from two great advantages. In the first place were the famous crusader castles that so bewitched T.E. Lawrence (of Arabia).[4] Including walled cities, there were more than fifty of these. Although their military role has been overplayed – they could not stop invaders, for example, and their purely strategic importance was largely over by 1140 – they were important both administratively and economically. Administratively they formed the heartland of Outremer and were often the focus for settlement and colonisation projects, while economically they provided the force that allowed castellans to extract a surplus from the working population locally. It is difficult to separate civic and military or public and private aspects of the castles, but in purely military terms it can be said they usually performed a negative rather than positive function: they allowed Christians to counter-attack Muslim forces sortieing on raids from their own strongholds and they afforded a base providing water, supplies and – in case of defeat – protection; it was always wise to encounter an enemy near a friendly fortress.[5] Finally, the best of the castles had a symbolic importance in that they betokened the indestructibility of Outremer. The great showpiece castle, supposedly impregnable, was Krak des Chevaliers (Hisn al-Akrad) in Syria.[6] Here successive obstacles of fosse, outer and inner walls and three great towers acting as redoubts, formed an overlapping system of defence. The inner defences were much higher than the outer yet were close to them so that an enemy could be simultaneously engaged from both positions, while round towers, closely spaced at intervals from both lines of the wall, provided security from the flank. So formidable was Krak des Chevaliers that Saladin himself took one look at it and decided not even to try to besiege it.[7] The other 'secret weapon' of the kingdom of Jerusalem was the two knightly orders that protected it: the Templars and the Hospitallers. The Hospitallers had developed from the hospices attached to a Benedictine monastery in Jerusalem in 1071, while the Templars were founded around 1119 to defend pilgrims travelling to the Holy Sepulchre. Having received papal recognition, the two orders added military roles to their functions, so that by the time of the Third Crusade they were the local backbone of the Christian armies in Outremer.[8]

The two obvious weaknesses of the Latin states were factionalism between the lords of the various castle-cities (especially Jersusalem,

Antioch, Tripoli and Krak) and the fact that they ruled largely Muslim populations whose loyalty was suspect, especially in wartime.[9] These disadvantages were played up by the rising star in the politics of the Middle East, Al-Malik al-Nasir Salah ed-Din Yusuf, known in the West as Saladin. Yusuf was the son of Najm-ad-Din, a Kurdish nobleman from northern Armenia, near Georgia. Najm-ad-Din migrated early in his career to Baghdad, the seat of the Abbasid caliphate, and was made constable of Takreet Castle on the River Tigris. Tradition said that Saladin was born on the very day in 1137 that Najm and his brother Shirkuh were disgraced and forced to relocate north in Mosul.[10] After many adventures, Saladin had his early formation in Damascus, where his father was in the service of Zangi, formerly ruler of Mosul but now the lord of Syria. When Zangi died, the new prince of Damascus was his son Nur al-Din, the major influence on Saladin's life, a man who had inherited Zangi's anti-Frank zealotry.[11] An ambitious Sunni, Nur al-Din set his sights on the detested Shiite caliphate of the Fatimids in Egypt and determined to destroy it; as commander of his armies he appointed Shirkuh, with his 26-year-old nephew Saladin as his aide. Nur al-Din's decision to launch his troops against Egypt was a courageous one, for it meant crossing territory dominated by the crusader states, but his gamble paid off. Although Shirkuh had to fight no less than three major campaigns in six years, and could not finish off the enemy even by the great victories at Kawm-al-Rish in 1164 and Al-Babain in 1167, finally, in 1169, he was triumphant and Nur al-Din's banner fluttered above the mosques in Cairo. The Egyptian campaign was the making of Saladin: a promising staff officer at the beginning of the war but a leader of men and Shirkuh's heir apparent by the end, he had also whetted his appetite for anti-Crusader warfare. The Franks, knowing the threat that would come from a united Egypt and Syria, intervened on the side of the Egyptian Fatimids but lost the third and final round of the struggle against Shirkuh.[12]

Shirkuh's triumph was actually too complete for Nur al-Din, for he had unwittingly raised up a rival in the new vizier of Egypt. Shortly afterwards he died, by poison it was rumoured, but maybe simply from obesity.[13] The removal of Shirkuh anyway did Nur al-Din no good, for Saladin promptly replaced him as vizier, being both acclaimed by the Army and then rubber-stamped by the Fatimid caliph. Saladin was in a ticklish situation in Cairo for, as a Sunni, he recognised the supremacy of the Sunni caliphate of the Abbasids in Baghdad, but in Egypt he was working for the Fatimids, its enemy. Until 1172 he walked a tightrope, surviving Fatimid conspiracies by the old guard of defeated malcontents who were prepared to ally themselves with the Franks to bring Saladin down. Knowing Nur al-Din's enthusiasm for *jihad*, he realised that to make Egypt subservient to Syria would simply give Nur the resources of Egypt for a Holy War against Jerusalem, so, while gradually suppressing the Fatimid caliphate, he did not immediately completely abolish it but used it as a pawn in his diplomatic struggle with the lord of Damascus.[14] The game was supremely dangerous, and a serious Fatimid rebellion in Cairo had to be suppressed, but Saladin, convinced that the Egyptian economy was not strong enough to weather the demands of Nur's anti-Crusader aims, continued to play both sides against the middle. When he at last formally reinstated the Abbasids in Egypt but would still not obey directives from Damascus, Nur al-Din lost patience and decided to attack. In vain did Saladin protest that to join Nur in *jihad* would simply expose Egypt to crusader counter-attacks. He added insult to injury by wasting Egypt's substance, as Nur al-Din saw it, in campaigns in Nubia, Libya and Tunisia. War between Saladin and Nur was imminent when the lord of Damascus died suddenly in 1174.[15]

The death of Nur al-Din produced a political situation similar to that in Egypt on the eve of Shirkuh's invasions, but with the roles of Egypt and Syria reversed. By 1175 Saladin was master of Damascus as well as Cairo. His political talents could scarcely be denied, for he had overcome the manifold problems that assailed Egypt in the late twelfth century: mob violence in Cairo and Alexandria, Norman naval attacks, revolts in Upper Egypt, famine and plague, even currency devaluations. He had risen to the top despite the underlying problems like the vicious Shia-Sunni conflict and the political fragmentation caused by the rise of the vizier class, independent of the caliphs to whom they paid nominal allegiance. The caliph-vizier divorce of ownership and control, as it were, also uncannily mirrored the situation in France, where more powerful Angevin rulers paid homage to less powerful feudal overlords. Now that he had established his power base in Egypt, harnessed its economic resources, its army and even its fleet, and integrated Egypt with Syria, Saladin had the scope to display his military talent. The situation faced by the Christian kingdom of Outremer was more serious than in its entire history, and the crisis was made worse by the absence of its normal allies. Ironically, in the very same year that the western emperor Frederick Barbarossa came to disaster at Legnano in Italy (1176), the eastern emperor Manuel sustained a stunning defeat at Iconium at the hands of the Saljuquids.[16] The Christian kingdom of Jerusalem could no longer look to Byzantium for support. In contrast to the situation ten or fifteen years earlier, Syria and Egypt now had little to fear from Outremer, especially as Venice, Pisa and Genoa, putative crusader allies, were trading with Egypt after meeting commercial resistance in Byzantium. Additionally, king Almaric, erstwhile scourge of Egypt, died in 1174 and was succeeded by the 13-year-old Baldwin, Jerusalem's leper king.[17]

Why, then, did it take a dozen years, between seizing power in Syria and 1187, before Saladin moved decisively against the Franks? In the first place, it took him that long to bring the whole of non-Christian Syria and Mesopotamia under his control. The long campaigns against the *atabegs* of Aleppo and Mosul occupied an unconscionable amount of his time and attention, even though Saladin made occasional forays against the Franks.[18] It was estimated that after 1174 Saladin spent thirteen months fighting the Christian states but thirty-three in battles against his fellow-Muslims.[19] All sections of his domains had specific grouses, with Egyptians in particular feeling that Saladin consistently neglected their interests in favour of Syria's. Some of his own table-talk was scarcely helpful, as with the much-touted saying: 'Egypt is a whore who has tried in vain to part me from my faithful wife, Syria.'[20] But even Syrians felt resentful. Cynics said of him: 'Saladin spent the revenues of Egypt to gain Syria, and the revenues of Syria to gain Mesopotamia.'[21] He was vehemently criticised within the Islamic world for wasting so much time in campaigns against Muslim states rather than against the infidel – exactly the criticism successive popes had made of Henry II and the French kings. Doubtless Saladin hoped for quick victories against Aleppo and Mosul, but these constantly eluded him. Additionally, the Aleppo ruler trumped his ace by calling in the radical sect of Islamic hitmen – the Assassins – to deal with him. There was a contract out on Saladin in 1176 until he bribed the 'Old Man of the Mountain' (the Assassins' leader) to desist, after which there was no more trouble with them.[22] Yet another problem was the rising power of Qilijarslan, the Saljuquid sultan who defeated the Byzantines at Iconium and was now looking covetously at the Euphrates. Saladin and Qilijarslan confronted each other once, in 1178, but the Saljuquids thought better of battle and withdrew.[23] Moreover, the Franks did not stand idly by while Saladin was thus preoccupied but raided into his territories. And Saladin was never entirely a free agent. He had to consult the interests of local warlords, who were apathetic about the idea of an anti-Christian *jihad*. Finally, there is the distinct possibility that Saladin himself was never that interested in Holy War, that his real preoccupation was a united Islam under a centralised Abbasid caliphate.[24]

During the years 1175–86 Saladin had many brushes with the crusaders. There were major skirmishes in 1177 and in 1179, when Saladin turned the screw by sending his fleet of 60 galleys and 20 transports on a raid along the coasts of Syria and Asia Minor which netted over a thousand prisoners. In 1183 Guy of Lusignan confronted Saladin with a Christian army, but both sides declined battle.[25] In general in these years, Saladin was preoccupied with Mosul and Aleppo and responded only to direct provocation from the Franks. Everything changed in 1186 when Saladin broke the power of Mosul (Aleppo had fallen in 1183) and he was finally able to devote his full-time attention to the kingdom of Jerusalem. Saladin's new bearing came at the worst possible moment for Outremer, deprived as it was of its traditional allies by the decline of Byzantine power and riven by factionalism.[26] By the early 1180s three major figures had emerged on the Christian side. Baldwin IV, affected by leprosy, was gradually turning the kingdom over to Guy of Lusignan but there was considerable resentment about this, since Guy was a 'new man', an interloper in the eyes of 'old Outremer', an adventurer who had made his mark by marrying Sybilla, the widowed sister of the king of Jerusalem, in 1180. Temporarily Regent in 1184 but meeting stiff opposition, Guy got his big chance when Baldwin died of leprosy in 1185 and his infant heir the next year. Despite intense unpopularity, Guy manoeuvred his way to the throne and was crowned in 1186 – a Poitevin king. Quite apart from religious considerations, Henry II and Richard now had a more immediate interest in Jerusalem, for Guy was nominally their vassal as a Poitevin subject of Richard, and Sybilla, as a member of the junior branch of the house of Anjou, was a cousin.[27]

The two other figures were bitter enemies of Guy of Lusignan, though they could not have been more unlike. Raymond of Tripoli would have been a more popular choice as king of Jerusalem, and he and his many supporters continued to brood about this setback. One of the 'old guard' of the Latin kingdom, a wiry man of medium height with a hawk nose and dark complexion, Raymond was a great warrior but a wise, solomonic and magnanimous counsellor and a great ally and promoter of the Hospitallers. He had suffered imprisonment at the hands of the Muslims but had learned to admire them, spoke Arabic and advocated peaceful co-existence with the heathen. He married the widow of the lord of Tiberias, whose territory, on the shores of lake Galilee and containing the New Testament locations of Nazareth and Mount Tabor, was the most vulnerable fief in the whole of the kingdom of Jerusalem and the first target for any invasion from Arabic Syria.[28] Mindful of this and resentful of Guy of Lusignan, Raymond established good relations with Saladin and even entered into a treaty of friendship with him. Utterly unlike Raymond in every way was the chief 'hawk' of the kingdom, Reginald (Reynald) of Châtillon, lord of Kerak, a classical crusader-adventurer from a minor family in northern France, who had come east in 1147 in search of wealth. Captured by Muslims in 1160, Reginald had spent fourteen years in captivity until ransomed for the enormous sum of 120,000 gold dinars. His years as a prisoner had left him with a fanatical, undying hatred of the Islamic world and all its works. Notorious for his cruelty, Reginald had been an eager warrior in the many clashes with Saladin in the period 1175–87. In 1182–83 his anti-Saladin zealotry bore fruit in a quixotic raid on the Red Sea, part of a grand design apparently conceived to sack Mecca and Medina and carry off the sacred black stone or Ka'aba. His piratical fleet was defeated by Saladin's navy off Medina, but Reginald escaped to fight another day. Saladin, who was heavily criticised for allowing the infidel to penetrate so close to the holy cities of Islam, swore a mighty oath that he would capture and behead the lord of Kerak. A wise man might have sought conciliation, as Raymond of Tripoli did, but in 1187 Reginald compounded his 'blasphemy' by attacking and slaughtering Arab pilgrims as they passed Kerak; among those taken for ransom from the caravan was Saladin's sister. Reginald had now insulted Saladin's family as well as the Prophet.[29]

Saladin at once appealed to Guy of Lusignan, as king of Jerusalem, to restore his sister and offer an apology and compensation for the attack on the caravan. Guy agreed that some such action was due, but Reginald of Châtillon, backed by the diehard leader of the Templars, Gérard de Rideford (another anti-Islamic fanatic), brutally rebuffed him, telling him in effect that events in the environs of Kerak were none of his business. Saladin methodically collected the largest army he had ever put in the field (some 25,000 strong), and then asked Raymond of Tripoli, his nominal ally, for permission to cross his territory so as to be able to strike back at Reginald de Châtillon. Raymond was thus in a terrible dilemma, bound on the one hand to an ally but on the other forced to betray his co-religionists if he honoured the alliance. The hawks, led by Châtillon and de Rideford, poured out all their venom on Raymond, alleging that he had 'gone native' and was a traitor to the Christian religion. Threshing around desperately to find a way out of this conundrum, Raymond hit on the idea of suggesting that Saladin's forces arrive in Tiberias by sunset but be gone by sunrise the next morning without any raiding en route.[30] He salved his conscience by warning Guy of

Lusignan that an attack was coming. But nothing could stem the Christian fanatics. When Saladin's forces crossed the River Jordan into Lower Galilee on 1 May 1187, a small force of Western knights, mainly Templars, engaged them at Cresson, two miles from Nazareth. Despite having merely hundreds to launch against thousands, Gérard de Rideford attacked. The Muslim army simply opened up like the biblical Red Sea, swallowed up the mailed knights, then closed up again, engulfing the Franks in frightful slaughter; miraculously de Rideford and four horsemen escaped, but they left behind over one hundred slain knights, the cream of the kingdom's chivalry.[31] The debacle meant the end for Raymond of Tripoli's fence-sitting diplomacy. His 'treachery', not de Rideford's folly, was blamed for the disaster, and he came under massive pressure, even from his own troops, to abandon his alliance with Saladin. Bowing to the inevitable, Raymond went to Jerusalem with his men and swore allegiance to Guy of Lusignan.

News of Cresson made even hesitant Arab warriors keen to join Saladin, who declared that this was a critical moment in the history of Islam, requiring a supreme effort. With an army of 25,000 men, Saladin at last had the manpower to offset the Franks' advantage in technology and discipline. But the Franks too were now waging Holy War. The remainder of the kingdom's 1,200 knights joined Guy's 20,000 foot to make up the most formidable Christian host yet seen in the Latin kingdom. Saladin next began by tempting Guy's army to move out of its secure rendezvous point at La Safouri. He laid waste the lands of Raymond, his erstwhile ally, even defiling the cone of Mount Tabor, the scene of the biblical Transfiguration. Since Raymond's wife had remained at Tiberias, that walled city was Saladin's next target, and soon the Arab army had breached the outer walls. At a council of war called by Guy of Lusignan, Reginald de Châtillon and Gérard de Rideford predictably urged immediate rescue but Raymond, the immediately injured party, advised waiting Saladin out and making a stand at Acre instead.[32] In the contest between the cautious and intelligent Raymond, backed by the Hospitallers, and the firebrand de Châtillon, backed by de Rideford and the Templars, it was perhaps inevitable that the hawks would prevail. But legend has it that it was only when de Rideford stole into Guy of Lusignan's tent after the council and accused him of arrant cowardice that Guy, seeing the issue as a point of personal honour, finally snapped and gave the order for an immediate attack.[33]

The crusader army proceeded to make every mistake in the book. Tiberias and the Sea of Galilee lay fifteen miles east of La Safouri, at first over the arid plain of Lubiya and then up onto the ridge of Hattin, with the final stage of the march over a waterless wilderness. Since it was only possible for a large, heavily encumbered force to march 6–7 miles a day in such conditions, the Christian army did not reach the village of Turan, with the last waterhole before the lake of Galilee itself, until noon on 3 July. They then set out immediately to march the nine miles to the lake, having to face the prospect of a battle without water if Saladin opposed them. As soon as they left Turan, Saladin sent riders to cut off their retreat. By nightfall Guy and his men were encamped in the middle of the desert, waterless and with the horn of Hattin, scene of the Sermon on the Mount, ahead of them. During the night of 3–4 July the Arab army surrounded them. Saladin positioned his archers carefully, telling them to aim at the horses for, without mounts, the fearsome Frankish knights were powerless. By morning, having spent a parched, thirsty night in great agony, the Christian troops were beaten before battle was even joined. Saladin could have finished his enemy off at dawn but, prolonging the agony, waited until the sun was high in the sky before attacking and destroying the Christian host piecemeal.[34] Defeat for Guy of Lusignan was total and the massacre fearful. Somehow Raymond of Tripoli escaped from the bloody battlefield, but Guy, de Rideford and Reginald de Châtillon were captured and brought before Saladin. After giving Châtillon the chance to convert to Islam, which Reginald contemptuously rejected, Saladin cut him down where he stood, leaving his guards to administer the *coup de grâce*. Guy feared a similar fate but Saladin shrugged and said to him: 'Real kings do not kill each other. But that man was no king and had overstepped the mark. So, what happened, happened.'[35]

Saladin was not so merciful towards the captured Templars and Hospitallers, whom he ordered executed to the last man. The True Cross, which Guy had brought from the Holy Sepulchre at Jerusalem to the field of battle, was sent on to Damascus. Saladin's armies then swept over the kingdom of Jerusalem. Acre, Beirut and Sidon surrendered without a fight. Only Tyre, whose defence was masterminded by Conrad of Montferrat, an adventurer who had made himself prince of the city, held out. Unable to make an impression on Tyre, Saladin moved on to take Caesarea, Arsuf and Jaffa. His next target was Ascalon, one of the five cities of the biblical Philistines. His idea was that he would barter Guy of Lusignan's freedom for Ascalon's surrender, but at first Guy returned empty-handed; fortunately for him, Ascalon soon afterwards had second thoughts and ran up the white flag. De Rideford gained his freedom in a similar way, after persuading the Templar castle of Gaza not to resist Saladin.[36] Instead of concentrating on strategic objectives, Saladin now decided that the propaganda coup of taking Jerusalem was irresistible. Jerusalem faced his coming with trepidation, for this was the scene of the massacre of some 40,000 Muslims by the Franks in the climax to the First Crusade in 1098. A vigorous defence of the Holy City by Balian of Ibelin convinced Saladin that a negotiated surrender was best; he knew reinforcements would reach the Franks from the West and he could not afford to lose manpower in a costly siege. Nonetheless, the terms of surrender were harsh. Those who could afford to pay steep ransoms were allowed to depart; those who could not were enslaved. Among the latter were many Christian women who suffered mass rape and enforced concubinage.[37] But atrocities were largely forgotten in the more general shock sustained by Christendom when Saladin entered Jerusalem on 2 October 1187. The archbishop of Tyre toured Europe preaching the crusade, while Pope Gregory VIII issued the encyclical *Audita Tremendi* on 29 October, calling on the faithful to rally to the rescue of Jerusalem and granting a plenary indulgence and other benefits to all who took the Cross.[38]

Dramatic and convulsive as these events were, they took time to make an impact on the feuding French and Angevins in Western Europe, where for a time it was still 'business as usual'. Tired of the entire running farce over Alice and determined to solve the issue once and for all, Philip next threatened an immediate invasion of Normandy unless Henry either returned Gisors and the Vexin or compelled Richard to marry Alice forthwith. But, in a surprise twist of events, at the supposedly 'final' conference at Gisors in January 1188, impassioned rhetoric from the archbishop of Tyre persuaded both kings to take the Cross themselves. Neither Henry nor Philip wanted to go on crusade – they regarded it as a tiresome diversion from the real arena of their interests in France – but they were increasingly being swept along by a force of public opinion that was more typhoon than tide.[39] Passions were running high, with those reluctant to crusade being sent 'womanly' tokens of wool and distaff – the twelfth-century equivalent of white feathers. Crusaders were offered important concessions: the freezing of all debt until return from the Holy Land; the protection of the Church for their property while they were away; and a plenary indulgence which wiped out all sin and removed the fear of Hell and Purgatory. Henry and Philip were caught in the whirlwind of history – Henry particularly, who had pledged himself to crusade since 1172 but had done nothing about it.[40] The two kings now had to raise the money for the expedition, and a special Saladin

Tithe was ordained in England – the first tax in English history levied on personal property other than real estate. But it was agreed that both monarchs would need at least a year to prepare a host sufficient to deal with Saladin, so that the proposed General Passage through Europe would have to be postponed into 1189. Nonetheless a major crusading conference was held at Le Mans in early 1188, where it was agreed that French troops would wear red crosses, the English white and the Flemish green. Philip sent advance envoys to the king of Hungary and the emperor at Constantinople to secure safe passage for the armies, while Richard, planning a seaborne approach across the Mediterranean, wrote letters to his brother-in-law King William of Sicily, requesting merchant shipping there. But the recruiting masterstroke among the many decrees at Le Mans was the exemption of all crusaders from paying the Saladin Tithe, which led many an ungodly knight to take the Cross.[41]

Even while these complex matters were being thrashed out at Le Mans, yet another rebellion broke out in Aquitaine, featuring Richard's old adversaries Geoffrey de Lusignan, Ademer of Angoulême, Geoffrey de Rancon and the Taillefers, who followed the rebel banner even though Richard had given up his original demand that Angoulême should be inherited by Vulgrin's daughter Matilda. The rising was something of a rerun of the events of 1179, with the castle of Taillebourg once more featuring as the centrepiece of the insurrection, but it was as futile as the one nine years earlier, for Richard simply hurried south and repeated his former exploits, taking all rebel castles and laying waste their territories with fire and sword. If the rebels had had any sense, they would have waited until Richard was safely on crusade in the Holy Land. But now, foreseeing that there would be another rising once he was out of the country, Richard pardoned the insurgents on the express understanding that they would all take the Cross.[42] Yet no sooner had he put this revolt down than he became involved in fresh hostilities with count Raymond of Toulouse; being duke of Aquitaine seemed like an everlasting game of Chinese boxes. Raymond had visited some atrocities on a party of Aquitaine merchants – either he blinded them or castrated them – and Richard, in a revenge raid, captured Raymond's right-hand man Peter Seillan. Raymond retaliated by taking prisoner two of Henry II's knights, on their way back from pilgrimage at Compostela. The stand-off soon turned into outright war – Philip of France tried to arbitrate but was rebuffed by both sides. Richard's Brabançon mercenaries assailed Toulouse while he himself took seventeen castles in a sweep to the north as far as Cahors. When Richard's combined army approached the gates of Toulouse, the citizens made it clear they were willing to do an immediate deal with him.[43]

Seeing disaster looming, Raymond appealed to the king of France. Philip did not want to fall out with his new friend Richard, and in any case that would leave Richard nowhere to go but back to Henry, which would defeat the point of Philip's anti-Angevin campaign. So, instead of replying to Raymond, he duplicitously complained to Henry about his son's behaviour at Toulouse. Henry replied that events in Aquitaine were nothing to do with him. In fact he was playing a double game, apparently with the intention of stopping Richard from going on crusade this year. He hated the idea of Richard's having an independent command that was proceeding ahead of the overland armies by sea, partly because he feared his son would win the renown as a general he felt should be his alone. Not only did he disavow Richard's actions, but Richard soon found evidence that his father had given moral and financial backing to both the Aquitaine rebels and Count Raymond. This was the end of the road for Richard as far as Henry was concerned.[44] Once Philip realised that Richard now harboured an implacable hatred for his father, he turned on his erstwhile friend and invaded Berry, in retaliation for the attack on Toulouse. Philip claimed, unconvincingly, that the attack on Toulouse was a breach of the January 1188 accord, but in fact Raymond had not agreed to take the Cross so was not covered by its provisions. Philip was being doubly disingenuous for Raymond, as a rebel against a declared crusader, should have been anathematised by the general decree of excommunication pronounced at Le Mans against all who hindered or delayed the General Passage. The real reason for Philip's intervention was that he regarded Toulouse as an integral part of France and could now be reasonably confident that Richard and Henry would not combine in the field against him. His invasion of Berry was a fully-fledged affair, with a full complement of siege engines. On 16 June he easily took the fortress of Châteauroux – so easily that it was reliably reported that a fifth column had treacherously delivered it to him. Once Berry switched its allegiance to Philip, the lord of Vendôme followed suit.[45]

Henry II was caught in the coils of his own double-dealing, for soon Loches and other key strongholds in the Angevin heartland were threatened as Philip's success became breakaway. Alarmed by the turn of events, Henry sent a deputation to Philip to protest against his invasion of Aquitainian territory. When this made no impression, he assembled an army, made ready to cross the Channel himself, sent out raiding armies on French dominions and began helping Richard to recover Berry. After

narrowly escaping destruction in a terrific Channel storm, he landed in
Normandy on 11 July 1188.[46] Wrongfooted as a result of a bad miscalculation – that Henry and Richard would never again make common
cause – Philip was forced to withdraw from Berry to protect his northern
border with Normandy, leaving Richard free to recover most of his lost
territories. Yet the fortress of Châteauroux stubbornly held out. While
in a scrimmage outside the gates, Richard was thrown from his horse
but quickly rescued when a giant of a man, a butcher by trade, plucked
him from the ground.[47] Meanwhile the Philip-Henry confrontation was
heading towards the inevitable stalemate. Henry simply camped on the
Normandy borders and made no attempt to invade France, as he feared
the prospect of a pitched battle. Philip struck south again but his
campaign ran into the sands when Richard moved into the Loire valley
to meet him. Philip retreated to Paris and Richard, seeing him gone,
rejoined his father in Normandy. The king of France was running out
of options, for his barons advised him he should not be making war on
the Angevins or any other fellow Christians at this juncture when every
last fighting man was needed for the crusade in the Holy Land.[48]

Yet another peace conference was arranged at Gisors. On the Feast
of the Assumption, 15 August 1188, Philip, Henry and Richard convened
under the eye of Holy Mother Church, with papal envoys frantically
beseeching the great lords to compose their quarrel so that the crusade
could begin. But this three-day conclave began badly and ended in farce
or bathos. On the second day a French knight made fun of a Welsh
archer in Henry's service for his strange accent and weird attire. The
Welshman fitted an arrow to his bow and shot the shaft into his taunter's
head. The wound was not fatal, but now, under the famous tree of Gisors
which was supposed to guarantee safe conduct and no blow could be
struck, the French knight showed King Philip the arrow sticking from
his skull and asked for satisfaction. Philip angrily declared the conference at an end. William Marshal, who was with Henry, hardly improved
matters by intervening to suggest that, although his liege lord accepted
responsibility for this crime, both sides should make up by a general
joust. When this was angrily spurned, he suggested a four-against-four
duel of champions; as he was the greatest knight in Christendom, this
was a contest he clearly expected to win.[49] Philip simply became more
angry at this absurd offer of 'compensation' and stalked away angrily.
Brooding in his tent, he finally found a way to avenge himself on Henry
for the egregious breach of traditional ceasefire terms at the tree of
Gisors. That night he sent out a party of axemen who cut down the

famous elm tree and used it as firewood. News of this 'sacrilegious' act caused a sensation, but Philip was making it clear that he had had enough of the endless deadlock at these colloquys and of Henry II's endless lies. He was in effect declaring that there could be no dealing with Henry and the only recourse was war to the death.[50]

On 30 August the Angevin army crossed the border and marched towards Mantes, burning and looting as it went in a particularly devastating raid. Richard was involved in a successful skirmish with a French knight, William de Barres, which further increased the diapason of ill-feeling caused by the Gisors conference. De Barres surrendered to Richard and was released on parole – the standard practice in both war and tournaments – but escaped on horseback, to Richard's great fury. The French then added chivalric insolence to injury by claiming that the real cheat was Richard because he had thrust his sword into William's horse, although, as William Marshal's career showed, this too was standard practice.[51] Clearly nerves were on edge on both sides, with the monarchs especially fretting at the burdensome costs of maintaining knights and archers in a combination of idleness and constant readiness. Then there were the calls of both harvest and vintage in the autumn, and the constant undertow of criticism, especially from the clergy, that putative fellow-crusaders should not be trying to kill each other. So, despite Philip's vow that there would be no more talk, circumstances forced him to agree to yet another conference on 7 October 1188, this time at Châtillon on the border of Touraine and Berry. Philip hoped to find a way to drive an entering wedge between Richard and Henry but began cautiously, offering to waive his conquests in Berry on condition that Richard handed back his gains in Toulouse to Count Raymond. Richard replied that he wanted the two matters kept separate, but offered to accept Philip as arbitrator between him and Raymond. Clearly he thought he could not trust Henry and suspected him of still wanting to cut him out of the succession in favour of John; an entente with Philip was therefore his insurance policy. This unilateral decision in turn enraged Henry, who felt he should have been consulted. When Philip escalated matters by asking for the surrender of a castle as an earnest of Henry's good intentions while he (Philip) arbitrated between Richard and Raymond, the Old King stormed out in a rage.[52]

Now that Richard was negotiating directly with him and was not part of an Angevin united front, Philip could deluge his ally with all the rumours, all the intelligence both hard and soft, that his spies brought him about Henry's future intentions. One circumstantial detail that nobody could argue round was that John had not taken the Cross. Why not? Was Henry simply waiting until Richard had left for the Middle East before making his move and naming John as his successor? Philip kept such suspicions at white heat. His agents claimed to have uncovered a plot whereby every vassal in Anjou and Aquitaine would be forced to pay homage to John; when Richard returned from crusade, with his own loyal forces depleted by a hard campaign against Saladin, he would find John installed in Aquitaine with the citadels of every castle there barred against him. On Philip's advice, Richard decided, despite his natural repugnance, that he would marry Alice as a point of policy, and in return Philip would press Henry to say before the whole world that he recognised Richard as his undoubted and indefeasible heir. Agreed on all points, Richard and Philip then demanded another colloquy with Henry, who could not refuse unless he was to stand forth as the man who prevented the Crusade from setting out; Henry had had enough trouble with the papacy over Becket to be unwilling to face a fresh threat of excommunication.[53] Accordingly, a fresh conference took place at Bonsmoulins on 18 November. Richard and Philip arrived together, rather ostentatiously making the point that they were now allies. They began with a kind of 'dumb show' where Philip suggested an exchange of conquests to Richard and he indignantly rejected it. Presumably this charade was meant to allay suspicions about their collusion, but it fooled no one. The atmosphere at the conference was notably tense. On the first day the parties managed to control themselves, but on the second day there were raised voices and angry exchanges, and by the third swords had been drawn. Richard made three demands that Henry found unacceptable: he must be proclaimed heir apparent to Henry in Normandy and England; he must immediately come into possession of all other Angevin fiefs; and he must marry Alice without delay. When Henry declared that these demands were simple blackmail, Richard replied: 'Now at last I must believe what I previously thought was incredible.'[54]

Without more ado Richard knelt and swore fealty to Philip. The breach between father and son was irreparable. That evening, when Richard rode off with Philip to Amboise, he began laying plans for calling out his vassals in Aquitaine for war against Henry. The Old King seemed bewildered and crushed by the turn of events. In his retinue he had Baldwin, archbishop of Canterbury and Hugh, bishop of Lincoln and now he turned on them, claiming that God had deserted him and, as his servants, they should have interceded for him. When the divines cautioned him against blasphemy, Henry whipped himself into new heights of execration. 'Why should I venerate and honour Christ,' he asked, 'who has allowed a mere stable-boy to insult and dishonour me?' When the bishops protested, he made obscene and atheistic references to the Christian God, so startling that Gerald of Wales, who reports the conversation, could not bring himself to mention the exact words.[55] What seems to have infuriated Henry most of all was that his bluff had been called and he had been outwitted by a son whose intelligence he despised. For years he had kept Alice in play as a political pawn, knowing very well that Richard would not marry her because she was a royal mistress. Now, prompted by the cunning Philip, Richard had stated openly that he wished to marry Alice. It was quite clear to Henry that Richard could not have thought up such a devastating change of tactics for himself and that he was now firmly in Philip's pocket. Gradually, though, his advisers talked him round. William Marshal said that the king owed it to himself and his realm to try to bring Richard back to his side. Henry tried the old ploy of bombarding his son with dozens of envoys, all pleading with him to return, but the Old King had cried wolf once too often and Richard was not impressed. William Marshal told Henry bluntly that the idea of 'turning' Richard was hopeless.[56] Hearing from his messengers that each new overture served only to make Richard indite another letter calling out further feudal levies, Henry bent his energies to securing his castles in Anjou. The agent for this mission was his faithful bastard son and now Chancellor, Geoffrey.

Henry was faced with a terrible crisis, worse than all he had endured with the Young King, as he no longer had the energy to deal tirelessly with it, as in earlier years. He was disconcerted to find that all the great knights of Aquitaine were declaring for Richard.[57] At root Henry was to blame: for his machiavellianism over the succession, his dishonesty over Alice, his partiality for John and his basic manipulative deviousness. It is possible, as some historians have maintained, that he was not planning to supplant Richard with John, that he believed too strongly in hereditary, indefeasible right for that, that he was simply the victim of his own deviousness. The historian W.L. Warren wrote. 'Henry had adopted the tactic of trying to discipline Richard by keeping him in uncertainty and had then become caught in the coils of his own deviousness.'[58] It is true that he made no overt steps in John's favour, except to prevent him from taking the Cross. One view is that Henry knew in his heart that Richard would succeed but refused to acknowledge him publicly because of the harm that had been caused when he announced the succession of the Young King prematurely.[59] Yet there is much that points the other way, towards a genuine desire to displace Richard in favour of his beloved John, and the endless vacillations and policy shifts may instead indicate a man determined that John should be king but uncertain how exactly to achieve that aim.[60] Certainly the analogy with the Young King was disingenuous, as Henry must have known. The Young King was an idler and wastrel who had eschewed responsibility and proven himself incompetent in government. With Richard the reverse was the case. And it is unconvincing to think that Henry was still playing manipulative games with no ulterior purpose in the years 1187–89, unless we conclude that he was stupid rather than cunning. Whereas he could have got away with sheer deviousness for its own sake or to control Richard before the Crusade became a pressing issue, once that loomed across the face of Europe, only an idiotic ruler would have continued in the same vein. The obstinacy in the face of pressure from the pope and Christian Europe in general surely points towards a grim determination to make John king, whatever the political cost.[61]

That Henry's star was fading was obvious at his last Christmas court, held at Saumur. Of his family only John was present; even more ominously most of his great barons stayed away, clearly awaiting the moment to transfer their allegiance to Richard or Philip. The truce agreed at Châtillon to last until the New Year 1189 was extended until Easter, but halfway through Lent Henry fell ill at Le Mans and took to his bed. The archbishop of Canterbury, the bishop of Tours and the archbishop of Rouen acted as a triumvirate of fathers-confessor and persuaded the Old King to confess his sins in a proper canonical form. Even close to death Henry remained devious and now he tried to con the Almighty, admitting to 'sins' that could be extenuated as *raison d'état* but denying graver ones of which he was obviously guilty. At first the bishops refused absolution on the grounds that Henry had not made a firm purpose of amendment; this was why they felt free to divulge his bogus confession. Yet in the end they were persuaded that Henry's fear of Hell was enough to make his confession genuine – quite how is a mystery, as Henry continued his atheistic ravings – and granted him the sacrament. Informed of Henry's illness, both Richard and Philip refused to believe that it was genuine and suspected some typically Henrician trick. Once the truce lapsed, they continued their raiding to the point where Britanny, seeing no counter-movement from the Old King, rose in revolt. The Angevin empire was starting to come apart at the seams.[62] Desperately Henry sent envoy after envoy to Richard, but the time for that had long gone; although many in the Old King's entourage were convinced that he was now genuinely sorry for the shabby way he had treated Richard, the harsh fact was that his eldest son no longer believed a word he said.[63]

Finally in June a papal legate named John of Anagni, under orders from the Vatican to compose the quarrel so that the Crusade could proceed, assembled an arbitration panel of himself and four bishops, two nominated by each side (the bishops of Rheims, Bourges, Rouen and Canterbury). The arbitrators met at La Ferte-Bernard in Maine, twenty-five miles north-east of Le Mans, secure in the pledge by both kings that they would abide by the decision. Many other bishops and abbots attended the conference out of curiosity, to the point where one observer said the gathering looked more like a synod of the Gallican Church than a peace conference of warring factions. But both sides arrived with armed guards, suspecting treachery. Richard and Philip once more demanded that Henry guarantee Richard's inheritance as heir apparent and immediately agree to his marriage with Alice. It may have been the irksome presence of John in his sick father's retinue that made Richard add a further condition: John was to take the Cross and depart overland with Philip before he, Richard, would set out for the Mediterranean. Henry retorted that he would accept all conditions but the one relating to Alice for, he now announced, he wanted her to marry John. Richard and Philip were outraged by this latest twist in Henry's serpentine schemings and rejected the idea angrily. But the papal legate and the panel now seemed to feel it was Richard who was being intransigent; the Old King's political skill had still not deserted him. John of Anagni threatened to lay a papal interdict on France if Henry's terms were not accepted; Philip, never one to take a direct threat lying down, replied haughtily that it was easy to see that the legate's bags were full of English silver. Yet another conference broke up in acrimonious chaos.[64]

Henry withdrew at once to Le Mans, but Richard and Philip attacked La Ferte-Bernard and quickly took it. A lightning campaign saw many more of Henry's castles – Montfort, Maletable, Beaumont, Ballon – fall into their hands. Henry was now in a desperate situation, for Aquitaine was wholly with Richard, England was dragging its feet about sending troops to the continent (and they would not be available for two months anyway), and Normandy was poised to receive an invasion from Philip. At first he hoped to make a stand at Le Mans and burned all the bridges over the River Huisne, thinking this would flummox Richard. But on 10 June his son rode with his knights in full armour into the middle of the stream, sounded the bottom with their lances and found a fording place. Still reluctant to abandon the town of his birth, Henry ordered the suburbs of Le Mans burned down, to provide a fire break between Richard's army and the defenders, but the blaze got out of control and began gutting the wooden houses around the citadel.[65] On the 11th Henry realised Le Mans was bound to fall and rode away northwards with his knights, towards Normandy; at the head of the column, surrounded by bodyguards so that he could come to no harm, was his beloved John. It is said that, two miles out of Le Mans, Henry mounted a hilltop to look back on his favourite city. When he saw it in flames he had another of his rants against providence. 'God, you have foully taken from me the city I loved best in all the world, the city where I was born and raised, the city where my father is buried, the city which holds the tomb of St Julian. I shall be revenged on you as best I can. I shall deny you my soul', were the words attributed to him. The vanguard rode without armour, but William Marshal and his followers provided a heavily-mailed rearguard. Richard meanwhile was pursuing his father on a fast horse so as to give him no respite, so rode armourless in his tunic. One of Henry's knights, William des Roches, charged into Richard's knights, despite curses and imprecations from both sides. Richard exhorted his men that the point of the pursuit was to harry Henry, not to get bogged down in a mini-tournament with William Marshal and his Poitevins. But he was too late. In the melee that followed, Richard suddenly realised to his horror that the greatest knight in the realm was bearing down on him with couched lance. As William Marshal's destrier thundered towards him, Richard cried out: 'By God's legs, Marshal, do not kill me! That would be wrong. I am unarmed.' Marshal replied: 'No, let the Devil kill you, for I won't,' and plunged his lance into Richard's horse instead.[66]

Meanwhile Henry made good his escape but, having got as far as Alençon, he seemed to give up the ghost, switched direction and went south to Chinon in Anjou. Richard and Philip took the opportunity to overrun Maine and Touraine. When Tours, the hub of the Angevin empire, fell on 3 July, the sick old man, probably suffering from dysenteric fever, had no choice but to bow his head. Next day, in such pain that he could hardly sit on his horse, he attended the last conference of his life, at Ballon, south-west of Tours. Sitting bolt upright on his charger while peals of thunder rolled around him in appropriate symbolism, Henry tasted the cup of bitterness to the dregs. He agreed to place himself wholly at the will of the king of France, to do him homage and swear fealty; he was to recognise Richard as his heir and pay Philip an indemnity of 20,000 marks; Alice would marry Richard on his return from the crusade and meanwhile three castles in Anjou would be handed over as surety; all Henry's subjects, in England and the continent were to transfer their allegiance to Richard and Philip; the crusade would commence at Lent 1190.[67] To seal the bargain Henry was forced to give Richard the kiss of peace. As he shammed the gesture, in a false embrace that somehow summed up his life, the Old King whispered balefully to his son: 'May God let me live until I can have my revenge on you.' Richard, full of contempt for his father, turned the empty threat into an after-dinner anecdote to enliven his followers, and soon the story was known throughout Christendom.[68]

Henry dragged himself back to Chinon, the physical pain of the fever compounded by the humiliation he had just been forced to undergo. That evening he sat alone by a window, brooding on the forced surrender and repeating the words: 'Shame on a conquered king.' But if he thought he had supped from a cup thrice full and overflowing, there was one further agony to endure. On 5 July definite word reached him that his beloved John had gone over to the enemy. John the realist had decided he had no choice but to submit and pay homage to Philip. When he heard of this final betrayal, Henry lost the will to live.[69] He died on 6 July, almost certainly unshriven. His rage against God was such that he was no longer interested in the flummery of the last rites and Extreme Unction. A messenger from William Marshal sped to Richard with news of the king's death. Richard arrived at the convent of Fontevrault next day as night was falling and entered the Church alone. He stood silently by his father's bier, looked down once at his father's face and fell to his knees to say a prayer. Then he stalked out.[70] There is no reason at all to believe Gerald of Wales's fanciful story that when Richard entered the Church the corpse began to bleed from the nostrils; this is simply an imaginative gloss on the old superstition that a murdered man will bleed in the presence of his killer and was barefacedly lifted from Chrétien de Troyes's Arthurian romances.[71] Richard had behaved nobly in the presence of his dead father, and he behaved even more royally once outside the chapel. He called William Marshal to him and reminded him pointedly that just the other day Marshal nearly killed him. 'If I had wanted to kill you, I could easily have done so,' Marshal replied, truthfully enough. Richard smiled grimly: 'Marshal, you are pardoned, I bear you no malice,' he said.[72] He could afford to be magnanimous for all his dreams had come true. The duke of Aquitaine was now lord of Normandy and Anjou and king of England.

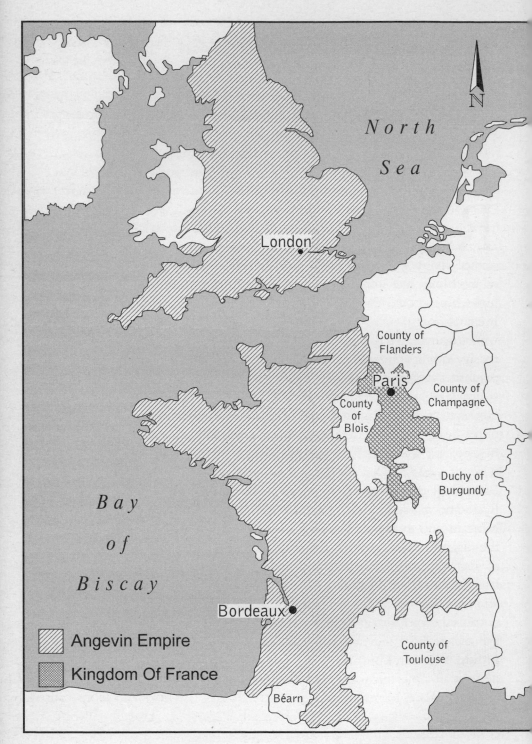

North
Sea

N

County of
Flanders

Paris

County of
Blois

County of
Champagne

Duchy of
Burgundy

Bay

of

Biscay

Bordeaux

County of
Toulouse

London

Béarn

Angevin Empire

Kingdom Of France

1. The Angevin Empire at the death of Henry II

6

◄◦►

RICHARD MOVED AT ONCE to consolidate his hold on the Angevin empire. First he dealt with the south. The key fortress of Châteauroux was given to his faithful knight Andrew de Chavigny, one of his most trusted followers. Another of his close aides, Baldwin of Bethune, then had to be compensated, for Henry II had promised him Châteauroux and a marriage to Denise of Deols to seal the bargain. Richard had to be at his most solomonic to avoid alienating Baldwin, who fortunately had not set his heart on the heiress and was content to receive other rich lands and and a rich bride as compensation. Richard made it a point of policy to promise something and then deliver it, in contrast to his father's way, which had been to make rash promises and then stall or wriggle out of them. He then met Philip of France to work out a deal on Tours, for the cathedral and the abbey there recognised France, not the Angevins, as its overlord. Evincing a gift for compromise that had eluded his father, Richard came to an agreement with Philip and then proceeded north to Normandy.[1] On 20 July 1189 at Rouen he was formally recognised as duke, confirmed John as count of Mortain and arranged some judicious dynastic marriages. He restored the disgraced Robert, earl of Leicester, to his lands and confirmed him as the bulwark of his defences against Philip in the duchy. Two days later he met Philip again at Gisors but the first of many bad omens that attended Richard after his father's death occurred: a wooden bridge collapsed under him and pitched him into a ditch.[2] The superstitious said this meant the Angevins were destined not to retain the Vexin, but Philip proved unusually conciliatory at the meeting and dropped his immediate demand for the territory when Richard told him he was now prepared to marry Alice. In return for a payment of 4,000 marks over and above the 20,000 the dying Henry had promised to pay at his final humiliating conference with Philip, the French king returned most of his recent conquests at the expense of the Angevins.

It has been suggested that Richard in 1189 was abnormally sensitive to the idea that he had betrayed his father, and was concerned with promoting the ethos of honour, making a distinction between principled opposition to a king who had gone off the rails – such as his to his father – and merely calculating, expedient treachery and turncoatery.[3] He dealt severely with those territorial magnates who had not supported him from the beginning but joined in on his side once they saw that Richard and Philip were bound to win the struggle against Henry. Such men found themselves disgraced and their lands confiscated. Some observers accused him of humbug – making a pharisaical distinction between types of betrayal – and were particularly incensed that John, whose treachery to his father had been last-minute, expedient, egregious and instrumental in killing Henry off – got clean away with it. But Richard cleverly blunted criticism by declaring a general amnesty for political prisoners, again advertising the fact that many men had languished in prison purely for opposing Henry but that his own methods would be different, emphasising justice rather than despotism. The most illustrious prisoner thus released – but again one vulnerable to the charge that Richard was making impossible distinctions among and between those who had opposed Henry – was his beloved mother Eleanor of Aquitaine.[4] Eleanor had been once again closely confined at the end of 1188, after some years of comparative freedom, once the great crisis between Henry and Richard loomed. Almost the first thing Richard did on Henry's death was to send the newly co-opted William Marshal to England with orders to release her. Not surprisingly, Marshal found that her jailers had accurately interpreted the shape of things to come and already set her at liberty. To liberate his mother was a natural filial action, but the wider amnesty provisions raised some eyebrows. Sceptics claimed that Richard was merely showing that he was 'soft on crime' but at first his apparent commitment to justice and mercy won him wide popularity.[5]

Richard sped from his meeting with Philip to Barfleur, to take ship for England. Again the superstitious shook their heads dolefully, for it was reported that William Marshal, Richard's harbinger in England, had fallen off the gangplank while boarding his ship for England, though cynics said it was because he was walking on air after Richard gave him the lordship of Striguil in the Welsh marches and the beautiful heiress Isabel Clare to boot.[6] Certainly Richard was remarkably magnanimous to a man who less than a month before had borne down on him with a couched lance. Apart from the Welsh territories, William had also received the vast holdings of Leinster in Ireland, and the combination of Wales and Ireland made him vastly rich. It seems that in his treat-ment of William Marshal, Richard was doing a number of things simul-taneously: displaying his magnanimity to a recent foe, ostentatiously displaying his gifts of patronage, showing kingly wisdom and shrewd-ness in making over the most important knight in the empire, and contrasting his own generosity, reliability and decisiveness with the dithering, prevaricating and manipulative Henry. What Henry had merely promised Marshal Richard gave, as he took pleasure in pointing out: 'By God's legs, he (Henry) did not! He only promised to do it. But I give her (Isabel) to you now.'[7] Marshal, once in England, set about his task with gusto. He raced to Winchester, where he found Eleanor of Aquitaine, at 67, 'more the great lady than ever'. He told Queen Eleanor that Richard had given her plenipotentiary powers until he arrived in England and that she should act the part of Regent. Eleanor rode directly to Westminster, where she tried to make straight the ways for her adored son, receiving oaths of fealty to him from the great barons, and spreading the gospel of royal mercy to political and social prisoners, among whom she included all felons who had fallen foul of Henry's draconian forest laws against poaching.[8]

Richard had John with him at Barfleur, but insisted that his brother disembark at Dover while he made a triumphal landfall at Portsmouth. Probably Richard wanted nothing to distract from his own pomp and glory; that the entire progress through England was being stage-managed became clear when he brought with him, like a Roman victor, an eminent captive in chains, none other than the widely unpopular Stephen of Tours, loathed and despised as Henry's most sycophantic servitor when he was seneschal of Anjou.[9] Richard posed as a Nerva, the merciful emperor succeeding after the tyranny of Domitian, the bringer of hope and light, the symbol of a new age. In the euphoria of the moment the people of England allowed themselves to believe the hype.[10] From Portsmouth he proceeded to Winchester, where John joined him. The royal procession continued via Salisbury and Marlborough to Windsor, where Geoffrey Plantagenet, the half-brother, joined him. Richard started as he meant to go on by dismissing the old justiciar Ranulf Glanville and making him pay a heavy fine to be reinstated in the royal favour. He then informed Geoffrey that he would be made archbishop of York but would have to pay 3,000 marks for the privilege. Then he completed the final lap of the journey to London. His coronation in Westminster Abbey on Sunday 3 September continued the purposive pageantry. After making a proces-sion from St Paul's Cathedral to Westminster Palace through beflagged and garlanded streets, where crowds cheered at the sight of Eleanor of Aquitaine in her robes of miniver, linen and sable, Richard entered the abbey. The archbishop of Canterbury anointed him on chest, head and hands before crowning him; Richard, anticipating Napoleon, picked up the Crown himself and handed it to the archbishop. Once again the superstitious shuddered at a bad omen, when a bat flitted around the throne in broad daylight.[11]

The supposed portent was ignored in the carousing and feasting that followed as a thousand or so earls, barons, knights and clergy gorged themselves on beef, venison and wine. Allegedly 'the wine flowed along the pavement and walls of the palaces'[12] but then it always does in medieval chronicles on such occasions. While the feasting went on, something happened outside the palace that would have grave repercussions throughout England. Some of London's wealthier Jews, eager to establish themselves with the new king, arrived bearing gifts. Somehow the Christian crowds at the gate got it into their heads that this was a blasphemous insult to the newly crowned king; this was, after all, an era in which Jews were doubly execrated – for being the killers of Christ and for usury, defined in canon law as the lending of money at interest, even the most microscopic amounts. Moreover, Jews were loathed for their conspicuous consumption, their sumptuary splendour and the ostentatious wealth that a few of the more incautious Israelites liked to display. Additionally, they were widely believed to murder Christian children for ritual purposes, and the well-known legend of 'Little St William of Norwich' was based on this canard. There were also many great aristocratic families, abbeys and religious houses in debt to Jewish moneylenders, people who would shed no tears if their debts were fortuitously wiped out by the death of their creditors.

Not surprisingly, in such a climate a riot developed, swords were drawn and soon Christians were slaughtering Jews. The rampaging crowd spread fire and sword into the city of London itself, killing, maiming, wounding, looting and gutting houses. To his credit, Richard dealt harshly with the rioters once order was restored; his motive was not philo-Semitism so much as aristocratic outrage that the vulgar mob had so defiled his coronation day. He hanged three of the ringleaders and ostentatiously conducted back into the bosom of his co-religionists a terri-fied Jew who had 'converted' the day before to escape death. He then sent orders to every shire in England that Jews were not to be harmed and, as an afterthought, extended the prescription to his domains in Normandy and Poitou.[13] Cynics said he cared nothing for Jews, but saw them as a rich source of funds and did not want to kill the goose that laid the golden egg. But it was difficult to convince the Crusade-happy mob that Jews should be left alone. If Saracens were to be slaughtered by European armies for occupying the holy places in Jerusalem, how much more deserving of death were the people who had actually cruci-fied the Saviour? This was the kind of fanatical feeling that lay behind the anti-Semitic riots that followed in East Anglia and the Wash (Stamford, Norwich, King's Lynn, Lincoln). Worst of all atrocities was the pogrom at York in March 1190 when Richard had already left the country. Here a mob, urged on by a twelfth-century Rasputin, began by slaughtering all Jews they could lay hands on and then pursued the pitiful remnants (about 150 souls) to the castle. When the Jews realised they could not hold out long in the citadel, they enacted a macabre rerun of Masada in AD 73: first they killed their wives and children, then committed suicide. A handful, not relishing such a death, foolishly believed prom-ises that they would be unharmed if they surrendered, emerged from the castle, and were massacred on the spot.[14]

Before he departed on crusade, Richard had five main matters to attend to: putting the Church on a sound footing; installing the men who would be de facto Regents in his absence; securing the Welsh marches; keeping Scotland quiet in his absence, and, above all, raising the vast sums of money needed to finance the expedition to Outremer. He began by appointing four new bishops, including his favourite William Longchamp, who was given the see at Ely, several new abbots and making a number of other changes in the senior ecclesiastical hierarchy. Once again there was an element of showmanship in all this, for Richard meant to distinguish his rule clearly from that of his father; Henry II had been infamous for his practice of keeping major livings vacant so that he could pocket the revenue.[15] Richard's most important church appoint-ment was also shrewd politics. In nominating Henry's natural son Geoffrey to the archbishopric of York, he was removing an important political player from the board. Geoffrey Plantagenet was rumoured to have ambitions to emulate William the Conqueror and become a bastard king. This was why he had resigned the see of Lincoln earlier, as he would have had to take Holy Orders and thus waive his political ambi-tions. Richard forced the issue, overcame theological objections to the appointment and even had it ratified by a papal legate. The reluctant Geoffrey was virtually carried kicking and screaming to his investiture as priest, but once ordained he ceased to be a possible pretender to the throne. Outwitted, he salved his anger by a career of defiance towards

Richard and the canons of his own cathedral.[16] Richard set the capstone on his ecclesiastical reforms by resolving a complex, tortuous but essentially arcane dispute between Archbishop Baldwin of Canterbury and the monks of his cathedral priory, which was essentially a clash between Cistercian (Baldwin) modalities and Benedictine sensibilities.[17]

The problem of civilian administration was a tougher nut to crack. The two key offices in England were the justiciar and the chancellor. Theoretically the justiciar was the chief legal officer, dispensing the king's justice, while the chancellor was a kind of primitive secretary of state, though over time the two offices tended to merge in function. Some authorities distinguish the royal household element (the chancellor) which moved around with the king on his travels, and the common administrative element (justiciar) which appeared in other parts of the Angevin empire as well as England.[18] Richard began well by removing Ranulph Glanville as justiciar and putting in his place a Church–civilian 'dyarchy' – the aged William de Mandeville, count of Aumale and the earl of Essex, and the oligarchic Bishop Hugh du Puiset of Durham. As Chancellor he put in William Longchamp, bishop of Ely and veteran administrator of Aquitaine, who thus combined the Church and civilian roles in one office. As his official heir Richard chose the four-year-old Arthur of Britanny, thus putting John's nose out of joint. But Richard expected that the liberality he showered on John would keep his younger brother quiet. Loaded with fiefs, titles and revenues, John also took a wife at this point – none other than the wealthy heiress Isabelle of Gloucester who had long been earmarked for him. There was some opposition to the marriage from the archbishop of Canterbury – on the grounds that John and Isabelle were second cousins without a papal licence to marry – but Richard steamrollered the match through anyway. He wanted John safely wed, so that the idea of his marrying Alice could never be resurrected.[19] John was now lord of Ireland, Mortmain and Gloucester and a number of other fiefs, including those he already held and new ones, such as Lancaster, that Richard added to his portfolio. Perhaps Richard's most stunning gift to John was a six-county benefice: Derby, Nottingham, Somerset, Dorset, Devon and Cornwall. Short of money for the crusade, Richard nonetheless allowed John to keep the entire revenues from all six counties, which would otherwise have accrued to the royal treasury; the only insurance policy Richard took out was to retain control of key castles in the territories. But in return for this largesse John had to swear that he would stay out of England for three years.[20] Richard's dispositions were essentially a balancing act, but the acrobats soon came toppling off the wire.

First Essex died, and Richard made the mistake of making Longchamp one of the justiciars as well. But if Longchamp was already too prominent and thus destroying the balance of power, Richard made the further error of listening to his mother's pleadings and partially releasing John from his oath to stay out of England: he made it dependent on Longchamp's say-so. Nonetheless the oath still stood: despite John's later lies, he had never been absolutely released from it.[21]

Wales was a permanent thorn in the Angevin side. For most of his reign Henry II had been content to accept the Welsh rulers' fealty – and in a few cases their homage also – and leave it at that; some historians have compared the situation to that of the independent princelings in India during the Raj. By and large the Welsh borders had been peaceful.[22] Henry, however, had used the security situation on his northern and western frontiers as the excuse for not going crusading; with Henry it was always falsehoods and deviousness, and he was the original man who could not lie straight in bed.[23] The much more straight-forward (naive, said his critics) Richard wanted open dealing on all sides and tried to get a permanent solution to Wales so that the Welsh would not go on the warpath as soon as he was out of the country. This was no confected fear: as soon as he heard that Henry II was dead the powerful chieftain Rhys of Deheubarth began raiding into English territory. He justified this on the grounds that, although he had sworn homage to Henry II, this was a personal oath that did not extend to the king's successors.[24] Richard sent John, now lord of Glamorgan, to deal with Rhys while he met the other Welsh chiefs and 'kings' at Worcester, who agreed not to attack England while he was away on crusade.[25] John's dealings with Rhys are much murkier. He met him and worked out an agreement, then took Rhys to Oxford to meet Richard. Informed by his spies that John had concluded a secret concordat with Rhys, Richard refused to meet the Welshman. For this Richard has been much criticised, particularly as Henry II regularly received Rhys, but the probability is that Richard was not being foolish so much as pragmatic. Rhys's status as Henry's 'man' had done little to dampen down anarchy and raiding in Wales, he had made a secret pact with John, the king's advisers counselled him that little could be looked for from Rhys, and moreover Richard calculated that the Welsh chiefs he had made over at Worcester were strong enough to contain Rhys and his turbulent sons.[26] The angry Rhys, smarting at the insult to his honour when Richard turned him from the door at Oxford, continued a form of guerrilla warfare for several years in south Wales. But the other Welsh leaders kept their promise to Richard, John was watchful of his interests as lord of Glamorgan and, very importantly, William Marshal, now lord of the Welsh marches, was a force any would-be leader of a general uprising in Wales would have to reckon with.

If Richard's dealings with Wales had produced only middling outcomes, his diplomacy with the king of the Scots produced spectacular and lasting results. In November 1189 Richard's half-brother Geoffrey persuaded King William to come south for talks and escorted him to Canterbury. There, in the famous Quit Claim treaty of 5 December Richard returned to William the castles of Roxburgh and Berwick – surrendered after the Young King's disastrous rebellion in 1173–74 – and formally acknowledged Scotland's independence from England. In return he received 10,000 marks for his crusading fund. Contemporary chroniclers, and advocates of a United Kingdom ever since, condemned this as a piece of egregious folly: Gerald of Wales denounced it as 'a piece of vile commerce and a shameful loss to the English crown'.[27] Scottish nationalists have, not surprisingly, seen the treaty in a very different light and have praised Richard as a second Daniel come to judgement. It is hard not to agree with the nationalists. Whatever our view of the crusades today, at the time people of all ranks accepted that regaining the Holy Land from Islam was a sacred duty; talk of the 'real English national interests' in such a context becomes metaphysical or theological. And the policy was a shrewd one. When John rebelled against Richard in 1193–94, the Scots did not join in. There is a strong case to be made that Richard's policies on the Celtic fringes provided a tranquil situation that contrasted with almost all other post-1066 periods. Certainly most contemporaries thought that during his short stay in England he had performed wonders of diplomacy and statesmanship.[28]

Yet the criticism of later generations over the deal with Scotland was as nothing compared with the contumely attracted by Richard in his ruthless quest for money to finance the crusades. For the first time Richard appears in the eyes of history to be no longer a knight *sans peur et sans reproche* driven to distraction by his father's duplicity but a ruthless militarist, the kind of fanatic who redoubles his efforts as he loses sight of his aims. For the first time it began to be whispered that here was a truly bad king: 'bad to all, worse to his friends and worst of all to himself', as Roger of Howden put it.[29] Henry II had left the English treasury in a healthy state, despite the huge expenditure on the wars in France: contemporaries estimated the surplus at anything between 100,000 and 900,000 marks.[30] Within days of his arrival in England Richard started running through this sum: first there was the 24,000 owed to Philip of France; then the huge cost of the coronation and associated ceremonies and banqueting; finally the massive and overgenerous amounts handed to John. On top of this he had to raise money for the crusade and, after the Saladin Tithe, another round of taxation would lead to serious civil unrest. A cynical student of human nature, Richard simply decided to mulct the rich, to seize and squeeze, to follow his father's example in never guaranteeing a steady revenue through taxation but through ad hoc profiteering. Henry II had always done this, to the point where one observer wrote: 'The King is like a robber permanently on the prowl, always probing, always searching for the weak spot where there is something for him to steal.'[31]

Richard's 'daylight robbery' project was made easier by the concentration of England's wealth into the hands of a few, all known to the king and his officials, all of them bound to him by feudal ties and politico-legal clientelism. There was no hiding place, no medieval equivalent of tax evasion. Ambitious nobles were willing to pay a lot for lucrative offices, titles, places and other privileges. Custom and tradition also made it easy for an unscrupulous king to make rich pickings from death or bequest. When the bishop of Ely died intestate, Richard helped himself to his 'portable property': not just 3,000 marks in coin but also gold and silver plate, horses, livestock, granaries, carpets, tapestries and other fine cloths.[32] The office of sheriff was particularly sought after, and in a 'sale of the century' Richard sold them off to the highest bidder. In order to gain control of local castles and become sheriff of Hampshire, Godfrey de Luci, bishop of Winchester paid out more than 4,000 marks. Hugh du Puiset, bishop of Durham, paid out 2,000 marks for the sheriffdom of Northumberland and another 1,000 for his recognition of the honour of being made justiciar.[33] But the royal scamming did not end just with the disposal of sheriffdoms, for a ruthless monarch would dismiss the incumbent sheriffs, fine them for malfeasance, nonfeasance or misfeasance (this could amount to 1,000 marks per sacking) and then make another appointment for another 2–3,000 marks. Given that levels of civil discontent were not high in Henry II's England, it was implausible that Richard really needed to dismiss twenty-two of the twenty-seven sheriffs in office when the Old King died. But every hiring or firing transaction brought in more money. However, it by no means follows that the new appointees were all rich sycophants: to his credit Richard required both money and ability before he would appoint a man to be sheriff.[34]

Another quick means of raising money, much copied by modern

states in modern combats, was to allow people to buy themselves out of military service in the Holy Land. Many people had taken the crusading vow in a moment of euphoria, uplift and hysteria and then realised next morning the potentially horrific implications of what they had done. For such people Richard offered a simple way out: pay for military exemption. It hardly needs to be said that such exemptions were not bought cheaply. It might seem that in a religious age buying oneself out would have been considered blasphemous or heretical, but the Pope himself provided a loophole by sanctioning this system of 'compounding' for those deemed essential to national security or stability at home while the monarch was leading armies abroad, or even for those deemed to be providing 'essential' administrative duties.[35] As with all such 'essential war work', the opportunities for shirking for those with a deep purse were almost infinite. Richard is often considered an obtuse warmonger, unalive to the nuances of administration and unversed in political subtlety, but there was much method in his apparent money-madness in 1189–90. At one stroke he could raise money and unseat all his father's old followers, as Roger of Howden pointed out: 'The king removed from office Ranulf Glanville, the justiciar of England, and almost all their sheriffs and officers; the closer they had been to his father, the more he oppressed them. Anyone who did not have as much as he demanded was immediately sent to jail where there was weeping and gnashing of teeth; then he appointed other sheriffs in their place. Everything was for sale – offices, lordships, earldoms, sheriffdoms, castles, towns, lands, the lot.'[36] One of his followers gently put it to Richard that he was overdoing the financial side of things. He replied dismissively: 'I would sell London itself if I could find a buyer.'[37]

Most modern criticisms of Richard as king of England focus on two things that were apparent in 1189: Richard cared little for England and he used it as a gigantic cash-cow. The first proposition is surely incontestable: he came to England on 13 August 1189 and left it four months later, on 12 December, then revisited it for two months in 1194 – six months in all during a ten-year reign. His preference for Aquitaine was overwhelming, and although he spoke Latin as well as his native French, he never spoke English. The criticism of using England like a bank is valid with hindsight, but Richard genuinely believed in the crusade and, if it was to be effective, he had no choice but to raise vast sums of money; it was either that or see his armies annihilated by better fed, armed and equipped Saracens. It is perfectly permissible for modern critics to say that, *sub specie aeternitatis*, the Frankish nations of the West should never have gone on crusade but, given the beliefs and ideologies of the time, it is an anachronistic judgement. It is significant that, of all contemporary chroniclers, only William of Newburgh raised the point that a king of England's proper place was to be in England, permanently, but in the light of the sensibilities of the time this would have been considered an eccentric point of view. It was only in the seventeenth century that the perception gained ground that an absentee king was the worst possible species. Hence the paradox that the one King Richard who was a paladin of chivalry and a military genius should ultimately have suffered in comparison with the two other King Richards, who died in abject defeat and disgrace.

Where both contemporary and modern critics are on surer (and unexceptionable) ground is their focus on Richard's absurdly myopic treatment of his brother John.[38] After granting him six whole counties, on top of the lordships he already held, Richard both shrank his own revenue base – for Nottingham, Derby, Somerset, Dorset, Devon and Cornwall contributed nothing to the exchequer until 1194 – and created a kind of kingdom within a kingdom, with John in possession of about a third of the kingdom of England. Richard of Devizes thought this was the wrong way to deal with John: his ambition was so evident that Richard should have moved in the opposite direction and taken him down a peg or two.[39] Defenders of Richard point out that he had little choice in his treatment of his brother, that harsher treatment would have made him certain to rebel. In terms of money John had all he could desire, but not in terms of power or prospects. If Richard had been generous in the power stakes, he might have given him Aquitaine or Normandy. As it was, John could legitimately complain that he had less power now that Richard was king than Richard or the Young King had had while Henry was alive. Some scholars even argue that, to head off John's ambitions, he should have given him *more* power. Perhaps the solution was to compel John to come on crusade? But Richard feared that the scheming John might do to him with Philip Augustus what he (Richard) had done with Philip to his father; the obvious way to deal with this was to make sure John and Philip never met. And it is true that a combination of Eleanor of Aquitaine and the ministers Richard appointed to serve in his absence should have been able to see off John quite easily.[40] But no one has satisfactorily explained why Richard rescinded his earlier demand that John stay out of England while the crusade was in progress. That was the truly cardinal error.

Having, at least to his own satisfaction, settled the affairs of England,

Richard made the eight-hour crossing from Dover to Calais on 12 December 1189, proceeded to Normandy and spent Christmas at Lyons-la-Forêt.[41] On 30 December he held another conference with King Philip at Nonancourt. A non-aggression pact was agreed, whereby an attack on the lands of one would be regarded as an attack on the lands of the other; since Richard and Philip were the only conceivable such aggressors in western Europe, the accord effectively guaranteed peace while the two monarchs were on crusade. More controversially, Richard renewed his pledge to marry Alice when he was already engaged in serious negotiations for the hand of Berengaria of Navarre – a duplicitous move which predictably aroused the selective fury of Bertran de Born.[42] Richard kept the Alice card in play throughout 1188–89, first to get Philip on his side against his father, and then to make sure the crusade proceeded, though he managed to avoid direct perjury on the issue. For his lies and half-truths on this matter he has been much pilloried, but if he blatantly stated that he would never marry Alice, war with Philip was the likely result. It needs to be reiterated that with Alice Richard was in a trap not of his own making. It by no means follows that he was homosexual, overly squeamish or absurdly fastidious in not marrying his father's mistress. The true cause of all this trouble was Henry. Like Louis XV of France and many another ruler, he had allowed his lusts to triumph over considerations of hard politics, and now his son was having to pick up the pieces. But the issue of Alice was a running sore between Philip and Richard, and made a poisonous and inauspicious start to the Third Crusade.[43]

The crusade was meant to be a tripartite effort by the German emperor and the kings of France and England. Aware that the aged emperor Frederick Barbarossa was proceeding overland to the Holy Land, via the Danube and Asia Minor, Richard went about his preparations in a leisurely way and spent six months touring his continental domains, appointing seneschals in Normandy, Anjou and Aquitaine and granting charters under the inevitable formula *teste me ipso* (with me myself as the witness).[44] There was another meeting between Richard and Philip at Dreux on 16 March – slightly overshadowed by the news of the death in childbirth of Philip's wife Isabel – to confirm the peace terms agreed at Nonancourt, with the added proviso that the Church would excommunicate anyone breaking the conditions of the covenant. The two kings agreed that, since preparations for the expedition were behind schedule, they should fix a departure date of 24 June.[45] Then Richard headed south, and by May was in the Pyrenees. He visited Bayonne, and made a brief foray into the county of Bigorre, where he hanged the lord of the castle of Chis for highway robbery, specifically the plunder of pilgrims passing through this territory to and from Santiago de Compostela.[46] Richard wanted to make his presence felt in this region, for his old enemy Raymond of Toulouse was the one great prince of France who had not taken the Cross. It did not require a genius to guess what Raymond's intentions might be once Richard was on the other side of the Mediterranean. Richard's obvious counterstrike was to strengthen his old alliance with Alfonso II of Aragon which had been so useful in the late 1180s. Since Alfonso was now in alliance with King Sancho VI of Navarre against Alfonso of Castile, it made sense for Richard to energise this new alliance against sleeping but not yet moribund dogs like Raymond of Toulouse. Hard *realpolitik* turned out to be the genesis of Richard's sudden marriage, just as it had hitherto been the reason for his stalling on the issue of Alice.

Since about 1188 there had been rumours that Richard intended to contract a Spanish marriage, with Berengaria, daughter of Sancho of Navarre. The rumours finally proved to be true, but there was much about the match that was puzzling. Most obviously there was the length of time it took to solemnise it: it was not until May 1191, in Cyprus, that Richard finally took Berengaria to wife.[47] The problem was, of course, Richard's pre-existing pledge to marry Alice of France. How could Sancho look kindly on a proposal for the hand of his daughter from a man who was already publicly committed to marry Alice? Richard already had a track record, with both Alice and Berengaria, of offering marriage (or seeming to) and then withdrawing the offer. Did this not mean that Richard was as double-dealing, devious and mendacious as his father? The why of the marriage – Sancho to shield Richard from Raymond of Toulouse and Richard to protect Sancho from the encroachments of Castile – was obvious but the how seemed impossible. The breakthrough came in Normandy in March 1190. Four days before Richard met Philip at Dreux, he had assembled a huge body of key nobles and churchmen – including Archbishop Baldwin of Canterbury, his brother John, his half-brother Geoffrey – to discuss the intricacies of canon law and the implications of dynastic marriage. The most significant participants, newly arrived from England, were Eleanor of Aquitaine and Alice herself. It seems clear that at the Dreux meeting four days later Philip promised to consider rescinding the proposed marriage of Richard to Alice, paving the way for Richard's dash to the deep south, although Philip did not formally relent on the issue for another year (March 1191). In the Pyrenees Richard met Sancho of Navarre, and some days of hard bargaining followed. Since Philip had still not formally consented to release Richard from his 'proposal' to Alice, Sancho was torn between the promise of a glittering match for his daughter Berengaria and his uncertainty about how far he could trust Richard. The details of the Pyrenean conference remain obscure, but Richard must have made some hefty private commitments and probably disbursed a lot of gold from his purse to make the Spanish king release his daughter.[48]

By settling on a wife, Richard was at least answering the charges that he had rushed off on crusade without even providing the Angevin empire with an heir apparent, leaving a possible chaos world to open up if he died and the ambitious John disputed the succession with the infant Arthur. Freed from the tortuous negotiations with Sancho, he headed north again to put the finishing touches to his crusading army. At Chinon in June 1190 he issued a series of draconian laws that would govern military and naval discipline on the way to the first rendezvous near Lisbon at the mouth of the Tagus. The 'ordinance' contained the following: 'Any man who kills another shall be bound to the dead man and, if at sea, be thrown overboard; if on land, he will be buried with him. If it be proved by lawful witnesses that any man has drawn his knife against another, his hand shall be cut off. If any man shall punch another without drawing blood, he shall be immersed three times in the sea. The penalty for abusive or blasphemous language shall be a fine of one ounce of silver for each occasion. Any man caught stealing will have his head shaved, be tarred and feathered and then put ashore at the first landfall.'[49] All this sounds severe, but the sequel shows clearly that Richard knew what he was doing. While he proceeded south overland for another meeting with Philip, sixty-three ships under Robert de Sable and Richard de Canville, full of crusaders who had embarked at La Rochelle and Rochefort, stood away from the Ile d'Oléron to brave the storms and snares of the Bay of Biscay. After a terrible storm, which allegedly only the interceding St Thomas Becket was able to allay, they reached the Tagus estuary safely but, during shore leave, the soldiers started a riot in Lisbon, at first targeting Jews and Muslims but soon burning and plundering everything in sight. The so-called soldiers of God indulged in an orgy of rape, and marked their passage with gutted buildings, trampled vineyards and devastated orchards. It says much for the forebearance of the king of Portugal that, when he eventually restored order, he merely jailed the offenders instead of hanging them as he would have been entitled to. The papal proscription against harming crusaders saved a pack of unworthy rapists and murderers from the gallows they richly deserved.[50]

After his decrees of Chinon, Richard moved to Tours (24–27 June) where he received the traditional pilgrim's staff, which broke when he leaned on it.[51] This was the second bad omen for the Third Crusade this year – the first had been the death of Philip's queen Isabella, which was immediately interpreted by the superstitious as a sign of God's displeasure. The third, news of the death of Frederick Barbarossa, was soon to follow. On 2 July Richard rendezvoused with Philip at Vézelay, on French territory, and made plans for a reunion of both armies in Sicily; Western Europe could not support up to 20,000 troops all travelling by the same route, and Messina was the only deep-sea port capable of sustaining the combined Anglo-French fleet.[52] At Vézelay the two kings concluded a further agreement and bound themselves to it by oath: that they intended to win new lands, new domains and new wealth and that whatever they conquered they should share.[53] Richard and most impartial observers sensibly concluded that the compact related to territories they conquered together, that Philip would not pretend a claim to anything Richard obtained unilaterally. Unfortunately Philip concluded (or said he did) that the accord meant a fifty-fifty division of any crusader acquisition; as usual with Franco-Angevin agreements, the two parties did not put their signatures to a written minute of the agreement, so that scope for misunderstanding remained as wide as it had been in the days of Henry II and Louis VII.[54] From Vézelay the two kings rode down to Lyons, travelling via Corbigny, Moulins and Belleville-sur-Saône, where the fourth of the year's ill-omened events occurred. A wooden bridge over the Rhône collapsed under the weight of mailed knights and pitched a hundred riders into the river; whether through luck or skill only two of them died.[55] At Lyons on 10 July Philip and Richard parted company, Philip bound for Genoa, Richard for Marseilles. On 13 July the English king began the 220-mile journey to Marseilles, travelling via Vienne, Valence and Montelimar, Orange and Avignon.[56] But the pattern of delays and plans going adrift continued. At Marseilles Richard expected to rendezvous with the seaborne army from the Ile d'Oléron, but the sixty-three ships were still labouring through the Straits of Gibraltar after the Lisbon debacle; this fleet would take a month to sail from the Tagus into the Mediterranean and along the Spanish coast to Marseilles.

Richard had not even quit European shores before his carefully-skeined reorganisation of England began to unravel. Immediately after dismissing Ranulf Glanville as justiciar, he had, as related, replaced him with the two-man rule of Hugh du Puiset, bishop of Durham, and William of Mandeville, the latter one of Henry's old faithfuls like William Marshal and, like him, promoted for fidelity on Richard's accession. Unfortunately he died on the very day Richard was crossing from Dover to Calais.[57] Hugh du Puiset naturally expected that, left as sole justiciar, he would be given the Small (Exchequer) Seal of the kingdom (Richard took the Great Seal with him) and wardenship of the Tower of London. But Richard not only gave these to William Longchamp, bishop of Ely, but appointed Longchamp joint justiciar, with instructions that he was to have full powers south of the Humber and du Puiset was to have them north of that river. This was a demotion in anybody's language. The proud and ambitious du Puiset took this hard. He was an aristocrat of ancient lineage, linked by kinship to any number of counts and princelings, a veteran of the wars of King Stephen, a man of wide culture with a vast library. Sheriff of Northumberland and connected through his wife Adelaide with the influential house of Percy, good-looking, handsome, regal, with natural authority and gravitas, du Puiset looked the part of great magnate and justiciar. Although Longchamp was no whit inferior in intellect or culture – he was the author of a learned treatise on civil war and much admired by the scholarly dean of St Paul's – he most emphatically did not look the part, and his unprepossessing physical appearance lent colour to the gibes of his enemies, who whispered that he was the grandson of a runaway serf. It was true that he came from humble origins and did not have du Puiset's pedigree but what told against him most was his dwarf-like stature – Gerald of Wales said he looked more ape than man.[58]

Richard favoured Longchamp against du Puiset because he trusted him utterly, and there is ample evidence that Longchamp repaid the trust with an energetic pursuit of the king's interests.[59] Unfortunately, he shared one of Richard's failings: as a Norman he had no real knowledge of England and its political nuances. Chillingly ambitious and nepotistic, he stuffed the offices of England with his kin: his brother Henry became sheriff of Herefordshire, his brother Osbert sheriff of Yorkshire, Suffolk and Norfolk; he used his power to secure rich heiresses and wardships for his extended family. He marginalised Hugh du Puiset and, by the time Richard left Marseilles, had all but eliminated him as a political force. He affected kingly graces and made quasi-royal progresses around the country, quartering a vast cohort of hangers-on in reluctant abbeys and priories. He made the Tower of London something of a personal fortress and brought in mercenaries from abroad.[60] Longchamp hardly helped his case by the elan with which he continued to raise money for Richard (to say nothing of himself) so that, less than a year after the king's departure from English shores, he was already wildly unpopular. As the holder of the three offices of justiciar, chancellor and papal legate he combined all powers in his person, but thereby made a threefold clutch of enemies. Clerks were reduced to ridiculing his brother by drawing funny faces inside the capital letter O of Osbert's name.[61] The barons despised him as a low-born, obscure foreigner; administrators and clerks hated him as a typical example of the here-today-gone-tomorrow jack-in-office; the other bishops deeply resented the power Pope Clement III gave him as papal legate in June 1190 (at Richard's urging).[62] As William of Newburgh, who detested him, remarked: 'The laity found him more than king, the clergy more than Pope, and both an intolerable tyrant.'[63]

Longchamp's short-term problem was his 'colleague' du Puiset, and he dealt with him with astounding ruthlessness. Using the excuse of an administrative error, that had led to an overdue payment from the county,[64] Longchamp first deprived his rival of the sheriffdom of Northumberland. Next, a meeting was arranged between the two justiciars at Tickhill, which ended with du Puiset being placed under arrest. Taken to London, and subjected to a variety of duress, du Puiset was then forced to surrender the castles of Windsor and Newcastle, plus the manor of Sadberge which he had recently bought from the king for 600 marks, and in addition was obliged to give hostages for his 'good behaviour'.[65] Not content with this, Longchamp had his brother Osbert arrest the ageing bishop on his way home to Durham. Imprisoned at Howden while Osbert helped himself to the sheriffdoms of the north, du Puiset then had the blame fastened on him for the anti-Semitic murders in York, on the grounds that the ringleaders were friends of his.[66] That was the end of du Puiset as a political force. But Longchamp's long-term and perennial problem was John, now officially count of Mortain. John bided his time in Angevin France, gleefully receiving news of Longchamp's growing unpopularity, calculating the right moment for the protracted campaign of usurpation he had in mind. His confidence was increased by the widespread feeling that Richard would never return from the crusades, that, as Newburgh put it, his return was not merely uncertain but against all laws of probability. Richard of Devizes described England without Richard as a land of gloom, chaos and instability, with every man for himself. 'As the earth grows dark when the sun departs, so the face of the kingdom was changed by the absence of the king. All the barons were disturbed, castles were strengthened, towns fortified, ditches dug.'[67] From France John directed a kind of rival administration in the counties Richard had given him, with his own justiciar, chancellor, seneschal and seal-bearer.

What forced John's hand and led him to land in England despite his oath was news that Richard, in a formal treaty with Tancred of Sicily in November 1190, had formally recognised Arthur of Britanny as the heir-presumptive.[68] So urgently did Richard need Longchamp to be informed of this that he sent another trusted follower, Hugh Bardolf, on the long journey from Sicily with secret instructions for his justiciar. Bardolf completed the journey in record time and a month later was at Longchamp's side in London.[69] Longchamp guessed what John's next step would be, but was in a difficult position. On the one hand Richard had bound John by oath not to return to England within three years; on the other he had semi-retracted the restriction and made it depend on Longchamp's discretion. Like many essentially weak men, Longchamp only liked battles he was sure to win, such as the struggle for supremacy with du Puiset. He did not relish having to be the one to deny John permission to land in England; John was frighteningly powerful with many secret friends in high places, and would make a dangerous and implacable enemy for life even if Richard did return. And what if he did not? The upshot was that, some time in the early new year of 1191, John crossed into England and Longchamp did not lift a finger to stop him. He had by this time taken his own precautions: two of his brothers had already travelled to Scotland to get the help of King William in the event that Arthur was proclaimed king and John contested the succession.[70] Naturally, John's spies kept him abreast of that development also. John then ingeniously claimed that Longchamp's failure to stop him entering the country was a de facto absolution by the chancellor of the oath sworn by him (John) to Richard.[71]

News of John's actions in turn reached Richard. In February 1191 he sent another emissary to England, together with letters directing that the new man be appointed a justiciar and admitted to the highest decision-making councils in London. This man was Walter of Coutances, archbishop of Rouen. A native of Cornwall, a scholar and administrator, Walter had served as archdeacon at Oxford (1175–82) and briefly been bishop of Lincoln before his appointment to the see of Rouen.[72] Richard gave him virtually plenipotentiary powers, for Walter carried two different sets of instructions: one made him Longchamp's colleague but the other allowed him to supersede and dismiss Longchamp if necessary for, as

Richard said, 'we have opened our heart to him and confided our secret thoughts to him'.[73] Clearly Richard had lost confidence in Longchamp: the order to admit John to England at his discretion, if indeed it ever existed, was obviously predicated on Richard's mistaken certainty that Longchamp never in fact would do anything so foolish. The new envoy took his sweet time about travelling to England – three months as against Hugh Bardolf's one; it seems that he stopped off in Rome to attend the consecration of Pope Celestine III and to get the new pope's endorsement of the consecration of Geoffrey as archbishop of York.[74] Accompanied by Eleanor of Aquitaine (who had been with him all the way from Sicily) he eventually headed north and reached England on 27 June. He arrived to find Longchamp and John at each other's throats. Temporarily popular as a reflex action against Longchamp's dimmed star, John had taken full advantage of the situation, seized castles and encouraged rebellion among the sheriffs; Gerard de Camville, sheriff of Lincolnshire, flatly told his nominal overlord, chancellor Longchamp, that he was answerable to no one but John. Roger Mortimer meanwhile raised the standard of revolt on the Welsh borders, and John seized the castles of Tickhill and Nottingham. When Walter of Coutances arrived, Longchamp had just completed the siege of Lincoln castle, for which he had hired mercenaries.[75]

The archbishop of Rouen called the warring parties to a conference at Winchester, held on 28 July. He managed, at least temporarily, to make peace between John and Longchamp. John agreed to surrender the castles of Nottingham and Tickhill, with the proviso that he would get them back if Richard died on crusade; Gerard de Camville was to be restored as sheriff provided he stood trial in the king's court; constables loyal to Richard would be appointed to all the main castles; and it was stipulated that if Richard refused to ratify the agreement, the castles of Nottingham and Tickhill would revert to John.[76] The archbishop of Rouen had halted John in his tracks, but hardly was the ink dry on this accord than Longchamp faced a challenge from yet another of the Devil's Brood. Geoffrey Plantagenet had finally been consecrated as archbishop of York in the most long-running will-he-won't-he ecclesiastical saga in England's history. Like John, he was bound by oath not to enter England for three years.[77] Nothing daunted, on 14 September he came ashore at Dover and sought refuge in the priory of St Martin. Having been humiliated by John once on this issue, Longchamp was in no mood to let Geoffrey get away with his oath-breaking. He failed in his first attempt, which was to bribe the countess of Flanders to stop him embarking in the first place. On 18 September Geoffrey was arrested and lodged in Dover Castle. The circumstances of the arrest raised a great éclat, and lost nothing in the telling: Geoffrey was said to have been dragged out from sanctuary by his arms and legs with his head bouncing along the stone pavings. But news of the arrest caused a sensation in priestly circles.[78] This seemed to be the Becket story all over again. Longchamp was denounced as a tyrant, pilloried as a simian paedophile, excoriated as a swindler and embezzler. John saw the chance to turn the uproar against Longchamp to his own advantage, and his effective propaganda machine, driven by men like Hugh Nunant, bishop of Coventry, went into overdrive. He raised an army, made Windsor his headquarters, then marched on London.[79]

The bishop of Coventry's scurrilous propaganda is worth dwelling on, showing the vicious contempt and hatred in which Longchamp was held by John's party. The main accusation was as follows: 'He (Longchamp) and his revellers had so exhausted the whole kingdom that they did not leave a man his belt, a woman her necklace, a nobleman his ring, or anything of value even to a Jew. He had likewise so emptied the king's treasury that in all the coffers and bags therein nothing but the keys could be found, after the lapse of these two years.' The circumstances of Longchamp's flight from London after being deposed are somewhat obscure but the bishop of Coventry presents a ludicrous picture of him roaming the beach at Dover, looking for a boat to take him to France.

> Pretending to be a woman – a sex he always hated – he changed his priest's robe into a harlot's dress. The shame of it! The man became a woman, the bishop a buffoon. Dressed in a green gown of enormous length, he hurriedly limped – for the poor little fellow was lame – from the castle heights to the sea-shore, and then sat down to rest on a rock. There he attracted the attention of a half-naked fisherman who was wet and cold from the sea and thought that the bishop was the sort of woman who might warm him up. He put his left arm around Longchamp's neck while his right hand roamed lower down. Suddenly pulling up the gown he plunged unblushingly in – only to be confronted with the irrefutable evidence that the woman was a man. The fisherman then called his mates over to have a look at this truly remarkable creature.[80]

Before this, finding his support melting away, Longchamp took refuge in the Tower on 7 October. Next day, at a great meeting in St Paul's attended by John's partisans, John and the archbishop of Rouen declared

Longchamp deposed as justiciar. John now thought his moment of supreme power had come but, to his consternation, William of Coutances suddenly revealed Richard's secret contingency instructions, allowing him to take supreme power if events warranted it. The archbishop duly became the new justiciar, and John was fobbed off with the title of summus rector, which gave him the trappings of Regent without the power, which William retained. John and all present then swore an oath of loyalty to Richard. The citizens of London gave John a consolation prize by agreeing to recognise him as king if Richard died without a direct heir; the star of Arthur of Britanny plummeted alongside Longchamp's. The ex-justiciar left the kingdom for France on 29 October, disguised as a woman his enemies said, as we have seen, and sent vociferous denunciations of John and the archbishop of Rouen to both Richard and the Pope.[81] Celestine III responded by reaffirming his predecessor's appointment: Longchamp remained the papal legate.[82] John meanwhile, like Longchamp before him, began making quasi-royal progresses around the country with armed men. He made no attempt to rebuke his followers when they said he would soon be king, for it was certain Richard would never return.[83] John was tempted to raise the banner of open revolt or to open secret anti-Richard negotiations with Philip of France.

This temptation was temporarily aborted when Eleanor of Aquitaine landed in England on 11 February 1192. She and William of Coutances together were able to restrain John for the present, with the result that 1192 was a relatively quiet year in England.[84] But John never stopped intriguing. Having used the archbishop of Rouen against Longchamp, he tried the same thing in reverse and accepted a bribe from Longchamp to allow him to return. Longchamp landed at Dover in March 1192, took refuge with his sister, wife of the constable of Dover Castle, and demanded a proper trial on the alleged charges for which he had been deprived of the justiciarship. The new justiciar William of Coutances and his assistants raised the ante and rebribed John to abandon the chancellor. After playing hard to get for some days, John came to London and swaggered into the justiciars' council. He made his position quite plain. 'The chancellor (Longchamp) will not fear for anything or beg favours from anyone if he has me as a friend. He offers me £100 within a week if I steer clear of the quarrel between you and him. You see, it is money I want. I think I have said enough for wise men to understand.' He then stalked from the meeting. The justiciar and his men were powerless unless they wanted the embarrassment of a public trial of the chancellor; John got his bribe. Longchamp was forced to flee a second time. With the money thus pocketed, John was able to suborn further castellans and constables. By the end of the year John had consolidated his position by gaining possession of the royal castles of Windsor and Wallingford.[85]

At Marseilles, meanwhile, Richard had leisure to ponder the implications of the great enterprise he was engaged on, and for which he had neglected the governance of England. Saladin's great victory at Hattin in 1187 should really have doomed the Christian kingdom of Jerusalem to extinction. Jerusalem itself had fallen, Acre, Beirut and Sidon had capitulated without a fight, and Saladin took Caesarea, Arsuf and Jaffa in quick succession. Even though Guy of Lusignan could not persuade Ascalon to surrender and thus fulfil the terms set by Saladin for his release, the city threw in the sponge anyway, as did the castle of Gaza. Soon all ports south of Tripoli except Tyre were in Arab hands, and only the fortresses of Margat and Krak des Chevaliers seemed proof against Islamic siege engines. But Saladin, albeit not entirely irrationally, made three cardinal errors. He freed Guy de Lusignan on the mistaken impression that he was a discredited force in Outremer, a paper tiger. He did not proceed to the siege of Tripoli and concluded an eight-month truce with Bohemond of Antioch. Above all, he sacrificed the obvious strategic target of Tyre to the glory of winning back Jerusalem for the prophet. Saladin had reasons for all three decisions. He was convinced that no Christian would ever again rally to the banner of the man who had lost at Hattin and, besides, he had bound Guy by oath never to fight him again. He proceeded to Jerusalem in the belief that this was the best way to rally the faithful for the final *jihad*. In fact his success there inflamed caliph al-Nasir in Baghdad against him – he resented the huge increase in the power of his 'vassal' – and very bad relations with his nominal overlord were the result.[86] Chafing at what he considered the arrogant and peremptory missives sent him from Baghdad, Saladin exploded: 'As for the claims of the Caliph that I've conquered Jerusalem with his army and under his banner – where were his banners and his army at the time? By God! I conquered Jerusalem with my own troops and under my own banner.'[87]

On the issue of the controversial truce with Antioch, Saladin was not really a free agent. His power depended on a constant juggling act: appeasing the caliph, satisfying the ambitions of his own rank and file and, most of all, conciliating the interests of powerful factions that might otherwise turn on him. His most important ally was Imad al-Din Zangi, the son-in-law of Nur al-Din, a prominent, turbulent warlord who had to be placated. Zangi had pressed hard for the eight-month truce with Antioch simply because he feared Saladin would otherwise become too powerful in his own sphere of influence.[88] Yet if reasons can be found that mitigate Saladin's 'errors', his decision to concentrate on Jerusalem rather than Tyre certainly does look like an egregious mistake. By the time he was ready to deal with this key port, a new Christian hero had arisen. Conrad of Montferrat, an adventurer who had made himself prince of the city, organised a masterly defence of Tyre, which led Saladin to postpone his assault. When he turned to deal with the problem after the fall of Jerusalem, he found it a nut too hard to crack. The city was virtually an island, surrounded on three sides by rip-tide waters and hidden rocks, connected to the mainland by a short and narrow causeway. Twenty-five-foot thick walls and twelve strong towers guarded the island city, and the causeway, facing the eastern land entrance was a crenellation of massive, high towers, set back to back. The only way to take the city was by a skilful amphibious assault or by the protracted business of starving it out. Tyre had taxed Alexander the Great's ingenuity, to the point where Napoleon himself later commented: 'He can have no idea of war who blames this prince (Alexander) for having spent seven months in the siege of Tyre. Had it been myself, I would have remained there seven years if necessary.'[89]

The siege of Tyre marked a turning point in Saladin's fortunes. His hitherto victorious army was in bad shape. Used to easy victories, walkover sieges and living on plunder, his soldiers were brought up short by the prospect of really hard fighting, to say nothing of having to spend their own money on food and fodder. Christian morale was meantime rising daily, as it became clear that no combined operations had been thought out by the Arabs. Seeing the cavalier way Saladin employed his navy for a blockade of the harbour, Conrad of Montferrat prepared a masterstroke and launched seventeen galleys and ten small ships against the blockaders. At dawn his sailors fell on the Muslim ships and found the crews asleep; the attack was a perfectly executed surprise. The remaining Arab ships were ordered back to Beirut, but Conrad's men intercepted them too.[90] This reverse confirmed all the pessimistic assessments of the defeatist faction on Saladin's war council. The rank and file soldiery were demoralised and Saladin lacked the funds to bribe them to stick to their task. A half-hearted cavalry assault on 31 December, the day after the naval defeat, was more in the nature of a face-saver than a serious attack, and when it failed Saladin's emirs were glad to have the excuse to disengage and raise the siege. It was Saladin's first serious military reverse since Hattin and he must accept the blame for the fiasco. He did not blockade effectively, had no plans to starve the garrison out, did not prevent reinforcements reaching the defenders and could not energise his own men. It is a moral certainty that if he had taken Tyre at the end of 1187, the Third Crusade would have been halted in its tracks.[91] It was becoming clear that Saladin could not trust his allies, his commanders or even his own relations. Meanwhile both the Almohad rulers of North Africa and the caliph of Baghdad had made it clear that they doubted his sincerity – had he not spent many years fighting against his co-religionists in pursuit of an expansionist vision of his own? He had shown no interest in a *jihad* – an attitude increasingly in evidence among the private soldiers, who wanted money and loot, not the triumph of the Crescent.[92]

The reverse at Tyre shook Saladin and the first six months of 1188 saw him unwontedly cautious, at first contemplating the siege of the Hospitaller castle at Kaukab and the Templar stronghold at Safad before moving off to Damascus in April. The question he had to answer by mid-1188 was whether he was strong enough to conquer the whole coast – a question the loose structure of his army, with men liable to drift away and a leader with no divine right to rule, seemed certain to answer in the negative. Having therefore opted to pick off some weak targets he easily captured Jabala, Latakia, Sahyun, Sarmaniya, Bursey, Darbsak and Baghras. The obvious next objective was Antioch, the capture of which would block the principal land route for Frankish reinforcements, but the eight-month truce, battle-weariness among his troops and the jealousy of rival chiefs like Zangi all dictated caution. Returning to Damascus in September, Saladin contented himself with diplomatic overtures to Byzantium, aimed at building a common front against the threatened crusade from the West. Byzantium feared the advent of Frederick Barbarossa and his German host as much as the Muslims did, so an informal treaty of alliance was concluded. Saladin was said to have sent emperor Isaac Angelus a large silver jar of poisoned wine and quantities of poisoned flour and more wine for use against Barbarossa's army.[93] By the end of 1188 Saladin could look back on a virtually empty year, clinging to empty promises like that of Reginald of Sidon, who pledged to hand over the castle of Beaufort provided Saladin spirited his family safely out of Tyre. Only the surrender of Safad, Kerak and Kaukab Castles lightened the gloom.[94]

The next year, 1189, was even worse for Saladin. Eighteen months after Hattin he was on the defensive, having to concentrate his forces on the coast against the Frankish counter-attack that was bound to come once the crusaders from the West arrived. And every day his ally in

Byzantium dinned into his ears the menacing stories about Frederick Barbarossa's careful and determined preparations. Saladin's failure to crush the Franks immediately after Hattin was now proving his biggest mistake, since his great victory there had done no more than rouse the sleeping tiger in Western Europe. He was now in a race against time, and he knew it. Ominously, at Tyre Conrad de Montferrat and Guy of Lusignan were reconciled, and Guy had been persuaded by his priests that the oath he had sworn not to fight against Saladin was not binding since 'an oath should not be kept when Holy Mother Church is in danger'. Once more a credible general in his own and others' eyes, Guy at once won a significant battle in July 1189 between Tyre and Sidon. Seeing the way the wind was blowing, Reginald of Sidon asked for a nine-month extension on his promise to deliver up Beaufort, on the grounds that his family was still within the walls of Tyre.[95] Then Guy of Lusignan made his great gamble. Helped by the fact that the first contingents of crusaders were starting to arrive from Denmark and Holland, he raised a new army of 700 knights, mainly Templars, and 9,000 foot and took it to Acre, where he commenced to besiege the city. Saladin in turn took the besieging army in the rear, so that Guy was hemmed in between a potentially sallying garrison and a relieving host, rather like Julius Caesar at Alesia in 52 BC during the Gallic War. Saladin tried to cut his way through Guy's army in September only to be thrown back in a bruising encounter. There was another inconclusive battle in October, when Guy and Conrad de Montferrat collaborated well (and Gérard de Rideford died). Saladin claimed a victory but any marginal military benefit was soon offset by plummeting morale in the Muslim army and mass desertions of troops carrying off loot, so that he could not capitalise on battlefield advantage. The fortunes of war had definitely turned in favour of Guy of Lusignan. At the beginning of 1189 Saladin had his pick of targets – Tripoli, Tyre, Antioch; by the end of the year he was fighting for survival.[96]

Ill throughout January 1190, Saladin had to devolve operations to his commanders, who were so devoid of new ideas that they tried to start an epidemic of fever by throwing Christian corpses into the River Belus. With the caliph in Baghdad lukewarm in his support, sending derisory financial contributions to the fight against the infidel, Saladin had to derive comfort from small victories like the final surrender of Beaufort Castle in April 1190. But he knew this could be the year when he was overwhelmed. With an army of 25,000 men (but rumoured to be ten times that size), Frederick Barbarossa moved down through Hungary, forced the Byzantine emperor to give him passage into Asia Minor and crossed the Dardanelles at the end of March 1190. Saladin still hoped that Qilij-Arslan, conqueror of the Byzantines, would be able to stop the Germans in their tracks, but Frederick defeated the Turks outside Iconium after a 33-day running battle and took the city.[97] The seemingly unstoppable German emperor was then destroyed by a freak accident when he drowned in the River Saleph on 10 June. Allah suddenly seemed to be smiling on Saladin and he accordingly won a victory on 25 July 1190. Once more he was unable to follow up, and the arrival of Henry of Champagne with crusader reinforcements three days later annulled any impact the battle had. Saladin's best piece of luck was that the German host was no longer formidable. Imploding after the emperor's death, it split into three divisions to make foraging easier but simply made itself easier prey for marauding Turks. Only about 5,000 under the command of Frederick's son the duke of Swabia limped into Antioch. The Germans had achieved little on their disastrous march through Asia Minor but they had forced Saladin to remain on the defensive for an entire summer.[98] Once he realised he had little to fear from them and tried to resume decisive operations against the besiegers of Acre, he found that the enemy had meanwhile grown stronger than ever with the arrival of fresh seaborne reinforcements. The most terrible threat, from Barbarossa, was no more, but, if the most powerful Christian monarch in Europe was dead, Saladin knew that close behind him trod the second- and third-ranking kings: Philip Augustus of France and the formidable warrior Richard I of England.

7

◄○►

AFTER WAITING FOR A week for the fleet that was then still labouring through the Straits of Gibraltar following its disgraceful behaviour in Lisbon, Richard divided his overland forces in two and sent one half directly to the Holy Land (we are not told where he got the shipping); in this force were such notables as Archbishop Baldwin of Canterbury, Ranulph Glanville and his nephew Hubert Walter, bishop of Salisbury. This party arrived at Tyre on 30 September and at Acre on 12 October.[1] The detachment Richard commanded embarked in ten large ships known as busses and twenty galleys on 7 August and began a leisurely cruise of the western coast of Italy, beginning in Genoa, where Philip of France had gone after the two monarchs parted company in Lyons. Philip's administrative arrangements looked more impressive than Richard's for he had already hired a Genoese fleet to take his army to Palestine, and the transaction was minutely and meticulously recorded: 650 knights with two squires per knight – some 2,000 men in all – were to be provided with transport to Outremer, food for themselves and fodder for their horses for eight months and even a four-month supply of wine for the total cost of 5,850 marks.[2] Even though many French knights had proceeded overland or gone on ahead by other means, Philip's total numbers were far less than Richard's host of an estimated 10,000. At Genoa Richard found Philip himself lying ill in the Church of St Lawrence from a mysterious malady, which cynics said was no more than a bad case of seasickness. Whereas Richard and Philip, political differences notwithstanding, had hitherto always enjoyed good personal relations, to the point where incautious writers today can still refer to them as 'lovers', it seems that it was at this juncture that they had the first of the serious disagreements which would terminate in a legendary feud. Philip asked Richard for the loan of five galleys, Richard responded with an offer of three, and Philip, choosing to take this as a personal insult, angrily refused.[3]

Richard's fleet then proceeded to Portofino (where the king rested for five days) and on to Portovenere, providing an opportunity to visit Pisa. The voyage continued past Cape Baratti to the castle of Piombino, thence via Portoferrajo on the island of Elba, the peninsula of Monte-Argentario, Porto Ercole and Civitavecchia to Ostia.[4] Though at the mouth of the Tiber and just 16 miles from Rome, he did not visit the Eternal City and to Octavian, cardinal bishop of Ostia, who came to meet him he coldly explained why. Angry at the 1,500 marks he had to pay to have the pope appoint William Longchamp legate for the English Church, he told Octavian that the papacy was a mere snakepit of corruption, the keys of St Peter in effect sold off to the highest bidder and the so-called Vicar of Christ no better than the moneylenders Christ drove out of the temple. He made it clear that his snub to the Pope had nothing to do with his haste to be in the Holy Land by proceeding to Naples (via Nettuno and Ischia) and then ostentatiously staying there ten days.[5] He then spent another five days at nearby Salerno, then considered the leading centre for European medicine. His leisurely progress had method in it, for he had left instructions for the main fleet to follow with all speed. This armada of cut-throats and reprobates actually arrived at Marseilles on 22 August and got under way again on the 30th. While Richard was at Salerno, he heard that it had leapfrogged him and was already off Messina.[6] He decided to complete the rest of the journey to Sicily overland, and his chroniclers logged the succession of dreary towns in minute detail: Amalfi, Conza, Scalea, Amantea, Santa Eufemia, Mileto. On the road from Mileto (where his overnight stopover had been the abbey of the Holy Trinity), he made a typically bad, impulsive Ricardian mistake. Having sent his servants ahead, he was travelling with just one companion when he heard the sound of a hawk coming from a village hovel. Indignant that anyone but an aristocrat should own a hawk, he strode into the house and seized the bird. This high-handed action soon had the entire village down around his ears. Pelted by sticks and stones, Richard drew his sword to chastise the contumacious villagers, only to see the blade snap when he smacked the boldest villager with the flat of the weapon. The proud king of England and lord of Aquitaine experienced the humiliation of conducting a fighting retreat with nothing more than the selfsame tools the villagers were using. He could easily have been killed for a moment of impetuous folly.[7]

That very evening he crossed the Straits of Messina, joined his fleet and, next day, made a triumphal entrance into Messina itself. The interview with Philip of France on 24 September was a sullen affair – Philip had been in Messina since the 16th, keeping a low profile and now he was outshone and piqued by the 'magnificent reception' given to his rival. The Sicilians seem to have been intrigued by the English fleet and its polyglot crews, as amazed by the olio of French, English and Flemish as by the bewildering variety of ships in Richard's armada. There were snacks, oared transport ships of a Scandinavian type, longer and narrower than the galleys or dromonds, then there were the bulkier and slower dromonds – galleys with either a single or double bank of oars and one or more masts with lateen or triangular sails, equipped with a ramming beak for immobilising an enemy ship or holding it fast while grappling and boarding tactics were attempted. Particularly admired were the destriers, for the Normans had acquired ever since the Conquest of 1066 a particular expertise in transporting horses by sea.[8] But the chronicler Ambroise said that the 'Grifons and Lombards' (Sicilians of, respectively, Greek or Latin descent) were angry at such pomp and circumstance, especially the caparisoned chargers and the flying pennants, which they considered a tactless slighting of their own king. Philip, angry that his arrival in a single ship had been so signally upstaged, announced that he was leaving his quarters in the royal palace and setting sail for Outremer at once. But Philip was as fearful a sailor as he was a warrior. Barely had he cleared Messina harbour when the sea began to make up and Philip, terrified by the waves, was forced to return to Messina and further 'humiliating' encounters with Richard.[9]

On his way to rescue the Christian kingdom of Jerusalem from crisis, Richard had fortuitously walked into another political maelstrom when he arrived in Sicily. A prosperous and affluent kingdom, with abundant agricultural wealth – apart from oranges, lemons, sugar cane and cotton, the island was still the breadbasket of the Mediterranean it had been in Roman times – Sicily, at the crossroads between Western Europe, North Africa and the eastern Mediterranean, had always been a cockpit for conflict over trade routes and strategic nodal points. The eleventh century saw it as a battlefield between Byzantines, Normans and Saracens – a conflict the Normans had largely won by 1090. The result was a syncretism of cultures and languages, with Greek, Latin and Arabic the languages representing the respective three combatants. A political crisis had arisen on the death of the childless King William II in November 1189. By the laws of succession the kingdom passed to the late king's aunt Constance, who was married to Frederick Barbarossa's son Henry. Since Barbarossa's career had largely been spent trying to assert German hegemony in Italy, it began to look as though the Holy Roman Empire might attain by dynastic marriage what it had failed to achieve by force of arms. The papacy, still scarred from the Guelph versus Ghibelline conflict, had no more desire to see Sicily fall into the German orbit than the Norman Sicilians had. Anti-German forces managed to instal Tancred of Lecce as the new king on the dubious grounds that he was an illegitimate cousin of the late king.[10] This blatant attempt at a kind of Norman super-hegemony triggered both a Muslim revolt and an invasion from Germany. The dust of civil war had only just settled when the crusaders arrived. Tancred feared it might not be only Saladin who felt the military lash from doughty warriors like Richard.[11]

For his part, Richard had a more immediate grievance. His sister Joan had been married to William II and, fearing trouble from her, Tancred had put her under house arrest and withheld the income from her dower, the county of Monte San Angelo. Moreover, William II had bequeathed his vast wealth in money, gold plate, grain, wine and warships to his father-in-law Henry II, but Tancred had used Henry's death as an excuse to declare the will null and void.[12] From Messina Richard dispatched envoys to Tancred in Palermo with a simple message: release my sister or face the consequences, and make good on William's legacy. Tancred immediately set Joan free but stalled on the issue of the dower, 'compensating' her with a large money grant.[13] Dissatisfied, Richard showed that he intended to pursue 'linkage' of both grievances by seizing the fortified monastery of Bagnara on the mainland side of the Straits of Messina and installing his sister Joan there. Irritated by the entire business over Alice, Richard thought he detected a flicker of interest in Joan from Philip and toyed with paying him back in the same coin by dangling the prospect of a dynastic marriage.[14] But he soon had more serious concerns to attend to. Warfare was already probable when an insurrection in Messina made it certain. The crusader rank and file had not even managed to live on friendly terms with the people of Lisbon, so it was not likely they could adapt easily to the complex multicultural society of Sicily. Misunderstandings and failure to communicate soon hardened into deadly hostility between the indigenous population and the interlopers. The issue of the local women and the lustful attentions of the crusaders immediately became a running sore. Moreover, with demand for the essentials of life outstripping supply, the presence of such large numbers of troops soon resulted in skyrocketing food prices, especially of staples. Local traders and shopkeepers welcomed the chance for some quick profits and cited the law of supply and demand, but for the crusaders rising food prices simply meant greed, exploitation and profiteering by the Sicilians.[15] Intemperate haggling led to crusaders refusing to pay prices asked, and the more ruffianly of them rode roughshod over the locals. The inevitable upshot was violence. Fearing rape, and, ultimately, enslavement, the Messinesi rose in revolt; Richard's seizure of another stronghold, the Greek monastery of San Salvatore, on 2 October was apparently the last straw. The word spread that Richard and his men intended to spend the winter in Sicily, so that there would be more rape, seduction, extortion, violence and bullying. Tancred's agents, and even his governors, obligingly fanned the flames.[16]

Even as Richard sat in conclave on 4 October with King Philip, Tancred's local governors and the archbishops of Monreale, Reggio and Messina, he received word that his men were coming under heavy attack by the people of Messina and that the quarters of Hugh of Lusignan, one of the barons of Aquitaine, had been selected as the first target. Richard at once broke up the conference and assumed command of his army. The only way to deal with this uprising was a systematic conquest of Messina, so he made his dispositions.[17] He began with a surprise uphill charge of the kind the locals had never seen before, which dislodged the defenders from their 'impregnable' position on high ground.[18] Then he battered down the city gates and stormed in at the head of bloodthirsty, vengeful troops; in their fear, the Messinesi had achieved a self-fulfilling prophecy and now faced the very hordes of murderous rapists they so feared. In such circumstances, the fighting was bitter and hand-to-hand. Losses were high, including twenty-five of Richard's household knights. To the fury of the English, Philip and the French remained neutral during the fighting, and Philip even seemed to favour the locals.[19] But Richard and his men needed no assistance. They were in their element in this bloody streetfighting, they were veterans of many a siege, and they could sense the plunder and the rape that awaited them at the end of operations. All too soon local resistance collapsed: Ambroise said Richard completed the conquest of Messina in less time than it would take a priest to say matins. Then came the inevitable aftermath when Messina got a taste of what Lisbon had suffered. Palls of smoke rose over the harbour as the victorious troops stormed down to the merchants' quarters to pillage and burn. Many a shopkeeper lived to regret the high prices he had charged, and many a shopkeeper's wife and daughter paid for the patriarch's profiteering by suffering the fate worse than death. As Ambroise put it in throwaway style: 'They acquired women, fair, noble and wise women.'[20]

Richard's swift victory infuriated Philip, who claimed to be insulted when he saw the banners of England and Aquitaine streaming from the towers and walls of Messina. Since the flying of banners implied the absolute dominion of the lord whose colours were flown, he demanded, absurdly in the circumstances, that Richard take down his own insignia and replace them with those of France. Not wishing to abort the entire crusade on a matter of protocol, Richard compromised by taking down his own colours and replacing them with the 'neutral' pennants of the Templars and Hospitallers, who would thus remain as keepers of Messina until Tancred agreed terms.[21] This was the second contretemps between Richard and Philip and some chroniclers said it was the crucial one, for Philip began to develop an obsession that Richard was flouting the terms of the 'all for one' agreement at Vézelay.[22] Richard meanwhile took hostages from the wealthy burghers and, to rub salt in the wound, built a wooden castle on a hill overlooking the town; to this structure he gave the undiplomatic name Mategrifon, or Kill the Greeks.[23] Faced with the possible permanent loss of Messina, Tancred agreed to pay Richard another enormous sum in gold, as full settlement of Joan's dower and Richard's other financial grievances. Tancred of Lecce may have been physically unprepossessing – ugly, simian and dwarfish – but he was a shrewd diplomat. In return for conceding Richard's demands, he got a treaty of alliance against any invaders of the island – whether the Germans of emperor Henry VI or the Almohads of North Africa – and a diplomatic revolution whereby the king of England became the enemy of the German emperor.[24] This was a rash step for Richard to take, and Philip Augustus, offered a similar deal earlier, had turned it down so as not to make an enemy of Germany. The value of Tancred's diplomacy was seen the following year. When emperor Henry VI launched an attack on Sicily, Richard engineered a revolt in Germany, led by his ally Henry, son of Frederick Barbarossa's old adversary Henry the Lion. Richard on the other hand was no diplomat since by his agreement with Tancred he alienated both the German emperor and his brother John. To cement the alliance with Tancred, it was expressly stated that Arthur of Britanny was the heir presumptive to the throne of England and that, when adult, Arthur would marry one of Tancred's daughters.[25]

Two days after the agreement with Tancred, on 8 October, Richard settled his differences with Philip by drawing up guidelines for the crusaders' stay in Sicily. He 'squared' the French king by giving him one-third of the monies received from Tancred, though the French later complained this should have been one-half, in accordance with the fifty-fifty rule.[26] Then he imposed a code of conduct for his own men. First, he insisted that all goods looted in Messina should be returned. Then he ruled that the moratorium on debts, allowable as a crusader's 'perk', applied only to debts contracted before the crusade. His target here was gambling debts, for the soldiers had taken to wagering huge amounts in the taverns of Messina and then, if they lost, repudiating the debts on the grounds that this was their privilege as crusaders. Additionally, a *total* ban on gambling, except in the presence and with the permission of officers, was imposed on the rank and file, with punishments for infraction severe: whipping through the army for a soldier (usually a fatal sanction) or triple keelhauling for sailors (even more decidedly so). These checks on high-handedness and indiscipline reconciled the people of Messina to occupation.[27] Richard's unsympathetic attitude to his private soldiers caused much muttering in the ranks, especially when he allowed knights and clerics to gamble up to twenty shillings a day. But bad feeling was to some extent assuaged by a price freeze: Richard and Philip fixed the price of bread at a penny a loaf, made it a criminal offence for merchants to raise the price of wine, and decreed that profits higher than 10 per cent on any transaction were illegal. Speculation and hoarding were punishable by death, no trading was allowed in dead meat, and in live meat only for slaughter by the army. A finance and discipline committee enforced these regulations and others, such as a tax of 50 per cent on the estates of crusaders who died, in order to further and finance the crusade, with the other 50 per cent being remitted to heirs and legatees in the home country.[28] These regulations were tough and even draconian but they preserved the peace for the next six months while the crusaders remained on the island.

It was probably at this stage that Richard had his first meeting with Tancred, for he spent a week away from Messina, in Palermo, during 9–16 October.[29] Roger of Howden was more interested in the king's encounter with the Cistercian abbot Joachim of Fiore, another of those mystics who claimed to be able to see hidden meanings in the Bible. Along with a lot of mumbo-jumbo about the Three Ages of History and the imminent coming of the Antichrist, Joachim was at least able to identify Saladin as the sixth of history's seven great persecutors of the Church (the seventh was to be Antichrist himself), and to predict that Richard, as God's chosen agent, would defeat Saladin and drive him from Jerusalem.[30] At the temporal level, Richard learned of the death at Acre of Archbishop Baldwin and, on Christmas Day 1190, entertained Philip of France to a magnificent banquet at Mategrifon – a sumptuous occasion of meat and wine served on gold and silver plate.[31] But his tarrying so long in Sicily puzzled many of his associates, particularly those who had been cooling their heels in Messina before he had even arrived. There were loud murmurings of discontent, with even oligarchic crusaders complaining of the damage to their purses caused by the long sojourn on the island. To quell the disaffection Richard was reduced to outright bribery: he distributed lavish cash gifts to his captains and there were even 'trickle down' payments made to the bored and fractious troops who were by now beginning to suffer from starvation and malnutrition. Many affected to query Richard's 'unconscionable' delay in Sicily, but his motives were simple and twofold. In the first place, he feared the elements and the state of the Mediterranean in winter; what would be the point in arriving at Acre with a shattered fleet? Secondly, he was allowing time for Eleanor of Aquitaine to bring his bride Berengaria to him. The women and their escort crossed the Alps in mid-winter and were at Lodi near Milan by 20 January 1191. There the 69-year-old Eleanor had a memorable meeting with Emperor Henry VI of Germany.[32]

By February 1191 it was clear that Richard and his men were at the extremities of boredom. They had drilled, they had manoeuvred, they had built siege engines and practised siege techniques, but now they really needed to sail to Acre and see action. Boredom and frustration must have been behind a notorious incident some time between 2–5 February when Richard took part in a tournament, not normally his favourite pastime. According to Roger of Howden, it was not even a properly organised tournament, just an improvised joust thought up on the spur of the moment when Richard, Philip and their retinues were out riding together. Finding peasants with a supply of long spear-like canes, the knights set about each other and, as bad luck would have it, Richard's sparring partner turned out to be his old antagonist William of Barres, France's equivalent of William Marshal. The details are confused and confusing, but it seems that Richard, having initially got the better of de Barres, tried to unhorse him only to find the French knight unwilling to admit defeat and clinging gamely to his horse's mane. Infuriated by this 'gamesmanship', and mindful of his previous encounters with de Barres, Richard lost his temper and ordered the Frenchman never again to come into his sight on pain of death. To make his rage even more potent, Richard insisted that Philip dismiss him from his service so that he would miss the crusade. Alarmed by Richard's volcanic outburst, Philip agreed, assuming that his fellow-monarch would eventually calm down. But when's Richard's wrath against de Barres continued at white heat, Philip had to play Agamemnon to his Achilles and play the suppliant. On his bended knees he and his knights begged Richard to grant at least provisional forgiveness to de Barres, so that he could continue on crusade. With great reluctance Richard agreed to allow de Barres to proceed to Acre, but made it clear that there would be no personal reconciliation between them.[33]

Maybe one factor disposing Richard to be 'lenient' to de Barres was the idea of an implicit deal with Philip over his sister Alice, the so-called fiancée of twenty years standing. By late February Eleanor of Aquitaine and Berengaria, accompanied by Count Philip of Flanders, had reached Naples, but there the problems started. Richard sent galleys to convey them the relatively short distance to Messina, but Tancred's agents forbade the women to embark on the ludicrous excuse that their entourage was too large; it was suggested that they travel overland to Brindisi first. With yet another reason for anger, Richard stormed down to Catania to demand an interview with Tancred. During a five-day conclave Tancred gradually revealed the reason for the insult he had offered to Richard's mother and bride. Philip of France had been playing Tancred like a violin, working on his fears that Richard intended to dispossess him and set up a permanent Angevin kingdom in Sicily. His motive was to save his sister Alice's honour from the shame of Richard's proposed marriage to Berengaria, but his methods were the old familiar Philippian ones of innuendo, rumour and dropping poison in the ear – the same ones he had used to such devastating effect when driving a wedge between Richard and his father Henry. Philip made particularly skilful use of the circumstantial features of Eleanor's meeting with Henry VI at Lodi: did this not hint at collusion between Richard and the Germans and was it not obvious that Richard intended to tear up the treaty of last October as soon as the emperor attacked Sicily? By patience and plain talking Richard convinced Tancred that he had been duped by Philip; he swore renewed friendship with Tancred and, to seal the entente, gave him what purported to be Excalibur, King Arthur's famous sword. Now convinced that he had been gulled by Philip, Tancred reciprocated by providing Richard with fifteen new galleys and four large transport ships. When Philip's agents protested that Richard was just trying to find a way not to marry Alice, as he was pledged to, and that he, not Philip, was the arch-manipulator, Richard was able to produce as a kind of surprise witness Count Philip of Flanders, who had come on ahead by ship from Naples. The fact that Count Philip backed Richard's version of events clinched matters for Tancred.[34]

So disgusted was Richard by Philip's duplicity that when the French king came to meet him and Tancred at Taormina, Richard refused to see him and returned to Messina. Grudgingly, the next day he allowed the count of Flanders to act as mediator between them, and some sort of amity was patched up. Richard told Philip bluntly that marriage with Alice was out of the question as she had been his own father's mistress and even borne him a son. He also offered to produce dozens of unimpeachable witnesses who could vouch for the truth of the accusation. That Richard was very angry about the entire Alice charade was clear from his explicit indictment of his father; as commentators have pointed out, to get out of the marriage all he had to show was the much easier-to-prove proposition that Alice had given birth to a child of which he was not the father.[35] Evidently Philip already knew something of his sister's liaison with Henry, or else he was simply not prepared for the shame and humiliation that would descend on Alice if a formal tribunal was called to establish the facts, for he quickly agreed to absolve Richard from his oath, salving his wounded pride by pocketing 10,000 marks in compensation. While they were in conference Richard and Philip also agreed to resolve all their outstanding territorial disputes over Gisors and the Norman Vexin (Richard to have it if he produced a male heir, otherwise it would revert to Philip). On the other boundary issues, a quid pro quo was hammered out: Richard was to have Cahors and the Quercy, while Philip got Issoudun, Gracy and Auvergne.[36] But defeat over Alice was a bitter pill for Philip to swallow even with the cash payment. He made his feelings clear by sailing from Messina for Acre on 30 March, a matter of hours before Eleanor and Berengaria arrived from Reggio in Richard's triumphant company.[37] For Philip this was the last straw: he had been humiliated over galleys, banners, William de Barres and now Alice. He sailed to Outremer with a heavy, angry, brooding heart. In his mind his bitter enemy was no longer Saladin but Richard.[38]

The tireless Eleanor of Aquitaine spent just three days at Messina before starting back on the long journey to Normandy. She left Berengaria with Richard's sister Joan, sailed to Salerno and thence went up to Rome to attend the new pope's consecration.[39] Richard was left to ponder his choice of wife. Politically, the match made sense, but was there any more to it than that, and should we discount the story that long ago, when count of Poitou, Richard had fallen in love with her and wanted her as his wife?[40] It is a moral certainty that she was a virgin, so there would be no Alice-style distaste this time on the part of the groom. William of Newburgh said she was both prudent and beautiful, though Richard of Devizes (who never saw her) thought she was more prudent than beautiful. The best eyewitness report is from Ambroise who said: 'She was a wise maiden, a fine lady, both noble and beautiful, with no falseness or treachery in her.'[41] Richard was keen to celebrate the wedding at once, but Church protocol forbade this as it was still Lent; whether he and Berengaria 'anticipated' marriage must be left in the realm of speculation. But the arrival of Berengaria concomitant with that of spring meant there was no further reason to remain in Sicily. The fleet was drawn up and loaded with provisions. The castle of Mategrifon was dismantled and stowed away in sections, ready for reassembly in the Holy Land. More than 200 ships, groaning with men, horses, armour, siege engines, food and fodder, stood away for the east on 10 April.[42] For once medieval and modern authorities are in rough agreement on numbers. Richard of Devizes's meticulous head count gives us 24 busses, 39 galleys and 156 other ships (219 in all) which on the usual basis of ships' capacity would provide a grand total of 17,000 soldiers and seamen, a massive force by the standards of the day and possibly the largest army any king of England had ever commanded to that date.[43]

Twelfth-century navigators were terrified of the open sea and liked to hug coastlines as far as possible. Dependent solely on the wind, they sailed the Mediterranean at a speed of little more than three knots – no more than walking pace – and even with the most favourable winds could not hope to complete the voyage from Marseilles to Acre in less than fifteen days.[44] It is therefore not entirely surprising that Richard's fleet took twelve days to reach Rhodes from Sicily. On the third day out, Good Friday 12 April, a gale hit the armada and scattered the ships, so that at the first staging point, Crete, on 17 April, no less than twenty-five ships were missing, including the one bearing Joan and Berengaria. The gales had not claimed them, merely pushed them ahead of the body of the fleet, so that by 24 April this detached flotilla was off the coast of southern Cyprus, near Limassol. Here the first casualties were sustained, for three ships were wrecked and their cargoes plundered. A number of soldiers and sailors drowned when the vessels ran aground, including Roger Macael, the king's vice-chancellor, who was carrying the great seal; this was recovered when Macael's body was washed ashore with the seal on a chain around his neck.[45] When the half-drowned survivors scrambled ashore, they were at once arrested, fleeced of their money and thrown in prison. A landing party attacked the fort where the imprisoned crusaders were held, which enabled the prisoners to sortie and join their comrades; together they then retreated to the ships standing offshore, including the vessel with Joan and Berengaria aboard. It took Richard another five days to complete the voyage from Rhodes to Cyprus, but, once arrived, he quickly secured a beachhead and drove the Cypriot defenders back. Richard had been enraged by his reception in Cyprus, and now announced that he intended to punish the island's 'tyrant' Isaac Comnenus, self-styled 'emperor'.[46]

The politics of Cyprus at this juncture were just as complex as Sicily's. Formerly the Byzantine governor of Cilicia, Isaac Ducas Comnenus had, by 1184, gained control of Cyprus in murky circumstances on which historians cannot agree. He immediately rebelled against the new emperor in Byzantium (Andronicus I), declared him a usurper and took the title of emperor on the grounds that he alone was the legitimate successor and all other claimants to the Byzantine throne merely usurpers.[47] He survived an attempt by yet another new emperor (for Andronicus lasted just two years) to overthrow him in 1186 but by the time of Richard's arrival was in a precarious position, since the death of his ally William II of Sicily in 1189 had left him friendless. Isaac's aggressive posture towards a huge crusader army seems the height of folly, unless his spies had already warned him that Richard intended to conquer the island. The probability is that Richard had this in mind all along. There are many circumstantial pointers in this direction: the fact that Joan and Berengaria and the others remained cruising off Cyprus while Richard was in Rhodes; the fact that Guy of Lusignan, his brother Geoffrey, Bohemond of Antioch and Raymond of Tripoli all arrived at Limassol on 11 May and swore fealty to Richard; Ambroise's cryptic statement, explaining Richard's tardiness in proceeding to Acre, 'He already had another plan in mind'; most of all, the obvious strategic imperative of securing the long supply lines from southern Italy to Outremer via Cyprus. Richard had a keen sense of logistics, and it seemed obvious to him that to have Cyprus in crusader hands simply reinforced the position of the struggling kingdom of Jerusalem.[48] Isaac Comnenus's seemingly mindless aggression may simply have been a reflex action to threat. From his point of view, the landing of crusaders without permission was an act of war, and their standing off the coast after an initial repulse spelled just one thing: they were awaiting the arrival of the main force.

When Richard arrived from Rhodes on 6 May, he was enraged to discover that Isaac had stripped Limassol bare of anything wooden and constructed beach defences that were partly improvised timber castles and partly great blocks of stone – he had to oppose the crusaders on the beach, since Limassol and all other Cypriot towns were unwalled.

Richard went through the pacific motions, demanding restitution and compensation for the goods seized from the wrecked vessels, but these demands were predictably rejected.[49] He then bruited through the army full details of Isaac's treacherous behaviour, including an alleged attempt to lure Joan and Berengaria ashore to captivity by false, forked-tongue words and, far worse, his alliance with Saladin, allegedly sealed in a ceremony of blood-brotherhood when they had actually drunk each other's gore. Ambroise stated that Isaac was more treacherous and evil than Judas, or Ganelon, who had betrayed Roland in the famous troubadour lay *Chanson de Roland*.[50] Having attended to morale, Richard then implemented the more difficult task of an amphibious landing on a defended beach, but his soldierly touch was as sure as ever. Showers of arrows from crossbowmen in the advancing landing craft forced the Cypriot defenders back from the shore, enabling Richard's commandos to wade through shallow water and then disperse the enemy by a well-timed charge up the beach. We even learn from Ambroise the names of some of the knights who distinguished themselves in this action, among them Roger of Harcourt from Brionne (Eure) and William of Bois-Normand, a Norman from Evreux.[51] The Greek and Armenian defenders melted away into the hills, leaving the crusaders to pillage Limassol, now virtually a ghost town after the inhabitants had abandoned it. Richard followed up his victory on the beaches with another next day, allegedly at Kolossi.[52] With local numerical superiority, Isaac was confident Richard would not immediately attack but he did so. The sources do not agree on the details, but it seems that the assault came as a surprise, that Isaac was nearly captured, and that the key to the second victory was the destriers. Isaac had known about the famed crusader warhorses but had either assumed it was too difficult to bring them from Sicily or, at worst, thought they needed to be fed and exercised before being used in battle. Ambroise's explanation is that Richard spent the night after the beach-head battle exercising his horses so that he could use them next day as a shock weapon.[53]

Isaac was vanquished but still not ready to concede total defeat. There was a short lull in the fighting, and in this interlude Richard turned his attention to two pressing non-military matters. In the first place, he finally married Berengaria, in a ceremony in Limassol performed by Nicholas, bishop of Le Mans. Then, in a separate ceremony, Berengaria was crowned queen of England by John, bishop of Evreux; other ecclesiastical dignitaries attended both events. Richard assigned to his queen as dower full rights in all territory in Gascony south of the River Garonne.[54]

Some observers queried the oddity of a Norman bishop crowning a woman queen of England in Cyprus, but there was method in Richard's eccentricity, since he wanted to arrive at Acre unencumbered by the possible embarrassment involved in an Outremer wedding with a peevish Philip of France hovering around like the proverbial spectre at the feast. Much more tricky was the issue involving Guy of Lusignan. It will be recalled that Saladin released Guy on condition he would no longer fight, but that Guy broke that pledge at the prompting of his clergy. Guy's daring, and even reckless, attack on Acre, which by now had petered out into stalemate after eighteen months of siege, had been an attempt to regain credibility as king of Jerusalem but he was under heavy challenge from the new Christian 'hero' Conrad of Montferrat. Guy of Lusignan's claim to be king had always been underpinned by his marriage to Sibylla, the acknowledged heiress of the kingdom, but in 1190 she and her two daughters died, victims of the plague that intermittently assailed Guy's camp. Conrad seized his chance to usurp the title and forced a marriage on Sibylla's younger sister Isabella. It was a classic case of duress: Conrad simply abducted the trembling woman and browbeat her to his will in a 'wedding' on 24 November 1190. But marriage by rapine was not even the worst of it, for Conrad was already married, bigamously, to Italian and Greek spouses, while Isabella was still married to Humphrey of Toron, who was still fuming impotently in the encampment at Acre. Moreover, it was later established by canon law that Conrad and Isabella constituted an incestuous coupling, because Isabella's sister had once been married to Conrad's brother, and no papal authority gave credence to the validity of Conrad's forced marriage to Isabella. He had found a couple of venal and corrupt churchmen to perform the ceremony, but a papal commission concluded that her marriage to Humphrey was never dissolved.[55]

The situation was black farce of the worst sort, particularly serious among men who claimed to be fighting for God and spiritual values and particularly dangerous at this juncture, since the Franks could scarcely afford a civil war when they were supposed to be warring against Saladin. A 'gentleman's agreement' was reached that the decision on who was truly king of Jerusalem should await the coming of the kings of England and France. But when Philip arrived at Acre on 20 April he immediately jumped the gun and recognised Conrad as king. In response Guy of Lusignan, his brother Geoffrey and the wronged husband Humphrey of Toron, together with Raymond of Tripoli and Bohemond of Antioch, set sail for Cyprus and arrived in Limassol the day before Richard's marriage to Berengaria.[56] Since the Lusignan sept were vassals of Richard as duke of Aquitaine, even though they (and especially Geoffrey) had caused him so much trouble in the past, he was bound to take their side in the dispute. Richard was also angered by Philip's attempt to steal a march on him by his unilateral declaration at Acre. Philip's action was controversial, provocative and divisive, but the runes on this could have been read by a perceptive observer, since it was his cousin the bishop of Beauvais who had been instrumental in arranging the phoney marriage between Conrad and Isabella. Philip proved himself a master of tactlessness by following up this insulting behaviour with a request that Richard make all haste to Acre. The envoy he sent with this request was none other than the corrupt bishop of Beauvais, accompanied by Dreux of Mello, soon to be Philip's choice as constable of France.[57] Richard pointedly treated the ambassador and his message with contempt, there were angry words spoken and Richard declared himself insulted; but he announced that he would proceed to Acre only when he had finally settled accounts with Isaac, and when he had secured Cyprus as a reliable provisioner for the crusaders in the Holy Land.[58]

For by now warfare had flared up again. The duplicitous Isaac agreed to Richard's peace terms and swore allegiance to him, thus gaining himself the time to gauge Richard's strength; maybe he thought the crusaders would at once respond to Philip's plea to proceed to Acre. But the terms he swore to were harsh: 20,000 marks compensation with an immediate down payment of 3,500 acres, his daughter to be at Richard's disposition to marry off as he saw fit, the surrender of his castles, and five hundred mounted men to serve in Palestine.[59] On second thoughts, he found them unacceptable and by now he had received envoys from Conrad of Montferrat asking him to delay Richard in Cyprus as long as possible. At any rate he suddenly stole away by night to Famagusta. This played into Richard's hands, as he had been hoping for a pretext to conquer the entire island. He divided his army, sending half with Guy of Lusignan to pursue Isaac while the other half he sent on a circumnavigation of the island, capturing towns and fortresses as it went. Intending to link up with Guy at Nicosia, Richard marched from Famagusta, and easily brushed aside an ambush Isaac had prepared at Tremetousha. Angry that the craven Isaac had not stayed to try matters with him in single combat, as he had offered, Richard took his anger out on the burghers of Nicosia and had their beards shaved. In the Byzantine culture of the twelfth century, this assault on the ultimate symbol of masculinity and power was the final insult. Isaac retaliated by blinding or mutilating Frankish prisoners or any of his own side that had offended him.[60] But the fall of Nicosia swung many Cypriots over to Richard's side, and it soon became apparent that Isaac was deeply unpopular, that the people had been merely waiting their chance to display their disaffection.

Isaac and his remaining forces were now confined to the castles of Buffavento, Kantara and St Hilarion in the mountains of northern Cyprus, playing a waiting game, hoping that Richard would depart for Outremer and allow them to reconquer the island. Hopes rose higher when it was learned that Richard was ill and detained in Nicosia. But when Guy of Lusignan captured the coastal stronghold of Kyrenia, eleven miles north of Nicosia, and Isaac's 14-year-old daughter, the 'emperor' lost heart and was consumed with grief.[61] Even while he digested this news, he learned that Richard had recovered from his illness and was now in possession of Buffavento Castle. Isaac fled to an abbey on Cape San Andrea, and pondered his dwindling options, but his love for his daughter proved to be the human frailty in this otherwise supremely unattractive man. On 1 June 1190 he surrendered, making only one condition: that he should not be put in irons. Richard fulfilled the letter of the agreement: he had Isaac bound in silver chains.[62] Isaac was lucky, as the usual penalty for failure in such circumstances in Byzantine culture was blinding or mutilation. Richard's campaign had been another brilliant feat of military organisation and imagination. Jealous rivals tried to belittle his achievement, and Saladin had it bruited about that Cyprus had fallen to treachery, but the truth was that Richard had proved himself a master of both strategy and amphibious operations.[63] His conquest brought him further wealth and resources, not just in the form of booty and confiscated property but from the swingeing 50 per cent tax he levied on every Cypriot. Securing the granaries and vineyards of Cyprus meant that the crusader army at Acre would never go short of food and supplies; news of Richard's victory visibly enhanced morale among the besiegers there. It is overwhelmingly probable that Richard always intended to conquer the island, but to his contemporaries he kept up the pretence that he had turned aside there by accident, simply to pick up survivors of the Good Friday storm, and that it was merely Isaac's cruel treatment of his shipwrecked sailors that had led to hostilities.[64]

To ensure that there would be no revival of Isaac's faction, Richard imposed an Angevin administration backed by garrisons. Robert of Thornham and Richard de Canville became co-governors of the island

(Richard always liked to divide power in this way, as his plans for the justiciarship in England in 1190 showed) while Ralf Fitzgodfrey became the personal jailer of the deposed Isaac. The ex-emperor languished in the crusader castle of Margat and, when released in 1193, spent the rest of his unhappy life warring against the Byzantine emperor Alexius III.[65] A decree was issued that Cypriot culture should henceforth be western, and that all beards should be shaved off. Disappointed that unrest continued in the island – for Isaac's cousin raised a revolt which was suppressed only when Robert of Thornham defeated the rebels and hanged their leader – and that Thornham seemed unable to temper main force with diplomacy, Richard sold Cyprus to the Templars for 100,000 dinars in Saracen money. This involved him in further trouble, as Philip of France then claimed a half-share under the fifty-fifty rule – though it seems he never got it.[66] Richard's critics then and now alleged that the sale of Cyprus was of a piece with his famous jest that he would have sold London to the highest bidder; in other words, it showed a man obsessed with short-term expediency and with no long view like that of his father or Philip of France who would throw away hard-won imperial possessions on a whim. Most of this criticism is once again the fallacy of viewing Richard through the prism of Victorian imperialism or, at least, from an exclusively English standpoint. In twelfth-century terms, Cyprus was not an appanage of some mythical empire but simply a strategic and logistical necessity in the reconquest of the Holy Land. Ambroise put the contemporary view explicitly: 'the king of England conquered all this in the service of God and to take His land'.[67] The critics, however, could scarcely fault Richard's treatment of Isaac's daughter. This girl, said to be 'most beautiful' but of unknown name (possibly it was Beatrice) became lady-in-waiting and constant companion to Joan and Berengaria. She accompanied them back to Italy and Normandy after the crusade and later became the fourth wife of Raymond of Toulouse and, later, Thierry, count of Flanders.[68]

Richard now prepared to sail to Acre. He had been receiving intelligence on the protracted siege, now nearly two years old, on a weekly basis ever since Guy of Lusignan made his daring and, many said, suicidal thrust towards the city in August 1189. Not strong enough to attack Jerusalem, Guy saw the psychological advantage in attacking Outremer's second city, a wealthy polyglot city which combined Byzantine pretensions with a high murder rate and, not coincidentally, the most thriving sexual trade and brothel culture in the Middle East.[69] But it was a tough nut for any besieger to crack. Triangular in shape, the city was protected on two sides by the sea while on the third, landward side there was a striation of defences: a double wall, towers a stone's throw apart, and a honeycomb of ditches and barbicans. The most vulnerable spot was the salient at the north-eastern corner of the city, where the walls came together at a right angle. Here a high tower had been built which the Franks called the Accursed Tower – because Judas Iscariot's thirty pieces of silver had allegedly been minted there. The walls gave Acre all-round protection, but they excluded the suburb of Montmusard in the north-west.[70] But the city's best known landmark was the forty-foot stone turret known as the Tower of Flies, which protected the seaward entrance to the city at the end of the break-water. Supposedly the Devil's tower – because Beelzebub is the Lord of Flies – it had really acquired its name from earlier times when, a place of human sacrifice, it attracted clouds of bluebottle flies. The inner and outer harbour, with capacity for hundreds of ships, lay just to the west of the Tower of Flies. When Guy of Lusignan arrived with his army in August 1189, he had made his base on a hill due east of Acre called Le Toron; from there Christian siege engines were deployed especially against the Accursed Tower and the damaged walls on this side. Across the neck of the peninsula on which Acre was sited they dug an immense trench to protect themselves from counter-attack by Saladin. He in turn pitched his camp east of Mount Carmel at Jebel el Kharruba, which afforded a view over the peninsula.[71]

The campaign settled into a pattern. Guy and his crusaders attempted a close blockade of Acre while fending off attacks from Saladin. The Franks immediately attacked the city on 29 August 1189 but had to fight two serious pitched battles against Saladin in the middle of September and the beginning of October. Saladin had the better of the two encounters, in the second of which the Templar leader Gérard de Rideford was killed, but found himself unable to follow up his advantage and score a knockout blow against the Franks, as his men scattered to plunder. The Franks responded by building a double line of trenches across the peninsula, isolating their encampment from both city and hinterland. By November Saladin went into winter quarters, contenting himself with a contemptuous surprise raid on the Christians' brothels and wine shops in December.[72] Winter saw a general de facto ceasefire and little naval activity either, since conventional opinion in the twelfth century held that the Mediterranean was too dangerous for shipping between November and March. Nonetheless, an enterprising Egyptian admiral managed to bring fifty galleys to Acre over Christmas 1189, significantly reinforcing the Muslim garrison and bringing new heart to the beleaguered defenders.

The war in this period tended to be a Homeric contest of individual heroes or a saga of freak and unusual occurrences: the miraculous survival of a Christian sergeant hit in the breast by a crossbow bolt which struck a metallic charm instead of flesh; the Arab defender of Acre who stood high on the wall to urinate on a crucifix and was transfixed with an arrow; the Christian squatting to defecate who was attacked by a Turk in mid-motion but still managed to kill his assailant with a stone; the single combat in which a Welsh archer defeated a Parthian counterpart who attempted treachery. Then there was the Arab captain who breached the Franks' naval blockade by posing as a Christian, complete with a shaved beard and a plethora of crosses and even displaying carcasses of pork on his vessel to 'prove' he was not a Muslim.[73] More realistic, and established from unimpeachable sources, were the accounts of Saladin's spy system. He maintained constant contact with the garrison in Acre in two main ways: by carrier pigeon and by expert swimmers who could brave the Mediterranean, swim in a huge loop and make landfall by the walls; some of these daredevils even carried pay for the soldiers in the garrison.[74]

For much of 1190 Saladin had been on the defensive, fearing the advent of Frederick Barbarossa and his host of Germans. In some ways his apprehension about the advancing Holy Roman Emperor was the least of his problems. The crusaders had many advantages, principally that they controlled the sea lanes, could therefore be provisioned from Italy, and were constantly being reinforced by new drafts from Europe. The first fresh troops on the scene were Italian, for Venice, and especially Genoa and Pisa, sent large contingents. Saladin's conquest of Palestine had threatened the Italian maritime republics with disaster, since much of their trade was with the Latin Kingdom of Jerusalem, and the Italian motivation for the crusades was overwhelmingly economic. A Pisan fleet of 50–60 ships had reached Tyre in early 1189 and was merely the harbinger of many more to come.[75] On the other hand, the crusaders were able to blockade Acre from the sea, even though this was only partially effective, and naval reinforcements from Egypt got through on four major occasions (June, September, October and December 1190).[76] On his own side, Saladin, heading a coalition, was beset by myriad problems. His chieftains insisted that their troops rest after every fifty days of campaigning so that he could not follow up on his victories; there were too many anti-Saladin intrigues by rival factions and too many desertions by troops disappointed by too few opportunities for plunder. The Zangids – followers of Zangi – were an important element in Saladin's army but they held him at arm's length and, when they departed for

Mosul and Aleppo in the winter, he could not be entirely sure they would return in the spring. Even Saladin's kinsmen were often too busy asserting their feudal rights to turn up for battle. His hopes for assistance from other Arab princes were in vain. The Caliph was uninterested in Saladin's *jihad* and, when he sent a promissory note for 20,000 dinars instead of the money itself, Saladin was so enraged that he sent it back to Baghdad. Similarly, he had petitioned the Almohads in North Africa to try to cut the crusader supply line between the West and Acre but they made no reply. One of the Saljuquid princes of Persia actually responded to his pleas for help by asking for help himself, against one of his own rivals, and an emir of Anatolia did the same.[77]

In April 1190 the crusaders began their spring offensive by wheeling out three huge mobile siege towers, so lofty that the attackers on the top could see into Acre. Each tower dominated the walls, was armoured with rope against artillery and swathed in vinegar-soaked hides against incendiaries. Each tower had a complement of five hundred men, including archers and auxiliaries. At first Acre's defenders could make no impression on these leviathans and contemplated surrender. Yet a coppersmith from Damascus refined the naphtha which had hitherto failed against the towers, adding a combustible mixture of gunpowder to the fiery brew; this new weapon succeeded in destroying the towers on 5 May 1190.[78] Meanwhile Zangi and the other emirs began trickling back and Saladin, heartened by the death of Barbarossa at this point, began planning a summer offensive to relieve the city. But first, on 14 June, there was a spectacular sea-battle when twenty-five Egyptian galleys were engaged by the Frankish fleet; the crusaders had the better of the fight, but enough Muslim ships got through to Acre to stiffen morale there.[79] On 25 July Saladin finally launched his land forces against the enemy and again achieved a technical victory but, as in the engagement the previous October, was not able to follow up his success because of the indiscipline of his troops. The Franks took severe losses in this battle but these were almost immediately repaired when Henry of Champagne arrived with reinforcements three days later; truly Saladin was involved in a hydra's head operation.[80] Henry was given command of operations and opted for a strategy of battering rams, with crews protected by an iron roof. The defenders' new naphtha-based combustible mixture proved just as deadly against the rams as the towers, and by October this line of attack too was abandoned.[81] Yet still fresh influxes of crusaders appeared. At the beginning of 1190 a huge detachment of Flemish crusaders led by James of Avesnes had joined the Christian host, together with a fleet of fifty Danish and Frisians with whom they had linked up in Messina.[82] In September it was the turn of the duke of Swabia, Frederick Barbarossa's son. Although the Germans were no longer formidable, and their great expedition had imploded after the freak death of Barbarossa, even after all the disasters in Asia Minor, Swabia still commanded 5,000 men. Met by Conrad of Montferrat at Tripoli, by late September the duke of Swabia was at Tyre, eager to pour his legions into the fray.[83]

Meanwhile Henry of Champagne had been busy with an artillery barrage on all the Acre fronts. Yet always the defenders seemed able to rise to the occasion. Several mangonels were destroyed during a sortie and a further two gutted in a sally on the night of 2/3 September.[84] The next attempted target was the Tower of Flies. Pisan soldiers and sailors headed this exploit, which was based on a floating siege tower built on two galleys lashed together. Built around the masts of the galleys, the tower was covered in the usual vinegar-soaked hides and equipped with a ladder. The Pisans came agonisingly close to securing their objective, and there was furious hand-to-hand fighting on the walls of the Tower but, supported by galleys from the city, the garrison finally turned the tide. The floating tower went the way of all Christian structures, being eventually consumed by the naphtha mixture.[85] A fireship attack on the boom of the harbour on 24 September also aborted, when the wind turned, blew the ships back and even helped to consume some of them with their own flames.[86] Saladin's spies told him there was discord in the Christian camp, with the duke of Swabia (who arrived at Acre on 7 October) being widely unpopular and an effective morale dampener. 'Would he had not come to us', was a typical sentiment. Sensing a break-through, Saladin threw everything into a last effort. On 13 November the fiercest battle since Hattin was fought near Haifa, but once again it was indecisive.[87] The crusaders were on some indices close to defeat by the end of the 1190 campaigning season, but their strategic and tactical cluelessness was offset by the steady stream of reinforcements that poured in from the West. Saladin, for all the reasons already mentioned, was unable to deliver the *coup de grâce*, and in some Muslim quarters the feeling grew that sooner or later the combined Christian land and sea forces must prevail over the heroic Acre defenders. At the very time the crusaders were close to total despair, having failed successively with battering rams, floating towers, fireships, trebuchets and mangonels, Saladin's allies demanded their right to go home for the winter. When he demurred, they started to go anyway; to save face, he was forced to authorise their furlough. Now with a severe manpower shortage, Saladin was obliged to abandon Jaffa, Arsuf and Caesarea. Despondent himself, he ordered all cities he was evacuating, including Sidon, Jubail and Tiberias, demolished. His many Arab critics said he was simply saving the enemy the expense of destroying places they would otherwise have had to besiege.[88]

The winter of 1190–91 was in many ways the grimmest experience of the entire siege of Acre. While Richard and his men lolled in Sicily, there was severe hardship among the crusaders at Le Toron. The almost total cessation of shipping in winter inevitably meant food shortages and rocketing prices: the price of an egg rose to sixpence, a single hen cost a year's pay and the flesh of a dead horse, invariably worth more than a live one, was considered the ultimate delicacy. By Christmas the food shortages had escalated to outright starvation. Offal and animal intestines, disdained in normal times, now became highly prized forms of meat. Bakers' ovens were overturned and bread plundered, a handful of beans cost a fortune, and men were prepared to commit murder for a square meal.[89] Moreover, since merchant shipping approached Acre from the north, following the coast past Tyre, the egregious Conrad of Montferrat took it into his head to intercept the supply vessels and hold the food in his city to bring leverage on the crusader leaders to accede to his demands (this was the time of the scandalous marriage to Isabella). Before long, even the nobility were reduced to eating grass, herbs and plants. The staple was the carob bean, the edible pods of the evergreen carob tree, which was found everywhere in the Mediterranean and known as St John's bread, though normally fed only to animals. Soon disease, the constant concomitant of starvation, made its appearance, exacerbated by the teeming winter rains.[90] Initially it was scurvy and gingivitis that caused the damage, but soon outright plague was raging through the Christian army and carrying off up to two hundred men a day. Exact statistics for the ravages of pestilence and disease cannot be retrieved, but an inference on generally high mortality can be made from the large numbers of Frankish 'celebrities' who died at Acre or from the consequences of the siege. These included the duke of Swabia, Archbishop Baldwin, Gérard de Rideford, Philip of Alsace, count of Flanders, Hellin of Wavrin, the seneschal of Flanders, Ludwig III, Landgrave of Thuringia, Henry, count of Bar-le-Duc, William Ferrers, earl of Derby, Thorel of Mesnil (a Norman magnate), count Theobald of Blois, Stephen, count of Sancerre, Ralph, count of Clermont and a host of lesser barons.[91] On 31 December 1190 an Egyptian flotilla made a sustained attempt to break the blockade around Acre but all seven vessels were lost to a combination of crusader counter-attack, reefs and storms. A week later part of the city wall collapsed, destroying part of the outworks. The Franks poured through the gap and were beaten back only with supreme difficulty; it was more the rain-sodden earth and the starved condition of their men and horses that beat them than the valour of the defenders. When the crusaders fell back exhausted, the Muslims were able to repair the breach by building a retaining wall. Conrad then made another assault on the Tower of Flies, which the Muslims again only just repelled.[92] Saladin's problems were multiplying. Already he was running short of weapons, and his appeals for reinforcement to the Caliph became increasingly strident, but to no greater effect than before. The Almohads, far from helping him, actually opened their ports to the Genoese. His most talented commander, Taqui al-Din, would shortly desert him to pursue his own interests in Armenia. Saladin's own health was deteriorating badly.[93] After nearly eighteen months of siege, in which both sides had exercised technical ingenuity to the limit, Christians and Muslims were stalemated. This was the context in which Philip of France arrived in Acre on 20 April with six large transports. Although the crusaders were initially disappointed at the small forces he had brought with him, he promised that this was merely a vanguard and that Richard would soon be with them. Philip had it trumpeted about the encampment that he was under a pledge to wait for Richard before the assault proper began, but he started a mangonel bombardment of the Accursed Tower. On 30 May Saladin had to make a forced march of fourteen miles to relieve the hard-pressed garrison.[94] With the military situation on a knife edge, it was obvious to both sides that Richard would tip the balance. Saladin still trusted in his God to see him through, but even he baulked at the thought of meeting Christendom's 'king of kings', reputedly the greatest captain in the West. The warriors of God were about to clash mightily.

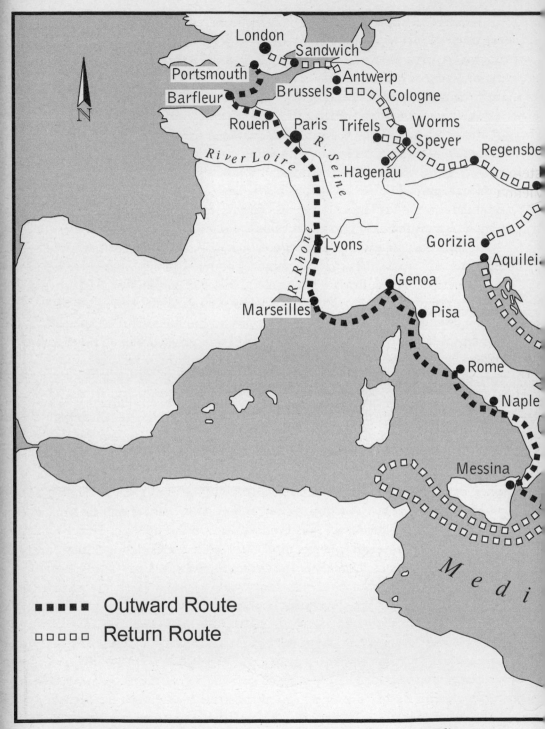

N

River Loire

R. Seine

R. Rhône

■■■■■ Outward Route

□□□□□ Return Route

M e d i

2. The Mediterranean and Palestine, showing Richard's
journey during the Crusade

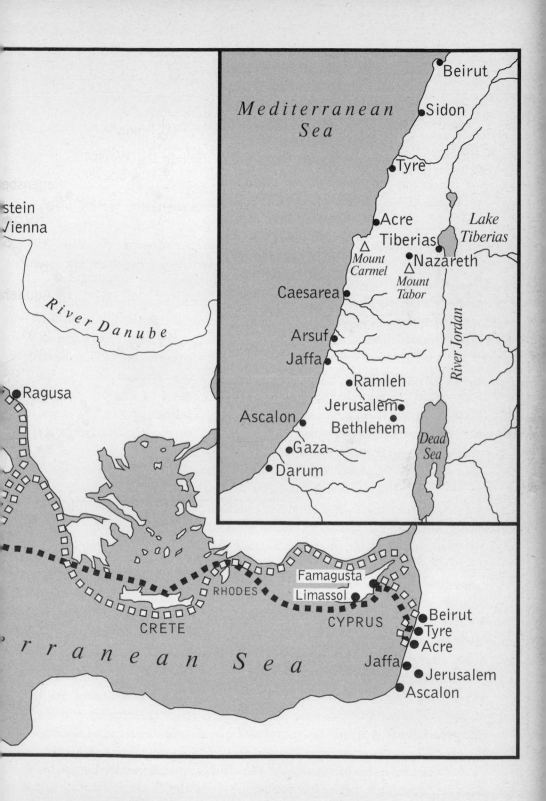

stein
Vienna

River Danube

Ragusa

Mediterranean Sea

Beirut

Sidon

Tyre

Acre
Tiberias
Lake Tiberias

△ *Mount Carmel*
Nazareth

△ *Mount Tabor*

Caesarea

Arsuf

Jaffa

Ramleh

Ascalon
Jerusalem
Bethlehem

Gaza
Dead Sea

Darum

River Jordan

RHODES

Famagusta
Limassol

CRETE
CYPRUS

Beirut
Tyre
Acre

Jaffa
Jerusalem

Ascalon

r r a n e a n   S e a

8

---◦◇◦---

ON 5 JUNE RICHARD and his knights, in company with Guy of
Lusignan and his entourage, set sail from Famagusta for the
short trip to the Asian mainland. He landed near the great
castle of Margat and handed Isaac over to the Knights of St John.
Continuing south, he was at Tyre next day, but the garrison, acting on
orders from Conrad of Montferrat, refused him admission.[1] On the final
leg to Acre, Richard's fleet intercepted a huge Muslim supply ship from
Beirut, a massive three-masted red and yellow buss. It was packed with
troops, said to number 350, and to have as cargo one hundred camel-
loads of weapons, quantities of Greek fire in bottles, and two hundred
poisonous snakes, which were to be used in the old Byzantine way as
missiles to be hurled at the enemy from catapults.[2] With a favourable
wind this vessel should easily have been able to evade Richard's twenty
galleys but, as luck would have it, the wind dropped, allowing the
crusaders to close with it. At first the Muslim ship inflicted losses through
greater long-range missile power, but Richard urged on his men, they
grappled, and soon the enemy vessel was sinking. The crusaders claimed
the credit, but Muslim sources allege that the captain simply scuttled his
craft once he saw that capture was inevitable.[3] Out of a large ship's
complement, maybe three hundred men when we have scaled down the
usual medieval exaggerations, only about thirty-five escaped drowning
when Richard chivalrously plucked them from the waves. There is no
doubt that this exploit lost nothing in the telling and was 'talked up' by
the chroniclers, to the point where it is alleged that Acre would not have
fallen if the ship had got through.[4] Yet the psychological effect was undeniable. In his first action against the Saracens Richard had scored a victory
and this augured well. Philip's arrival two months earlier with an exiguous
force had greatly encouraged the Muslims, and he had not made much
of an impression thereafter, despite the ludicrous assertion of his propagandists that Acre would have fallen by his efforts alone had he not

chivalrously decided to delay the final assault until Richard's arrival.[5] The plain truth is that Philip's attack on the Accursed Tower was a failure, with the defenders managing to burn some of his siege engines. Even filling up the ditches on the city's approaches cost the Christians dear, and they were reduced to throwing their dead into the fosse to make a more solid foundation. Philip as augur of ill-fortune seemed confirmed by a singular bad omen: his rare and magnificent white falcon, his pride and joy, flew away from him, ignored calls to return and perched defiantly on the walls of Acre.[6]

Richard's arrival at Acre on 8 June, with twenty-five ships, heartened the Frankish attackers and dismayed the Saracens. Since Arab historians say that each one of the vessels was 'as big as a citadel', scholars wonder whether he had not re-equipped his fleet in Cyprus and even built a new kind of ship, maybe something like the galleys of the fifteenth century.[7] But the simple fact that he had secured a supply line to Cyprus, arrived with massive reinforcements, and won a naval battle into the bargain, pitched the Christians into euphoria. The night of 8–9 June saw the crusader camp a riot of celebration, as drunken soldiery danced dizzily by the light of flambeaux or flickering bonfires. The spirits of the Saracens drooped correspondingly.[8] Yet Richard still awaited most of his transports carrying the siege engines, and for this reason declined the French king's proposal that they launch a joint attack immediately. Sullenly Philip ordered the offensive anyway; Richard's troops simply guarded the flanks and outer trenches against any Muslim counter-attack. As Richard had foreseen, the unilateral French assault failed, even though Geoffrey de Lusignan distinguished himself in the action and won a reputation as the finest knight in the field.[9] Meanwhile Richard's fleet intercepted a Saracen flotilla from Beirut bringing supplies and 700 fighting men; the destruction of these ships cast the Arabs further into despondency. There were ferocious attacks on Acre on 9, 14 and 18 June by Philip which petered out in the midday heat, but finally Richard's siege engines and trebuchets arrived from Tyre, and the pressure on the city intensified. Richard even had a new kind of stone he had brought from Cyprus which did not shatter on impact and was thus a more lethal artillery. His tactics were twofold. While his offensive concentrated on demolishing the Accursed Tower by artillery bombardments and undermining, he aimed to demoralise the defenders by sheer attrition, since the crusaders now had superior numbers and equipment. By 24 June the Acre garrison was desperate and on the point of surrender.[10]

Suddenly Acre had an eleventh-hour reprieve when Richard went down with a serious illness, followed shortly by Philip. The chroniclers refer to the malady that struck down both kings as *Arnaldia* or *Leonardie* and speak of a fever that caused hair and nails to fall out, which has led some historians to mention scurvy or trench mouth. But Vincent's disease or trench mouth is a fairly minor disease resulting from poor diet and lack of Vitamin C, and the same applies to scurvy. Since Richard had recently been living off the fat of the land in Cyprus, a land rich in meat and fruit, this diagnosis seems unlikely. It was probably either some form of the plague that had devastated the Christian armies at Acre or, in Richard's case, a recurrence of a chronic illness that manifested itself in the form of pallor and swellings.[11] Whatever the aetiology of the illness, by 28 June it had taken an acute form and Richard's life was thought to be in danger. He spent his invalid days parleying with Saladin about a possible face-to-face meeting, both of them alone and without followers. At first Saladin brushed this aside, saying that kings who talked together could not afterwards fight one another. When Richard persisted with the idea, Saladin replied enigmatically: 'He does not understand my language and I do not understand his.' When Richard offered, through his envoy-interpreter, to send Saladin a gift of falcons and hunting dogs, in return for chickens, the Saracens began to suspect that the rumour that the English king was stricken with a serious illness were true, for the demand for chickens signified a concern for an invalid's diet.[12] By 6 July Richard was sufficiently on the mend to ask to be carried to the front line on a litter so that he could direct siege operations. By now he was anyway convinced that Saladin was stalling and playing for time. Two days earlier three of his envoys had been taken on a grand tour of the 7,000 cookshops and 1,000 baths that Saladin provided for his troops – a clear case, in Richard's mind, of obfuscation of the issues through concentration on unnecessary detail. But in reality both sides were play-acting and shadow-boxing. As the Arab historian and eyewitness Baha al-Din rightly remarked: 'The object of these frequent visits was to ascertain the state of our morale and we were induced to receive the enemy's messages by the same motive that prompted them.'[13]

Once returned to health, Richard pressed the assault on Acre with even more vehemence. A major attempt on the city on 2 July forced Saladin to attack the crusader camp to relieve the pressure. The Christian kings responded by making Richard's men responsible for warding off attacks from Saladin while the French concentrated on bringing Acre to its knees. Next day, Philip's miners finally brought down a section of wall next to the Accursed Tower, but French troops, crossing sharp, piercing rubble, could advance only at a snail's pace, which allowed the

Saracens to regroup and beat them off with heavy losses.[14] But it was a short-lived pyrrhic victory. By now Frankish numerical superiority was such that they could 'spell' their combat troops, resting one regiment while another attacked, yet the Arabs in Acre had no such luxury and had to fight non-stop. A garrison commander came out under a flag of truce to discuss surrender terms but Philip either acted in a high-handed manner or his interpreter portrayed him as doing so, for the commander ended by storming back to Acre in disgust. By 4 July the defenders were so desperate that they tried to cut their way out and link up with Saladin, but the crusaders were forewarned and nipped this attempt in the bud.[15] Saladin refused to give up, though his situation was increasingly parlous. He had to deal with a mutiny when some of his regiments refused to continue with the futile assaults on the strongly-defended crusader camp and accused him of ruining Islam itself by his fanatical preoccupation with Acre. Others inside Acre were voting with their feet: on the night of 3 July three high-ranking emirs in the city simply panicked, deserted their posts and escaped in a small boat. Nevertheless, Saladin still retained his core of fanatics. Yet another French attack on the Accursed Tower on 7 July was thrown back with heavy losses, and the triumphant defenders sent a message to Saladin that they would fight to the death.[16] Richard and the Pisans tried their hand at the Accursed Tower on 11 July, yet even they were beaten off, though coming very close to success. But this proved to be Acre's last hurrah. As Baha al-Din expressed it: 'The breach in the walls was now very large and they feared that every one of them would be put to the sword if the city were carried by storm.' On 12 July Acre surrendered.[17]

The terms of surrender were precise and had been the subject of some agonised and protracted discussions even while the siege was in progress. The garrison commander who had been so brutally rebuffed by King Philip asked for the lives of the defenders to be spared, pointing out that quarter had always been granted to Franks in previous battles; obviously his nervousness was caused by Saladin's brutality towards the Templars and Hospitallers after Hattin. This point was now conceded, provided the Acre men accepted Christian baptism, and the lives of all women and children were spared, on condition that Acre paid 200,000 dinars in ransom, and that Saladin released 1,500 Christian prisoners and two hundred named individuals and restored the Holy Cross.[18] This was an improvement on Saladin's previous 'final offer' which merely proposed a one-one exchange of garrison members for Christian captives, but it stopped short of the crusader 'impossibilist' demand that Saladin restore all the lost lands of Outremer. The Christian baptism proviso turned into farce when the released Arabs went through a nominal conversion, then joined Saladin and denounced their forced apostasy, after which Richard and Philip agreed it was pointless to continue with this charade.[19] Probably the break-through condition negotiated by Richard and Philip was that Saladin hand over the whole of his fleet at Acre, some seventy ships – an inference strengthened by the fact that the Egyptian crews intercepted at sea did not burn or scuttle their ships. By this action Saladin conceded that control of the Mediterranean would be totally Christian and that his attempt to contest Italian hegemony in the eastern areas of the sea was a mistake.[20] Yet other chroniclers maintain that Saladin and the defenders of Acre were not in contact over the agreement of the final surrender terms and that these conditions – which he had no choice but to accept as a fait accompli – came as a severe shock to him. It is hard to see how Acre itself could have implemented the surrender of the intact Egyptian fleet without consulting Saladin but, under pretence of the need for 'clarification' Saladin asked for time in which to approve and ratify the hastily agreed terms. The clause whereby Conrad of Montferrat was to receive a commission of 10,000 dinars for his services as 'mediator' seems, however, to have been an ad hoc agreement between Conrad and the garrison.[21]

While Saladin considered what to do about these steep surrender terms, Richard and Philip pondered the military implications of their victory. Although the capture of Acre was a triumph of war by attrition, Christian siege engines had played a notable part in grinding down the opposition. By far the most successful artillery pieces were those brought by Richard from Sicily – as mentioned, he even brought his own high-density rocks from Cyprus for them to fire – and here again we see that perennial motif: Richard's military genius.[22] His ability to improvise is seen clearly in the way he snapped up the men from the French artillery crew dismissed by Philip because they had protested about low wages. On 17 June their replacements failed to prevent the gutting of the portable shields and armoured roofs on his siege engines; predictably Philip blamed this mishap on Richard's 'perfidy'. The hiring of the dismissed men was of a piece with Richard's relentless 'oneupmanship' campaign against Philip: when recruiting mercenaries, Richard offered three gold pieces to anyone who would join his service.[23] Richard's sappers and miners were also much more successful in their undermining of the Accursed Tower than Philip's men had been and again this may have been due to his instinct for human psychology, since he once more upstaged Philip by offering, at first one gold piece, then two, then three and finally four gold pieces for each stone extracted and brought back from the Tower.[24] Richard knew how to use siege engines. He had studied the campaigns of the First Crusade, but in addition to this research he knew how to improvise and adapt to new conditions and fresh circumstances: hence his use of counterweight machines and counterweight and traction engines, which were much more effective than the traditional use of mangonels and trebuchets. Richard took his engines closer to the walls than earlier leaders like Henry of Champagne had done. In this position his men were much more vulnerable to missile fire from the garrison, to sudden sorties, sallies and counter-attack, and it is a tribute to his leadership that his men were prepared to follow him there. The contrast with Philip's sacked siege engineers is marked. The most detailed recent study of the siege of Acre stresses the originality of Richard's contribution. 'Crusader poliorcetics at Acre involved techniques and machinery characteristic of twelfth-century operations *and also some which foreshadow developments for later periods* (italics mine) . . . the effectiveness of artillery at Acre anticipates developments in thirteenth-century poliorcetics . . . Heavy artillery was effective not only against Levantine cities, but also against less accessible positions and others less vulnerable to other methods of attack. In this regard, the siege of Acre can be seen as ushering in the great age of pre-gunpowder artillery in the West.'[25]

Politically Richard was less successful at Acre. As soon as Philip Augustus arrived, he recognised Conrad of Montferrat as king of Jerusalem. But Richard's coming, with vastly superior forces, made the machiavellians among the crusaders (and there were plenty of those) go where the power was and worship the rising sun. Both the Genoese and Pisans immediately offered Richard their services. He accepted the Pisans but turned down the Genoese on the grounds that they had already pledged allegiance to Philip and Conrad. Geoffrey of Lusignan thereupon claimed the Crown for his brother and accused Conrad of treason; Conrad fled to Tyre on 25 June, fearing that Richard would arrest him.[26] There was already bad blood between Richard and Philip over Conrad but, when Acre fell, the bad relations were exacerbated. On 13 July the city was divided – its stores, artillery, ships, wealth and prisoners – between the two kings, in accordance with the fifty-fifty agreement. So far, so good, but then Philip raised the issue of Cyprus. He demanded half of the island and half of all Richard had taken from there, pointing to the wording of the Messina protocol. Richard replied that the fifty-fifty provision clearly applied only to conquests in Outremer itself, not territories acquired on the way, and most authorities agree this is how the kings' agreement should have been construed.[27] But there was ambiguity in the idea of Philip's having half of all that Richard acquired 'on God's service'. If Richard had planned the conquest of Cyprus, that premeditation alone should qualify as 'on God's service', which was why Richard disingenuously claimed that the hostilities on the island were the purely contingent results of the shipwreck of his advance vessels. Even so, Richard said, he would share his Cyprus conquests with Philip if Philip in turn would share the rich lands of Artois, which he had inherited on 1 June when Count Philip of Flanders died at Acre, plus the lands bequeathed to him by the late castellan of St Omer.[28] Even in the Holy Land the two kings still perceived the struggle for France as the key issue in international politics.

Worried that the Franco-Angevin factionalism was threatening to affect the outcome of the crusade itself, on 20 July Richard suggested to Philip that they issue a declaration of intent: both of them would remain in Outremer for three years or until Jerusalem was taken. Two days later Philip revealed his hand by answering that he intended to return to France forthwith, to safeguard his inheritance from Count Philip of Flanders. Many of his own nobles were aghast at this and pressed him to stay on.[29] He replied that he would do so only if Richard agreed to apply the fifty-fifty rule to the Cyprus conquests. Richard refused adamantly. But now Conrad, deprived of the French king's protection, was out on a limb. On 26 July he prostrated himself at Richard's feet and craved pardon for the offences committed against Guy of Lusignan. Next day the two claimants to the throne of Jerusalem put their respective cases before the two kings and, on 28 July, Philip and Richard returned their verdict. Guy would remain king for his lifetime but on his death the Crown would pass indefeasibly to Conrad, Isabella and their heirs, regardless of whether Guy married again and had issue. The kingdom's revenues would be split between the two claimants and Conrad would further be compensated with Tyre and – assuming they could be reconquered – Sidon and Beirut; to balance this, Guy was also granted the lordship of Jaffa in the south. Philip then merged the Conrad issue with the fifty-fifty arrangements by making over his half of Acre to Conrad.[30] Having received his half of the Muslim prisoners, Philip set out for Tyre with Conrad, but first he swore a mighty oath that he would neither harm the king of England's lands while he was away on crusade nor permit anyone else to do so and that he would regard an attack on the Angevin domains as an attack on his own realm.[31] But already he was instructing his agents to spread the word that Richard was an unChristian liar: he had attacked a Christian island (Cyprus), insisted on completing its conquest before proceeding to Acre and, most of all, had needlessly attacked innocent co-religionists in Cyprus when he could have been killing Saracens in Outremer.[32]

Philip's withdrawal from the Third Crusade was highly controversial at the time and has been so ever since. His own nobles were disgusted and disillusioned with the decision and, of the great French magnates, only Peter of Nevers went back with him. The others, including the most powerful noble, Hugh, duke of Burgundy (who became commander of the French forces) and Richard's old adversary William de Barres, stayed on in the Holy Land. There seems little doubt that pure pique at seeing himself outclassed, out-generalled and out-thought by Richard played a large part in Philip's decision. As the chronicler Richard of Devizes put it, it was a case of the hammer tied to the tail of a cat.[33] Philip and his propagandists immediately went into overdrive trying to explain the withdrawal, alleging that it was all really Richard's fault. The French envoy to Pope Celestine III claimed that Richard had humiliated him by suborning his courtiers, knights and even his kinsmen, but he did not explain how Richard had managed this, and it was obvious that these Frenchmen had all stayed on to make it clear what they thought of Philip. To obfuscate all this, Philip and his chroniclers alleged, absurdly, that Philip had achieved more at Acre than Richard, that the Lionheart had done nothing at all, and had lain on his palliasse, ill, for most of the time. They insinuated that Richard had been systematically deceitful, uncooperative and treacherous towards Philip – in fact the reverse was the case. Other 'reasons' given for Philip's withdrawal from the crusade were, sometimes confusingly, blended into a 'grand slam' argument: that Philip had been seriously ill; that Richard had been intriguing with Saladin behind his back (the 'proof' was the exchange of gifts between Richard and Saladin); that Philip had left behind huge sums to finance the French contingent that stayed on at Acre; that he feared assassination (the later murder of Conrad was adduced as circumstantial evidence of the correctness of this fear).[34] Most of these arguments are remarkably flimsy: Richard had been more ill than Philip; the exchange of gifts was a commonplace of chivalry; and in fact Philip left Hugh of Burgundy *nothing* in the way of money, so that Hugh had to borrow 5,000 marks from Richard. Philip's most severe critics say that he cynically encouraged the cream of the French feudal nobility to remain in Palestine so that their position at home (and hence their potential threat to him) could be nullified, and that he always intended to break his oath to Richard and use the Lionheart's absence in Outremer as a golden opportunity to seize Gisors and the Vexin and other disputed territories.[35]

Philip made a swift return to France. On 3 August he embarked at Tyre and travelled via Tripoli, Antioch, Rhodes, Crete, Corfu and Otranto to Rome. In Rome he met Pope Celestine III and then in Milan Emperor Henry VI. Crossing the Alps, he was back in Paris by 27 December 1191.[36] Richard's attitude is likely to have been 'good riddance' and he undoubtedly had a strong case to mount against the French king's philippics (the pun is irresistible). But he showed far less diplomatic and political skill in his cavalier treatment of the other grandees who left Acre in Philip's wake. In some cases, it was simply that they had backed the wrong horses – Philip and Conrad, instead of Richard and Guy – and Richard was less than magnanimous (arrogant, his enemies said) about their feelings and anxieties, with a certain triumphalism in evidence once Philip had left.[37] But in the case of the senior German noble present he made a worse mistake and made a deadly enemy. Barbarossa's second surviving son, Duke Frederick of Swabia, died at Acre in January 1191, leaving Leopold of Austria as the leading German crusader. Leopold was a proud and touchy man, who felt that his pedigree – he had family connections with the Hofenstaufen and Comneni dynasties and could thus boast of being related to both the western and the eastern emperors – was second to none. When Acre fell, Leopold had his standard carried into the city alongside Richard's and Philip's. Whether on Richard's direct orders or simply with his tacit consent, the Anglo-Norman contingent seized these colours and trampled them in the dust.[38] This was a mortal insult, but there was method behind Richard's apparent madness. If the two kings had allowed Leopold's standard to be displayed, this would be tantamount to admitting that he deserved a share in the booty, yet Philip and Richard greedily insisted on sharing everything between themselves.[39] Leopold, together with many other nobles and barons who had been at the siege of Acre from the outset, felt that Richard and Philip were johnny-come-latelies, that they themselves had endured the agonies and travails of a siege that lasted almost two years, and yet the kings of France and England had so finessed their arrival at the eleventh hour that they now claimed to be the true victors. It was the parable of the vineyard with a vengeance. Huge discontent centred on this issue and on the perception of the two kings as being greedy, insensitive and ungrateful. Wittingly or unwittingly, Leopold made himself the focus for this discontent, and his resentment further smouldered as he fancied himself a worthy member of a triumvirate, like Lepidus ground down between an Octavian and a Mark Antony.[40]

Philip was just as truculent as Richard in rejecting the pleas of these lords for a share of the plunder. But, machiavellian as he was and a superior politician, he escaped censure on the issue; instead, the entire opprobrium fell on Richard. There was something about Richard's swaggering public persona that alienated those outside his magic circle and, besides, lesser men do not like to acknowledge the superior talents of a military genius. Leopold too quit Acre in anger once Richard failed to indulge him. He departed for Germany, nursing a deep and abiding hatred of the Lionheart, and many of the frustrated and disappointed minor barons of Christendom went with him. Richard decisively lost the propaganda war for hearts and minds in Europe, for now both Philip and Leopold were riding through the continent, spreading the word that the king of England was a monster, a deceitful ingrate, a poisoner and assassin.[41] The absent are always wrong, as the French proverb tells us, and Leopold and Philip's tales lost nothing in the telling. Ambroise said that envy was merely the least of the evil visited on Richard because of his heroic feats on crusade.[42] In Rome Philip falsely claimed that he had wanted to stay on in the Holy Land but that Richard had insisted on his departure. He then manipulated Pope Celestine III into absolving him and his followers from all oaths sworn in Palestine on the strength of their status as 'Jerusalem pilgrims'. This meant that Philip could invade Richard's domains without incurring the charge of being foresworn, or at least so Philip claimed, for Celestine made it clear that the overriding prescription still held good: that no Christian could invade the lands or harm the property of a lord who was still on crusade.[43] Having maligned Richard to the Pope, Philip notched up a major triumph in his propaganda war against the Lionheart when he met emperor Henry VI in a summit conference at Milan. Initially suspicious, since Philip had been on good terms with his enemy Tancred in Sicily, the emperor allowed himself to be charmed and gulled. Whatever doubts he had about Philip's version of Richard's personality were dispelled by the complementary account he received from Leopold of Austria, which backed the French king in detail. Philip, who initially hoped simply to dupe Henry VI so that he could have safe passage through his dominions and over the Alps, lied about his relations with Tancred so successfully that he ended by securing a fully-fledged alliance with Henry.[44]

When Philip left for Tyre with Conrad at the beginning of August, he unaccountably took his half of the prisoners with him. Here is clear proof of Philip's pique-driven bad faith, for this action was inexplicable except on the basis that he wished to complicate and muddy Richard's negotiations with Saladin. There was no administrative or military reason for the removal of the French-owned prisoners, for Philip could easily have left them with Hugh of Burgundy, whom he had nominated as his military successor. Philip succeeded in his desire to vitiate the peace negotiations. After protracted discussions, on 2 August Richard accepted Saladin's latest offer: that on the thirty-first day after the surrender of Acre he would deliver up the Holy Cross, all his Christian prisoners and one-half of the agreed ransom, i.e.100,000 dinars. But when the due date (11 August) came, Saladin insisted that all the Muslims taken at Acre be released, and hostages be given against the payment of the second instalment of the ransom. Failing that, Richard himself should give hostages, to be returned when all the money was paid and all the Muslim prisoners freed.[45] Here Saladin was being disingenuous. The blunt truth was that, impoverished as he was, he could not even raise the first instalment of the money. But, hearing of Philip's boorish behaviour with his half of the Muslim prisoners, he grasped at a straw and insisted that by not surrendering *all* the Muslim prisoners (knowing full well that half of them were at Tyre), it was Richard who was in breach of the agreed terms. Indignantly Richard lost patience with this blatant attempt to rewrite their agreement, seeing it (rightly) simply as a stalling tactic. Saladin's defenders say he did not trust the Franks and feared that, once they received the first tranche of the cash, they would renege on the accord. Meanwhile Richard sent a delegation headed by Hubert Walter and Robert, count of Dreux, to fetch back the rest of the Muslim prisoners from Tyre.[46] Whether primed by Philip or simply acting on his own account, Conrad refused to comply, adding the absurd demand that if he sent back Philip's half of the captives he should in return receive half of the Holy Cross.[47] Angry now with Conrad as well as Saladin, Richard sent a second delegation headed by Hugh, duke of Burgundy, to tell Conrad that if he did not obey orders, he himself would come to Tyre and finish off Conrad once and for all. On 12 August Burgundy duly returned to Acre with the prisoners, though Conrad did not accompany him.[48]

Richard reopened negotiations, but Saladin spun them out until 20 August. By then it was not just Richard who was angry.[49] The other crusaders had had enough of Saladin's obvious stalling and prevarication, clearly designed to frustrate and demoralise the Christians who were eager to march south. As nerves frayed, tempers snapped and military skirmishing became more frequent, with rumour and counter-rumour flitting through the Frankish encampment – such as the canard that 600 Christian prisoners in enemy hands had been poisoned – Richard faced a crisis of credibility and a test of his leadership.[50] He could not allow Saladin to make a fool of him indefinitely. Suddenly, on 20 August, he took a decision. It seems doubtful that this was done in hot blood, despite the chroniclers' constant stressing of the king's anger and rage. Royal anger was a ritualistic, formulaic and almost ideological reaction in medieval society, denoting the metaphorical 'feelings' of the state; we may doubt that Richard was personally incensed.[51] But military necessity, credibility and *raison d'état* all pointed in the same direction: he must call Saladin's bluff. Accordingly, on the afternoon of the 20th he marched his soldiers into the middle of the plain of Acre, shepherded the 3,000 Muslim prisoners into their midst, and ordered the slaughter to begin.[52] Furious Franks set upon the heathens with sword and lance, scything and butchering. Realising too late that he had overplayed his hand, Saladin ordered his army to attack but the attackers were held at bay in bitter, bloody fighting that went on to dusk. Overnight the Franks withdrew from this fresh Golgotha. When the Saracens inspected the human abattoir on the plain, they recognised many of their dear comrades but noted grimly that the great Arab magnates and the rich merchants of Acre had been spared. In revenge they slaughtered their own Christian prisoners, except those who would command a rich ransom or could still perform prodigies of labour as human workhorses.[53]

Richard's killing of the Muslim prisoners has always been as controversial as the similar action by another military genius in the same land some six hundred years later. In February 1799 Napoleon at Jaffa had more than 3,000 prisoners executed by cold steel, and the uncanny parallels continue for, like Napoleon, Richard claimed that the main reason for the massacre was that he could not leave so many heathen prisoners – men whose parole of honour meant nothing – behind when he marched south, and that he did not have enough food to feed them.[54] Modern historians have condemned Richard's actions as barbarous and stupid – why, it is said, did he not accept Saladin's hostages and release the hungry mouths which he would then not have to feed; he would still have had the Holy Cross and the money? Probably he calculated that Saladin would then welch on the deal and accept the slaughter of a small number of hostages rather than the 3,000 in Richard's hands, so that he (Richard) would end up without the second instalment of the 200,000 dinars.[55] Whatever the criticisms from the twentieth and twenty-first centuries, contemporaries were more forgiving and accepted the killings as a necessity of war. Christian chroniclers regarded it as a natural and even necessary consequence of Saladin's failure to keep to the surrender terms, and Ambroise stated it was a just requital for the many thousands of crusaders who died during the siege of Acre, to say nothing of the Hospitallers and Templars Saladin had butchered after the battle of Hattin.[56] Baha al-Din conceded that Saladin had invented difficulties and prevaricated and that Richard was within his rights to consider the agreement broken. But he insisted that in that case Richard should have formally enslaved the prisoners and sold them to the highest bidder, not massacred them, and it is interesting that the Christian commentator Sicard of Cremona agreed with him on this point.[57] Others simply thought that war was war, that it made no sense for Richard to spare men who might one day fight against him again. Still others stressed the wider connotations of 'credibility': it was not just that Richard had shown he was not a man to be trifled with, that he had regained the confidence of his troops by his 'toughness', but he had also sent a message to the garrisons of the coastal towns – Haifa, Caesarea, Arsuf, Jaffa, Gaza – that they should look for no quarter if they did not surrender.[58] Whether intended or not, this message certainly made an impact on the Saracen garrisons, who did not stay to test the theory. Yet another view was that Saladin himself had lost caste by allowing such a disaster to befall his own people, so that his credibility took a nosedive. The crudest view was that Saladin had cold-bloodedly sacrificed his men so as not to have to pay the money (assuming he had it, which is doubtful) and, on a cynical cost-benefit analysis, saving 200,000 dinars may have meant more to him than the lives of 3,000 wretched of the earth (significantly all men of substance and influence survived the hecatomb of slaughter).[59]

Richard's reputation would forever be tarnished by this act of brutality, whatever the arguments from military imperatives. But the fact that Acre had fallen to him after just five weeks in Outremer gained him additional kudos as a master of siegecraft; in retrospect his achievement was all the more noteworthy as, in the long Crusader-Muslim struggle that went on for another hundred years after Richard, sieges were to be the crucial decider of the contest and all other military activities would be incidental.[60] Both Richard and Saladin were at the cutting edge of siege technology, and at this date there was little to choose between the two sides technically. Both used both the mangonel and the *ballista*. The mangonel was a swing-beam machine that unleashed stones or other projectiles by rocking a giant arm; by the time of the Third Crusade, a swing-beam machine, using a heavy counterweight, was in use by both sides. The *ballista* was a lighter siege engine better designed for the mobile campaign Richard now contemplated, as it could be moved around, unlike the mangonel which was too heavy to transport once assembled.[61] Yet though Saladin could match Richard when it came to siegecraft, he failed woefully to keep pace with him in seapower. With very little direct knowledge of the sea, except for a handful of Channel crossings, Richard had demonstrated that his military genius extended to naval matters by getting most of a fleet of 216 ships safely to landfall in Outremer after a voyage of 5,000 miles, including 125 days at sea, and routing Saladin's flotilla into the bargain. Crusader superiority at sea was indeed so marked that some historians have portrayed Saladin as a kind of early version of Napoleon frustrated by Nelson, dumbfounded and clueless when it came to blue-water strategy. To Saladin's credit, he was the only Muslim leader to make any real attempt, albeit vain, to combat the Franks at sea.[62]

A genius at siegecraft and naval warfare, Richard was about to add to his laurels by showing that he had a total mastery of strategy and logistics. To march south to Jerusalem from Acre entailed myriad problems: Richard commanded a multinational force with poor training and discipline; it had no experience of mobile warfare, having been effectively lamed by the long siege of Acre; and it would be necessary to keep Saladin at bay during the onward march. Richard had to be cautious, since a single defeat might mean the loss of the entire Christian presence in Palestine, but he could not simply do nothing when all crusader factions clamoured for an advance on Jerusalem. Most of all, Richard as commander-in-chief had to think through every stage of the coming campaign, to establish a supply base on the coast and keep the supply lines between that base and his army open. He had to get his army down to the Holy City through difficult terrain, to keep it fed, watered and supplied, and also to transport all the impedimenta and engines necessary for the eventual siege of Jerusalem. His first business, therefore, was to decide on the itinerary. The inland route ran from Acre to Nazareth, then south past Mount Tabor, the Pools of Jacob and Ramallah. The objections to going this way were several: because of the huge baggage and supply train, the army would have to keep in the valleys, vulnerable to Saracen attacks from the hills; the route was 150 miles long, stretching the supply lines dangerously taut; and the army would be proceeding at a crawl, making the march a matter of months, and increasing the likelihood that fate or contingency would intervene adversely. A better option was to march the 80 miles down the coast to

Jaffa before striking inland to Jerusalem: this way he would have the sea to protect his right flank and the supplies and siege equipment could be carried by ship for the first leg of the march; moreover, he could worry Saladin by suggesting that perhaps his destination was not Jerusalem after all, but Egypt.[63]

Next Richard reviewed the forces at his disposal. Numbers are notoriously a problem in medieval historiography, but a reasonable estimate of the crusader army can be attempted from the numerous scraps of circumstantial evidence. From England and Normandy Richard had brought around 9,000 men (900 knights and 8,100 foot); from France he had the men left behind by King Philip, probably some 7,000 (700 knights and 6,300 foot); from Outremer itself about 2,000 men (maybe 200 of them knights) remained, plus around 1,000 Templars and Hospitallers, whom we can suppose to have been divided into the usual 9:1 infantry/cavalry ratio. There were also the Pisan and Genoese cohorts, the Danish/Norwegian expeditionary party, a handful of Germans (most had gone home with Leopold), and even a Hungarian contingent, plus a sprinkling of mercenaries.[64] To face Richard's 20,000-strong force Saladin had an army of perhaps 25,000 men, with both sides very evenly matched. The days of the First Crusade, when the Muslims fielded enormous armies of low quality, were long gone, and Saladin could match Richard in most departments, except perhaps his heavy cavalry.[65] Crusader tactics depended heavily on the shock charge of the heaviest destriers, delivered with devastating force at a moment when the Saracens could not retreat before it and leave the knights puffing impotently like beached whales, but Saladin was alive to this threat and countered it with mobile cavalry retreating beyond normal missile range and then unleashing a shower of arrows in Parthian shot manner. To bring these horsemen to battle, Richard in turn depended on his light horsemen, the turcopoles, traditionally recruited from baptised Turks and native Palestinians of mixed parentage (usually a Christian father and a local mother).[66] By the time of the Third Crusade, the Saracens had largely closed the technological gap in weaponry between the West and the Arab world, though there was still some inflexibility in Saracen ways of making war. They preferred spring campaigns, had a fondness for ambushes, and liked to have their backs against a mountain, river or hill, with the sun shining into the enemy's eyes and the wind at their own back. They were also overly dependent on the personalities of generals and tended to become disconcerted if the leader was killed. Conversely, Saladin's presence was worth a regiment. Both sides liked to avoid pitched battles, the Saracens for fear of losing leaders, the Franks for fear the crucial heavy cavalry charge would not work and they would be left without further tactical options.[67]

Yet essentially a battle between Crusaders and Saracens was a contest between heavily armoured cavalry and mounted archers. Anna Comnena, the Byzantine princess and historian, related at the time of the First Crusade that the charge of Norman knights could knock down the walls of Jericho, and the judgement remained valid one hundred years later. With reins and shield held in the left hand, and the couched lance held rigid beneath his right arm, using the horse's charging speed for momentum, the Frankish knight could easily smash through a cloud of Saracen horsemen, and then turn to use his secondary weapons of sword and mace. Everything was in the timing. If this was wrong, the Saracen cavalry could disperse and reform, finding the Franks suddenly vulnerable because they had lost their tight formation. In such a situation the mounted archers would swarm round the crusaders like angry bees or wasps or, as Ambroise preferred it, gadflies.[68] Unless shot at very close range, Muslim arrows could not penetrate the thick chain mail worn by the knights, so the knights could often be seen charging around a battlefield like porcupines, stuck with shafts that had penetrated the armour far enough to stick in but not far enough to reach flesh. The knights' horses were more vulnerable, so the Saracen mounted archers tended to concentrate on them. Coordination between infantry and cavalry was thus the key to Frankish success, for the foot soldiers had to protect the cavalry with a shield-wall until the precise moment for a charge arrived, so that Saracen arrows could make no impact. These tactics were effective, since Saracens liked to pincushion their enemies with arrows before moving in for the *coup de grâce*. But their horsemanship was so expert and their mobility so pronounced that it was very difficult to pin them down so that they would be an effective target for the heavy crusader charge. It was always a cat-and-mouse game, or rather agility and cunning ranged against brute strength and the killer instinct.[69]

As a military genius, Richard felt equal to any strategic or tactical challenges and his personal courage was known to inspire his men. But only careful and meticulous planning could solve logistical problems, and the impressive thing about the Lionheart was that he proved himself just as much a master of this crucial aspect of the military arts. He made sure that all 20,000 men under his command had ten days' rations and water before setting out. Living off the land would be difficult in such desolate terrain, where the Saracens were awaiting every opportunity to annihilate stragglers or foragers, so for a ten-day march each man carried 30 lbs of provisions, two pounds of food and one of firewood daily – the timber was necessary for lighting fires and boiling water. The normal crusader diet was hard, dry biscuit, a soup of beans and a little salted pork or bacon, supplemented by fresh fruit, vegetables and horsemeat, eaten with the fingers from wooden or clay bowls. It should be stressed that the 30 lbs was carried in addition to the infantryman's normal complement of helmet, hauberk, sword, shield, eating utensils and extra clothes. The water ration of four gallons a day per man was carried in animal skins by porters or in barrels by horse-drawn carts. The normal expectation for an army was that water rations could be topped up from rivers and streams, but in desert landscapes Richard was taking no chances, especially as he expected the Saracens to poison all wells. There was a particular problem about the knights, for each horseman additionally needed 15 lbs of fodder and five gallons of water a day for each horse. Six thousand horses accompanied Richard's army on the march, for most knights had three horses: either the warhorse proper, or destrier, weighing 1,800–2,400 pounds, used for the shock charge, expensive, and thus available only to the wealthiest knights, or the courser, weighing 1,300–1,500 lbs and similar to the heavy dragoon horse of the nineteenth century; the palfrey, weighing around 1,000 lbs for normal riding and travelling; and the rouncey, used by squires and knights' servants or sometimes as a pack animal. For a twenty-day march, Richard's army needed 1,340 tons of food and 800,000 gallons of water.[70]

For three days, from 22–25 August, Richard waited in his camp outside the Acre trenches for his forces to muster. It was a slow process, in part because Richard had decreed that no women at all, except elderly laundresses, were to accompany the army, and his men were reluctant to leave the stews and fleshpots of a city notorious for its lubricious excesses.[71] Leaving his wife and sister behind in the city, he eased the army by gentle stages to the River Belus and the coastal plain, marching just two miles a day at first, so that his men could shake off the effects of a week of debauchery and dissipation and adjust to a new, austere regime, then lengthening the pace on the third day to eleven miles.[72] There was nothing to fear on the right flank, which was protected by the sea and the crusader fleet, but on the left flank Saladin's army marched in parallel, just out of range. Richard alternated flank duties, spelling his infantry with tours of duty on the dangerous left and the secure right. Between the two flanks of infantry rode the knights, in three divisions, stirrup-to-stirrup, the horses nose-to-tail. The vanguard and rearguard were provided by the Templars and Hospitallers, who rotated this duty on a daily basis. But on the very first day the Saracens took advantage of a gap in the rear left by the boorish duke of Burgundy, commander of the French contingent and in a permanent sulk about having to take orders from Richard. The Muslims broke through and attacked the wagon train and were beaten off only when Richard and his men rode back from the van and charged. One beneficial spin-off from this brisk action was that Richard's old enemy William de Barres so distinguished himself that Richard decided to forget his long-held grudge and commended the Frenchman for his gallantry.[73] He also honoured another old foe, Geoffrey de Lusignan, appointing him governor of the great harbour fortress of Ascalon which was his first military objective on the coast. He explained to Geoffrey that this was a long-term appointment, that if he conquered Jerusalem its future security would depend on crusader control of the coastal route between Egypt and Syria.[74]

The first stop for the army was Haifa. Already the scale of what they were attempting had sunk in. They were marching in the scorching heat of August, with the temperature ranging from a low of 27°C to a high of 40°C – the heat all the more trying since they wore armour and chain mail. As the days went on, more and more men fainted in the heat. The lucky ones were loaded on ship and taken to the next bivouac; the unlucky ones were left to die where they fell. The stench and foetor from an army on the march in such conditions were unspeakable, with the odours of stale sweat mingling with those of horse dung and human excrement. The soldiers found the going very hard, since they were marching on tracks that had not been proper roads since Roman times, and the path was in many places overgrown with bushes and scrub. It was particularly irksome for the rearguard since the way was churned up by those in front, leaving only loose sand and sometimes mud to walk on. Thorn bushes and prickly scrub tore at the men's skin and clothing. And always alongside them were the Saracens, sometimes discharging another shower of arrows towards the Franks. Baha al-Din, an eyewitness, was amazed at the fortitude and discipline of the crusaders: 'I saw some of the Frankish foot soldiers with from one to ten arrows sticking in them, and still advancing at their usual pace without leaving the ranks . . . One cannot help admiring the wonderful patience displayed by these people, who bore the most wearying fatigue without having any share in the management of affairs or deriving any personal advantage.'[75] Richard tried to ease the burden on his troops as much as possible by making early pre-dawn starts, marching only until noon, and interspersing a day's marching with a day's rest. But even on the rest days there was little peace. Apart from the danger from poisonous snakes, the crusaders had to deal with the reliable menace of tarantulas which infested the camp-sites and gave painful, though non-lethal, bites. The rumour spread that noise would ward off these predators, so that a crusader encampment at night sounded like bedlam, with the shouting and yelling, the beating of pots, pans, shields and helmets.[76]

Tuesday 27 August found the crusader army toiling along the 12-mile route to Athlit. They headed west on the old Roman road which took them round the foot of Mount Carmel and then south, protected this time on the left flank by the steepness of the hills. Pausing at midday at Caphamum, already demolished by the Saracens, and exhausted after a morning of hacking through thick undergrowth, they pressed on after a short meal break to the so-called Castle of the Narrow Ways at Athlit, arriving in the late afternoon. Resting for three nights and two days, the crusaders were resupplied by sea. On Friday 30 August they set out on the longest stretch so far – 13 miles to Merla.[77] Already men were dropping dead from the heat and, in addition, the Saracens chanced an attack. Richard led a charge to clear the way and, as so often before in such circumstances, came within an ace of being captured. Ambroise suggested that the king was nearly taken because apathy, lethargy and exhaustion were consuming the army.[78] At Merla Richard encamped on the so-called River of the Crocodiles, then pressed on next day to Caesarea. This was the worst day's march so far, the heat exceeded anything yet experienced, and many men dropped dead in their tracks from sunstroke. When they camped that night, ships arrived from Acre with further supplies and reinforcements to replace the dead, in the shape of the 'lazy folk' who had tried to avoid service and clung on in the brothels of Acre.[79] On 1 September the army moved on another three miles to the Dead River. Again the Saracens harassed them and in one furious skirmish one of their emirs, Ayas Estoi (Ayaz the Tall) was killed.[80] Buoyed by this minor success, the Franks were then depressed on arrival at the Dead River to find the watercourse almost invisible under a dense matting of reeds and rushes, which they construed as camouflage devised by the Saracens – but for what end no one bothered to explain. In the stress of the march even natural phenomena were being interpreted as sinister manifestations by the enemy.[81]

On Tuesday 3 September the crusader army found the going so impenetrable that the troops diverted inland to find a road running parallel to the coast. Here the Saracens launched a heavy attack, and the Templars lost a large number of horses in the scrimmage, as did another group under the Count of St Pol; Richard, heading a rescue mission, was slightly wounded by a crossbow bolt. The attacks continued throughout the seven-mile march to the night's bivouac at the Salt River and, to add to the difficulties, food was again discovered to be running short. With the men ravenously hungry, the price of meat from the day's dead horses was rocketing. Morale was plummeting, so Richard announced that if his knights killed horses and gave them to the troops for food, he would make good the loss from his own stock of horses.[82] It was doubtless to play for time and gain a breathing space that he opened negotiations with Saladin on the afternoon of the fourth, while the army rested. Next morning at 3 a.m. the army moved out for the 10-mile trek to the River Rochetaille while Richard went to a rendezvous with Saladin's brother Safadin, taking Humphrey of Toron with him as interpreter to discuss peace terms. The meeting broke up quickly without agreement: Saladin himself was simply stalling and had told his brother to try to spin the negotiations out until reinforcements came up, but Richard announced peremptorily that his terms were nothing less than the return of the whole Latin kingdom thus far conquered, which gave Safadin nothing to talk about, still less an excuse to prevaricate. Meanwhile the crusaders toiled through the forest of Arsuf, anxious because of rumours that the Saracens intended to set light to the forest and consume them in a hecatomb of fire as they marched.[83] Nothing happened but, when they emerged into the open, they found the enemy drawn up ready for battle. The crusaders pitched camp on the north bank of the River Rochetaille, in sight of the campfires of the enemy. The tense night of 6–7 September, with battle certain the next day, has been compared by some to the English armies before Agincourt in 1415 and Waterloo in 1815, also within sight of the enemy, and there is the additional consideration that Saladin, like Wellington in 1815, had selected his battleground some time before.[84]

The plateau of Arsuf overlooks a natural harbour guarded by sandstone cliffs. On the morning of 7 September the army moved out cautiously, crossed the river, and followed the coast road, aiming to reach the town of Arsuf by midday. Richard laid his plans well, with his usual three columns, that with the baggage nearest the beach, the cavalry in the centre and on the left a dense infantry screen commanded by Count Henry of Champagne. In the van were the Templars, next came the Bretons, Angevins and Poitevins, followed by the fourth division in the centre comprising the English and Normans guarding Richard's dragon standard. Behind them came the French and, bringing up the rear in the position of maximum danger, were the Hospitallers. The troops were drawn up in such a tight formation that, as Ambroise relates, it was impossible to throw an apple into the ranks without hitting a man or horse.[85] Saladin brought up a vast force of 25,000 men to track them, and Richard and the duke of Burgundy rode up and down the line of march, checking for the merest flicker from the Saracens. Standing orders were that no knights should charge until Richard gave the signal, which was to be a simultaneous blast on six trumpets scattered along the column in two pairs. It was 9 a.m. when Saladin made his move. He launched a determined assault on the rearguard, deluging it with showers of arrows so that once again the foot soldiers bristled with shafts, their padded *gambesons* or protective tunics looking like pincushions.[86] The job of the valiant infantrymen was to absorb the enemy's arrows, always keeping them out of range of the valuable and vulnerable cavalry horses. Even so, horse losses began to mount, the heat was becoming unbearable, and the Hospitallers made the first of their many requests that day to Richard to be allowed to charge. He refused.

Saladin threw more and more men into his bid to crack the crusader rearguard, and the pressure mounted intolerably, with the Hospitallers having to make their horses walk backwards to keep up with the column while they faced about to confront the attackers. This time the Grand Master of the Hospitallers galloped up to Richard to ask permission to charge, but again this was refused. Richard spoke enigmatically and, to the Hospitallers, maddeningly: 'Put up with it, Master; no one can be everywhere at once.'[87] The Hospitallers' feeling was that it was the enemy that was everywhere, with horsemen charging and wheeling, performing pirouettes and braking turns in front of them. Some said, echoing Leonidas at Thermopylae, that the cloud of arrows was so dense it at least provided shelter from the blazing sun. All seemed chaos, with a deafening throb of drums and clashing of cymbals cutting through the shimmering heat. The Hospitallers, hard pressed at all points, sent several more despairing messages to Richard, begging to be allowed to charge the enemy, but each time Richard told them to hang on a bit longer until the Saracen horses were tired. The Hospitallers began to mutter among themselves that the king never intended to give the signal and that history would judge them cowards for submitting to this ordeal without making a fight of it. Finally they could stand it no longer and two of their principal knights, the marshal of the order and Baldwin Carew, snapped, broke cover and charged.[88] At this the entire rearguard, both Hospitallers and French joined in, the infantry screen parting in wonder to allow the thunderous cavalcade to gallop past them. This was a critical moment. If this premature charge was not supported, the Hospitallers would soon be surrounded and cut off by the enemy. Scarcely missing a beat, Richard sized up the situation at once and ordered a general assault. Angevins and Poitevins joined the king and his knights in the headlong charge.[89]

Richard, following his usual practice, steered his horse towards the thick of the fighting. Luck was with him, as many of the enemy had by chance dismounted to get a better aim with their bows; the crusaders knocked them to the ground, leaving them to be finished off by the infantry coming up fast behind them. Saladin's men were taken by surprise. Having moments before had everything their own way, they now found themselves taking the brunt of the one thing they feared most: the sustained charge of heavily-mailed knights on destriers. Most of them buckled at once and many were cut down or threw themselves from the 80-foot cliffs to escape; there were even reports of panic-stricken Arabs climbing trees to escape the fury of the Franks.[90] Rout for Saladin was averted only by a misunderstanding. The disciplined Norman and English troops, forming the reserve and clustered around the standard, tried to position themselves close to the king, but their movement temporarily confused the Angevins and Poitevins, who broke off the chase to rally round the flag. Saladin at once saw his chance and ordered a counter-attack, committing the crack troops of his household regiment.[91] For a while there was intense fighting, but then Richard ordered another charge with his squadron. William de Barres led another, and the two fresh attacks finally broke the Saracens. As they withdrew, Richard led three more charges, pausing only at the edge of the woods in case Saladin had troops concealed there and was trying the feigned retreat ploy. The king then ensured that no small groups of knights were lured away to their doom in the excitement of the chase, for he knew this to be another favourite Saladin stratagem. He was left in possession of the field, where his men counted some 7,000 enemy dead; the Franks had lost barely one-tenth that number. The only notable killed on the crusader side was James of Avesnes, a celebrated French knight who was said to have killed fifteen Saracens before being surrounded and cut down.[92]

The battle of Arsuf was a superb military achievement. Within three months in the Holy Land Richard had proved he had every talent: a master of siegecraft, tactics, strategy, logistics; an outstanding battlefield commander; and a man of personal bravery and charisma who could inspire courage, loyalty and admiration in his followers. Unsurprisingly the Saracens were depressed. Saladin was their greatest general, yet Richard had swatted him aside like a tiresome mosquito. The Muslims took to referring to him as Melek Richard (Richard the true king) and Ambroise reported their despondency, with one of Saladin's emirs telling him bluntly that the western knights were unbeatable, and Saladin so depressed that he could scarcely eat.[93] It already seemed to be the case that he could not defeat the Franks when they were entrenched, as at Acre. Now it transpired that he could not defeat them in mobile warfare either. Saladin took consolation from the fact that his defeat had not been a total rout, that there was factionalism among the crusaders (he was thinking particularly of Conrad), and that he might be able to outlast Richard in a war of attrition. It was essential to save face, so he made a point of challenging the crusader army with skirmishers when it got under way again on 9 September. To Zangi and his other emirs he declared that the Franks would never get to Jerusalem, as their column proceeded like a tortoise and had taken seventeen days over a journey his own army could have accomplished in two.[94] Richard avoided all obvious triumphalism but evinced the true confidence of a man who knew his own worth and realised that he had scored a great victory. On 8 September he commended all who had performed so valiantly in the battle – the duke of Burgundy, Robert, earl of Leicester, Hugh de Gournai, William de Borris, Walkelin de Ferrers, Roger de Tosny, Robert, count of Dreux, William de Garlande, Drogo de Mello, Robert Trussbut and, especially, Henry, count of Champagne and William de Barres. On 8 September, together with King Guy, he attended the funeral of James d'Avesnes (whose body had been found on the battlefield) and received the plaudits of his captains.[95] There could now be no serious doubt that Richard Coeur de Lion was both the greatest warrior in Christendom and the greatest that had been seen in the West for three hundred years.[96]

9

THE SARACENS MADE ONLY token resistance to the crusaders' entry to Jaffa, by staging a half-hearted ambush by the River al-Awjah but then fading away after a brief skirmish. The contrast between the constant aggression before the battle of Arsuf and the caution afterwards suggests both that Saladin considered the occupation of Jaffa inevitable and that his men had little stomach for a fight. The Christian army took a day to plod over the remaining ground and began to enter the town on 10 September only to find it virtually demolished. They quickly made camp in the surrounding orchards and olive groves and began to unload supplies from the fleet, which arrived in the afternoon. Trying to read Richard's intentions, Saladin thought that Ascalon rather than Jerusalem must be the next objective for a great military commander. Since he and his emirs did not have enough troops to defend both Ascalon and Jerusalem, the Saracen council took a decision that Ascalon should also be demolished, though a minority took the view that this was an act of arrant cowardice, a short-term measure dictated purely by the shaken morale of the rank and file after Arsuf.[1] To the dismay of the inhabitants, the work commenced. Saladin hoped that he could get favourable peace terms if he surrendered the coast to the crusaders, thus avoiding a siege of Jerusalem, but was worried that Richard would learn of the destruction of Ascalon and hasten to prevent it. Hearing rumours to this effect, Richard sent Geoffrey of Lusignan, who had been named lord of Ascalon, to learn the truth. Coasting down by galley, Geoffrey observed the demolition and reported back.[2] Richard called for an immediate march south to attack Saladin's men, but the besetting sin of the Third Crusade at once manifested itself. In short, the crusaders were divided between those who were primarily religious pilgrims and those who stressed military realities. To Richard and the captains, Ascalon was the obvious target, but to the pilgrims it had to be Jerusalem, and at a meeting of the army council it was the devout party that carried the day. They argued that the obvious route to Jerusalem was inland from Jaffa, that Ascalon was an irrelevance. Richard argued eloquently that the crusader supply line would be in danger once they left the coast, since the Franks could no longer be supplied by sea, that a march to Ascalon was what Saladin feared most, and that it would keep him guessing, but he was overruled and reluctantly acquiesced in the majority view.[3]

Making the best of a bad decision but privately incensed that he was merely first among equals in an unwieldy coalition, Richard set the army to rebuilding the fortifications of Jaffa. Word came in that Saladin's men had completed the destruction of Ascalon in ten days, so some rationalised the decision not to march south by alleging they would not have got there in time anyway. Saladin then set up a road block at Ramleh on the Jaffa-Jerusalem road and left a covering force under his brother Safadin at Ibelin, twenty miles south of Jaffa, with orders to harass the Franks at every turn. Next he returned to Jerusalem, put its defences in order and then, on 4 October, withdrew his army to Toron des Chevaliers (Latrun), ten miles beyond Ramleh and about halfway between Jerusalem and Jaffa.[4] Richard meanwhile was concerned about the continuing baneful effect on his army of the whorehouses, stews and bordellos of Acre, which still housed hundreds of deserters, absentees and malingerers. He sent Guy of Lusignan north to round up these miscreants but he came back empty-handed. The Lionheart himself then lent a hand, stormed up to Acre and, with a mixture of threat and cajolery, fire-eating oratory and silver-tongued eloquence, half-coaxed and half-forced the reluctant soldiers to accompany him to Jaffa. One consequence was that most of the ladies of the night shifted the base of their operations to Jaffa too.[5] Always energetic, always resourceful, Richard was almost too prodigal with his energies, for he habitually paid too little attention to his own security; indeed Saladin was later to pinpoint this as the English king's worst fault. While out hawking on 29 September he was caught up in a skirmish with the Muslim advance guard and was nearly captured. The valiant knight William de Preaux called out that he was Melek Ric' and was taken by the Saracens, while four other knights were slain when they placed themselves between their king and Saracen lances. Publicly criticised by the duke of Burgundy and others for his rashness in placing himself needlessly in peril, Richard shrugged off the criticisms and remained impenitent. He knew the value of impressing his men with his personal bravery and, besides, he liked fighting and liked spying out enemy positions for himself.[6]

On 1 October Richard wrote a long letter to the abbot of Clairvaux, hoping to capture Jerusalem shortly after Christmas and depart from Palestine by Easter 1192. He did not expect a long siege of Jerusalem but knew from the Acre-Jaffa march that he would take a long time to reach the Holy City. With no fleet to resupply them, the crusaders would have to be meticulous in their logistics, advancing slowly, never pressing on until all problems of food, water and forage had been solved. But what worried the king was that he lacked the money and above all the personnel to make a conquest of Jerusalem stick. For this reason he told the abbot of Clairvaux that what was most needed was an influx of Christian souls; he asked the prelate to preach a new crusade that would bring Christians out in swarms, so that his conquests could be consolidated. Time was of the essence, for he, the duke of Burgundy and the count of Champagne would run out of money by next Easter.[7] But some Lionheart experts think Richard was being disingenuous, that he was actually contemplating the conquest of Egypt. For this reason, although he had hitherto tended to support the Pisans, the allies of Guy of Lusignan, against the Genoese, who had been backed by Philip of France and Conrad, he now made overtures to the rulers of Genoa to entreat them to cooperate with Pisa and back his scheme for an amphibious attack on Egypt; as a sweetener he promised to pay half the expenses of the fleet from the moment it left port and pledged that Genoa would receive a share of the conquered lands proportionate to the size of the armada sent.[8] Others again think that Richard was bluffing, that he wanted Saladin to think he really intended an outright conquest of Egypt, so that the enemy leader would come to terms. Certainly it is significant that two days after the sheaf of letters dispatched to Clairvaux, Genoa and Pisa Richard sent an envoy to Saladin at Ramleh.[9]

Ostensibly Richard went up to Acre in early October to round up his reluctant and dissolute soldiers and to bring back Berengaria and Joan with him. But he was also concerned about the intrigues of Conrad of Montferrat, who had already put out feelers to Saladin suggesting an alliance: he would attack Acre while Richard was in the south and in return Saladin would give him Tyre and Sidon. Saladin did not trust Conrad and doubted his ability to deliver Tyre as promised – a suspicion that seemed confirmed when an apparently insouciant Richard returned from Acre on 13 October with a large fleet.[10] Richard replied to Conrad's intrigues by intensifying his own negotiations with Safadin (al-Adil). On 17 October Safadin sent his secretary Ibn an-Nahlal to Richard at Jaffa, and prolonged talks followed. Richard gave the secretary a message for Saladin, pointing out that the war was futile and cost too many lives. There were only two points at issue: Jerusalem and the Cross. 'Jerusalem is for us an object of worship that we could not give up even if there were only one of us left . . . The Cross, which for you is simply a piece of wood of no value, is for us of enormous importance. If you will return it to us, we shall be able to make peace and rest from this endless labour.'[11] He proposed that the land between the River Jordan and the Mediterranean, including Jerusalem, should be recognised as the Christian kingdom of Outremer. Saladin rejected this approach and replied: 'Jerusalem is as much ours as yours. Indeed it is even more sacred to us than it is to you, for it is the place from which our Prophet made his ascent into heaven and the place where our community will gather on the day of judgement . . . As for the Cross, its possession is a good card in our hand and could not be surrendered except in exchange for something of outstanding value to Islam.'[12]

Richard next proposed that Safadin should marry his sister Joan and that Saladin and Safadin should divide Palestine between them, with Safadin as the guarantor of a Christian presence in Outremer. Safadin accepted the idea with alacrity, asked for further details, and then sent them on to Saladin with another envoy, the historian Baha al-Din. The 'further and better particulars' contained the following: Safadin would marry Joan who would be established as queen at Jerusalem; Richard would cede to the Safadin-Joan dynasty Acre, Jaffa and Ascalon; Saladin would make over to Safadin all the lands between the River Jordan and the sea and recognise him as king of that country; the villages in the territory would belong to the Templars and the Hospitallers but Safadin and Joan would possess the castles; the Holy Cross would be handed over to the Christians; and all prisoners, both Muslim and Christian, would be freed; finally, the king of England would return to his own country.[13] It is quite clear that Richard was trying to play Saladin's duplicitous game with Conrad back at him and had struck the right psychological note by involving the ambitious Safadin. Saladin evidently considered these proposals chimerical but wanted to keep the ball in play so accepted them as a basis for further talks, though he told his intimates Richard's proposals were either a joke or, if serious, would not be carried through. His scepticism seemed warranted when Saladin's envoy arrived at Jaffa only to be told by Richard that his sister had exploded with anger when she heard the proposals; perhaps, he suggested, the only way around Joan's categorical refusal to marry a heathen would be for Safadin to be baptised as a Christian.[14] Saladin took the news calmly and left the draft treaty on the table as the basis for continuing talks. The farcical idea for Joan's marriage aside, the proposals were not far from those eventually agreed almost a year later, but more blood had to be spilled before the great warriors would see sense and conclude a realistic peace.

While the talks went on, the war of skirmish and counter-skirmish continued, with Richard forever itching to be in the fray, at the centre of the action. The Muslims alternated daylight attacks with night-time raids, using Arab irregulars in Saladin's pay, men expert at murder, kidnap and horse-stealing. Scarcely a day passed without mayhem or manslaughter of some kind. On 31 October Richard left Jaffa and occupied the two ruined fortresses of Yasur, the 'Castle of the Plains' and the 'Casal Moyen' and began rebuilding them while throwing his men out on foraging raids and scrimmages. On 1 November, while out riding near Ramleh, he saw some enemy scouts, charged straight at them, killed one, wounded a couple more and put the rest to flight; this was dangerous folly for a king and leader. On 6 November there was a sharp passage of arms at Ibn-Ibrak, two miles from Yasur, when the Templars, guarding a foraging party, ran into superior numbers and sent back a plea for help. Richard, supervising the reconstruction at the Casal Moyen, sent off the earl of Leicester and the count of St Pol with a company of knights, only for the so-called reinforcements to fall into an ambush which the Saracens had carefully baited with the initial attack on the Templars.[15] Two separate detachments were in danger of annihilation and, when Richard exhorted his men to follow him, on the rescue, they cautioned him against, as it were, throwing good men after bad, for the two Christian parties were surely doomed; besides, the king himself was too valuable, for if he was slain the entire Crusade would collapse. Richard would have none of it. 'When I sent them there and asked them to go, if they die there without me then would I never again bear the title of king.'[16] Richard's courageous intervention turned the tide, and the Saracens were put to flight. As Ambroise described it: 'He kicked the flanks of his horse and gave him free rein and went off, faster than a sparrowhawk. Then he galloped in among the knights, right into the Saracen people, breaking through them with such impetus that if a thunderbolt had fallen there would have been no greater destruction of their people. He pierced the ranks and pursued them; he turned and trapped them, hewing off hands and arms and heads. They fled like beasts. Many of them were exhausted, many killed or taken. He chased them so far, following and pursuing them, until it was time to return.'[17]

Richard spent the rest of November in negotiation with Saladin's envoys. He stressed that he had an ancestral claim to Outremer, since his kinfolk had originally conquered it, and was therefore obliged by considerations of family honour to hold out for the restoration of the kingdom and the payment of tribute from Egypt. The continuing talks led some Franks to mutter that the Lionheart was 'soft on Islam', and he took to returning from patrols with the severed heads of enemies as 'proofs of toughness'. On 9 November he sent his ambassador and interpreter Humphrey de Toron to Saladin with the following message: 'Your friendship and affection are dear to me. I told you that I would give these parts of Palestine to your brother, and I want you to be the judge between us in the division of land. But we must have a foothold in Jerusalem. I want you to make a division that will not bring down on your brother the wrath of the Muslims or on me the wrath of the Franks.'[18] Richard was certainly dealing with thorny realities here. In many ways his statesmanship provided the basis for an agreement with Saladin, who was seriously worried about the morale of his troops and the decaying civic virtue in Egypt, as reported by his chief administrator Al-Fadil, who spoke of unparalleled vice, fornication, sodomy and perjury among all classes from the emirs downwards.[19] But the relationship was poisoned by suspicion on both sides. Richard's advisers constantly harped on the theme that Saladin was merely playing for time, and Saladin's emirs likewise thought Richard untrustworthy. A further complication was that Conrad of Montferrat was still pressing Saladin for a treaty of alliance against Richard and his old rival Guy of Lusignan. His envoy Reynald of Sidon had an interview with Saladin on 9 November but was told crisply that Conrad would have to take the field openly against the crusaders if his proposal was to have any chance of success. Saladin put the rival proposals to his council on 11 November. The emirs decided that if it was to be peace, this could only be with Richard, since it seemed inherently implausible that Muslims and Christians could coexist peacefully in Palestine and they had no security against possible treachery by Conrad. If they had to choose between Richard's ideas for the partition of Palestine or alliance with Conrad, a man who was both a former enemy and known to be routinely perfidious, then Richard and partition it should be.[20]

Saladin informed Richard that they should continue talks, since he now had the backing of his emirs. Richard at once introduced a new complication (or stalling device) by saying that Christian priests had been vociferously denouncing the idea of marrying Joan to Safadin; he therefore had to appeal over their heads to the Pope to approve the match, but it would take three months for his envoy to reach Rome, confer with the pontiff and then return. He then raised the possibility of marrying his niece to Saladin's brother, if the Pope vetoed the union with Joan.[21] Whether the idea was ever serious, either in Richard's mind or as an objective possibility, remains problematical, although the best authorities are inclined to credit it as plausible.[22] After mid-November 1191 there were few serious moves, either military or diplomatic, for the rest of the year. On 17 November Saladin went into winter quarters at Jerusalem and three weeks later Richard did the same at Ramleh. By now the weather had broken, so that both armies were sorely assailed by rain, snow, hailstorms, mud and slush. Food was soggy, salt pork rotted, clothes soaked, arms and armour rusting in the claggy wetness. By Christmas Saladin had disbanded his army and had no plans to campaign actively again until May the following year. Ambroise reported that the Muslims had decamped to the mountains and left the plains to the Christians.[23] The bulk of the crusader army remained at Ramleh until the end of December, but on 23 December Richard moved his headquarters to Latrun, where he celebrated Christmas in his usual grand style, holding an improvised Yuletide court where the star attractions were the two queens and Guy de Lusignan. But it was impossible ever to relax completely, for skirmishing and raids by irregulars and guerrillas continued, including one Muslim probe at Tel es-Safi on 20 December when they nearly succeeded in capturing the Lionheart.[24] The new year opened with more such probes and counterprobes. The Saracens managed to ambush a Christian caravan on 3 January but were themselves nearly caught in a counter-ambuscade planned by Richard (who was said to have lain in wait all night long), which inflicted considerable losses.[25] Some time after Epiphany, probably on 11 January there was a meeting of the crusader army council to decide on the next step. Richard asked the Templar and Hospitaller leaders and the leaders of the Christian kingdom of Outremer to give their opinion on the feasibility of a siege of Jerusalem. They advised against it, on the grounds that a besieging army could be caught between the defending garrison and a relieving army and that the lines of communication to Jaffa would be too brittle. Besides, even if Jerusalem was taken, they did not have enough settlers to hang on to it; there would be a great influx of pilgrims in the short term, true, but having achieved their purpose, these people would go home to Europe. What was lacking was a core of Christians ready to live in the Holy City permanently and to defend it against all Muslim comers. Richard backed the case of the knightly orders by asking for a map of Jerusalem to be drawn. When presented, the map showed clearly that the Franks simply did not have enough troops to invest it properly, since the circumference of the city's walls was so great; the defenders would easily be able to pierce the line of attackers stretched thinly around the walls.[26] With ferocious weather to contend with as well, the crusaders faced mission impossible. Richard took the sense of the meeting and ordered a return to the coast, where he intended to rebuild

Ascalon. The mood in the army was one of total dejection. The soldiers had been euphoric over the New Year, confident that they were proceeding to Jerusalem and had the equipment and supplies necessary to do the job. Richard's orders cast them into profound gloom. The barrack-room lawyers among them argued that – hail, snow and flash-floods notwith-standing – the crusader army should press on, for were not the Saracens also at the mercy of the elements? Ambroise reported, with his usual hyperbole, that never since the beginning of time had there been an army so demoralised.[27]

Richard's arguments, and those of the knightly orders, were compelling, yet many in the crusader army took the line that they had not crossed the seas to rebuild Ascalon but to take Jerusalem, and this should be a do-or-die objective. The consequence was that as the Frankish forces withdrew from Ramleh to Ascalon, the united crusader army began to break up. The French in particular refused to serve under Richard any longer and dispersed to Jaffa and Acre, that reliable fleshpot magnet; the more extreme anti-Richard faction joined Conrad at Tyre. Only the contingent led by Richard's nephew Henry of Champagne remained loyal.[28] Relieved by the withdrawal of the crusaders, for condi-tions in Jerusalem were bad, and many horses and mules had been lost in freak weather, Saladin set about strengthening the defences of Jerusalem, using 2,000 Christian prisoners of war as slave labour.[29] On 21 January Richard's men reached Ascalon, where they spent a depressing week, bowed down by the scale of the reconstruction task ahead of them and the bad weather, which prevented resupply by sea. But there was no more determined character in the twelfth-century world than Richard, and he held his followers to their task, presiding over a four-month building programme that eventually made Ascalon the strongest fortress on the coast. Meanwhile he sent out forces to prey on Muslim cara-vans on the road between Egypt and Syria which he now controlled, and managed to free hundreds of Christian captives.[30] The surly Conrad of Montferrat held aloof from all operations and categorically refused a summons to come to Ascalon, while, naturally, not waiving his rights to the revenues of the kingdom, and Richard's only contact with his Christian opponents was a visit from the duke of Burgundy in early February; but Burgundy did not stay long once Richard told him he could not afford to add to the 5,000 marks he had already loaned him.[31]

In February Richard spent more time worrying about his own side than Saladin. Chaos threatened to overwhelm Acre as the Pisans and Genoese energetically joined in faction-fighting on behalf of Guy of Lusignan and Conrad respectively. The hard-pressed Pisans, in danger of being expelled from the city, appealed to Richard who made another of his lightning rides with his knights, which scared Conrad and his aider and abettor the duke of Burgundy out of Acre. Richard patched up the feud between Pisans and Genoese, then rode north for an interview with Conrad. The meeting, at Casal Imbert on the road to Tyre, was acrimonious and intemperate, with Conrad once more point-blank refusing to join the army at Ascalon. Richard then presided over a council meeting which formally deprived Conrad of all share in the kingdom's revenues, although sceptics doubted this could be implemented if Conrad retained the support of the French.[32] Conrad and Hugh (the duke of Burgundy) then trumped Richard's ace by sending envoys down to Ascalon, reminding all French troops that King Philip was their overlord and he had pledged his support to Conrad. Despite Richard's pleas, 700 Frenchmen announced they were leaving for Tyre; Ambroise cynically remarked that they were drawn to that city by the opportunity for drunken carousal and unlicensed fornication.[33] It was more than ever necessary for Richard to play for time, so he reopened negotiations with Saladin, who was similarly happy to stall and sent his brother Safadin off again for further talks. The only new proposal Richard put forward was a piece of fine-tuning on the general idea of partition; he proposed that the city itself be divided, with the Rock and the citadel in Muslim hands and the Christians controlling the rest.[34] Saladin's emirs considered this gesture enough to warrant a definitive peace, and Saladin told his brother to tell Richard the terms were acceptable. Safadin journeyed to Acre, where Richard supposedly then was (27 March) but the English king vanished before Safadin could speak to him. Some say this was a mere coincidence, since Richard had to be with his troops at Ascalon for the Easter festival, but it is much more likely that he was being machiavellian. Either he had heard from his spies that Saladin's position was parlous, making it likely the crusaders could get even better terms, or he wanted to hook Saladin definitively by suggesting that the offer for the partition of Jerusalem would not stay on the table for long. It is significant that there was no longer any talk of Joan's marriage.[35]

Skirmishes continued, including major brushes on 27 March near Jaffa and on the next day at Darum. After spending Easter Sunday, 5 April, at Ascalon, Richard went on a major reconnaissance of Gaza, demolished the year before by Saladin, and Darum, which was still occupied by the Saracens. It was his intention to besiege Darum as soon as the campaigning season began but, on his return to Ascalon, he found Robert, prior of Hereford, waiting for him with complaints about Prince

John and news of his intrigues with Philip of France.[36] Since it was clear that John intended to usurp the Crown, and William Longchamp had sent letters begging him to return, Richard considered it essential to settle the issue of the kingship of Outremer as soon as possible, for otherwise he could never leave the Holy Land without undoing all that he had already achieved. On 15 April he summoned a council and announced that he might soon have to return to England. It was necessary that the crusaders choose a leader to take his place once he was gone and that man had to be someone who could hold his own with Saladin; it was no time for sentiment and *realpolitik* had to prevail. Since Conrad was the only real man of blood and iron, the only tried and tested warrior and politician, it had to be him, even if this meant that Richard had to dump Guy of Lusignan. Craftily Richard led others to take the decision so that he could feign shock at the outcome, but it was obvious what the result was going to be, if only because any other choice than Conrad would still leave him in the field as a 'third force' and one, moreover, who was already in secret talks with Saladin.[37] There may have been duplicity, also, in the appearance of Henry of Champagne as a third candidate considered by the council, in addition to Conrad and Guy of Lusignan, for Richard's nephew would hardly have thrown his hat into the ring without the king's say-so.[38] Some say there was still further duplicity in Richard's attitude, for hitherto Guy, the supposed king of Jerusalem, was in reality Richard's puppet. Significantly, when Richard wanted a real leader he sacrificed his friend and chose his erstwhile enemy, and indeed, the summoning of the council makes no sense unless Richard had really wanted a change at the head of Outremer. The truth is that Guy had never really lived down his reputation as the man who lost the battle of Hattin, and it was not lost on his critics that Acre fell after a two-years' siege only when Richard appeared. Conrad was confident that once Richard left for England he would be top dog – so confident in fact that he made it a point of understanding in his talks with Saladin that, if he (Conrad) succeeded as king of Jerusalem, he would enjoy the full benefit of any treaty signed between Richard and Saladin.[39]

Nowhere is Richard's subtlety as a politician – and a clear sign that he was a true son of Henry II – more in evidence than in his treatment of the dispossessed Guy of Lusignan. The Lusignans were a powerful family, well capable of causing all kinds of problems in Poitou, as Geoffrey of Lusignan's track record showed, and the insult to their honour of Guy's dethronement would have been palpable – and they would clearly have held Richard responsible – if substantial compensation was not made. Just before he summoned the council, Richard learned from a courier sent by galley that a revolt against Templar rule had broken out in Cyprus, and that the Templars increasingly doubted their ability to hold down the island. They still owed Richard money for the purchase of the island, but their problem was that to pay the balance owing they had to raise taxation, and it was the tax hike that had precipitated the rebellion. Caught in a vicious circle, the Templars were happy to renegotiate the unwise sale, and Richard's brilliant idea was that Guy of Lusignan should swap the kingship of Jerusalem for a more trouble-free throne in Cyprus.[40] Guy accepted the idea with alacrity and repaid the Templars the 40,000 marks they had already paid Richard. On paper he still owed Richard the remaining 60,000 of the purchase price but Richard colluded in the fiction of a 'loan' and in effect gifted the island to his friend as compensation. This meant that he still had a foothold in the eastern Mediterranean and also that the turbulent Geoffrey would not be seen again in Poitou, raising the standard of revolt.[41] Geoffrey had already been chafing at the fact that his lordship of Ascalon was another fiction, since Richard was the real power there, and had been considering his options, including a return to France. At one stroke the Lionheart solved the problem of both brothers. The Lusignans would rule Cyprus for another three hundred years.

Richard sent Henry of Champagne to Tyre to tell Conrad the good news. Conrad was overjoyed and, in a histrionic gesture, fell to his knees and asked God not to allow him to be crowned if he was not worthy. It was agreed that the coronation would take place at Acre within the week, and count Henry proceeded there at once to make straight the ways.[42] At last, it seemed, there was light at the end of the tunnel and Richard could see his way clear to departing for England, possibly when he had wrung a few more concessions from Saladin – who was disconcerted to hear from Conrad that all negotiations between the two of them were naturally broken off forthwith unless Saladin agreed immediately to the peace terms already proposed.[43] But, as so often on the Third Crusade, fate dealt an unexpected hand. On the afternoon of 27 April 1192 Conrad was awaiting the return of his wife from the baths so that they could dine together. Impatience got the better of him, and he set out with two friends for the house of the bishop of Beauvais, hoping to make his meal there. When it turned out that the bishop had already eaten, Conrad decided to return home to see if his tardy wife was available yet. Turning into a narrow street, he was accosted by two men he recognised. One of them handed him a letter and, when Conrad reached down from his horse to take it, one of the men stabbed upwards with a knife while his comrade leapt on the back of the horse and stabbed Conrad in the back. The man who would be king fell to earth and bled to death in the street. Conrad's men killed one of the assassins on the spot, but the other was taken back to the palace and tortured.[44] Breaking under the pain of rack and fire, the second man confessed that he was indeed a member of the feared murder-cult, the Assassins, the scourge of the twelfth-century Middle East and a major factor in its politics until the sect was wiped out by the Mongols in the middle of the following century.[45]

Since the Assassins were a secret society devoted to murder, rather like Japan's more famous *ninja*, it is not surprising that historians still find them controversial. Even the derivation of their name, supposedly from the Arabic *hashishiyyin* or dope fiends, allegedly because they carried out their slayings while high on hashish, has not commanded universal assent. All that can be said for certain is that the Assassins were a break-away Shia sect. When the Shi-ites, originally a splinter group from the Sunnis, themselves further split into a mainstream cadre and the new cult of Ismailis, founders of the Fatimid caliphate overthrown in Egypt by Saladin, fragmentation and factionalism became the order of the day. One of the more prominent deviant groups was the society of Assassins, founded by Hassan as-Sabah at the end of the eleventh century. Hassan promised his supporters the delights of paradise if they would risk a martyr's death to wipe out the enemy of the true faith and allegedly showed them a vision of Heaven when they were suitably drugged.[46] From a base in northern Persia the leader of the Assassins, always referred to as 'the Old Man of the Mountains', directed his followers in a calcu-lated campaign of terror and murder; the Assassins were the nearest thing the twelfth-century world had to international terrorism. Among the scalps their dagger-men claimed were two Grand Viziers in Persia (1102 and 1127), the Fatimid Caliph in Cairo (1130), the Caliph of Baghdad (1139), Count Raymond II of Tripoli (1152), and many lesser princelings (princesses too were on their hit-list). Saladin had barely survived two attempts on his life by the Assassins and had been compelled to come to terms with the Old Man of the Mountains.[47] The Assassins were secular, in that they would strike at any target that seemed good to the Old Man, though his particular targets tended to be located in Mosul and Aleppo rather than Outremer. By the time of the Third Crusade the ultimate logical absurdity had occurred, and the Assassins had them-selves split, with one Old Man directing operations in Persia and another, named Rashid al-din Sinan, based in the mountains. It was Sinan who was responsible for the murder of Conrad.[48]

But why had the Assassins killed Conrad? Some said Saladin had hired Sinan to 'take out' both Richard and Conrad but Sinan objected to Saladin's 'giving him laws' and therefore slew Conrad alone; alternatively he was said to have feared that if he got rid of Richard, Saladin would be left in too powerful a position and potentially dangerous to the Assassins.[49] But the Arab sources are adamant that Saladin had no interest in seeing Conrad dead and indeed trusted him enough to have signed a draft treaty with him just before Conrad was elected king. It is possible, however, that Saladin was so angered by the abrupt volte-face whereby Richard and Conrad suddenly became allies that he decided to lash out at the 'perfidious' Conrad.[50] Philip of France and the anti-Richard faction in the West naturally asserted that the Lionheart had had him killed out of pique at his election, but this does not square with his machiavellian actions at and after the council. It was true that both the assassins had 'fingered' Richard as their paymaster, but the Old Man always provided his acolytes with a cover story in case they were captured after the assignment and, besides, the Old Man, on the famous 'need to know' principle, never told his hit-men who their ultimate employer was.[51] Another circumstantial factor working against the idea that Richard put out a contract on Conrad is that the interrogators of the tortured Assassin at Tyre, especially Hugh of Burgundy and the bishop of Beauvais, were Philip's men through-and-through, and would see the obvious chance to make mischief through black propaganda, working from the known fact that Richard and Conrad had enjoyed a turbulent relationship. All obvious candidates as the 'hidden hand' behind the Old Man and his killers fail to convince on one ground or another, so that historians have been led to look for more and more abstruse possible authors of the atrocity.[52] The person with the most obvious motive would appear to be Guy of Lusignan. The most likely explanation is that Sinan himself had a personal grudge against Conrad. The story was that Conrad had seized a ship belonging to the Old Man, stolen its cargo, and drowned his agents. Moreover, when the paranoid Philip of France became convinced that Richard had hired Assassins to kill him, he took the extraordinary step of writing to the Old Man of the Mountains to try to learn the truth. Sinan's successor (Sinan died in 1193) was happy to reassure him. The leader of the Assassins wrote back, categorically denying that Richard had anything to do with Conrad's murder.[53]

Conrad's murder threw crusader politics into turmoil. All the carefully planned arrangements put together since the beginning of April now seemed questionable. Who was to be the next king of Jerusalem and who would be the decision-makers? Ambroise says the French faction under the duke of Burgundy tried to preempt the issue by seizing Tyre, but Conrad's pregnant widow Isabella foiled them by fleeing to the citadel and shutting herself up there with the garrison. There she announced that the French could have Tyre only if Philip returned from France to claim it; meanwhile she would obey Conrad's dying request and hand the keys of the city to Richard.[54] Guy of Lusignan would presumably have had a good claim to resume his kingship had he not already accepted Richard's more lucrative offer of Cyprus and, initially at least, the Pisans urged him to reclaim his title. The position of Isabella and her first husband Humphrey of Toron was particularly chaotic. Theological diehards said that Conrad had been punished for his 'unlawful' marriage and that Isabella should return to her first (and only true) husband. At this juncture Henry of Champagne returned from Acre, and influential people begged him to accept the Crown and seal the compact by marrying Isabella.[55] Henry dithered both about the Crown and the marriage, and asked Richard for the final decision. Richard evidently gave him the nod very quickly for, in what seems an extraordinarily rushed affair, Henry married Isabella on 5 May. Some said he should not have married a woman pregnant with another man's child, while others asserted that the bride was under duress.[56] Whatever doubts might have been entertained about the match in canon law, in terms of *raison d'état* Richard now had exactly what he wanted: neither a weak, unpopular ally like Guy of Lusignan nor an over-independent loose cannon like Conrad, but a faithful and deferential servant. It was the very convenience of the outcome of the dispute over the kingship of Outremer that convinced the sceptics that it, and Conrad's death, were all part of a devious, long-prepared, master plan by Richard. In many ways the elevation of Henry was a stroke of political genius – either that or the ultimate in serendipity – for Henry was Philip's nephew as well as Richard's. The outcome for Henry was less happy, for he was never crowned king of Jerusalem, was constantly assailed by doubts about the validity of his marriage, and in 1197 he stepped backwards through an open upper-storey window and was killed. There was clearly something jinxed or ill-starred about Isabella, because her fourth husband died 'of a surfeit of fish' in 1205. She thus achieved the dubious distinction of being widowed three times and divorced once by the time she was thirty-three.[57]

Henry's position as titular leader of Outremer satisfied the duke of Burgundy, who at last returned to full cooperation with Richard. With the whole crusader force now once more under his command, Richard was able to widen the scope of his military activities. Until the chaos caused by Conrad's murder and Henry's succession, Richard had been out every day on horseback in the country between Ascalon and Jerusalem, once more involved in skirmishes, patrols, night attacks and, when no Saracens appeared, hunting; his horsemanship during the pursuit and killing of a wild boar was especially praised.[58] But once he had the duke of Burgundy's troops under his aegis, he ordered an assault on Darum, twenty miles south of Ascalon, another coastal target that, when taken, would put additional pressure on Saladin and further menace the trade routes between Egypt and Syria. The impetuous Richard did not wait for the French to muster but rushed ahead with his vanguard of knights, secured a beachhead and began supervising the ferrying of supplies from the fleet. Saladin sent reinforcements to the Darum garrison, but its commander seems to have been spectacularly incompetent, since Richard encountered little resistance when he unloaded three engines brought from Ascalon by sea.[59] Richard did not have enough men for a close investment of Darum, but his brilliant military mind had detected a weak spot in the principal tower (one of sixteen). After enduring three days and nights of accurate artillery fire, covering a meticulous sapping operation, the garrison, which remained unsupported by the so-called relieving force, surrendered on 22 May on condition that they, their families and their property would be spared. When Henry of Champagne and the duke of Burgundy finally arrived, Richard made a point of handing over his conquest to the new overlord of Jerusalem – an action which performed wonders for morale in the coalition.[60]

Leaving a Christian garrison in Darum, the crusaders advanced to al-Hasi (the 'Cane Brake of Starlings') on 28 May, fanning out in a wide circle to catch all Saracens within the net. The Saracens tried to play down the success of these operations, but the truth is that Saladin was hard pressed, with all his men not yet back from their winter furlough. His hopes of a diplomatic alliance against the crusaders had been stymied when an envoy from the Byzantine emperor at Constantinople arrived in Jerusalem on 15 May with a demand that Saladin restore the Cross to him, allow Christian priests in the churches at Jerusalem and join him in an attack on Cyprus. Saladin impatiently refused all the demands.[61] But luck was with him, for Richard was simultaneously receiving the same kind of bad news. The envoy John of Alençon arrived with the latest instalment of Prince John's treachery in England, including the disquieting news of an alliance with Philip of France directed against Richard.

The Lionheart immediately wondered whether he should throw up the crusade and return to England with all speed. He summoned a council, attended by the leaders of all the regiments: English, French, Norman, Poitevin, Angevin. This time there was little wrangling, and a unanimous decision was taken to advance on Jerusalem a second time, whether Richard stayed with them or went home.[62] Rumours spread through the camp about a possible crisis when a new leader was chosen to replace the Lionheart but, after a week's depressed and gloomy reflection in Ascalon, where he withdrew the army for supplies and remustering, Richard sent his personal confessor with a message that he would stay in Palestine until the following Easter (28 March 1193) and would lay siege to Jerusalem if this proved practicable.[63] All the indications are that Richard was unconvinced about the ability of his army to take Jerusalem, but feared his sudden departure would lead the crusade to implode. His reasoning was that of a master chess player. If he was able to take the Holy City in the summer, when there was no more mud and rain to impede his army, he would cut the ground from under the feet of Philip and John and so square the circle involved in the either-Crusade-or Angevin-empire conundrum. He then returned from Ascalon to al-Hasi, rested two days, then began the march on Jerusalem. The mood in the army was optimistic, and in some quarters euphoric.[64]

Even so, the desertion level continued high, and Richard sent Henry of Champagne back to the fleshpots of Acre to round up the latest quota of skrimshankers and backsliders. He then set up his headquarters at Beit Nuba, 13 miles from Jerusalem, where he would remain for a month.[65] The advance to Beit Nuba saw the euphoria continuing, for the crusaders ambushed a Saracen raiding party on the way, and congratulated themselves on having accomplished in five days a march it took them two months to complete the year before. The only Christian losses during this period were two deaths from snakebite. On 12 June the fighting took a more serious turn when a large party of Saracens attacked the Franks near Beit Nuba, gradually sucking in more and more French troops, Hospitallers and Templars by feigned retreat until they were ready to spring the trap. Vicious hand-to-hand combat ensued, and the Hospitaller knight Robert de Bruges distinguished himself in single combat with the Arab champion, but things were going badly for the crusaders when suddenly the bishop of Salisbury and the count of Perche arrived with reinforcements and swung the balance.[66] Richard was absent from this fracas, as he himself was turning the tables on a party of would-be ambushers at the Pool of Emmaeus. He killed twenty of the enemy, captured Saladin's herald and bagged a number of horses and mules. Traditionally, it was said to be during his pursuit of his outwitted foes that he rode to the top of a hill called Montjoie and saw his first and only sight of Jerusalem. Legend has embroidered the incident.[67] It seems just too pat that this should be the selfsame hill from which the men of the First Crusade should also have first seen the Holy City, while the story that Richard collapsed in tears and begged God not to allow him to glimpse a city he could not deliver to him is almost self-confessedly apocryphal; it does not square with the known personality of Richard, who was no-nonsense and avoided histrionics, and it is also too obviously a variant on the story of Moses viewing the Promised Land from Pisgah but destined never to enter it.

The prime aim of Saracen raiding parties was to intercept supply convoys between Jaffa and Beit Nuba. On 17 June there was a major assault on a Christian caravan near Ramleh, commanded by Baldwin de Carron. Another large-scale engagement escalated from the primary assault, involving French nobles named as Clarembaud de Montchablon, Ferric de Viane (Henry's deputy), Manasser de l'Isle, Richard de Orques and the knights Theodoric, Philip and Otho.[68] A well-timed attack by Turkish horsemen on the rearguard caused initial panic, and then the attackers moved in, wielding great iron clubs to deadly effect. Once again the French were rescued from a tight spot, this time by the arrival of the earl of Leicester, who put the enemy to flight.[69] The increasing severity of Saracen attacks and the non-appearance of Henry, who seemed, said the grumblers, to be taking an unconscionable time about rounding up deserters in Acre, began to affect morale. Perhaps it is not being overly cynical to query the fortuitous appearance at exactly this juncture of yet another fragment of the True Cross, whose authenticity seemed guaranteed to Ambroise simply because its location was divulged by an old hermit with a grey beard.[70] But the real situation was more accurately signalled by yet another grand council convened by Richard to reconsider the decision to march on Jerusalem. Richard made an impassioned speech, pointing out the crusaders did not have enough men to invest the city properly, stressing the fragile supply lines and underlining that, once in the hills around Jerusalem, the Franks would be as vulnerable to Saladin's counter-attacks as the Athenians had been at Syracuse in 414–413 BC, and everyone knew that that venture had ended in consummate disaster. In a pointed jibe at the French, he said he was well aware that he had enemies in Europe (Philip), and maybe in the present assembly, who wanted him to fail and to blame him for the fiasco of an aborted crusade. Once again Richard revealed himself a master politician. Ostensibly keeping out of the decision-making process he appointed a committee of twenty to decide the matter once and for all. Five Frenchmen were appointed, five Hospitallers, five Templars and five representatives of the kingdom of Outremer. Richard knew perfectly well from all past experience that this would provide a 15–5 vote in favour of abandoning the march and concentrating on a campaign against Egypt; and so it proved.[71]

When the decision was announced, Richard greeted it with enthusiasm, dilating on the possibilities of besieging Cairo and sending a fleet up the Nile. Yet the French instantly disabused him of such high hopes. For them it was Jerusalem or nothing and to them the Egyptian campaign was a meaningless irrelevance. In vain Richard remonstrated that, even if Jerusalem fell, it would have to be abandoned soon afterwards, since most of the crusaders would simply complete their pilgrimage and return to Europe. But the duke of Burgundy and the other French nobles refused to cooperate.[72] Richard tried to compromise: he was quite prepared to accompany the French as a private soldier but he could not in all conscience proceed there as their commander. The French remained adamant and obtusively unreceptive to all overtures. Matters had reached an impasse when suddenly the logjam was broken by external events. Richard's spy system was efficient, and the lure of *baksheesh* had seduced many Arabs from ideological allegiance to Islam. In addition, if we may believe Ambroise, a Syrian Christian named Bernard had anticipated Sir Richard Burton by seven hundred years, and moved freely in disguise through the bazaars and markets of Cairo.[73] From a number of different sources the Lionheart now learned that Safadin's half-brother Falak al-Din was bringing up a fresh army, with hundreds of horse and mules, new supplies and a plethora of trade goods, to relieve the hard-pressed Saladin in Jerusalem. It must be remembered that, although the wiser heads in the crusader army doubted their ability to take the Holy City, the enemy did not know of their doubts and indecisions, and were seriously dismayed at the prospect of facing the great Melek Ric and his army. Saladin, aware that the issue of morale was crucial, set great store on the arrival of the new army from Egypt. Richard, with his lightning reflexes for strategy, saw at once that Falak al-Din's caravan might be the hinge on which the whole war turned. He made rapid preparations for an attack.[74]

Taking 500 knights and 1,000 picked troops with him, Richard left the camp at Beit Nuba on the evening of 21 June, accompanied by the duke of Burgundy and some French troops, who had successfully bargained for a one-third share of the expected loot, even though their numbers did not warrant such a figure. A night's forced march in the moonlight brought the task force to Galatie, where they rested and waited until supplies of food and drink arrived from Ascalon.[75] But on the 22nd Saladin's spies told him a crusader host had moved off southwards; it was not difficult to guess the target. He therefore sent a large force of reinforcements to aid the caravan. On the 23rd, while Richard's force was moving towards al-Hasi, Falak al-Din made the fatal decision to take the shortest route to Jerusalem and camp at Tel al-Khuwialifia, 14 miles from al-Hasi. Not even the arrival of the relieving force could make him change his mind, since he reckoned that during a night march the caravan would break-up in confusion, leaving the separate detachments easy prey for the Franks. He stayed where he was.[76] At first, when this was reported to Richard, he could scarcely believe his luck, and sent out a body of scouts, disguised as Bedouin, to verify the information. After making sure both men and horses were well fed and watered, he ordered another night march. Minutes after dawn's first gleaming, as the cursing camel drivers were loading their charges, Richard's horsemen swept over them like a tsunami. The Saracen convoy had camped in three detachments, and one of them was cut to pieces, with the loss of all animals and impedimenta. The remaining two cohorts scattered into the desert, pursued by frenzied crusaders. Among those seen hewing, cleaving and scything at the foe were the king himself, the earl of Leicester, Alexander Arsic and two Frenchmen Gilbert Malmains and Stephen de Longchamp.[77] The slaughter, though short-lived was frightful: the crusaders claimed 1,300 dead that they counted on the battlefield and many more ridden down and trampled in the half-light, or who crawled away into the desert to die of their wounds; five hundred prisoners were also taken. Perhaps even more significantly, the Franks netted 4,700 camels and dromedaries and thousands of mules and asses together with their loads of gold, silver, arms and armour, clothes, spices, medicine, money, tents and ropes; even Baha al-Din conceded a loss of 3,000 camels.[78] This was yet another massive triumph for Richard, as Saladin's defensive strategy lay in ruins and now even Egypt itself was highly vulnerable.

The French, with their share of this immense booty, no longer depended on Richard for funds, and more than ever clamoured for an advance on Jerusalem. In a sense they had a case, for Saladin was seriously rattled by this setback. Baha al-Din was in the sultan's tent when the news of the disaster came in and he reported: 'Never was the sultan more grieved or made more anxious.'[79] Saladin saw at once that many of the obstacles to a crusader invasion of Egypt had been removed for, with so many pack animals captured, the logistics of an Egyptan campaign eased. On the other hand, the Franks might ride the crest of the wave and immediately assault Jerusalem. But which would it be: Egypt or Jerusalem? On the hunch that the Franks must surely strike at the Holy City, Saladin prepared to pull out, leaving his grand-nephew to defend it, and it was reported that he prayed in the mosque on Friday 3 July with tears in his eyes, certain that his departure was imminent.[80] But when Richard returned in triumph to Beit Nuba on 29 June, the entire vexatious question was once again aired in council. The return of Henry of Champagne from Acre with many deserters in tow seemed to provide the opportunity, finally, for an advance on Jerusalem, but Richard objected that his cavalry could not do an effective job in a siege there, for Saladin in despair had poisoned all wells and waterholes near the city and destroyed all cisterns.[81] This meant that the horses would have to be watered in relays in a river some distance from Jerusalem, with half on active duty and half drinking their fill at any given moment. Richard pointed out that Saladin could then easily deal with the truncated cavalry force, leading eventually to disaster. The French accused Richard of defeatism, and the duke of Burgundy added that it was quite clear the Lionheart had never had any serious intention of besieging Jerusalem. To rub salt in the wounds he composed some scurrilous verses about the English king, to which Richard replied in similar vein. But this verse-writing contest did not solve the essential issue. For the last time the question was put to the council. A 'grand jury' of 300 men was chosen, which was then whittled down to a dozen, from which a shortlist of three was to be chosen, with the proviso that the decision of the three just men should be final and irrevocable. Not surprisingly, they opted for the Egyptian campaign rather than the siege of Jerusalem.[82]

Yet the French were people who believed in majority decision-making only when it concurred with their own wishes. Despite the 'irrevocable' commitment, the duke of Burgundy announced that the French would never campaign in Egypt. The crusaders were caught between the rational dictates of grand strategy – indicating an attack on Egypt – and the irrational siren calls of pilgrim ideology. The French never answered Richard's crushing point that, without Christian settlers, the Franks could not hold Jerusalem, and made no attempt to do so, merely insisting peevishly that everyone knew this was the goal the crusaders had signed up for. Some say Richard should have made an audacious bid for Jerusalem anyway, as this was the one objective on which the entire army would have united behind him. But Richard was a great captain first and foremost, an ideo-logue second. His argument was that pressure on Egypt, particularly an expedition up the Nile which would turn Saladin's flank, would force him to disgorge Jerusalem, that there was more than one way to skin the cat. Yet this meant taking the long view, and the French commanders lacked all strategic vision. The failure to recapture Jerusalem led to massive disap-pointment and severe recriminations in Europe, with scapegoating and blame-shifting much in evidence. Richard scored a great propaganda triumph in largely winning the game of *cherchez le coupable*. Such was the reluctance to criticise Christendom's great military hero that the most absurd canards and legends arose, strong enough to infect serious history. It was alleged that the real fault for failure to take Jerusalem lay with the duke of Burgundy, who had secret orders from Philip to make sure that the king of England did not get the kudos and glory accruing from the recovery of the Holy City.[83] This is absurd, as the historical facts have amply demonstrated. The truth is that both Richard and the French badly wanted to wrest Jerusalem from Saladin, that Richard always regarded himself as a failure for not having achieved this supreme prize, but that he and the duke of Burgundy could never agree a sensible common strategy for achieving the ultimate aim of all crusaders.

With the crusaders once again dejected and despondent, it was time for Richard to reopen negotiations with Saladin. Arguing, like so many before and since, that his retreat was merely a 'strategic withdrawal', he cautioned Saladin not to draw any false conclusions from the movements of the crusader army: 'Do not be deceived by my withdrawal. The ram backs away in order to butt.'[84] But both commanders were war-weary, so that the Lionheart was relieved when an envoy came from the Sultan with some constructive proposals. Saladin offered Richard the Church of the Resurrection and free entry for pilgrims into Jerusalem; to divide the country with him, with the littoral towns remaining in crusader hands and the interior remaining with the Saracens, saving only that the land 'between the mountains and the sea' would be partitioned between them.[85] Referring to Henry of Champagne as 'your sister's son', Saladin wrote: 'Since you honour us with your trust and one good turn deserves another, the Sultan will treat your sister's son like one of his own sons.' But then he produced the sting in the tail: in return for all these 'concessions', Richard must promise to demolish Ascalon.[86] This was a condition too far for Richard. He had spent a fortune on this coastal fortress and made it the axis of his strategy. His answer to Saladin was to send even more troops there, to remind him of the military threat to Egypt. His formal message on 19 July was that the crusaders had to retain the entire coast from Antioch to Darum before peace could be considered. Both leaders reluctantly accepted that the campaigning had to go on. Saladin took heart from the fact that by 26 July the main Frankish army was back in Acre, having retreated all the way from Beit Nuba.[87] Although there were garrisons in Jaffa, Ascalon and Darum, in one sense Richard and the crusaders were back where they started.

Encouraged by the turn of events, and informed by his spies that Richard was planning an assault on Beirut in the north, Saladin launched a surprise attack on Jaffa on 27 July. Fortified by the arrival of reinforcements from Aleppo and Mosul, he saw a golden opportunity to win back much of what he had lost since Arsuf.[88] His miners and sappers went to work with gusto while his trebuchets and mangonels pounded Jaffa. But he was taken aback by the vigorous defence made by the crusaders, who stood their ground dauntlessly even when the Saracen artillery brought down a large section of the walls on 31 July. The only black sheep in the story was the castellan Aubrey de Reims, who took refuge on board a ship in the harbour and had to be shamed into returning to his post. Bristling with lances, spears and pikes like a nest of porcupines, the Franks retreated only when heavy stones came crashing down on them from the mangonels, but they retired in good order to the citadel, leaving the town to the enemy.[89] At this point the Saracens dispersed throughout Jaffa, seeking for plunder, women and prisoners for ransom. In vain did Saladin try to restore order for, as Baha al-Din sagely commented: 'It was a long time since our troops had taken any booty or won any advantage over the enemy; they were therefore eager to take the citadel by storm.' The last factor was particularly annoying for Saladin, as he wanted to talk the garrison out of their eyrie without sustaining further casualties. Seeing an outside chance of retrieving something from the fiasco, the newly elected Patriarch of Jerusalem audaciously proposed to Saladin that the troops in the citadel be given until 3 p.m. next day (1 August) to surrender. Saladin agreed, partly, it is alleged, out of quirky and intermittent quixotry but mainly because he was confident Richard could not possibly get down from Acre in time to relieve the garrison. Saladin took hostages for the deal (the defenders insisted on including the cowardly Aubrey de Reims) and settled down to wait for the deadline. But to his consternation early next morning he heard the blare of Frankish trumpets. With a sickening feeling he realised that Richard had arrived on the scene.[90]

Richard got news of Saladin's attack on 28 July. Characteristically

The Seal of Henry II:
symbol of the power of the Angevins

Henry VII at his coronation

Eleanor of Aquitaine:
powerful even in death

A royal adventuress: the controversial marriage of Eleanor and Louis VII of France

The wages of rebellion: Eleanor on her way to captivity after the rising of 1173

The idealised
Young King:
nothing in life
became him like
the leaving of it

Bertran de Born:
the Young King's dark angel

Richard as icon:
where history and Hollywood meet

Emperor Frederick Barbarossa: a less successful version of Richard the Lionheart

Richard and his sister with Philip of France at Palermo, 1190

Gustav Doré's quasi-Biblical view of Saladin

Saladin as his own people saw him

Saladin lays waste the Holy Land

A Saracen warrior
on caparisoned steed

Crusader with destrier:
God is invoked to bless the bloodshed

The Crusaders at their most fearsome:
the pursuit of Sultan Nureddin
of Damascus

Crusader castles at their apogee:
the impregnable Krak des Chevaliers

Seapower: another area where
Richard and the Crusaders had the
edge over Saladin and the Saracens

Medieval siegecraft:
the desperate struggle for Acre

The fall of Acre

la doubte de la traison le roy trichart.

Audis come ces choses suin

Surrender of Acre to Richard
and King Philip of France

Richard's darkest hour:
the massacre of the Saracen prisoners
according to Gustav Doré

The artist imposes order on murderous chaos:
another view of Richard's massacre
of the Saracen prisoners

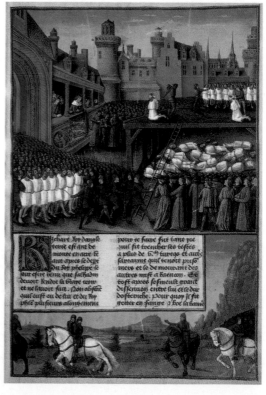

Richard's cynosure:
Chateau-Gaillard or the 'saucy castle'

History as Germany would like it to
have been: a cowed Richard allegedly
fawns overs Emperor Henry VI

Durnstein Castle:
where Blondel is supposed to have
found his friend and fellow troubadour

quick-thinking, he assembled a task force (mainly the Pisans and Genoese foot with English and Angevin knights) and set off by sea in fifteen galleys. Equally characteristically, Hugh of Burgundy and the French refused to help, but Henry of Champagne proved most royal and set off overland with a force of Templars and Hospitallers; this detachment was halted in its tracks at Caesarea by a report that another Muslim army stood astride the road ahead. Meanwhile Richard's fleet encountered heavy contrary winds off Mount Carmel, so he did not arrive off Jaffa until the night of 31 July/1 August with just seven of his ships, the others having been scattered by the light gale.[91] At first he thought he was too late, for the shore was lined by Saracens firing arrows, but a priest, showing more physical courage than is usual in one of his cloth, dived from the citadel's battlements into the sea, swam to the royal galley and explained the situation. It seemed that some fainthearts in the garrison had agreed to leave before the deadline but, after paying over their ransom money, were immediately seized and beheaded; the others shut themselves up in the citadel and prepared to sell their lives dearly.[92] Exhorting his men to follow him and declaring that a curse would light on anyone who faltered, Richard steered his galleys into the shallows and sprang ashore. No more than eighty knights and a handful of infantry landed, but in a remarkably short time, using accurate crossbow fire, they secured a beachhead. Offering surprisingly little resistance to this landing party, Saladin instead concentrated on trying to persuade the knights in the citadel to surrender before help reached them. Some sources suggested that the mere sight of the red-headed monster Melek Ric, with his red ship, red shield and red tunic simply demoralised the Saracens, showing once again the huge psychological effect of a solid reputation for invincibility.[93]

Once in command of the beach, Richard ordered his men to collect wood and build a temporary palisade, which would act as a rallying point if things went badly for them in the town. Then he ordered an advance into Jaffa. His arrival seems to have confused and paralysed the Saracens, some of whom were still mindlessly plundering even as the wrath of God swept down on them. Still others, thinking the garrison had already surrendered, faced around to deal with the newcomers, only to be taken in the rear when the crusaders sortied from the citadel. The Muslims withdrew in a shambolic panic not far short of rout, with crossbowmen harrying them all the way. They left behind practically everything they had retrieved from the defeated caravan so, infuriatingly, were once more back at square one.[94] The Lionheart had scored yet another notable victory. Saladin's surprise attack on Jaffa had been a brilliant stroke, but still more brilliant was the king of England's counterstroke – an exploit, as some of the troubadours later pointed out, well worthy to be ranked with Roland's last stand at Roncevaux. Both sides now badly needed a breathing space, and a truce was arranged while peace talks resumed yet again. Once more the sticking point was Ascalon, which Richard categorically refused to surrender or demolish. He told Saladin that if Ascalon was guaranteed to the Christians, the war would be over within a week and he himself would return to England. Saladin made the obvious retort that Richard would have to stay through the next winter 'since if he goes everything he has conquered will fall into our hands'. Saladin even attempted psychological warfare, pointing out that Richard had concerns in Europe which were bound to take him away sooner or later while he, Saladin, was in his native land and could stay another ten summers and winters if necessary. Richard stalled the talks long enough to get reinforcements; by the time hostilities resumed, Henry of Champagne and part of his force had arrived from Caesarea by sea.[95]

For three days Richard himself, Henry of Champagne and the other great nobles laboured alongside the ordinary soldiers, trying to repair the walls of Jaffa. By midnight on 4 August the king and his comrades were just preparing to bed down in a makeshift camp outside the town. Alerted by his spies to the Lionheart's vulnerability, Saladin prepared an elaborate commando raid. Picked Turkish and Mamluk veterans were earmarked as a snatch squad to seize Richard while he slept, and there would be a showy diversionary attack on the town meanwhile. The Saracens, however, were never as good as the Franks at irregular operations during the Third Crusade, and this time the scheme went wrong because the Turks and Mamluks could not agree among themselves which should form the infantry and which the cavalry. The grave delay caused by this contretemps meant that dawn was breaking when they finally made their kidnapping bid.[96] A Genoese mercenary, answering a call of nature, by sheer chance detected the approach of the commandos and raised the alarm. Richard just had time to get his men into battle stations, though many were asleep or half-dressed when the first alarum went up. His defence formation was solid, with the front rank composed of kneeling men, each protected by his shield, with the butt of the lance on the ground and the shaft facing upwards like a sharpened stake. Behind this close-packed phalanx were archers, each with a bow positioned between the heads of the kneeling infantry. The archers worked in pairs, one loading and the other shooting, exchanging weapons all the time so that there was a continuous fire.[97] Heavily outnumbered, this steel hedgehog broke up charge after charge from the foe, who became discouraged and began veering off into the town. After eight hours of this inconclusive fighting, the Franks sensed a faltering in the pulse of the Saracens and went over to the attack. Once again the Muslims broke and fled. Lovingly Ambroise registered the names of the aristocrats among the 'happy few' that stood with Richard that day: count Henry, the earl of Leicester, Bartholomew de Mortimer, Ralf de Mauleon, Andrew de Chauveney, Gerard de Furnival, Roger de Sacey, William de l'Etang, Hugh de Nevill and Henry Teuton.[98]

The crusaders claimed 700 enemy dead and 1,500 horses slain in the battle, for a handful of dead in their own ranks; they did, however, admit to large numbers of wounded. Contemporaries thought Richard's victory at Jaffa miraculous and at this point in his career he definitively became a creature of legend as well as a figure in history. Baha al-Din testified that Richard rode the entire length of the Saracen army in full view of his foes, and not one of them dared to attack him. Ambroise reported that Safadin sent him two Arab steeds as a token of his admiration.[99] Throughout the battle he was often only a hair's breadth from defeat, but his energy, commitment and acumen saved the day. He seemed to be everywhere, both in the thick of the fighting and directing operations with a serene Olympian detachment. Richard possessed a clear aura of invincibility for whenever he was matched against Saladin – whether at the siege of Acre, in the mobile battle of Arsuf, attacking the caravan at Tel el-Hesi, or in the two very different battles of Jaffa – the Lionheart always emerged on top. Nonetheless, his victories were not miraculous and are rationally explicable. He was a military genius who was a master of every last one of the arts of war and he could enthuse his men by charisma and success, so that they felt themselves to be part of an ever-victorious army. It has been well said that the brilliant defence at Jaffa was the beginning of the legend of the 'thin red line' in the English army, the foundation of a spirit and ethos that would afterwards manifest itself at Crecy, Poitiers, Agincourt, Blenheim, Minden and Waterloo.[100] The Saracen position, on the other hand, was disastrous. Saladin had briefly seemed to possess the same martial attributes as Richard after Hattin, but he was only an average captain and by 1192 increasingly plagued by factionalism, indiscipline, dissent and low morale in his army. Saladin rode off in a fury after hearing how badly his troops had behaved in battle, refusing to charge and ride down the Christian lines even though repeatedly urged to. After the second defeat at Jaffa there was nothing for it but further negotiations, for another attempt at battle might lead this badly mauled army to disintegrate from mass desertions.[101]

Predictably the talks again foundered on the immovable rock of Ascalon. Richard was desperate to return to Europe but he had to save face, for otherwise his enemies could say that all his successes in the field were a mere smokescreen to mask the essential utter failure of the Third Crusade. He tried bluff and sent a message to Saladin as follows: 'How long am I to make advances to the Sultan that he will not accept? More than anything I used to be keen to return to my own country, but now that winter is here and the rain has begun, I have decided to remain.'[102] The poker hand the Lionheart was playing was actually a double bluff, for he fell ill, perhaps not fortuitously after summoning the French to his side and learning from Henry of Champagne that they would not come and refused ever to serve under him again. Superstitious souls who spoke of divine anger liked to link this refusal to the sudden death of Hugh, duke of Burgundy, in Acre that very month.[103] It did not take Saladin long to learn both of the French refusal and of Richard's illness. His hopes rose, but he was chivalrous enough to reply to a request for peaches and pears from the English king by sending him groaning bowls of fruit, and snow with which to make a primitive fruit salad. Saladin's spies further brought him news of despondency in the crusader camp and apparently shrinking numbers in Jaffa. Saladin thought the time was ripe for another attack and got his army on the march. But on 27 August he received another message from Richard, conveyed through the official envoy. Richard laid his cards on the table and virtually admitted that he needed a face-saver by asking what compensation the Sultan was prepared to offer him for the loss of Ascalon. Saladin immediately realised that Ascalon was not non-negotiable after all, that Richard might be prepared to give it up for a suitable consideration. The chance of getting rid of the Franks's greatest asset was too tempting. He halted his army's march and sent a secret envoy with fresh proposals. Yet even as he sought some way around the Ascalon problem, the weary Richard unilaterally decided he would give up the citadel without compensation.[104]

Perhaps it was his illness that led a drained Richard to make this crucial concession which has been so much criticised, then and now. Certainly he was still very ill at the end of August and seemed uncertain from day to day whether he had given up Ascalon without compensation or whether peace depended on the generosity of Saladin's offer; there is circumstantial evidence that he was hallucinating and may not have been entirely clear about the day-to-day drift of events. At any rate Saladin pounced and after conferring with his emirs, declared that the following would produce an immediate peace: Ascalon would be demolished and not rebuilt until three years from the following Easter, 28 March 1193 (i.e. in 1196); the crusaders would be allowed to hold Jaffa and the coastal strip up to Acre without let or hindrance; there would be no fighting and both sides would be allowed to travel freely; and Christian pilgrims would be allowed to visit the Holy Sepulchre in Jerusalem and trade in the Muslim territories.[105] These terms were simply a recognition of necessity: long-term the crusader army would shrink while Saladin's would augment; the French refused to lift a finger to help Richard while pharisaically condemning him for betrayal of the crusade; most of all, events in England called the Lionheart home; for all he knew, his brother John might already have usurped the kingdom. To save face, Richard sent a message to Saladin that this was merely a three-year truce, not a permanent peace, that when he had settled matters in the Angevin empire he could come again with a new army to try conclusions with the Sultan. Saladin accepted this gracefully in the idiom of a sporting wager and wrote back: 'He entertained such an exalted opinion of King Richard's honour, magnanimity and general excellence, that he would rather lose his dominions to him than to any king he had ever seen – always supposing that he was obliged to lose his dominions at all.'[106]

The peace was ratified and the rival rulers departed, Richard to Acre, Saladin to Jerusalem. Needless to say, Richard's enemies converted a piece of *realpolitik* into a black legend of treachery and venality. French writers and chroniclers roundly asserted that Richard had been bribed to give up Ascalon, though more perceptive European observers saw clearly that there were no other realistic options in Palestine, that Ascalon would have been lost anyway sooner or later.[107] A middle-of-the road faction pinned the blame for the 'disaster' on Richard's illness, asserting that he was not *compos mentis* when he agreed to Saladin's terms, that whereas Turks, Arabs and Mamluks could not defeat the Lionheart, the diseases of the Middle East had, thus depriving the crusaders by ill-luck of the prize they had secured by their martial prowess. There is some truth in this, for Richard was extremely ill, even close to death at times, and was too weak to do much more than be carried up to Acre.[108] Some stated, more pragmatically, that Richard was running out of money and that his treasury was exhausted, not least through having to subvent the ungrateful and unco-operative French. Richard did not himself journey to Jerusalem, although many crusaders did take advantage of the pilgrimage offer made in the treaty. It was speculated that Richard wanted to lead by example, that if he went to the Holy City every last soldier would follow him, so how then could he ever raise 'pilgrims' for the intended Fourth Crusade?[109] For precisely the same reasons, Saladin rejected Richard's request that he apply a quota system on Christian pilgrims to Jerusalem and only allow in those he (Richard) approved. Saladin knew that a peaceful pilgrimage was in itself a disincentive for a Christian to serve in a crusading army again.[110] But if Richard was machiavellian in this matter, he was an upright paladin elsewhere. Not only did he pay all his debts but he took the trouble to ransom William de Preaux, who had been captured in the ambush a year before, releasing ten Muslim lords in exchange.[111]

The peace formalities took a month to be tied up completely, since Henry of Champagne and the French lords, who took a pacific oath independently of Richard, demanded in turn that all the leading emirs, not just Saladin, should do the same. Then envoys were sent to Bohemond of Antioch and Muslim lords in far-flung locations. But finally there was nothing to stop Richard departing. The two queens Joan and Berengaria had sailed from Acre on 29 September and Richard followed in their wake two weeks later on 9 October.[112] He had time to reflect ruefully that neither side in the Third Crusade had won and that each had fought the other to a standstill, with the crucial factors perhaps being Muslim numbers on one side and Frankish command of the sea on the other. Given the divided command, the intransigence of the French and the massive logistical problems Richard faced, the amazing thing was that he achieved as much as he did. Yet it is certain that the Lionheart's exploits prolonged the life of the crusader states for another century.[113] Lovers of drama will always regret that Richard and Saladin never met, but then neither did Elizabeth I and Mary Queen of Scots or General Gordon and the Mahdi. Certainly no two captains of such prestige ever clashed again in the Middle East until Tamerlane's fateful encounter with Bayazid on the field of Angora in 1402. Ironically, having repelled the Frankish invader, Saladin died very soon afterwards, on 4 March 1193, almost as though with the departure of Richard his life's work was over. Alternatively one can speculate that it was the very stress of having to deal with the most brilliant Western commander in the entire period 1000–1300 that brought on his sudden death. Richard and Saladin had both on occasions acted with ruthless brutality, but their chivalric effusions and mutual admiration won the pagan many friends in Christendom, to the point where Dante included him in the pantheon of virtuous unbelievers in the *Inferno*, alongside Hector, Aeneas and Julius Caesar. It was Saladin's fate to depart the vale of fears almost the moment Richard had departed. But Richard, having endured his Iliad, was now to face his Odyssey.

10

ALTHOUGH BERENGARIA AND JOAN had an uneventful passage to Brindisi and then proceeded to Rome, Richard's voyage had all the travails of Odysseus's homeward journey. One of the great mysteries in Richard's life, about which professional historians have been unaccountably silent, is exactly what happened to his crusading army at the end of the campaign in Outremer. The host that had terrorised Lisbon, laid waste Sicily and convulsed Cyprus, seems to have been no more, or else Richard could surely have cut a swathe with fire and sword through Europe just as he had on the outward journey. The inference is that losses in the Holy Land, more from disease than battle, must have been catastrophic; one estimate is that only one in twelve of those who had left England remained.[1] But the mystery does not end there. What happened to Richard's battle fleet? Ships cannot travel overland, as Richard now proposed to do, and in any case his manpower losses would not have enabled him to man them all. The only warranted conclusion is that Richard's army by and large made its way back to England on a *sauve qui peut* basis, and that the warships, once beached in European ports, were simply abandoned. The central fact Richard had to contend with was that neither he nor his fleet could return via the Straits of Gibraltar. The great Arab geographer Edrisi had already cautioned the unwary about what awaited anyone foolhardy enough to venture into the Atlantic in winter, but the plain fact was that even if Richard had been prepared to take the risk of facing 60-foot waves in galleys that would be overwhelmed by waves one-quarter that height, medieval technology ruled out that possibility. East-flowing currents through the Straits were faster than the speed of any twelfth-century vessel plying in the opposite direction.[2] For Richard's troops, the outgoing voyage through the 'Pillars of Hercules' had been a one-way ticket in more senses than one.

What, then, were Richard's options? The leisurely outward procession through France was not a feasible scenario, given King Philip's hostility, but at first Richard thought he could land somewhere on the southern coast of France, probably Marseilles, and make his way to England overland. An overland route via Spain was also apparently suggested, but making for Spain on too southerly a track would mean risking interception by Barbary corsairs and, if they headed too far north, they risked running into naval forces commanded by Raymond of Toulouse. In any case Spain was now in turmoil. One of the many envoys who arrived in the Holy Land in 1191–92 informed him that his old enemy Raymond of Toulouse had fomented another rebellion in Aquitaine. Sancho of Navarre had immediately helped the seneschal of Gascony to suppress this uprising. Infuriated, Raymond intrigued with the king of Aragon and Catalonia to make common cause against Navarre. With Aragon in the enemy camp, most of the coast of Provence and northern Spain, including Barcelona, was closed to Richard. An educated man, Richard might have pondered the words of Virgil describing the Underworld: 'The way down is easy . . . but to come back and regain the outer air, that is the task, that is the problem.' Nevertheless, he was initially determined to land in Provence and fight his way through if necessary. At midnight on 9 October he sailed from Acre on a large buss capable of housing 1,000 men.³ Even a Mediterranean voyage in winter at this date was a terrifying ordeal for sailors. Navigators had not mastered the currents and were largely baffled by the unpredictable winds: sirocco, ghibli, mistral, bora. In Roman times sailors had been advised never to put to sea after 14 September, and even the daring Pisans in the Middle Ages thought 30 November the absolute limit for safe seafaring. The result was that in the winter the Mediterranean was more a dead sea than the Roman 'lake' of old. Richard's buss, a two-masted ship with a 75-stong crew, was going in harm's way, not really equipped for the Mediterranean winter at any level. Navigation was crude – latitude determined by an astrolabe but no means of fixing longitude – pilots steered mainly by the stars, and conditions on board were noisome: water brackish, latrines non-existent, food poor and hygiene woeful.⁴

Whether because the master of the buss was fearful of heading into the open sea or because Richard wanted to give a boost to Guy of Lusignan, the ship anchored in Limassol harbour three days after leaving Acre. Then, after another midnight start, it headed for Rhodes where, after a brief landfall, the voyagers threaded their way out through the Dodecanese islands, with Karpathos on the starboard, heading south-west for Crete. Once at Crete they hugged the southern coast before striking north along the west coast of Greece. Taking a risky track through the Zakynthos Channel between the mainland and Corfu, Richard landed on the island for the first time on an unknown date. Corfu was one of the great trading crossroads, a meeting point of merchants from Italy, the West, Byzantium and the Arab world. It was a hive of spies and secret agents, and it was here that Richard first heard of the meeting between Philip Augustus and Henry VI, and Henry's threats to seize the English king. Both Philip and Leopold of Austria had returned from Palestine angry, vengeful and malicious towards Richard for the reasons already mentioned (see pp.176-77). Leopold added 'spin' to his grievances by alleging that Richard was anti-German and had insulted German soldiers by doubting their courage.[5] The ostensible pretexts for hostility seem relatively trivial, except to men with a prickly sense of honour, but there was something else. Richard was exceptionally decisive and quick-thinking, and this quality comes across as arrogance to the ditherer and waverer, of whom Philip Augustus was a prime example. Whatever the rights and wrongs of the case, Leopold and Philip had defamed and traduced Richard all over Europe, and a new twist to the catalogue of calumniation was provided by the bishop of Beauvais, who returned from the crusade roundly asserting that the king of England had betrayed Philip to Saladin, had had Conrad of Montferrat murdered, and then capped his exploits by poisoning the duke of Burgundy.[6]

Richard's options were narrowing. We cannot follow all the agonising and prevarication and the stressful conferences with his followers that must have taken place, but the king evidently decided to throw his enemies off the scent. He initially sailed north and came close enough to Brindisi to be spotted by watchers on the shore, as was his intention.[7] He then changed direction, went round Cape St Maria di Leuca and crossed the Gulf of Taranto to Sicily, intending to pick up currents off the North African coast that would waft him north to Marseilles without the necessity of hugging either the Spanish or Italian coasts. The probability is that he put in to a port in southern Sicily to obtain further intelligence about political events in Europe. What he learned confirmed his worst fears. Philip and Raymond of Toulouse had barred the entire southern coast of France against him, and Emperor Henry had done the same in Italy. Genoa was firmly in the Franco-Imperial camp and the territory of Piedmont was controlled by the relatives of Conrad of Montferrat, who remained convinced that Richard had had Conrad murdered; to cap all, Richard's erstwhile allies in Pisa had signed a treaty with Heny VI, pending his invasion of Sicily. Richard's homeward journey looked more and more impossible. The only good news was that the Angevin empire itself was holding firm. His marriage to Berengaria had paid off, and Sancho of Navarre was at the very gates of Toulouse.[8] Nevertheless, literally at sea and on a stormy winter Mediterranean, it was clear that Richard had to think quickly. He ordered the buss put about for Corfu, intending to make landfall in the Adriatic. After a dangerous voyage in and among the shifting currents of Sicily and southern Italy, the buss struggled to the top of the Ionian Sea and the most northerly of the Ionian islands. Fortune had been with them so far, and they had avoided storms. It is not clear whether 11 November, the date mentioned by the chroniclers, was the date of the first or second landing in Corfu (probably the latter).[9]

The second approach to Corfu involved yet another mysterious episode about which professional historians hesitate to express a definite opinion. According to some versions, Richard's ship had an encounter with the notorious pirates in the Ionian Sea, who had already intercepted his mother during the Second Crusade, but Richard unfurled his colours and browbeat the sea rovers. Much more plausible is the more prosaic version that Richard, concerned about the weatherliness of his sea-battered buss, decided to switch ships and therefore chartered two privateer galleys and their crews for a fee of 200 marks.[10] Perhaps the idea of the Lionheart hiring corsairs did not appeal to the romancers, so they had to turn it into a rewrite of Julius Caesar's famous browbeating of the pirates. Richard's chartering of the two galleys from irregulars was sensible, for it turned away a plethora of awkward questions and gave little away to Corfu's espionage community. Most of Richard's men were paid off or otherwise discharged at this point, and he went on with just twenty companions, divided into two groups on the two galleys, so that potential marauders would not know which vessel to target. Coggleshall gives the names of some of the happy few: William de l'Etang, Baldwin of Bethune, Philip of Poitou, Robert de Turnham (his admiral) and his chaplain Anselm. They were engaged in a desperate endeavour at two levels. In the first place, galleys could not survive in gales higher than Force Five, and they were already in the storm season.[11] In the second, their objective seemed chimerical to all but the most optimistic. Richard had decided to head north to Ragusa (modern Dubrovnik) but his ultimate destination was either the north-east of Germany (the lands of his brother-in-law Henry the Lion), or Saxony, where the duke was his nephew, or even Bohemia, whose ruler Ottokar had recently had a major falling-out with German emperor Henry VI – historians still dispute his real intention. The safest way to accomplish this was a round-about route through the territories of Bela III of Hungary, a man whose feud with Leopold of Austria was legendary.[12]

So far Richard's luck had held, for all the evidence suggests his enemies still thought he was heading for the southern coast of France.[13] But the passage up the Adriatic proved stormy; under heavy battering from the feared Adriatic wind, the bora, the galleys could not even run into the safe anchorage of Ragusa harbour but were forced to put ashore at the island of Lokrum, about half a mile out to sea at the entrance to the harbour. Salvation from the storm had been a close-run thing, and there is a powerful tradition that Richard, momentarily despairing, promised to spend 100,000 ducats building a church if he was saved; and so, according to the story, he became the founder of the cathedral of Ragusa.[14] Proceeding up the coast past Pola and Zara early in December, he ran into another storm, which drove the galleys ashore somewhere between Aquileia and Venice. The sources speak of a landing in a deserted area of swamps and forests, maybe somewhere in the estuary of the Tagliamento.[15] Longhaired, bearded, in need of clothes that would make them inconspicuous, the crusaders halted to take stock. Richard decided to press on incognito, having no confidence that anyone in these parts would give him a safe-conduct, taking with him only a handful of hand-picked comrades: Baldwin of Bethune, William de l'Etang, Philip of Poitou and the chaplain Anselm being the most notable. It was bad luck that he had landed where he did, for this area was the domain of Meinhard II of Gorz (Gorizia), who represented double jeopardy – as a close ally and loyal subject of the German emperor and also the nephew of Conrad of Montferrat. Richard decided that his original idea of travelling disguised as a Templar was not such a good one. The story now would be that he and his party were pilgrims returning from Palestine and that Richard was a wealthy merchant named Hugo.[16] There had to be some covering fiction, for this was not an era in which a traveller could proceed in privacy; at every town and castle you were expected to reveal your identity, your destination and the purpose of your travels.

The wayfarers headed north-east towards Gorizia and Hungary. The first day on the road gave them a taste of the travails to come, for medieval travel was no affair of the faint-hearted, being more the stuff of Grimm's fairy stories than feudal reality; voyagers could expect to run risks from brigands and wild animals, quite apart from the obstacles of nature (winds, mountains and flood) and the hardships of a bitter winter.

Few roads or bridges had been constructed since Roman times and, by common consent, those undertaking unnecessary journeys in the Middle Ages were on a fool's errand.[17] At the end of the first day on the road the 'pilgrims' came to Gorizia, a crossroads for the cultures of Italy, Germany and Slovenia. Richard asked the town authorities for safe passage, a guide and the Truce of God for crusaders, but he was no actor and foolishly sent a messenger ahead with a rich ruby ring as token of his good faith – an appropriate gesture for a great king but scarcely for a money-grubbing Hugo. Engelbert III, lord of Gorizia, immediately became suspicious at such munificence and questioned the envoy closely. At the end of the interview he told him he knew full well, from all kinds of circumstantial evidence, that 'Hugo' was Richard the Lionheart. In awe of the great king or secretly sympathetic to his plight, he returned the ring and sent a warning to the Lionheart to be on his way with all speed. When this was reported to him Richard grew alarmed, concluded Hungary was beyond his reach and set his course instead for Bohemia, where he knew Duke Ottakar was locked in a bitter dispute with the emperor.[18] The new itinerary would involve crossing the mountains to Vienna and thence traversing the Danube to Moravia (ruled by Ottakar's brother Ladislaw), then Bohemia itself, Saxony and home to England.

Accordingly Richard and his companions set off north-west towards Udine. Engelbert, meanwhile, playing a double game, sent a messenger to his brother-in-law Meinhard, the emperor's ally and bearing the title of hereditary 'Advocate' of Aquileia, to tell him that Richard was at large in his domains. Meinhard sent his aide Roger of Argentan to search the inns and taverns of Udine for pilgrims. It was a simple matter for Roger to run such conspicuous travellers to earth, but Meinhard had made a bad mistake in his choice of henchman. Roger was a Norman with divided loyalties. He confronted Richard and forced him to admit who he was, but then let him go, informing Meinhard that he could find no one answering the description of the wanted pilgrims. Meinhard found this the tallest of tall stories and in a fury sent out a fresh search party, but by the time they reached Udine the birds had flown.[19] It must be admitted that no historian has ever been able to pin down the precise sequence of events in Udine. It seems that, even with Roger of Argentan's blessing, the travellers had a hard time of it and were set upon twice by predatory locals, who noticed the contradiction between the apparel of the 'pilgrims' (they were travelling in disguise) and their lavish and conspicuous expenditure; it is not an easy thing for a prince to play the pauper. It is not clear whether the 'killed and wounded' referred to in some of the sources refers to the assaults here or the later one at Friesach.[20]

Heading north from Udine, the travellers joined the Via Julia Augusta, the main road from Aquileia to the Alps. Realising that he was too tall, distinguished and well known to pass muster convincingly as a merchant, Richard reverted to the original Templar disguise, trying to avoid attention by travelling with caravans and merging with crowds in the towns. The 22-foot wide stone highway ran past the fortified town of Venzone and then turned east into the valley of the eastern Alps known as the Val Canale. Although twelfth-century winters in central Europe were warmer than our own, Richard's spirits must have drooped as he saw the higher peaks of the Alps looming ahead, for by this time he was exhausted and suffering from fever – perhaps a recrudescence of the malady that had laid him low in Palestine. The probability is that the travellers stopped at the monastery of Moggio to allow the king to rest, and maybe it was here that they picked up the boy who spoke German and who features so prominently in the annals. On 13 December the pilgrims recommenced the journey through the Val Canale and soon passed Pontebba (Pontafel), usually regarded as the frontier between Italian and German-speaking peoples. Once past Tarvisio they were in the dangerous country of Carinthia. Everything now seemed to conspire against them, and they spent an entire day slipping and sliding in the snow before limping into Villach. Next day they galloped along the northern shore of the Ossiacher See, past the Benedictine monastery at Gerlitzen and then into the deep valleys of Carinthia, following a track through Feldkirchen and St Veit to Friesach.[21]

News of their coming had preceded them. Friesach, a silver-mining boom town and fief of the bishop of Salzburg, turned out to be honey-combed by the troops of Friedrich III of Pettau, one of Leopold's leading barons. Matters were desperate, so Richard agreed with Baldwin of Bethune that his faithful knight would have to be the sacrificial scape-goat. Baldwin and the main party would stay in Friesach, spend lavishly and generally draw attention to themselves, while Richard with just William de l'Etang and the German-speaking boy, would make a dash for Vienna.[22] Friedrich duly took the bait and arrested Baldwin and the rest of the party; the confused sources hint that they may have resisted arrest and sustained casualties as a result. The larger diversionary plan worked only up to a point. Richard and William got as far as Erdburg (now a suburb of Vienna) after a three-day, 145-mile ride (past Forchenstein castle near Neumarkt, north-west to cross the River Mur just after Teufensbach, crossing back to the south bank near the Magdalenkirche at Judenberg, and then at full tilt across the plains of what is now the Viener Neustadt before dropping down to Vienna), and rented a room. There Richard collapsed with fever. Unfortunately, while the king slept off the fatigue of his recent exertions, the boy went out for food and was recognised by the emperor's secret police; his arrogant manner in the Rochus market to say nothing of an expensive silver cross he wore almost invited attention. The story is that the boy went to the market on three successive days and on the third took with him Richard's ornate gloves as the day was so cold. The police either seized him on the spot and put him to torture or followed him back to the house (once again the sources are unclear) and arrested Richard; the date was either 20 or 21 December.[23] Some say the king was asleep when taken, others that he put up a fight, but the persistent legend that he was caught in the kitchen while masquerading as a chef and cooking meat over a spit may well be the truth. In the end Richard agreed to be apprehended but insisted he would surrender only to Leopold in person. International law was then in its infancy and the grounds for arresting a king who was travelling incognito seemed shaky, but the Austrians claimed that the selfsame *ius gentium* that established the reality of piracy was the basis for a charge against Richard of what we would nowadays call 'crimes against humanity'. More specifically the following counts in the indictment were mentioned: the unlawful abduction of Isaac of Cyprus and his wife; insults offered to Duke Leopold at Acre; and the murder of Conrad of Montferrat. However, in general, educated and informed opinion in Europe, and even in France, where people had reason enough to hate Richard, concurred in finding the Austrian action an outrageous injustice, a crime made more outrageous by its humbug, for the jailers had kidnapped a king on the pretence that he himself was an abductor; rarely was the principle of *tu quoque* more appropriate.[24]

Delighted to have his old enemy in his power, Leopold sent Richard to the castle of Durnstein, perched high up the Danube forty-five miles above Vienna, where the castellan was Hadmar of Kuenrig, one of his most reliable vassals. The Lionheart arrived there either on Christmas Eve or Christmas Day.[25] Richard's sojourn in this fortress was the basis for one of the most enduring but, alas, apocryphal legends about the Lionheart. The story goes that Blondel was a wandering minstrel and troubadour, who had collaborated with Richard in Aquitaine on some *aubades*. Richard on his return from the crusades vanished into thin air, and it was feared he was being held for ransom by some desperate kidnappers, probably aided and abetted by some powerful continental magnate. When he learned of Richard's arrest, Blondel at once wandered the length and breadth of Germany, searching for his lord. Outside all known prisons, dungeons and fortresses he would sing the first verse of the joint composition, hoping one day to hear his adored co-author respond with the second verse. Finally, as in all good stories, the inevitable happened, and Blondel heard Richard's powerful voice wafting from the castle of Durnstein. He was thus able to return to England with news of the king's whereabouts.[26] One hardly needs to dwell on the manifold absurdities of the legend. Richard was held in Durnstein for just two weeks before being taken to the German emperor at Ratisbon. Even if the Austrians had been trying to conceal his whereabouts, and even if this was discovered immediately, it would have taken two weeks for the news to reach England. By the time Blondel was setting out on his quest, Richard would no longer be in Durnstein anyway, so would not have been there for him to discover. Besides, the motivation ascribed to the abductors is that valid only in the normal criminal case, where the kidnappers have to keep the hiding place of their prize secret, so that the celebrity's family will pay the ransom money before the police can discover the hideout. But the whole point about the imperial seizure of Richard was that everything was out in the open. This was the coup of the century, and Henry VI of Germany *wanted* it known that he had Richard as a prisoner, so that he could extract the literal king's ransom. It is a matter of historical fact that the emperor wrote to Philip of France on 28 December, virtually trumpeting the news that he had the Lionheart in his power, and soon all the civilised world knew it.[27]

Yet since human beings are swayed more by myth than historical fact, it is worth probing a little more deeply into this extraordinary legend. Its first appearance is in a Reims prose chronicle written about 1260, yet it really started to take off in the eighteenth century, especially after the 1785 comic opera *Richard Coeur de Lion*; this work, with words by M.J. Sedaine and music by Gretry, premiered in Paris, and features a rescue of Richard from Durnstein by Blondel in league with Margherite, countess of Flanders. In the nineteenth century Blondel appeared in Sir Walter Scott's *The Talisman* and he attracted the interest of the composers Robert Schumann and Joaquim Raff. In the twentieth century, following the fad for turning as many historical figures as possible into bisexual or homosexual personalities, Blondel tends to appear, inevitably, as Richard's male lover.[28] Although the story of Blondel at Durnstein is as clearly apocryphal as any story could be, the astonishing thing is that a troubadour named Blondel de Nesle did exist and was a contemporary of Richard's. A native of Picardy, he was a mediocre composer of melodies and words which showed the influence of Gregorian chant, and twenty-three of his songs (seven of them with their music) have come down to us. He is sometimes tentatively identified with the minor nobleman Jean de Nesle of Picardy (though even here the attributors cannot agree whether it is Jean I or Jean II), but this is unlikely; more plausible is the notion that he was a member of the minor gentry or even a commoner. This Blondel de Nesle probably died around the age of 50 at the end of the twelfth century, and it is highly unlikely that he would ever even have met Richard. It is tempting to think the legend has been so enduring in part because an entirely fictional minstrel called Blondel was conflated with an actual troubadour of Picardy.[29] Yet the myth of Blondel is extraordinarily tenacious, to the point where many writers seem reluctant to consign it to a fictional limbo. One recent valiant attempt to keep the flame alive ingeniously suggests the story may have been a transmogrified version of a real event, possibly involving troubadours as secret agents; the Blondel legend would thus be an elaborate smokescreen to hide the real story of England's super-efficient espionage system.[30]

The capture of Richard I of England was like manna to the troubled Henry VI, beset as he was by grave problems in every part of his realm. The German emperor faced the kinds of problems that would later bedevil Richard's brother John: rebellious barons, breakaway provinces, local nationalism challenging imperial centralism, even Church-state collisions. Late twelfth-century Germany was a natural federation and should have been ruled as such, but Henry VI had autocratic tendencies and blundered into esoteric disputes between his vassals where he had no business.[31] When Liège had to choose a new bishop in 1191, and two rival factions appeared, headed by the duke of Brabant and the count of Hainault, Henry chose to stick his imperial oar in and support a third, so-called *tertius gaudens* candidate. On 24 November, just a month before Richard's capture, the Brabant candidate, Albert, was murdered and Henry was accused of having hired the hit-men. The Church in the Rhineland responded by raising the princes of the Rhineland in revolt against the emperor, and the Church leaders, the archbishops of Cologne and Mainz, proposed the assassinated man's brother Henry, duke of Brabant, as the next emperor.[32] With revolts brewing in the north and east of his domains as well, Henry faced the possible break-up of the Holy Roman Empire. This was the context in which Providence delivered Richard into his lap. It was the classic instance of the external dimension serving as a diversion from internal problems – a transparent but perennially effective ploy that has served rulers well down the ages. Besides, a gigantic ransom obtained from the Angevin empire for the Lionheart would so swell the imperial coffers that Henry would literally be able to buy off his rebels by one means or another.

Richard was now in effect a trophy to be auctioned off to the highest bidder. The despicable Henry VI had already shown how much store he set by the Church – and indeed to some extent he was following in Frederick Barbarossa's Guelph v. Ghibelline footsteps. It did not bother him that he was in flat defiance of canon law and papal bulls by detaining a crusading king who was supposed to be under the protection of Holy Mother Church. Leopold of Austria, however, was more cautious and genuinely feared excommunication. This was not the only point of difference between the two men, for both were pursuing very different agendas. Not surprisingly, the first bargaining round in the cattle auction did not produce results. Leopold took Richard under heavy armed guard to Ratisbon to exhibit the prize to the emperor, and king and emperor had a brief and, one imagines, intemperate meeting.[33] Unable to strike a deal, Leopold began to fear that Henry would simply seize his human cash-cow, so suddenly returned to Austria to an unknown destination – it was most unlikely to have been Durnstein, for the emperor's spies had already scouted the location against a possible order to snatch the English king. While Henry and Leopold contemplated their next step, Philip of France entered the fray, writing in early January 1193 to Leopold to enjoin him on no account to release Richard until all three men – Philip, Henry and Leopold – had held a summit conference to decide the next step.[34] Despicably, he sent a message to the helpless Richard that all bonds between them were severed and that he should regard this communication as a declaration of war. Even more despicably, he contacted the emperor and offered to match and then outmatch any sum paid for Richard's release, stating clearly that he wanted the Lionheart kept in Germany as a prisoner for life. This was too much even for Henry's venal advisers, who advised the emperor that to accept the offer would make him the pariah of Christendom. The peevish Philip contented himself by invading Normandy instead.[35]

It took six more weeks of haggling before Leopold and Henry finally hammered out an agreement. The contract was signed in Würzburg on 14 February; Richard was not present and was rumoured to be held a close prisoner at Oschenfurt. The ransom for Richard was set at

100,000 marks, to be split by the emperor and Leopold on a fifty-fifty basis. Half the sum was to be handed over at Michaelmas to Henry and Leopold on the occasion of the marriage of Richard's niece Eleanor of Britanny (daughter of Richard's late brother Geoffrey), and the other half at the beginning of the following Lent (23 February 1194). Additionally, Henry would provide Leopold with 20 hostages as surety that, should the emperor die while Richard was in his hands, he would be given back to Leopold; if Leopold died in the same period, the contract would be fulfilled by whichever son was chosen to marry Eleanor. Personal spite and vindictiveness are apparent in the clause requiring Richard to provide fifty galleys fully equipped for war plus one hundred knights as an outright gift to Henry before his departure on a campaign against Sicily, and the further provision that Richard in person had to accompany the emperor on the campaign, bringing another hundred knights at his own expense; truly Richard's alliance with Tancred of Sicily was bearing bitter fruit. Further, as surety for his performance, Richard would provide twenty hostages of the highest calibre, who would also be detained until Richard obtained the Pope's absolution of Leopold for breaking his crusader's vow. The king of Cyprus and his daughter had to be freed before Richard himself could be released. If all these conditions were not fulfilled by Lent 1194, Leopold had the right to demand the return of the king to his custody. If Richard died while in the emperor's power, Leopold would hang on to the 200 imperial hostages until he received full payment of the agreed ransom.[36] Even by the standards of the Middle Ages, this was one of the most scandalous documents ever committed to paper. It was victor's justice with a vengeance, and a coward's charter to boot.

The gleeful Philip of France passed on news of the treaty to his new-found ally Prince John. As soon as Philip returned from the Crusade he began intriguing with Richard's disaffected younger brother, promising him Normandy in exchange for marriage with Alice. The dauntless Eleanor of Aquitaine nipped this in the bud by threatening John with confiscation of all his estates if he took ship for France.[37] But John continued to tour England, telling anyone who would listen that Richard was dead. Matters seemed to swing decisively in his favour with the stunning news from Philip that Richard was a prisoner in Germany. This time nothing could stop John, and he sped to France. In Paris he did homage to Philip for the entire Angevin empire – an express act of treason. He promised to marry Alice and to hand over Gisors and the Vexin to France. He then put a toe into Normandy but was quickly rebuffed when the Norman barons, meeting at Alençon, told him bluntly they would never accept him as their lord.[38] When Philip's forces arrived, they swept through the Vexin, took Gisors and moved on Rouen, but there they were vigorously repelled by the returning hero of the crusade, the earl of Leicester. Even so, Philip felt he held all the cards in his struggle with the Angevin empire. Delighted with the turn of events, he even contemplated an invasion of England and sent John back there to foment rebellion. He asked William king of Scotland for an alliance but William, remembering the generosity of Richard in the 1189 Quitclaim of Canterbury, turned him down contemptuously. Eleanor of Aquitaine and the justiciars raised an army to defend the south-east coast, so John withdrew into the castles of Windsor and Wallingford which he had managed to capture with Flemish mercenaries. He then proclaimed himself king as the legitimate and indefeasible heir of the dead king Richard. But John's claim that Richard was dead was refuted in spectacular fashion when a letter arrived in England from Emperor Henry VI, asking for the 100,000 mark ransom. Accordingly, Walter of Coutances summoned a great council of the realm to a meeting in Oxford on 28 February 1193.[39]

The justiciars of the realm debated all the possible means for securing the king's release. Savaric, bishop of Bath, told the conclave he had already put out feelers to the emperor, his kinsman, on Richard's behalf; the Council ordered the oath of fealty to Richard to be renewed throughout the realm; and the abbots of Boxley and Robertsbridge were chosen as delegates to go to Germany and communicate first-hand with the king. It was 28 March before the envoys discovered Richard at Oschenfurt on the Main, ten miles from Würzburg, where Leopold had him securely lodged pending the final offer from the emperor. Boxley and Robertsbridge found the Lionheart in good spirits; he was openly contemptuous when they told him of Prince John's intrigues: 'My brother John is not the man to conquer a country if there is anyone to offer even the feeblest resistance,' he said dismissively.[40] On 20 March the emperor met Richard again, and the king flatly refused the extortionate terms offered. Henry's response was to charge him formally with betraying the Holy Land to Saladin, breaking his promises to the emperor (presumably by his treaty with Tancred of Sicily) and compassing the death of Conrad of Montferrat. A 'trial' duly took place at Speyer on the 21st. The ordeal of appearing before a panel of German princes shook Richard but he responded in a typically spirited way, rebutting the charges confidently, with such eloquence and forensic skill that even his enemies were impressed; the mood of the German princes began to shift decisively in his favour.[41] Second thoughts prevailed on both sides, the indictment was dropped, and, presumably as a quid pro quo, Richard agreed to pay the ransom of 100,000 marks, on condition that Henry VI acted as peacemaker between him and Philip of France. Thereupon Leopold handed Richard over to Henry, and king and emperor continued on their way to Speyer. Here Richard was joined by Hubert Walter of Salisbury, his faithful companion and adviser in the Holy Land, a splendid mixture of soldier, administrator and diplomat, who was returning from the crusade; having got as far as Sicily he heard the news of the king's capture, went up to Rome to lobby the Pope for support, and then hastened to Germany to be at his side. Richard sent Hubert back to England, with a letter for his mother Eleanor, in which he commended Hubert and suggested they work together for his release; Hubert's reward for his fidelity was to be the archbishopric of Canterbury, vacant since Baldwin of Canterbury's death in November 1190.[42]

Confidently expecting he would soon be released, Richard sent to England for hostages and ships to take him across the Channel. But Henry distrusted Richard as a slippery eel and was taken aback by the facility with which he had won the German princes round at his 'trial'. His first response was to send the king under armed guard to the castle of Trifels in the mountains west of Speyer, where it was intended that his imprisonment be harsher than the initial confinement at Durnstein. Fortunately for Richard he spent no more than a couple of days in this spartan fortress, for William Longchamp, no great success as justiciar in England, now proved his mettle by appearing at the imperial court and persuading Henry VI to ease the terms of the king's captivity.[43] Consequently Richard was moved back to the itinerant German court, now at Hagenau. Longchamp achieved a further breakthrough by getting the emperor to agree to release Richard once an initial payment of 70,000 marks was made. Longchamp then returned to England with letters from both Henry and Richard, urging the justiciars to raise the money as soon as possible. Hubert Walter and Longchamp both proved able advocates once back in England, although the scale of their task should not be underestimated.[44] 100,000 marks or £66,000 – maybe £2 billion in today's money – was an enormous sum for any medieval state to raise, as may be seen from some everyday comparisons. At the time a sheep cost one penny, a pig sixpence, the normal rent for a cottage was sixpence a year, and soldiers were paid twopence a day; the ransom was three times the annual expenditure of the English government. Moreover, this extra sum had to be found in a society that had already been mulcted by the Saladin Tithe and drained by other taxes to pay for the Third Crusade.[45]

It was fortunate for Richard that England was the financial jewel in the Angevin empire. Not only was the taxation system itself superior in efficiency to those in Normandy, Britanny and Aquitaine, but the English economy itself was robust, swimming in silver coins that had flooded in from abroad to pay for English wool and the products of water mills and the lead and tin mines in the West Country. The justiciars, at Eleanor of Aquitaine's urging, issued a decree levying a 25 per cent tax rate on income and moveable property and began by requisitioning gold and silver plate from churches as well as the annual wool crop of the Cistercian monks. But soon it was decided that the justiciars should be excluded from the actual process of collecting the ransom. Instead the business was given over to four trustees who would lodge the collected silver in the vaults of St Paul's Cathedral pending its shipment to Germany: Hubert Walter, Richard Fitzneal, bishop of London, William, earl of Arundel and Hamelin, earl of Warenne were the quartet appointed – on the basis that they were the only members of the English elite not involved in the ousting of Longchamp in 1191.[46] The systematic means of uplifting money centred initially on the 25 per cent tax on revenue and portable property, but this produced disappointing returns, raising only £7,000 instead of the expected £12–25,000 (as a result of corruption?).[47] Other means of raising money in England were via the scutage on the knight's fee, and through special ad hoc taxes, some of them fines on localities that had seemed sympathetic to the rebellious Prince John; there were also retrospective taxes in 1194 and 1195 to celebrate Richard's eventual release.[48] Churches and abbeys were gradually forced to disgorge all their wealth; carucage (a tax of two shillings per hide per landowner) was levied; there was a new additional toll imposed on anyone with property worth more than ten shillings; and individual contributions were invited (demanded?) from all the great lords, who responded variously, with William king of Scotland in pride of place with a donation of 2,000 marks.[49] The worst burden of new taxation fell on the Jews who were visited with a special new tax of 5,000 marks. It has been well said that the raising of the ransom money was eloquent testimony to the soundness of English finances and administration, not to mention general economic prosperity. Similar letters were sent to the other parts of the Angevin empire, and we can catch glimpses of the response in, for example, the amount of £16,000 paid over to Germany from Normandy in the financial year 1194–95.[50]

Despite the momentary threat of the dungeons of Speyer, the real enemy Richard had to worry about was not Emperor Henry but Philip of France. Richard moved quickly to neutralise Philip's influence in England by taking his brother John off the chessboard. The justiciars soon went over to the offensive and confined the rebellious John to the castles of Windsor and Tickhill. John and his party were in desperate straits by April 1193, when Hubert Walter suddenly returned from Germany and saved them by the unexpected offer of a truce – unexpected because Richard and the loyalists had the rebels on the ropes. But Richard reasoned that the enormous ransom he had to raise could not be gathered in while the realm was rent by virtual civil war. He proposed a six months' truce, and John leapt at the offer. The justiciars were secretly glad of the outcome, for it was still possible that Richard's enemies would find ways to detain him forever in Germany, in which case John would become king; what would their own position then be worth? The terms of the truce laid down that John could retain the castles of Nottingham and Tickhill, but had to surrender those at Windsor, Wallingford and the Peak in Derbyshire.[51] Meanwhile Richard checkmated Philip on another front, when his mother and loyal forces in Aquitaine defeated a rebellion there by Ademar of Angoulême aided and abetted by Philip.[52] Finally, he brokered an agreement between his putative allies in Germany (the duke of Saxony, the duke of Louvain, the archbishops of Cologne and Maintz, and other nobles, all still angry about the murder of Albert of Louvain) and the emperor. He knew that Henry VI was due to meet Philip at Vaucouleurs on 25 June and feared that the emperor, still anxious about the possible implosion of his kingdom, might ally himself with the French king against his own recalcitrant barons; the price of such an alliance would almost certainly be that Philip would demand the surrender of Richard into his custody, which would mean lifetime imprisonment. When Richard managed to bring about a reconciliation between Henry and the dissidents, the emperor in gratitude abandoned the proposed meeting with Philip.[53]

Normandy was the one failure Richard had to confront by mid-1193 but, under arrest as he was, there was little he could do about it. The reason Philip had been able to take Gisors and the Vexin with such ease was precisely because the lords who held the land on the borders between Normandy and France could not be certain that Richard would return as king; their position vis-à-vis Philip was therefore much like that of the English justiciars when dealing with John. It was fortunate indeed that the defence of Rouen had been in the hands of an authentic hero of the war with Saladin – Robert earl of Leicester. Philip's humiliation outside Rouen was so striking that he destroyed his own siege engines in a classic example of displaced rage.[54] He turned from campaigning to diplomatic pressure, and on 15 August married Ingeborg, daughter of Cnut VI of Denmark, who himself had a tenuous claim to the English throne that went back to the days before 1066 when King Svein Estrithson was a pretender to that crown. But Philip with Ingeborg proved to be a pre-echo of Henry VIII of England and Anne of Cleves in the sixteenth century. After one night with her, Philip declared he was sick of the sight of his wife. He repudiated her and demanded that the Danish envoys who had accompanied her to France take her back with them. When they refused, Philip got some tame and sycophantic bishops to dissolve the marriage on spurious grounds, though the Pope refused to endorse their actions; need one add that among the ecclesiastical toadies was Richard's old enemy the bishop of Beauvais? Philip had contracted the Danish marriage in the first place simply and solely to gain access to the large Danish fleet, which he hoped to use for an invasion of England. But the imbroglio with Ingeborg turned him into the laughing-stock of Europe. By winter 1193 he was desperately scratching around for a German marriage, proposing himself as husband to the daughter of the Count Palatine of the Rhine, himself Emperor Henry VI's uncle.[55]

After two months at the imperial court at Worms, where he divided his time between composing songs and supervising from afar the election of Hubert Walter as archbishop of Canterbury, Richard faced a moment of truth there when a grand conference was held on 25 June to decide his fate. Among those present, as well as the emperor, were the dukes of Louvain and Limburg and Hubert Walter, newly consecrated in Canterbury, who had sped to Germany immediately after his coronation.[56] By 29 June the final terms of Richard's ransom were hammered out. It was agreed that the emperor's envoys would accompany the English king's messengers back to London, and there receive 100,000 marks of pure silver; Richard would also provide a further 50,000 marks for Leopold of Austria. Hostages would be taken and released when two-thirds of the total ransom (i.e. 100,000 marks) was paid. Some details of this accord are obscure. Why the increase in the total sum? Some speculate that the extra 50,000 marks were a quid pro quo in exchange for releasing Richard from the initial pledge to campaign alongside the emperor against Tancred of Sicily. Subordinate clauses appeared to suggest that if Richard was able to bring about a lasting reconciliation between the emperor and Henry the Lion, formerly duke of Saxony, Henry VI would waive the payment of half of the money due to him, reducing the ransom once again to a total of 100,000 marks. If Richard was unable to reconcile the two Henrys within seven months, he would have to pay the 50,000 marks originally waived. Moreover, also within seven months, Richard undertook to marry his niece Eleanor of Britanny to the duke of Austria's son.[57]

Sober historians say that Richard got a good political deal at Worms in that he effectively stymied Philip of France, but only at the cost of further financial burdens for his long-suffering subjects. Henry VI was determined to hang on to Richard until the last possible moment and play out the hand Providence had dealt him for all it was worth, but he took a perverse delight in playing on Philip Augustus's fears. The famous message he sent to Philip after the agreement at Worms was sealed – 'Look to yourself; the devil is loose'[58] – anticipated reality by a good six months, for it was not until February 1194 that the devil finally gained his freedom. Henry further tantalised Philip by letting him know of the 'intimacy' he how enjoyed with the king of England and of the easy terms of Richard's confinement: he was allowed to transact the business of his kingdom; his friends and advisers could come and go without let or hindrance (and did so in large numbers); he even had his favourite hawks sent from England so that he could enjoy hunting. Sufficiently alarmed by this diplomatic upset, Philip hastened to make peace with Richard so that he could retain his recent conquests on the Norman border; the treaty of Mantes signed on 9 July secured Philip Gisors, Loches and Châtillon.[59] Undoubtedly Philip scored a paper success with this treaty, for additionally it stipulated that Richard would pay Philip 20,000 marks in four instalments, that Prince John's estates on both sides of the Channel would be secure, and that Count Ademar of Angoulême would be given amnesty for his recent rebellion. Richard could only grit his teeth and bide his time, knowing, as Philip did not, that his release was by no means imminent.

Yet neither Philip nor his unsavoury ally John stopped intriguing. John crossed to France soon after the treaty of Mantes, having spent much of the year so far skulking in Dorset (at Wareham and Dorchester).[60] He went first to Normandy to claim his castles there in accordance with the treaty, but the castellans so despised and distrusted him that they refused to hand them over, even when presented with writs in Richard's own hand. Angrily he went to visit Philip, and was temporarily consoled by being given the castles of Drincourt and Arques – which according to the treaty should have been granted to the archbishop of Reims.[61] In pique at the unravelling of all his schemes, he barefacedly signed a treaty with Philip in January 1194, ceding further portions of the Angevin empire to the French king. All of Normandy east of Rouen was handed over; as were the lands of Vaudreuil, Verneuil and Evreux, plus the castles of Moulins, Bonmoulins, Vendôme, Tours, Azay-le-Rideau, Ambroise, Montbazon, Montrichard, Loches and Châtillon-sur-Indres.[62] It was the giveaway bonanza of the century; John all but said in so many words that he hated his brother so much that he was prepared to destroy the Angevin empire if need be. Even Philip, the beneficiary of John's treacherous largesse, despised him for so signally selling out his own country. In his mind he must have been prepared for John to betray him in time, just as he had already betrayed his father and brother.[63]

For the moment, though, Philip was prepared to employ this treacherous turncoat for his own purposes. The Angevin empire was slow in assembling the huge quantities of silver needed to pay the ransom, so that it was November before Henry VI's emissaries arrived in England to check the weight and fineness of the monies, and arrange for the onward transport to Germany. Assured of his loot, Henry announced that Richard would be released on 17 January 1194.[64] Philip and John had to act quickly. Together, in January 1194 immediately after their disgraceful treaty, they approached Emperor Henry VI with a new proposal: they would pay 80,000 marks if Henry was prepared to detain Richard until the autumn, or a proportionate sum for every month he kept him captive beyond the January date.[65] Henry dithered, uncertain whether to take the bait. His effusiveness towards Richard, most in evidence in December when he announced a quixotic project to make him king of Provence as his vassal (even though he did not control Provence) seems to have dissipated by the New Year, possibly because he blamed Richard for the secret marriage of his cousin Agnes to Henry the Lion's son (contracted some time between November 1193 and January 1194) – which he construed as an act hostile to him. Even though the true reason for the marriage was Agnes's desire to be taken off the marriage market before Philip of France could get at her – she knew about the farce with Ingeborg of Denmark and wanted no repeat performance – instead of blaming Philip for the contretemps, Henry chose to blame Richard.[66]

For the second half of 1193 Richard was mainly at Worms, though he spent Christmas at Speyer.[67] There were now some grounds for anxiety, since Henry had put back the date of his release until 4 February at the earliest and convened a summit conference at Mainz two days before to

discuss the final terms of Richard's release. A massive crowd of notables crowded into the imperial halls, including, on Richard's side chancellor Longchamp, Walter de Coutances, archbishop of Rouen, Eleanor
of Aquitaine and Savaric de Bohun, bishop of Bath. In the enemy corner
were Leopold of Austria, Conrad, duke of Swabia and the tame bishops
of Worms and Speyer; official neutrals were represented by the duke of
Louvain, Conrad Hohenstaufen, Count Palatine of the Rhine and the
archbishops of Cologne and Mainz. 'Anxious and difficult' (Walter of
Rouen's words)[68] negotiations then ensued, but one clearly hopeful sign
was that, just before the meeting, Henry signalled his willingness to bind
up imperial wounds and compose the Welf and Hohenstaufen factions
by accepting the marriage of Henry of Brunswick (Henry the Lion's
son). The other auspicious sign for Richard was that among the so-called
neutrals were his old friends the archbishops of Mainz and Cologne,
who had headed the anti-emperor faction in 1192–93. This meant that
a powerful coalition of German princes was exerting maximum leverage
on Henry VI; to listen to the siren voices of Philip and John might mean
finally plunging the empire into civil war.[69]

By 4 February the final terms were agreed and ratified: Richard would
pay 100,000 marks to Henry VI and 50,000 to Leopold and do homage to
the emperor. Hostages, including the son of Sancho of Navarre, the two
sons of the duke of Saxony, Longchamp, Savaric of Bath and the archbishop of Rouen were taken for Richard's performance of the terms,
though a minor sensation was caused when Robert de Nunat, brother
of the bishop of Coventry, was named as a hostage and refused to serve
on the ground that he was Prince John's man; instant imprisonment was
his punishment.[70] On the advice of Eleanor of Aquitaine, Richard
formally divested himself of the kingdom of England and granted it to
the emperor as the 'lord of all men'; following a pre-arranged rigmarole,
Henry then gave back the kingdom to Richard in front of witnesses,
subject to a yearly tribute of £5,000 sterling. This was a humiliation for
the Lionheart but a necessary face-saving formula for Henry, who was
being taunted by Leopold of Austria for conceding too much. On paper
it meant that Richard was now Philip's vassal for that part of the Angevin
empire that lay on the continent and Henry's for England.[71] To save
Richard's face this part of the Mainz settlement was hushed up. It
remained a dead letter, and on Henry's death (28 September 1197) the
payment of the £5,000 was remitted.[72] The emperor and all his magnates
then sent a letter under their seals, requiring Philip and John to restore
to Richard all castles and towns seized by them during the king's captivity,

and pledged the full resources of the empire to Richard if the king of France refused; this clause, too, remained a dead letter.[73]

Richard was finally a free man again, having been in captivity for one year, six weeks and three days, but his freedom had cost the subjects of the Angevin empire dear. 100,000 marks was twice Richard's annual income from England, though naturally as master of the Angevin empire he did not receive income only from England. All the duchies and provinces of the empire, particularly the monasteries, felt the effects of raising such an enormous sum, and Exchequer Rolls bear eloquent testimony to the gigantic hole made in the respective accounts of England, Normandy, Britanny and Aquitaine.[74] Quite how much of the ransom was actually paid to Henry VI remains controversial to this day. Some say that when the German emperor waived the payment of 17,000 marks in November 1195 (in order to prevent Richard from making peace with Philip of France), that was the only part of the debt to the emperor left outstanding, and this seems plausible.[75] It was this massive influx of cash that enabled Henry to ride high in 1194. Aided by the sudden death of Tancred of Sicily in February 1194 (historians have often remarked on the almost supernatural run of good luck Henry enjoyed in 1193–94), he swept across the Alps, down into Sicily and had himself crowned king of the island at Palermo on 22 November 1194. All this was made possible at root because of his hoard of Angevin silver. Yet there are many aspects of the actual money handed over which remain puzzling. The official ransom contracted for was 100,000 marks to the emperor and 50,000 to Leopold of Austria, yet it seems that in the end Austria never received a penny. Somehow, in all the final financial negotiations, Henry must have beaten Leopold down to a final payment of 25,000 marks, for unimpeachable evidence established that by the end of 1194 only 4,000 marks had been paid to Austria and 21,000 were still owing.[76]

The undaunted and secretly defiant Richard made his true feelings clear by writing to Henry of Champagne in Outremer to promise that he would soon be back with the crusaders in the Holy Land, once he settled with Philip of France, and provided God allowed him vengeance against his enemies.[77] God certainly seemed to be on the Lionheart's side when Leopold of Austria was humbled. First, the Pope excommunicated him for having imprisoned a crusader and ordered him to repay the ransom money. Leopold waved aside the anathema and refused to return any money; it appears that the 21,000 marks outstanding were due to arrive with Eleanor of Britanny when she came to Germany for the forced marriage with his son.[78] Richard attempted to stall on this part of the release agreement, and seven months after his departure from Germany there was still no sign of Eleanor. At this point Leopold threatened to execute the hostages if the bride was not produced. One of these unfortunates, Baldwin of Bethune, Richard's old comrade on the mad attempted dash across Germany, took the news to Richard and informed him that the dreadful Leopold was not bluffing. Reluctantly Richard bade farewell to Eleanor, who began the journey back to Germany with Baldwin. Yet even as they were on their way, miraculous tidings overtook them. On 26 December 1194 Leopold was injured when his horse threw him and fell on top of him. Next day his foot was a hideous black, and his surgeons advised rapid amputation, while declaring themselves incompetent to perform the operation. When no one could be induced, forced, cajoled or bribed to cut the gangrenous foot off, Leopold ordered his servants to chop it off with an axe. After three agonising strikes they succeeded, but it was too late. On 31 December Leopold died. On his deathbed he recanted his actions, made peace with the Church and promised to repay every penny mulcted from Richard. The hostages returned home.[79] The devout drew the moral that this was what happened to evil men who tried to interfere with God's holy work by imprisoning a crusader.

Just before Richard departed for his own lands, Henry VI reiterated that it was his firm policy to make Philip of France a vassal of the empire and to curb his overweening ambitions.[80] This policy was the genesis of the alliances, at first sight gratuitous, that Richard made with a whole host of German princes, making them pensionaries of the Angevin empire into the bargain. The lucky beneficiaries of yet more money from Angevin empire taxpayers were, among others, the dukes of Austria, Swabia, Brabant and Limburg, the marquis of Montferrat, the Count Palatine of the Rhine, the count of Holland, Baldwin the son of the count of Hainault, the archbishops of Mainz and Cologne and the bishop-elect of Liège.[81] Although there is doubt about how many of these pensions were in fact paid – except to those who had actually been instrumental in securing his release – Richard's German alliance endured and was a fixed feature of English foreign policy until 1214. As with so many of Richard's dealings with German princes, there is much in the detail here that is obscure. The magnates had to pay homage to Richard in return for the nominal pensions, but is it really credible that his mortal enemy the duke of Austria should have gone through such a charade, to say nothing of the implausibility of Richard's promising to pay him even more money? Similarly, there is confusion about Richard's policy in the Low Countries. On the one hand, he was supposed to be detaching Philip from his most valuable ally, Baldwin VIII, count of Flanders, yet on the other he was pledged to help the duke of Brabant (Louvain) in his feud against Baldwin.[82]

Richard's first major stop on the journey back to England was Cologne, where he spent three days as the guest of his friend the archbishop. The sung mass in the cathedral on 12 February contained the pointed words: 'Now I know that God has sent his angel and taken me from the land of Herod.' He was at Louvain on 16 February and at Brussels on the 25th.[83] At Antwerp next day a flotilla of ships from England met him, but Richard tarried in the port for a week and then spent another five days in Zwin, ostensibly delayed by the weather but really, the best historians think, scouting out the estuaries, inlets and islands of the Low Countries, assessing the plausibility of Philip Augustus's oft-made threat of an invasion of England and charting the waters.[84] At last, on 13 March, he landed at Sandwich, from where he hastened to Canterbury, declaring that he did not want to visit any other church in England until he had visited the seat of St Thomas Becket of blessed memory – proof in itself that Richard was an able ecclesiastical politician.[85] Although one may doubt whether Richard, always more a Frenchman than an English king, really did say that he did not consider himself truly freed from the yoke of Henry VI until he had trodden English soil, there is no doubt that in the month of his homecoming he enjoyed a honeymoon relationship with the Anglo-Norman realm.[86] The explosion of joy, at any rate among the literate classes, seems genuine. William Marshal, often at cross-purposes with Richard in the past, missed the funeral of his brother John so that he could greet the king in person.[87]

Making his way to London via Rochester, Richard was feted at a thanksgiving service in St Paul's, where Ralph of Coggleshall, in a justifiably hyperbolic moment, claimed that the heavens themselves rejoiced. Even the normally sceptical French received glowing reports from their spies about the enthusiastic popular reception of the homecoming king. The impatient Lionheart stayed just one day in the capital, then rode north to Nottingham by way of Bury St Edmund's and Huntingdon.[88] It was time to deal with his treacherous brother and indeed, while the king was still on his way to England, the great Council had declared all John's estates forfeit and the assembled bishops excommunicated him.[89] By now John's supporters were panicking. It was said that the castellan of St Michael's Mount in Cornwall dropped dead of fright when he heard the Lionheart had landed. Once the constable of Tickhill castle ascertained that King Richard really had returned from the crusade, he and the garrison surrendered without a fight on the promise that their lives would be spared. Only Nottingham castle held out, and it was this that Richard immediately besieged on his arrival there on 25 March, commencing operations with just a few hours of daylight left. Such were his military talents that he took the outer bailey and the barbican before dusk came on. When the garrison burned down the castle's outer works during the night, Richard retaliated by bringing up two pieces of equipment: siege engines with which to batter down the citadel and gallows, on which the previous night's prisoners were ostentatiously hanged, to show the defenders what was in store for them. On the 27th he gave a safe-conduct for two knights from the garrison to visit his camp, and showed them his scars, as if to a doubting Thomas. What the envoys reported back did the trick: fourteen knights left the citadel at once, and the more recalcitrant rump of defenders threw in the towel next day.[90]

In accordance with the chivalric code – which was to protect men of high birth and sacrifice all commoners – Richard pardoned the aristocratic rebels, on payment of hefty ransoms, but punished their foot soldiers severely, hanging all the sergeants.[91] Yet he was very angry about the rebellion and decided to make an example of two of the oligarchs who had supported John in his treason. He flayed one of them to death and ordered that another be starved to death in prison. This unfortunate, Robert of Brito, was a marked man as he was the brother of that Hugh de Nonant who had so enraged Richard by refusing to be a hostage in Germany on the grounds that he was John's man.[92] Next Richard turned to administration, involving his council during an exhausting four-day session commencing on 30 March in shaking up the system of sheriffs, both appointing new ones and making them pay more for their office-holding.[93] Richard liked to reward the faithful by granting them these lucrative offices, but he was not above neutralising potential troublemakers like his half-brother Geoffrey, appointing him sheriff of Yorkshire. For all that, he still had to spend valuable time at the council trying to sort out the multitudinous feuds and quarrels Geoffrey, a true scion of the Devil's Brood, had become involved in, principally with the chancellor and Hubert Walter; it was enough that someone enjoyed Richard's favour for Geoffrey to find a reason to assail him.[94] On the second day of his council, Richard discussed the legal implications of the case against John and his partisan Hugh de Nonant, bishop of Coventry, making watertight arrangements for the disposal and running

of the forfeited estates. Nonant was ordered to submit 'to the judgement of bishops in that he was himself a bishop and to the judgement
of laymen in that he was a sheriff of the king'. Deprived of his three
sheriffdoms (in Stafford, Leicester and Warwick), he was later allowed
to buy the king's pardon for 2,000 marks but was effectively disgraced,
retiring to Normandy where he died in 1198.[95] The third day was taken
up with budgetary and fiscal matters, introducing new taxes and varying
the rates and conditions of existing ones and their exemptions. Day four
saw a demand from his councillors to a reluctant Richard that he should
make a public display of kingship at Winchester on 7 April, so that
everyone could know that he had returned from crusade and captivity
stronger and more powerful than ever.[96]

Richard was destined to become a legendary figure on three main
counts: his duel with Saladin in Palestine; Blondel's fictitious 'finding' of
him at Durnstein castle; and his alleged connection with Robin Hood.
It was on 29 March, just before the four-day council, that Richard
approached the realm of myth most closely, for on this day he made a
visit to Sherwood Forest. Legend makes this the day he met and pardoned
the outlaws of Sherwood but sober history, alas, records no such
encounter. The quest for a historical Robin Hood is as entertaining, but
just as fruitless, as the search for a historical Arthur. Robin is clearly a
creature of syncretism, part woodland spirit, part a confused recollec-
tion of some historical figure. It is tempting to see him as an entirely
mythical creation, and the circumstantial evidence for this is compelling.
Both outlaws and fairies live in the forest, both wear green, and Robin
is a name for spirits, as in Robin Goodfellow. Robin Hood was the traditional figure of the medieval summer festival, of May Day rites and
Morris dances. The story of the apple shot off a human head by expert
archery is a motif common to William Tell and Norse legend. The
character of Maid Marian underlines the link to fertility cults, even though
she is a later accretion to the Robin Hood ballads (like Lancelot in
the Arthurian cycle). Whether mischievous woodland sprite or more
profound fertility symbol, Robin would therefore link with Herne
the Hunter and the legendary King Arthur in terms of ontology.
Some researchers go even further and assert that Robin, or Puck, was
really a warlock leading a coven of witches (the Merrie Men).[97] But the
difficulties of (literally) spiriting away Robin into the ether of pure legend
and mythology are legion. Many aspects of the Robin Hood ballads –
our only reliable source for the entire story – make no sense or become
even more mysterious if not granted some kind of historical basis. What

is the meaning of the persistent 'topos' of yeomanry against noblemen – an issue which becomes even more problematical if Robin is considered historically? Does not the theme of Saxon versus Norman (which so influenced Sir Walter Scott), making Robin a kind of latter-day Hereward the Wake, suggest something more than mere pagan fertility rites? And how do we explain the archetype of Robin as master of the longbow, given that the longbow came to the fore only in the years 1333–1453, roughly between the battles of Halidon Hill and Chastillon?[98]

For this reason it has usually been argued that there must be some historical tincture to the story of Robin Hood. Many are the candidates as the possible 'real' Robin. One of the prime sources for the legend, Fordun's *Scotichronicon*, places Robin Hood firmly in the period immediately after Simon de Montfort's defeat at Evesham in 1265; here he features as a mere cut-throat (*siccarius*), one of the dissident 'primitive rebels' (or on some fanciful views a proto-parliamentarian in the de Montfort mould).[99] William Stukeley, the famous eighteenth-century antiquarian, was adamant that he should be identified as one Robert fitz Ooth (1160–1247), earl of Huntingdon, but others locate him around the year 1322, involved in the rising of Thomas, earl of Lancaster.[100] Another favourite candidate as Robin Hood is the Robin Hod, aka Robin of Loxley in Barnsdale Forest, who appears in the records of York Assizes and in the Wakefield Rolls and is tentatively assigned dates of 1290–1347. But the truth is that there are so many possible Robin Hoods spreading over a two-hundred-year period, ranging from such unlikely characters as Sir Robert Foliot (1110–65) and Robert de Kyme (1210–85), that the historian must throw up his hands in despair.[101] Possibly the most cogent historical argument yet made is that Robin Hood may be the man mentioned in the 1230 Pipe Roll and also involved in the rebel movement led by Sir Robert Twing in 1231–32 – an inference strengthened by the fact that the ballads overwhelmingly place Robin in the first part of the thirteenth century.[102] The tradition (which has now become the 'hegemonic' one in popular culture) that Robin was extant in the 1190s and led the opposition to John while Richard was on crusade, was first mooted by the Scottish historian John Major in 1521 and was later heavily promulgated by writers as diverse as Sir Walter Scott, Augustin Thierry and L.V.D. Owens.[103] Unfortunately for those who prefer romance to fact, this notion has less real historical authority than most of the other candidates. If there was a 'real' Robin, he should almost certainly be sought somewhere in the years 1215–1381. One of the core problems concerning an historical Robin Hood is that there is no consensus on where he should be located geographically. Sherwood Forest near Nottingham is the traditional abode of the 'Merrie Men' but Barnsdale Forest in Yorkshire has many powerful backers and in some ways makes more sense of the ballad evidence: roughly speaking, we can say that a thirteenth-century setting favours Nottingham and the four-teenth century Yorkshire.[104] Yet even these waters are muddied, for some sleuths contend that the said Barnsdale Forest refers to the Forest of Barnsdale in Rutland (whose lord was the earl of Huntingdon) rather than the Barnsdale Forest in Yorkshire. As for chronology, the issue of the longbow argues for the latest possible dates, since even in Simon de Montfort's time this weapon had not been invented. The most plausible overall suggestion is that the ballad cycles are concerned with two very different men, possibly a nobleman in Sherwood and a yeoman in Barnsdale, conflated to form 'Robin Hood' and thus like the two different stories of Odysseus and Ulysses in Homer's *Odyssey*.[105]

We must return to the world of documented historical fact. On 4 April, at Southwell, Richard met King William of Scotland, who had come south to ask to have the counties of Northumberland, Westmorland, Cumberland and Lancashire restored to him, as in the days of Scottish kings of yore. For eighteen days the two monarchs were together, with Richard charming and accommodating, but forever finding reasons not to grant William's request. He had a difficult balancing act to perform, as William's demand was unacceptable, but Richard owed him for past services and, besides, did not want to alienate him and thus set his northern frontier alight. Richard fobbed off his fellow king by speaking earnestly of the need to discuss the matter in a grand council of all the English nobility. Meanwhile he flattered, cajoled and feasted William as the two of them wound their way slowly southwards, spending nights in Melton Mowbray, Geddington and Northampton. Finally, in Northampton, where they remained four nights, Richard could stall no longer. Summoning an ad hoc council to paper over a foregone conclu-sion, he then told William that what he asked was impossible at present, but sweetened the pill by inviting him to the second coronation that the council at Nottingham had insisted on, adding that he would have some-thing advantageous to tell him there. Cutting across country via Silverstone, Woodstock and Fremantle, he arrived in Winchester, the coronation venue.[106]

On the Sunday after Easter (17 April) Richard was recrowned in the presence of his mother and all the notables of the realm. The king of Scotland, Ranulf, earl of Chester, and Hamelin, earl Warenne carried the three ceremonial swords, while four other earls bore the canopy.[107] The evening was rounded off with a great feast but, before banqueting, Richard did two significant things. First, he sent envoys to the Pope, asking the Holy Father to demand the release of the hostages held in Austria, the return of all monies paid to Leopold plus a substantial sum in compensation for the injuries and insults inflicted on him in captivity.[108] Then he granted William of Scotland a charter paying all his expenses whenever he visited England. William was taken aback: he expected more from the cryptic promise made to him at Northampton on 11 April. Noticing Richard's acute sensitivity on matters financial, as evinced by the embassy to Rome, a few days later he offered 25,000 marks for Northumberland alone, with all its castles. Richard replied that he would sell Northumberland for that price, but without the castles. A disconsolate William departed on 22 April, having achieved nothing, but by no means bitter or scheming, as John or Philip Augustus would have been; his extremely good relations with the Lionheart continued.[109] Indeed, the good relations England enjoyed with Scotland during his reign were a major achievement when one ponders the turbulent and bloody relations between the two nations before and after. In 1195 King William went so far as to propose marrying his daughter Margaret to Richard's nephew Otto and making him heir to the Scottish throne. Although the scheme foundered when William's queen suddenly became pregnant and he began to hope for a male heir, the mere fact that the Otto-Margaret match was broached in the first place shows the warmth of Anglo-Scottish relations in the 1190s.[110]

As William made his way dejectedly north from Winchester, Richard moved rapidly south towards Portsmouth, intending to cross the Channel as soon as possible. There was bad news from France, for Philip Augustus had found a pretext to denounce the truce, which should have lasted until 5 June. Pausing only at Bishop's Waltham, where he thought it best to conciliate the peevish archbishop of York, his half-brother Geoffrey (Geoffrey had pointedly stayed away from the coronation at Winchester), by restoring him to his lands in Anjou, Richard, in company with his mother Eleanor, arrived in Portsmouth on 24 April. But the elements were against him, so that he had to wait for fair weather for three weeks; an impatient attempt to clear for France in a gale had to be aborted with loss of face.[111] Fuming with frustration, Richard spent a day hunting at Stansted, then rationalised his compulsory sojourn by the great natural harbour by deciding to make Portsmouth the site of a great naval base; Richard was always interested in sea power, and some scholars are even

prepared to date the first glimmerings of Britain's eventual naval hegemony to this decision. Portsmouth as an arsenal also made sense in terms
of the geopolitics of the Angevin empire, for troops could be rushed
from England to troublespots in Normandy, Poitou and Aquitaine.[112]

On 12 May Richard finally set sail and landed the same day at Barfleur
in Normandy. No one had any reason to think he would never see
England again, as turned out to be the case. He has been much criticised for his alleged neglect of his island kingdom, and his dismissive
remark is often quoted that he cared 'not an egg' for England. Richard
spoke no English and undoubtedly had no particular sentimental attachment for the country, as he had for Aquitaine. It is also true that England
seems to have borne a disproportionate share of the financial burden
of his ransom from captivity, though, if the hyperbolic boasts of Hubert
Walter can be believed, this soon came to seem almost a drop in the
ocean; Hubert claimed in 1196 that in the last two years he had raised
over a million marks for him.[113] In light of the oft-heard criticism that
Richard neglected England and treated her simply as a cash-cow, it might
be appropriate to highlight four specific areas of achievement, where
it can be proved that Richard performed right royally. The first was in
his relations with the Celtic fringes: with a few marginal exceptions,
England had no trouble with Ireland, Scotland or Wales during his
reign.[114] The second was in his military reforms. Having observed the
calibre of French knights on the crusade and (to his own satisfaction at
least) having established that this was because they trained hard by
jousting, Richard decided to follow their example and ignore the papal
interdict on tournaments. He designated five venues (in Warwickshire,
Northamptonshire, Suffolk, Nottinghamshire and Wiltshire) as tournament sites, all licensed, taxed and directed from the centre by administrators close to Hubert Walter (his brother was appointed collector of
tournament fees). William Marshal later testified that the quality of
English knighthood increased exponentially in just five years (1194–99).[115]

Yet it was the overall excellence of English administration and the
efficiency of tax-collection that was probably most impressive in
Richard's reign. Some say that Richard was lucky, that he inherited a well-
oiled machine from Henry II, which was why England was able to sustain
the burden of the 150,000 mark ransom. Others push beyond this to
the assertion that Richard was a mindless warmonger with no interest
in economics or administration, that he was lucky in having in his service
an organiser of genius like Hubert Walter.[116] The best scholarship,
however, reveals Richard as a highly intelligent monarch who knew

exactly what he was doing when he delegated authority in England. The introduction of customs duty – a new tax that substantially enabled him to make war on Philip Augustus for the five years of 1194–99 – shows both ingenuity and imagination.[117] One must, however, concede a partial role to contingency and luck, for in Hubert Walter Richard found a rare jewel. Having caught Richard's eye on crusade and further enhanced his prospects by his diplomatic skill in Germany, the new archbishop of Canterbury turned out to be in reality what Henry II had only been able to dream about in the case of Thomas Becket. Longchamp had been loyal but lacking the essential political skill and administrative gifts. Hubert, appointed chief justiciar in succession to Walter of Coutances at Christmas 1193 and made a papal legate two years later, was a brilliant combination of all the talents needed to govern England as Richard's right arm.[118] Naturally the combination of offices in Hubert's hands attracted great envy and jealousy and he was therefore much maligned by hostile critics, especially the more saintly bishops who thought him a wordly cleric, but no one has seriously questioned his credentials or his role as Richard's cynosure. It is sometimes insinuated that England without Richard worked on a kind of automatic 'cruise control', but it must never be forgotten that, for all Hubert's brilliance, it was the shrewd Lionheart who had talent-spotted and headhunted him for his dominant role.

11

RICHARD'S ARRIVAL IN BARFLEUR was an occasion for joyous celebration and feasting by his subjects, who were proud of their
king, acknowledged throughout the Western world as the greatest
warrior in Christendom. William Marshal testified that even in a long
career of witnessing royal triumphs and processions, he had never seen
anything quite like it.[1] Richard brought with him a hundred ships, men,
arms, siege engines and money, but he was under no illusions about the
scale of the task in front of him. Ever since the fall of Gisors in April
1193 Philip Augustus had carried all before him, and now held large slabs
of conquered territory in eastern Normandy, including the port of
Dieppe. Most of the frontier lords on the marches between Normandy
and France had gone over to Philip once they heard of Richard's imprisonment in Germany and believed the widespread propaganda that he
would never be freed. Having acquired Artois from Flanders in 1192,
while Richard was still on crusade, Philip was already the most powerful
king of France since Carolingian times, and some assessed his combined
wealth and resources as greater than that of the Angevin empire.[2] A host
of rebel lords in Aquitaine had raised the banner on Philip's behalf and,
in northern France, he still possessed what looked like an invaluable asset
in the person of Prince John, here acting in his capacity as count of
Mortain. On paper Richard had few assets: the loyalty of the ex-crusader
Earl Robert of Leicester, who had lost lands and castles through being
true to his liege lord, and the dependable alliance with Sancho of Navarre,
which had saved his position in Aquitaine.[3]

Part of Richard's careful preparations for the coming titanic conflict
involved assembling a totally professional army. Since feudal levies
following their lords were limited by custom to military service of no
more than forty days, Richard tried to dispense with technically feudal
service altogether so as to create something resembling a standing army.
This he did partly by requiring knights to serve for twelve months, partly

by recruiting professional troops from Wales, and partly by the use of mercenaries. The regulars were well paid: a knight received one shilling a day, while Welsh men-at-arms got 4d a day if mounted and 2d a day if infantry. The mercenaries were of two kinds: the Genoese cross-bowmen and others brought back from the crusade; and the despera-does and adventurers generically known as Brabançons or routiers, recruited by his famous captains of irregulars like Mercadier or Gérard de Athée.[4] Since the routiers were a byword for savagery, even Henry II had restricted their use in England to the single occasion of the 1173–74 revolt by the Young King, though the justiciars had employed them in Richard's absence in 1193 to deal with John's rebellion.[5] Barbarous rapists and murderers who struck terror into every civilian's heart, the Brabançons happily slaughtered old men and women, children, young women (after ravishing them), priests, civilians, traders – it mattered not, so long as they were in the path of the whirlwind. The use of routiers had been forbidden by the fifth canon of the Lateran Council in 1179, but the mindset denoted by the later famous question – 'how many divi-sions has the pope?' – was already in evidence in feudal Europe. Richard had scruples in warfare, but they did not extend to men who in his eyes were traitors and perjurers and those who abetted them; since this included Philip Augustus and all his allies, the luckless townsfolk of eastern Normandy and the Aquitaine were clearly in for a thin time from May 1194 on. Moreover, Richard had brought back from the Middle East new technologies acquired from the Saracens or refined in warfare against them, such as the dreaded Greek fire (a combustible mixture of sulphur, pitch and naphtha) first used in England at the siege of Nottingham in early 1194. He had even recruited some Saracen fighters – surprisingly this did not provoke the outcry in Christian Europe one might have expected – and they are recorded as being in the thick of fights at Domfront and in the forest of Le Passeis.[6]

There was supposed to be a truce in the whole of north-eastern France, but Philip had engineered a breakdown on the basis of some dubious raiding by a party of bandits allegedly from England.[7] On 10 May he began the siege of the castle of Verneuil, and it was news of this action that made Richard champ and chafe in Portsmouth.[8] Overconfident, presumably because they knew the Lionheart was on his way to relieve them, the defenders mocked and ridiculed Philip in crude burlesques, but this simply made him more determined to force the stronghold's surrender. While storms and gales kept Richard hemmed in Portsmouth harbour, Philip brought up his strongest siege engines and

managed to demolish part of the castle walls.[9] It was 21 May before
Richard arrived in the vicinity, and at Tuboeuf he met a knight who had
managed to breach the blockade and ride for help. With his customary
rapidity of thought, Richard devised a twofold stratagem: a picked force
of knights, Welsh infantry and crossbowmen was sent to break through
the French lines and relieve the garrison; while a larger force was sent
round to the east of Verneuil to cut Philip's communications. On 28
May Philip split his forces and rode off with half to Evreux, leaving the
other half to continue the siege; but the detachment left behind, demoralised by their king's sudden departure, promptly abandoned the task and
fled. Richard's forces, soon in hot pursuit, captured Philip's entire siege
train, and on 30 May the Lionheart himself entered the castle.[10] So pleased
was he by the garrison's valour and steadfastness that he kissed each man
in turn and marked them down for huge financial rewards, large enough
to figure prominently in the 1195 Norman exchequer role.[11]

Why had Philip broken off a promising siege so abruptly? The answer
lay with his untrustworthy ally John. Once Richard arrived on the soil
of Normandy, John went to pieces, sped to Lisieux (where Richard was
staying at the house of John of Alençon), and gambled on securing his
brother's forgiveness. Eyewitnesses reported John as being in a high state
of nervous agitation before he went in for the interview but he was reassured when John of Alençon told him: 'The king is merciful and straight-
forward, and kinder to you than you would be to him.'[12] John entered
the royal presence and fell at his brother's feet. Richard raised him up
and said soothingly, but with an oceanic subtext of patronising contempt,
'Have no fear, John, you are but a child. It is those who led you astray
who will be punished.'[13] Richard's merciful treatment contrasts strikingly
with the brutality he could evince at other times, most notably to
the Saracen prisoners after the fall of Acre. Some speculate that, like
Napoleon, who demonstrated similar brutality in the very same theatre
of war, Richard was excessively family-minded, that the up side of
the ultra-competitive spirit among the siblings of the Devil's Brood was
a Mafia-like solidarity towards kin. We know that Eleanor of Aquitaine
was at Lisieux, and her instinct was always on the side of patching up
quarrels between John and her beloved Richard, if only because, if
Richard died, she did not want the Crown passing out of the family.
William Le Breton simply stated that, although Richard hated John for
his cruelty, treachery and weakness, he still loved him as a brother
should.[14] Certainly John fared far better at Richard's hands than he
deserved to. John's next action was typical of the man. Presumably to

show his gratitude to his brother, John hastened back to Evreux and ordered all the French civilians there slaughtered, while announcing that he held the town now for Richard, not Philip.[15] It was volcanic rage at this atrocity that led Philip to ride off to Evreux, leaving the investment of Verneuil to peter out. When he heard that John had compounded his treachery by inviting the principal French commanders to a meal and then having them cut down as they sat at table, Philip joined the epidemic of mindless fury by forcing John to retreat and then methodically sacking Evreux, as if it were the burghers who had been the treacherous ones. Coming on top of the Ingeborg fiasco and the previous outburst of rage when he had burned his own siege engines, even the official French historians were aghast at the crazed behaviour of their king.[16]

Philip next laid siege to the castle of Fontaines, just five miles from Rouen, to cock a snook at Richard and dent his credibility – by investing a stronghold so close to the capital of the duchy of Normandy. Outnumbered and outmatched, John and the earl of Leicester lurked in Rouen and did not try conclusions with the French. But it was a case of trebuchets to squash a mosquito, for it took Philip four days to reduce and demolish an insignificant fortress.[17] Yet the French king had a stroke of luck as he turned away from the siege, for the earl of Leicester, out on a foray, fell into his hands. Philip thought this an opportune moment to propose another truce, but Richard was adamant that those lords of Normandy who had committed treason against him should not enjoy the luxury and privileges of a ceasefire.[18] Treason and treachery were evidently still on his mind when he reached Tours, and the city must have harboured many a turncoat and trimmer, for the city fathers made the extravagant gesture of contributing 2,000 marks to the English war chest provided there were no reprisals for earlier 'mistakes'.[19] The Lionheart hit back at Philip's pyrrhic victory at Fontaines by besieging and taking three truly important castles – at Loches, Montmirail and Beaumont le Roger. These strongholds were a huge distance apart, and Richard demonstrated once again his mastery of logistics and strategy by dividing his army temporarily and sending a detachment to each of the three corners of his empire.[20]

The capture of Loches was materially aided by the armies of Sancho of Navarre, who proved a hammer of those southern rebels Ademar of Angoulême and Geoffrey de Rancon. But it took Richard to achieve the fall of Loches. Sancho returned to Spain on news that his father was dying, yet his forces remained outside Loches, though without making much impression on the castle. On 13 June, in one colossal assault, the

Lionheart took it by storm in a single day.[21] Concentrating now on Aquitaine and the crushing of all the southern rebels, he moved on to besiege Vendôme. Although Philip's army was within striking distance, the French king himself did not relish a pitched battle with a man so manifestly superior in arms. He turned his army round and began retreating, but Richard fell on his rearguard at Fréteval on 4 July and added another easy victory to his tally. The Anglo-Norman army pursued, with Richard on horseback desperate to catch up with Philip and make him a prisoner. Mercadier and William Marshal particularly distinguished themselves that day. Disappointed in his objective, Richard turned back to survey the fruits of his success. Philip had been forced to abandon his entire wagon train, containing vast amounts of treasure, horses, tents, siege engines and, most interestingly, the French royal archives, wherein Richard was able to find documentary evidence of all the Norman lords who had betrayed him.[22] Together with the 2,000 marks donated by Tours, on this campaign alone Richard was well on the way to recouping the vast sum spent on his ransom.

Striking out from his temporary base at Vendôme, in the first three weeks of July Richard fought another blitzkrieg campaign, smashing the rebels Geoffrey of Rancon and the count of Angoulême, capturing Taillebourg and many other castles, culminating in a glorious victory at Angoulême, where he captured the city and citadel in a single evening and scooped up 300 knights and a large number of infantrymen (Richard claimed the impossible number of 40,000). Verneuil, Loches, Fréteval, Taillebourg, Angoulême: the list of important Lionheart victories seemed endless.[23] In the south Richard carried all before him but in the prolonged struggle for dominance in the crucial marches of Normandy, between Rouen and Paris, the English king found the going much harder. Philip's strategy was to retire before Richard in the south but then to dig in and not yield an inch in the Seine valley, where his true interest lay.[24] He elected to make his stand at Vaudreuil, controlling the Seine bridges ten miles south of Rouen. Formerly one of John's castles in his capacity as count of Mortain and ceded as a token of fealty by John to Philip, Vaudreuil soon found itself besieged by forces commanded by John and the earl of Arundel, while Richard attended to matters in Aquitaine. Confident now that he faced only the militarily unimpressive brother and not the Lionheart himself, Philip made a forced march and arrived outside Vaudreuil with the cream of his forces. His attack on John was completely successful: while the Norman cavalry fled, Philip captured the Angevins' siege artillery and made most of their infantry prisoners.[25]

This setback in the north, plus simple war-weariness and financial exhaustion, led Richard to agree to a ceasefire. The truce of Tillières, signed on 23 July 1194, was supposed to run until 1 November 1195 and froze both sides on an 'as is' basis with regard to territory. Philip retained Vaudreuil, Gisors and Vexin and a host of other castles (effectively most of north-eastern Normandy), while Richard was only allowed to rebuild four of the many fortresses the French had devastated.[26] Since Richard's representatives negotiated the truce in ignorance of his victories in the south, and consequently extended amnesty to the major Aquitaine rebels, it was not surprising that Richard was reported very angry at the fait accompli his ambassadors had forced on him, and particularly the fact that 'treasonable rebels' were to enjoy all the benefits of the truce. The temporary peace was far too favourable to Philip, considering that Richard had won a string of victories. He also objected to the prominent role of the Church in brokering the agreement, sharing his father's distaste for ecclesiastical meddling in politics.[27] It seems that he made many representations to the German empire to petition the anti-Philip military aid vaguely promised in the release agreement at Mainz, but in vain. Richard's anger must have increased as he heard repeated reports of Henry VI's great successes in Italy, first in Apulia and Salerno and finally in Sicily where he overthrew the dynasty of Tancred.[28] Richard realised he was in for a long hard slog in the Seine valley if he was ever to restore the Angevin empire to its position when at the apogee under his father Henry II.

There followed a year of 'phoney peace', with both sides skirmishing, jockeying for position, building castles and generally waging a war of attrition in all areas from unofficial border 'incidents' to simple propaganda. Everyone knew the peace could not hold, for too many essential issues, especially concerning the Franco-Norman marches, had been swept under the carpet. The Lionheart, having inherited his father's restlessness, was almost constantly on the move. Based at Rouen, where he spent Christmas 1194, he spent time in Alençon, Tours, Poitiers, Chinon, Le Mans and elsewhere.[29] Richard used the interlude to patch up the many feuds and rows in his own family. In May 1195 he moderated his cold contempt towards John to the extent of restoring him to the counties of Mortain and Gloucester (his forgiveness the year before had obviously been partly a piece of theatre) and the living of Eye, and granting him a handsome income in Angevin livres in lieu of his other lands; significantly, though, he drew the line at restoring him his castles. John had to be content with witnessing charters and signing himself count of

Mortain.[30] In some ways an even more serious quarrel, with Richard's half-brother Geoffrey, archbishop of York, was also patched up. Here Richard's ire had been aroused by Geoffrey's high-handed use of the royal seal, on Henry II's death and without permission from Richard. He had dealt with this in the first instance by simply annulling the benefices made by Archbishop Geoffrey, but now he summoned him to France to effect a reconciliation, which seems to have been finalised very soon after the rapprochement with John.[31] The month before, Richard achieved his third family 'breakthrough' by a reconciliation with his wife Berengaria, capped by joint purchase of a country house near Sarthe.[32] We do not know the details of the estrangement, but it is clear that an uxorious man would not have sent his wife on by separate ship from the Holy Land. Scholarly ignorance about the rift between husband and wife has, naturally, encouraged speculators to assert that it 'must have been' because of the king's alleged homosexuality.[33]

Richard was by no means idle in this limbo period. Desultory peace talks, as also talks about talks, continued through the first half of 1195. One bizarre suggestion mooted was that all outstanding disputes be settled by a duel of champions, with five knights from each side deciding the issue. Philip seemed interested until it turned out that he and Richard were supposed to be two of the ten knights.[34] The scheme was hastily shelved. It was probably a pure propaganda exercise, like today's perennial proposals in Britain, likewise summarily turned down, that heads of political parties should debate face-to-face on television. During the year when he was free from major hostilities, Richard also followed international affairs closely, noting the safe return of all the hostages from Austria following Leopold's dramatic and untimely death, the return of Henry VI from Sicily to Frankfurt via Como, the death of Henry, duke of Saxony (his brother-in-law) at Brunswick, and of Baldwin V, count of Hainault at Mons, and also the demise of Isaac the deposed 'emperor' of Cyprus.[35] Yet it was only when Henry VI was back in Germany that the international dimension impinged to the point where France once again became a battleground. In June Henry sent Richard a golden crown and charged him 'by the fealty which he owed him' to invade the domain of the king of France, this time promising that he really would send military aid.[36] Alerted to this by his spies and alarmed by what it portended, Philip denounced the truce and ordered most of the castles he held in Normandy demolished – a kind of Ascalon in reverse, informed by the conviction that he could not beat Richard on the battlefield. The story is told that Richard and Philip met to parley at

Vaudreuil but were overwhelmed by dust and debris as Philip's engineers managed to bring the castle walls tumbling down even as Richard was supposed to be negotiating its eventual fate. 'By God's legs I will see that saddles are emptied this day!' cried an enraged Richard. Philip barely escaped from the conference with his life and evaded pursuit by Richard by having the bridge over the Seine at Portjoie pulled down behind him.[37] General war was at once resumed, and Richard's great captain Mercadier, now promoted to general, captured Issoudoun in the important county of Berry.[38]

A major conflict was just about to be waged on all fronts, when more dramatic international news halted the war in its tracks. Terrible tidings were received from Spain that the king of Morocco had invaded and inflicted a signal defeat on a Christian army at Alarcos.[39] This conjured ancient memories of Islam and Charlemagne, of Charles Martel at Tours, of El Cid and the Almohads a century before. Most of all, it inevitably suggested a crusade in reverse. It was clearly necessary for the two powerful monarchs of Western Europe to lay down their arms and compose a permanent peace at such a critical juncture. Accordingly, another truce was called, and there were further parleys. Initial terms proposed included the return of Alice to Philip (at long last) and a marriage between Philip's son Louis and Eleanor of Britanny, Arthur's sister – the woman Leopold of Austria had earmarked for his son before his sudden death changed everything. Philip would renounce his claims in the counties of Angoulême, Aumale, Eu and Arques and return to Richard the castles he had seized during the Lionheart's captivity; more significantly, in exchange for 20,000 marks he would give back the Vexin.[40] The shorthand version of this proposal was that the Vexin would be given to Richard as a dowry for Eleanor, provided she married Louis. As a further sweetener, Philip publicly declared that Richard had had nothing to do with the assassination of Conrad of Montferrat.[41] All seemed set fair for a long-running truce, but Richard insisted that he first had to consult his 'liege lord' Henry VI. Philip meanwhile married his sister Alice to William, count of Ponthieu. Since he provided as her dowry the county of Eu and the town of Arques already pledged to Richard in the draft treaty, there are grounds for suspecting Philip of arch-machiavellianism.[42]

Richard certainly made a meal of his consultation with the emperor, sending his chancellor to the German court (as his opposite number went the archbishop of Rheims, representing France). Predictably, Henry VI refused to ratify the peace proposals, and it was on this occasion that he waived the final 17,000 marks of Richard's ransom, as a douceur.[43] All signs had anyway pointed to a renewal of hostilities before that, from the intriguing of William of Ponthieu to the arrival at the end of August (at Barfleur) of a fresh army from England. A further circumstantial pointer is that Longchamp's brother, abbot Henry of Croyland, found Richard uninterested in administrative and church matters, but preoccupied with military planning.[44] The sober conclusion is that both sides were preparing for war once the day set for a firm conclusion of the truce (8 November) arrived. It was Philip who jumped the gun, leading a dashing raid on Dieppe (which he had given back to Richard in July) that ended with the sack of the town and the gutting of the harbour with Greek fire.[45] The mind behind the raid, however, was the turbulent William of Ponthieu, who had more than one reason to hate Richard; Alice apart, Richard was even then besieging Arques, supposedly part of Alice's dowry but also promised to the Lionheart in the truce and which had never been handed over. It was never wise to try to outpoint Richard in wars of rapid movement, as Philip and his six hundred triumphant knights learned on their way back through the northern forests; with another lightning movement, Richard formed his Welsh veterans up in ambuscade and mauled the victors of Dieppe severely.[46] By the end of the year Richard had both Dieppe and the fallen Arques in his possession.

Piqued by this setback, Philip switched fronts and made another probe in the south. News had come in that there were two separate revolts in Aquitaine, one in the Perigord and another, more familiar manifestation, involving treasonous border lords in collusion with Raymond of Toulouse. Seeing a unique chance opening up, Philip appeared before the town of Issoudoun in Berry and took it after a very short siege; the garrison in the castle, however, continued to hold out. This was the kind of challenge at which Richard excelled. Leaving orders for his army to follow him with all speed on forced marches, he and a picked company of knights rode south at great speed, covering three days' journey in a single day. At Issoudoun Richard and his company broke through the French besiegers and appeared in the castle to the joy of the defenders. Philip thought that by his quixotry Richard had placed himself in a trap and continued with the siege, hoping soon to do with the Lionheart what Henry VI had done the year before. Suddenly the main Anglo-Norman army appeared in his rear, and he realised to his horror that he was caught between two fires; the hunter became the hunted. Out-thought, outclassed and outgeneralled, Philip swallowed hard and accepted the humiliation of an imposed truce on 5 December.[47] It was agreed that

all troops would go to their homes, that the truce would last until 13
January 1196, and that the two kings would then meet again to see if
the temporary peace terms could be made more permanent.[48] Richard
spent a satisfied Christmas at Poitiers, sufficiently relaxed to take an
interest in the election of a new bishop of Durham.[49]

The peace conference at Louviers in the Seine valley in January 1196
showed clearly that in the struggle for northern France Richard currently
held the advantage. He had expelled the French from all Channel ports,
regained all of Normandy except the Vexin, and got Philip to agree that
in the south Raymond of Toulouse was no more than a warmonger, and
his allies illegitimate rebels against the count of Aquitaine, to whom in
feudal law they properly owed homage and service.[50] The French
consoled themselves by the thought that in the treaty of Louviers Richard
had implicitly abandoned for all time his claim to the Norman Vexin.
Naturally Richard himself did not construe the treaty in that way at all;
for him it was merely a means of buying time until the time came to
renew the peace in June.[51] The common rallying point of the two
monarchs was their joint dislike of the archbishop of Rouen, in their
eyes yet another turbulent priest. The archbishop had grievances against
the two kings because of the damage done by both to his churches in
Normandy, and even tried to place Philip's lands under interdict. Richard
tried to silence the archbishop by making him surety for a payment of
2,000 marks to Philip, but the divine refused and fled to sanctuary with
the archbishop of Cambrai, where the two ecclesiastics devised a kind
of mutual assistance pact, to protect themselves against powerful
temporal lords. But Richard was before him. As soon as the archbishop
withdrew from the Louviers conference, Richard decreed that if the
churchman refused to act as his surety for the 2,000 marks, he would be
banished from Normandy and not allowed to return until he had either
paid the 2,000 marks or secured King Philip's permission to come back.[52]
Richard demonstrated on this occasion that he could be just as tough
as his father on any prince of the Church who overstepped his due
bounds.

That the peace of Louviers was shaky was immediately demonstrated
when Philip changed tack on the affair of the archbishop of Rouen.
First he issued safe-conducts for him and his confederate the archbishop
of Cambrai. Then he promised to make restitution of all the losses
sustained by the bishop. Seeing himself in danger of being marginalised
as an enemy of the Church, Richard then wrote to Rouen, assuring him
of his benevolence and releasing him from the onus of being a surety

for the 2,000 marks. In return he asked that the archbishop help him get the earl of Leicester (still a prisoner in Philip's hands, even though he had promised, in the treaty, to release him) freed by offering as a quid pro quo the withdrawal of the episcopal interdict.[53] When Rouen proved amenable, this particular headache seemed ended. But an even greater one almost at once supervened. Ever since Henry II's death, Britanny had been a weak link in the Angevin empire, so Richard decided to summon to his court his late brother Geoffrey's wife Constance, who had since remarried (to Ranulf of Chester) in a bizarre marriage of convenience, where the husband lived in England and the wife in Britanny. Apparently Richard had decided that holding Constance's daughter Eleanor as his ward was not enough for effective control of Britanny, that he needed Constance too. But this turn of events was too much for the absentee husband. Suddenly he appeared in Britanny and kidnapped his wife even as she prepared to obey Richard's summons.[54] Perplexed by this enigmatic sequence of events, Constance's Breton advisers appealed to Philip on the grounds that their duchess had been kidnapped by the Lionheart. Philip loved fishing in such troubled waters and engineered a virtual coup in Britanny, whereby the duchy revoked its allegiance to the Angevin empire. Richard could not stand idly by and tolerate such a signal threat to his sea power and cross-Channel communications, so invaded Britanny and swept all before him (in the Easter week of 1196).[55] The defeated Breton oligarchs responded by whisking Richard's heir-apparent Arthur off to Philip in Paris. When Philip publicly granted Arthur asylum, he made a virtual declaration of war against Richard. The English king responded by writing to Hubert Walter, urgently calling for more knights for a long campaign against France.[56]

The Arthur affair was a straw in the wind. By summer 1196, the diplomatic advantage seemed to have shifted to Philip. He had persuaded Baldwin IX, the new count of Flanders and Hainault, to join his anti-Angevin alliance, and with Baldwin and his (Philip's) brother-in-law the count of Ponthieu, he launched an attack on Aumale in July.[57] Richard retaliated by seizing Nonancourt, suborning the castellan so that it surrendered without a fight. From there he marched to Aumale but now, for the first time ever in his career, the God of war deserted him. Richard sustained his first serious reverse at the hands of Philip's forces — a defeat so embarrassing that the English chroniclers of his reign prefer to pass it by in silence. It seems that Richard failed to realise how gravely he was outnumbered and, once he did, faced the unpalatable choice of retreating and losing face or pressing on against impossible odds.[58] There was only one possible course for a Lionheart, but the dice was loaded against him, as events proved. On 20 August Aumale fell, and Richard had the further humiliation of having to pay 3,000 marks to ransom the garrison.[59] Although the French had taken heavy losses during the siege and from Richard's diversionary attack – which seems to have been directed at particularly strong French entrenchments – they completed the Angevin shame by not leaving one stone of Aumale standing on another.[60] That summer, 1196 turned into a disaster for Richard. Philip recaptured Nonancourt, the Lionheart himself was wounded by a crossbow quarrel and, as if to add insult to injury, the despised John took the fortress of Gamaches in the Norman Vexin.[61]

Once again both sides paused for breath. Increasingly convinced that his reconquest of the Vexin – his abiding aim – was not something that could be achieved by the previous strategy of lightning campaigns, however flamboyant and spectacular his individual victories might prove to be, Richard settled in for the long haul. His new project was the construction of a fortress in the Seine valley that would rival for impregnability the great crusader castles like Krak des Chevaliers. Château-Gaillard, as the new castle was called, was Richard's version of the Arthurian Joyous Garde. Built on a limestone rock 300 feet above the Seine and its companion new town Les Andelys, the castle had a most elaborate network of defences: outworks linking it to the town, which in turn was protected by bridged waterways and a stockade built across the river on the south side of the rock. A veteran of dozens of sieges, Richard knew all about the blind spots that allowed attackers to get inside the guard of defenders and be secure from their missiles – the so-called 'dead angles' – and combated them with curvilinear walls. Château-Gaillard turned out to be a mathematical gem: citadel, fortifications, crenellations, embrasures interlinking and in turn interpenetrating with the island town and the stockade so that the whole had the pleasing symmetry of a Bach sonata.[62] This was Richard the mathematician at work, in this, as in so much else, anticipating Napoleon. Throughout the winter of 1196, into the new year, and well into 1198 Richard kept his architects and builders, his masons and engineers, his soldiers and his civilian labourers hard at work completing his masterpiece. Chroniclers reported an anthill of activity, with water-carriers, carpenters, quarrymen, woodmen, miners, blacksmiths, hodcarriers and stonecutters all competing against each other for piece-work bonuses. Delighted with his handiwork, Richard declared that he would eventually be able to hold Château-Gaillard against all comers; the layout permitted a concentration of force at any locality such that he felt confident of defending the walls, as he put it, even if they were made of butter.[63]

Nothing could halt the frenzied pace of the building work on the fair castle of the rock (bellum castrum de Rupe). On 8 May 1197 there was a fall of red rain, which the superstitious interpreted as a shower of blood. Richard brushed aside the ill omen and said the work would go ahead even if an angel descended from heaven and ordered him to stop.[64] Château-Gaillard became something close to monomania with him, and its cost was astronomical – £12,000 in two years as against £7,000 spent on all other castles for the whole of Richard's reign. Even Henry II had not spent more than £7,000 on his showpiece, Dover Castle, which took twelve years to complete (1179–91). It is likely that Château-Gaillard was the most expensive castle built in all Europe until that date; it was certainly the most famous fortress in the Middle Ages.[65] Richard's obsession with his Camelot had some rational basis, for the castle was designed both as the ultimate in defence, blocking the direct route to Rouen, and as a command post from which he would launch an offensive to regain the Vexin, when the time was ripe.[66] In tandem with Château-Gaillard, which provided the funnel through which troops from Rouen could be poured into the marchlands of eastern Normandy, Richard developed his inchoate ideas on sea power, tested on the Mediterranean and against Saladin's fleets on the Seine, building a fleet of 'galleys' (probably versions of the Viking longship) with shallow hulls, designed for speed and riverine warfare.[67] Under the protective shelter of Château-Gaillard Richard built a port in the new town of Les Andelys for his pilot version of the flyboat. There was thus an elaborate network of sea power extending from Portsmouth to Rouen and up the Seine. To set the capstone on his great achievement, Richard built a palace in the town, which became by far his favourite residence.[68] For the rest of his life he was absent from the urban complex Les Andelys-Château-Gaillard only when campaigning.

The one snag with Château-Gaillard was that the territory of Les Andelys was technically the manor of Richard's old gadfly the archbishop of Rouen. The problems with this fiery cleric, which had only just been damped down, flared up once more as the archbishop strenuously objected to Richard's despotic and 'illegal' action in so contemptuously riding roughshod over his (Rouen's) prerogatives. To the archbishop it seemed the last straw that the king of England, who had devastated so much of his church property during the late war, should now filch the jewel in his episcopal crown – for the toll-house at Andeli, collecting dues from ships plying up and down the Seine, was one of his principal sources of income. Richard made the archbishop many tempting financial offers, but the stubborn divine turned them all down.[69] Angered and frustrated, Richard simply moved in and started the building work anyway. The archbishop thereupon laid Normandy under an interdict and set out for Rome to lay his case before the Pope.[70] Not wishing to share Leopold of Austria's fate at the hands of the papacy, Richard sent his own rival embassy, principally the troika of Philip of Poitou (bishop elect of Durham), the bishop of Lisieux, and his old warhorse, the faithful William Longchamp. Richard's mission began badly when Longchamp suddenly died at Poitiers, having barely begun the long journey.[71] In Rome the ambassadors fared better, since Pope Celestine and his cardinals were sympathetic to Richard; as many of them said, the entire war and castle-building programme was only taking place because Philip had defied a previous papal bull and seized the Vexin while Richard was on crusade. Celestine additionally thought that the archbishop of Rouen was being greedy and had been offered a fair price for Les Andelys, and moreover was guilty of the sin of pride, leaving the bodies of the dead in Normandy unburied simply because of a wrangle over filthy lucre. In April 1197 he raised the interdict and sent the fire-eating bishop back to Normandy with instructions that he was to agree a settlement with the Lionheart. The litigious archbishop did not do badly out of the settlement, netting a net annual revenue of £1,405 (a vast fortune in those days) from the agreement signed with Richard.[72]

Richard's diplomacy was successful on several other fronts in 1196–97, once again refuting the absurd canard that he was nothing but a tunnel-vision soldier. By brilliant manipulation, in a very short span of time he deprived Philip of France of both his major allies. It had always been his hope that matters in the south of his empire could be stabilised so that he could concentrate all his resources on the struggle in the Seine valley, but now events in Spain forced his hand. Following the death of his ally Alfonso II of Aragon in April 1196, the new rulers in northern Spain became involved in fratricidal conflict of their own, leaving them unwilling or unable to intervene in the affairs of Gascony, Aquitaine and Provence. King Sancho of Navarre was engaged in war with Castile, and Richard could no longer rely on him.[73] Faced with these new currents, and licking his wounds over the setbacks in Normandy in the summer of 1196, Richard decided to think the unthinkable and aim for a total diplomatic revolution. In short, he set out to conciliate the count of Toulouse, whose forefathers had waged a forty-year war against the

Angevin empire. In a generous package designed to win over the new count Raymond VI (Raymond V died in 1195), Richard renounced all claims to Toulouse, gave back all disputed territory to the count, and offered his sister Joan in marriage, with the county of Agen as dowry.[74] Raymond VI jumped at the terms for, quite apart from the benefits to himself, Toulouse could now enjoy uninterrupted trade through Bordeaux and have unimpeded access to the Garonne river. In Rouen in October 1196 Richard presided over the marriage of his sister (given her full honorific title of queen of Sicily) to the young count of Toulouse.[75] The elaborate wedding was a particular slap in the face for Philip of France, since Philip had defied papal and public opinion that summer by taking a wife, even though the fiasco involving his Danish spouse Ingeborg had not been resolved. Agnes, his new wife, was the daughter of Berthold IV, count of Meran in the Rhineland, a Hohenstaufen supporter and ally of the duke of Swabia. The papacy never recognised Philip's third marriage, and Anglo-Angevin chroniclers delighted in referring to Agnes as 'the adulteress'.[76]

Having secured the south of his empire, Richard next proceeded to turn Philip's flank by another and, some think, even more important diplomatic about-turn. Just as economic imperatives made sense of an Aquitaine-Toulouse accord in the Garonne basin, so did the prerequisites of the important English wool and corn trades point towards a Flanders alliance. The densely populated manufacturing centres of Bruges, Ypres, Ghent and Lille were the classic secondary producers of the Middle Ages, with England as their complementary primary producer, but hitherto politics had cut across the natural lines of comparative advantage, with trade embargoes, tariffs and sanctions the order of the day.[77] Once again it was the opportune death of a representative of the old order that opened the door to diplomatic revolution – with the succession of Baldwin IX – and once again one can observe the synchronicity that Baldwin VIII of Flanders died in 1195, the same time as Raymond V of Toulouse. Richard's envoys prodded away at an old Belgian wound – the loss of Arras, St Omer and Douai to Philip Augustus in 1192. Richard secretly promised not just an end to all trade embargoes and the payment of full arrears on his truncated pension (consequent on the loss of Artois to Philip) but also an ex gratia emolument of 5,000 marks. In the summer of 1197 Baldwin IX came to Normandy to sign a formal treaty. One of the significant straws in the wind was that three of the Norman lords of the Vexin marches, who had previously been most wobbly and ambivalent about the Angevin cause, now stood surety for Richard's end of the treaty. Both the pact and the action of the Norman lords were a serious blow to Philip and to France.[78]

If 1197 was a year of spectacular military triumphs for Richard, it also saw the revival of his military fortunes. In April that year he raided Ponthieu and singed Alice's husband's beard by sacking the port of St Valery. The gutting and looting of the town was notable for one incident, showing the harsh side of Richard. When he found an English ship in the harbour, caught redhanded trading with the king's enemy (the count of Ponthieu), he hanged every last member of the crew as an example.[79] The next month he captured the castle of Milli, in an action where William Marshal distinguished himself. When Richard gently rebuked his most famous knight for recklessness, doing a job that younger men should be doing, Marshal reminded the king of his own bullheadedness, for his captains had had to restrain him from leading the charge during the siege.[80] Yet if Richard's right-hand man, the greatest knight in England, *sans peur et sans reproche*, was winning golden opinions, the Lucifer on his left surpassed him, for Mercadier, dauntless leader of the routiers, hauled in an even greater prize than Milli by capturing Philip, the bishop of Beauvais.[81] The bishop, another fiery cleric, who had been a reliable thorn in Richard's side for years and was largely responsible for the black legend that he had hired the Assassins to murder Conrad of Montferrat, was now in his power and, as William Marshal saw, 'was one of the men Richard hated most in all the world'.[82] Richard threw the bishop into a dungeon and refused to release him. To protests from the Church Richard replied that he was holding Beauvais not in his capacity as a bishop but as a military prisoner, since he had imprudently sprung to arms when hearing of the siege of Milli and had been taken by Mercadier in full armour, helmeted and caparisoned. Richard knew that it was Beauvais's lobbying that had led to a temporary worsening of his conditions while the emperor's prisoner in Germany, and determined to exact a grim vengeance, but the pleas of the invaluable Hubert Walter made him soften his stance.[83] Convinced that fortune was with him – he even vaingloriously told William Marshal that the capture of Beauvais proved that God was on his side and against Philip – Richard spurred on, took the castle of Dangu, just four miles from Gisors, and even sent outriders to threaten the outskirts of Paris itself.[84]

After the alliance with Baldwin of Flanders was concluded, Richard was able to indulge his dream of a two-pronged offensive against Philip. While Baldwin invaded Artois in late July 1197, Richard swept through Berry, capturing ten castles.[85] Philip took his time about responding, evincing the perennial obsession with the Vexin by recapturing Dangu, and only then advancing to the relief of Arras.[86] Baldwin tried the oldest trick in the world – the feigned retreat – and the angry and intemperate Philip fell for it. Having stretched Philip's supply lines thin, Baldwin got his troops round behind him, broke down the bridges and cut his communications and food supplies. He then opened the sluices and flooded the country so that the French were trapped, unable either to advance or retreat, and still less to receive supplies. Surrounded and starving, the French at first tried to live off the land, but their depredations merely aroused the peasantry against them as armed guerrillas to add to their woes. Philip was at last forced into an abject surrender; he offered to give Baldwin whatever he asked if he would only break with Richard. Baldwin rejected the offer brusquely and instead summoned Philip to a peace conference to be held in September.[87] Although Richard was riding high and certainly felt no inclination to make a permanent peace with Gisors and the Vexin still unconquered, he and Baldwin met Philip at a venue between Gaillon and Les Andelys in the week of 9–16 September and agreed a truce of 16 months, to run until New Year 1199.[88] Baldwin departed on a pilgrimage to the shrine of St Thomas Becket in Canterbury, while Richard cemented the alliance by getting John to agree that, in the event of Richard's death, he would make no peace with France without Baldwin's consent and in the event of Baldwin's death would not do so until he had consulted Baldwin's brother and heir presumptive. John's letters patent to this effect were issued under his titles of lord of Ireland and count of Mortain.[89] The significance of the covenants made by John with Baldwin and his brother, witnessed as they were by the most important civil, military and ecclesiastical dignitaries in the Angevin empire, was that for the first time Richard implicitly recognised John as his heir. Arthur of Britanny's wardship with the king of France, so 'cleverly' devised by Constance and her husband, now looked like the gravest of errors.[90]

Diplomatic matters now returned to the fore with an election of a new German emperor, after Henry VI died of a fever in Messina on 28 September 1197, aged only 32. The devout said that God had once again punished a malefactor who had abducted the crusader king, just as he had previously punished Leopold of Austria, though on his deathbed Henry promised to repay Richard all the money he had extracted for the ransom. Indeed Pope Celestine expressly forbade Henry's burial until all this money was repaid.[91] Henry's son, the future Frederick II, was only three years old and so out of the running, but a fierce contest developed between the Hohenstaufen and their Welf enemies that once again threatened to tear the empire apart; since the rivals were backed by Richard and Philip, respectively, the German election campaign of 1197–98 turned out to be Franco-Angevin warfare by other means. Richard's allies were all the friends who had backed him in the dark days of early 1194: principally the archbishop of Cologne and the princes of the Lower Rhineland.[92] Though invited to come to Germany to take part in the election, Richard declined – the psychology here is surely obvious – and instead sent his old comrade from the grim 1192–93 kidnapping, Baldwin of Bethune (now count of Aumale), plus Philip of Poitou, the bishop of Durham and other old faithfuls. Richard's inclination was to support his nephew Henry of Brunswick, though he was inconveniently absent on crusade. This happy chance averted a potential conflict with the archbishop of Cologne, who was unhappy at the thought of Henry the Lion's heir as emperor. When an assembly of princes chose Henry VI's younger brother Philip of Swabia as the Hohenstaufen candidate, the archbishop, with Richard's blessing, opted for Henry of Brunswick's younger brother Otto, whom the Rhineland princes thought would be a cipher. Richard was happy with Otto, whose education and cultural formation had been in Aquitaine, and he became known as the 'English' candidate.[93] In June he was elected king at Cologne and crowned at Aachen the following month, with Baldwin of Flanders and his brother as Richard's representatives. Philip of Swabia bitterly refused to accept the outcome, and signed a treaty with Philip Augustus, identifying Richard, Otto, count Baldwin and the archbishop of Cologne as his mortal enemies.[94] The treacherous Prince John must have been tempted to join his erstwhile ally, for Richard's enthusiasm for Otto threatened his own position; there was talk that Richard intended to name Otto as his heir in England.[95]

Yet the dissentient stance of both Philips virtually received its *coup de grâce* when the new Pope Innocent III (elected on 8 January and consecrated on 2 February 1198), having maintained an official posture of neutrality, openly welcomed the new emperor's election in the most effusive terms. In fact he and Richard had been working together to get Otto elected.[96] Once again Richard had decisively outpointed Philip Augustus in the diplomatic stakes. The new pontiff proved energetic and interventionist, determined to mediate in the long-running dispute between Angevin and Capetian kingdoms but reserving his judgement until he had visited both countries; in expressing such a wish the Vicar of Christ showed himself an innovator, for by tradition the pope never left the environs of the Vatican.[97] In April Richard sent the bishop of Lisieux to Rome to get Innocent's backing for his attempt to get the entire ransom repaid from the heirs of Henry VI and Leopold of Austria. Innocent replied sympathetically, promising to do all in his power to bring pressure on Leopold's son and the duke of Swabia. For all that, at the same time he lifted the interdict on Henry VI and allowed his body to be buried. When the duke of Swabia was so bitterly disappointed at failing to become the new German emperor, Innocent let him off the hook by failing to press him for the return of the money.[98] This was a blow to Richard, but Innocent made good his complaisance in this regard by two hard-hitting decisions that clearly favoured the English king. In the first place, he took an even tougher line than his predecessor Celestine on Philip Augustus's marriage to Agnes, condemning it out of hand on two counts: he, the pontiff, stood forth as the protector of 'persecuted women' like the discarded Ingeborg; and Philip had been contumacious in not awaiting the Church's permission before entering a third union. When Philip predictably failed to respond to the Pope's demand that he restore Ingeborg, Innocent placed an interdict on France; it was, however, only partially obeyed by the French clergy, as Philip viciously persecuted any priests who obeyed the pontiff's orders rather than his own.[99] The second papal move favouring Richard also concerned wives, this time Berengaria. As long as the king of Navarre was Richard's ally, it hardly mattered that he had not in fact handed over the castles of St-Jean-Pied-de-Port and Roquebrune, promised to the English king as Berengaria's dowry. But now that the new king of Navarre, Sancho VII, had other concerns and was no longer any use to Richard, it was imperative that Richard gain possession of the strongholds. Innocent wrote to the new king in the strongest terms, requiring him to make good his father's pledge on the dowry.[100] It was clear from this development that Berengaria's reconciliation with her husband had been only partial, and that her childlessness was now perceived as a major problem. Berengaria had failed to produce an heir, and had a brother who was now insouciant about Richard's diplomatic concerns. The cynic might say that, in a loveless marriage, the queen had outlived her usefulness.[101]

Richard's run of diplomatic successes continued with many notable defections from Philip's camp: the Bretons, the barons of Champagne and many other notable local magnates (including those of Blois, Perche, Brienne, Guînes and St Pol). By far the most spectacular catch for the Angevins was Count Renaud of Boulogne, regarded as the best warrior among Philip's vassals; the French king's tit-for-tat alliance with the rebel lords Aimar of Limoges and Ademar of Angoulême, long-term malcontents, was poor compensation for these losses.[102] Naturally, most of Richard's converts came over not through ideology or personal loyalty but for money. Like a more famous cold war eight hundred years later, the 'phoney war' of 1198 turned into a massive spending contest, where the Angevin coffers seemed deeper.[103] At last, in September that year Richard thought the time was right to make the cold war a hot one. Baldwin invaded Artois, always disputed territory between France and Flanders, captured Aire and, together with the new ally Renaud of Boulogne, laid siege to St Omer. The burghers there sent word to Philip that they would surrender if he did not come with all speed. Philip promised he would be there by the end of the month, but was distracted when Richard opened his Normandy offensive as part of a two-pronged strategy. Since both the Angevin and Capetian kings were perennially obsessed with the Norman Vexin, it was not surprising that, faced with the threat on his western flank, Philip Augustus soon forgot about Flanders. After a six-week siege, St Omer capitulated, and Baldwin marched in on 13 October.[104] Philip Augustus could not even boast successes in Normandy to set against this, for he had sustained two serious defeats at Richard's hands. In the first of these, Richard had retreated before the French, waiting for reinforcements to come up. When these arrived, led by Mercadier, the Lionheart fell on the French rear, whose soldiers were overconfident as they had been looting without being disturbed. The tally from this attack was thirty knights and one hundred horses captured and a number of French troops killed.[105]

The second defeat of Philip by Richard was a notable achievement, but written up and absurdly exaggerated by all the English king's hagiographers. By the end of September Richard was closing the ring on Gisors by capturing the nearby fortresses of Dangu and Courcelles. Not knowing that it had already fallen, Philip set out with a large army, including 300 knights, to relieve Courcelles. Richard's patrols picked up the movement of the French army – and it may even have been the English king himself who noticed it, as he still went out on patrol just as he had done in the Holy Land.[106] He decided on an immediate attack, before Philip realised that Courcelles was in enemy hands and started withdrawing, but was short of numbers for a full engagement. He therefore sent for reinforcements from Dangu. But when Philip's army continued on the march at a good clip, Richard feared the day would end before his own army was at full strength. He therefore ordered an immediate assault. The element of surprise, and the impetuous charge Richard directed – William Marshal said it was like a starving lion scenting prey – threw the French into confusion. It takes time for a marching army to get into battle formation, and time was what Richard did not allow the foe.[107] Philip panicked and ordered a withdrawal to Gisors, but the retreat soon became a rout. In the mad scramble to get back into Gisors, the leaderless and panic-stricken infantry crowded over the bridge to the town in such numbers that it broke beneath them, pitching large numbers to their death, including twenty knights. Others were left outside when the gates were closed before them. Richard and his men rode many of them down with their lances but took more than a hundred prisoners, presumably the valuable ones who could be ransomed – an inference strengthened by other figures that speak of French losses of ninety knights and 200 horses. Mercadier alone notched up thirty knights in his tally of captives. Philip, having initially fallen into the waters of the river Epte, scrambled back to safety, concealed, it was said, by the clouds of dust churned up on the dry roads; the high tally of knights captured was allegedly because they had remained behind to hack out an escape path for their king. Lacking siege engines with which to make an impression on Gisors, Richard withdrew to Dangu to count his prisoners and their likely ransoms.[108]

The French had lost the flower of their chivalry, with many famous names among the slain, including William de Barres's brother. Passions ran high on the French side after this major setback. There were many disloyal murmurings in the Capetian camp, with many opining that the disaster was so egregious it stood in need of some special application. The devout explained it as God's punishment for Philip's persecution of priests and his defiance of Pope Innocent III's interdict; as the penalty for setting aside Ingeborg and living with the 'whore' Agnes; or for tolerating Jews and allowing them into his domains.[109] Philip struck back at the enemy by declaring *guerre à outrance*, with no quarter asked or given. Atrocities began to mount. Philip routinely blinded enemy prisoners as if he was in Byzantium; under pressure from his own men to retaliate in kind, a reluctant Richard did so; needless to say, French propagandists then falsely alleged that Richard had started the escalating cycle of barbarism. Both sides began to target objectives *in terrorem*, without regard to their military or strategic value. Philip sent a force of incendiaries to burn down Evreux, south of the Seine, to which Richard responded by dispatching Mercadier and the very worst of his cut-throat band of routiers to plunder the town of Abbeville during a trade fair.[110] Even so, Richard was clearly winning the war and it was evident that Philip did not have the resources to wage a two-front war. If he wanted to regain

Artois, then clearly he had to give ground in Normandy. In October he therefore proposed peace terms on the basis that he gave up all conquests in Normandy except for Gisors; the future of that castle would be determined by a panel of six Norman barons chosen by Philip and six by Richard. But when Richard insisted that Baldwin and his other allies must be included in any treaty, the talks broke down. Finally, in desperation, Philip agreed these conditions, but only for a short truce, to last until 13 January 1199.[111]

After spending Christmas at Domfront, on 13 January Richard duly appeared at a rendezvous on the Seine, between Les Andelys and Vernon, for the talks with Philip supposed to secure a lasting peace. In yet another uncanny Napoleonic pre-echo (this time foreshadowing Napoleon's famous meeting with Czar Alexander on a raft at Tilsit in 1807), the two kings conferred aboard Richard's galley in the middle of the river. A vague five-year truce based on the status quo, but with no minutiae clarified, was agreed, pending more detailed negotiations to feature a papal legate as mediator. Innocent was more than ever anxious to see an end to the feuding between Capetians and Angevins – for him the interminable struggle for Gisors and the Vexin really was two bald men fighting over a comb – since he had just proclaimed the Fourth Crusade. Unfortunately the go-between he appointed was not a happy choice for the job. The papal legate Peter of Capua displayed from the very first a pronounced pro-French bias, and his oily prolixity particularly angered William Marshal, who described him as a French puppet with a sickening aura of unctuous rectitude, physically unappealing to boot, with a complexion as yellow as a stork's foot.[112] Richard's position was quite simple: in the interests of peace he was prepared to forgo all indemnities and reparations for war damage provided Philip returned all the lands he had illegally filched through conquest. Peter of Capua made the mistake of trying to get him to soften his stance, on the grounds that the kingdom of Jerusalem was in deadly peril from the Saracens. This was teaching grandmothers to suck eggs, with a vengeance. Angrily Richard reminded the legate that but for Philip's departure to France from the Holy Land, Jerusalem would probably already be in Christian possession; he himself had left Outremer only because Philip, in defiance of God's law, papal edict and his oath as a crusader, had begun attacking the Angevin empire even while its king was fighting Saladin. Richard then launched into a vehement attack on Philip's treacherous behaviour during his captivity in Germany. Peter of Capua merely added insult to injury by spouting bland nonsense. 'Ah, sire,' were his reported words, 'how true it is that no one can have everything he wants.'[113]

Worn down by the monotonous prattling from the legate about the Holy Land, Richard finally agreed to an 'as-is' five-year truce. But the foolish legate could not count his blessings and leave well enough alone. He then raised the issue of Philip's cousin, the bishop of Beauvais, still languishing in an Angevin dungeon, and began waffling and prating about men of the cloth who were both anointed and consecrated. At this Richard exploded. With many a 'by God's legs!' he reiterated that the bishop of Beauvais had not been wrenched from an altar like Thomas Becket but had been captured in full armour, for all the world a warrior. Cursing Peter as a fool and humbug, he told him that if he were not the papal envoy, he would send Innocent back something he would not soon forget. At the implied threat of murder or castration, the legate went weak at the knees, but Richard had not finished. 'The Pope! The Pope did not raise a finger to help me when I was in prison. And now he asks me to free a robber and arsonist who has never done me anything but harm! Get out of here, you liar, hypocrite, scoundrel and bought-and-paid-for so-called churchman, and never let me see you again.'[114] Paroxysmic with rage after this interview, and now more than ever recalling his father, he stormed to his chamber and left word he was not to be disturbed. For a long time he lay fuming on his bed, in the dark with the shutters closed, unable to contain his rage at the monstrous impertinence of the legate. He was finally roused by the only man in the empire who had the gravitas and prestige to risk the royal wrath. William Marshal, who had by no means always seen eye to eye with Richard, had in the later years of the king's reign become a trusted counsellor, and on this occasion his advice was sound. He put it to Richard that Philip was in financial straits, and that his retaining the castles he had illegally obtained would simply stretch his meagre resources to snapping point. Richard's best course was harassment: close investment of these castles so that the castellans and their men could not sortie to collect feudal revenues or even reprovision; Philip would thus have a full-time logistical task simply keeping his garrisons in the illegal fortresses in being.[115] Richard accepted the advice. Some have speculated that Richard's anger was totally histrionic, a gallery touch used to manipulate the French, to make them think he was more discontented with the terms of the truce than he really was. The most plausible explanation is that Richard's outburst contained both rage and controlled anger. If rage is a purely negative emotion while anger, properly channelled, can be used constructively, it may well be the case, as the shrewdest scholars have concluded, that Richard's anger was both genuine and calculated.[116] And yet this is the man who, according to his detractors, was a militaristic blockhead!

12

───────◇───────

THE TRUCE BETWEEN RICHARD and Philip was no sooner signed than broken. Still plagued by revolts in the south, Richard sent Mercadier and his routiers to deal with them in their usual brutal way, but on the march down to Aquitaine they were ambushed by some French counts and their levies. Richard immediately claimed that the interceptors must have been working in collusion with Philip Augustus. Naturally Philip denied it, but as soon as Richard himself went south to retrieve the situation, he began fresh castle-building on the Seine in defiance of the ceasefire terms. Richard's chancellor Eustace of Ely gave due warning that unless this activity ceased, a state of war would automatically exist, and the shaken Peter of Capua warned Philip that he would be unable to cover for him unless he observed the truce conditions strictly. The papal legate then got down to work on a draft treaty to ensure that the peace really would hold. This time the dynastic inter-marriage proposal was for a match between Philip's son Louis and Richard's Spanish niece, daughter of the king of Castile, to be cemented by a grant of 20,000 marks from Richard and the castle of Gisors donated in perpetuity. In return for this generous marriage, Philip would pledge himself to abandon Philip of Swabia and work for German unification under Otto of Brunswick.[1] While a draft of these proposals was sent to Richard, Philip showed clearly that he was unhappy with them by some spectacular stirring of the pot. He informed Richard that John had deserted to the French side and sent him some documentary evidence of a circumstantial kind. Although John had kept his head down for five years and served Richard faithfully on the battlefield and in the council chamber, his previous sins came back to haunt him. Knowing how untrustworthy his brother was, Richard not unnaturally believed the bad news and ordered John's property seized. The old John might have stormed off to Paris in dudgeon, but the 32-year-old was no longer the 'child' of 1194 and calmly refuted Philip's 'evidence' which turned out to be paper-thin. Richard restored his estates, though his suspicions were not entirely assuaged.[2]

Leaving Chinon on 15 March 1199, Richard headed for Limoges to link up with Mercadier, intending to extirpate once and for all the rebellious sept of Aimar, viscount of Limoges and his son Guy. He and Mercadier then proceeded to besiege the viscount's castle at Châlus-Chabrol, south of Limoges. For three days he directed a close investment of the fortress, having his bowmen shower the battlements with cascades of arrows while his sappers, protected by a 'shield' of thick canvas, undermined the walls. Since the garrison was tiny, with no more than forty defenders, there could only be one outcome to the siege. But Saladin, who had warned Richard that his Achilles heel was the gallery touch – the obsessive need to undertake minor operations which did not require his presence yet endangered his life – proved a true prophet. At dusk on the evening of 29 March, Richard left the comfort of his tent for the trivial pleasure of taking potshots at the castle walls with a crossbow – for the king fancied himself as an expert archer. He wore no armour and relied for protection simply on a large rectangular shield. There was only one man on the castle parapet, a bowman who liked to fire off quarrels at the besiegers as a token gesture of defiance. Fascinated by the man's marksmanship, Richard either did not see the shaft heading towards him in the gloom, or overrated his own reflexes. At any rate, the bolt found its mark and buried itself in the king's flesh, in the left shoulder. It was a serious wound but it should not have been a fatal one. Perhaps Richard's mistake was not to ask one of his men to pull the missile out there and then, but maybe he feared the effect on their morale. Staggering back to his tent with remarkable stoicism, he tried to pull the bolt out cleanly – clearly it was a job for a skilled physician – but botched the job. The wooden shaft snapped off, leaving the iron barb still deeply embedded in his flesh. Finally a surgeon arrived and with great difficulty and much gore managed to remove the bolt; it is speculated that in the bad light of sundown the ham-fisted physician prodded around inexpertly with his scalpel, causing fresh wounds. Finally, the badly butchered shoulder was patched up and bandaged, but septicaemia, that reliable scourge of medieval battlefields had already taken a hand. Gangrene set in, the wound worsened and Richard, veteran of so many fatal encounters, knew the end was near. He sent for his mother, allowed only four trusted comrades to know the reality of his situation, and waited for the inevitable. The castle fell while he lay dying, but Richard barely took this in. Having received the last rites of the Church,

he expired in the early evening of 6 April, the Tuesday before Palm
Sunday, around 7 p.m. Abbot Milo of the Cistercian abbey of Le Pin
near Poitiers heard his last confession, gave extreme unction and closed
the dead man's mouth and eyes.[3]

Richard left exact instructions for the disposal of his body. His brains
and entrails were buried at the abbey of Charroux on the Poitou-
Limousin border, probably because Charlemagne was said to be the
founder of the abbey. His heart went to Rouen to be buried next to the
Young King; here at last we depart from Napoleonic comparisons, for
the king's heart was said to have been unusually large, whereas the examin-
ing physicians on St Helena found all the French emperor's organs to
have been on the small side.[4] The rest of his remains, together with the
Crown and regalia he had worn at the second coronation at Winchester
were buried at Fontevraud, at his father's feet. The effigy on the tomb
declares the glory of the Lionheart: a king in gorgeous apparel, scep-
tred and crowned, his Excalibur-like sword at his side.[5] Hugh, bishop of
Lincoln, was the man chosen to conduct the Fontevraud service on Palm
Sunday, 11 April. For reasons not entirely clear Berengaria did not attend
the funeral, so bishop Hugh visited her at Beaufort on his way to the
funeral. Those present at the funeral included Aimeri, viscount of
Thouars and his brother Guy, William des Roches, Peter Savaric, Maurice,
bishop of Poitiers, William, bishop of Angers, Miles, abbot of Le Pin
and Luke, abbot of Torpenay.[6] But the most significant presence was
that of Eleanor of Aquitaine, at the side of her beloved son in death
as in life. She had been with him during the last days, and five years later
would follow him into the family vaults at Fontevraud.[7] It is difficult not
to contrast the dominant role of Queen Eleanor, present at the second
coronation at Winchester, present at Richard's deathbed, present at his
funeral, with the unexplained absence of Queen Berengaria from all
these events.[8]

The deaths of great men are nearly always swathed in mystery and
legend; we see this clearly in the case of Alexander the Great, Julius
Caesar, Napoleon and Lincoln, and the virus also infects the not-so-great
but celebrated (William Rufus, Hitler, John F. Kennedy). It was scarcely
to be expected that a celebrity as famous as Richard the Lionheart would
be allowed to die a pointless death, as the result of mere chance. Modern
mindsets do not appreciate raw contingency, and medieval sensibilities
liked it even less. It followed, then, for his contemporaries, that his death
had to have an ulterior or profounder meaning. The story the Lionheart's
contemporary chroniclers liked to tell was that he met his end through

greed, while engaged in a demeaning hunt for treasure.[9] The quest for hidden gold, silver or other riches is a staple of medieval mythology and fairy tale, and continued to fascinate down the ages; the conquistadors' conquest of the Americas, the downfall of the Jacobites, the last days of the Jesuits and the Nazis – all are allegedly concerned with buried treasure; tales of hidden treasure are a favourite device for explaining the otherwise inexplicable; and in psychological terms Jung has written extensively about the Nibelungen hoards as metaphor – 'the treasure hard to attain'.[10] The men of the Middle Ages were similarly awestruck. Roger of Howden's version was that the viscount of Limoges found a hoard of gold and silver on his land, offered Richard his liege lord a share, but that the avaricious Richard saw no reason why he should have merely a cut when he could have it all. The same story, with some name changes, occurs in the French chronicles of Rigord and William the Breton. The siege of Châlus-Chabrol then becomes a story, not of putting down rebellion, but of sordid treasure hunting. Howden named the bowman who fired the fatal bolt at Richard as Bertrand de Gurdon. He goes on to tell how Richard forgave him on his deathbed after he had heard how Angevin armies had killed his father and two brothers. Howden thus gets across a hamfisted fable about an allegedly wicked king showing repentance and contrition on his deathbed, pointing a Christian moral.[11] Ralph of Coggleshall indicts Richard for his financial greed, laments the burden of taxation placed on England by Richard, and says that God struck him down because of his avarice. However, since Richard was always a loyal son of the Church and had never sought to make money out of ecclesiastical preferments, there was every reason to think that his stay in Purgatory would be a brief one and that he would attain the kingdom of Heaven.[12]

Medieval writers naturally conceived of human life as fulfilling a pattern – the aleatory, the contingent, the adventitious, and the chaotic were to them manifestations of the Devil. The pattern was either Aristotelian – what could, might and even *ought* to have happened, rather than what actually did in brute fact – or providential, evincing God's purposes; it followed that a random death of a king was outside the medieval writers' universe of discourse, for this would make God appear a jester or a dice-player. French chroniclers were particularly confused on the issue: William of Breton said Richard's death showed clearly that God was on Philip's side and had come to the aid of France by striking down her most dangerous enemy; but Rigord thought that Philip's imprisonment of Queen Ingeborg after repudiating her was the decade's real sin crying to Heaven for vengeance, and was therefore puzzled as to why Richard, not Philip, was the monarch who was stricken.[13] By contrast, the English view was more one-dimensional. Although both Coggleshall and Howden are invaluable as historical sources when their preconceptions and *parti pris* do not intrude, clearly in this case they did. There may well have been a minor incident involving treasure which aroused Richard's wrath – in that simulated but serious mode we have already discussed – but that was not his motive for the siege of the castle where he received his death-wound. That was a simple case of suppressing a rebellion.[14] Medieval historians, and some modern ones who follow them uncritically, like the story of treasure trove as it fits the picture of an irresponsible king; not surprisingly, this story has always been popular among the anti-Lionheart school of history. Yet the most serious strike against the treasure story is that it is not mentioned in the most authentic account of Richard's death, by Bernard Itier, a monk in the Benedictine abbey of St Martial in Limoges, who had access to all the most reliable eyewitnesses.[15] Many historians, even until recently, knew nothing of Itier's account, partly, the historian John Gillingham suggests plausibly, because they still cleave to the old fallacy that Richard is important only as king of England, and therefore totally ignore Aquitaine and its local historians.[16] At least three other major sources follow Itier and make no mention of treasure.[17]

The tenacious hold of legend on Richard's death can be seen from a number of different angles. Freudians, who like to link Eros and Thanatos, will doubtless relish the persistent canard that Richard disregarded the advice of his physicians and weakened himself still further by a prolonged bout of lovemaking as he lay dying; unfortunately, it is only the pedlars of tall stories who insist that this last sexual fling was with boys rather than women.[18] Christian apologists spread the rumour that Richard had not attended Mass for seven years, since his hatred for Philip of France was so strong he could not in conscience take the sacraments or even witness the Consecration, though this sounds like an obvious riff on the old Melusine and 'Devil's Brood' stories.[19] Mythmakers, determined to rewrite his somewhat depressing and meaningless death into something more like romance, liked to transfer his death away from Châlus to more glamorous and well-known sights, to Chinon, Loches or Château-Gaillard.[20] Confused as to the identity of the king's killer, the chroniclers opt for a number of different names for the crossbowman: in Itier's account he appears as Peter Basil, in William the Breton's verse epic he is Dudo, while in Roger of Howden's history he is confidently assigned the handle Bertrand de Gurdon.[21] There seems to be agreement that Richard did forgive the man on his deathbed, but less consensus on what happened afterwards. One plausible version is that the dying king's instructions were set aside and that Mercadier had him flayed alive. Another story is that Mercadier thirsted for the man's death but did not dare disregard the Lionheart's last wishes openly, so sent him secretly to Joan (now wife of Raymond of Toulouse) who put him to death in some gruesome way.[22]

So passed the most famous king in English history. Whatever final judgement historians reach on the personality, reign and achievements of the Lionheart, no other English or British monarch comes close to him in terms of his impact on the wider world, and hence his status in myth and legend. Comparisons with the historical and mythical great are almost commonplace in the writings of posterity about Richard I: Alexander, Augustus and Charlemagne figure most prominently as examples of the former, with Arthur, Gawain and Roland as favourites in the latter category.[23] The legendary stories told about Richard are legion.[24] Apart from Blondel and Robin Hood, two especially stand out. In one fable Richard fights Saladin in single combat and worsts him. In another, significant in that it shows the Lionheart entering legend as a heterosexual rather than as the homosexual beloved by twentieth-century mythographers, Richard falls in love with the German emperor's daughter during his famous captivity. Angry at the real or imagined seduction of his daughter, the emperor releases a lion into Richard's cell, but the king kills the beast by distracting its attention with forty silk handkerchiefs received from his lady fair, putting his arm down the lion's throat and ripping out its heart; actually, in mythical terms, the emperor was a fool for, by the canons that governed medieval fiction, lions cannot harm anointed kings.[25] Although there are passing references to Richard in Chaucer and Shakespeare, it is generally considered that Richard was too much of a colossus to be a manageable subject even for a genius like the Bard, who preferred (when not dealing with the remote Ancient World) to base his dramas on obscure or little-known rulers; though some allege that there is a lost Shakespearean play about Richard.[26] In literature Richard's great significance is his massive influence on Arthuriana in general and in particular the medieval literature of Spain and Germany.[27] In the wider world of Islam, Richard was regarded as a greater figure than Saladin. As with Napoleon centuries later, mothers would frighten their babies with talk of the English ogre who would come and eat them if they misbehaved.[28]

It took a while for Europe fully to grasp the legendary dimensions of Richard, for in the immediate aftermath of his death all his contemporaries were shocked, convulsed, paralysed and incredulous. England lurched into temporary chaos, with an epidemic of crime and lawlessness, while the barons fortified their castles, uncertain what would happen next, eager to be on the winning side in any dispute over the succession but perplexed about who the new king would be. The barons of Anjou, Maine and Touraine declared for Arthur of Britanny, Geoffrey's son, while Philip of France invaded Normandy. But John had powerful backers, with his mother Eleanor especially important.[29] Whether on her advice or on his own initiative, he acted quickly. Ironically he was staying with his nephew and rival Arthur when the news of Richard's death came in. At once he rode south to Chinon and seized the Chinon treasury, thus providing himself with the sinews of war.[30] The fact that Richard had nominated John rather than Arthur as his heir (and given him all his castles and three-quarters of his treasure) was a factor deciding the great lords of the empire which way to jump, but it was scarcely conclusive. If Richard had had a son, he would have succeeded him; since Geoffrey was older than both Richard and John, it seemed to follow logically that his son had precedence. Moreover, Richard's judgement of John in 1194 when he patronisingly forgave him his sins, and waived a trial only through the intercession of Eleanor of Aquitaine, allowed the Arthurian party to assert that Arthur had always been accepted as Richard's heir, and it was only the weakness of his mind when he lay on his deathbed that led him to nominate John as his successor.[31] But logic had little to do with the situation in 1199. Medieval law, feudal custom, precedent and, most of all, the differential mores and folkways of England, Normandy, Aquitaine and the other constituents of the Angevin empire, all conspired to make the succession a muddied and turbid affair; it was clearly going to be main force that decided the issue.[32]

The barons of Aquitaine adopted a 'wait and see' policy by simply rendering homage to Eleanor of Aquitaine, leaving open the question of who the next king would be; Eleanor passed on the duchy to John, while retaining a life-interest.[33] Anjou, Maine and Touraine, who opted for Arthur, were dominated by feudal lords who wanted the least possible interference in their internal affairs, and that clearly indicated Arthur, a boy king and therefore a weak king; William des Roches was the key figure in marshalling pro-Arthur support.[34] Hubert Walter, Richard's financial and administrative genius, initially favoured Arthur, and a famous conversation with William Marshal at Vaudreuil on 10 April, four days after Richard's death, shows that key magnate devoted to *realpolitik*. Walter stressed that the matter of a new king could not be left in abeyance and warmly supported Arthur. 'To my mind that would be bad,' replied Marshal. 'Arthur is advised by traitors, and is proud and haughty; if we put him over us, he will ruin us, for he does not love the people of this land. John, on the other hand, was clearly the choice both of his father and of Richard.' 'Are you sure this is really what you want?' asked Walter. 'Yes,' said Marshal, 'it is the only just way. A son is surely more entitled to a father's lands than a grandson.' Walter sighed. 'So be it. But remember my words. You will never regret anything in your life as much as the step you are now taking.'[35]

From Chinon John rode to Fontevraud to inspect Richard's tomb, then on to Beaufort-en-Vallée, where he interviewed Berengaria and bishop Hugh of Lincoln. But he found the tide of opinion running against him in the Angevin heartland: on Easter Sunday the barons of Anjou, Maine and Touraine met in Angers and chose Arthur as Richard's rightful successor.[36] Moving on to Le Mans, which he also found hostile to his cause, John narrowly escaped capture when a pincer movement of the Breton army and Philip Augustus converged on the town.[37] Once over the Normandy border, John experienced a dramatic change of fortune, for under Norman law a younger son was nearer heir to his father's estates than the child of an elder brother who died before the father.[38] At Rouen on 25 April John was invested as duke of Normandy and garlanded with a coronet of golden roses. While his mother Eleanor and Mercadier kept armies in the field in Aquitaine to contest the Arthurian coup in Anjou, and John raised a force with which to raze Le Mans for its 'treason', William Marshal slipped across to England to whip up support for John.[39] The justiciar Geoffrey Fitzpeter backed John, and the trio of Marshal, Fitzpeter and the archbishop of Canterbury summoned the English barons to a conclave at Northampton. There was little enthusiasm for John, but the alternative, Arthur, seemed to presage weak rule, anarchy and possibly civil war. Grudgingly the barons agreed to take an oath of fealty to John. Leaving his mother and Mercadier to deal with the Arthurian factions on the continent, John crossed the Channel to Shoreham on 25 May, and two days later was crowned king of England at Westminster Abbey, on Ascension Day 1199.[40]

Faced with the perilous situation on the continent – for by now Constance of Britanny had made formal homage to Philip Augustus for all the lands currently possessed by Arthur – John did not dare to tarry long in England. Constance's actions were an implicit statement that she cared nothing for the Angevin empire and did not mind if it broke up, so long as her son came into his own and was protected; it was revenge for the English barons' action at Northampton. In part too it was a recognition of necessity, for the military successes of Mercadier and Eleanor of Aquitaine in Poitou had put the Arthurian party on the back foot.[41] Three weeks after landing at Shoreham, John was back at Dieppe with reinforcements from England. Maine, Anjou and Touraine were still largely in Breton hands, and enemy possession of the great Angers-Tours crossroads meant that Philip and his allies had effectively sliced the Angevin empire in half. But John could not proceed south while Philip still menaced him in Normandy. After some half-hearted skirmishing, the two kings met for a parley in August, both aware they needed time to think through their respective strategies. John played the injured innocent and enquired peevishly why Philip had attacked him; Philip replied that it was because he had had himself acclaimed duke of Normandy without doing homage to his feudal overlord (Philip).[42] When John offered to give satisfaction, Philip replied brusquely that his terms were simple: cede Anjou, Maine and Touraine to Arthur and abandon the disputed territory along the Seine to France.[43] It was a call for surrender that John could not possibly accept. Fortunately for him, he inherited a large, well-drilled army that Richard had been preparing for the next strike against Philip Augustus. Even more crucially, he inherited Richard's network of alliances and, for the moment, this held firm. On one day he was said to have received fifteen counts at his court, and among them were the counts of Flanders, Boulogne and Bar, the key players in Richard's assault on Philip's northern marches.[44] Eleanor of Aquitaine meanwhile turned the screws on the Arthurian party by declaring John her heir and expressly repudiating all claims on her from Arthur. To cap this run of success for John, envoys arrived from Otto IV of Germany, promising support.[45]

Feeling confident now that he had both the Pope and the emperor on his side (Otto IV was backed by Innocent III) – a very rare event, given the protracted Guelph-Ghibelline dispute) – John headed south, dogged all the way by Philip's forces. All parties in the struggle for the succession kept a keen eye on the slightest change in political weather, and at this juncture the Arthurian commander of the Breton forces and the most powerful baron in Anjou decided that the tide was turning away from Philip Augustus. All William des Roches needed was an excuse to change sides. This Philip duly provided by invading Maine and razing the castle of Ballon. Des Roches claimed that the castle was his and demanded an explanation from the French king. Arrogantly, Philip said that he would deal as he pleased with any castles he captured, and bogus claims from the Arthurian party would not deter him. Angrily des Roches sent secret envoys to John, offering to surrender Arthur if John offered him suitable terms. John took the bait, and on 22 September at Le Mans des Roches brought in Arthur and his mother Constance.[46] Arthur and his mother made their submission, but something about John's demeanour alerted them that he would not treat them as Richard had treated him. That very night Arthur and Constance, protected and escorted by Aimeri of Thouars, stole away from Le Mans. John, having gained an ally in des Roches and seemingly also captured a great prize, found himself back to square one, simply through stupidity; he had alienated the viscount of Thouars by peremptorily demanding the return of Chinon. The refugees sought sanctuary in Angers. John's reputation was already catching up with him. Here, after all, was a man who had betrayed his father in 1189, betrayed his brother in 1193–94 and betrayed Philip Augustus in 1194; such a man was a byword for treachery and would surely act treacherously again, this time at the expense of the 12-year-old Arthur.[47]

Arthur's flight, immediately after he had come in to make his peace, seriously affected baronial opinion and, besides, Richard's allies had not been impressed by their first contacts with the new king, so unlike his late brother.[48] By the end of 1199 Richard's carefully constructed system of alliances was in tatters. There were no violent ruptures, it was just that Richard's old allies largely abandoned John by voting with their feet and taking the Cross: Baldwin of Flanders, Louis of Blois, Stephen of Perche, the marquis of Montferrat and others forsook European politics and departed on crusade. The unravelling of Richard's alliance can be fairly precisely dated to November 1199, when the count of Champagne held a great tournament at Evry-sur-Aisne. Thibaut and his brother Louis of Blois together with many lesser lords and their followers formally laid down their arms and announced that they were heeding Pope Innocent's call for a new attempt to regain Jerusalem.[49] The trickle of would-be crusaders, which had so disappointed the Pope before the November tournament, now became a flood. The real slap in the face for John was the treaty signed by Baldwin of Flanders with Philip of France on 2 January at Péronne, which at a stroke destroyed the two-front military strategy Richard had used so successfully against the French. This more than compensated for the more or less simultaneous papal interdict imposed on Philip and France by Innocent for his egregious treatment of Ingeborg. Nonetheless, Philip was hard pressed by war with the Angevins on top of a political struggle with the papacy, so he responded with alacrity to John's peace feelers. The two kings met on the Norman frontier on 15 January, embraced warmly and signed preliminary articles of an accord.[50]

Such was the genesis of the peace treaty signed between Philip and John at the town of Le Goulet on the Seine on 22 May 1200. This treaty enshrined many of the articles earlier negotiated with Richard at Louviers in 1196, but with significant new additions which demonstrated the high price John had to pay to secure his succession against the claims of Arthur of Britanny.[51] Philip recognised John as Richard's lawful heir and endorsed his right to the Angevin empire, except that Arthur was to hold Britanny as John's 'man'. Disputes between Arthur and John were to be settled by John's court, but John recognised Philip anew as his liege lord. The treaty was to be cemented by a marriage between John's niece Blanche, daughter of Alfonso of Castile and Philip's son Louis; this marriage actually did take place, the day after the peace of Le Goulet was signed.[52] In return for these 'concessions', John allowed Philip to keep all his recent gains in Normandy, yielded ground in Berry, agreed to pay Philip 20,000 marks and, crucially, abandoned the alliance with Otto IV.[53] It should be remembered that in January 1199, while Richard was still alive, it was Philip who had promised to abandon his German alliance with Philip of Swabia. Now the whole of Richard's carefully assembled diplomatic network lay in ruins, with both his German and Flanders allies discarded or lost. Sceptical observers also noted that the terms negotiated by John were far inferior to those Henry II used to extract from his so-called overlord. Moreover, the 20,000 mark 'relief' was also a humiliation. This was a soi-disant succession duty, payable by a vassal to a feudal lord, and it was the fact of the demand by Philip, and its payment by John, which were truly salient.[54] Once again the contrast with Henry and Richard was clear, for they had always merely paid the ritual homage to the kings of France, but never a cash sum. Finally, John agreed that the counts of Boulogne and Flanders were properly vassals of the king of France, so that it was against international law for an Angevin monarch to try to seduce them from their feudal loyalties, as Richard had done. The much weaker kingdom of France had always tried to drain the Angevin empire of its power by setting father against sons and brother against brother, but many historians consider that in the treaty of Le Goulet, France for the very first time asserted itself as a de facto as well as de jure superior to the Angevins.[55]

Superficially, an era of peace seemed to have descended. Philip referred to the new king of the English as 'our dearly beloved John'.[56] John toured his continental dominions, from Caen in Normandy to St Sever in Gascony (June–August 1200), and visited Philip in Paris, where he was made much of. Philip appeared willing to accept the reality of a powerful neighbour on his doorstep, but those who knew the French fox were only too aware that he was merely awaiting the next family dispute, border quarrel or tussle over local sovereignty to show his teeth again. Only the truly naive could not have been suspicious about the many trips Philip made in the year 1200 to the sensitive marchlands of Normandy.[57] Indeed many English chroniclers thought that John was a classic dupe for having concluded a treaty on terms so advantageous to France; Gervase of Canterbury dubbed him 'John Softsword', and the nickname stuck.[58] Apologists for John, however, say that he had no real choices. The Angevin empire was geared for defence, not mobility and attack, as the system of castles in Normandy showed quite clearly.[59] To counter the lightning martial probes Philip favoured and to get round the obstacles imposed on military action by feudal custom, Richard had been forced to introduce a standing army in all but name. This, plus his innovation of campaigning all year round, placed enormous strains on the exchequer, and provoked in his critics the familiar charge that he was a monomaniac or military fanatic.[60] The truly costly item in the accounts was the hire of mercenaries, routiers and Brabantines. Richard's heavy taxation had caused many rumblings, and even a rich realm like the Angevin empire could become overstretched if it had simultaneously to defend frontiers from the Cheviots to the Pyrenees. Critics of Richard said he simply borrowed money from international banks or Jewish moneylenders, then left it to underlings to work out how to make the repayments.[61] There is no need to get snarled up in the heated debate about the exact state of the empire's finances in 1199 – had Richard left his realm virtually bankrupt or was this simply 'spin' put on the situation by John's propagandists (and his later admirers)?[62] The fact is that John, rightly or wrongly, thought he could not afford protracted warfare against Philip, and this was the deep subtext of the treaty of Le Goulet.

The extent to which Le Goulet has become a battleground for modern historians is little short of astonishing. One of John's most prominent modern defenders has this to say: 'The contrast with Richard's gusty bravado and reckless resort to expensive adventures no doubt justified to small minds the epithet 'Softsword', but if John had tried a firm sword it would have shattered in his hands.'[63] This follows the familiar pattern of the pro-John faction, which, on a purely *a priori* basis, dubs all chroniclers hostile to John 'unreliable' – a very good example of 'the enormous condescension of posterity'. Gervase of Canterbury's famous (or notorious) judgement on John merely echoes what other chroniclers thought. Ralph of Diceto criticised the peace of Le Goulet severely, and especially the size of the dowry given to Blanche of Castile. Andreas of Marchiennes, another excellent source, said that in the Le Goulet treaty John made the entire war against Philip meaningless by giving to the French king the very things for which the campaign had been waged in the first place. Roger of Howden also took a 'jaundiced though discreet' view of the peace terms.[64] So, although the most balanced interpretation of John's actions at Le Goulet is in terms of his false perception of the differential resources available to both sides, there are grounds for interpreting his actions even more pessimistically, in terms of sheer cowardice or incompetence. Some say that John was shaken by the sudden death of Mercadier, his most able captain, at Bordeaux on 10 April 1200. Others, like Diceto, stress the sheer quantity of bad advice John received: 'less than prudently'; 'on the advice of evil men'; 'in a manner unworthy of the royal majesty' – these are some of the phrases Diceto predicates on John's actions in 1200.[65]

But Le Goulet was not John's only failure in the first year of his reign. He also showed the lack of a sure touch by his less than subtle treatment of two people Richard had dealt with tactfully and diplomatically. John decided to assert himself against his half-brother Geoffrey, who as archbishop of York seemed overmighty and arrogant. While Geoffrey was away in Rome, John kept back the rents from the archiepiscopal estates for his own use and then, on his return from Rome, summoned him to court to explain his high-handed actions.[66] While his attitude to his half-brother (to whom he owed a moral debt for past services) may be regarded as merely petty, his dealings with William, king of Scotland, are more suggestive of bad-tempered incompetence. It appears that 'William the Lion' originally favoured Arthur for the succession and had even intrigued along these lines with William Longchamp.[67] On Richard's death, William offered fealty to John in return for the northern earldom for which he had petitioned Richard in vain. John detained William's envoys at court and instead sent back one of his own, counselling patience. When the Scottish envoys pressed the matter immediately after John's coronation in England, John replied by brusquely summoning William to meet him at Northampton.[68] The Scottish king responded angrily, threatening that if the earldom was not handed over within forty days, he would invade England. John called William's bluff, ignored him, went to France and returned to the issue only in March 1200 when he again summoned William to meet him, this time in York. Again the summons was refused, and it was only in October 1200, when John sent a seven-man embassy north of the border with letters patent, guaranteeing safe-conduct, that William finally came south, to Lincoln, to do homage. John got his way, postponed consideration of the northern counties indefinitely, and engendered a period of strained relations with Scotland.[69]

John's first year as king had hardly been auspicious. It did not help that he had ascended the throne just before the year 1200, when the superstitious forecast an apocalypse, as they always did at a century's end; this time the canard was that Antichrist had been born in Egypt and the world had entered the final days.[70] Famine, dearth and pestilence stalked both France and England; crime was at epidemic levels throughout the Angevin empire, with the saintly bishop Hugh of Lincoln experiencing a succession of footpads, highwaymen and brigands on his 1199 journey to Aquitaine to see Richard.[71] The laws of chivalry seemed in abeyance, both as a result of the Lionheart's year-round campaigning and the new savagery: one half Brabantine atrocity, one half Philip's Byzantine liking for blinding prisoners. John was distrusted by his fellow princes, despised by his barons and deeply unpopular with the common people. It was not just that he walked in the shadow of the great Richard; he was widely regarded as cruel, treacherous, cowardly and politically inept; had not Philip made him an international laughing-stock with the terms of Le Goulet? He had no charisma that would bind men to him, no track record of success in war, and he had a reputation for meanness withal, that contrasted markedly both with the perception of Richard as an openhanded king and the reality that he was lavish with money when it came to buying allies.[72] The great lords who abandoned John in the winter of 1199 and set off on crusade were essentially saying three things: they would be more secure, richer and in every way better off in the Holy Land than in Western Europe while John was king; they could not be sure that he rather than Philip was going to win the struggle for power in greater France; and they regarded John as a morally unsavoury character, who had tried to harm his nephew and would doubtless do the same to them if given a chance; moreover, he was now in alliance with a wife-beater and anti-crusader in the form of Philip Augustus, which rather proved the point.[73]

Contemporary chroniclers and observers were virtually unanimous in finding John an unprepossessing monarch. Aged 32 when he ascended the throne, he always evinced remarkably consistent character traits, few of them, unfortunately, very appealing. He cut a poor figure physically, being no more than 5ft 5ins tall.[74] Contemporaries thought him a poor general and even a cowardly one, though modern historians have not usually been willing to share that view.[75] But not even modern revisionism can shake the universal consensus that John was a deeply unpleasant individual: cruel, miserly, extortionate, duplicitous, treacherous, mendacious, suspicious, secretive, paranoid and lecherous. There can be no serious doubts about his cruelty, for even if we discount the many accounts from hostile witnesses, there are simply too many well attested instances of barbarous behaviour that cannot be argued away. Men were hanged by the thumbs and the hands, roasted on gridirons and tripods, and prisoners were blinded with salt and vinegar. Roger of Wendover tells the story of one Geoffrey of Norwich who was thrown into jail and then weighted down with a cloak made of lead or iron, so heavy that the unfortunate man quickly expired.[76] Even more repulsive was John's treatment of Maud of Saint-Valéry, wife of William de Braose, at one time John's chief henchman in Ireland. When John finally broke with de Braose, he captured Maud and her son and (in 1210) starved them to death in a dungeon at Windsor Castle.[77] John had no compunction about mistreating or murdering women and children, and the comment of the historian Nicholas Vincent hits the nail on the head: 'The chivalric code of honour was never much more than a light veneer, a superficial application of courtesy and civilization to what was, underneath, a far grimmer and more violent reality. At the court of King John the veneer appears to have worn perilously thin.'[78] John indeed always liked to starve people to death, and he visited the same fate on forty knights captured at Mirebeau. Modern defenders of John, unable to deny his cruelty, try to deal with it by ahistorical and anachronistic attenuation, principally through what has been termed the argument *ad Hitlerum*; that is to say, they insinuate the idea that his atrocities were small beer alongside those of Hitler, Stalin or Pol Pot, conveniently ignoring that John lacked both the technology and the political culture for mass killing; there is simply no way of telling how a particular individual temperament would react in an entirely different milieu, but the circumstantial pointers are scarcely favourable.[79] That there was a morbid side to John's cruelty seems clear from his Nero-like delight in bloodshed in the arena – in John's case in the judicial combats that he would often defer to a time and place of his convenience, so as not to miss any nuance of the gory spectacle.[80]

It is almost a stereotype of the despotic personality that cruelty goes hand in hand with extreme suspicion and paranoia, and the paradigm certainly worked out in John's case. He liked to exact an oath from his staff that they would report immediately any comment made about him, especially if it was negative.[81] Treacherous himself, he expected treachery in others. There are those who cannot afford to trust because they cannot afford to fail, but such a defence is scarcely possible for a man who had inherited the Angevin empire and was therefore, by definition, already a success. In John's case pathology rather than circumstance provides the answer. Unpredictable, quick-tempered, capricious, a nurser of grudges and a brooder over ancient wrongs, John liked to lull his victims into thinking themselves secure in the king's affection before making lightning strikes that compassed their downfall. His action at Evreux, when he pretended to be on Philip's side, gulled his way inside the citadel, but then slew the men of the garrison and paraded their heads on poles, is typical of the man.[82] John's defenders are once again on shaky ground, and they usually attempt to palliate his worst excesses by tracing them to an unhappy childhood and then blaming that on Eleanor of Aquitaine. Yet even his most zealous modern defenders tend to give up when faced with the catalogue of his two-faced crimes. One of them finds John 'secretive and suspicious, over-sensitive to the merest flicker of opposition', while another agrees on his 'inability to manage his magnates . . . his suspicion of them contributing to their distrust of him'. Kate Norgate, John's first modern biographer, went further and spoke of his 'almost superhuman wickedness'.[83] The combination of cruelty, suspicion and paranoia receives its most eloquent testimony in the story of his treatment of Peter of Wakefield in 1213. Peter, a harmless crank regarded by fellow rustics as a prophet, made the mistake of prophesying that John would no longer be king by Ascension Day. John imprisoned Peter at Corfe until the due date had passed, then dragged him 'at the horse's tail' to Wareham, where he was hanged. John then meted out the same fate to Peter's son just in case he shared his father's views.[84]

John was avaricious, miserly, extortionate and moneyminded. Like Philip Augustus, he preyed particularly on the Church, exhibiting clear signs of insensate greed and cupidity. Some go so far as to say that his notorious quarrel with the papacy was ultimately actuated by his lust for abbey lands and monastic wealth, rather than personal or political ideology.[85] He begrudged money spent on anything other than his personal pleasures, though as a hedonist he could be lavish and profligate. He liked to live high on the hog and measured his own magnificence by a groaning board, such as the one provided for the Christmas feast in 1206 at Winchester, where 20 oxen, 100 pigs, 100 sheep and 1,500 chickens were roasted, and 1,500 eggs consumed.[86] He liked to spend on gorgeous raiment and gold-trimmed robes and, like many epicureans, was fascinated by jewellery, of which he kept a vast collection; whenever he saw someone with a precious stone he desired, he tended to fine the person and stipulate that the fine had to be paid in the form of the coveted jewellery. He also liked to spend money on gaming and betting, though he was a very poor gambler.[87] Yet most of his money was spent on his mistresses, for John was a notoriously unfaithful husband and ran a veritable harem of lemans, concubines and *grandes horizontales*. Occasionally the names of the mistresses surface in the official records, especially the financial ones. Thus we can identify Clementia and Suzanne, the widow Hawize, countess of Aumale, and a fair unknown to whom in 1212 he sent a chaplet of roses from the justiciar's garden.[88] The names of his known bastards were Joan, daughter of Clementia, Geoffrey and Richard (both of whom had military careers), Oliver and Osbert; Oliver and Richard were born to 'noblewomen who had scandalous liaisons with John'; and there were certainly others, whose names escaped the official records.[89] Some say that lechery was not unusual in a medieval king, and five not a particularly high tally of natural children, especially when set alongside someone like Henry I, who sired at least twenty-one illegitimate offspring. But this defence ignores two crucial factors. There are hints in the sources that John's sexual tastes ran to perversion, possibly sado-masochistic. And John sacrificed political aims and the well-being of his empire to his personal lusts, in that he alienated his barons by pursuing their wives and daughters.[90] As the historian Nicholas Vincent has well said: 'A king who dallied with the wives and daughters of his leading barons was likely to excite far more bitter resentment than a king who confined his extra-marital entertainments to low-born courtesans.'[91]

Another pronounced characteristic of John was restlessness – a quality that was inevitably traced to his father. He became irritated and even angry with priests who said Mass slowly or waffled through sermons, on one occasion sending a servant to tell the preacher in the pulpit that he was bored and wanted his dinner.[92] John also resembled Henry II in his peripatetic court and the speed with which it moved around the realm. The triumphal progress through France in June–August 1200 shows a man dedicated to haste – and this would have had his opponents in the Church nodding their heads, as John perfectly exemplified the old patristic formula that all haste was the work of the devil (*omnis festinatio ex diabolo est*). Starting at Caen, he took in Falaise, Le Mans, Chinon and Loches in under two weeks. On 18 June he was in Angers, at the end of June in Tours, at the beginning of July in Poitiers, on the 14th in Bordeaux, then to St Sever in Gascony, and finally on a zigzag course back north, through Agen, Périgeux, Angoulême and Poitiers (again) before returning to Angers at the end of August.[93] Yet these bursts of frenetic energy alternated with periods of indolence, such as the famous occasion in 1203 when, according to Roger of Wendover, John stayed in bed until midday and spent the rest of the day feasting and carousing even while Philip Augustus overran Normandy.[94] The lazy workaholic is not an unknown phenomenon, and indeed interpreting John is a bit like biblical exegesis in that virtually any proposition can be sustained by picking out certain tendentious passages in the writings of the chroniclers. One historian gave up and concluded: 'Almost any epithet might appropriately be applied to him in one or other of his many and versatile moods.'[95] Yet when all allowances for the bias of hostile witnesses have been made, what remains is a clear indication of manic-depressive behaviour, bipolar affective disorder, cyclothymia – a diagnosis which would also account for the violent mood swings and tempestuous rages.[96]

Three aspects of John particularly appeal to a modern sensibility. First, his love of books. He had a small library which he carried round with him on his restless travels and often swapped titles with the abbot of Reading; we hear of John's interest in Pliny and in the history of England – not something one can ever imagine Richard bothering with.[97] In an age when attention to personal hygiene did not rank as one of the human priorities, John was positively oriental in his liking for baths and cleanliness; the records show that between 29 January and 17 June 1209 he took eight baths at different places on his itinerary and even possessed a dressing gown.[98] Yet what most intrigues the historian of the early twenty-first century is John's alleged atheism. The circumstantial evidence for John's status as unbeliever is strong – he did not attend Communion as an adult – and is explicitly declared by Matthew Paris.[99] The counterarguments designed to make out John as devout are unconvincing. True, he kept up outer show and paid lip-service to official religion, but for purely prudential reasons; John was far from a stupid man and realised that religion was a kind of social cement, in terms of which a sceptical king was in an exposed position. True, he occasionally made donations to religious foundations, but this was merely giving back with the left hand part of the vast sum he had extorted with the right. And would a true believer really have dug in for a long war of attrition with the papacy, as John did? Not even Henry II nor Richard, two men much more audacious and dauntless than John, went so far as this. It is interesting that the one man in English history to go farther down the anti-papal path than John did was Henry VIII, like John a despot who recognised no authority superior to his own will, and like him with a contemporary reputation as Europe's new Nero. Professional historians determined to have John as a loyal son of the Church insist that we should be able to find documentary proof of his atheism, as if John would have been foolish enough to state in a charter or other official document that he did not believe in God. Desperate to find real evidence that John was a devout Christian, his apologists have sometimes tried to cancel out his atheism with his greed, alleging that he preyed on Church wealth out of cupidity, not ideology.[100]

John's apologists like to say that he was a man plagued by bad luck, but it was arrogance and stupidity rather than ill-fortune that characterised his next significant move after the treaty of Le Goulet. John decided to make a dynastic marriage that would cock a snook at Philip of France, but the initial problem was that he was already married. It will be recalled that in 1189 he married his cousin Isabella of Gloucester, related to him in the third degree of consanguinity. This meant that according to canon law the couple could not be legally married unless the Pope relaxed the ruling.[101] Archbishop Baldwin clashed mightily with John by forbidding the pair to cohabit and summoning John to appear before his ecclesiastical court. John allowed no one who was not his feudal superior to 'give him laws', and contemptuously ignored the summons; Baldwin responded by laying an interdict on his lands. John outwitted the archbishop on that occasion by appealing to a papal legate who was visiting England, and got the interdict lifted, pending the Pope's decision on granting a dispensation for the marriage. The papal legate made the would-be solomonic decision that John's marriage was lawful until the Pope decreed otherwise. But Archbishop Baldwin died in the early stages of the appeal to Rome, and no one thereafter had the interest or the energy to pursue the matter. John and Isabella remained in marital limbo, their union neither declared null and void nor valid and indissoluble. This twilight state of affairs suited John very well, especially as he gained Isabella's dowry and the earldom of Gloucester, but he had no special feeling for Isabella and even toyed with a marriage to Alice in 1191.[102] Although John and Isabella were probably still cohabiting in 1196, they had no children. Possibly for this reason, or because his vaulting ambitions already directed his gaze to farther horizons, this was also the year John started taking soundings about an annulment.[103] The matter became more urgent when John became king in 1199, and at the end of that year he demanded that the bishops of Normandy declare the marriage void. The tame clerics complied, and their lead was followed by the even more influential trio of bishops in the south, those of Poitiers, Saintes and Bordeaux – with the Gascon primate the prime mover in John's marital schemes.[104] Pope Innocent III rightly took the view that all six diocesan lords were acting out of sycophancy and looked about for a way to bring John to heel. It required Isabella to appeal to the Vatican, but this was the one thing Isabella did not do, almost certainly because John had bought her off.[105] This divorce by mutual consent irresistibly recalled John's mother's separation from Louis VII, especially as in both cases the royal personages initiating the divorce had hidden agendas of their own.

It was during the tour of his French dominions in the summer of 1200 that John took his fateful decision to remarry. While staying with Hugh the Brown (Hugh Le Brun) at his ancestral seat of Lusignan in early July, John summoned Ademar of Angoulême and Guy of Limoges to pay homage to him.[106] At this stage John seemed determined to stick with the Angevin-Lusignan alliance that Richard had pioneered. It will be recalled that the Lusignans, lords of lower Poitou and doughty crusaders, had waged a forty-year war with Henry II and Richard, which came to an end only when Richard struck up a notable friendship with Hugh of Lusignan in the Holy Land. Hugh had even visited Richard during his captivity in Germany, and in return Richard had elevated the Lusignans at the expense of their territorial rivals, the Angoulême family, headed by Ademar.[107] South of Poitiers the Angevin empire had a shaky existence, with scattered Plantagenet garrisons and outposts vying for hegemony with the local feudal aristocracy who held the real power on the ground. The Angevin rulers had total control only along a narrow coastal strip running from La Rochelle through Oléron and Saintes to Bordeaux. The phantom nature of much 'imperial' control in the south was the origin of the tedious and wearisome wars (in 1167–69, 1173–74, 1176, 1178–79, 1183, 1188, 1194) waged by Henry II and Richard in the south.[108] Simplifying, one can even say that the reigns of Henry and Richard centred on two main themes: the never-ending war in the south and the struggle against the kings of France for the Vexin in Normandy. An Angevin ruler, lacking the military force to impose proper centralised control, had to play divide-and-rule in the south, encouraging the lords of Angoulême and Lusignan to struggle between themselves for the much coveted rich county of La Marche (an Angevin possession since 1177), to which they both laid claim. Alarmed by the chaotic and rapidly changing scene following the sudden death of Richard, Hugh of Lusignan realised that John would not necessarily feel bound by the purely personal ties of friendship that had united him and Richard. Taking matters into his own hands, in January 1200 Hugh actually kidnapped Eleanor of Aquitaine and released her only when John made a solemn promise to assign La Marche to him and reject the claims of Ademar of Angoulême.[109]

Hugh of Lusignan can have feared nothing from the meeting of John and Ademar, for the count of Angoulême had recently added to his de facto independent status (in feudal theory he was supposed to be a vassal of the dukes of Aquitaine but had always enjoyed semi-autonomous status) by the de jure stance of accepting King Philip of France not the duke of Aquitaine (John) as his overlord.[110] But Ademar brought an intriguing, secret proposition from Philip which the devious John listened to eagerly. Philip suggested that the way forward was for John to marry Ademar's only daughter Isabella, as this dynastic match would solve both John's problems in the south and the complications of overlapping homage and feudal duties owed by the count of Angoulême.[111] There was an obvious problem straightaway, which was that Isabella was already engaged to Hugh of Lusignan himself. But Ademar was not pleased with the prospect of this wedding, which he saw as a patronising sop from Hugh because the Lusignans were already nine-tenths of the way towards winning the struggle for La Marche. John was no fool and he saw immediately what Philip's game was: to alienate the Lusignans from the Angevins once more. Yet the alternative was potentially an even worse prospect. If the Lusignans and Ademar of Angoulême made common cause and Lusignan, La Marche and Angoulême all became one bloc, the new alliance would control the valley of the Charente between Poitou and Gascony, dominate the crossroads of central France and occupy all the Roman roads south, especially from Poitiers to Bordeaux; Aquitaine, in short would be cut off from the rest of the Angevin dominions with its survival as part of the empire in serious doubt.[112] The alienation of the Lusignans was therefore a gamble John would have to take, and perhaps it appealed to the gambling side of him. Others have speculated that John always hated the Lusignans, associated them with Richard, deeply resented their kidnapping of his mother, and saw a chance to destroy them once and for all.[113] There was certainly something defiant and deliberately confrontational about the way John planned his elaborate double-cross.

There was yet another twist in the complex skein John was now weaving. At Le Goulet John had told Philip he was thinking of taking a wife, and had sent envoys to the court of Portugal. His thinking was obvious: Richard had done very well politically out of his marriage to Berengaria, but the changed situation in Spain now (with Castile, Aragon and Navarre at war) made a Spanish marriage much less attractive. But a Portuguese union held some of the advantages of Richard's brilliant diplomacy in 1198, potentially menacing Philip in regions where he thought himself secure. To Lisbon, then, his envoys sped in the early summer of 1200, before the fateful meeting between John and Ademar. The negotiations reached an advanced stage, with an exchange of ambassadors.[114] Suddenly everything changed: the Portuguese marriage was off, and John was to marry Isabella of Angoulême. The about-face was so rapid that John's emissaries, still bargaining earnestly in Lisbon, were left out on a limb.[115] Historians have struggled to make sense of the rapid sequence of events. Some accuse John of having had the Angoulême match in mind even while parleying with Philip at Le Goulet, and see the embassy sent to Lisbon as a blind, designed to hoodwink the French king.[116] But this makes no sense if it was Philip himself who suggested the match with Isabella. The overwhelming likelihood is that John was serious in his quest for a Portuguese bride and abandoned it only when he faced potential disaster in the form of the Lusignan-La Marche-Angoulême axis, at which point he abruptly changed tack and married Isabella. There was clearly something rushed about the entire episode. On 5 July John was holding preliminary talks with Ademar of Angoulême; on 24 August he married his daughter in Bordeaux.[117] At the beginning of October the newly-weds crossed to England, where they were crowned together at Westminster on the 8th. Isabella accompanied her husband to the meeting with the Scottish king at Lincoln, then, in the new year to the Scottish border, returning via Cumberland and York to a 'second coronation' at Canterbury at Easter (25 March 1201).[118]

Almost everything about John's union with Isabella has invited controversy: his motives; the murky circumstances of the engagement; the status of the marriage in canon law; the balancing of competing political goals; the personality of the new queen; and the reason for the excessive wrath of the Lusignans.[119] Some historians have alleged that concupiscence marched together with *raison d'état* – in a word, that John lusted after his young bride – but there are substantial difficulties with this notion, as will shortly appear. Politically, John alienated the Lusignans, but he must have known this would happen and he may anyway have regarded them as unreliable allies. In any case, many of his advisers endorsed his decision to break with the Lusignans – William Marshal for one, who loathed them for the murder of his uncle earl Patrick and their humiliation of him when they took him prisoner in those far-off days.[120] Moreover, for a brief period after the marriage, John was at last able to bring Angoulême under effective Angevin control. By the normal rules of expediency and self-interest the marriage made sense, for Isabella's kinship links bound her and John to most of the ruling families of Christendom; her mother was a member of the Courtenay family – a crusading sept – and was descended from the kings of France.[121] Isabella herself was, like most medieval queens, a plaything and puppet of powerful males – her father and her husband – but she was every bit as controversial as her own wedding. She had a difficult role to play – and if she was as young as some scholars allege – an impossible one, not least in that she was merely the third queen of England to come onto the stage, with Eleanor of Aquitaine and Berengaria already ensconced as dowagers.[122]

Oddly enough, it turns out that Lusignan rage and canon law are organically connected in the case of Isabella. Naturally, the Lusignans were angry that John had double-crossed them and snatched Isabella as a bride from under their very noses, particularly since Hugh of Lusignan may have initially condoned the release of Isabella from her betrothal with him on the understanding that John would grant him clear title to the country of La Marche – an expectation John predictably confounded, thus adding a second double-cross to his initial breach of all known feudal custom. In his usual way, he then stoked up the anger of his enemies by gratuitously promising his wife the lordships of Saintes and Niort, two of the richest in Poitou and thus a natural magnet for the Lusignans.[123] Yet there was an 'overplus' in Lusignan anger that suggests some other factor may have been at work, and the probability is that it was John's utterly ruthless lack of squeamishness or regard for the proprieties that so disgusted them. John had not just exhibited a kind of Angevin repetition compulsion by having major problems with his wife, as Henry and Richard had done; he managed to go one better by having problems with both wives. Whereas degrees of consanguinity vitiated the earlier match with Isabella of Gloucester, with Isabella of Angoulême the obstacle to happiness was that canon law laid down a clear age of consent for sexual congress, namely twelve for girls.[124] The suspicion arises that Isabella may have been under the age of consent when John married her, but certainty on this point is difficult, for the chroniclers estimate her age as anywhere between nine and fifteen, with twelve being the favoured option. Henry II's daughter Eleanor had been married to the king of Castile at eight, but the marriage was not consummated until she was fifteen. What enraged the Lusignans was that John had been prepared to marry an under-age girl, where count Hugh had shown more sensitivity towards her. Since it is hinted in many dark corners that John's sexual tastes ran to perversion, it seems that paedophilia may possibly be added to his many crimes. At the very least he was a cradle-snatcher.[125]

From the Lusignan point of view, John had added perversion to treachery and double-cross. Roger of Howden relates that Isabella was betrothed to Hugh of Lusignan in Richard's lifetime, and that the Lionheart approved of the match. Marriage vows were exchanged by proxy, according to the medieval *verba de presenti* formula, whereby it was accepted that a couple was legally married, but the marriage had not yet been consummated.[126] Hugh of Lusignan did not wish to consummate until his bride was legally of age, which provided John with a legal loop-hole but he did not bother to obtain a divorce on these grounds for Isabella but rushed into the marriage as if possessed. The haste of the marriage has led even sober scholars to speculate that he was besotted with Isabella, but if she was not even twelve, John's passion seems abnormal, to say the least. Nicholas Vincent has argued that, since she did not give birth to her first child until October 1207, she may indeed have been around nine years old at the time of her wedding.[127] This would make Matthew Paris's story of John's lust for his wife in 1203, which kept him in bed when he should have been in the field waging war against the French, even more disturbing – if true.[128] Once again historical inter-pretation is vitiated by lack of hard evidence; the charitable (for John) version might be to assume that Coggleshall's estimate that Isabella was twelve in 1200 is the correct one, which would make John's lust for her at fifteen more natural. The fact that Isabella did not conceive until around Christmas 1206 does not necessarily mean that sexual relations between her and John had only just begun. But the consensus seems to be that, once launched on sexual life, Isabella enjoyed it. Matthew Paris, always a hostile witness to both John and Isabella, said that the queen was a shrewish, adulterous, incestuous woman who practised the black arts – 'more Jezabel than Isabella' was his famous description.[129] Although Paris's view of Isabella is usually dismissed as nonsense, both in her particular case and because all medieval royals were routinely described as lecherous and dissipated, there may be fire behind the smoke. Nicholas

Vincent has pointed out that she had several kinsmen in England who could have been her lovers, and the main suspect was her French half-brother Peter de Joigny.[130]

John remained married to Isabella for the rest of his reign, and it has sometimes been assumed from her relative absence from the historical record that the marriage must have been, if not strong, at least serene. This seems doubtful. The only direct evidence of discord is Gervase of Canterbury's statement that John imprisoned her at Devizes in 1209, but even this has been disputed on the ground that the Latin word used to describe the alleged jailing (*includitur*) could mean house arrest or even 'confinement' before a birth.[131] And it is certainly true that Isabella attracted wild rumours and outlandish gossip, such as the absurd story that she was raped at Marlborough and her younger son murdered.[132] Yet it is clear that John continued his extramarital escapades, whether or not he was sexually besotted with Isabella. In 1204, when one of his mistresses wanted to go to bed with her husband instead, an angry John fined her 200 chickens for the privilege. There must be something in the story, for the wronged husband Hugh de Neville showed he had a grievance by appearing in rebellion later.[133] John's taste for cruelty and semi-psychotic caprice also appears in his treatment of the first Isabella, his discarded wife. To keep Isabella of Angoulême in her place, he seems to have kept his first wife in a style as lavish as the queen's and even on occasion forced the two women to be under the same roof, to provide him with some sick enjoyment.[134] On the other hand, there is no such mystery about John's marriage as attaches to the union of Richard and Berengaria. He and Isabella clearly enjoyed normal marital relations, and he sired five legitimate children on her in the years 1207–15. The real problem in the marriage seems to have been that John routinely demeaned and disparaged his wife by not allowing her the sorts of privileges enjoyed by Eleanor of Aquitaine or even Berengaria. The suspicion arises that John, always meanminded and avaricious, refused to pay her normal expenses once he had begotten a male heir.[135]

The official records certainly bear this out, for we see a marked difference in the way Isabella was treated. John played true to form by double-crossing his wife almost instantly. Having angered the Lusignans even more by promising the richest lordships in Poitou (those of Saintes and Niort) to Isabella as a wedding present, he then blatantly failed to make good on his promise. His method was to farm out the lordships nominally assigned to the queen to powerful local magnates and then pocket the rents himself.[136] The contrast between Isabella's position and that of Eleanor, who had real power and real ownership of her dower estates, could scarcely be clearer. Yet Isabella had an even more poignant financial grievance, relating to the so-called Queen's Gold – monies traditionally paid to the royal consort from the taxes, levies and fines on transactions with Jews and other bankers.[137] Whereas Eleanor of Aquitaine always received this income, neither Berengaria nor Isabella did, even though custom ordained that a king could waive a fine but never the taxable percentage of it due as Queen's Gold.[138] What is worse, it is likely that John did in fact levy the money but simply pocketed it himself or – another favourite scam – wrote it off against his personal debts. What is clear is that John kept Isabella in a lamentable state of financial subjection, dependent for everything on his handouts. She received no income from her dower lands or from the Queen's Gold and did not even enjoy Angoulême in her own right. And whereas Eleanor of Aquitaine had brought a huge household of kinsfolk and clients to England, John prevented this is Isabella's case, imposing his own placemen in her household and preventing her from bringing over fellow natives of Angoulême.[139] It is not surprising that in her later years Isabella, who survived John by a full three decades, evinced no fond feelings whatever for her royal husband. John, though, made her a scapegoat for his own failings. It is a known characteristic of the authoritarian personality that such an individual can never acknowledge his own mistakes; errors must always be someone else's fault or the result of a 'conspiracy'. When John lost Normandy to Philip of France in the years immediately after his marriage, it was entirely predictable that he blamed his wife for an outcome that was purely the result of his own weakness.[140]

13

I T WAS SOME TIME before the backlash from the Lusignans manifested itself, so that John must sometimes have wondered if, against all the odds, he had got away with his latest double-cross. Eleanor of Aquitaine, whose political antennae were always much sharper, knew better. At 78 very tired after her latest political mission – a journey to Spain to fetch her grandchild Blanche of Castile for the marriage with Philip Augustus's son – she retired to her favourite anchorage, the abbey of Fontevraud in Anjou. Seeing the way the wind was blowing, she identified Aimeri of Thouars as a key player in the dispute between the houses of Angoulême and Lusignan and invited him to Fontevraud. Aimeri's past was chequered and he was the classical political trimmer: having originally supported John in the spring of 1199, he veered away later in the year into the camp of Arthur and Constance of Britanny, doubtless nudged in that direction by the fact that his brother Guy became Constance's third husband then, but also virtually propelled thither by John's inexplicable action in first making him seneschal of Anjou and Touraine and then rescinding the offer.[1] In February 1201 Eleanor entertained Aimeri at the abbey, and extracted from him a solemn promise that he would remain faithful to John; Aimeri confirmed the pledge in writing to John, in a letter warning him of looming trouble on the continent.[2] John seems to have paid no attention. The Lusignans seem to have been waiting to see if John was prepared to offer any compensation for the affront to their honour, but it was not the new king's way to be gracious in victory. Even one of his defenders concludes ruefully that John liked 'to kick a man when he was down'.[3] He responded to Eleanor's warning by sending his officials to take over La Marche, actually turning the knife in the wound.

By feudal law, John should have denounced the Lusignans in his court before proceeding to despoil them, but a regard for legal niceties was never his strong point when his own interests and desires were concerned. The Lusignans therefore appealed over his head to the nominal feudal overlord Philip of France. Philip proceeded cautiously. He was not eager for another war with John at this time, while he was locked in conflict with the papacy over the bigamous marriage to Agnes of Meran, and his inclination was to pour oil on troubled waters. In a would-be solomonic judgement he tried to 'part the combatants', on the one hand telling the Lusignans to desist from their siege operations in Poitou, on the other inviting John to a conference and rolling out the red carpet for him.[4] He went in person to meet John at the Normandy frontiers, where John had recently arrived from England, flushed with another of his perfidious triumphs. The king of England had just perfected a new financial scam. Having ordered his feudal army (not the mercenaries) to assemble at Portsmouth for a campaign in France, telling his lords to bring all their power and the money for campaigning expenses, he promptly dismissed the knights and their host, but first he relieved them of their expense money and proceeded to hire mercenaries.[5] John congratulated himself on taking a shortcut through the usual resistance to taxes and levies, but his actions were regarded by his own barons as shifty and underhand. He felt himself to be on a winning streak, and was flattered and gratified when an emollient Philip invited him to a state visit to Paris in June. On this occasion Philip Augustus once more laid it on with a trowel and appeared, if anything, over-accommodating, even vacating the royal palace so that John could be lodged there.[6] He told his guest he would disregard the Lusignans' appeal if John did his feudal duty and heard their case in his own court. Unfortunately, John was one of those personalities who regard compromise and statesmanship as weakness. He concluded that Philip must be hiding some weakness that prevented him from being 'strong' and resolved to solve the Lusignan problem in his own repressive way.

John so clearly felt he was the master of events in the summer of 1201 that he even displayed momentarily the flickering generous touch, intermittently in evidence, that his defenders always pounce on with gusto. He settled a generous widow's dowry on Berengaria and, on the strength of this magnanimity, started negotiations for an alliance with Sancho of Navarre.[7] Feeling overconfident, he showed his true character next by the way he dealt with the Lusignans. They had asked for the exhaustive processes of feudal custom to be set in train; very well, he would show them there was pain as well as gain in making feudal appeals. Using the letter but not the spirit of feudal law, he invoked the procedure whereby trial by combat would decide an accusation of treason. He formally charged the Lusignans with long-standing treachery against the Angevin dynasty and offered to prove the truth of his words by a duel to the death with royal champions, issuing individual challenges to dozens of members of the Lusignan family. John then provided a list of his champions, from which it became clear that he had simply bought the services of all the premier duellists and specialists in man-to-man combat in Western Europe. The Lusignans quite rightly declined to play with such a rigged deck, and appealed once more to Philip, pointing out the incontestable fact that John was denying them justice and making a mockery of the very notion of trial by their peers.[8] Credibility required that Philip acted, but he patiently exhausted the repertoire of peaceful conflict resolution. He secured a promise from John that a proper trial, not a travesty, would he held, but then John went back on his word by endless prevarication. He fixed a date for the trial and a venue, then switched both time and place. When Philip continued to press him, he fixed a definite date but then refused to offer the Lusignans a safe-conduct to attend their trial.[9] Becoming more and more irritated, Philip told John that there was no way out of this maze: a feudal overlord like himself *had* to guarantee due process. To underline his seriousness, he insisted that John give him three castles as an earnest of his intentions. John responded to this by sending the archbishop of Canterbury to Paris with an entire rigmarole of specious verbiage and bad faith.[10] By Easter 1202 Philip had had enough of the stalling and evasions. He ordered John to appear before a court of barons in Paris to answer a charge of default of justice. Not yet done with his logic-chopping, John replied that by ancient custom the duke of Normandy was obliged to attend a French court only if it met on the boundaries of France and Normandy. But Philip was fully the equal of such casuistry. He replied that he had summoned John, not in his capacity as duke of Normandy, but as duke of Aquitaine, count of Poitou and count of Anjou.[11] Finally cornered, John made clear the contempt he had been disguising: he refused either to surrender the three castles or to attend the hearing in Paris. In feudal terms he was now a contumacious vassal.

When Philip's barons met, they quickly confirmed that John was, in international law terms, an outlaw. The penalty for contumacity was forfeit of his fiefs of Aquitaine, Poitou and Anjou. Philip now had the perfect excuse he needed to complete the task he had long looked forward to: destruction of Angevin power outside England.[12] Prince Arthur was already a key player in the drama, especially when the death of his mother Constance in September 1201 drove him ever deeper into Philip's orbit. Philip knew which power levers to pull, summoned Arthur to do homage and promised him the hand of his daughter Mary. He also knighted Arthur and declared him John's successor in all fiefs save Normandy, which he retained for his personal domain.[13] The fact that Normandy had expressly not been included as a subject for the decision of the court, so as to checkmate John's prevarications, nonetheless gave John the excuse he needed to present Philip's actions as aggression. He launched into a propaganda offensive to portray himself as the injured party, particularly targeting religious houses.[14] Yet in all other ways he was on the defensive. Philip's position improved immeasurably between 1201 and 1202. Under papal interdict for the bigamous marriage to Agnes, Philip was saved by Agnes's fortuitous death in July 1201. Moreover, in 1201 he had been constrained by the presence in Europe of Richard's old allies on his eastern flank, Baldwin of Flanders and the German princes, who could conceivably make common cause with John. By 1202 these powerful magnates had all departed on crusade. The Fourth Crusade, a notorious shambles that never even reached the Holy Land and ended with the disgraceful sack of Constantinople in 1204, took a raft of putative anti-Philip pieces off the diplomatic chessboard. Baldwin of Flanders fared even worse than Richard by becoming a short-lived emperor of Byzantium and then ending his days as a prisoner of the Bulgarians. Even those German princes who remained at home were no use to John, for they were sucked into the vicious faction fighting between the new Holy Roman Emperor Otto and his deadly rival Philip of Swabia.[15]

The war between John and Philip that now commenced was to be a disaster for the Angevins. No amount of special pleading, purporting to show that France was now richer and commanded more resources than the Angevin empire, can disguise the fact that the years 1202–04 show John simply outclassed by a better general and a more astute politician. Since Philip had no reason to feel jealous of John, as he had of Richard, or patronised and overawed, as he had been by Henry II, his personal feelings for John were probably warmer than for his predecessors, as evinced by the sumptuous reception in Paris in 1201; it may have helped that the two men were roughly the same age (Philip was a year senior), though critics are divided on the impact of kinship (John's mother having been married to Philip's father).[16] Like John, Philip was quick-tempered; like John, Philip had his fair share of conflicts with the Church and the papacy; like him he was a bon vivant; like him he had turbulent relations with women and he was also something of a sexual oddity, though no stories of perversion sully the image of Philip. But there the similarities end. Philip may have been a cold fish, but he was never cruel as John was, and there was nothing 'manic' or bipolar about his steady, plodding, patient and focused march towards his political goals.[17] Alongside Richard he may have seemed cowardly and timid as a warrior, but he was more than a match for John. Above all, he had been tempered in the fire, annealed by exposure to Henry II and then Richard. He had spent an entire adult life contending with Angevin monarchs, and John was the third, and least considerable, of those he encountered. While John was playing the buffoon in Ireland in 1185, or indulging in petty intrigues while Richard was in the Holy Land, Philip had been learning his craft, pitting his wits against Henry II, Saladin and the Lionheart. While John was in obscurity during 1194–99, Philip, though on the back foot against Richard, was building up his strength and learning valuable political and military lessons. Already bald, Philip by now looked the part of an elder statesman, while the chroniclers still tended to view John as an immature playboy, a spoiled brat who had ascended to the purple through luck, essentially a child raised to man's estate.[18]

Philip began the war in his usual unimaginative way, concentrating on the Seine valley and laying siege to the frontier fortresses of Normandy. It was left to Arthur and the Poitevins to display flamboyance by a thrust into the Loire valley, but their energy alarmed Eleanor of Aquitaine, who feared they meant to capture her, so she sent urgent messages to John in Le Mans, pleading for rescue. Fortunately John was in the energetic phase of his bipolar cycle, and he responded with unwonted rapidity and imagination. Taking his army of mercenaries on a forced march of eighty miles in forty-eight hours, he achieved total surprise as he fell upon the enemy unawares. Arthur had urged caution and the need to wait for reinforcements, but the Lusignans argued that if they captured Eleanor of Aquitaine, John's position in the entire south would collapse.[19] With Eleanor now trapped in the keep of Mirebeau castle, Arthur and the Lusignans were complacent, leisurely preparing the *coup de grâce* against the citadel. A force one thousand strong, including Arthur's 200 knights, had no answer when John and his ally William des Roches (seneschal of Anjou and John's right-hand man in the south) swept in on them in the early hours of 1 August. Panic overtook the bleary-eyed or still somnolent men; and Geoffrey de Lusignan was actually breakfasting off roast pigeons when he was taken by John's men. Completely surrounded, the entire enemy force was caught in John's net; no one of any significance escaped.[20] It was probably John's finest victory, the more unexpected for being out of character with his usual martial achievements, and the only time he showed the Lionheart's elan in the field. It was the greatest success for English arms until Crécy, and Philip was momentarily stunned. John permitted himself some public boasting about his exploit, while William Marshal went out of his way to send taunting messages to his old enemy the Lusignans.[21] Philip broke off his campaigning in Normandy and headed south to see if he could retrieve anything from the disaster but he was too late. John made a slow and triumphant progress back to Normandy, exhibiting his heavily manacled prisoners to the people of the towns through which they passed as if they were part of a freak show. The prize catch was Arthur, and he and Geoffrey de Lusignan were imprisoned at Falaise. The Lusignan patriarch Hugh was lodged in a dungeon at Caen, while the non-ransomable prisoners were shipped over to England and held in Corfe castle and other Dorset strongholds. The disaster of Mirebeau might have led anyone less determined than Philip Augustus to sue for peace immediately.[22]

By the autumn of 1202 John was in a dominant position, but if ever there was a time when the moral prevailed over the material it was now. The aftermath of Mirebeau was a test of character that Richard would not have failed, but John managed to do so, evincing distinct self-destructive tendencies withal. He began by alienating William des Roches, the real brains behind the triumph at Mirebeau. Des Roches had given his best advice and employed his best strategy and tactics on the clear understanding that he would decide Arthur's fate if the young prince was captured.[23] John agreed, but then, predictably, went back on his word once he had Arthur in his power. This was fatuous folly. True, des Roches was ambitious, but his ambition could easily have been contained by granting him local hegemony in the Loire valley. The despotic John construed des Roches's reasonable demands concerning Arthur as 'giving him laws' and cast about for ways to take the strut out of his over-mighty vassal. The removal of Arthur to Falaise was a slap in the face to des Roches, and could not have been read in any other way by anyone who was not a milksop. The result was predictable. Des Roches at once abandoned John and persuaded Aimeri de Thouars (previously won over at great cost by Eleanor of Aquitaine) to go with him.[24] The upshot was that John faced continuing warfare in northern Poitou with formidable enemies, when by a scintilla of statesmanship he could have concentrated all his military resources against Philip Augustus in the Seine valley. Trying to paper over the disastrous cracks he himself had caused to appear in his anti-Philip alliance, he did an about-face and tried to curry favour with the Lusignans — the exact thing he should have done two years earlier. Magnanimously he released them from jail on their oath that they would remain loyal – he took pledges and castles as security – but once the birds had flown the coop, they made plain their contempt for John by joining des Roches and Aimeri of Thouars.[25] William Marshal was stupefied at John's naivety and folly in allowing the anti-Angevin party in central France to emerge from the debris of Mirebeau even stronger than before. But it is sometimes observed that treacherous personalities can never quite imagine that anyone else could ever be quite as perfidious. Maybe it was thus with John. It is even more likely that, once he realised his error, he gave short shrift to the less useful prisoners. The story of an attempted mass break-out by twenty-five prisoners at Corfe, which ended with their being surrounded and then starved to death, has more than a whiff of 'shot while trying to escape' about it.[26]

By acquiring a reputation as a cruel, despotic fool John had already gone a long way towards 'losing hearts and minds' but he set the capstone on his malign reputation by his murder of Arthur. In an ominous pre-echo of modern times Arthur suddenly 'disappeared' and for a long time no one knew whether he was still alive. Whenever John tried to open negotiations with the king of France, Philip Augustus sent back the same formulaic answer: first abandon your continental possessions or deliver up Arthur.[27] For the rest of his reign John escaped explicit censure for the murder of Arthur (though most intelligent people suspected what had happened), and spread the disinformation that Arthur had died of fever in prison, had fallen from the battlements while trying to escape or had drowned in the later stages of an escape bid; even Matthew Paris, John's most severe critic in the immediate post-1216 period confessed himself at a loss to know what had really happened.[28] The entire gruesome story began when John, persuaded by his advisers that the 16-year-old 'pretender' to his throne was too dangerous to be left alive, compromised by deciding to have him castrated and blinded. Hubert de Burgh, the castellan at Falaise, baulked at this barbarity and also thought it was stupid, since the whole of Britanny would immediately explode into revolt at news of such an atrocity to its beloved prince. He therefore prevented John's two hired thugs from carrying out their savage mission. This is the famous moment in Act Four Scene One of Shakespeare's *King John*:

> *Well, see to live: I will not touch thine eye*
> *For all the treasure that thine uncle owes.*
> *Yet I am sworn, and I did purpose, boy,*
> *With this same iron to burn them out . . .*

Your uncle must not know but you are dead:
I'll fill these dogged spies with false reports;
And, pretty child, sleep doubtless and secure
That Hubert, for the wealth of all the world,
Will not offend thee.

The historical Hubert was certainly a man who took too much on himself, for he decided to announce that Arthur was dead of natural causes, but the Bretons exploded anyway, convinced that their prince had been murdered. Backtracking feverishly, Hubert then admitted that Arthur was alive, but by then nobody believed him anyway.[29] Britanny was in a ferment, for the cult of King Arthur, sedulously promoted by Henry II, was almost a religion there, and the Bretons regarded the young son of Geoffrey and Constance to be *Arturus Redivivus*. The killing of Arthur was therefore akin to deicide, and his murderer was regarded as a second Mordred, the very avatar of evil and the destruction of the hopes of heaven here on earth. The only thing that remains uncertain is whether the solemn assembly convened by the Bretons in 1203 to condemn John for Arthur's murder was a consequence of Hubert's hamfisted vacillation or whether they had harder evidence of the crime.[30]

Although many people knew the true story of Arthur's death, there was a curious conspiracy of silence about it in the work of the major chroniclers. Only the peculiarly well-informed Cistercian Abbey of Margam in Glamorgan was able to reproduce the grim sequence of events in its annals. It seems that John, furious that Hubert de Burgh had disobeyed him, transferred Arthur to a dungeon at Rouen. The annals continue: 'After King John had captured Arthur and kept him alive in prison for some time, at length, in the castle of Rouen, after dinner on the Thursday before Easter (i.e. 3 April 1203), when he was drunk and possessed by the devil, he slew him with his own hand and, tying a heavy stone to the body, cast it into the Seine. It was discovered by a fisherman in his net and, being dragged to the shore and recognised, was taken for secret burial, in fear of the tyrant, to the priory of Bec called Notre Dame des Prés.'[31] Everything about the story rings true: John's rage, the drunkenness, the cruelty, the cowardice in facing up to the consequences of his own actions. In strictly legal terms, it could be argued that John had every right to put Arthur to death since he was a traitor to a lord to whom he had sworn homage, though Arthur could have pleaded duress in answer to that charge.[32] As a betrayer of a feudal lord, Arthur could have been put to death without trial, which doubtless accounts for the subdued tone of the papal reaction to Philip's formal indictment in 1216. From the vantage point of the Vatican, which had experience of murders of kings and by kings going back over the centuries, Arthur's death was a 'little local difficulty', not something that raised fundamental ethical and theological issues. It must be remembered that the cult of Arthur as the reincarnation of the mythical king Arthur of England was something confined to Britanny; his murder would only have been perceived as a sin crying to heaven for vengeance in the Celtic fringes imbued with the legends of the Round Table. For all that, even in an age inured to brutality, John's callous making away with his nephew touched a nerve. It is no accident that, as soon as Arthur's death was regarded as a moral certainty, many major Norman barons deserted John, including the count of Evreux, Hugh of Gournai, Peter of Meulan and Guy of Thouars.[33]

Yet John had to undertake a major task of damage limitation, and engaged his favourites in an elaborate cover-up. He realised that his best move was to leave Arthur's fate in a limbo of uncertainty, for the Bretons would not move against him in force until they were sure Arthur was dead. As in all such cases, the accessories were themselves in danger. John's key henchman on this occasion was William de Braose. When he fell from favour in 1207, John demanded his sons as surety for his good behaviour; he realised that de Braose knew too much and was dangerous. William's sharp-tongued wife refused to hand over her sons to a man who was a known murderer, one who had not scrupled to assassinate his own nephew.[34] John had to wait a few years before he could take revenge on the de Braose sept and when he did he was as merciless with them as with Arthur (see below, pp.344, 347) Philip Augustus meanwhile showed a curious insouciance about Arthur's fate. While using him as a bugbear ('first produce Arthur') in his dealings with John, he did not milk the murder for its real propaganda worth, and the truth is that Philip had no personal, as opposed to political, feelings about Arthur. Although it is often claimed, and with justification, that the death of Arthur was one of the factors that ultimately lost John Normandy, Philip's strategic and tactical planning proceeded without regard to Arthur. It is sometimes falsely stated that Philip began his campaign of 1203 to avenge Arthur, but the reality is that for a long time Philip could not be sure the young pretender was dead – and hence the phrase 'if he still lives' used in documents dated that year which refer to Arthur.[35] Probably it was only in 1204 that Philip knew for certain of the passing of Arthur, yet it was not until 1216 that John was widely acknowledged in Europe to be the prince's killer. By this time the poets and chroniclers were embellishing and adding ornate touches to the basic story: William le Breton's tale that John took Arthur out on the Seine in a boat, killed him and then tipped him overboard, sounds more like Theodore Dreiser's *An American Tragedy* than the sad story of the death of princes.[36]

The murder of Arthur was, moreover, more effect than cause of John's military collapse. As a result of his folly, mismanagement and incompetence, by autumn 1202 John faced war on three fronts: in the east with Philip in the traditional theatres of Normandy and the Vexin; with the Bretons in the west; and with the powerful coalition of des Roches, Thouars and the Lusignans in the south. John's reconnaissance trips revealed an overall situation even more serious than his worst estimates. Depressed and confused, John did not need much more to tip him over into outright defeatism, and the trigger seems to have come in January 1203. Hastening south to rescue a beleaguered Queen Isabella, John found himself cut off by the count of Alençon, who suddenly declared for the other side after wining and dining the king of England in apparent friendship just two days earlier. There was no second Mirebeau, no second lightning dash south; John retreated to Le Mans, tail between legs, leaving the ticklish task of rescuing Isabella to his mercenary captain Peter de Preaux.[37] It was during the limbo period of inactivity that followed that John, raging in his cups, slew Arthur. The situation in the south deteriorated to the point where Philip Augustus was able to coast down the Loire in perfect safety for a meeting with his southern allies.[38] Bottled up in Normandy, John soon found that the allegedly impenetrable carapace of Angevin defences was no such thing. Mere fortifications cannot bolster morale, and the mood throughout Normandy in early 1203 was vehemently anti-John, with more and more barons going over to Philip every week. Le Mans, Angers and Alençon were soon in enemy hands, as well as the strongholds of Beaumont-le-Roger and Conches.[39] The great fortress of Vaudreuil on the left bank of the Seine surrendered to the French without an arrow having been shot, creating a sensation throughout the land.[40] John seemed paralysed by the course of events; the usual restlessness collapsed into lethargy, apathy and sensualism. Roger of Wendover claimed that John was consumed by lust for his wife and therefore neglected the great affairs of state, but even those historians who reject the story are hard put to suggest other explanations, unless the alternative theory of bipolar disorder (equally unpopular with straitlaced analysts of his reign) is brought into play. When told that Philip had led away the castellans of surrendered castles tied to the tails of their horses, he remarked insouciantly: 'Let him alone; I will win back all his booty some day.'[41] The only rational interpretation that favours John asserts that he was awaiting papal intervention, thinking Innocent III was on his side; Innocent might have been, but John misunderstood the political realities, which were that Philip was prepared to risk a papal interdict if it meant that he could conquer Normandy.[42]

The crisis in Normandy reached a climax in August 1203 when Philip brought up his heavy siege engines and opened the siege of Château-Gaillard, Richard's cynosure, his 'Saucy Castle' – the pride of Angevin Normandy and hitherto thought so far impregnable that it was not even worth investing it.[43] For once John felt proof against treachery, as the castellan, Roger Lacy, was an Englishman with no territorial or political interests in Normandy. But Château-Gaillard, with its large garrison, was vulnerable to hunger, and the Angevin supply lines had to be secured. John planned a twofold approach: running supplies through Philip Augustus's blockade while preparing a smashing counteroffensive to destroy the French mangonels and trebuchets. On paper at least by August John was back in an energetic phase, for his scheme for blockade running was a return to Mirebeau conceptions and, if successful, would have done credit to Richard himself.[44] John devised an ambitious amphibious stratagem. Seventy supply vessels laden with provisions and guarded by marines – the first fruit of Richard's inchoate attempts to make England a naval power – would move up the Seine at night, flanked by routiers. Meanwhile William Marshal would lead a mixed force of cavalry and infantry up the left bank, ready to fall on the French camp at dawn. While the French were fighting for their lives, the marines and routiers would demolish the pontoon bridge Philip had built across the river to prevent the arrival of enemy reinforcements and, free from interference, ferry the supplies to the castle. Amphibious operations are difficult at the best of times, especially night-time ones, and require meticulous coordination and split-second timing. Unfortunately, John's naval captains had not properly factored in the strength of wind and current, and the rowers on the supply vessels found themselves beating up against a hostile current, losing time all the while. Marshal's attack force struck the French as planned, but at dawn the naval party was still not at Château-Gaillard. The result was that the French were able to deal with the attacks piecemeal. First they beat back Marshal's army with heavy losses, then turned to deal with the second threat.[45] The marines and Brabantines tried to smash their way through on their own but were heavily routed by the combined French forces. Blocks of wood, arrows and even Greek fire rained down on the attackers from the heights. Angevin losses that night were grievous, and it was said that the Seine ran red with the blood of courageous but doomed marines and mariners.[46]

The siege of Château-Gaillard lasted from the end of September 1203 until 6 March 1204, but thereafter John made no attempt to relieve it. Instead he swung west to deal with the Bretons, apparently hoping that if he defeated them, Philip Augustus would raise the siege of Château-Gaillard and march westward. But Philip was not to be tempted. John's forces took Dol, and his mercenaries had a field day, running rampage, gutting the cathedral, sacking and looting to their heart's content, yet nothing militarily significant was achieved.[47] Returning slowly to Rouen via Falaise and Lisieux, John spent the autumn of 1203 in another furious lather of indecision and dithering, where mere energy substituted for thought or planning. On one occasion in October he rode all day from dawn to dusk, covering an immense distance but for no discernible reason. After a drinking bout in Caen, he then returned to Rouen, the entire reason for the journey still a mystery.[48] John was inclined to give up the ghost and flee to England, but credibility demanded that he save face and make some kind of showing. Yet already his councillors were picking up the contagion of defeatism. William Marshal tried to talk some sense into him: 'Sir, you have too few friends, and if you challenge your enemies to fight, you will be crippled.' John made one of those offhand, cavalier and almost delphic replies that so infuriated his followers: 'Whoever be afraid, let him flee. I shall not go for a year.'[49] But he was whistling in the dark, and he knew it. The moment of truth came in December when he announced that he was going to England 'to consult his barons' but would return immediately; the fact that he took Queen Isabella with him made his advisers doubt the exact truth of the last remark. The preparations for the flight to England – for no other word than flight will do – show a secretive, panicky, paranoid mind at work. Fearing betrayal and scenting treachery everywhere, he gave out that he was going to sleep in the castle of Bonneville on his way to the coast, but slept in the town instead, lest he be apprehended. At the next stop he went to bed, told William Marshal and his barons to wake him at dawn, then got dressed and rode on through the night with his most trusted admirers; when Marshal and the others came to his chambers at daybreak, John was already twenty miles away. He rode to Bayeux via Caen, then headed for Barfleur, where he embarked for England on 5 December.[50] As many in his entourage had suspected would be the case, he never returned to Normandy.

John spent Christmas of 1203 at Canterbury, and the rest and security seem to have enabled him to recover his nerve. Early in the new year he met his barons at Oxford and outlined the options.[51] Eastern Normandy had passed out of his control, though there were glimmerings of hope elsewhere. Château-Gaillard still held out – and while it did so Rouen was safe – and Chinon under Hubert de Burgh, Loches under the mercenary captain Gérard of Athée, and the powerful garrison at Tours provided beacons of light for the Angevin cause. John argued strongly that a major expeditionary force was needed and for that he required money, taking the opportunity to chide the barons for their tightfistedness hitherto. Now John announced a new war levy via 'scutage' or shield-money, the process whereby feudal landholders paid a lump sum to an overlord for military service owed and then reclaimed the amount from their knights.[52] Since most magnates in England held their land in return for military service, they could not avoid scutage, which on this occasion was levied at a rate of two and a half marks for every knight they would otherwise have to bring into the field. John topped up the scutage income with a plethora of new or amended taxes: tallage uplifted from towns; a 7 per cent tax on all mercantile goods in ships in English ports; privileges, prerogatives, titles and lifetime concessions sold off to the highest bidder.[53] The universal mulcting irresistibly recalled Richard and the 'Saladin tithe' but that had been for the 'noble' purpose of expelling the heathen from the Holy Land, while these latest taxes were designed merely to recoup territories a wiser and better king would not have lost in the first place. John's hopes of reconquest rose, and on 6 March he gave detailed orders for the transport of animals – dogs, horses, falcons as well as prey like deer and boar – for the hunts he proposed to hold in France.[54] By a choice irony, on this very date the situation in Normandy reached the point of no return when Château-Gaillard fell. Philip Augustus was not a military natural as Richard had been; but time proved that he was a stayer, capable of learning from more talented men and absorbing lessons learned at Acre and elsewhere. By 1203 he had become as much a master of siegecraft as the Lionheart. The defenders contested every inch of ground tenaciously, but Philip's sappers and miners over the months gradually succeeded in weakening the castle walls; the English made the mistake of countermining, hoping to frighten off the French burrowers, but this simply made the foundations even more tottery. When he was convinced that the wall was seriously undermined, Philip brought up his most massive trebuchet and hurled gigantic boulders at it until it collapsed. Vicious hand-to-hand fighting ensued until the weary English survivors in the citadel, by this time reduced in number to 156, finally surrendered.[55]

The news of the fall of the 'impregnable' Château-Gaillard sent shock-waves across the Angevin empire; the reaction in Normandy was closer to panic. It now seemed distinctly possible that Rouen might fall before John could get his relieving army over the Channel. Efforts were switched to building up an enormous granary and storehouse of provisions in the Norman capital, so that it could not be starved out. Within its strong walls and triple fosse, John's faithful lieutenant Peter de Preaux remained confident he could hold out until John's new army crossed over from England, for there were already enough supplies to feed the garrison for a year and Rouen, unlike the other towns in Normandy, really did owe its wealth and prosperity to the special favours received from John; since its burghers had nowhere to go but down under any new dispensation, they were immune to the virus of turncoating sweeping across the duchy.[56] John allowed himself to relax and lay plans for a huge counteroffensive, using Caen and the Cherbourg peninsula (hitherto unravaged by the war) as his launch-pads. Meanwhile John tried to exhaust all his diplomatic options, even forlornly sending to Germany to see if there remained any Rhineland lord who had not left on crusade. He placed many of his hopes on papal intervention, and fortuitously a papal legate was in England, charged with the very task of achieving a cease-fire between Angevins and Capetians. In the second week of April a high-powered delegation (including William Marshal, the archbishop of Canterbury, the earl of Leicester and the bishops of Norwich and Ely) accompanied the nuncio on a visit to Philip in Paris. Philip was affability itself but he would not be budged on his main demands: John must hand over Arthur and surrender all his continental claims.[57] The insistence that Arthur's sister Eleanor (whom John had, paradoxically, treated well) also be handed over must have struck a sour note, for John had just lost another Eleanor – his mother. She died at 80 on 1 April 1204, already foreseeing the loss of Normandy. Richard had always been her favourite son, but she had also performed for John tasks that went way beyond the call of either maternal or queenly duty.[58]

Faced with the prospect of a gruelling siege of Rouen, Philip revealed his true intelligence. He simply turned away and left it to stew, instead concentrating on targets on the periphery of Normandy. He reasoned that if all the rest of Normandy were lost, it would be futile for Rouen to try to stand alone, an Angevin oasis amid a wilderness of enemies. He marched up the River Risle and took Argentan; the next objective, Falaise, birthplace of William the Conqueror, resisted half-heartedly for a week then capitulated. Caen then surrendered without a fight, and barons and nobles flocked in from all sides to worship the rising sun and pay their homage to the new conqueror.[59] Meanwhile in the west his Breton allies swept over Mont St Michel and Avranches; the Bretons and the French then converged and mopped up the Cherbourg peninsula.[60] With most of Normandy in his hands, Philip then allowed himself a leisurely progress through Lisieux, bound for Rouen. The Rouenais were now surrounded and pondered their options; it was one thing to be the jewel in the Angevin crown and to receive all the trading and financial privileges that went with that status, but what happened if there was no longer an Angevin ruler to protect them? If they were to salvage anything from the wreck, the burghers had to look to their own salvation and make what terms they could with the new dispensation. Philip piled on the pressure by granting 'most favoured' status to towns already conquered, which raised the possibility that Rouen, once top of the heap, would soon be the bottom-most. Peter de Preaux, seeing how the minds of the civilians were working, sent frantic messages to John, saying that without the swift advent of a relieving army, he stood no chance.[61] To save destruction from mangonels and the barbarities that would accompany a sack of the city, on 1 June 1204 de Preaux came to sensible terms with Philip: it was agreed that if John did not come to his aid in thirty days, his duties to his feudal lord would have been fully discharged and an honourable surrender could follow. Peter de Preaux wrote to John again, stressing the urgency of his situation. John sent back one of his cavalier messages, that everyone should do what ever seemed best. It was *sauve qui peut*. De Preaux saw no point in prolonging the misery and surrendered on 24 June, a week before the deadline.[62] Philip spent August and September mopping up Angevin fortresses in the Loire, adding Niort, Tours, Amboise, Saumur, Poitiers, Loudun, Montreuil and Parthenay, plus the fortresses of Loches and Chinon, to his victorious tally.[63] The entire duchy of Normandy, save only the Channel Islands, was lost to the English crown.

Why did John lose Normandy so spectacularly, when his father and brother had easily held their own against the French? The proximate cause was the epidemic of treachery that beset him, with literally dozens of barons going over to Philip; one scholarly study lists thirty-eight names, while admitting that they are the tip of an iceberg.[64] Many of the most important magnates changed allegiance once it became clear that John had murdered Arthur, including Count Amaury of Evreux, Hugh of Gournai, Peter of Meulan and Guy of Thouars. The contemporary chroniclers were quite clear in their own minds that John was unable to resist Philip's incursions or relieve besieged castles because he could not trust his own Norman vassals.[65] Treachery, then, had both an objective and subjective aspect: objectively, it robbed John of vital resources and fighting men, while subjectively it increased his tendency towards paranoia and left him paralysed, unable to take any firm decisions as he could never be certain who were the men he could truly rely on. The situation in Normandy in 1203–04 was overwhelmingly John's own fault: he had no natural powers of leadership or charismatic personality, he could not enthuse men and make them work for greater purposes than immediate self-interest, and he had the aura of a loser – 'John Softsword' was a tag that did a lot of damage – in clear contrast to Richard, who always had the psychological advantage over his enemies of appearing to be invincible. John could be tough, ruthless and even cruel, but he could not inspire love, admiration or devotion, he was liable to panic when the going got tough, and his risk assessment was poor, doubtless heavily influenced by his 'bipolar' oscillation between hypertrophied optimism and black pessimism. William Marshal's poet biographer put the issue very clearly: 'The Normans were not asleep in the day of the Young King. Then they were grain but now they were chaff, for since the death of King Richard they have had no leadership.'[66]

John's defenders claim that Normandy was anyway slipping from the Angevin grasp by the time he came to the throne and that not even Richard could have arrested the process. This argument tends to be three-fold, subdividing into what one might call political, cultural and structural aspects. The political proposition is that the dukes of Normandy, once they became kings of England after 1066, put England before Normandy, treated the duchy as an appanage of the kingdom, and took over modes of tyranny and despotism which were native to England but not to Normandy. In modern terms, we might say that the Angevin rulers had lost political legitimacy. The idea that the descendants of William the Conqueror had absorbed an allegedly Anglo-Saxon tendency towards authoritarianism, as it were by osmosis, seems a curious argument, but there was undoubtedly a widespread perception in Normandy that their rulers had become more dictatorial and had flouted many of the older Norman customs, mores and folkways. Gerald of Wales drew attention to the paradox that while they were simply dukes of Normandy, the rulers easily held their own against the French but, once they acquired the kingdom of England as well, with much greater resources, they performed far less impressively against the Capetian monarchs of France. Gerald thought that ordinary Normans had responded to the increase in despotism of their rulers by, as it were, working to rule and he put a new 'spin' on the hardy perennial, beloved of students of the Ancient World, that Persian slave levies could never defeat free Greeks. 'How can they raise necks trodden down by the harshness of notorious tyrants to resist the arms and fierce courage of free Frenchmen?'[67] Gerald topped up this political argument by a quite different, cultural, one. He correlated the rise of France under Philip Augustus with an artistic and intellectual renaissance based in Paris, which was by now streets ahead of Rheims or Chartres as an academic and creative powerhouse. In modern terms we might say that the France of Philip Augustus, who was consciously presenting himself as the new Charlemagne, was becoming culturally 'hegemonic' in all francophone areas.[68] Notions like legitimacy and hegemony, which have a peculiarly twentieth-century resonance, actually work perfectly well in explaining political change in the early thirteenth century.

Yet the main argument purporting to show that the loss of Normandy should not be laid at the door of John personally is that Normandy was already becoming disaffected as early as the reign of Henry II, simply because Normans resented the continual warfare between Capetian and Angevin and the financial cost of this that they were called on to bear. Normandy was already in debt in 1194, because of the vast sums raised for the Crusade and then the ransom money paid to Germany for Richard's release, with instalments of debts contracted for this purpose still being paid off in 1203–04. When sustained warfare began again in 1194 in Normandy, the financial exactions rose to meet its costs, but the duchy was having to run to stay in the same place, for the more revenue-yielding regions that fell to Philip Augustus's conquest, the less the tax yield and the greater the consequent Norman expenditure on defence. Old taxes – scutage, tallage, carucage or the Norman equivalents thereof – were levied at higher rates while new taxes were introduced, on bailiwicks and towns especially. John compounded the problems by financial mismanagement, and when Philip Augustus's military probes bit off larger and larger lumps of Normandy, the duchy managed to keep going only with the injection of funds from England.[69] Normans had to endure hefty taxation as well as the horrors of war – rape, atrocity, looting, the murder of civilians and the sacking of towns – in a campaign that they increasingly thought could not be won. Everyone perceived the balance of power to be swinging in favour of Capetian France; that kingdom seemed to be almost visibly waxing while Normandy waned, and the days when a William the Conqueror could habitually defeat the king of France were long in the past. Since Philip Augustus was the rising power it made sense for both masters and men to come to terms with him and abandon John. John, on this view, was simply unlucky; neither his father nor his brother had to contend with a France with its present level of resources, and the intrinsic weakness of the Angevin empire, which had been there for fifty years for the really shrewd to discern, suddenly became apparent to everybody. John, in short, was the victim of historical inevitability.[70]

Naturally there is much merit in this 'structural' argument but there has been in recent years a tendency to push it too far. The relative strengths and weaknesses of the Angevins and Capetians can be debated, if inconclusively, but the logic of historical process cannot explain or excuse the contingent actions John took in Normandy, unless we accept the quasi-Marxist argument that the 'privatisation' of John's realm was happening because feudal relations in general were already weakening and being replaced by a money economy. On this view, there might well be a correlation between the rise of a cash nexus and the rise of John's personal retainers, the 'knights bachelor', and his consequent detachment and alienation from his barons.[71] But it is very difficult to see how any overarching historical process can excuse or mitigate John's egregious stupidity in farming out large sections of Norman administration to his mercenary captains. It is true that Richard had introduced the practice in exceptional circumstances, but John made it the norm throughout his francophone empire. The idea of an administrative cadre being headed by bloodthirsty buccaneers in itself suggests why Normandy was lost; Philip may have used mercenaries but he never made them senior civil servants. Among John's appointments were Martin Algais as seneschal of Gascony, Gérard of Athée as seneschal of Touraine and Brandin in the same office in La Marche.[72] John openly declared about Algais: 'Know that the service of Martin Algais we esteem more highly than the service of any other person.'[73] The most controversial of all such appointments was that of Lupescar aka Louvrecaire ('The Wolf') to a Norman baili-wick. The most rapacious of all John's profit-obsessed mercenary captains, Lupescar alienated great swathes of Norman society by his barefaced rapacity. The abbess of Caen was reduced to paying John protection money to ensure that Lupescar did not despoil the abbey's estates further, after he had siphoned off vast chunks of the estate as his own personal rents.[74] The lupine depredations of Lupescar became a black legend in Normandy, to the point where William Marshal's biographer recorded the following judgement: 'Do you know why King John was unable to keep the love of his people? It was because Lupescar mistreated them and plundered them as if he were in enemy territory.'[75] Things reached the pass where John had to bind his Norman barons with an oath that they would defend and protect the hated Lupescar in return for his own pledge to rein him in; left to themselves, the barons would gladly have killed The Wolf.[76]

It is difficult to overstate the reign of terror unleashed throughout the Angevin empire when John foolishly let these mercenary captains off the leash. The routiers swarmed over the land like locusts, preying on all and sundry without distinction of rank: neither churches nor monasteries nor even large towns were safe from their depredations.[77] It was fortunate for John that the mercenary leaders never made common cause, or they might have posed the threat to his kingship that the Praetorian Guard did to the Roman emperors. Too greedy, self-centred and blinkered to cooperate, these thugs led atomic existences, each in his sphere of influence with his band of desperadoes. Their non-parochial ambitions were largely directed at each other: Richard's favourite routier captain Mercadier was assassinated in the streets of Bordeaux by a henchman of Brandin, and one is tempted to see this murder of Richard's right-hand man by one of John's minions as a kind of transference of sibling wishes from younger to elder brother.[78] A weak ruler, John never kept an iron grip on these unruly elements, as Richard always had. Mercadier summed up thus his service for Richard: 'I fought for him loyally and strenuously, never opposed his will, was prompt in obedience to his commands, and because of this service I gained his esteem and was placed in command of his army.'[79] But in John's reign the routier captains were not just subject to only the most nominal suzerainty from the centre, but they demanded, and received, all kinds of special privileges and perquisites: special protection for their booty which was almost sacrilegious in the quasi-sacramental status it gave to ill-gotten goods; the right to keep and ransom their own prisoners; the right to govern their castles and estates according to their own lights rather than in accordance with local laws and customs.[80] Whereas Richard had valued Mercadier because of his military talent, John liked the company of routier captains like Martin Algais precisely because they were cruel and nihilistic and shared his contempt for religion and the normal feudal regulations that bound a liege lord to his vassals; John wanted all the rights of an overlord but none of the duties. It is hard not to be pleased that the biter was often bit; the detestable Lupescar, a psychotic thug with no redeeming graces, repaid the multiple benefits he had received from John by deserting him and surrendering Falaise to Philip in 1204.[81]

Nonetheless, John's apologists both ancient and modern, have always clung to the consoling argument that Normandy was already effectively lost to the Angevins before John ever ascended the throne, though naturally they disagree on the reasons.[82] For some, the rot had already set in during the reign of Henry II; for others, Richard is the villain, for having allegedly impoverished Normandy.[83] But the most influential argument is that, in ways largely unexplained, Philip Augustus became much more powerful financially than the Angevin empire in the decade of the 1190s. The best research, however, fairly conclusively establishes that Capetian resources had *not* overtaken those of the Plantagenets by 1202–03; it is conceded that Philip's revenues had increased but not by nearly enough to provide a decisive advantage over John. As the historian V.D. Moss points out: 'King John was almost certainly extracting more revenue from Normandy than King Henry II did in 1180.'[84] The more ingenious defenders of John therefore concede that Philip had no significant advantage in economic and financial resources overall, but that he was able to employ the principle of concentration of force: he was able to deploy his energies much more effectively in the war zone of Normandy, which was geographically contiguous to the kingdom of France; clearly no Angevin ruler could harness all the wealth of Aquitaine and England purely to defend Normandy.[85] Moreover, once Normandy was lost and its resources started accruing to France, Philip's local superiority became even more pronounced, making the prospect of a campaign of reconquest chimerical. Yet even the concentration of force argument relies heavily on the hidden premise that Richard really had bled Normandy dry, and this too has been effectively contested. The allegation rests on economic naivety. As the most careful student of the loss of Normandy has shown, vast sums of money from England and the king's creditors were spent in Normandy, so that if anywhere was being bled dry it was England. And taxation and war-spending lavished on projects like Château-Gaillard were not a one-way drain on Normandy's resources, since the extra employment and income thus generated in turn stimulated the Norman economy.[86]

The great historian of Richard's reign, John Gillingham, has made two further crucial points. A direct comparison of the resources available to John and Philip might just, on the concentration of force argument, show that Philip had greater power in Normandy, on the basis that the wealth of England and Aquitaine could not be *entirely* mobilised to defend Normandy. But such a comparison would be unreal, ignoring as it does the clear and obvious fact that Richard in 1198–99 had powerful allies on Philip's eastern flank (in the shape of the German princes and Baldwin of Flanders), and that the *combined* resources of this coalition easily outweighed Philip's.[87] The overwhelming consensus of all the most reliable contemporary chroniclers was that in 1198–99 Richard was richer than Philip.[88] Even if, for the sake of argument, we accept the proposition that in 1203–04 John had inferior resources to Philip's, this could only be, as a matter of pure logic, because he had alienated the allies Richard cultivated so assiduously, so that they departed on crusade and deprived John of the Angevin's second front. Gillingham's second argument in effect turns the 'concentration of force' thesis on its head. If it is accepted that it is not just a question of resources, but the *direction* and deployment of those resources, then we can easily appreciate that in 1197–98 Richard both outspent Philip in buying key allies but also won the propaganda war by being more generous.[89] In short, even if we exclude the factors of treachery and mercenaries from the count against John, we discern a clear pattern of a successful Richard and failing John that has nothing whatever to do with revenues, resources or structures. It is surprising that the financial argument purporting to favour John has been given so much consideration, for Richard's position in Normandy in 1194 was far weaker than John's ten years later, as vast amounts of money had to be diverted from the war zone to pay the huge ransom in Germany. 1194 comes into the picture in another way, for it was John's willingness to surrender most of upper Normandy to Philip in January that year which so alienated many of the Normans and led to the fracturing of the duchy, with ducal power only really strong thereafter in the central and western areas, from Rouen to the Cotentin.[90]

In the propaganda war between Richard and Philip Augustus, Richard was always the winner, and indeed in the late 1190s Philip was widely regarded as an oppressive ruler.[91] Only someone with an even worse reputation would lose a propaganda war against the French king, and John duly obliged. William of Newburgh made the important anti-deterministic point that personal charisma could transcend resentment caused by heavy taxation, and this Richard was always able to do; John clearly was not.[92] Widely perceived as a great Christian hero, Richard was given the kind of leeway never permitted to John, as Ralph of Coggleshall pointed out.[93] Yet even without the uneven personality contest, John never matched Richard. V.D. Moss roundly asserts: 'John's failure to match Richard's fiscal performance as duke of Normandy must carry significant weight in any explanation of the duchy's fall.'[94] Of course, financial performance and propaganda persona can never entirely be considered separately, for John's murder of Arthur affected his revenue collection as well as his general credibility. John lost control of the eastern marches of Normandy very early in his reign, and it was because of his own weakness that he eventually lost the entire province. It was his incompetence and double-dealing that alienated William des Roches and the rest of the great Norman magnates; it was his poor showing as a monarch that led Baldwin of Boulogne and the German princes to depart on crusade instead of allying themselves with him; it was his brutal and cowardly murder of Arthur that completed the process of disgust and disillusionment.[95] Add to that his morbid fear of betrayal, his tendency to panic, the objective fact that most Norman nobles did betray him, plus the depredations of his mercenaries and it is truly staggering – and certainly against any conceivable version of Occam's razor – that historians should have sought financial and structural reasons for his failure in Normandy.[96] The brutal fact is this: John and John alone, because of his vices and failings, lost Normandy. Richard would never have done so – and indeed he held the whip hand against Philip until the end of his life and was clearly winning the Normandy war. Normandy would never have become part of Capetian France while Richard was alive, which is not to say that it could *never* long-term have suffered such a fate.[97] We are concerned only with Richard and John, and it is as clear as anything can be that Richard was a winner and John a loser. Nothing succeeds like success, and men knew that Richard won battles and campaigns and could therefore be followed with confidence. With John the reverse was the case.

Fully to trace the manifold consequences of the loss of Normandy would take one too far away from a dual biography of Richard and John. Among the many byways are those concerning the impact of 1204 on English law, and particularly the development of laws against treason and aliens. Under a system of divided loyalties, where barons did homage to both the duke of Normandy and the king of France under the complex system of overlapping fealty already noted, the notion of treason was both absurd and otiose, and vassals were still allowed to rebel against lords without incurring the dread charge of traitorous behaviour. This situation began to change after 1204, much more rapidly in England than in France.[98] Because of divided loyalties, it was not easy to prove a charge of treason, but it started to become simpler once Philip and John were ruling distinct and non-overlapping realms. It was only much later in the thirteenth century that the French monarch St Louis insisted on an absolutely clear distinction between fealties. But the loss of Normandy did throw the issue of land tenure into sharper focus. In 1205 Philip Augustus confiscated the lands of all knights with property in Normandy who lived in England unless they returned by a given date; John retaliated by a similar order expropriating lands in England held by Norman knights who threw in their lot with Philip.[99] Magnates faced a stark choice: they must decide whether their future lay in England or Normandy, for there was no halfway-house. This was a tough decision for the many barons who had lands in both countries, but at least their position was easier than that of the sub-tenants, wards, widows and others, whose feudal future depended on the judgement or whim of overlords, guardians or former husbands. At least it was possible to change one's mind if the initial choice of lords and lands proved misguided; on payment of a suitable sum (officially a fine), barons could buy back their forfeited lands and change residences. It was only in 1244 that St Louis ended this free-and-easy system and insisted on a once-for-all choice: one must either be French or English with no backsliding.[100] The only notable exception to the either-or binary land system imposed by John and Philip seems to have been the great paladin William Marshal, who retained a foot in both camps. He was allegedly given John's permission to do homage to Philip for lands he continued to hold in Normandy, though Marshal angered John by telling him that this meant he could not make war on the French king, who was thereby a liege lord.[101] It seems that the special status accorded to Marshal was resented by his less prestigious and powerful fellow-barons. The ageing Baldwin of Bethune advised John that he had been foolish to make such a concession and that he should make no further exceptions.[102]

The schism between England and Normandy, after nearly 150 years of convergence, sharpened the distinctions between Frenchmen and Englishmen, so that in John's later reign a tradition of hostility to France and all things French grew up; to some extent this was mirrored in Normandy where, as one of its distinguished scholars has remarked: 'England suddenly became a forbidden land.'[103] One obvious consequence of the loss of Normandy was that England began once more to be a sea power. Since England controlled the northern and western coasts of France after the Conquest of 1066, the Channel was secure, especially as for most of the twelfth century the other littoral powers (the counts of Boulogne and Flanders) were at least nominal English allies. Since John had to face the possibility that Philip Augustus might now mount an invasion of England, and also that he needed a fleet if he was to retain contact with Aquitaine, it is not surprising that the years after 1204 saw a dramatic increase in naval activity, with more warships being built, more sailors hired and trained, and significant technological improvements coming on stream, including a primitive mariner's compass, better rudders, lighthouses and more deadly armament on the war galleys, including Greek fire and boarding ladders and bridges.[104] The naval preparations also connected organically with John's long-term strategy, for he had not given up all hopes of a war of reconquest in Normandy. Many studies show John after 1204 building up his revenue steadily, against the day when he might challenge the French king to a rematch.[105] Since the power of France really took off after the acquisition of Normandy, it is tempting to see these parallel developments as a skeletal form of the much later paradigm, perhaps not seen clearly until the Second Hundred Years War of 1689–1815, whereby a great land power confronted a great sea power – the elephant against the whale – although these tendencies were very much inchoate in the Middle Ages proper.

Yet the most salient consequences of the loss of Normandy for John were those occurring in England. Deprived of the battleground in Normandy that had occupied so many years of the life of his father and brother, John naturally looked around for military glory nearer to home, and so he became more closely involved in the affairs of the Celtic fringes than either of his two successors had ever been. It is often cast up at Richard that he spent almost no time in England, as against John, who spent most of his reign there, but what is forgotten in the comparison is that John had no real choice. John was indeed the first king of foreign stock to travel widely in England, to make a real impact on the country, and to leave his traces in many different English localities, but he did not have northern France as his playground, as Richard did, and lacked the sentimental regard for Aquitaine that Richard possessed.[106] Philip Augustus's triumph in Normandy spelled trouble for Scotland, Wales and Ireland. If the flight of John's barons from Normandy consequent on Philip's land settlement there was in some ways a pre-echo of the flight of the Jacobite lords after the Williamite land settlement in Ireland in 1691, with severe losses occurring on both occasions, at least in the years after 1204 the dispossessed Normans had alternative lands to conquer in compensation.[107] But there was trouble in store for John too as a result of the flight of the barons. Having given up (or been forced to give up) their Norman lands, the new barons domiciled in England had more time to concentrate on the affairs of the island, with unpleasant consequences for John, especially as this development went in tandem with a growing body of opinion that argued that feudal obligations did not include the duty of English men to serve on the continent. There are even those who say that the discontent and troublemaking among the Norman barons marooned in England had a cultural tinge, since they yearned for the ethos of jousting and the troubadours, yet England was very far from being a centre of tournaments but rather of pedestrian, picayune and peace-loving pursuits.[108] At all events a yawning gap soon opened up between the barons and John, increasingly cocooned with his household knights. The events of 1204 lit a fuse that would eventually explode with Magna Carta in 1215.

14

◄○►

F OR A YEAR JOHN pondered his military response to the loss of
Normandy. Logic pointed to an expedition to Poitou, since
Eleanor of Aquitaine's death in 1204 removed the legal obstacle
to Philip's expansion in that direction. Sure enough, once he had mopped
up in Normandy, Philip sent William des Roches on the invasion of
Poitou with a strong army of mercenaries under Cadoc. Des Roches
gained marked early success: the dithering barons like the viscount of
Thouars threw in with Philip, and the entire territory was soon in French
hands, except for the port of La Rochelle and the castle of Niort.[1]
Saumur, Poitiers, Loudun, Chinon, Loches, Tours and Amboise were all
in Capetian hands, and Philip rubbed it in by making a triumphal tour
of his conquests.[2] Further French expansion was problematical, for
Angoulême was held by Isabella in her own right and not simply as John's
wife (Count Aymer died in 1202), but that might not have stopped Philip
Augustus. What gave him pause was the sudden stiffening of resistance
in the far south, as Aquitaine made it plain that it preferred a distant
English king as overlord, one who would not interfere too much, to a
strong centralising French monarch. John decided to seize the moment;
28,000 marks were raised from scutage, and the money was sent to
Bordeaux to prepare and equip a host of 30,000 Aquitaine loyalists against
John's expected disembarkation there.[3] But now John faced the Richard
factor in reverse. If England had been nothing to Richard, who neglected
it in favour of his beloved Aquitaine, by the same token Aquitaine was
nothing to the English barons who were now being asked to pour blood
and treasure into a major venture in south-west France. For them the
prime concern was Normandy. Many of them had lands in Normandy
that looked certain to be lost irretrievably unless John waged a war of
reconquest there. It was the lesser nobility, owning but a few manors,
who were hardest hit and pressed most vehemently for a campaign in
Normandy. It was only a handful of them who were able to pull off the

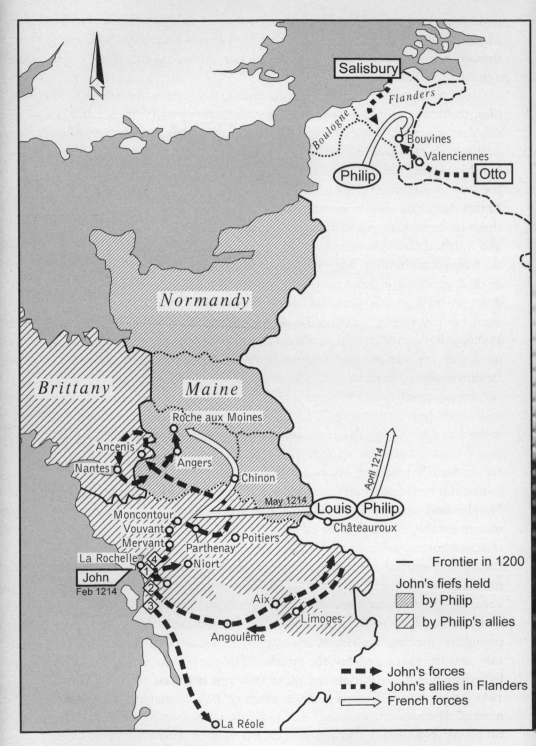

N

Salisbury

Flanders

Boulogne

Bouvines

Valenciennes

Philip

Otto

Normandy

Brittany

Maine

Roche aux Moines

Ancenis

Nantes

Angers

Chinon

April 1214

May 1214

Louis

Philip

Moncontour

Châteauroux

Vouvant

Poitiers

Mervant

Parthenay

La Rochelle

4

John

1

Niort

Feb 1214

2

3

Aix

Limoges

Angoulême

La Réole

— Frontier in 1200

John's fiefs held

▨ by Philip

▨ by Philip's allies

▰▰▰► John's forces

•••••► John's allies in Flanders

⇨ French forces

3. The French Campaigns

ingenious kind of swap arranged by Ellis of Wimberville and Alan Martell; since Martell had lands in England and Wimberville in France, though both had their main abode in the other country, they simply agreed to an exchange.[4]

It is clear that in the year 1205 John and his barons were in serious disagreement about the strategy to be adopted against Philip, and some scholars say that the discord went beyond military matters, that the outlines of 1215 were already in sight. The three great lords of Chester, Pembroke and Leicester, with massive land holdings in Normandy, led the way into conflict with John by coming to a private agreement with Philip Augustus: for a payment of five hundred marks from each of them he agreed not to confiscate or expropriate their estates for a year and a day; if these were still under his control by that time, they would do homage to him.[5] It was quite clear to everyone that there had either to be a rapid reconquest of Normandy by John or a permanent settlement with Philip, and that this expedient was simply to buy time. John grudgingly agreed to the temporary arrangement made by the trio with Philip, and the earls of Chester and Leicester confidently looked forward to a war of reconquest. The position of William Marshal, earl of Pembroke, was different. He had long regarded himself as the equal, if not superior, of anointed kings, and seems to have hoped for a settlement with himself as *tertius gaudens*, somehow owing allegiance to both kings and serving two masters, and with all his estates intact. It followed that William Marshal headed those who advised a campaign in Aquitaine rather than Normandy, but it also followed that the barons who stood to lose out heavily if John did not reconquer Normandy resented William Marshal and whispered to John that here was an overmighty subject who was unreliable.[6] The details of court life in 1204–05 are notoriously obscure but acrimonious exchanges were frequent. In some men's eyes the factionalism at court and the uncertainty about the future seemed mirrored in the chaos principle at large in Nature, for the winter of 1204–05 was extraordinarily severe. The Thames froze after Christmas, and snow and ice took such a toll that the rock-hard soil could not be ploughed until late in March. Meanwhile crops were destroyed wholesale, and the spectre of famine loomed. The cost of foodstuffs became hyperinflationary, with oats ten times the pre-Christmas price by March 1205 and a handful of vegetables fetching half a mark on the open market. The superstitious said that God had punished John for his sins by taking Normandy from him and was now extending his wrath to England.[7]

But John's problems did not even end there. While he and his barons argued about the most rational military response, they could by no means assume that Philip Augustus would simply loll in idleness on the other side of the Channel. The possibility that he might invade England was real and deeply troubling, exciting all John's latent paranoia and tendency to panic. At a council in London in January 1205 John decreed that the whole kingdom was to be organised into a giant commune for defence of the realm, and all persons above the age of twelve had to take an oath of allegiance to the commune. Constables would be appointed in every borough and hundred and they would serve under the direction of the chief constables of the county and bring their levies at their command; anyone failing in duty to the commune was to be regarded as a public enemy;[8] there was indeed a whiff of the French revolution about the panic of 1205. A quota system for national defence was adopted: nine knights were to equip and pay a tenth at the rate of two shillings a day. Anyone failing to rush to arms when the enemy landed on English shores would be visited with the most condign penalties: those with land would be disinherited forever, while those without would be reduced to perpetual slavery.[9] No ship was allowed to leave any English port without the express permission of the king. It is difficult to know whether all this was hysterical overreaction. Certainly the dukes of Brabant and Boulogne (Henry and Renaud respectively), formerly enemies but now allies and supporters of Philip, had often claimed lands in England as the true property of their wives (on the grounds that they were granddaughters of Stephen and Matilda, barefacedly robbed of their property by Henry II) and for once seemed to have an opportunity to enforce their claims.[10] Some have speculated that John's insistence on oaths of loyalty and dire penalties for treason show that he really feared a stab in the back from his own barons more than an invasion by Philip, and the lack of confidence between king and baron was almost overtly evinced at a council at Oxford held on 27–29 March 1205. John insisted on yet another oath of obedience and the barons agreed, but first they in turn compelled the king to agree that he would, with their advice, maintain the rights of the kingdom inviolate, to the utmost of his power.[11] The entente between John and his magnates hardly sounds like a marriage made in heaven.

One of John's problems was that, although he had a personal household of sycophants, hangers-on and yes-men, he had no close relationship with any noble of repute and, moreover, disliked most of them. He positively hated Ranulf, earl of Chester, and suspected him of treason,

mainly on the specious grounds that he had married the widowed
Constance of Britanny, Arthur's mother. But this marriage was entirely
the product of political circumstance, not sentiment and had no deep
roots. Ranulf cared nothing for Arthur, nor Constance for him, it seemed,
as she shortly decamped to yet another marriage (with Guy of Thouars)
without even bothering to get a divorce. Yet Ranulf evidently knew too
many of the dirty little secrets of John's court (probably also about the
murder of Arthur), so he became a favourite scapegoat for John's paranoid rages.[12] In April 1203 John accused him of plotting with the Bretons
but was forced to back down when Roger Lacy, commandant of Château-
Gaillard, backed Ranulf's protestations of innocence in every detail. In
December 1204 John suddenly took it into his head that Ranulf had
been plotting with some Welsh rebels led by Gwenwynwyn and ordered
his estates seized, and once again unimpeachable witnesses forced John
to stay his angry hand.[13] John could blow hot and cold with Ranulf and
keep him in a state of nervous tension but he had few options when it
came to another of his hate figures: Hubert Walter, the archbishop of
Canterbury. Hubert was Richard's man and had governed England
expertly in Richard's absence during 1194–99, and it was probably this
that most rankled with John. But because Hubert had been treated with
respect by greater men than John, and could not abide the new king's
shallowness and duplicity, he probably treated him with less than the
deference John thought his due. It was also one of Hubert Walter's ambitions to achieve a permanent peace between John and Philip Augustus –
yet another issue that made him anathema in John's eyes.[14]

Trying to divide and rule, John decided that it would be the lesser
of two evils if he could encourage William Marshal's ambitions – if that
also meant he could cock a snook at Hubert Walter. He therefore pointedly cut Hubert out of the loop and sent Marshal (together with vice-
chancellor Hugh of Wells) on a secret mission to Paris. Marshal took
the opportunity to make it a point of understanding with John that,
while in Paris, he could press his own plans to safeguard his Normandy
lands, even if that meant paying homage to Philip.[15] John grudgingly
consented but then almost immediately repented, for word got out in
the court that William Marshal had been granted this 'dispensation' and
other, more minor and therefore more hard-pressed barons, lobbied to
have the same privilege extended to them.[16] Marshal and Hugh of Wells
met Philip at Compiègne and seem to have put forward some phantom
peace proposals which, in Marshal's mind at least, were merely the diplomatic prelude to his real purpose – getting Philip to guarantee his

Normandy lands. Philip asked for time to consider all John's proposals but went for the jugular by pointedly reminding Marshal that the said period of grace of a year and a day had almost expired. 'You may find it the worse for you if you do not do me immediate homage,' were his reported words.[17] Marshal thereupon went through the form of homage. Meanwhile Hubert Walter had learned of the secret mission and sent his own envoy to Paris to warn Philip that according to the laws of England Wells and Marshal had no power to conclude a treaty. Philip then humiliated his two guests by pointing this out at their next meeting, at Anet. Meanwhile Hubert Walter's special agent (Ralf of Ardenne) further stirred the pot by speeding back to England and telling John that the terms of the homage sworn by William Marshal compelled him to side with the French king in any dispute with the English monarch.[18] John, in another of his paranoid rages, declared that the lords of England would be assembled to hear a charge of treason against Marshal. John had some justification for his anger. The formula by which Marshal tried to avoid having to take sides was that he offered Philip Augustus 'liege homage on this side of the sea'. As one of John's biographers rightly remarks: 'It is a curious formula for which no precedent can be found in feudal law, and its precise meaning is not clear.'[19]

The collision between John and William Marshal was in many ways an accident waiting to happen. Richard had his differences with Marshal but he knew how to distinguish the political and the purely personal, as John did not. Although John did not in Marshal's case harbour the extreme dislike, and even hatred, he felt for Hubert Walter or Ranulf of Chester, nonetheless he was always uneasy around him. Although he turned to him for advice, particularly on the affairs of Normandy, on which he considered him expert, confirmed him as earl of Pembroke and permitted him a degree of frank speaking rarely vouchsafed to other courtiers, John was always cool towards Marshal. He resented his gravitas, his proud bearing, his poise and dignity, his prestige as a warrior and jouster, his reputation as a counsellor, his skill as a negotiator and the way people spoke of him as the most loyal servant of the Angevins. Marshal for his part thought John wrong on almost every issue of policy and secretly despised him; he went through the motions of being King John's man but his heart was not in it; he yearned for the halcyon days of the Young King, the only Angevin he had ever truly loved.[20] The contretemps over the homage to Philip brought all the latent antagonism to the surface. On paper John had a case in his suspicion of Marshal. In feudal law it was recognised that one could hold fiefs from different lords and even that one could do homage to them in respect of these fiefs, but there was no precedent for Marshal's attempt to have it both ways and to owe personal service to two masters. Marshal was in effect trying to evade the law of excluded middle by claiming that in France he was Philip's man and in England John's – a position that raised theological and philosophical possibilities. If Marshal was travelling with John's fleet to France and the vessels were intercepted by Philip's warships in mid-Channel, on what side would Marshal fight then? On the other hand, John had clearly been foolish in (out of spite for Hubert Walter) granting Marshal permission to do homage to Philip without thinking through the implications of such a step.[21] The issue remained in limbo for the moment but would burst out again with a vengeance later in 1205.

By the early summer of 1205 John was becoming increasingly confident that Philip would not invade England; all his military actions seemed to be concentrated in central and southern France. John therefore strained every nerve and harnessed all possible resources to mount a dual counteroffensive against the French; this was his way of cutting the Gordian knot, the paralysis created by two opposite groups of advisers counselling very different strategies.[22] One expedition was destined for Poitou, to be commanded by John's shadowy bastard son Geoffrey, and this was to have its jumping-off point at Dartmouth in Devon. Meanwhile a much larger army and navy were being assembled at Portsmouth, ready for a strike across the Channel and a landing in Normandy. The pincer strategy thus envisaged required colossal feats of organisation, planning and logistics. A quarter of the revenue for the year was spent solely on military and naval preparations.[23] The entire kingdom hummed and pullulated with the sights and sounds of a realm stretched to maximum capacity for war-fighting. Wagons and carts streamed across the country en route to the south coast, their cursing and sweating drivers enduring traffic jams, road bottlenecks and tailbacks. With bacon, venison, wool, sailcloth, wood and iron on board the groaning wagons, destined for use during the manufacture of everything from ships to crossbows, the country resembled a gigantic itinerant fair. Some observers said that John's preparations eclipsed even Richard's preparations for the crusade.[24] Even when we allow for the exaggerations of the chroniclers, who provided an impossible tally of 1,500 ships, it is clear that in 1205 John assembled the greatest force yet seen in English history, with a total of some 30,000 men, all allegedly 'ready and willing to go with the king over the sea.'[25] He held a preliminary muster of the land forces at Northampton in May, declared himself satisfied and arrived at Porchester Castle on the Solent on the last day of the month. For ten days he commuted between Porchester and Portsmouth, overseeing fleet preparations, then on 9 June announced that all had been done to his satisfaction and that he was ready for the great enterprise.

John's preparations show a keen interest in sea power, but it must be emphasised that he was building on foundations laid by Richard. When he set out for the Holy Land, Richard assembled a fleet drawn from all the ports of the English and Bristol channels: 33 of the more than one hundred vessels came from the Cinque Ports, three each from Shoreham and Southampton, and the rest from Brixham, Dartmouth, Plymouth, Bristol and divers other ports.[26] There was thus a pre-existing administrative apparatus for fleet assembly that John could draw on. Moreover, in 1196 Richard built seventy *cursoria* – seaworthy vessels primarily used on patrol along the Seine, and which John had used in his abortive attempt to raise the siege of Château-Gaillard in 1203. It was Richard too who had founded Portsmouth, under the protection of the royal castle at Porchester, as an embryonic naval dockyard. It was therefore Richard rather than John who was the true father of English sea power.[27] Yet because of the loss of Normandy, John had perforce to exceed in degree anything Richard achieved as a naval planner. His originality lay in extending the idea of the mercenary force into the maritime area, with forty-five galleys being built in 1203–04 to patrol the waters around southern England. Galleys – equipped with both sails and banks of oars to secure independence from the wind – were always the principal type of warship, but they were expensive and John soon found the need to supplement them from other sources.[28] In effect he decreed a nationalisation of all shipping, ordering the constables in southern ports to seize all vessels that could be converted for war purposes, even if the craft could carry no more than half a dozen horses. In his energetic moods John could be a dynamo, and he had his own early version of the Churchillian 'Action This Day'. The Patent Rolls habitually contain the injunctions 'Hasten immediately' or 'Work day and night.'[29] The rise of sea power under John helped some of his favourites, who attained high positions in the navy. William of Wrotham and Reginald of Cornhill became in effect the very first lords of the admiralty,[30] while John's half-brother William Longsword, earl of Salisbury, became the first admiral of the fleet. Longsword was the only great magnate who was a genuine crony of John's. John liked to carouse and roister with him and even paid his gambling debts.[31]

It was during these days at Porchester that John tried to settle accounts with William Marshal. In the presence of the assembled barons, he revived the charge that in paying homage to Philip Augustus, Marshal had acted treasonably. Marshal calmly replied that he had done no more than John had given him permission to do. 'In that case,' said John, 'come to France with me and fight for the recovery of my inheritance against this king to whom you have rendered harmless homage.' Marshal replied that feudal law made this impossible: one could not with honour fight against an overlord to whom one had paid homage. John turned to his barons in triumph: was this not express treason, he asked? Before they could answer, Marshal cut in with a stirring appeal: 'Let this be a warning to all of you. What the king is planning to do to me he will do to all of you once he becomes powerful enough.' The words struck home. To John's horror and fury the barons began to back away, shuffling uneasily, mumbling and muttering excuses that they had other pressing business. 'By God's teeth,' John exploded, 'it is plain to see that none of my barons are with me in this: I smell treason, the whole thing looks ugly and I must take counsel with my bachelors.'[32] His young henchmen naturally agreed that Marshal could have no cogent reason for not accompanying his liege lord to France. The problem was: who was to bell the cat? One of the more intelligent household knights pointed out that if William contested the justice of John's decision, the issue could be decided only on the field of combat, by a judicially sanctioned duel, and which of them had the prowess to beat Marshal in single combat? There was a general murmur of agreement, and a general consensus emerged that the best action was to take no action. Seeing that no one was prepared to stand forth as his champion, John stormed away to dinner in high dudgeon. After a couple of days fuming in impotent fury, he finally decided to let the matter drop and to adopt correct and civil, if frosty, relations with the overmighty William Marshal.

But the barons were not at odds with John only on the issue of Marshal. Their reluctance to support the king against him derived from their general reluctance to take part in the expedition in the first place. Despite the many straws in the wind indicating that he might have a rebellion on his hands, John ignored the evidence and waited only for the one wind he really cared about: the favourable breeze that would carry him to Normandy. Seeing that winks and nods were unavailing, the two men with the greatest prestige in England, Hubert Walter and William Marshal, decided to take the bull by the horns, with the enthusiastic backing of virtually the entire English aristocracy. They began by urging John to think again and to abandon the 'quixotic' expedition to

Normandy, piling argument on argument until the king could stand it no longer. Philip Augustus was too powerful, they said, he had over-whelming local superiority; the English and the king himself could end up trapped like the Athenians at Syracuse in 413 BC; to trust the Poitevins as allies was folly as they were notoriously treacherous. Besides, if the expedition cleared from Portsmouth, England would be left undefended, inviting a counterstrike from the count of Boulogne, who would never have a better chance, since any campaign would be a walkover with the entire English army abroad. A king should not be a gambler, they advised, and especially one who had no heir and could easily die in Normandy. John listened but gave no indication that he had heard anything he wanted to consider even for a moment. In desperation the two envoys fell to their knees in tears, beseeching him to see reason. When John still remained obdurate, they showed the steel beneath the deference: 'if he would not listen to their entreaties, they would forcibly detain him lest the entire kingdom be thrown into chaos by his departure'.[33] Walter and Marshal were actually demonstrating statesmanship, trying to head off a situation that would lead to civil war or constitutional crisis, for they foresaw that a direct order from the king to embark would be met by almost universal refusal by the barons. In tears of rage and frustration John was hustled away to Winchester by his closest advisers to sleep on it and come up with second thoughts.[34] But there were none. Next morning John was back at Portsmouth, this time apparently trying to whip up the 'patriotic' feelings of the ordinary soldiers and sailors against their 'cowardly' masters. He actually boarded the royal galley with his household knights and cruised up and down the Channel for three days, trying to shame the barons into joining him. But it was all in vain. He finally realised that both he and the expedition were going nowhere. In a rage he put into Studland at Dorset and announced the indefinite post-ponement of the Normandy expedition.[35]

The subsidiary expedition from Dartmouth to Poitou did, however, manage to clear from English shores, as did a small force under the earl of Salisbury, sent to shore up the garrison at La Rochelle. The only imme-diate result was the ransoming of two of John's cronies taken captive after the fall of Loches and Chinon, Hubert de Burgh and Gérard d'Athée, two men, not coincidentally, cordially loathed by the English barons.[36] But John began patiently to lay the foundations for a great campaign in Aquitaine that would take advantage of local antipathy to Philip Augustus. First he strengthened the defences of the Channel Islands – a major way-station on the seaborne route to the Bay of Biscay. In the winter of

1205–06 he built eight huge transport ships and sent chests of treasure to Poitou to consolidate the loyalty of the magnates there.[37] Next he undertook an extensive tour of northern England to win hearts and minds in the early months of 1206, successfully whipping up support from the northern lords; the itinerary took him first to Yorkshire and then to Cumberland, Lancashire and Cheshire.[38] Finally, he assembled another armada of warships and transports, though on a less spectacular scale than for the ill-fated Normandy expedition of 1205; once again the Cinque Ports were the principal providers. Again the rendezvous was at Portsmouth, though this time there was no foot-dragging by the barons, mainly because the great lords who sailed with him were largely the barons of the north he had so effectively conciliated in his charm offensive a few months earlier.[39] John was in good heart, for Niort and La Rochelle still held out, the former courageously defended by Savary de Mauléon, one of the few prisoners taken at Mirebeau and released under a promise of fealty who had actually kept his word.[40] With a formidable fleet John and his army sailed for La Rochelle on 29 April and arrived there on 7 June.

John was further encouraged by the influx of Aquitaine vassals eager to fight Philip, but wisely decided he was still not strong enough to try conclusions with Philip in a pitched battle. He therefore marched out to Niort and relieved the defenders there, then feinted towards Poitiers before turning abruptly south towards the Garonne. His objective was the supposedly impregnable castle of Montauban, said to be so secure against attackers that not even the great Charlemagne had been able to breach its defences. John was back to his military best on this campaign. As if in emulation of his legendary brother he took just fifteen days to reduce Montauban, using powerful siege engines. The spoils from Montauban's fall on 1 August were impressive: not just horses, arms and money but a quantity of wealthy noble prisoners, whose ransom would bring him another small fortune.[41] Confident that his position in Aquitaine was now secure, he headed north and was back at Niort by 21 August, whence he proceeded to raid across the Poitou/Berry border. That John was on a winning streak was clear when the ace trimmer, the viscount of Thouars, once more changed his allegiance and returned to John's fold. As if this was not enough, from England came the news of the death of his old enemy Hubert Walter. John exulted in his usual brutal manner: 'Now for the first time I am king of England!' he exclaimed with typical hyperbole.[42] With northern Poitou under his control, John next aimed at Anjou, aiming his thrust at the precise point

on the Loire where Anjou, Poitou and Britanny meet. After fording the
Loire in a histrionic and melodramatic manner, implying that he was a
God-endorsed saviour (in reality he took advantage of unusually low
water levels), he fought his way into Angers and held court in the home
of his ancestors.[43] In September he pressed on as far as the border with
Maine, all the time emphasising his credibility but taking care not to
encounter Philip's main army. Finally Philip was stung into action and
led his host to the borders of Poitou. John, who had achieved all his
propaganda objectives, was anxious not to be sucked into a pitched battle
and put out peace feelers. Philip's ready acquiescence seemed to signal
that, as long as his position in Normandy was not threatened, he was
prepared to tolerate John's hegemony in the south.[44] The truce agreed
between the two monarchs on 13 October 1206 was to last for two years.
During that time each sovereign would retain the homage and services
of the lords who had fought for him in 1206, and disputes were to be
settled by a tribunal of four barons, two from either side. Trade and
communications were to continue as normal.[45] John had reason to be
satisfied. He had secured his mother's inheritance and retrieved his
situation in Poitou, while gaining invaluable experience in seaborne and
amphibious operations. But he may have realised that he had been lucky,
both in that Philip's aims in the south were not expansionist and that
the perilous voyage around Ushant and into the Bay of Biscay had
proceeded without mishap. A decisive campaign against Philip would
mean bringing a larger army by that route, and the potential for disaster
by shipwreck and storm was clear.[46]

John realised that another trial of strength with Philip would require
years of careful planning and preparation. He therefore turned away
from the affairs of France and began to interest himself in his own
Celtic fringes. The easiest to deal with of the three non-English regions
in the British Isles was Scotland, since the overall cause of problems
between that nation and England was the Scots' demand for Northumbria
and this the English kings adamantly refused to give up. From the very
earliest days John's relations with William of Scotland had been far more
fractious than Richard's and the pattern of shadow-boxing evident from
early in the reign persisted into the first decade of the thirteenth century.
John met the king of Scots at York in May 1207, and even set up a
further meeting for 11 November that year, but William claimed the
notice given was too short, and temporised so successfully that the two
monarchs did not meet again until 1209.[47] In that year John sent William
a friendly invitation to meet in Newcastle, possibly because, being in

Northumberland, it was 'neutral' territory, possibly because William was ill and John wanted to save him the trouble of the extra journey to York.[48] Either way, the ensuing meeting was very short, as William was genuinely ill. There was enough time for John to demand that William restore the castles of Berwick, Roxburgh and Jedburgh and that William's son Alexander be sent into England as a hostage. Evidently William did not make a satisfactory answer to this demand, for we next find John in hostile mood towards the Scots.[49]

Why the sudden enmity in summer 1209? One explanation is that William had reacted angrily and intemperately when John built a castle at Tweedmouth to destroy Berwick. Another is that William made the mistake of harbouring some of John's enemies, especially recalcitrant bishops caught up in the great crisis with the Pope (see Chapter 16). Yet a third is that there was a conspiracy of northern barons against John that year in which William was implicated. Needless to say, all these explanations have had their passionate scholarly expositors and detractors.[50] But probably the profoundest underlying cause of tension was that John got wind of Philip Augustus's attempt to bring Scotland into his orbit by offering a dynastic marriage. The much-married serial monogamist Philip was once again tiring of his current wife and seeking to get an annulment of the latest marriage.[51] What is much clearer is the upshot. Hearing that John was assembling an army south of the border preparatory to full-scale invasion, William sent him a more emollient message, but John continued grim and implacable and advanced as far as Bamburgh by the end of July 1209. Matters were now very serious but William was too ill to organise effective resistance and so was forced into a shameful climb-down. Wishing to buy time, he was forced into the humiliating treaty of Norham in August 1209. This stipulated that William was to pay John an indemnity of 15,000 marks, to send thirteen hostages into England and to agree to the marriage of his daughters to John's sons. For the sake of peace John accepted the Scots king's disingenuous denial that he had ever negotiated a marriage with Philip. Finally, William's son Alexander was to hold William's lands in England from John; William's hope was that, whereas John could not stomach ceding Northumbria to him, he might be prepared to do so in future to his son – a hope that was almost certainly vain.[52]

For two years the Scots lay low. The instalments of the agreed indemnity were paid on time, although the means remains a mystery since the king of the Scots was already heavily in debt to Jewish moneylenders and owed the estate of 'Aaron the Jew' the sum of £2,776.[53] John and

William met again, at Durham in February 1212; each swore to protect the other in all just quarrels. This was more than just empty diplomatic protocol, for William was beginning to be hard pressed within his own dominions.[54] A serious rebellion in Scotland had been engineered by a formidable pretender, Guthred McWilliam, challenging the Anglo-Scottish 'culture creep' in the name of Gaeldom. The ageing William went to Durham determined to secure the succession for his son Alexander at all costs, but John made it plain that the price of his support would be high. The powerful English baron Eustace de Vesci fled to Scotland when John nipped one of the many baronial revolts in the bud, but John told William that he required Alexander to come south of the border and be held as hostage until the Scots gave Vesci up. Under pressure from his Scottish nobles, William refused the request, arguing that John already held his hostages from the treaty of Norham in England, a surety for Scotland's good faith in the matter of Vesci. The record until December 1214, when William died, is far from clear, but it does not appear either that Vesci was surrendered or that any significant concession was made, even though John sent an army of mercenaries into Scotland to suppress the rising by Guthred McWilliam. Alexander succeeded his father without any help or hindrance from John, and the most plausible inference is that John made no move in Scotland as he already had his hands tied with a full-blown war in Wales.[55]

Wales presented John with far more problems than Scotland. Stability there during the reign of Henry II had been guaranteed by Henry's alliance with the uncontested supreme native ruler Rhys ap Gruffyd, who bestrode Welsh history of the second half of the twelfth century like a colossus. But when Henry died in 1189, succeeded by a man who had no interest in Wales, the older pattern of factionalism and chaos reasserted itself, even more so when Rhys himself died in 1197. As earl of Gloucester and lord of Glamorgan during his obscure years, John knew all about the turbulence of Welsh politics, and he knew from bitter experience that it was a reflex action of discontented marcher lords and border barons to make common cause with Welsh princes. At his accession there were no less than three rival claimants as ruler of South Wales: Rhys's sons Griffith and Maelgwyn and the more impressive Gwenwynwyn, son of Owen Cyfeiliog, prince of Powys. With English help Griffith seemed to have won the struggle by 1198 but he died in 1200, when Gwenwynwyn's star definitely started to ascend. But at this very moment a contender burst onto the scene, later to be acknowledged as Rhys's true spiritual successor: Llewellyn ap Iorweth, prince of North

Wales. In a few years Llewellyn made all of South Wales his virtual appanage while John looked on, content to stir the pot occasionally and play divide and rule from a distance.[56] He eventually decided that an alliance with Llewellyn was the best policy, an idea in which the Welsh prince readily acquiesced. In July 1202 he promised to do homage to John as soon as he returned from Normandy, in 1204 he was betrothed to John's illegitimate daughter Joan, and in 1206 he married her.[57]

John had eliminated the main opposition to Llewellyn by confining Gwenwynwyn in an English prison, but he was released in 1208 after doing homage to the English king. John's overall triumph seemed secured when all the princes of North and South Wales did homage to him at Woodstock in October 1209[58] but, as so often in John's reign, auspicious omens were merely the calm before the storm. The very next year saw a serious rift between John and Llewellyn when the Welsh prince decided to support the recreant William de Braose, who fled to Wales from Ireland just as John was setting sail across the Irish Sea (see below, p.344–45). In May 1211, fresh from what then looked like a military triumph in Ireland, John summoned Llewellyn's rivals as allies and crossed the border into Wales at the head of a formidable army. He took the castle of Dyganwy but soon got bogged down in the mountain country of the north. While Llewellyn proved a master of guerrilla warfare, logistics and commisariat defeated John, whose army was soon starving and on the brink of collapse. John withdrew to re-equip his forces and make more methodical preparations for a tough campaign; he returned to the fray in July that year. Alarmed by John's pertinacity, Llewellyn sent his wife (John's daughter) to negotiate terms. John insisted on draconian terms for peace. Mid-Wales was reserved as an English enclave, thirty hostages were taken, and Llewellyn had to pay heavy reparations in the form of cattle and horses.[59] Following hard on the treaty of Norham with William of Scotland and the campaign in Ireland in 1210, this triumph at first seemed to set the seal on John's achievements in the British Isles. Walter of Coventry boasted: 'In Ireland, Scotland and Wales there was no man who did not obey the nod of the king of England – a thing which, it is well known, had never happened to any of his forefathers.'[60]

This was premature, for the wily Llewellyn was merely playing for time. The following year he pulled off the stroke that William of Scotland had tried and failed, namely securing an alliance with Philip Augustus.[61] Secure in this powerful pledge of foreign support, Llewellyn denounced the treaty his wife had negotiated the year before. Angrily John took to

the field once more. He diverted an impressive host assembled for a
projected campaign in France to Chester and made such thorough preparations that no less than 8,500 men were dragooned into service as
labourers for a massive castle-building project he had in mind. So determined was John that eighteen galleys and other naval craft were
earmarked for an amphibious assault on Wales.[62] Yet another baronial
conspiracy distracted John so that he was unable to advance into Wales
for the fire-and-sword chastisement he had intended; frustrated and
therefore in a state of homicidal anger, he hanged 28 of the Welsh
hostages. This was a bad mistake: Welsh princes who had previously
been suspicious of Llewellyn's ambitions now came to suspect John of
wanting to have the whole of Wales under his dominion – a return to
the situation under Henry I a hundred years earlier. When Llewellyn
raised his standard as the purported saviour of Wales, his rivals joined
him against the 'English tyrant'. John perfectly verified the description
by putting a price on the head of every Welshman delivered to him.[63]
While the barons and a new war with Philip Augustus preoccupied John,
Llewellyn seized his chance and by the end of 1213 was again dominant
in most of Wales. His real moment of glory came in the year 1215. While
John and the barons argued and agonised over Magna Carta, Llewelyn
swept all before him; Shrewsbury, Cardigan and Carmarthen all fell to
his armies.[64] It is amazing that some historians still seem impressed by
John's dubious achievements in Wales. His policy there was characterised
by myopic short-termism, and he made the particular mistake of taking
Gwenwynwyn out of the political equation, allowing Llewellyn to become
over-powerful.

John was no more successful long-term in Ireland. Since his ill-starred
voyage there in 1185, much had happened but even to a wily politician
like John most of it must have seemed esoteric and obscure. Richard I
has often been blamed for having no interest in England but he had
even less in Ireland, and did not even deprive John of his title of Lord
of Ireland when his other fiefs were taken away from him in 1194. The
result was near-chaos, with bloodshed, mayhem, revolt, rebellion and
mini-civil wars the norm, and native Irish princes and English interlopers
making a series of ad hoc indiscriminate alliances. It has been suggested
that one factor in the chaos was that nearly all the leading actors in the
English invasion of Ireland died young (Strongbow, Hugh de Lacy the
elder, Robert FitzStephen, Maurice FitzGerald, Ramond le Gros, Miles
of Cogan), leaving minors, heiresses or indirect descendants as successors; consequently the fiefs were temporarily administered by Crown

agents who were woefully ignorant of conditions in Ireland.[65] Meanwhile feuds between the native O'Conors and O'Briens weakened the position of the indigenous Irish in Connacht and Munster, making straight the ways for the English conquerors; Rory O'Conor, the last high king of Ireland, died in 1198. When Henry II died the dominant English figure in Ireland was the swashbuckling adventurer John de Courcy, who had conquered Ulster, Cortes-like, with a handful of men and been appointed justiciar by Henry. In circumstances that remain obscure de Courcy fell foul of Richard and was removed as justiciar in 1191 but, so murky are the sources for this decade, we do not know who, if anyone, succeeded him in this post. As de Courcy's star dipped, another energetic Norman conqueror moved into the power vacuum. This was William de Burgh, who conquered most of modern Limerick and Tipperary and began meddling in the affairs of the all-Irish province of Connacht. Meanwhile the sons of Hugh de Lacy allied themselves with John de Courcy and attempted the conquest of Munster and Leinster.[66]

John the great centraliser tried to rationalise the chaos in Ireland and began by appointing Meiler FitzHenry as justiciar.[67] He neutralised John de Courcy in Leinster by strengthening the position of William Marshal, who had extensive holdings there, although he had never visited Ireland. He cajoled, bribed or persuaded the de Lacy brothers to jettison de Courcy and work closely with Meiler instead, and broke de Courcy by transferring the lordship of Ulster to Hugh de Lacy in 1205.[68] Most of all, he employed accelerated promotion to boost the position of his favourite William de Braose. Scion of an ancient Norman family that had come over with William the Conqueror after the conquest of 1066, de Braose came to the fore around 1180 when he succeeded his father as a lord of the Welsh Marches and acquired the reputation of being tough, fearless and ruthless.[69] Richard had liked his martial qualities and John appreciated them too, though there was always a time-bomb ticking away in the John–de Braose relationship, since de Braose knew the full facts about the murder of Arthur, and John knew that he knew.[70] In the early years of John's reign de Braose prospered mightily: he quickly became the most powerful English baron in South Wales, rich marriages were arranged for his children and one of his sons was given a bishopric; John even wrote off his extensive debts to Henry and Richard.[71] A man of chilling ambition, he persuaded John to make him lord of Limerick in Ireland also, which brought him into immediate collision with William de Burgh, who was still governor of Limerick city.[72] At first de Braose had difficulty enforcing his new land grant, as de Burgh and other Leinster grant holders did not relish their demotion from tenants-in-chief of the king to undertenants of de Braose and initially de Burgh and the other recalcitrants were supported by the justiciar Meiler. But in 1203 clear orders went out from John in England; the justiciar was ordered to ally himself with the de Lacy brothers and expel de Burgh from Limerick, which was duly accomplished.[73] Evidently John then had second thoughts, or his machiavellian instinct for divide and rule got the better of him, for he restored all his Irish lands to him (except the ones in Connacht he did not control but which de Burgh, typically, still laid claim to).[74]

John wanted to control Ireland personally and he wanted deputies he could rely on, which meant that at first he leaned on de Braose and William Marshal, but John's almost reflex instincts of mistrust meant that he encouraged the English adventurers in Ireland to engage in a 'potentially deadly game of snakes and ladders'[75] in which treachery, murder and hostage-taking were reliable constants. Apart from the internecine struggle for dominance in Ulster, Leinster and Munster, all the Norman adventurers had their eyes fixed farther afield, on Connacht, the only province still under native Irish rule.[76] The death of Roderic O'Conor in 1198 was the signal for civil war in Connacht between his sons, in which the English took an avid part. John de Courcy and the Lacys (Walter and Hugh, whose power base was in Meath) supported Cathal Crovderg O'Conor while William de Burgh and his Limerick acolytes backed Cathal Carrach, who was at first victorious. Then the new justiciar Meiler FitzHenry led the cohorts of Leinster against Cathal Carrach and turned the tables in a campaign in which Carrach was slain and his brother emerged triumphant.[77] De Burgh then tried to stage a coup against Crovderg but was himself expelled. Yet the unfortunate Irish ruler had no illusions about the ambitions of the Normans to cross the Shannon and reduce him to vassalage. Crovderg would eventually 'solve' his problem by ceding two-thirds of Connacht to John himself, leapfrogging over his adventurer-barons, in return for the sum of one hundred marks a year, on the sole condition that the remaining third was guaranteed to him and his heirs in perpetuity. John accepted this deal but overegged the pudding by insisting that Meiler FitzHenry chose the two-thirds to be ceded. Not surprisingly, Crovderg refused these humiliating terms, and there the matter rested until John came to Ireland in person in 1210.[78]

Meanwhile in the rest of Ireland the faction-fighting and semi-civil war between the English adventurers continued. The six-headed dragon of discord comprised de Braose, de Burgh, John de Courcy, the Lacy brothers and Meiler FitzHenry. When Meiler and Walter Lacy fell out, having cooperated earlier to dish John de Courcy, John tried to punish both by granting the entire custody of Limerick to de Braose. John at various times dealt with the adventurers he did not favour by summoning them to England; this was the fate both of John de Courcy and Walter Lacy.[79] But Meiler FitzHenry upset John's plans by promptly falling out with de Braose; in exasperation John privately vowed to replace his justiciar. The already cloudy Irish waters were further muddied when William Marshal insisted, against the wishes of a most reluctant king, on visiting his Irish domains in 1207 – Marshal was lord of Leinster by virtue of his 1189 marriage to Isabelle, Strongbow's daughter. Marshal was a big fish in the Angevin empire considered as a totality and in Ireland he was more like a leviathan in the power stakes. Predictably the turbulent justiciar especially resented his coming and appealed to John. John did what he always did in such circumstances, which was to summon both men back to England. This would-be clever move solved nothing for both the followers of Marshal and Meiler FitzHenry carried on a war by proxy, ranging from intrigue to battlefield encounters. Meanwhile John made his preferences clear by welcoming Meiler and cold-shouldering Marshal.[80] John then detained Marshal in England and sent Meiler back to Ireland, roundly declaring that no one had a right to question his justiciar's rights to sieze fiefs if he (John) commanded it; he also ordered Marshal's knights to return to England.[81] This ukase was aimed at Marshal, but Meiler saw the chance to use it to strike also at de Braose. This was a bad miscalculation, for de Braose was still John's special favourite, and when Meiler moved against the de Braose interests in Limerick, John sharply rebuked his justiciar.[82]

William Marshal often sailed close to the wind when dealing with the Angevin monarchs and never more so than when dealing with John. So far from recalling knights from Ireland, he sent more over as reinforcements; secret messages had reached him from his followers in Ireland adamantly insisting that if they crossed the Irish Sea, Meiler would seize their lands. Marshal decided to present John with a fait accompli. He urged his men to an all-out effort, which turned out successfully when with the help of Hugh Lacy the Marshal faction defeated Meiler and took him prisoner.[83] Meiler had already poisoned John's mind against Marshal so John thought of a characteristic way to take revenge. One day at the end of January 1208, as John and Marshal were riding out of Guildford together, the king said he had just heard dramatic news from Ireland. Marshal immediately knew this was a lie, either because he knew John so well and could read his body language or, more likely, because he knew that the stormy Irish Sea was at its most tempestuous that winter, with alarmingly high wave heights reported, so that it was impossible for any courier to have crossed to England. John made up a story that Meiler had heavily defeated Marshal's knights near Kilkenny, hoping to cast his too-mighty subject into despondency. The poker-faced Marshal simply replied: 'Certainly, sire, it is a pity about the knights. They were after all your subjects, which makes the affair only more regrettable.'[84] But when John finally learned the truth and realised that Marshal had the whip hand in Ireland, he bowed to necessity and allowed him to depart for Ireland, this time in semi-disgrace. From April 1208, for five years, Marshal remained in Ireland while John's fit of the sulks continued, finally bringing peace to Leinster where all John's lieutenants had failed.[85]

Meiler FitzHenry's poison against Marshal, assiduously poured into the king's ear, availed him nothing, but the similar dose of venom directed at de Braose finally worked. Gradually John came to feel that de Braose had abused his trust by unilateral conspiracy with the Lacys and the Welsh rebels. Disillusioned with de Braose, stuck with Marshal and exasperated with Meiler's ineffectiveness, the pragmatic John made it clear that Marshal's hegemony in Ireland had his blessing, confirmed Walter Lacy as lord of Meath (April 1208), and put in four royal commissioners over Meiler in Ireland; FitzHenry lingered on in this lame-duck capacity until John put him out of his misery at the end of 1209 by replacing him as justiciar with John Gray, bishop of Norwich.[86] But Meiler's shirt of Nessus had at least put paid to de Braose. No one has ever satisfactorily explained why John turned so viciously on his erstwhile favourite – though the sources tend to indicate that de Braose's habitual and persistent financial dishonesty was at the root of it – but there was no mistaking the savage vindictiveness when he did so. John broke decisively with de Braose and ordered all his Welsh lands forfeit. The desperate de Braose tried to head off utter disgrace by promising he would pay his debts, offering castles as payment and pledging his grandson as hostage.[87] But de Braose's strong-minded wife Maud refused to hand over this hostage, saying publicly that John had murdered Arthur and could not be trusted with the custody of minors. Already furiously angry when this was reported to him, John virtually exploded when he heard that de Braose had surrendered the agreed castles and was now trying to retake them. He proclaimed him outlaw and foul traitor.[88]

Although John had many motives for going to Ireland in 1210, undoubtedly the de Braose affair was one of the principal ones, especially when he learned that William Marshal was protecting him and that the Lacys had offered him asylum. In 1209 de Braose had fled to Wales and embarked there for Ireland. When he arrived in Wicklow, William Marshal entertained him hospitably for three weeks. John Gray protested vociferously that Marshal was harbouring a traitor, but Marshal replied in a rather sibylline way that he was compelled by feudal law to shelter his 'lord'.[89] It is not clear what Marshal meant by this, and the suspicion arises that he was merely twisting John's tail to show the king the limits of his power, but it is just possible (though unverifiable) that Marshal held a fief in Wales that was technically in de Braose's lordship; as has been remarked before, the complexities of feudal tenure made almost any form of hierarchy, however ludicrous, credible in terms of the overall system. Yet finally Marshal was faced by a direct order from Gray, in the king's name, to give up the traitor, whereupon Marshal sent him on to safety with the Lacys and when they in turn were threatened, de Braose fled back to Wales on John's promise of a meeting and a safe-conduct.[90] At the meeting John told him the true villain was his wife, and they should go together to Ireland to sort it out. De Braose refused to budge from Wales, but John thought he would run Maud to earth in Ireland once and for all; while he was there, he would try to rationalise the confused situation that decades of faction-fighting had brought about.[91]

And so John returned to the land from which he had retreated so ignominiously twenty-five years before. Elaborate preparations were made, with an impressive commissariat, drawing supplies from the four corners of the kingdom, from Sussex, Devon, Somerset, Lancashire and Yorkshire. The large number of knights and Flemish mercenaries the king took with him suggests not so much that he feared heavy fighting as that he was planning a dress rehearsal of future campaigns against Philip Augustus. In June 1210 he crossed from Pembroke to Waterford, then proceeded via Newbridge and Thomastown to Kilkenny, where he and his army were entertained by William Marshal.[92] On 28 June he reached Dublin, intending to advance into Meath to chastise the Lacys for having sheltered de Braose. Some of the Meath barons came to him to intercede for their lord, but John was in no mood for compromise. He dispossessed Walter Lacy, who was immediately inclined to bend the knee, but his brother put up initially stiff resistance in the mountains of Mourne until John's army made its numerical superiority felt. Evidently relishing the campaigning, John seized Carlingford Castle, then threw his army across Carlingford Lough on a bridge of boats, outflanking the enemy; John himself, travelling by sea, surprised and took the castle of Dundrum. Hugh Lacy and Maud de Braose fled to Ulster and, when pursued, to Galloway (Scotland).[93] Lacy left a fighting remnant behind at Carrickfergus at the entrance to Belfast Lough, but the garrison took one look at John's formidable siege preparations and surrendered. Preening himself on his triumph, John lolled at Carrickfergus from 19–28 July.[94]

The inclination of the native Irish princes was at first to do homage to John. Cathal Crovderg joined his host and marched north with him. At Carrickfergus a northern Irish prince, Aed Meith Ua Neill, came to John to enquire what would be the terms if he consented to vassalage. John raised the issue of hostages that always so bedevilled his negotiations with would-be vassals. Ua Neill went away to think about this, but shortly sent word that he was not prepared to send hostages.[95] John then made the same demands of Cathal Crovderg. On the pretence of consulting his council, Crovderg returned to Connacht, telling John he would be returning in a fortnight with his son and heir, Aed. But Cathal was advised by his wife that it was not safe to deliver their beloved son into John's mercies; evidently the story of Arthur was known all over Europe by now. When Crovderg accordingly returned without his son, John flew into one of his rages and arrested four of Crovderg's officers whom he took to England with him as the replacement hostages.[96] John then moved down to Dublin, where a week's leisurely stay (18–24 August) brought his Irish expedition to an end. While in Dublin John had another meeting with William Marshal and could not resist bringing up once more the subject of de Braose and Marshal's having harboured a traitor. Marshal replied that if anyone was prepared to make this charge publicly, he must prove it in combat.[97] Not surprisingly, as on previous such occasions, there were no takers. John contented himself by 'humiliating' Marshal, insisting that he take hostages for his future good behaviour.

On paper John's 1210 expedition to Ireland was a great triumph. Meath, Ulster and Limerick were all forfeit to the Crown, he had put his rebellious barons in their place, snubbed Marshal and reinforced the authority of the justiciar John Gray.[98] His one clear and incontestable success was the destruction of the de Braose sept. Even while he was in Ireland, John's lieutenants captured Maud de Braose and her son in Scotland. Maud offered the surrender of all her husband's lands and a fine of 40,000 marks but, when John accepted, compounded her folly by repudiating this and driving the king to a fresh diapason of anger.[99]

Threatened with dire punishments, Maud next offered to honour her original agreement and to pay a further 10,000 marks indemnity for having reneged. John agreed, on condition she remained in custody until the full amount was paid. John had another face-to-face encounter with de Braose himself in England, and the disgraced favourite reiterated and confirmed Maud's terms. But the day before he was due to pay the first instalment, he fled. John with calculated cruelty asked Maud what she intended to do next; she broke down and admitted she could not pay. While her husband was outlawed, the luckless Maud and her son were starved to death in a dungeon at Windsor.[100] As has been well said, this was 'one of the grimmest examples of the king's merciless love of cruelty'.[101] John always made a great play of his interest in justice, but he could hardly temper it with mercy, as he did not know the meaning of the word.

However, as so often with John, a short-term triumph masked long-term failure and showed the king once again indulging his taste for papering over a problem rather than solving it. On John's departure relations between the justiciar and the native princes immediately soured, as instanced by the orders to Gray to build no less than four castles in and around Connacht. Gray also organised a two-pronged invasion of Connacht, from Meath and Leinster in the north and from Munster in the south, as further punishment for Cathal Crovderg's failure to hand over his son and heir as hostage.[102] But Crovderg and his wife were right, for John as all-devouring Moloch of wards and hostages soon manifested itself once more. To save his kingdom from annihilation, Crovderg finally handed over a younger son as hostage, but the boy was cast into a dungeon in England and died there some years later.[103] Ua Neill was also punished for his 'contumacity' but Gray's Ulster campaign of 1212, ambitiously planned as an amphibious operation, finally bogged down in failure. The idea of John's 1210 expedition to Ireland as a glittering triumph must therefore be considerably modified. In terms of chastising his Anglo-Norman barons and settling accounts with de Braose the enterprise had been a success, but as a long-life conciliation of Ireland, with native princes accepting John's overall suzerainty, it was a failure. Some claim that the great revolt in Wales under Llewellyn torpedoed John's plans in Ireland.[104] The only thing certain is that it was almost another two hundred years before an English king took an expedition to Ireland: the doomed Richard II. Ireland survived John's attempts to master it and remained as a thorn in England's side for the rest of the Middle Ages.

15

◄◊►

JOHN WAS LIKE HIS father in his incessant journeyings. Partly a function of his personal restlessness, partly an aspect of his control-freakery but also partly a necessity of medieval kingship, his rovings took him to all parts of England. One scholar has linked John's peripatetic lifestyle to the exigencies of a primitive economy: 'in the days when rents were tendered in kind it was often simpler to go to eat them where they were produced than to transport the food itself'.[1] John had no central residence like Louis XIV's Versailles or Queen Victoria's Balmoral, but simply a set of favourite castles, like those at Windsor, Winchester, Nottingham and Marlborough. In London he had apartments at the Tower and a palace at Westminster, but at any of the sixty-plus royal castles in the realm it was a case of 'watch and wait for you know not the hour when the master cometh'. John had a number of fortified residences which fell short of the status of palaces, such as those at Freemantle in Hampshire, Clarendon in Wiltshire, Feckenham in Worcestershire, Brill in Buckinghamshire, Geddington in Northamptonshire, Clipston and Kinghaugh in Nottinghamshire, but he also had stopover hunting lodges, the medieval equivalent of motels.[2] He was almost constantly on the move: he visited Winchester sixty times during his reign and Clarendon over forty. Probably John's favourite county was Dorset. He was a frequent visitor to Dorchester and Cranborne Chase, and had hunting lodges at Corfe, Bere Regis and Powerstock Common.[3] He rarely stayed more than two or three nights in any one location. An inventory of his travels in 1207 finds him at Geddington on 3 March, on the fourth at Kimbolton in Huntingdonshire, on the fifth at Southoe and on the sixth at Huntingdon. On 7 March he was in Cambridge, on the 9th at Newport, Essex and on the 10th at Bardfield in Essex. After two days spent in Hallingbury (Essex), he arrived in London where, after two days at Lambeth, he moved on to Farnham in Surrey (15–16 March). He was at Freemantle in Hampshire for three days, at Winchester from 20–22nd March, followed by three days at Clarendon and then a further three at

Cranborne in Dorset. He was at the Powerstock hunting lodge in west Dorset on 29–20 March, and ended the month's peregrinations at Exeter.⁴ Much the same picture emerges from a detailed study of other years. Here is one three-week period from 1209: 10 May, Bristol; 13–14 May, Bath; 16–18 May, Marlborough; 20–22 May, Winchester; 22–23 May, Southampton; 24 May, Portchester; 27 May, Aldingbourne (Sussex); 28–29 May, Knepp.⁵

All these residences had to be kept in a state of good repair, and each had a keeper paid at anything from the rate of a penny a day for the least significant to the £10 a year paid at Westminster or the £15 paid at Woodstock. When John was in the territory of special favourites like Peter des Roches, the bishop of Winchester, who had a magnificent pile at Farnham, he liked to stay there.⁶ But it is clear that John spent much of his reign on the road, accompanied by a veritable travelling circus of horsemen, wagons, carts and pack animals, bearing wardrobes, bedding, treasure chests, documents and charters and even a urinal and bathtub. Since his household knights numbered around one hundred, it is clear (and verified by other evidence) that not all his knights accompanied him at any one time, and speculation has grown that there must have been some kind of duty roster.⁷ Some officials must have been present from the very nature of their duties, as for example the Seneschal, the Chamberlain, the Marshal of Bodyguards, the Clerk in charge of household expenses, the Butler (in charge of food) and his assistants such as the Master Dispenser of the Bread and the Master Dispenser of the Larder, plus a host of servants to wait at table or work in the kitchens encountered en route, the royal bedmaker, the royal laundress, the master tailor, the king's bathman, and so on. We can infer numbers from the more than 150 Christmas presents distributed by the king to his staff, and the lesser perquisites given to a host of hangers-on.⁸ The itinerant caravan or cavalcade had to be constantly resupplied with ready cash brought from London by a senior official under a cavalry escort; since silver pennies were the only currency recognised as tender in all normal transactions (the marks and pounds of the world of taxation and subsidies were units of account rather than media of exchange), such posses travelled slowly with heavily-laden sacks. One of John's innovations was to try to simplify this cumbersome system by collecting money in the various localities and giving the debtors a chit for presentation at the London exchequer. Soon the idea was expanded into that of having money dumps (cash caches, so to speak) in the provinces, so that 'area treasuries' evolved, as at Nottingham and Rochester and, above all, in John's beloved West Country, at Bristol, Devizes, Marlborough, Salisbury, Exeter and Corfe.[9]

Since to maintain formation in this wagon train would mean going at the pace of the slowest member – and the pace of the baggage cart was very slow indeed – John often rode ahead of the main body of his travelling court and went hunting at the stopover location, giving the baggage time to catch up. Even though specially-bred heavy horses pulled the carts – since it had been found they could go half as fast again as oxen – they could not achieve much more than two and a half miles per hour even on the best surfaces. Consequently, the absolute maximum the king's travelling court could achieve in a day was fifteen miles, though the daily average was usually less than half that when stopovers are taken into account. It is an extraordinary fact about English history that, until the coming of the turnpikes in the eighteenth century, successive rulers still largely relied on the old Roman roads – Watling Street, Ermine Street, the Foss Way and the Icknield Way – which were wide enough for two wagons to pass each other or for sixteen armoured knights to ride abreast.[10] When the king's mobile court left these main roads, the rate of progress slowed to a crawl, for thereafter the 'roads' were no more than tracks between one village and another. Although medieval kings baulked at actually emulating the Romans by starting a proper road-building programme, they came down very hard on any one foolhardy enough to dig up or otherwise tamper with the old Roman roads, as we know from Henry II's reign.[11] Local communities were under standing orders to make good any pitting or holes in the surface made by excessive traffic. John frequently suffered from the inadequate infrastructure. In 1212 a boat had to be hired to carry the royal baggage across the Thames as London Bridge was broken down; and in the same year carts carrying John some of his favourite wines from Southampton to the north were delayed at Nottingham because the Trent was in spate.[12] This highlighted the principal difficulty about land transport: although rulers could struggle on with antiquated roads so as to avoid capital investment (truly there is nothing new under the sun), the real problem was bridges. Here John did make an effort: hundreds of new structures were built and old wooden bridges replaced with stone ones. So important was the bridge-building programme that Clause 23 of Magna Carta was devoted to it.[13]

With so many mouths to feed, the itinerary of the travelling court had to be planned meticulously. The Butler had to bring wine from the cellars at Bristol or Southampton, and the Baker had to have supplies of flour ready at the overnight castle or hunting lodge. The problems were compounded because John had none of his father's austerity while on the road, but demanded a high level of creature comforts. The level of spending on clothes for himself and his wife almost suggests that he was consciously compensating for the rigours of travel by conspicuous consumption. Gorgeous garments and ravishing raiment for his courtiers showed John virtually imposing a sumptuary law between the inner circle of his court and the outer circle of the barons. John showered his wife Isabella with gowns, robes and cloth, trimmed with ermine and other precious furs and, in his periodic fits of generosity, would suddenly decide to buy an entirely new wardrobe for the wives of his crossbowmen; when he was in this mood, he would suddenly remember his first wife, Isabella of Gloucester, and extend his largesse to her in the form of expensive gifts of cloth and wine.[14] But he did not neglect himself, and among his sartorial innovations was the first royal dressing gown.[15] All the time he built up his collection of jewels and precious stones, importing rare items or accepting sapphires and rubies as payments or part payments for debts owed him. Before he lost patience with John and cast him into anathema, Pope Innocent III sent him four rings set with an emerald, a sapphire, a topaz and a garnet. Although John, displaying his habitual mania for secrecy, liked to secrete parts of his jewel collections at monasteries whose locations only he knew, he was so besotted with the fire and lustre of jewellery that he always had to have some with him on his travels; special treasure chests increased the groaning loads carried by the heavy horses.[16]

Food and drink also had to be of high quality for John, who lacked his father's indifference to such matters. John evidently had a sweet tooth, for the official records and accounts make frequent mention of sugar, cinnamon, nutmeg and ginger; other culinary items often featuring are pepper, cumin, galingale and cloves. He shared too the medieval monarchs' fondness for fish, with herrings, whiting, haddock and lampreys appearing in large numbers as the staple for Chistmas and Easter feasts.[17] Certain fish such as the sturgeon were reserved for royal consumption alone, and to this list were added other animals classed by the rudimentary zoology of the time as fishes, such as porpoises and whales. With meat largely off the peasant menu for financial as well as class reasons, fish was highly prized and people would often throw nets across rivers to catch them, impeding river traffic; Richard the Lionheart himself had to take time off from his weighty military and diplomatic plans to pass a law banning all such fishnets on the River Thames.[18] John and his court were naturally not limited to fish. A week's shopping list made out for Eleanor of Britanny (sister of the unhappy Arthur), shows the high protein and sugar level of the aristocratic diet of the time:

> *Sunday: bread, ale, sole, almonds, butter, eggs*
> *Monday: mutton, pork, chicken, eggs*
> *Tuesday: pork, eggs, egret*
> *Wednesday: herring, conger, sole, eels, almonds, eggs*
> *Thursday: pork, eggs, pepper, honey*
> *Friday: conger, sole, eels, herring, almonds.*[19]

At John's table wine was perceived as a necessity. The wine trade was England's principal commerce with France and the king had a preferential role: not only could he fix the prices of wine but he was entitled to take a certain amount of wine from imported cargoes at a discounted rate. Wine was drunk young, and the cheaper varieties were either home-grown (average temperatures were one or two degrees higher in medieval England) or from the Rhineland; but grandees and monarchs like John could afford the best vintages, from Poitou, Gascony and Auxerre.[20] When he first came to the throne, in 1199, John tried to win favour at his wine assize by fixing the price of wine very low. Not only did this enrage the wine merchants, whose profits were eaten into, but, according to Roger of Howden, the result was that the whole of England 'was filled with drink and drinkers'.[21] Howden must have been exaggerating, for the English already had a reputation for heavy drinking. The French chronicler and anecdotalist Jacques de Vitry said that each European nation had distinct characteristics: the French were proud and womanish; the Germans furious and obscene; the Lombards greedy, malicious and cowardly; and the English were drunkards who had tails like the devil.[22] Other observers endorsed this judgement. John of Salisbury reported that the English were notorious abroad for their drinking, while some were even prepared to correlate high crime rates in England with levels of intoxication.[23]

As a relaxation while he travelled John liked to play chess, which had been introduced to the West by the Arabs and then, via Sicily and Normandy, to England after 1066.[24] His other main pastime was reading from his extensive mobile library. John fancied himself as an intellectual, and collected theological works, including Hugh of St Victor on the sacraments, the *Sententiae* of Peter of Lombard, and St Augustine's *City of God*, a particular favourite. He liked to read French historians like

Wace, who wrote a history of Normandy from earliest times to the Conquest and also had a copy of Pliny.[25] How good his Latin was, and whether it enabled him to enjoy the contemporary craze for Aristotle, whose work (though written in Greek) was now widely available in that language, is uncertain, but he must have had a good working knowledge, as Latin was the language of Church, the Courts and government.[26] It is likely that he had a smattering of Anglo-Saxon though John, like all the Angevins, thought in his native tongue, French. Yet, when he was not in the doldrums in one of his bipolar moods, John was above all a man of action. He loved hunting and kept a large mixed pack of dogs for the chase. He used a liam hound – a massively built canine – and greyhounds for hunting by sight and ordinary hounds for following the scent.[27] A devotee of falconry, he would pay premium rates for prize hawks, such as the two marks he paid to one man who brought him two goshawks from Ireland and the sixty shillings to King William of Scotland's falconers, who provided him with three top-of-the-range falcons. Ever on the lookout for some stunning bird of prey to add to his collection, John cultivated contacts in Scandinavia expressly for this purpose. King Sverrir Birkebein of Norway became a friend purely on this basis, and John would trade shiploads of corn for his best birds. It was said that he waived all customs and import duties due on produce brought to England by the Danish merchant Nicholas Dacus on condition that the Dane made him annual tribute of a hawk.[28] John had a favourite gerfalcon called Gibbun, whose name has puzzled scholars perhaps fruitlessly pondering its meaning, and was devoted to it – 'we have none better than him', he wrote.[29] So great was John's falconry mania that he habitually hunted on holy days though forbidden to do so by canon law; he salved his conscience, such as it was, by giving alms to the poor. On the feast of St Mary Magdalen in 1209 he threw a feast for a hundred paupers to atone for his hunting on a proscribed day; and in 1212 at Elwell, after hunting cranes and herons with his birds of prey, he made amends by hosting another fifty needy souls.[30]

It was partly because of John's hunting mania that there arose one of the great trans-class grievances against the king, culminating at Magna Carta in 1215. Part of the royal prerogative under the Angevin kings was the power to declare lands 'Forest' and as such subject to the special laws of the Forest, in many cases no more than the arbitrary will of the monarch. During John's reign no less than a third of England was 'Forest' – not in the modern sense of densely wooded areas (though there were far more of these than in the modern era) but in the sense that the whole territory,

towns, villages and farms as well as the wilderness proper, was in the exclusively royal domain.[31] When John was king, it was possible to travel from
the Wash to Oxford or from Windsor to the Hampshire coast without
ever leaving the Forest; the county of Essex was wholly Forest, and so
was much of Hampshire, Berkshire and Wiltshire. The inhabitants of Kent,
Norfolk and Suffolk thought themselves especially fortunate as there was
no Forest there. A thirteenth-century Somerset jury claimed that John had
'afforested' all England[32] and there was a smidgin of truth in the claim,
for John liked to take great swathes of land into the ambit of 'Forest'
partly so that he could make huge sums of money by selling it back to
individual or communal takers. But John also enjoyed the brutal exercise
of kingly power, taking into his own management and control what had
previously been owned by local lords or tenant farmers. The entire 'Forest'
scam had been started by William the Conqueror, who set up massive
game reserves for deer and ordained brutal penalties of mutilation and
blinding for anyone who killed a hart or hind without royal permission; it
was said that William had the same mania for deer that John later had for
falcons. Even Richard I himself, a man with no interest in hunting, promulgated an Assize of Forest in 1198, ordaining that the penalty for killing
deer was to be castration and blinding.[33]

The 'Forests' served a twofold purpose for the Angevin kings: they
were a place for rest and recreation, and they were a source of revenue.
In the Forest the king alone could hunt deer and boar. The official line
on the Forests was summed up thus by a royal functionary:

> They are the private places of kings and their great delight. They go
> there to hunt and to enjoy a little peace, away from the cares of
> government. There, away from the continuous business and inces-
> sant hubbub of the courts, they may for a while draw breath in
> Nature's glorious freedom. That is why those who despoil it are
> subject to a unique royal censure . . . The king's forest is a safe
> abode for wild animals, not of every sort, but of the kind that lives
> in woodland and not everywhere but only in suitable places . . . in
> the wooded counties, where wild beasts have their lairs and abun-
> dant feeding grounds. It makes no difference who owns the land,
> whether the king or the barons of the realm; the beasts have
> freedom and protection, and wander wherever they will.[34]

This was pious cant, and neatly sidestepped the point that the arbitrary
forest laws of the Angevins had no sanction in habit, custom, folkways

or even Roman Law. The learned Church fathers of the reign of Henry II, Richard I and John knew perfectly well that according to Roman Law wild animals were nobody's property and that by the law of nations they belonged to whoever captured them, whether on the hunter's own land or someone else's. John of Salisbury was particularly scathing about the Forest Laws: 'Human presumption dares to claim for itself things that are wild by nature and become the property of whoever captures them . . . you had heard that the birds of the air and the fish of the sea are common to all, but those that are hunted, wherever they fly, belong to the royal estate.'[35] How far the Angevin Forest Laws were from Roman Law can be gauged from one simple fact: the latter said that anyone could hunt on a landowner's land, but the former said that not even the landowner could hunt on his own land.[36]

The draconian Forest Laws laid down that only the king could kill red deer, fallow deer or wild boar. Occasionally the monarch might allow ecclesiastical tenants to take small game – hares, rabbits, foxes or wild cats. Roe deer inhabited a legal grey area: sometimes they were reserved for the king, but sometimes tenants were allowed them. Peasants had limited grazing rights in designated Forest, being allowed to take dead wood for fuel but not to cut down a tree or even lop a bough or branch. No one but the king's men could carry a bow and arrow or keep a dog unless its front paws were mutilated so that it could not run after game. If a deer was found dead contrary to the 'peace of the king's venison', a forest inquest, similar to a coroner's inquest, had to be held; circumstantial evidence was allowed, the poachers treated harshly and, if no individual could be identified as the poacher, the entire locality was punished for harbouring him.[37] The indictment that the Monk of Eynsham made against Henry II applied equally to his favourite son: 'In revenge for wild animals that lack reason, which ought by natural law to be available to everyone he had either punished by death or cruelly mutilated in their limbs human beings who possess reason, are saved by the same blood of Christ and share the same nature in equality.'[38] The Church was virtually unanimous in condemning the Forest Laws and another monk, Nigel Wireker of Canterbury thought that the Angevin kings' higher regard for animals than humans was particularly reprehensible: 'Although Man is created in the image of Him who made all things from nothing, kings regard the beasts of the earth more highly than men and think of the human race as more vile. How many wretches have they hanged on the gallows for taking the flesh of wild animals!'[39]

Compounding the basic tyranny was the attitude of the royal officials appointed to enforce these vicious game laws. The Chief Forester
had at his command foresters and verderers – forest police, in effect –
regarders (inspectors) and justices of the forest who tried offences against
the Forest Laws. In return, these officials got the right to hunt animals
not on the proscribed list: hare, fox, wild cat, badger, otter, marten,
squirrel, but *never* deer or wild boar.[40] Clearing and cultivating land in the
Forest could be done only with royal permission, and woe betide anyone
who broke the rules. A woman who dug an unauthorised ditch round
her land had the land confiscated, and she had to pay £100 to get it
back. Boundary lines between the royal forest and private forests had to
be marked by a path, and the costs of making the path, needless to say,
had to be paid by the private landowner; anyone refusing to pay was
fined anyway.[41] A well-known case in Shropshire in 1209 shows John's
draconian laws in action. Venison was found in the house of a man
named Hugh the Scot. He fled for sanctuary to the nearest church and
confessed to the priest that he had killed a hind. Sheltered in the Church
for a month, he finally made his escape dressed as a woman and presumably fled to the woods, there to end his days as an outlaw.[42] Yet the most
bitterly contested cases usually involved the clergy in their own right. If
John was baulked in his endless quest for money, one of his responses
was to use the Forest Laws against those who had 'wronged' him. When
an extortionate demand to the Cistercians was not met with immediate
compliance, John stopped the monks and their workers pasturing flocks
in the royal forest, which had been a customary right for decades. The
case proved that anybody could be deprived of rights and privileges in
a trice, purely on John's whim.[43]

The clergy had a particular general grievance, which was that John's
foresters treated them with contempt – treated them in short as they
treated laymen – and that John had trampled on all the customary rights
they had built up since the days of King Stephen. It was a festering
grievance that, as part of the delicate trade-off between Henry II and
the Vatican in the attempt to resolve the crisis over Thomas Becket, a
papal legate had expressly allowed Henry II to visit the full rigour of
the Forest Laws on the clergy, both secular and regular, with no exceptions.[44] The biographer of the saintly St Hugh of Lincoln put it like this:
'The worst abuse in the kingdom of England, under which the country
groaned, was the tyranny of the foresters. For them violence took the
place of law, extortion was praiseworthy, justice was an abomination and
innocence a crime. No rank or profession indeed, no one but the king

himself, was secure from their barbarity, or free from the interference of their tyrannical authority.'[45] Walter Map, close enough to Henry II's elbow to know what he was talking about, confirmed the judgement. He despised the foresters and thought: 'they eat the flesh of men in the presence of Leviathan, and drink their blood . . . They fear and propitiate the lord who is visibly present: the Lord whom they do not see, they offend without fear. I do not mean to deny that there are in this vale of misery some merciful judges. It is of the wilder majority that I speak.'[46] Part of the cruelty and cynicism of the foresters may derive from their own treatment by the Angevin kings. The Neville family were the hereditary chief foresters, but their relationships with Henry and John were always fractious. When Alan de Neville died, some monks asked leave to bury him. Henry replied dismissively: 'I shall have his wealth, you shall have his corpse, and the demons of hell his soul.' John's chief forester Hugh de Neville did not fare much better. Based at Marlborough, he rose high in John's favour but made his first mistake in 1210 when he allowed the bishop of Winchester to enclose a park at Taunton without the king's permission. Suspecting Neville of having taken a bribe, John fined him 1,000 marks. Although John later let him off the payment, the rot had set in. By 1212 Neville had clearly lost favour, and it is not surprising to find him, in 1216, among the rebels against the king.[47]

Yet John's selfish monopoly over the Forest was not exercised purely because of the pleasure principle. There was big money to be made in this area, and John knew it. Although the king had the right to exact capital punishment for infringement of the game laws, he chose wherever possible to exact fines and mulct offenders instead. Once again it was Henry II who had blazed the trail: his records show one hundred men being sentenced in Hampshire to a total of £2,093. 10s.[48] Even apart from fines, there were rents for pannage and pasturage, the sale of privileges and exemptions and the revenue that could be raised from the sale of fresh or salted venison to favoured barons or garrisons. Wood from the Forest was another source of income. Timber was supplied for building, while licensed charcoal burners changed wood into fuel for iron-smelting, and hence for iron arrowheads, arrows, crossbow quarrels and roofing shingles. But the greatest source of revenue for John was the machiavellian process of 'de-afforestation'. Just as the Forest could be created by arbitrary royal fiat, so it could be unmade by the same process. Charters freeing woods and manors from the Forest Laws were available at anything between 30–150 marks, depending on the value of the land. In 1204 Cornwall paid £2,000 (3,000 marks) and twenty palfreys for the disafforestment of the whole county, except for two woods and two moors, and in 1215 bought these up too for a further 1,200 marks and four palfreys.[49] De-afforestation did not even exhaust the potential for revenue-raising. Although the wardenships of the royal forests were hereditary, they were subject to the usual feudal 'reliefs' and fees. Whenever an heir inherited, he had to pay John a huge fee for being 'confirmed' in the office — usually the fee was between 100 marks and £100. Moreover, in the case of heiresses John could sell their marriages to the highest bidder. He did well out of the de Lucy family, accepting 500 marks for a marriage in 1202, and another 900 marks and nine palfreys for the same heiress two years later.[50] By using various means to rescind marriages already agreed and paid for, the crafty John was often able to sell the same wardship twice.

Although Richard is often indicted for being an absentee king of England, there must have been many in the land who wished that John would spend more time in France, so that he did not have the leisure to oversee the Forest so ferociously; this was yet another consequence of the loss of Normandy. Once again the moral is clear, so evident elsewhere in John's reign and so damaging to those who would rehabilitate his reputation, that his much-touted administrative efficiency was a function of his overwhelming greed.[51] Although Magna Carta would later indict the entire Angevin attitude to the Forest, not just John's, the Lackland monarch's stance on the game laws affected not just the economy but the landscape itself.[52] As far as the economy was concerned, it was a running sore with financial officers of the Crown that all questions about the administration of the Forest had to be referred to John or his chief forester, and even a minion as loyal as Peter des Roches chafed under this inflexible regime.[53] For yeomen and local lords the main grievance was 'the law's delays'. The bureaucracy associated with the Forest Laws was fearsome, and the petty frustrations legion: one had to attend forest courts under the 'guilty until proved innocent' dispensation, even while the king acted as a fetter on economic development by preventing the cultivation of virgin land or the improvement of one's existing plot. But what united all the critics — clergy, barons, peasants — was the perception that the Forest statutes were a travesty of real law. Henry II's treasurer Richard FitzNigel had long ago zeroed in on this crucial issue: 'The whole organisation of the forests, the punishment, pecuniary or corporal, of forest offences, is outside the jurisdiction of the other courts, and solely dependent upon the decision of the king, or of some officer specially appointed by him . . . The Forest has its own laws based, it is said, not ón the common law of the realm, but on the arbitrary decision of the ruler; so that what is done in accordance with that law is not called "just" without qualification but only "just according to forest law".'[54] In a context like this, it is easy to see how the legend of Robin Hood arose.

John, like his father and like Emperor Frederick II (*stupor mundi*) but unlike his brother Richard and his son, the future Henry III, was besotted with hunting and the chase. His interest extended to all wild animals, and especially wolves, which still roamed England in the late twelfth and early thirteenth centuries.[55] It has been established from place-name evidence that wolves were common in Anglo-Saxon England, but the Anglo-Norman obsession with the Forest and the forest properly so-called, rapidly cut down their numbers. In the reign of Henry I there were specially designated royal wolf-hunters, who used traps partly to cut down on lupine predation against horses and sheep but also partly to swell the tally of wolf-pelts and hence the king's prestige.[56] Alexander Nequam's view that wolves could be tamed and kept as dogs was very much a minority perspective.[57] Yet hunting wolves was not a task for the unskilled or fainthearted and considerable financial inducements were necessary before England's most dangerous animal (Man) would move systematically against the second most dangerous; the going rate under Henry II seems to have been three shillings a head for a wolf, but by John's reign this had increased to five shillings.[58] Where wolves were a menace to his favourite hunting grounds, as in the network of forests and hunting lodges in his beloved Dorset and nearby (Gillingham, Bere, Blackmore, Powerstock, Purbeck, Milcet, the New Forest and Clarendon), John was prepared to pay even more. In 1209 two wolf catchers were given fifteen shillings for two wolves taken at Gillingham and Clarendon.[59] By the middle of the thirteenth century wolves were on the list of endangered species. Beavers had already become extinct by John's reign, so that prized beaver pelts had to be imported from Scandinavia and the Baltic lands but, as if in compensation, the rabbit, originally restricted to Spain, broke out of the species cordon and reached the west and south of England by the time Richard was ascending the throne; the hare was already there, being a native of England. In John's time rabbits were still a rarity: they do not appear as an item in a royal banquet until 1240 and continued to be a luxury food, costing four or five times as much as a chicken.[60]

Mention of wolves brings one by an inevitable association of ideas to sheep. Owners of sheep were among the wealthiest people in England, which was why abbeys habitually kept flocks as large as 2,000. While skins could be used as parchment and writing paper and their milk for making cheese, it was sheep's wool that was the chief source of England's wealth. When the abbey of Melrose in the East Riding disgorged 300 marks for Richard's ransom in 1193, much of it was as wool (the rest being plate or cash).[61] Most of the wool was exported to Flanders where it was worked into cloth, and the English wool trade was a constant factor in Flemish politics; the Flemings' motivation for joining the Young King in his rebellion of 1173–74 was the hope that if young Henry displaced his father he would let them have cheaper wool.[62] Although the intrinsic interests of Flanders may always have been opposed to those of the Anglo-Normans and Angevins, the Low Countries depended on the import of corn and wool from England, so had limited room to manoeuvre. The Flemings' dependence was not absolute, since the cloth trade could (and did) in an emergency use coarser wool from northern France, Scotland and Ireland, but for the production of the finest quality cloths there was no substitute for the English strain of sheep.[63] The rotation of crops practised in the agriculture of medieval England involved three courses: in the first, winter-grown crops, such as wheat and rye; in the second, spring-grown crops such as barley and oats; and in the third, the fallow period, when animals would graze. The open-field system was often used, whereby arable land was divided into three fields, one of which would be fallow at any given time.[64] In this way, even agriculture yielded to the pastoral priority, predicated on the realisation that crops meant survival but sheep meant real wealth.

There is no evidence that John had any interest in animal husbandry, but there is controversy about the role of sheep in his economic policy and about the general trends of the economy during his reign. Two salient propositions have been advanced in support of a general thesis that the 1180s marked some kind of economic watershed. One is that the rising demand caused by a population reaching the limits of subsistence allied to the influx of new silver brought into England by the wool trade caused rapid price and wage inflation during John's reign.[65] The other is that the same period saw landlords beginning to produce for external markets rather than local consumption and thus starting to concentrate on wool and grain for export.[66] Against this is the view that true economic take-off, with the accompanying inflation, occurred only after 1220. Counterbalancing a natural inflationary tendency were John's exactions – the surpluses he extracted really were massive, and his revenue in 1211 was *six* times what he had received in 1199 – which had a deflationary effect and thus brought the economy back to something like equilibrium. Indeed, many economic historians argue that John's fiscal policies would have been even more deflationary but for an increase in the velocity of circulation of coinage and the growth in population.[67] This, in turn, involves the vexed question of population levels in early thirteenth-century England. Some authorities put the figure as low as two and a half million, but it is probable that there were already that number of inhabitants of England at the time of Domesday Book in 1086, and that by 1215 the figure was at least three and a half million and possibly as great as five million. On this view the Black Death was the great divider. By 1300 England had a population of six million – as many as in the eighteenth century – but in the years 1377–1540, plague and pestilence held the numbers at Domesday levels.[68] Summing up on economic trends during John's reign, it is probable that the switch to a market economy was more gradual than the '1180 watershed' school contends, and that there was too much uncertainty in the years 1199–1216 for a smooth switch to production for export markets; this is to leave on one side the debate about whether inflation is always the prime motor of an economy. The sagest conclusion is that John's economic problems did not come from inflation but from the tax burdens he imposed to build up a war chest.[69] As the economic historian John Bolton (arguing that economic take-off occurred *after* John's death) has commented: 'Henry III's military ineptitude, indeed his general ineptitude and resistance to royal exactions in his reign, may have been just what an uncertainly expanding and commercialising economy needed.'[70]

John's lust for money and his personal interventions always had a distorting economic effect even when, on paper, his projects were commendable. A very good example is provided by his attitude to urban development, and once again we see him continuing traditional Angevin policies. Between 1066 and 1235 more than 125 towns were founded in England. A miscellaneous list produces the following: Arundel, Boston, Chelmsford, Devizes, Egremont, Harwich, Hull, King's Lynn, Morpeth, Newcastle-upon-Tyne, Okehampton, Portsmouth, Reigate, Salisbury, Truro, Uxbridge, Watford and Yarmouth (Isle of Wight). This was the most important historical era for new towns and cities until the Industrial Revolution. Between 1180 and 1230 fifty-seven new towns were founded, many of them in John's reign.[71] John's most famous creation was Liverpool, on an empty site on his own demesne. The letter patent, creating this new borough, was issued on 27 August 1207. All who took up the king's offer of plots of land in the new town were exempt from labour services and many tolls, dues and other taxes, and were allowed to have their own ovens and handmills, instead of having to use the feudal lord's for a fee; additionally, John undertook to build a castle and a chapel.[72] There was no largesse or generosity about John's actions. He liked to found new towns so that he could tax them. Although the initial privileges seemed generous, the burghers soon found that there were hidden snags. All markets and fairs, which arose naturally if the settlement was a success, required a royal charter, which had to be paid for; and there were further fees payable for the enfranchisement of serfs (villeins) or for the renewal of charters. Moreover, John liked to found his towns on the coast so that they could function as ports and thus be subject to import and export duties. He always valued his royal right of prise and preemption, which gave him first choice of all luxury imports and a free gift of wine; additionally he could charge fees for licences given to foreign merchants.[73] In 1203–04 John found a new means of getting revenue, by setting customs duties at one-fifteenth the value of imports. He collected over £2,000 from Newcastle, Hull, Boston, Lynn (King's Lynn) and Hedon alone; Boston paid 15.7 per cent of the total uplifted and Lynn paid 13.1 per cent as against the 16.8 per cent paid by London, the 14.3 per cent by Southampton and the 13.3 per cent by Lincoln.[74] These ports were all close to the great medieval fairs and the areas that produced most wool and wheat. John's experiment with urbanisation can thus be seen as barefaced exploitation, but at least one expert warns against a machiavellian interpretation, on the ground that the king rode a commercial wave but did not create it.[75]

The rise of towns encouraged fairs and markets. There were only two markets in Oxfordshire when Domesday Book was compiled but a dozen by the 1220s. The requirement that markets had to be held on different days in different towns created a circuit, allowing merchants to buy in one place and resell in another, thus avoiding some of the tolls and taxes the new towns tried to impose on their trade.[76] The growth of fairs encouraged foreign merchants to visit England, stimulated rural enterprise and encouraged the wider use of coinage in the countryside. Silver coins were starting to become widespread in John's reign, as the money supply increased; this was a 'spin-off' of the discovery of new silver-bearing ores in the 1160s, in the Alps, in Tuscany and above all in Germany, near Meissen.[77] Towns created entirely new social sectors: merchants, goldsmiths, clothworkers, weavers, shoemakers, tanners, bakers, butchers. Forming themselves into guilds, some of these trades became so powerful that they were virtually independent of town authorities, which in turn caused jealousy and resentment, so that boroughs tried to deprive weavers, in particular, of their civil rights.[78] Yet for all the new groupings that emerged, England under John remained an overwhelmingly rural and agricultural society, with nine-tenths of the population living in the countryside. The steepness of the social pyramid can be appreciated from one simple statistic: in a population of some four million in John's reign, there were only twenty earls, two hundred barons and 5,000 knights.[79] The historical records do not show John in any way interested in the plight of this vast majority of faceless toilers, the nuances of local custom, the relation of freemen to villeins, or the complexities of land tenure and the virgate (peasant smallholding). The lot of the peasant in thirteenth-century England was, to use the classic Hobbesian formulation, 'nasty, brutish and short'. Surviving on strips of land while they owed feudal labour service to the feudal lord, the wretched of the earth would have impinged on John only as objects of curiosity when they occupied their minimal leisure hours with wrestling, cock-fighting, bull-baiting or (in the winter) skating on frozen lakes and meadows.[80]

One important group he could never ignore, if only because relations with the Church occupied so great a part of his reign, was the religious. When John came to the throne there were around seven hundred monasteries and convents, housing some 10,000 monks and 3,000 nuns. The period from the death of William the Conqueror to the accession of John was the golden age of monasticism, with more religious houses founded than at any other time – nine a year in the middle of the twelfth century.[81] At the time of the conquest monasticism based itself on the rule of the Benedictines, which meant taking vows of poverty, chastity and obedience. In theory, no monk could own private property, have sex or raise any objection to severe discipline from a superior, including corporal punishment. The trade-off was security, the opportunity to gluttonise and the access to vast communal wealth. Monks were recruited as oblates – children 'offered' to the religious life by their parents, or as adults with a real or alleged vocation. For a family man to enter the contemplative life meant abandoning his wife and family to strangers. What most impressed contemporaries was the plethora of regular clergy. There were monks properly so called, following the rules of St Benedict, and there were 'canons' who followed the precepts of St Augustine and were more evangelical and prepared to engage with the world.[82] There was also a reformed order of Benedictines, the Cistercians who were, as it were, Marxist-Leninists to Benedict's Marx: that is to say, they accepted the basic rules of the Benedictines but added variations and refinements of their own.[83] It was only after John's death that the neat tripartite division into monk, canon and nun was further complicated by the addition of friars, members of the newly founded Franciscan and Dominican orders. Most contemporaries distinguished the regular clergy by the colour of their clothes. Thus the black monks were the Benedictines, the white monks the Cistercians, the black canons the Augustinians, the white canons the Premonstratensians, the black nuns Benedictine sisters and the white nuns female Cistercians. After the arrival of the Franciscans and the Dominicans there were, additionally, Grey Friars and Black Friars respectively.[84]

Although monasticism was supposed, by definition, to be other-worldly, the great religious houses became economic and even political powers in the areas they dominated. The orthodox Benedictine establishments swam most sturdily into John's ken, based as they were at Winchester, Canterbury and Westminster Abbey. The chronicler Jocelin of Brakeland, a monk of Bury St Edmund's, reveals that the day-to-day concerns of the Benedictines were more worldly than they should have been: promotion, relations with the abbot, and relations with the civil authorities or with bishops.[85] Both Richard and John had problems with the Benedictines, and in dealing with these turbulent monks Richard proved himself a notable diplomat and negotiator.[86] The Cistercians lacked the pride and snobbery of the Benedictines, being prepared to take in 'lay brothers' (uneducated auxiliaries) to do the heavy labour on their estates and in general opting for a more austere lifestyle than the Benedictines. Mariolatry was their unique selling pitch, and a successful one, for it was to the Cistercians that would-be novices tended to gravitate. The growth of the Cistercians in the twelfth century was spectacular. Their showpiece monasteries were the great foundations at Fountains Abbey and Rievaulx in Yorkshire and Waverley Abbey in Surrey.[87] I have referred, semi-facetiously to the Cistercians as Marxist-Leninist, but there was something seriously communistic about their cell-like organisation. Every Cistercian abbey had a mother house, which in turn would have a mother house and so on, until the end of the chain was reached with headquarters at Cîteaux in Burgundy. It was the austerity and other-worldliness that impressed potential temporal benefactors and, before his clash with the papacy, John was an admirer of the order; he himself founded a Cistercian house at Beaulieu in Hampshire and, when locked in conflict with Philip Augustus, felt the need to justify himself to two leading Cistercian abbots.[88]

John cared nothing for most other people, so one should not expect from him any great interest in social class or the social composition of England, beyond the function of the population as fruit to be squeezed dry. Given that his domestic record was as dismal as his showing in foreign affairs, his apologists are forced back on the defence of last resort: that his administration and legal system were peerless. Part of the defence is sound. John's reign sees the burgeoning of official records and archives to an unprecedented degree, so that historians are able to follow the king's actions on a virtually day-to-day basis. It was in his time that the Chancery adopted the system of enrolling copies of all letters and charters issued under the rubric of Charter Rolls, Close Rolls and Patent Rolls.[89] Hubert Walter, chief justiciar and bureaucrat par excellence is usually given the credit for this reform, but we should remember that many of his reforms were already well under way while Richard was on the throne, so that John simply continued the tradition of efficient central administration instead of initiating it. John's justiciar Peter des Roches was also in this tradition of bureaucratic modernisation.[90] There is truth in the assertion by one of John's modern defenders that the personality of John is writ large on the records that survive.[91] The efficiency of the civil service was an aspect of John's desire for control. The Angevin administrative and legal system worked perfectly well without royal intervention and could survive a monarch's lengthy absence – how else could England have been governed under Richard, who spent almost his entire ten-year reign out of the country? – but a 'hands off' approach was not John's way. He wanted to direct from the centre and to be seen to be doing so.

John stood at the apex of a legal and administrative pyramid. Immediately below him were the chancellor, in charge of Chancery, and the justiciar, the supreme law officer.[92] Next in line came the sheriffs (shire-reeves), the chief agents of the Crown in local government, at the head of the fiscal, judicial, administrative and military organisation of the shires, and thus each analogous to a governor under an imperial or federal system. Sheriffs accounted to the Exchequer twice yearly for the shire revenues, executed the king's orders, mobilised the local militia, and presided over the shire court. Originally most sheriffs had been barons, but gradually a class of professional administrators arose to take their place. At the beginning of his reign John had 46 sheriffs, of whom seventeen were barons, twelve knights, and the rest professional royal officers and administrators.[93] The trick in appointing sheriffs was to 'balance the ticket' – to appoint men with sufficient standing locally to be able to exercise authority but not with so much local power that they became unbiddable and unaccountable. The office of sheriff had originally been hereditary, but Henry II put a stop to that with his 1170 Inquest of Sheriffs. Competition for the office was intense, and kings were paid high prices for the position, but the quid pro quo was supposed to be that, once in office, sheriffs could recoup from the local population far more than they had paid out. Henry found out exactly what kind of surplus the most rapacious sheriffs were extracting and began the move towards professional royal administrators.[94] In 1204 John added a refinement to the system by moving away from fixed twice yearly payments due from the sheriffs to a percentage share of all they had uplifted, which increased his revenue from the shires by 30 per cent.[95]

Since under the old system abuses had been frequent and the sheriffs mostly venal and corrupt, the reforms instituted by Henry and John, using professional civil servants rather than local magnates, secured both better government and higher revenues. Another innovation, begun under Longchamp, was to stop sheriffs becoming entrenched in one locality by sending them out on circuit.[96] John also increased the professionalisation of the lower administrative ranks: the sergeants, something like modern chiefs of police, and the bailiffs, in charge of the divisions of the shires known as the hundreds. A new class of local coroners was set up, investigating murder, manslaughter, foul play and sudden death. An embryonic form of a modern legal system can be discerned and even more so in John's highlighting of the jury system. Juries were originally bodies formed solely by royal prerogative, and jury trial was unavailable to lords using the normal, private feudal courts. Since the jury system dispensed rapid justice and was preferable on a number of levels to the old system of ordeals and penalties, more and more people were encouraged to bring their disputes into royal courts.[97] Since a mass of litigation had previously been dealt with in local or feudal courts, the new inflow of cases into royal courts made the legal system more subject to central control – exactly what John wanted. The other beneficial aspect of jury trial for John was that it generated revenue. From the beginning of his reign, defendants could opt for jury trial, but on the strict condition that they paid the necessary fee. John, in short, enlarged the scope of royal jurisdiction at the expense of feudal courts, simply to make more money.[98]

In general John continued in the direction first posted by his father in the area of legal and administrative reform. In his reign we can see in inchoate form a public prosecution service, the growth of a legal profession, a system of circuit judges – the so-called 'eyres' or visitations by between two to nine royal judges – and a Court of Common Pleas at Westminster. The scope of the eyres was all-embracing: they heard pleas dealing with tenancies, wardships, criminal cases, the sale of land, the sale of wine, the election of coroners, taxes, local dues and loans made by Jewish moneylenders.[99] New legal procedures or assizes had been instituted to deal with cases where a landowner had been illegally dispossessed or an heir wrongfully disinherited (the famous assize of novel disseisin and mort d'ancestor).[100] Yet it would be a mistake to think of John as a medieval Solon or Lycurgus. Although he was something of a barroom lawyer himself, with a taste for the pettifogging pedantry of the law, his main interest was always money. During his reign ten baronies passed from brother to brother and, in adjudicating in these cases, John made himself richer by an average 'fine' of 1,575 marks per case, with the colossal figure of 10,000 marks being his highest fee.[101] As one student of his methods has caustically remarked: 'Smallholders' petty pleas held little interest for John, apart from the revenues that they generated.'[102] Nonetheless, in his own mind John was sincerely interested in law courts and the administration of justice. He had authoritarian views which he attempted to validate by reference to the works of St Augustine.[103]

The other reason for scepticism about John's commitment to justice was that he was keen on the traditional ordeals and wanted them to continue. It was only when Pope Innocent III, at the Fourth Lateran Council, forbade the clergy to take part in these procedures that they began to wither away. Settling disputes by ordeal was supposed to involve an appeal to God, who would see that the innocent party prevailed. Ordeals were of two kinds: bilateral, where the litigants or their champions fought duels or mini-battles; and unilateral, where the accused submitted to the ordeal by iron or water.[104] The ordeal by iron meant that the accused had to walk an agreed number of paces holding a heated iron; the hand was then bound and inspected after three days; innocence or guilt was determined by how well the hand was healing. The ordeal by water (never used against women, allegedly for reasons of sexual decorum) meant being thrown into cold water in a lake, pool or pit; if the accused sank, he was innocent, but if he floated he was guilty. Two-thirds of those who underwent the ordeal emerged not guilty. In Launceston in 1201 fifteen cases involving twenty-seven individuals were decided by ordeal, and the system was widespread in John's reign; John oddly saw the ordeals as a way of boosting royal power.[105] But it was

John's old adversary Innocent III who dealt the death-stroke to his primitive method of deciding guilt or innocence. Since the ordeals had to receive ecclesiastical sanction (the iron, for instance, was blessed and consecrated) in line with the theory that God would decide the outcome, the participation of priests was essential to the system. This was, in sum, a form of punishment that hinged on theology, and at the Lateran Council in 1215 Innocent and his learned doctors (more than a thousand bishops and abbots attended the conclave) knifed through to the essential fallacy of the ordeal. The theological basis of ordeals was that God was required to work a miracle on each occasion but, since a miracle is a free act of God unless automatically triggered by the sacraments, the blasphemous logical entailment must be that the ordeal was a sacrament. Innocent's prohibition of ordeals followed, and churchmen everywhere obeyed it.[106]

Summing up on John and justice, one may be sceptical as to this particular monarch's real commitment to the principle. John's defenders tend to make three main points: the barons lost out under his system but the social classes below them did well; corrupt courts and judicial venality were not a serious problem until the reign of Henry III; and it was now clear that minor tenants could win lawsuits against the gentry.[107] Sometimes John's over-eager apologists lurch into outright hyperbole: 'there is no doubt that his royal duty of providing justice was discharged with a zeal and a tirelessness to which the English common law is greatly indebted'[108] is one such judgement. But against these points are three even weightier. One is that John's energy and intervention in legal and administrative matters was a consequence of his control-freak paranoia; he could not trust anyone, he could not delegate so (as he saw it) his finger had to be in every pie. Moreover, it was a contingent fact that feudal custom in England allowed a king to regulate the lives of his tenants-in-chief (and hence his subjects in general) more closely than a French monarch could.[109] The second is the simple and incontestable point that John's main interest in the legal and administrative sphere was always the raising of money; the more unsuccessful he became in foreign warfare and diplomacy, the more frenziedly he taxed and mulcted. It may not be quite an example of Santayana's definition of fanaticism – redoubling efforts when one has lost sight of the aim – but it is heading along that way. Thirdly, the much-lauded extension of jury trials in England turned out to be a function either of John's lust for the fees payable in royal courts or, more directly, Innocent III's ban on ordeals, which caused a reflex switch to jury trials in the years 1216–17.[110] There is certainly no justification in domestic policy for the new revisionism of 'good King John'.

16

RELATIONS BETWEEN THE VATICAN and sovereign nation-states in modern history are simplified by the stark fact that the Church of Rome is a spiritual power dealing with temporal lords. In the Middle Ages there was no such simple contrast. The Church was itself a temporal power and the higher clergy were major players in the politics of the day in all western societies. As the titanic struggle between Henry II and Becket had shown, the apparently straightforward matter of a nomination to a vacant archbishopric could set in train events that convulsed kingdoms. It was in his dealings with the Church that John most clearly revealed himself a true son of Henry II. All the kings of England since 1066 wanted a situation where, to use Walter Bagehot's terms, the papacy was merely the 'dignified' aspect of the Church in England while the monarch was the 'efficient' aspect, the real power. In other words, they were prepared to acknowledge the Pope's nominal position as eccesiastical overlord, but wanted all the real decisions about preferment to bishoprics and other high offices to be in their own hands.[1] The *locus classicus* of this tendency was Henry II's 'Constitutions of Clarendon', adopted in 1164, which attempted to exclude papal authority by recognising the pontiff's suzerainty 'saving only the king's royal rights and liberties.'[2] This proviso contained so many exceptions and opt-outs that the basic acceptance of papal authority was rendered meaningless. One of the more notorious utterances by Henry was that reported to the Pope by the Young King during his rebellion: Henry told the monks of Winchester in 1173: 'I order you to hold a free election, but I forbid you to elect anyone except Richard my clerk, archdeacon of Poitiers.'[3] Henry had learned after the martyrdom of Becket and the failure of his conflict with Rome that it was wisest not to confront the papacy head-on. Richard the paladin had no quarrel with the Church so long as it did not impede his martial glory. The foolish John, however, allowed a relatively trival slight to his dignity to escalate into a full-blown crisis with one of the most determined popes of the Middle Ages. Although some historians have tried to commend John for his 'patriotism' and 'defence of England' and made him a kind of forerunner of Henry VIII, the truth is that John miscalculated badly and then redoubled his efforts when he had lost sight of his aim. It was John in typical mode, exhibiting all the bad-tempered despotism which was characteristic of him. Comparisons with Henry VIII may be more apt than some of his uncautious modern admirers would care to admit.[4]

A charitable view might be that John was unlucky in that his reign almost exactly coincided with that of Pope Innocent III, whose pontificate is widely regarded as the apogee of both the spiritual and temporal power of the Roman see. Innocent presided over the birth of the Franciscan and Dominican movements, held the famous fourth Lateran Council in 1215, and adjudicated between rival emperors in Germany, deposing Otto IV. The Latin conquest of Constantinople in the Fourth Crusade (1204) destroyed his Christian rivals in the East, while his ruthless extirpation of the Albigensian heresy in south-western France eliminated the radical threat in the West. John's relations with the papacy had been brittle from the very beginning. Innocent III was exasperated with both John and Philip Augustus, because their dispute over Normandy impeded his plans for a fourth Crusade.[5] Nonetheless, as long as the German imperial throne remained vacant and the succession undecided (that is to say, until about 1207), Innocent treated John with remarkable indulgence. Despite John's despotic policy towards the Church, Innocent allowed him considerable leeway, not interfering when the bishops of Normandy and Aquitaine authorised the annulment of his first marriage; this was in pointed contrast to the Pope's martinet attitude when Philip Augustus discarded his wife Ingeborg of Denmark.[6] When Philip Augustus triumphed in Normandy, however, the Pope washed his hands of the affair and instructed his Norman bishops to follow law, custom and their consciences. This de facto acceptance of the Capetian conquest of Normandy rankled with John and it may have been a factor in his later attitudes to the papacy. Even before this, though, John had been marked down in the papal book as a man with despotic tendencies. Once crowned king in 1199, John continued the feud he had waged as 'lord of Ireland' against John Cumin, archbishop of Dublin; having once before driven him into exile, he repeated the medicine in 1203, drawing from Innocent a stinging rebuke and a warning that if he did not readmit Cumin, he would place John's lands under papal interdict. But Cumin was just the tip of an iceberg. John offended the Pope over a range of arbitrary actions and preferments, pogroms and persecutions, in Normandy, Limoges, Poitiers, Lincoln and Winchester.[7] While John was locked in conflict with Philip Augustus over Normandy, he could not afford a fight on another front and was compelled to accept unwelcome papal orders and decrees, but John, secretly fuming at the insult to his 'honour', bided his time and awaited a suitable opportunity to retaliate.

It was the death of Hubert Walter in 1205 that was the precipitant to a decade of battle with the papacy. Whether John secretly loathed and resented Walter, and suspected him of being too friendly to Philip Augustus, as some of the chroniclers allege, is still a subject on which scholars debate.[8] Yet of Hubert's talents as a bureaucrat there can be no reasonable doubt; after all, it is due to him that we possess a swathe of documentation for John's reign unavailable for the Richard era: chancery documents, charter, patent and close rolls; the appearance of official archives as an aid to administration is almost entirely due to Walter.[9] A master of administrative efficiency, he introduced set tariffs for fees and fines, invented the oath of peace, the office of coroner and much else. He regulated the fees payable at the Chancery for the issue of documents under the Great Seal – a process that had degenerated into a financial racket in Richard's times, with exorbitant tariffs almost inevitably engendering elaborate forgeries.[10] He was a great civil servant, but as archbishop of Canterbury was scarcely in the Thomas Becket mould. The monks of Canterbury complained to the Pope that he was far too obsessed with affairs of state to be an efficient or even credible primate. He was no respecter of religious punctilio or even the rights of sanctuary, and on one notorious occasion gutted the Church of St Mary-le-Bow to smoke out a would-be Robin Hood named William FitzOsbert and his nine companions; seized as they made their fuliginous exit, the alleged rebels were bound to horses' tails and dragged to Smithfield, where they were hanged in chains.[11] Hubert Walter was also a venal and extortionate man, who extracted large sums of money for private purposes as well as for the exchequer, and was not over-scrupulous about how he raised the cash. It is certain that he died owing £1,000 – an enormous debt for the thirteenth century.[12]

Nonetheless a new archbishop of Canterbury had to be appointed, and according to canon law the electors were the monks of Christ Church; usually the country's bishops also had a say in who was to be head of the English Church. The situation was complicated by tensions between secular and regular clergy in early thirteenth-century England, largely on the grounds that the monastic orders had departed from the

vows of their founding fathers in favour of money-making and involvement in worldly pursuits; the Cistercians were a particular butt of criticism.[13] Yet it was virtually axiomatic that no archbishop could be elected
who did not have the king's approval. Foreseeing that hotheads among
the monks might precipitate a crisis by holding a snap election, John
sped to Canterbury and persuaded the chapter to postpone their
choice for six months (until December 1205). Meanwhile both the king
and the monks separately lobbied the Vatican.[14] After consultation with
the bishops, John sent envoys to Innocent III with instructions to use
all means (diplomacy, cajolery, bribery) to persuade the Pope simply to
order the monks to fall in line with his wishes, which were that his friend
and confidant John de Gray, bishop of Norwich, should be the next
metropolitan. Historians are divided about Gray. For some he is no more
than a sycophant and yes-man: 'He was a man of purely secular interests – a competent captain and efficient civil servant. There was no man
in England whom John trusted so completely and so consistently as he
did John de Gray.'[15] For others, he was a lesser version of Hubert Walter
but still one whom the monks would have been wise to accept, as he
was easy-going and would have given them what they wanted.[16] But John's
action in sending secret agents to Rome played into the hands of the
die-hard faction among the Christ Church monks. Angered by the king's
intrigues they chose their subprior, Reginald, on the understanding that
the choice required papal sanction, and sent him to Rome under an oath
not to reveal his provisional election unless Innocent III seemed to be
bending to the lobbying of John's agents.

The ambitious Reginald had a high opinion of his own abilities and
decided to 'bounce' the Pope into proclaiming him archbishop. Once in
Rome he told Innocent the monks had already elected him and sought
his confirmation. Innocent was no more likely to be gulled by an oppor-
tunistic cleric than by John's agents, so he ordered a cooling-off period
while he examined the merits of the possible candidates. News of the
contretemps was carried back to England by a relay of couriers. Hearing
of the election of Reginald in defiance of his explicit wishes, the irate
monarch stormed down to Canterbury to confront the recreant monks.
An Angevin ruler in a rage was not a pretty sight, and everyone knew
that the 'Devil's Brood' was notoriously unpredictable in such a situation. The monks therefore disingenuously denied that they had elected
Reginald and were forced to make good their words by 'electing' bishop
Gray on 11 December; John rubbed in the monks' humiliation by ostentatiously awarding Gray five hundred marks for the 'necessary expenses'

of his investiture.[17] The bishops took no part in any of this but were simply required by John to add their approval. All that was needed now for Gray to become archbishop of Canterbury was papal ratification; accordingly a second delegation of monks set off for Rome with the king's consent to obtain it. But their arrival simply made matters worse for, faced with 'inputs' from three sectors, John, the bishops, and the cathedral chapter, Innocent was becoming both perplexed and alienated. Reginald, still clinging to his golden dream, told the Pope, plausibly enough, that the second delegation of monks were handpicked stooges who had been bullied and browbeaten by John and did not represent the true views of Canterbury Cathedral.[18] There now seemed to be at least four viewpoints. John's agents claimed that no election involving Reginald had ever been held; Reginald and his coterie of monks insisted that he was the true archbishop according to canon law and had been duly chosen in a genuinely free election, not the charade organised by John on 11 December; the second delegation of monks argued that Reginald had been elected but only provisionally, and that this was rescinded by 11 December; and meanwhile a bishop's proctor had arrived representing the English dioceses and claiming that their voices too must be heard.[19] Innocent tried to cut the Gordian knot by quashing the election of both pretenders (Gray and Reginald), ruling the bishops out of court and insisting that all Canterbury monks then in Rome should hold a new election under his own impartial auspices, to be held in December 1206. When this suffrage produced a tied result as between the supporters of John de Gray and Reginald, the Pope announced a compromise candidate, one who had his personal backing. This was Stephen Langton, cardinal priest of St Chrystogonus, a native of Lincolnshire in his late forties, with a distinguished academic record in Paris. At the Pope's urging the monks proceeded to elect Langton unanimously.[20]

Innocent consecrated Stephen Langton at Viterbo on 17 July 1207, but Langton was unable to proceed to England as the furiously angry John declined to confirm his appointment. Ominously he remained for six years at the Cistercian abbey of Pontigny, Becket's old refuge during the stand-off years with Henry II. To show his contempt for the Pope's decision, John expelled all the monks of Canterbury (except for a handful of the aged and infirm) and seized the cathedral's property, expropriating revenues of nearly £1,500 a year.[21] John's rage against organised religion extended even to his half-brother and one-time confidant Geoffrey, archbishop of York, long a thorn in John's side for objecting to the king's barefaced robbery of the Church. After excommunicating all collectors and payers of royal taxes on Church property, Geoffrey fled to the continent, where he died in 1212. With no incumbent archbishops in either Canterbury or York John had a clear field for his depredations. It has sometimes, absurdly, been claimed that John was conventionally pious, and some lame circumstantial evidence has been adduced, as for instance his acting as pallbearer at the funeral of St Hugh of Lincoln.[22] More convincing is the evidence of Adam of Eynsham, the biographer of Hugh, who knew the true situation; he reports that John never took communion after he came of age, not even at his own coronation.[23] The truth is that John made obeisance to the forms and myths of Christianity when it suited him and when he could extract a political or propaganda advantage. No true believer could have lived with the burden of Arthur's murder on his conscience. John's negative attitude towards organised religion was probably partly cerebral, the product of his reading, and partly derived from his meanness and avarice. Piety in a monarch meant generosity and almsgiving, and this was never John's strong suit. John was supposedly devoted to St Hugh but, when his alleged hero was celebrating Mass at Fontevraud in 1200, John was observed to be reluctant to make the customary offering of twelve gold coins.[24] Again, immediately after his coronation, John went to Bury St Edmunds, where the monks looked forward to some royal munificence. John donated merely a silken cloth which he had borrowed from the sacrist and never paid for; then at Mass on the day of his departure he left only twelve pence for all the hospitality he had enjoyed.[25] Employing what E.P. Thompson called 'the enormous condescension of posterity', John's modern-day defenders simply sweep aside all the evidence of John's atheism and impiety in Matthew Paris, Adam of Eynsham and other chroniclers and boldly assert that an irreligious John 'cannot' have been the case.[26]

John's quarrel with the Church, then, was not something reluctantly taken up as a result of miscalculations and ineptitude but a crusade he, at least initially, entered on with enthusiasm. Innocent patiently explained to John why he had chosen Stephen Langton and given him a cardinal's hat, but all John could understand was that *he* had not got his way. Furiously and intemperately, with never a thought for the consequences, he fired off a blistering reply that Langton was quite unacceptable, on the grounds of his long residence in Paris and his French connections – 'consorting with his enemies', as John put it. Innocent was not accustomed to such insolence. He rebuked John as a headmaster might a cheeky schoolboy, pointing out that his letter was contumacious, impertinent and muddled: for one thing Langton's reputation was second to none, and for another John himself had congratulated him on his cardinal's hat (before he knew of his elevation to Canterbury) – the king, then, was being a humbug. Innocent also pointed out, justifiably, that he had given John every leeway, that he had waited an unconscionable time to hear from him, even though he was under no obligation to consult him on a matter wholly within papal prerogatives; John should realise that the Pope had already treated him above and beyond the levels of consideration normal in such matters, and he could scarcely expect that canon law should yield to the caprices of an earthly and therefore ephemeral ruler.[27] Moreover, once a proper election had been held, as it had in Rome, not even the Pope had the authority to rescind it or declare its provisions void. John sulked and fumed, telling his intimates that he might not be able to depose a bishop but he could certainly ensure that the said bishop never managed to exercise his functions in England. To make the point pellucid, he decreed that anyone calling Langton archbishop was guilty of high treason.[28]

As early as August 1207 Innocent warned John (through the medium of the bishops of London, Ely and Worcester) that he might place England under an interdict if John did not admit Stephen Langton.[29] John, an exponent *avant la lettre* of the alleged Stalinist 'how many divisions has the Pope?', took no notice. On Sunday 23 March 1208 Innocent made good the threat. The original document containing precise details of the scope of the interdict does not survive, but we know from the sequel, and indeed from *a priori* principles, that a papal interdict meant a suspension of all normal activities of the Church – what has been called a 'general strike of the clergy'; Confession went into abeyance, the sacrament of Extreme Unction was denied to the dying, the dead did not receive Christian burial but were interred in woods and ditches, marriages were not solemnised in Church, and the baptism of infants had to be performed by parents under the time-honoured emergency rubric.[30] For six years the faithful of England languished in metaphorical limbo (and the dead presumably in the actual one), deprived of one of the few solaces the ordinary peasant, labourer or journeyman could aspire to. Only certain arrogant and worldly sectors of the regular clergy, the Cistercians for example, defied the Pope and carried on as normal. The bishops of London, Ely, Worcester and Hereford left the country, joining Langton and Archbishop Geoffrey of York in continental exile. Very few pastors were left in the dioceses, since the sees of Lincoln, Chichester and Exeter were currently vacant, and the bishops of Durham and Coventry were on their deathbed. Of the higher clergy, only John de Gray, the cause of all the trouble, and Peter des Roches, bishop of Winchester, were openly defiant of the pontiff, while the bishops of Bath, Salisbury and Rochester kept a low profile, trimming and tergiv-ersating, until Innocent's excommunication of John in October 1209 finally brought them down off the fence.[31]

The interdict saw John and Innocent in a ferocious struggle for hearts and minds, with the English king employing all the resources of black propaganda and primitive spin-doctoring. John was initially successful in putting over his line that a tyrannical Pope had deliberately insulted him and bishop Gray, and put in his own nominee, a man who was little better than a spy for Philip Augustus.[32] Appeals to custom and tradition rightly stressed that it was unheard of for popes to intervene in the appointment of bishops, but John's propagandists neglected to mention that this was only because of the high-handedness of the Angevins, faced with weak or short-lived popes. John cleverly played on the theme that he was being persecuted, when the only people actually being perse-cuted were those, like the monks of Canterbury and Langton himself, who had had the courage to stand by the Pope. John also used his favourite stratagem when he could not get the result he wanted by main force: he stalled, played for time and went through a dishonest charade of talks and negotiations. He invited Langton's brother Simon to come to Winchester for discussions, and sent his own envoy, the abbot of Beaulieu, to Rome to try to snarl the Pope up in casuistry. Even one of his most prominent modern defenders admits: 'John was merely trying to gain time: he offered concessions and then slithered out of them.'[33] He made mendacious public announcements to the effect that Simon Langton had told him the only terms the Pope could agree to were unconditional surrender; 'he said he could do nothing for us unless we put ourselves completely at his mercy.'[34] Every time the Pope thought he was on the brink of an agreement, John would insist on adding the words 'saving only his royal rights and liberties' to the protocol, thus taking away with the right hand what he had appeared to give with his left, and returning the situation to the Becket-Henry II stalemate over the Constitutions of Clarendon.[35] Innocent did his best to combat this tide of mendacity, while suffering from the obvious disadvantage that he could make almost no inroads in England, for any pro-papal commu-nications rendered the utterer liable to the penalties for high treason. He tried to appeal to John's barons, stopping short of an actual incitement to rebellion but urging them 'Do not fear displeasing him temporarily in the name of justice.'[36] But the barons had their own agenda as far as

John was concerned and did not intend to get caught up in what was to them an irrelevant quarrel. Innocent grew increasingly frustrated and bewildered. When he laid interdicts on Laon in 1198, on France in 1199 and Normandy in 1203, they had proved remarkably successful. Philip Augustus caved in after just a few months of the interdict pronounced when he defied the Pope over his marriage.[37] What was wrong with England?

John was confident he could ride out any turbulence from the interdict and in many ways actually welcomed it, since it gave him the excuse he otherwise lacked to expropriate Church property and grow richer – always a consideration in the brain of this most moneyminded of kings. As soon as the clergy downed tools in obedience to the interdict, John sent his officers to seize their property in the king's name. The efficient administration of Hubert Walter and John de Gray gave John the ability to confiscate clerical property with ease; sheriffs were appointed as administrators of the forfeited estates and lorded it in abbeys, bishoprics and parishes.[38] Having wielded the big stick, he then spoke softly and offered compromise: the clergy could have their property back on payment of appropriate fines and provided they made themselves personally responsible for paying future revenues to the king. Only a machiavellian like John could think of impounding property, getting the owners to pay for the 'privilege' of having it administered by royal officers, having them pay fines to retrieve their position and then, in many cases, agreeing to remit a portion of the retrieved revenues to the king as 'thanks' for his magnanimity. This was John's way of avoiding tangling up his civil servants in long-term administration of church lands and benefices, while still retaining the money so mouth-wateringly offered by the original seizures.[39] He got many takers for his barefaced scam and made huge sums of money from the fines; the abbot of St Albans, for example, paid 600 marks to regain his property, while the abbot of Peterborough recovered control of the abbey's estates but had to pay an ongoing sum of £600 per annum to acknowledge the king's 'generosity'.[40] By 1213 it was estimated that John had made more than 100,000 marks (the crippling sum levied for Richard's ransom in 1194) from the interdict,[41] which to him was big business.[42] As a fraudster John had few medieval rivals, and only modern 'privatisations' can compare for barefaced audacity. In this, as in so many ways, John anticipated Henry VIII. His hatred of organised religion also surfaces in his scheme for fining clergy for failing to keep their vows of celibacy. The Middle Ages were notorious for unchaste priests, with some parochial houses more akin to crèches or bordellos than abodes of God.[43] John noted with glee that Henry I had fined clergy for disobeying the Church's decrees on celibacy and then sold them licences to marry, thus making two lots of money from self-contradictory transactions.[44] John finessed this by ordering his officials to seize all priestly mistresses, concubines and courtesans, allowing them to be released only on payment of a ransom; his low estimate of human nature proved correct when the clergy flocked in to bail their women out.[45]

By 1209 Innocent III had lost patience both with John's relentless stalling and bogus offers of talks and with the failure of the interdict to have much impact on England. Sterner measures were clearly called for, so in the summer of that year he instructed Stephen Langton to pronounce a sentence of excommunication on King John whenever he thought fit.[46] Langton tried one last time, sent his brother on a further mission and even crossed the Channel himself under a safe-conduct to confer with John's ministers at Dover. But the king's insincerity was patent, so in November Langton, safely back in France, formally promulgated the decree of excommunication, placing John beyond the Christian pale.[47] Excommunication was an altogether more serious matter than the interdict. Although the general strike by the clergy caused inconvenience, hardship and disturbance, by and large people could live with it. But excommunication, in effect an ecclesiastical sentence of outlawry, meant that nobody could aid or abet the king without suffering the loss of their immortal souls. If the thirteenth century really was an age of belief, the effect should have been immediate and catastrophic. To be sure, hitherto collaborationist bishops like Jocelin of Bath concluded that the game of fence-sitting could no longer be played and withdrew abroad, but once again the immediate impact of the Pope's escalation of the crisis was disappointing. Scholars are divided about the reason: some say it is simply that fear of John and his easy way with a hanging rope overrode the fear of eternal damnation; others that the Church had cried 'wolf' too often in the past, using excommunication for trivial reasons and thus undermining its credibility.[48] Probably, disappointed at the impact of the interdict, Innocent had revised his expectations and hoped rather that the sentence of excommunication would have a steady, drip-drip, erosive effect: political dissidents, economic malcontents, wavering barons, rebels in the Celtic fringes and indeed anyone opposed to John could 'legitimate' their stance by arguing that John was no longer a Christian king and that the Pope had removed all grounds for allegiance to such a person.[49] The Scottish campaign of

1208–09, for instance, was marred by fears that John's troops would desert once they heard he had been excommunicated.[50] Moreover, the effect on morale had to be considered. How could John hope to combat Philip Augustus in Europe when Philip now stood forth as the champion of the Pope and Christianity while John was an outlaw and apostate? As a moral leper, John was, in the eyes of Christendom, in no better case than Saladin faced by Richard.

John's response to the excommunication was to lift the mulcting of the Church up another notch. From phoney 'fines' and 'fees' he moved to outright plunder, seizing ecclesiastical plate and melting it down. He also ran a neat line in extortion, for instance blackmailing the monks of Montacute that he would reinstate the prior they had just deposed unless they paid the 'consideration' of sixty marks.[51] It has been estimated that the sums paid into the exchequer from Church sources rose from only £400 in 1209, before the excommunication, to £24,000 in 1211.[52] Ecclesiastical friend and foe were swept alike into John's ravening maw. Even after the excommunication, two Cistercian monks stayed loyally in attendance on the king, one of them, the abbot of Bindon, acting as his almoner.[53] But this did not help the wider Cistercian movement, which seemed to have suffered more grievously than the rest of the regular clergy; more than 15 per cent of the revenue extorted by John from the Church came from the Cistercians, and many of their monasteries were dissolved, with the monks seeking refuge with other orders.[54] John acted particularly ruthlessly towards the clergy who fled after the decree of excommunication, expropriating their property without compensation and expelling proxy prelates appointed to their benefices by the exiles. In two especially vindictive acts, the woods of the archbishop of Canterbury were sold, and the bishop of London's castle at Stortford destroyed.[55] Defenders of John like to say that 'only' £11,000 a year was extracted from the Church over six years, in addition to the income from vacant sees and abbeys which would have been taken by the Crown in normal circumstances, and that this sum must be set in a context where the total annual income of the English Church was some £80,000.[56] Another common defence is that when the great abbeys were allowed to manage their own property on payment of a fine, they were allowed to keep back very generous sums for their own subsistence when returning the accounts to the king's officers.[57]

But – very appropriately in this instance – not by bread alone . . . Religious life suffered badly, to the point where by the end of 1211 only one bishop was left in England.[58] Once John de Gray was sent to Ireland to be justiciar (February 1208) and the other bishops fled after the decree of excommunication, there remained only Peter des Roches, bishop of Winchester. The irony about des Roches was that he had himself been the centre of a disputed election in 1205; on that occasion when the hostile parties held a fresh election under the Pope's eyes, he emerged as the unanimous choice.[59] It was a poor return for the lavish privileges Innocent III had showered on him that des Roches should have emerged as the most disloyal divine of all in the eyes of the Vatican. Beyond the absence of the Church's princes was the paucity of religious life at the grass roots. Some attempt was made to keep up the tempo of devotion, with sermons being preached in churchyards, and Innocent made some concessions to a liturgically challenged faithful by allowing monks to celebrate Mass once a week behind locked doors; in 1212 he even allowed the dying to receive the *viaticum*[60] But the ordinary parishioners were denied the sacraments, church weddings and burials in consecrated ground. What was worrying for the Church was that nobody seemed to mind; if this continued, religion might cease to exert its grip altogether. Increasingly, the common people murmured and wondered why they had to pay church tithes if the Church was doing nothing for them.[61] The Vatican meanwhile grew increasingly concerned at the behaviour of priests who, having no work to do, spent their time in brothels and taverns or dallied with the world in business or money-making; having let the genie out of the bottle with the interdict and the excommunication, it might not be so easy to get it back in again.[62] For John there were hidden worries too. If he could shrug off the authority of the Pope and Holy Mother Church with no other moral authority than his will and his say-so, might it not occur to the toiling masses that there was then no reason why they should not jettison a purely instrumental and pragmatic ruler as well? This was doubtless the reason why John tacked in and out of hatred and contempt for the Church and upholding its moral authority as a necessary corollary to his own. One story has it that John encountered a sheriff's officer in charge of a handcuffed prisoner and learned that the man had slain a priest on the highway. 'Loose him and let him go,' said John, 'he has slain one of my enemies.'[63] That was John in irreligious, atheistic mood. But the cunning self-serving John was the one who issued orders that anyone speaking evil against the clergy should be hanged from the nearest oak tree.[64]

This is another way of saying that John had perforce to weigh short-term gains against long-term implications. In the short-term the quarrel with Innocent had made him rich and his coffers were overflowing; the

ordinary taxpayer had meanwhile been relieved of the heavy financial
burden of the expeditions to Scotland, Wales and Ireland in 1210–12.
This was what led contemporary chroniclers to say that John was both
happy and successful, going about with whistling insouciance, devoting
himself to hunting and other pleasures: 'he haunted woods and streams,
and greatly did he delight in the pleasure of them'.[65] Yet in the long term
his sights were set on the recovery of Normandy, and he was aware that
he could scarcely fight Philip Augustus with force of arms while he was
waging a bitter battle of wills with the Pope, especially as that enabled
Philip to portray himself as the protector of Christianity, civilisation and
spiritual values. That was why John never entirely suspended negotiations with the Vatican, and envoys continued to travel back and forth
from Rome.[66] In the summer of 1211 he allowed a papal legate, Pandulph,
to enter England and argue the Pope's case before a royal council at
Northampton. Pandulph's terms for an end to the interdict/excommu-
nication were that John should finally accept Stephen Langton, reinstate
the exiled bishops and clergy and restore their confiscated property. John
summarily rejected these terms.[67] But a year later events at home and
abroad had weakened his position to the point where he sent a fresh
embassy to Rome under the abbot of Beaulieu to accept on his behalf
the terms refused the year before. Innocent decided to make John sweat
and at first said that the offer of 1211 was no longer on the table; since
John had turned down the terms then, it was his fault that peace had
not been restored; moreover, since then, John had committed fresh
outrages against the Church and shown himself unworthy of generosity.
Nevertheless, Innocent concluded, 'so that we may overcome evil with
good' he was prepared to stretch a point and allow John to sign up to
the 1211 deal, provided it was ratified in a watertight way. Moreover, in
addition to receiving back the exiled prelates, John must show his good
faith by readmitting Robert FitzWalter and Eustace Vesci, the exiled
leaders of the disgruntled barons with a full pardon; as a first instalment
on the peace plan, John would also be required to pay over £8,000.[68]

   John's embassy narrowly averted the next stage in the Pope's
campaign against John, which was to declare him formally deposed
as king and his subjects released from any allegiance. Innocent
was prompted to this apocalyptic course by exactly the same developments that led John to accept the Pope's terms: on the one hand Philip
Augustus was at last preparing his long-threatened invasion of England,
and on the other John's barons had finally lost patience with him and
were beginning to break rank. Stephen Langton had actually left Rome

with Innocent's bulls declaring John deposed, which he intended to publish in France, but was overtaken on the road by Pandulph, who explained the changed situation.[69] John was to be given until June 1213 to ratify the terms agreed with the Pope by his envoy, failing which Langton was to promulgate the bulls. This time, however, John was not stalling and really intended to submit. To ensure no eleventh-hour contretemps – perhaps he did not entirely trust Langton's discretion – Innocent sent his legate Nicholas of Tusculum to recover the papal bulls from the archbishop and burn them.[70] Nevertheless, Innocent remained deeply suspicious of John and laid contingency plans in case he reneged. He wrote to Langton as follows: 'It often happens that a ruthless foe, finding himself cornered, treacherously pretends peace and after the peace attempts treachery, in order to outwit by guile those he could not by force. Wishing, therefore, with careful precaution to guard against such treacheries, by the authority of this letter we grant you this power: if King John should violate the peace that has been restored between him and the English Church, then (unless after due warning he makes amends to you) you will, after consultation with the Pope, reduce him and his kingdom, by apostolic authority, to the state of excommunication and interdict that they were in before the restoration of peace.'[71]

Beset by multitudinous problems, John was in Kent waiting nervously for the return of his envoys. One of them, Brother William of Ouen crossed the Channel to confer with John, then recrossed to confirm to Stephen Langton that the king had ratified.[72] Finally Pandulph came over for the formal treaty signing and met John at Dover on 13 May. The king reiterated his acceptance of the deal negotiated in Rome, and three of his barons (the earls of Salisbury, Warenne and Ferrers) plus the count of Boulogne stood as guarantors of his good faith.[73] Two days later, at the house of the Templars at Ewell near Dover, John pulled a rabbit out of the hat. He issued a charter making England and Ireland feudal fiefs of the Holy See, with himself as the Pope's vassal. Technically, he resigned the kingdoms of England and Ireland to Innocent and received them back under the bond of fealty and homage, on a pledge to pay 1,000 marks a year to the Holy See, 700 for England and 300 for Ireland. This charter was witnessed by John de Gray, by Geoffrey Peter, the justiciar, the count of Boulogne, and the earls of Salisbury, Pembroke, Surrey, Winchester, Arundel and Derby as well as three members of his own household.[74] It was then ratified in St Paul's Cathedral on 3 October in a solemn ceremony in the presence of Nicholas, cardinal-archbishop of Tusculum and sealed with a golden bull. John's formal release from excommunication was, however, delayed until the following July when Langton finally returned. The interdict took even longer to be rescinded because John, typically, haggled about the reparations due to the English Church. Once in England, Langton set up a commission to assess the clergy's losses, which took time, and there were many disputes, principally arising from the fact that John had bullied monasteries into giving him quittances for what he had taken from them.[75] Yet in Innocent's eyes, in the euphoria of victory, all this was mere detail. He was delighted with the unexpected turn of events which so enhanced the prestige of the Apostolic See, and sent off a fulsome letter to John, praising him for having known how to turn evil into good.[76]

John was lucky in that Innocent did not extract the last pound of flesh. Bowled over by John's submission, the Pope swung from over-suspicion of the English king to over-trust, and wrote to him with a warmth and enthusiasm he seldom evinced to others. In sending Nicholas of Tusculum as his personal representative, he described the legate as 'an angel of salvation and peace'.[77] He gave Nicholas secret instructions to go easy on John in the matter of reparations, so Nicholas cut through the acrimony over what John actually owed to churches and monasteries by compounding the debt at the round figure of 100,000 marks, over the angry protests of the English clergy that John was getting away with financial murder and that the true debt was at least half as much again. So unswayed was Nicholas by these remonstrations that he actually allowed John to pay the 100,000 marks in instalments: he was to make a down-payment of 40,000 and pay the rest off at 12,000 a year. When the interdict was lifted, Nicholas allowed John to get away with a down-payment of just 13,000.[78] But if the clergy thought John had gulled the Pope and his representatives, many thought Innocent had humiliated the English nation and its king. John was overcompensating for his former excesses, and many who had previously criticised him for dragging England into an unnecessary conflict with the papacy now attacked him for having sold out the true interests of England.[79] Interestingly, many of the critics were themselves churchmen, and even Stephen Langton thought John had gone too far in allowing papal power to extend to England; he particularly resented Nicholas of Tusculum's high hand in making appointments to vacant sees and benefices which he saw as his own prerogative.[80]

The high point of John's new entente with the Pope came on 20 July 1213 in a solemn ceremony at Winchester Cathedral when John welcomed as archbishop the man he had vowed would never occupy that office. Stephen Langton for his part formally absolved the king of excommunication. John then swore on the Gospels that he would defend the Church at all times and revive the good laws of former times, and especially the codes of Edward the Confessor; moreover that he would abolish all bad laws and hear all issues in his courts with justice as the ruling principle, guaranteeing human rights to all men.[81] By thus appearing as the patron condescending to a suppliant, Langton regained some of the prestige lost to Nicholas of Tusculum. Innocent had given Nicholas plenipotentiary powers which the legate had exercised injudiciously and with some want of tact. It particularly incensed the ultramontane clergy, who had been steadfastly loyal to the papacy, that Nicholas, with the Pope's blessing, rewarded the trimmers, apostates and royal lickspittles, so that those who had lacked the courage and integrity to break with John now received the glittering prizes: among those so despised were William Cornhill, who became bishop of Lichfield, and Walter Gray who was appointed to the archbishopric of York, left vacant by Geoffrey. John's half-brother was never recalled from exile, as might have been expected.[82] The most scandalous case of papal betrayal of his faithful occurred at Durham. Here the chapter assumed from John's submission that it could now exercise the ancient canonical right to elect a new bishop, and chose the saintly Richard Poor, dean of Salisbury. Yet, with Nicholas's connivance, John imposed his old henchman John de Gray, lately justiciar of Ireland.[83] Once again Innocent seemed to be letting the king get away with the ecclesiastical equivalent of daylight robbery. Innocent evidently considered that *raison d'état* and his new Concordat with John meant far more than justice, meritocracy or canon law. Langton hit back by dragging his feet, seemingly in no hurry to restore England to full Christian status; it was only pressure from Nicholas that finally got the interdict rescinded in July 1214. With stunning predictability, the reparations immediately began to dry up. A further 6,000 marks was paid in August–November 1214, but thereafter John 'forgot' about the balance, pleading the pressure of other concerns.[84]

The political implications of John's entente with Rome were spectacular since, once the king had deferred to Innocent and accepted him as overlord, he simply could do no wrong in the pontiff's eyes; Innocent thereafter connived at the most flagrant despotism on John's part. The diplomatic revolution this entailed was akin to Richard's reversal of alliances in the late 1190s but perhaps even more striking, for here now was Innocent allied to the man he had recently excommunicated, who in turn was allied to the Pope's bitterest enemy, the excommunicate German pretender Otto, while ranged against them were the Pope's erstwhile allies Philip Augustus and Frederick of Hohenstaufen.[85] The implications of all this would become dramatically manifest in 1214. Meanwhile the period of bitter enmity between Innocent and John, followed by the close bonding subsequent to the lifting of the excommunication, had more immediate implications for another important group: the English barons. Relations between the Angevin kings and their barons had always been brittle – this was, after all, one of the deep undercurrents of the Young King's rebellion against Henry II in 1173–74[86] – but it may be that by their constant wars, and the opportunities thus held out for enrichment, Henry and Richard warded off the worst of the baronial backlash. The loss of Normandy and John's ceaseless quest for more money brought the struggle between king and barons back to centre-stage. Whereas under Richard the levy of scutage or shield-money had been occasional and intermittent, John converted it into a virtual annual tax.[87]

In the struggle of king versus barons, the monarch held nearly all the cards. Henry II had specialised in increasing the Crown's executive power, using ad hoc agents instead of the barons and extending the scope of royal courts while taking as many castles as possible into the regal orbit, where they could be controlled by loyal castellans. While not neglecting any of these methods, John's preference was for the financial scam, especially the vagueness surrounding succession duties (that early form of inheritance tax) due from an heir succeeding to a barony. As the official guide to these taxes put it: 'there is no fixed amount which the heir must pay to the king; he must make what terms he can'.[88] John liked to set these 'reliefs' at a very high level, forcing the new fief-holder into a permanent cycle of indebtedness. The going rate was supposed to be £100, but John increased the 'norm' to six hundred marks. And since the amount taxed was entirely at the whim of the king, John liked to punish anyone who had displeased him by levying an enormous amount: sums of 7,000 and even 10,000 marks (one-tenth the ransom for Richard in Germany) were recorded.[89] Since the average baronial income was around £200 a year, any extraordinary rate of relief plunged the unfortunate baron into lifelong debt-bondage. The only hope was that, in return for excessive sycophancy or sterling military service, John might remit the debt or at least part of it, but in general he preferred to keep the barons under his thumb rather than allow them the freedom which debt liquidation would bring.[90] And he would certainly have regarded all modern notions of insolvency or bankruptcy with contempt: if you could not pay the debt, you forfeited your lands.[91] It was not even possible to escape the royal tentacles by borrowing and transferring the debt to a less grasping creditor. The only way out was to use Jewish moneylenders, since lending money at interest was forbidden to Christians under medieval canon law. But, quite apart from the consideration that one was still subsidising John, who allowed the Jews to operate on the sole condition that he could raid their funds whenever he felt like it by the system of 'tallages', the law ordained that the king was every Jew's heir, so that when a moneylender died the monarch inherited all his cash, property, promissory notes and IOUs. To escape from John's coils via Jewish credit, therefore, ran the risk that one could pay out a fortune in interest and still end up back at the start as the king's debtor.[92]

John's main tactic, then, was to burden the barons with such heavy debts that they were effectively gelded both by the repayments and the threat of expropriation if they failed to make them. But he also encouraged a cash nexus whereby barons were expected to pay for an entire range of 'goods and services'. He would let a man know that he was out of favour but could be reinstated on payment of a certain amount, usually hundreds of pounds; he would fine one local lord for allowing an outlaw to escape, another for marrying without permission, yet another for putting a fish-weir in a river without going through the necessary bureaucracy, and so on.[93] On the other hand, greedy and corrupt barons would approach John with cash offers to secure particular favours: a fief, the wardenship of a forest, the position as constable of a castle, the guardianship of a minor's estate. One of John's favourite wheezes was to control the supply of rich heiresses as brides, releasing them onto the marriage market only when the appropriate funds had changed hands. He was not above accepting money for favours and then not granting them.[94] Always a master of the double-cross, John was said to prowl the country sniffing out so-called crimes and misdemeanours for which he could levy a fine. John made it clear that all who were not for him were regarded as being against him and should expect to pay the consequences; why should enemies have the same access to courts and royal justice as friends and loyal subjects, he reasoned.[95] Above all other considerations was the fact that the royal will acknowledged no superior tribunal. If the monarch wanted something badly enough, that was the end of the matter, and this was why so many contracts, warranties and guarantees contained the escape clause: 'save in the case of royal violence'. If John wished to seize and expropriate, he liked to have specious reasons for doing so but, at the limit, he was quite prepared for the brutal exercise of blatant power, based only on his will: *fiat pro lege voluntas*.[96] However, even John realised that to subvert the entire system of custom, law and tradition in favour of arbitrary despotism might eventually drag down the institution of monarchy itself, which was why he was mindful of rumblings of excessive discontent and thought better of levying scutage in the years 1207–08; fortunately his conflict with the Church in these years enabled him to shift the financial burden from the barons to the bishops and abbots.

In addition to heavy taxation, arbitrary fines and 'reliefs', expropriations and forfeitures, new taxes on chattels and ploughlands, the tenants-in-chief of feudal England had specific and personal grievances relating to the destruction of their castles, the corrupt disposal of manors through tame courts and tribunals appointed from John's yes-men and heavily overseen by the king himself, the asset-stripping of estates while in wardship and the indignity of forced marriages of widows and heiresses.[97] John expected unquestioning obedience and faithful commitment to duty from his barons while ignoring their rights. It is often lamented that in the modern world people demand rights without duties but in John's England it was the other way round. When the barons expected rewards for their uncomplaining acceptance of John's arbitrary fees, taxes and reliefs and their support for him in the never-ending wars, they found instead that his favours were bestowed either on his household knights or, even more alarmingly, on alien mercenary captains.[98] Names like those of Fawkes de Bréauté, Savary de Mauléon, Peter des Roches and, especially, Gérard d'Athée – all men John had brought with him from France to England – loom large in contemporary annals. These were the men who did John's dirty work for him, who enforced his tyranny at the point of a sword and whose presence so close to the throne was so bitterly resented.[99] Gérard d'Athée it was who acted as John's spearhead when he finally compassed the destruction of William de Braose. So highly did John think of him that he paid 2,000 marks for his ransom from Philip (who had captured him when the castle of Loches fell in 1205), brought him to England and made him master of the county and castle of Gloucester – the action that decided William Marshal to self-exile himself in Ireland. The ruthless d'Athée, who had made his name in the brutal suppression of Touraine, visited his special methods on the Welsh marches and was John's strong right arm there for many years. He died in 1213 but was so universally loathed that he was the only adventurer explicitly and expressly named in Magna Carta as the scourge of England.[100]

There were good reasons, then, why John should have feared the possible reactions of the barons during his conflict with the Church. As Roger of Wendover put it, he had 'almost as many enemies as he had barons'.[101] His immediate instinct was for hostage-taking. The return of the paranoia of 1204–05 was evident in the way he took hostages not just from the barons but from his own mercenary captains. In 1212 he decided to haul in a fresh batch of the sons, nephews and kinsmen of his hard-pressed magnates and once again most of the barons meekly rolled over and gave him what he wanted. Two notable exceptions were Eustace de Vesci and Robert Fitzwalter who fled, respectively to Scotland and France, after the failure of a plot to murder John.[102] Yet John had little to fear from the barons during his struggle with Rome. Politically it would have made sense for them to increase the pressure on John when he was engaged with the Pope, yet they seem to have feared that a capitulation to the Vatican would break down the natural spheres of influence: the Pope had his, the king had his, the barons had theirs. In modern terms one might say that John's magnates favoured the pluralism of civil society, and that in supporting the autonomy of the king of England from the Pope they were also asserting their own autonomy from him. Neither John nor Innocent III saw it that way. For John the barons' attitude meant they were weak, which in turn meant he could pile further humiliation on them. For the Pope the barons' attitude was rank betrayal of their Christian duty, and he commented acidly on their failure to do anything for the Church.[103]

When the dust settled and John had accepted papal overlordship of the British Isles, the barons thought again and concluded they had backed the wrong horse. During the interdict and excommunication John had pulverised the clergy, coerced, browbeat and bled them dry to a degree they would have thought impossible. Custom, habit, charter, religious mores and folkways had all gone out of the window. The Church, on paper the most stable part of the entire political system, had been convulsed and all but destroyed by a spectacular demonstration of despotic willpower, and seventeen monasteries had virtually ceased to exist.[104] Ecclesiastic properties had been confiscated, exploited and sold off, wealth, lands and benefices seized, and senior divines had cravenly bowed the head. If John could do this to the Church, brushing aside excommunication and anathema, what might he not be able to do to the far less securely entrenched barons? There seemed no end to John's arbitrary government, and the awful example of William de Braose, a favourite one day, a refugee outlaw the next, seemed to portend what might be in store for the rest of them.[105] Moreover, to get his deal with

'We fight only for Richard, sire.' The mythical meeting between the Lionheart and Robin Hood in Sherwood Forest.

English triumphalist revisionism: King Richard salutes the land for which he cared 'not an egg'

How the other half lived
in the era of the Crusades:
peasants harvesting corn

'Nasty, short and brutish'.
Everyday life of English woodcutters

'I am the heir of every Jew': John's diabolical
treatment of the chosen people

An early pogrom:
Jews under the cosh
in Angevin England

William
Marshal
unhorses a
French
knight

The Royal Seal provides an
idealised picture of John the Warrior

King John: the image may be fanciful but the
cruel demeanour expresses an essential truth

The mania for the forest: John hunts a stag with hounds

The one living thing for which John probably did care: the royal Nimrod with his dog

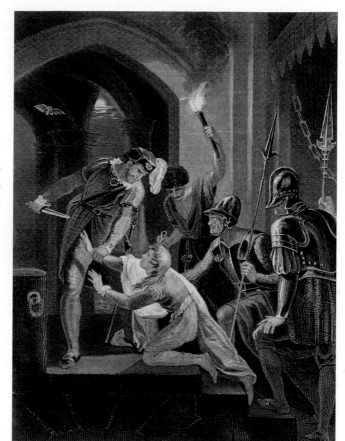

An Arthur not destined to come again: John murders his nephew at Rouen Castle

A cynical meeting: John plays for time by doing homage to Philip of France

Bouvines: where John's grand coalition came apart at the seams

Applicat Lodolbrcus.

A Bayeux Tapestry rerun: Prince Louis of France crosses the Channel to invade England, 1216

John brought to bay
at Runnymede

Magna Carta: the Charter of Liberties

Disaster in the Wash: John loses his treasure and his nerve

Rome, John had waived the principle of lay rights in ecclesiastical appointments, which was in effect a serious truncation of baronial power. The
magnates had backed John against the Pope but now, to their horror,
they found that the Pope was backing John against them; they had
muffed the opportunity to catch him between two fires by making themselves the papal allies in 1207. Even worse, Innocent III was still fuming
at their 'perfidy' and determined to punish them. When they broke into
rebellion in 1215, they were immediately condemned by Rome in pointed
terms. Innocent wrote: 'The enemy of the human race who hates good
impulses (sc. the Devil) has stirred up the barons with his cunning wiles
so that, with a wicked inconsistency, the men who supported him (John)
when he was injuring the Church rebelled against him when he turned
from his sins and made amends to the Church.'[106] With John seemingly
stronger than ever, the outlook for the barons seemed dire in 1212–13.
They could not defeat John, and their only hope was that he would self-
destruct. This he now obligingly proceeded to do.

JOHN NEVER ACCEPTED THE loss of Normandy as a permanent feature of the political landscape but, preoccupied as he was with other matters, principally the struggle with the papacy, it took him almost ten years to prepare his counterstroke against Philip Augustus. His abiding ambition was to build a European confederacy that would gradually tighten the noose on France, which was why the continuing German civil war and events in the Holy Roman Empire were top of his foreign policy agenda. The empire that had humiliated Richard the Lionheart collapsed into anarchy after the death of Emperor Henry VI in September 1197.[1] The late emperor's brother Philip of Swabia claimed the Crown, but the majority of electors in the empire favoured Otto of Saxony, son of Henry the Lion and Maud, Henry II's daughter. As Otto IV, Henry II's grandson enjoyed a precarious hold on the empire from 1198 to 1212 – precarious not only because the new duke of Austria backed the Swabian prince but because Philip Augustus did too.[2] All the best observers thought that Otto was a poor choice as ruler. Physically large, with a much-noted resemblance to Richard the Lionheart, whose favourite he was, Otto was by common consent an unreliable braggart, a rather stupid, bungling, inefficient but arrogant man, who let his tongue run away with him and made lavish promises he had no intention of keeping.[3] John initially regarded him with suspicion as a possible rival for the English throne, but Otto's preference for the German crown removed that problem. But it cannot have helped after 1199 that whenever John looked at Otto he was reminded of Richard and, moreover, that Otto claimed Richard had bequeathed his jewels and two-thirds of his treasure to him; he was correct about the jewels, but the treasure story was a fantasy.[4]

It was typical of Otto that he continued to claim the revenues due to him as putative earl of York (Richard had apparently promised him the earldom) even when he was king of Germany. Not surprisingly,

John had no compunction about double-crossing him when it suited his book. But in foreign affairs John was constrained by *realpolitik* not personal predilections. The alliance of the two Philips, Capetian and Hohenstaufen, was as much a feature of international relations as the contrary alliance of Otto with John, Welf and Angevin.[5] Although John occasionally had to ditch Otto because of the requirements of treaties with Philip Augustus, the deep currents of European affairs drew them together. John showed his awareness of where Angevin interests naturally lay by letters, loans, gifts and presents to Otto and by granting commercial and trade preference to the German and Flemish cities that supported him.[6] Otto curried favour with John by offering to make a truce with Philip of Swabia so that he could concentrate his attentions on attacking Philip Augustus and seizing Rheims and Cambrai.[7] This was hubris since, although Innocent III had recognised Otto as the legitimate emperor-elect, Otto had not yet been formally crowned and the civil war in Germany still raged. But Otto set a lot of store on the endorsement by Innocent, and the Pope for his part saw Otto as the future for Germany (certainly in the early years) and in a letter of March 1202 even pressed John to make over to Otto the monies promised by Richard; needless to say, John ignored the papal request.[8]

In 1204 both John and Otto sustained terrible reverses. While John lost Normandy, Otto suffered a series of hammer blows. First his brother the Count Palatine went over to the enemy, followed shortly by the archbishop of Cologne and the duke of Brabant, thus shattering Richard the Lionheart's carefully constructed Rhenish confederacy. Then in 1206 Cologne, the city whose commercial interests were so tightly bound up with England's and which had received 'most favoured' status from John, capitulated. Deserted by most of his powerful backers (even the Pope opened negotiations with Philip of Swabia), Otto fled to Denmark and thence across the North Sea to England.[9] There he was given a hero's welcome and accorded all the honours of a state visit, even being received in audience by John at Stapleford. He and John jested about how they would carve up Philip Augustus's realm; Otto gave John a great golden crown and John gave Otto six thousand marks.[10] How Otto was supposed to regain his position in Germany was unclear, but suddenly fortune dealt him a hand when Philip of Swabia was assassinated (21 June 1208).[11] Even for the doubters Otto now seemed a better bet than anarchy and chaos, so he was invited to resume as king of Germany. Otto next ingratiated himself with the Pope by interceding with John on behalf of

Stephen Langton and in 1209 sent his brother the Count Palatine to England for the same purpose. Although John was not yet in the mood to heed these overtures, he cemented the German alliance by making the count a 1,000-mark a year pensioner of England.[12] By this time John was dreaming of a great coalition of the northern European powers directed at Capetian France. He stepped up the diplomatic momentum by sending his new favourite the earl of Salisbury on an embassy to the German princes.[13]

In November 1209 John received the news that Pope Innocent III had crowned Otto Holy Roman Emperor in Rome the month before.[14] The ambitious Otto requited this papal favour by conquering Tuscia, Apulia and Calabria and then invading Sicily in blatant defiance of the Pope's wishes. By one of those amazing twists which typified international relations in the Middle Ages, a year later the very same pope who had crowned Otto excommunicated him.[15] The Pope and Philip Augustus together now raised up a new rival to Otto: the young Hohenstaufen prince Frederick. Meanwhile John and Otto, both now under sentence of papal excommunication, hit back at Innocent and Philip by assisting yet another ruler who had fallen under the papal anathema: Raymond of Toulouse, married to John's sister Joan. Raymond was backing the Albigensians of south-western France, the Gnostic movement denounced for heresy by Innocent III. The Pope had sent an army of 'crusaders' under Simon de Montfort against the Albigensians and they began by besieging Toulouse. Otto and John poured money and materiel into the defence of Toulouse and their kinsman, and Raymond made such a good showing that the 'crusaders' lost heart and raised the siege (1211).[16] John seemed to be riding the crest of a wave now with Otto and Raymond as confrères; it occurred to him that he could do even better if the princes of the borderlands of France and Germany – Boulogne, Flanders, Lorraine, the Netherlands – could also be brought into the alliance, giving him the grand coalition he had always dreamed of.

John was now aiming to rebuild the coalition of princes in the Low Countries that Richard had managed so triumphantly and that had been allowed to lapse only through his (John's) fecklessness. His chief agent in the complex negotiations that followed was Renaud of Dammartin, count of Boulogne, an ambitious soldier-scholar-diplomat, as much at ease in the company of troubadours as on the battlefield.[17] Renaud had joined the long list of those who loathed Philip Augustus when the French king seized his fiefs of Mortain, Domfront and Aumale in Normandy. Renaud then took a mighty oath that he would spend the rest of his life compassing Philip Augustus's downfall.[18] The task was difficult, for Philip Augustus dominated Flanders after 1202, following Count Baldwin IX's capture at Adrianople and subsequent death in captivity. In the power vacuum Philip successfully manipulated the regent, Baldwin's brother Philip of Namur and even became ward of Baldwin's daughters. So inept was Philip of Namur and so easily dominated by his more powerful namesake that it was said he practised an idiosyncratic form of wearing sackcloth and ashes, parading through the streets of Valenciennes with a notice attached to his neck which read: 'I ought to die like a dog.'[19] Philip controlled the regent partly through lavish subsidies, and for a while he and John tried to outbid each other by raising the ante for the castellans of the key fortresses: St-Omer, Bruges, Ghent, Lille, Cassel. Count Renaud decided to leave Philip of Namur till last and began his campaign by enlisting his kinsman Count Théobald of Bar (Lorraine).[20] Together Renaud and Théobald achieved their first coup by getting Otto's brother Henry (the Count Palatine) to travel to England and engage in a formal anti-French alliance with John; the count sealed the bargain by doing homage to the English king.[21] Another Lorrainer persuaded into the coalition was Henry, duke of Limberg. The temporary adherence of the slippery duke of Brabant, a man who was said to be unable to lie straight in bed, was more trouble than it was worth.[22]

By 1212 Renaud was ready for his greatest stroke: the winning of Flanders for John's coalition. Here the key figure was Ferrand, duke of Flanders, one of Philip Augustus's placemen. When Philip of Namur died, the French king imposed Ferrand, son of Sancho I of Portugal, and gave him the Flemish heiress Joan as his wife, thinking this was certain to cement Ferrand's loyalty. But for all Philip Augustus's cunning, he had an Achilles heel in the shape of his impulsive son Louis, the classic spoiled royal brat. Philip understood his son's weaknesses but was too much the doting father to rein him in. He paid heavily for his paternal indulgence. In an evil hour Louis took it into his head to seize the fiefs of Aire and St-Omer (in Ferrand's domain) for himself, claiming that they were his mother's dowry.[23] Unable to proceed against the interloper without making war on Philip himself, Ferrand had to endure the taunts of his subjects, who accused him (rightly) of being a French poodle and suggested he return to Portugal.[24] Stung by these reproaches and angry with Philip for having allowed this humiliation to develop, Ferrand was receptive to the feelers put out by Renaud. After much hesitation, Ferrand joined John's coalition and this proved a popular move in Flanders, where the English wool trade was so important. The crisis came in April 1213 when Philip Augustus was preparing an invasion of England. He asked Ferrand to take part but the duke refused. Philip invaded Flanders forthwith and at first won a series of victories. Tournai, Cassel, Lille, Bruges and Ghent all fell to French arms, and Ferrand was forced to take refuge in Zeeland.[25]

Even before his coalition was complete, John had been aching to land forces in France and reverse the verdict of 1204. His initial intention had been to take an expedition to Poitou in 1212 for an invasion of Normandy. With five years of looted Church money in his coffers, John faced the problem not so much of revenue as of manpower. Utilising methods similar to Domesday Book, John's officials held an exhaustive census of available manpower in every shire of England, and extra cash was raised by an official investigation into offences against the Forest Laws, with the inspectors-general given wide powers to fine and punish.[26] But the revolt under Llewellyn in Wales (see p.339) threw all John's plans into disarray. To deal with the Welsh threat he ordered the host assembled at Portsmouth for the voyage to Poitou to muster instead at Chester.[27] As previously mentioned, the Welsh expedition in turn foundered on alarming rumours of baronial conspiracy and even more hair-raising canards of royal assassination and the rape of Queen Isabella. So seriously did John take the reports that he put his five-year-old son and heir Henry (later Henry III) into safekeeping in a heavily garrisoned castle.[28] The flight of the would-be rebellion's ringleaders, Robert Fitzwalter and Eustace de Vesci, handed the initiative to John. He destroyed two of Fitzwalter's castles (Benington in Hertfordshire and Castle Baynard in London), and broke up Vesci's network of followers in the north.[29] But as the scope of the revolt he had nipped in the bud became clear, John realised he had had a narrow escape. For purely prudential motives he ostentatiously began a charm offensive, curtailing the powers of his Forest commissioners and other over-mighty officials. He relieved traders and foreign pilgrims of many irritating taxes and 'fees' imposed at seaports, and held himself forth as a protector of widows. In a word, he aimed at the reputation of 'Good King John'.[30]

John was almost too late. For a month or two the future of his kingdom seemed to hang in the balance, as wild talk of deposition, abdication and a new monarch swept the realm. Nothing better illustrated the twilight state of England than the prophecies of the gaunt, half-mad seer named Peter of Wakefield, who lived on bread and water. As we saw earlier, Peter prophesied that John would be gone by Ascension Day 1213, and he found ready listeners.[31] Wandering all over the north country, Peter told his audience that it had been vouchsafed to him in a vision that only fourteen years were allotted to John, after which 'one who is pleasing to God' would ascend the throne; it was not clear whether John was to die a natural death, be murdered, exiled or forced to abdicate. Initially dimissed as no more than a crank and a nuisance, Peter of Wakefield eventually worried John so much that he had his sheriffs arrest him and bring him before him. Given a chance to recant, Peter refused and reiterated his message: 'Know thou for sure that on the day which I have named thou shalt be king no longer; and if I be proved a liar, do with me as thou wilt.'[32] John clapped him in a dungeon in Corfe, but this proved to be a bad mistake as Peter attained martyr's status once he was imprisoned and his credibility was enhanced. This particular bubble burst only when the date of 23 May (Ascension Day) came and went. John held a day-long party to show his contempt for the prophecy and was of course vindicated.[33] The lovers of the supernatural, baulked of their miracle, then claimed that the fourteenth anniversary of John's coronation (27 May) was the date Peter really meant. When that too passed without mishap, the poor prophet was finally discredited. On 28 May Peter and his son were dragged at the horse's tail all the way from Corfe to Wareham and there hanged.[34]

In this turbulent and uncertain maelstrom, when John did not know whom to trust, the support of William Marshal came as a godsend. Out of favour for six years, Marshal once more rescued the Angevin house he had served so loyally by getting twenty-six fellow barons in Ireland to renew their oaths to John and to swear to fight for him till death. In return he strongly advised John to make peace with the Pope.[35] Although John blustered in reply about his royal prerogatives and the dignity of England faced with papal encroachment, Marshal's words were just one more factor leading him towards rapprochement with Rome. Perhaps even more pressing was the rumour that Innocent III had declared him deposed and invited Philip to take over as king of England. By 1213 all kinds of different factors compelled John to endure the unendurable and to submit to the pontiff: baronial revolt and conspiracy, the policies of Otto IV in Germany, and most of all the factor of Philip Augustus lay behind the momentous volte-face of 1213.[36] John knew that Philip was even then preparing an invasion of England. His advisers were divided between those who thought that he should remain in England and deal with this threat and those who thought that the best way to make Philip back off from his English design was to land in Poitou. For his part, Philip seems to have taken the old line that Rome must be defeated in Rome. This, or possibly simply an irrational hatred of the Angevins, lies behind the at first-sight puzzling decision to go for the difficult option (a hazardous sea-borne landing on the English coast) rather than the easy one (an overland invasion of Aquitaine).[37]

Sustained by the effusive demonstrations of loyalty by Marshal and aware of the danger across the Channel, John for once demonstrated both sagacity and energy. Although he liked to poke fun at William Marshal with his intimates and accuse him of the most far-fetched acts of treason and treachery, in his heart John knew that William Marshal was the best friend the 'Devil's Brood' had ever had. Accordingly in 1213 he recalled him to England and restored to him his two sons taken as hostages for his good behaviour some years before.[38] Meanwhile he summoned to a rendezvous at Dover all available soldiers and archers, and ordered the fleet to convene at Portsmouth. Every single earl, baron, knight, freeman and sergeant was required to attend on pain of 'culvertage' and perpetual servitude. Not surprisingly, hosts of knights and ordinary soldiers converged on the southern ports; one annalist reported that 'If they had been all of one heart and one mind for king and country, there was no prince under heaven against whom they could not have defended the realm of England.'[39] That 'if' conceals a multitude of sins; no one knew how many of the magnates would remain loyal if Philip landed and how many would immediately go over to his side. Even without this question-mark, John had his problems, for his commissariat was overwhelmed by the sheer numbers of men arriving in Kent in answer to the minatory summons. In desperation the army's marshals dispersed the host to other ports, to Faversham and even as far away as Ipswich, sending the lightly armed troops to these locations as a reserve and retaining the knights, archers and better-armed freemen.[40]

John realised that rapprochement with the Pope would not make Philip halt his military plans, that they were independent of the hitherto existing Franco-papal diplomatic alliance, but he hoped long-term to drive a wedge between the two most dangerous enemies he had encountered so far. As with John's plans for the reconquest of Normandy, Philip's project for the invasion of England was of long gestation. The French king thought of implementing it in 1209 but his preparations too had taken a long time to mature. But finally, at almost the precise moment

John effected his reconciliation with the Pope, Philip was ready. At a council at Soissons in April 1213, in a classic of chicken counting before egg-hatching, he drew up detailed plans for relations between England and France when his son Louis was sitting on the English throne.[41] He put to sea from Boulogne with his invasion fleet on 10 May 1213, and coasted up to Gravelines, where he began embarking his army on the 22nd. News of John's submission to Innocent spiked his guns; he was reported furiously angry, but called off the invasion while he considered his next move.[42] The propaganda advantage of invading England while claiming to be waging a holy war against an excommunicate king had now vanished, and meanwhile, by his alliance with the Flanders princes, John had turned his flank. Like Napoleon seven hundred years later, Philip decided to shelve the invasion of England and deal with his continental enemies first.[43]

At this stage it should be appreciated that, even after John's reconciliation with Pope Innocent, Philip held most of the cards. In Aquitaine Simon de Montfort and his brutal crusaders were gradually turning the screws on the Albigensians, threatening John's ally Raymond of Toulouse with utter ruin.[44] Even more seriously Otto IV was beginning to look like a liability. John's obstinacy in his struggle with the papacy had led Innocent to look for ways of subverting his friends and allies, and he found the perfect answer in the young prince Frederick Hohenstaufen, the future Frederick II of Germany. On 5 December 1212 Frederick was elected king of Germany in Frankfurt and crowned thus in opposition to Otto.[45] In vain did Otto try to use the dead Philip of Swabia for his dynastic purposes by marrying the late duke's daughter; she died a few days after the marriage. The really significant development at the beginning of 1213 was the treaty of alliance signed between Frederick and Philip Augustus, which increased the personal rancour Otto had always felt towards the French king. In the welter of diplomatic manoeuvrings and *realpolitik* tergiversation and duplicity, we should not forget the influence of raw human emotions in this arena. Otto always hated Philip Augustus viscerally. In the spring of 1212 he wept with rage in front of witnesses when the subject of Philip was raised, and this was far from the only occasion when his fury towards France was made manifest.[46] Renaud Dammartin, the architect of the Flanders alliance and John's henchman, also alienated many by his attitudes. Looked at askance by some of John's courtiers and cordially loathed by the French because he lived openly with a courtesan, Renaud was in many ways a man after John's own heart. He laid elaborate plans for sharing out the domains of defeated France and had his own scheme, modelled on John's seizures, for dissolving French monasteries and expropriating Church wealth. He and John shared an atheistical outlook and a contempt for priests, whom Renaud denounced for 'their useless lives whose sole occupation is to devote themselves to Bacchus and Venus and to fill their stomachs'.[47]

Faced with Philip's increasing power, John decided, wisely, to use his newly constructed navy as his first line of offensive tactics. As Roger of Wendover reported: 'The king decided to engage his enemies at sea, to drown them before they landed, for he had a more powerful fleet than the French king, and it was there that he thought his greatest hope of resisting the enemy lay.'[48] While John mobilised his army on Barham Down, between Canterbury and Dover, he unleashed his navy from Portsmouth for damaging raids on the French coast. One amphibious operation ended with the gutting of Dieppe and the taking of a number of prisoners; in others French shipping was badly mauled in the Seine ports and at Fécamp.[49] When Philip Augustus swept into Flanders with his invading army, Count Ferrand appealed to John, whose response was prompt, though, typically, he spoiled the effect of his generosity by chiding the counts of Boulogne and Holland for tardiness: 'Had you sent to us sooner, we would have sent you greater help'[50] – presumably a reference to the men he had demobilised because of the pressure on commissariat. Ferrand's envoy arrived on 25 May 1213, John called a conference that night at Ewell, and by the 28th a large fleet of 500 ships commanded by the earl of Salisbury, with 700 knights and a large body of mercenaries, cleared from the English coast. Battling offshore winds, the fleet fetched the Flemish coast on 30 May and began to thread its way up the estuary of the River Zwyn.[51]

Suddenly at the harbour of Damme, then the port of Bruges, a few miles inland but connected to the Zwyn by a narrow channel, they found the entire French fleet anchored unawares, complacent in Philip Augustus's early and easy Flanders triumphs. No fewer than 1,700 vessels lay at anchor, laden with arms, materiel and provisions; even more amazingly, there were few defenders, since most of the French knights and heavy infantry were elsewhere, at the siege of Ghent or simply bent on the routine plunder and rapine of medieval warfare.[52] The French were sitting ducks, and the English mariners, mercenaries and knights swept in for the kill. Those French sailors who had the ill-fortune to be standing guard over the ships were butchered, and most of the ships were burnt, disabled or taken in tow; those who managed to escape could not reach the open sea and were later gutted on the direct orders of Philip Augustus.[53] It was about as overwhelming as any naval victory of the era could well be, but it bred overconfidence. When Ferrand arrived next day to treat with Salisbury, the English knights disembarked to harry the French in the town of Damme, but ran into Philip's advancing army, received a severe check and were lucky to escape back to the ships before annihilation.[54] But Salisbury had ended the threat of invasion and stymied Philip's offensive in Flanders; he took his prizes back across the Channel in triumph, able to report to John that the new royal navy had acquitted itself brilliantly in its first major test. The plunder brought back to England created a sensation: 'never had so much treasure come into England since the days of King Arthur' was one vainglorious verdict.[55] Perhaps as nemesis for such hubris Salisbury himself was ship-wrecked on the coast of Northumberland, but survived.[56]

In a state of euphoria John now hoped to catch Philip Augustus between two fires, pincered from Flanders and Poitou. Once again it was his barons who scuppered his plans. They came forward with a variety of excuses as to why they could not follow the king to Poitou. The first was that they could not follow him while he was still excommunicate (Langton had not yet arrived to release him from the anathema).[57] Then they claimed they could not go on any expeditions as they were broke, having spent all their money preparing to resist the French invasion; it followed that they could go to Poitou only if John paid their expenses. Finally, the northern barons tired of prevarication, threw off the mask of punctiliousness and revealed their hand: not only were they exhausted, they said, after John's relentless campaigning in the Celtic fringes but they were anyway not bound by their feudal oaths to serve abroad and would not do so.[58] In a bizarre example of repetition compulsion, John responded by replaying the events of 1205. He put to sea in a fury before he had properly thought through what he was doing, cruised as far as Jersey, then realised the futility of what he was doing and put back into port. His initial fury having hardened into a cold anger, he proceeded to make preparations for a northern campaign to rival William the Conqueror's famous 'harrying of the north' in 1068; he fully intended to let his mercenaries off the leash once he reached the territories of the contumacious barons.[59]

It was at this juncture that Archbishop Stephen Langton arrived at Winchester where (on 20 July) the papal ban on John was lifted, on the express condition that he renewed his coronation oath and promised to uphold the ancient laws of the kingdom. Langton moved on to St Albans and London, unaware of what was in the king's mind. Once he realised he hastened after the northbound John, caught up with him at Northampton and remonstrated with him, pointing out that his precipitate action was contrary to the oaths sworn at Winchester.[60] A duel of wills developed all the way from Northampton to Nottingham, with John still adamant that he intended to chastise the North, and Langton warning him and his troops that they risked re-excommunication. Finally John saw sense: the folly of breaking with the Pope again after having just patched things up was too much even for him. As a face-saving device he marched farther north before announcing that the expedition to Poitou was now postponed until the spring of 1214. With Langton as mediator, the northern rebels were formally reconciled at Wallingford on 1 November, on the strict understanding that John pledged himself to maintain the laws of Henry I and his charters, and the liberties contained therein;[61] Langton had actually been working on a scheme to curb John's power by means of these charters when he had to break off and race to Northampton.[62] But it was an uneasy peace, a truce of convenience, agreed by John only because he was desperate to sail to Poitou. All the underlying problems remained.

Although the Poitou expedition had now been postponed twice, John was determined it would finally take place in 1214. Throughout the winter the usual (and by now almost formulaic) naval and military preparations went ahead. John showed his distrust of the barons by summoning them to a council at Oxford in November to discuss the coming campaign but ordering them to come unarmed.[63] At Christmas John held court at Winchester, trying by a display of sumptuous magnificence to keep at bay the misgivings he must have felt about leaving England in such a turbulent condition.[64] At Canterbury in January he received Count Ferrand of Flanders, who did homage to him, though scholars do not agree whether this means he was accepting John as overlord of Flanders.[65] We may infer that John made him another hefty subsidy, for about this time he was obliged to subvent Count Raymond of Toulouse, another short-staying visitor to England, to the tune of 10,000 marks to keep alive the flickering Albigensian defence against Simon de Montfort. Raymond's position after de Montfort had defeated the king of Aragon at Muret in September 1213 was truly desperate, but John could do little more for him, for the papal legate at once demanded the removal of this 'heretic' from England.[66] In January too John announced his plans for the government of England while he was away. Peter des Roches, bishop of Winchester, was appointed justiciar, in place of Geoffrey

FitzPeter who had died in October, and was to have another of John's favourites, William Brewer, as assistant justiciar. This appointment was deeply unpopular both with the barons, who despised des Roches as a foreigner and John's lickspittle, and with the hierarchy, who remembered his role during the interdict.[67] But John admired des Roches, whose name indicated his nature – 'hard as a rock' said one annalist.[68] It was the wrong appointment to make if he wanted to conciliate the barons, whose uncertain attitudes continued. In the event, many of the earls and magnates did not come to John's final muster and failed to send their knights, leaving in the air the question of whether they would consent to pay fines and scutage in lieu of service. To John's continuing irritation, William Marshal made it plain he would not accompany John to wage war on his (Marshal's) other overlord, Philip Augustus. But by this time John desperately needed Marshal; he instructed des Roches to ensure that all new measures ordained for the good of the kingdom were carefully discussed for their religious implications with Stephen Langton and for their political ones with Marshal.[69]

On 2 February 1214 John embarked at Portsmouth with his queen, his elder son Richard, his niece Eleanor of Britanny and a large treasure chest ('an incalculable treasury of gold, silver and precious stones') to pay the expenses of the campaign in Poitou. With him went his household knights, his mercenaries and the lesser knights of small fortune who could not afford to defy him.[70] Adverse weather delayed the expedition in the Solent for a week, so that it was 15 February before he arrived in La Rochelle, his intended base during the campaign. At about the same time William, earl of Salisbury set out for Flanders with a crack regiment of English troops, a large number of mercenaries and money enough for lavish subsidies to the northern allies. Opinions are divided about Salisbury. An illegitimate son of Henry II (and thus John's half-brother), he was tall, massively built, and considered a good soldier (he was nicknamed Longsword – an obvious contrast to John's soubriquet), though modern historians tend to see him as a braggart and blusterer.[71] But he enjoyed John's confidence, and the energy displayed in equipping and sending two large expeditions to the Continent simultaneously shows John at his best. It was said that he had been secretly setting aside money for years for this grand design of catching Philip Augustus between two massively powerful armies, with Poitou as the anvil and Flanders the hammer; and that the secrecy was such that his clerks were not allowed to note in the official archives the names of those who had received bribes and sweeteners for this purpose.[72]

John at first achieved striking success. His welcome in La Rochelle was cordial, not only because it was an 'English' town that depended for its prosperity on English trade but because the magnates of Poitou had become alarmed at the growing power of France and were willing to set one ruler against another so as to regain their old independence; French chroniclers cynically said that treachery was in the lifeblood of the Poitevins – 'affection will no more hold a Poitevin than chains will bind a Protean' was William the Breton's gloss.[73] Despite criticism for Fabian tactics – remaining so near to the La Rochelle seaboard for so long – the truth was that John could not advance against Philip until he was sure of the loyalty of all the Poitevin magnates along the proposed line of march; for this reason, if no other, it seems absurd to credit John with a 'grand strategy' of cutting through France from south-west to north-east to join his Flemish allies. The fact that a local lord held the castle of Milecu, a few miles from La Rochelle, against him was hardly an auspicious omen; John had to reduce this stronghold before going any farther.[74] John's itinerary can be followed in sketchy outline, though not all the details are clear: Mervant (20 February); Niort (25 February); the siege of Milecu (2–4 March); Angoulême (15 March); Saint-Junien (17 March); Aixe (18 March); La Souterraine (23 March); and thence through the Limousin again to the Charente, passing through Limoges and Angoulême.[75] In April he marched into Gascony as far as La Réole to reassure himself that his southern flank was secure. His boasts in dispatches to England – 'immediately on our arrival 26 castles and fortified places were restored to us'[76] was belied by the reality on the ground.

Yet Poitou could not be made solid pro-John territory simply by marches and countermarches. In May John brought diplomacy into play by trying to placate the hostile Lusignans, even offering his daughter Joan in marriage to Hugh of La Marche (Hugh of Lusignan). But when the powerful clan continued to drag its collective feet, John decided on stronger measures. He quickly took Geoffrey of Lusignan's castle of Mervant, then moved against the stronger fortress of Voucant, where Geoffrey and two of his sons had barricaded themselves. A three-day assault by trebuchets brought Geoffrey to heel; he and his sons surrendered themselves to the English king's mercy.[77] John's thrust against the Lusignans finally brought the French into the field against him, for Geoffrey's third and most easterly castle at Montcontour, the toughest nut to crack of the trio, was suddenly reported to be under siege from Louis, Philip Augustus's son. On 25 May John made rendezvous with the three Lusignans (Geoffrey and his brothers the counts of La Marche and Eu) at Parthenay, where John confirmed the marriage contract of Hugh with his daughter Joan, stressing what a great favour this was, as Philip Augustus, playing his usual diplomatic games, had tried to spike the proposal by offering his son as a husband for Joan instead.[78] A plethora of Poitevin barons attended and witnessed the marriage contract at Parthenay (like so many of these proposed dynastic marriages it was fated never to take place), indicating that John's campaign had been successful so far. Heartened by this showing, he decided to attempt the recapture of Anjou, lost to Philip in 1204–05.

This was the crucial moment when, if operations on the two allied fronts really had been coordinated, John might have been able to score a glittering victory. Even though Philip could raise an army estimated at some 20,000 in all (including 3,000 knights),[79] he would still have been stretched thin if the army of the north under Salisbury, Ferrand and Otto IV had been ready to invade France the instant John struck north into Anjou. As it was, Philip had to divide his army to deal with the dual threat; he faced north, leaving his son Louis to confront John in the south. It was a supremely perilous moment for France, for if the allies were victorious in the north the momentum of victory would almost certainly sweep John back across Normandy and possibly even into Paris itself. It was therefore in a jaunty mood that John struck north-west across the Loire on 1 June, having first feinted in the direction of Louis's army.[80] He captured Ancennis (on the Anjou-Britanny border) easily, feinted again, this time towards Angers, before doubling back and besieging the seaport of Nantes – a far more convenient base for operations against Britanny and Normandy than La Rochelle. The garrison at Nantes sortied against John but they and the citizen levies were badly defeated on the bridge outside the city. John took several important prisoners, among than Philip Augustus's cousin Peter of Dreux, count of Britanny. This victory seems to have struck terror into the burghers of Anjou's capital Angers, for they immediately opened their gates to John's Anglo-Poitevin army; on 17 June he entered the erstwhile capital of the Angevin empire in triumph.[81]

The triumph was soured by Philip Augustus's Anjou seneschal William des Roches, who still defiantly held the castle of Roche-aux-Moines, a few miles from Angers. Instead of ignoring this and working round it, or because he thought it too great a threat to the Nantes-Angers road, John proceeded to waste two weeks on a futile siege of this stronghold. While he was so engaged, word came in that Prince Louis, hitherto as elusive as a phantom, had at last put in an appearance and was marching to the relief of the fortress, probably as a result of direct orders from his father.[82] From the reports of his scouts John learned that he had a clear numerical advantage over Louis; he was keen to offer battle and the headstrong Louis, when this challenge was officially made, was just as keen to accept.[83] But now at last John discovered just what his conquest of Poitou was worth, for the Poitevins flatly refused to risk themselves and their fortunes in pitched battle. The ringleader of the Poitevin opposition was that habitual trimmer and turncoat Aimeri of Thouars, who mocked and ridiculed John's pretensions as a warrior. Raging, fuming but impotent, John had no choice but to return in humiliation all the way back to La Rochelle; faced with the treachery of the Poitevins and with all his old paranoid fears revived, it was the first place where he felt genuinely safe. There was no disguising the fact that his 'retreat' was more like a panic-stricken rout; in the general shambles he abandoned siege engines, tents, baggage and materiel. Louis pursued the English as far as Thouars, causing the demoralised Anglo-Poitevins to sustain further losses through drowning when crossing the Loire.[84]

John had already dispatched so many boasts to England about his glittering military triumphs that he was in a quandary about how to 'spin' the latest debacle. It is hard not to have grudging admiration for the effrontery with which he presented the ruin of his entire campaign. After licking his wounds for a week in La Rochelle, he summoned up the energy to indite the following pack of lies, beneath whose surface, however, it was possible for the discerning to perceive the king's true plight:

> The King to the earls, barons, knights and all his lieges in England,
> greetings. Know that we are safe and well and that everything, by the
> grace of God, is prosperous and happy with us. We return manifold
> thanks to those of you who have sent us your knights to serve in the
> preservation and recovery of our rights, and we earnestly entreat
> those of you who have not crossed with us to come to us without
> delay, being assiduous for our honour, to help in the recovery of our
> territory (save for those who in the opinion of our reverend fathers
> the lords Peter bishop of Winchester, our justiciar, and of Master
> Richard Marsh and William Brewer, should stay in England), doing
> so much in this matter that we are bound in perpetual thanks to you.
> Assuredly, if any of you should have understood that we bore him
> ill-will, he can have it rectified by coming here.[85]

Three weeks after John's return to La Rochelle, the allied army in the north at last got under way in its offensive against Philip Augustus. Otto, starting from Aachen, had taken an unconscionable time getting into the field, finally taking a route to Flanders through Maastricht, Nivelles (near modern Brussels) and Valenciennes in Hainault, where he met his confrères: Salisbury, the counts of Flanders and Boulogne and other notables, including the dukes of Brabant and Limburg, the lord of Mechelin and Hugh, count of Boves.[86] There is no way of knowing the exact strength of the allied army, partly because medieval chroniclers routinely exaggerated numbers, but an 'educated guess' would put it around the 9,000–10,000 mark (at least 1,500 knights and 7,500 foot). Numerically the allied force had the advantage over Philip Augustus's Frenchmen, who may have numbered only 7,500 – roughly the same number of knights but only some 6,000 infantry. But Philip's military reforms, albeit partial, had made his army a more professional force, and his urban battalions were a particular innovation.[87] The sources are somewhat confused, for some speak of the French as having 2,000 knights and 2,000 other warriors. Roughly speaking, though, the French had the edge in cavalry and the allies in infantry.[88] Motivation on both sides was high, for Philip, menaced on two fronts, was fighting to save France while for Otto this was the last chance to regain the imperial throne.

Philip had several other advantages: by the time the allied army made its move, he knew he was secure on the southern front and could concentrate all his energies against Otto, and he enjoyed the secret services of the duke of Brabant, a spy at the very heart of allied decision-making. On the other hand, the much-touted idea that he harboured a military genius in the shape of bishop Guérin de Glapion has recently run into strong criticism as an absurd exaggeration.[89] Philip's initial strategy was to march into Flanders and cut off the Anglo-Poitevin force under William, earl of Salisbury whose subsidies were the sinews of war, but he was too late; by the time he marched, Salisbury and the Flemish lords had already met Otto. Then he attempted to take the enemy by surprise from the north, but when the allies marched south the two armies ended up passing each other in the night, both now with extended lines of communication in danger of being cut. On the evening of 26 July, learning that the enemy was at Mortagne, and there was no suitable ground near there for giving battle, Philip held a council of war at which it was decided to retreat at least as far as Lille, about twenty miles away. From Tournai Philip turned back west towards Lille, Douai and Cambrai, trying to stretch the allies on the rack, hoping that either the ramshackle alliance would disintegrate through personality clashes or that John's subsidies would run dry.[90] When Otto's scouts brought him this news, the foolish ex-emperor thought it indicated a panic retreat like John's from La Roche-aux-Moines and set off in pursuit. Absurdly overconfident he told his men in a rousing battle speech that the allied knights outnumbered their French counterparts three to one. Only Renaud de Dammartin, by far the best military mind in the allied camp, urged caution, but for this he was roundly berated by Hugh, comte de Boves, who accused him of cowardice.[91]

Philip's army, marching with carts over flat land and in fine weather, set a blistering pace of about four miles an hour. Confident that a Christian enemy would not attack on a Sunday, Philip ordered his men to cross the River Marque at the bridge by the village of Bouvines, and settled down to a picnic lunch on the far side, with the rear column of his force still strung out over about two miles to the east of the bridge. Otto, though, was equally confident he could cut the enemy off before they reached the bridge and marched his men at the double; yet by the time he made contact with the French most were already on the other side of the river. As the imperial troops began rushing into the fields on the eastern side of the Bouvines bridge 'like a plague of locusts',[92] a running fight developed with the French rearguard, which was forced to turn around and beat off attacks from Otto's vanguard. Bishop Guérin de Glapion, bringing up the rearguard and half-blinded by the whorls of dust thrown up by the onrushing Germans, realised Otto meant business when he saw Otto's banner of the golden eagle and dragon being unfurled.[93] He quickly sent word to Philip, who at once grasped the gravity of the situation. With commend-able presence of mind, he ordered his army to traipse back across the bridge and form battle stations with the river at their back. With amazing rapidity the French took up position. Philip just had time for a short speech of exhortation, pointing out that the enemy were largely excommunicate heathens; why else would they choose to fight a battle on a Sunday?[94]

Philip seized the initiative by taking his cavalry back across the bridge to aid the hard-pressed viscount of Melun in the rearguard.[95] In some ways this was the critical action in the entire battle, for if Philip had not maintained presence of mind, a massacre of the French might have ensued. More and more horsemen appeared, including Guérin who, prohibited by canon law from shedding blood, neatly solved that conun-drum by going into battle wielding a mace. Philip drew up his forces in three divisions. On the right were the men of the rearguard who were already battle-scarred, grouped around bishop Guérin and the duke of Burgundy, supported by the levies of the great French counts: Beaumont, Montmorency, St-Pol, Melun and Sancerre. The king himself commanded the centre and clustered around him most of the crack corps, including his household knights and redoubtable warriors like William de Barres, famous from the Third Crusade.[96] On his left he placed his kinfolk, the lords of Dreux, including the bishop of Beauvais, and the counts of Dreux, Ponthieu and Auxerre. Opposite him, commanding the allied centre was Otto, still fuming that his scouts had told him Philip was in full retreat, in company with the dukes of Brabant, Louvain and Limburg; on his left were Ferrand and the count of Holland and on the right most of the men with a true martial reputation, as for example Salisbury, renowned for his physical strength and Hugh de Boves, infamous for his cruelty.[97] With the numerical disadvantage, Philip was forced to weaken his left by extending it to prevent outflanking, but otherwise his ground was well chosen: his right was protected by marshy ground – particularly boggy this Sunday afternoon as the wet winter and spring of 1214 had exacerbated the basic wetland problem (the Rivers Escaut, Scarpe, Deule and Marque all drained here) – and in front of him was a mile-wide plateau suitable for cavalry charges. His men fought with their backs to the river, which meant there was no escape route in case of defeat; to reinforce the point Philip destroyed the Bouvines bridge once his men had crossed back over.[98] Finally, and not unimportantly, the allies were forced to fight with the sun in their eyes.

A lesser commander might have thrown all the cavalry at the enemy before they were properly formed up, but Philip could see the danger that his horse might be sucked into a melee beyond infantry protection and then cut down piecemeal. Guérin used the cavalry initially to harass the enemy as if deployed off the road and onto the battlefield in a confused and time-consuming manoeuvre but this move was checked by Flemish cavalry screening the situation. It may have been as late as three in the afternoon when the first real clashes took place. The battle began more as a gigantic joust, with knights on either side performing heroically if inconsequentially. First the French sent forward their non-knightly cavalry force, which the Flemings beat back with ease.[99] Bishop Guérin next tried to group the French knights together for a charge but this was beaten off by the Flemish horsemen, who responded by issuing individual man-to-man challenges to the French, as though to imply that a massed cavalry charge was against the laws of chivalry.[100] French grandees named as performing doughtily in these actions were the count of Beaumont, Duke Odo of Burgundy, the viscount of Melun, Matthew of Montmorency and the count of St-Pol, who claimed to be utterly exhausted by his efforts; his enemies whispered that he was secretly in Otto's pay.[101] This stage of the battle petered out when the leader of the Flemish horse was killed in such an encounter. Meanwhile Philip was greatly encouraged when his men seemed to be having the upper hand in the weakest sector, the French left. Already the French were acting more as a coordinated force and the imperial army as a number of separate contingents.[102]

Seeing the allies making little progress, Otto ignored his obvious option – outflanking the French left – and ordered his cavalry to charge at Philip's standard, sending his infantry forward at a run to take care of the French foot. The fighting was bloody and furious, with the infantry using long slender knives to try to pierce the knights' armour; an unlucky Frenchman, Stephen of Longchamp, died when such a knife thrust through the eyehole of his helmet and pierced his brain. Eustace of Melenghin, a Flemish knight, was another killed in this way. French infantrymen surrounded him. One man grabbed his head, holding it between his arm and chest, pulled off his helmet and exposed him to the thrusts of his comrade, who knifed him under the chin. These tactics were initially successful, and the imperial infantry had the upper hand in the slugging match on the ground but Philip cleverly withdrew his horse in face of the initial impact, regrouped, then launched them in a counter-attack.[103] The climax of this stage of the battle came when a large force of German infantry, armed with spears, iron hooks and long curved knives, crashed into Philip's division grouped around the royal golden fleur-de-lis standard. Furious fighting followed, during which Philip was unhorsed and would have been killed had an enemy lance not been absorbed by his heavy armour. One of his knights, Peter Tristan, jumped off his horse and covered the king with his body until more and more French knights arrived, slaughtering the lightly armoured German foot. Gradually the French forced the Germans back, but not without taking heavy casualties. Losses among the French knights were especially severe as the enemy continued to use their long thin three-bladed knives designed to slice through gaps in armour.[104] The sanguinary mayhem in the centre was effectively ended when the bishop of Beauvais, seeing the French left unexpectedly free to manoeuvre, ordered it to roll back the supporting action from the allied right. The Germans had almost succeeded in breaking the French cavalry and they failed only because their attacks were uncoordinated. One scholar indeed suggests that the action around Philip's standard was a battle within a battle, that this encounter took place at the southern end of the battlefield while a general melee was being fought to the north.[105]

After the great allied effort in the centre, the pulse seemed to go out of their attack. The bishop of Beauvais had a surprisingly easy time of it when dealing with the allied right, doubtless helped by his good fortune when he clubbed down Salisbury, allegedly the strongest man on the field, with a mace.[106] When Salisbury was captured, his back-up Hugh de Boves, who had taunted Renaud de Dammartin with cowardice, turned and fled. Ironically, it was the man de Boves had accused of cowardice who displayed the greatest military talent that day. Early in the battle Renaud had used the very effective device of drawing up his 700 pikemen into a circular formation – a primitive square – from which cavalry would emerge for sudden charges before retiring once more into the protective fold.[107] As the fight in the centre became more intense and Otto called for every last cavalryman, this tactic had to be modified. Suddenly the struggle in the centre was over. The key event was the unhorsing of Otto himself. A French knight grabbed at the bridle of his horse, while another lunged at him with a knife. The first blow rebounded off the emperor's heavy armour, but a second pierced the eye of Otto's rearing horse; maddened with pain the steed bolted carrying Otto with it before collapsing. The great French knight William de Barres came within an ace of capturing Otto after he was unhorsed. Unhinged by this calamity, Otto lost his nerve and fled.[108] His flight demoralised the imperial troops, who soon began to disengage and stream away off the battlefield. Soon the gallant Renaud and his pikemen were left to fight on alone. Although French troubadours ungallantly jeered that Renaud resisted and would not surrender only because he feared prison would be the end of his life of amatory dalliance, the truth is that he fought on courageously, his squares still bristling like porcupines, defying the French cavalry to approach them. Freed of anxiety in the centre, Philip ordered his infantry and archers to make an end of the defence. Sheer weight of numbers told; the French knights, their blood up, scythed down the Flemish pikemen to the last man, as knights were wont to do in battle with their social inferiors. Renaud was cut down and his life spared only by the rapid intervention of bishop Guérin.[109]

Although a terrible experience by the contemporary standards of

Western Europe – where feudal leaders liked to avoid pitched battles – the battle of Bouvines was a relatively brief affair, lasting no more than three hours.[110] But it was as decisive as such a battle could well be. The French captured 130 knights and five nobles (Boulogne, Flanders, Salisbury, Dortmund and Tecklenburg) who were taken to prison in Paris. The fate of the noble prisoners depended entirely on Philip Augustus's personal attitude to them. Salisbury, as an honourable enemy, was released almost instantly, but the fate of Ferrand and Renaud was grim indeed. Ferrand spent thirteen years in captivity, was released only in 1227, and then died soon afterwards from disease contracted in jail. Because Philip was angry with Renaud for supposed treachery, his gallantry on the battlefield availed him nothing. He was granted his life but chained in a dungeon like a dog for thirteen years. When Ferrand was released, the French taunted Renaud by telling him he never would be; the unfortunate man thereupon committed suicide.[111] The most despicable of the allied leaders, Hugh de Boves, tried to flee to England but was caught in a storm off Calais and drowned. Otto escaped but politically was finished. After his defeat all significant Germans switched their support to young Frederick, who was crowned at Aachen in 1215. Otto retired to Brunswick, impoverished, and died there of a drug overdose in 1218.[112]

The greatest triumph was Philip's. France was now the major power in Western Europe, Flanders was its appanage, and John's ambitions to restore Normandy and Poitou to Angevin rule now seemed the merest chimera. Whether it was intrinsic French military superiority, and particularly their greater mobility, a combination of inspired moves by Philip and bishop Guérin, or simply the incompetence of Otto and the allied commanders, nobody could deny that by his victory at Bouvines Philip Augustus had established the Capetian monarchy as an unassailable institution in the western world – at any rate unless some fearsome force were to appear from the Orient. As has been well said, Bouvines was the Austerlitz of the French Middle Ages.[113] Parisian university students went wild with joy and feasted, wenched and caroused for seven days and seven nights when the news reached the French capital.[114] King John's supporters like to say that he was defeated in 1214 by action-at-a-distance, that he was the hapless victim of events. But John had shown defective strategic insight. The two-front strategy was one of those grandiose plans that look fine on paper but are only practicable if the most meticulous coordinated timing is applied. This may well have been something beyond the reach of medieval tech-nology and communications, and the question arises why John did not opt to sail to Flanders with his entire army and confront Philip there. The need to shore up Poitou is a non-starter as an answer, since if the allies had defeated Philip in a pitched battle – if they had done to him what he did to them at Bouvines – the future of Normandy and Poitou would have lain with John anyway.

As it was, a decade of diplomacy lay in ruins and hundreds of thousands of marks in subsidies had been spent pointlessly. At first John still hoped to continue the war in the west, and sent to Peter des Roches for another three hundred Welsh archers in August.[115] It was probably fortunate for John that Innocent III entered the fray at this juncture. The Pope was planning a new crusade, and the last thing he wanted was further weakening of Christendom by a second Bouvines. He ordered his legate in France to bring about an urgent truce between the French and English kings, to run until 1 November 1215, pending the convening of a council to discuss a fifth crusade.[116] While diplomacy slowly got under way, the euphoric Philip Augustus was advancing westward, having added the army of his son Louis to his mighty host. He got as far as Loudun when he received the submission of the Poitevin barons, led by the slippery Aimeri of Thouars. John meanwhile, seventeen miles away at Parthenay, was in another of his periods of paralysis, uncertain which way to jump, having nowhere to flee to, but knowing that either fight or flight would probably be disastrous. Once again the barons came to him and advised him that offering battle was not a realistic option, that they would not support him if he did.[117] On 30 August John told the papal legate that he would agree to a ceasefire. To save face, he withdrew under cover of the truce towards La Rochelle. On 13 September, by letters patent, he pledged himself to observe whatever terms his envoys negotiated with Philip.[118] The French king, for his part, was persuaded not to try conclusions with John both by personal letters conveyed to him from the Pope and, more cogently, by, it was whispered, a 60,000-mark sweetener from John.[119] Finally, on 18 September, a definitive truce was agreed to run until Easter 1215, and then to be ratified for another five years.[120] Early in October John sailed from La Rochelle for England, making landfall at Dartmouth. His reputation was in tatters.[121] With the king stricken, the English barons saw their chance. As has often been remarked, the road from Bouvines to Runnymede was to be a short and inevitable one.

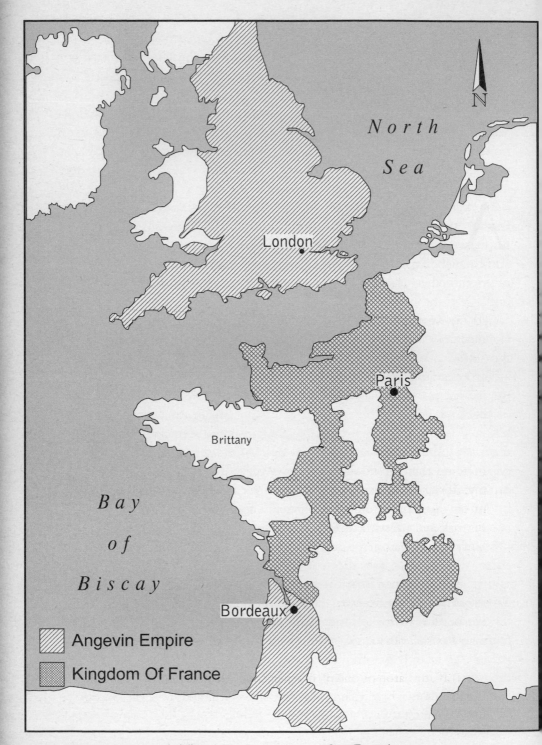

North
Sea

London

Paris

Brittany

Bay
of
Biscay

Bordeaux

Angevin Empire

Kingdom Of France

4. The Angevin Empire after Bouvines

18

_{◄○►}

ALTHOUGH THE DEFEAT AT Bouvines brought John's conflict with the barons to a crisis, it was a clash long in the making and for a long time masked by the troubles with the Vatican. A famous 'Unknown Charter of Liberties' was circulating in 1213–14, before John crossed to the continent, and ran as follows:

1) King John concedes that he will not take men without judgement, nor accept anything for doing justice, nor perform injustice.

2) And if my baron or my man should happen to die and his heir is of age, I ought to give him his land at a just relief without taking more.

3) And if the heir is under age, I ought to put the land in charge of four knights from among the lawful men of the fief, and they with my official ought to render me the proceeds of the land without sale of anything and without releasing any man, and without destruction of park and beasts; and then when the heir comes of age I will let him the land quit of payment.

4) If a woman is heir to land, I ought to give her in marriage on the advice of her relatives, so that she is not disparaged. And if I give her once in marriage I cannot give her a second time, but she can marry as she pleases, though not to my enemy.

5) If my baron or one of my men should happen to die, I concede that his money be divided as he himself willed; and if he dies intestate through war or illness, his wife or his children, or his parents and close friends, shall divide it for the good of his soul.

6) And if his wife shall not have to leave her house for forty days, and then she shall have her dower decently, and she shall have her marriage.

7) Furthermore, to my men I concede that they should not serve in the army outside England, save in Normandy or Britanny and this properly; and if anyone owes thence the service of ten knights, it shall be alleviated by the advice of my barons.

8) And if a scutage should be imposed in the land, one mark of silver will be taken from a knight's fee; and if a greater army shall be needed, more will be taken by the advice of the barons of the realm.

9) Then I concede that all the forests which my father, and my brother, and I have afforested, shall be disafforested.

10) Then I concede that knights who have their grove in my ancient Forest, shall have their grove henceforth as to their dwellings and as to clearance; and they shall have their forester; and I only one who protects my beasts.

11) And if any of my men shall die owing to the Jews, the debt shall not gain interest while their heir is below age.

12) And I concede that no man shall lose life or limb for Forest offences.[1]

The Unknown Charter is clearly a draft drawn up by a baron or baro-nial clerk trying to imagine the concessions that could be wrung from John; although the exact phraseology leaves something to be desired, and the switch from third to first person shows it is not an actual Charter, it provides a lucid account of the magnates' chief grievances: feudal reliefs, wardship and marriage, feudal military service and scutage, the operation of the Forest Laws. The barons were sick of having to attend Forest courts to hear the adjudication of a Forest Law they detested; they were sick of John's requirement that so many civil suits could be heard only in his presence; they were sick of his interventions between themselves and their vassals; and in general they were sick of the man himself and his arbitrary acts of tyanny.

John's return from La Rochelle in October 1214 plunged him

immediately into a sea of troubles. Alongside the blow to his prestige from the unravelling of his 'Grand Alliance', particular animus had been aroused by the high-handed actions of his justiciar Peter des Roches, a man detested as much for his foreign provenance as his financial exactions.[2] Yet these two issues merely exacerbated an already tense situation. In May at La Rochelle John promulgated writs for the collection of scutage of three marks per fee from all tenants-in-chief, royal demesnes, vacant bishoprics and lands in royal wardship.[3] The northern barons who had previously refused to serve in France now refused to pay, alleging that the terms of their feudal tenure made them exempt from foreign service.[4] The claim has universally been held invalid, as fiefs in northern England were no different from those elsewhere and, in any case, if there had been such a precedent, no Angevin king would ever have been able to campaign on the continent in defence of Britanny, Normandy, Anjou, Poitou, Aquitaine or anywhere else. John quite clearly had precedent on his side, but the fact that the barons were prepared to trail their coat on such a flimsy pretext shows they had had enough of John's money-grubbing, greed and general corruption, to say nothing of the lustful lunges the king made in the direction of their wives and daughters. Roger of Wendover suggested that the breakthrough moment for the barons came when Archbishop Stephen Langton held a secret conference with them in autumn 1213 and revealed to the ignorant the precise royal obligations laid on a monarch by Henry I's coronation charter.[5] It was clear from all they read and heard that John's system was a miasma of financial extortion and corruption.

Shortly after John's return, the barons met at Bury St Edmund's under the pretence of making a pilgrimage there and swore on the high altar that they would force John to sign a new charter like Henry I's, guaranteeing their key demands.[6] They then presented a document to the king which he promised to consider 'in the New Year'; when they pressed him again for an answer on the feast of the Epiphany (6 January 1215), he again stalled and said his considered reply would be ready by Easter.[7] It seems that the new charter was almost wholly concerned with feudal reliefs, wardships, marriages and debts to the Crown, which suggests that the original grievance about foreign service was a feint, to pin John down so that they could then present the demands over the things that most seriously concerned them. The barons had in effect lured John into a trap: by providing him with the 'straw man' argument about exemption from foreign service, which John leaped on eagerly as it was so easy to refute, they had embroiled him in their secondary but most profound argument: that all discussion about foreign service was predicated on the assumption that the king was acting justly over, say, reliefs and wardships, and it was precisely this point that they were now disputing.[8] In response John tried the old trick used by William the Conqueror to stifle opposition to his plans for the conquest of England in 1066: he held individual interviews with each of the barons and tried to bribe, browbeat or otherwise suborn them from the general cause. He asked for a written promise that the interviewee would never again demand such 'favours and liberties' from him or his successors. Doubtless primed as to John's likely tactics, the barons stood firm, with just three of them (the earl of Chester, the bishop of Winchester and William Brewer) prepared to break rank.[9]

Since many of the greatest magnates, such as William Marshal, the archbishop of Canterbury and the bishop of Ely held aloof from the fray, the question must be posed: who were the barons who opposed John? Were they all northerners? Were they all motivated by the same considerations? It would be misleading to see the movement for the charter in 1215 as an exclusively northern phenomenon; the problem has arisen because the chroniclers used the word 'northerners' as a short-hand tag for baronial rebels and in turn thought of them this way because one of their prominent ringleaders was Eustace de Vesci, lord of Alnwick, now in the forefront of opposition to John alongside his former fellow exile Robert Fitzwalter, lord of Dunmow and hereditary holder of Barnard Castle in the city of London; both of them had headed the 1212 rebellion.[10] Vesci and Fitzwalter had been expressly named by Innocent III as lords against whom John was not allowed to take reprisals, as part of the settlement which ended the papal interdict and excommunication. The ingenious duo of barons, who had actually planned to murder John, duped Innocent III into believing that they had fled abroad (not, as in fact they did, because the king discovered their conspiracy) because they could no longer stomach the persecutions of the Church by an ungodly king. The Pope regarded them as martyrs, accepted that his cause and theirs were one and the same, and insisted on their restoration to full wealth and honours in England as an earnest of John's sincerity.[11] The reality is that there was bad blood between both Fitzwalter and Vesci on the one hand and John on the other, and this was a long-standing affair, which had nothing to do with John's struggle with the Church. The fact that Vesci and Fitzwalter pulled the wool over the Pope's eyes and those of the papal legate Pandulph, has nothing to do with the core issue. Vesci's main grievance seems to have been John's lecherous designs on his wife,[12] but Fitzwalter's animosity was over-determined. Some say John tried to seduce his daughter, others that Fitzwalter defied the king by bringing five hundred armed men in a show of force to a trial for murder by Fitzwalter's spoiled and roughneck son-in-law Geoffrey de Mandeville. It is quite within the realm of possibility that John had offended Fitzwalter in both ways but he was certainly no noble rebel fighting for freedom, as in the absurd legend, but a deeply unpleasant thug with a well-documented track record for cowardice, treachery and ingratitude.[13]

Vesci and Fitzwalter, the two highest profile rebels, were profoundly rebarbative individuals, but this in no way vindicates John nor does it affect the merits of the campaign for the Charter. Evil men may, intentionally or otherwise, support good causes, and vice versa. There were others in the Vesci/Fitzwalter mould among the barons, notably Saer de Quincy, who had collaborated with Fitzwalter in cravenly opening the gates of Vaudreuil in Normandy to Philip Augustus in 1203 and was William Marshal's bête noire.[14] Yet there were others who had good grounds for their hatred of John. Giles de Braose, bishop of Hereford, had never forgotten the dreadful fate meted out by John to his brother and sister-in-law. Nicholas Stuteville had been mulcted by John for no less than 10,000 marks as the 'relief' for his inheritance. William Mowbray had even deeper grounds for hatred. John had demanded 2,000 marks to hear a case concerning his barony and had then barefacedly given judgement against him – all this in the case of a man who had spent four years in Germany as a hostage for the payment of Richard's ransom in the 1190s.[15] For some, adherence to the rebels was a simple function of family loyalty. Geoffrey de Mandeville, earl of Essex, was in the Fitzwalter orbit (only fitting, as he owed him his life), as were the other members of this extended clan: Henry Bohun, earl of Hereford, Robert de Vere, earl of Oxford and Geoffrey de Say. Since these were southern magnates, it is clear that, even if the rebellious spirit first flickered in the north, it was fanned into flame farther south. The northern faction of the rebellious barons contained few great earls, and leadership quickly devolved on the lords of East Anglia and the south.[16] The rebel spirit was also very strong in John's beloved West Country: the earl of Salisbury led an army against the men of Dorset and Devon but was forced to retreat because of his inferior numbers.[17]

On paper the rebels' endeavour seemed a desperate venture, as the really big baronial guns held firm and stayed loyal to John. The earls of Salisbury, Chester, Albemarle, Warren and Cornwall, plus William

Marshal, earl of Pembroke, all lined up behind the king. So did the lords of Aubigny, Vipont, De Lucy, Basset, Cantelupe, Neville and Brewer; all these had pointedly paid the scutage demanded by John which the 'northerners' so vehemently objected to.[18] Although numerically inferior to the rebels, John's loyal barons carried far more weight in terms of power, land, money and prestige. The two most notable were William Marshal and Ranulph de Mandeville, earl of Chester. Though with no illusions about John, and in some instances having suffered just as much objective damage as the rebels, these men took the view that only egregious tyranny could outweigh their feudal oaths of allegiance, and in their view John had not yet crossed the invisible line separating an authoritarian monarch from a despot; it would be a mistake to underrate the medieval fear of chaos as Satan's work. The prestige of Marshal and Mandeville was particularly important: Marshal brought the senior Irish lords in his wake, while the earl of Chester attached William Ferrers, earl of Derby, and other important lords to John's standard. The open adherence of the earls of Warwick, Devon, Arundel and Surrey to the king also helped to tip the balance of power in his favour.[19] There were also perhaps a hundred neutral or undecided barons. Gradually it seemed most intelligent for the more far-sighted of the king's party to make common cause with these neutrals and try to hammer out a peace formula. It was not just that if John completely vanquished the rebels, he might not be able to resist the temptation to make himself an absolute ruler by turning and rending his erstwhile allies; it was also that the ever-present fear of the chaos principle accelerated daily, once it was realised that sons were taking up arms against fathers and brothers against brothers.[20] Not even William Marshal's gravitas saved him from this fate, since his eldest son joined the rebels. There was a generational tinge to the conflict also, since young men and heirs tended to join the rebels while their fief-holding fathers clung to the status quo. Bit by bit, then, it was the middle-of-the road centrist opinion that prevailed over the outright advocates of civil war, whether Eustace de Vesci and Fitzwalter on the one hand or the fire-eating reactionaries in John's entourage on the other. Vesci, in particular, sustained a personal check when Innocent III singled him out and warned him not to vex or trouble the king.[21]

John had not been idle after the Epiphany meeting with the rebel barons. His reflex action to all challenges to his authority was to use force so, while pretending diplomacy, he began assembling an army. His first step was to order a nationwide renewal of the oath of allegiance, trying to manipulate the modalities of liege homage so that each subject taking the oath would bind himself to 'stand by him against all men'. This was at once construed by the rebels (correctly) as the opening shot in John's campaign against the charter.[22] He sent commissioners to the ostensibly 'loyal' counties in the south and Midlands to rally their support, and called in knights from Poitou and Ireland. On 19 February John was persuaded to sign a safe-conduct allowing the 'northern' barons to travel to Oxford to confer with William Marshal, Stephen Langton and a quorum of other bishops who fancied themselves peacemakers.[23] The conference took place on 22 February but, whatever tentative proposals were made then were soon overtaken by two dramatic new developments. In an act of consummate cunning, on 4 March John took vows as a crusader. He had not the slightest intention of travelling to Outremer but he knew that his father had taken the Cross without actually going on crusade, and could see the potential of such a manoeuvre to obfuscate issues and confuse the opposition. Moreover, by taking the Cross John put himself and his cause technically under the protection of the Church and, as a crusader, he was allowed three years' grace before fulfilling his secular obligations.[24] John's act gives new meaning to the word machiavellianism. Meanwhile at the end of April there was good news from Rome. Both sides had lobbied the Vatican: John's agent William Mauclerc reached the Eternal City on 17 February and at the end of the month Eustace de Vesci himself arrived with written representations to Innocent III from his confederates.[25] The Pope quickly decided in favour of John.

Gone were the days when Innocent III forced John to make special exceptions for Vesci. His former protégé was now firmly in the rebel camp, and Innocent doubtless took a grim satisfaction in disappointing the hopes of those who had so grievously disappointed his during the interdict. Although the documentary evidence Vesci produced of John's stalling, prevarication and duplicity was compelling – and archbishop Stephen Langton himself was fuming at John's wriggling tergiversation – for Innocent in 1215 the overriding consideration was that John had placed himself in the papal camp twice over: by making himself a papal vassal and England a papal fief; and by taking the Cross. Innocent had already shown which way the wind was likely to blow by prohibiting the election to the archbishopric of York of Simon Langton, Stephen's brother, purely because that was what John wanted.[26] On 19 March 1215 he wrote his formal pronouncement on the dispute in England. A letter to the barons condemned leagues and conspiracies against King John, especially since they would have the effect of delaying his holy purpose of going on crusade.[27] The same day Innocent wrote to Stephen Langton to rebuke him for failing to mediate between the king and the rebels, and for having allegedly given succour and comfort to the northern barons.[28] Innocent followed up this initial salvo with a fresh barrage on 1 April. He ordered the barons to pay for the Poitevin scutage of 1214, again citing the imminence of the crusade as the reason; if the barons wanted justice he added naively, they could seek it from the Vicar of Christ himself.[29] Finally on 7 July he reprimanded the English bishops for their lukewarm support for King John and their sympathy for the rebels, declaring that they were indulging in a wicked conspiracy against God's holy work and a 'worthy' king who was prepared to carry the fight for the true faith to Outremer; if they did not themselves wish to be dismissed from office, they should immediately excommunicate the rebels.[30]

It infuriated Stephen Langton that Innocent either could not or would not see through John's obvious ploys, and the disingenuous pretence of going on crusade. But John played his machiavellian hand to perfection. Until the shoal of letters from Innocent arrived in England, John was the very model of a meek son of the Church, appearing conciliatory at all points and even rescinding the order to the knights of Poitou to join him.[31] Needless to say, when Easter came there was still no answer to the barons from the king: John stalled shamelessly, keeping Stephen Langton and William Marshal closeted on detailed negotiations he had no intention of honouring, while he waited for the papal letters to come in. For the barons Innocent's intervention was the last straw. They responded defiantly, first mustering at Stamford then meeting at Brackley near Northampton and issuing a fresh sheaf of demands, presumably a hardening of their initial conditions, since the next we know is that John rejected them outright. 'Why do these barons not ask for my kingdom at once?' he said scornfully. 'Their demands are idle dreams, without a shadow of reason.' There followed the customary John tantrum, in which he claimed the barons were trying to turn him into a slave. In vain did Langton and Marshal represent to him that he ought to make some concession. Raging and frothing, John insisted that the two 'mediators' return and repeat to the rebels word for word what he had said.[32] The barons then decided that the time for diplomacy was past; on 3 May they formally renounced their homage and fealty, in effect declaring that they no longer recognised John as king. Fitzwalter was appointed commander-in-chief of rebel forces and assumed the grandiose title of 'Marshal of the army of God and Holy Church'. They marched back to

Northampton, occupied the town and besieged the castle, held for John by Geoffrey of Martigny, kinsman and protégé of the notorious and much feared mercenary leader Gérard d'Athée.[33]

The rebels soon realised that John was a tough nut to crack. Perhaps they had underestimated how many mercenaries and well-fortified castles he had under his aegis. At all events they found Northampton Castle to be impregnable, at any rate given the absence of trebuchets which they did not possess; they raised the siege after a fortnight and switched their attentions to Bedford. Here they had better luck, for its constable William de Beauchamp surrendered it to them.[34] John meanwhile was not idle. He ordered a general muster at Gloucester and, on 30 April, ordered his forces to proceed to Cirencester for a further rendezvous. Reassured that the fortresses in London, Oxford, Norwich and Bristol were all unassailable and as soon as he received the good news from the Pope, John renewed the request for help from the knights of Poitou and Flanders, and based himself in London, granting the city the right to elect its own mayor in future as a guarantee of its loyalty.[35] But if John thought he had thereby secured the capital, he soon received a rude awakening. On Sunday 17 May rebel forces were secretly admitted to London by a powerful dissident faction, acting with speed and precision before the implications of John's charter of privileges became common knowledge.[36] The euphoric rebels then plundered all known royal partisans and instituted a mini-pogrom against the Jews, confiscating their money and tearing down their houses. They then issued a general declaration, calling on all undecided magnates to come off the fence or risk the loss of their property. Fire-eating threats were made to all neutrals that the rebels would 'direct their banners and their arms against them as against public enemies, and do their utmost to overthrow their castles, burn their dwellings and destroy their fishponds, orchards and parks'.[37] Some have interpreted this declaration as a sign of rebel weakness, but for John it was a devastating blow that convinced him that some accommodation with the barons was inevitable.[38]

John hit back with a mixture of threats, cajolery, promises, bribes and sweeteners. On 9 and 10 May he published letters promising to submit all points of difference between him and the barons to papal arbitration, doubtless now confident that Innocent would back him to the hilt. He also offered a concession: 'Know that we have granted to our barons who are against us that we shall not take them or their men, nor disseise them, nor go upon them by force or arms, except by the law of our realm or by the judgement of their peers in our court.'[39] John tried to put flesh on these bones by offering to have two particularly controversial reliefs, those imposed on the earl of Essex and the bishop of Hertford (significantly relating to inheritances from two of John's most hated families, the Mandevilles and the Braoses) reviewed by a jury of their peers.[40] *If* John could be trusted, this was a significant concession, as it was an implicit admission that the barons had genuine grievances and that he himself had acted arbitrarily and unjustly, but could he be trusted? Might this not simply be a ruse to get the barons to disarm, whereupon the 'concession' would be at once rescinded? What guarantees was the king offering? Also, it seemed just too transparent a ploy to abandon the general demands of the charter for the satisfaction of a few particular ones on an ad hoc basis. But the offer was speciously reasonable, deliberately made to seem attractive to waverers, and some of the barons took the bait, influenced no doubt by John's 'carrot and stick approach': alongside the silky purr of diplomacy the king applied the resounding thwack of main force by granting rebel lands to his favourites. Some of the less obdurate rebels began to buckle at this point. When Henry Braybrooke had two manors seized, he secured a safe-conduct to come and talk to John about the terms on which he could be reconciled. Even more dramatic was the coming to heel of Simon Patishall. On 15 May John alienated his manor of Wasden to one of his placemen; within a week Patishall had used the good offices of the abbot of Woburn to make his peace with the monarch.[41]

Stalemate and stand-off, almost 'phoney war', seemed the main feature of the civil war by mid-May, with the rebels entrenched in London and John based at Winchester (but even now pursuing his peripatetic existence – Fremantle (Wiltshire) 17–19 May, Silchester 19 May, Winchester 19–20 May, Odiham (Hampshire) 21–22 May, Windsor 22–23 May, Winchester 23–24 May). While the king sent a plethora of negotiators and mediators to treat with the rebels, with Stephen Langton always foremost, he tried to extinguish baronial hopes in the west, so that he would not be threatened by a two-front war. There seem to have been two (and possibly three) expeditions to the West Country under the earl of Salisbury. One was supposed to relieve the rebel siege of Exeter, but the city fell before the royal troops could get under way properly. It was either on this or a subsequent occasion that the embarrassed Salisbury, believing the enemy were preparing an ambush near Sherborne (Dorset), crept back to Winchester with his tail between his legs, claiming that he was hopelessly outnumbered.[42] John is said to have remarked scornfully that Salisbury's approach was no way to take fortresses. It

seems that the earl was indeed unduly fainthearted, for when John sent
him back with reiterated orders to relieve or retake Exeter, boldness won
the day. Once again Salisbury's scouts brought him alarming news of an
ambuscade near Sherborne, but this time the earl preferred to take his
chances with a concealed enemy rather than return for another shaming
tongue-lashing from John. Salisbury's army was mainly composed of
Flemish mercenaries and their ferocious reputation preceded them, to
the point where the rebels in Exeter did not relish trying conclusions
with them and lamely evacuated the city.[43]

John's strategy now was to tighten the noose around the rebels in
London while he waited for reinforcements to come in from overseas.
Hubert de Burgh was put in charge of the new army to be formed from
the foreign knights, and meanwhile John tried to close the ring by
mustering forces at Marlborough and Reading and then ordering them
to a general rendezvous between Odiham (Hampshire) and Farnham
(Surrey). That John was thinking of investing London from both sides
is clear from the instruction to Stephen Langton on 26 May that he
should hand over Rochester castle (in Langton's custody by right of his
being the archbishop of Canterbury) and allow the king to garrison it
with his own men; the subtext is clear – John had no confidence in
Langton's ultimate loyalties.[44] John indulged himself in his favourite
stalling tactics by negotiating interminable truces and safe-conducts with
the barons, under the guise of an earnest quest for peace.[45] The stalling
extended to the papacy. John kept Innocent III warm by writing that it
was only the rebellion that prevented him setting out on the much-desired
crusade.[46] But the first week in June saw a major setback to his plans.
Northampton Castle suddenly collapsed under the fury of the townspeople, who massacred some of the garrison. Then simultaneous news
came in that Lincoln had fallen to the rebels and that the garrison still
holding out in the Tower of London was likely to capitulate at any
moment.[47] There were four rebel armies in the field but, even more seriously, England had lurched into financial and administrative anarchy.
Taxes were no longer being paid or courts attended, while debtors and
criminals awaited the outcome of the civil war.[48] To some of John's more
thoughtful advisers, the slide towards anarchy was ominous. It was not
inconceivable that the political void would lead to total social breakdown,
with a peasant rising as the ultimate nightmare. The king might well find
that, even if he defeated the barons, he had a rural *jacquerie* on his hands.
He would certainly not get any money in the future. It was time to bow
to the inevitable and strike a deal with the rebel magnates.

On 8 June John issued a safe-conduct for the rebel leaders, enabling them to make a journey to and from Staines between 9–11 June. On 10 June he himself came down from Windsor to the water meadows near Staines to meet rebel leaders and commit himself to a draft schedule.[49] A preliminary version of Magna Carta (the Great Charter) known as the 'Articles of the Barons' was haggled over, but in the end John agreed to affix his royal seal to it, to show that he had agreed the provisions in principle.[50] He then sent William Marsal and an embassy to London to tell the dissidents there what had happened: 'that for the sake of peace and for the welfare and honour of his realm, he would freely concede to them the laws and liberties which they asked; and that they might appoint a place and day for him and them to meet, for the settlement of all these things'.[51] When both sides had discussed the terms among themselves, a formal ceremony of acceptance took place at Runnymede on the 15th. Both sides pitched their tents a short distance from each other on a long level stretch of grassland that ran down to the riverbank. The barons came with a large party of well-armed knights, perhaps still not quite trusting John.[52] It was an impressive assembly, with anyone who was anyone in English politics present: Stephen Langton, Pandulph, all the senior bishops, the Master of the English Templars, William Marshal, Hubert de Burgh, the earls of Salisbury, Warren and Arundel and a host of other dignitaries and warriors.[53] Magna Carta concludes with the words 'Given in the meadow that is called Runnymede between Windsor and Staines, 15 June'. Several more days were to elapse, however, while the Chancery clerks and their rebel equivalents hammered out the exact wording. Finally, when copies had been made and distributed on all sides, there was a further ceremony on 19 June, when the rebel barons formally renewed their oaths of allegiance to the king. This was a necessary quid pro quo, for a solemn grant by the Crown could not be made to rebels still in the field against that selfsame royal authority.[54]

The towering reputation of Magna Carta seems at first sight puzzling, since the sixty-three clauses of the Charter overwhelmingly deal with medieval and feudal matters. Much predictable mirth has been expended by the cynics and sceptics on clauses like number 33: 'Henceforth all fish-weirs shall be completely removed from the Thames and the Medway, and throughout all England, except on the sea coast.' For convenience Magna Carta may be considered under four headings: purely baronial grievances; wider issues touching on the law; clauses benefiting the rebels' allies; and those aspects which really do bear upon the common good and 'liberty' as it would be understood today. Reliefs, wardships, marriage, the position of widows of tenants-in-chief, and the payment of debts to the Crown were the most vexatious matters oppressing the barons, and the sought-for protections were assured in clauses 2–9. Clauses 10–11 covered debts due to the Jews. There was an important concession about scutage in clauses 12 and 14, where it was declared that this would be taken 'only by the common counsel of our kingdom'. This meant, in future, not just rubber-stamping by handpicked royal advisers but the actual consent of the tenants-in-chief, who would be summoned to give it either individually, if they were great lords, or collectively, in the case of lesser barons. John promised to abolish the 'evil customs' of the Forest once a commission of enquiry had reported, and to disafforest all the land he had afforested in his reign (clauses 44, 47, 48 and 53). He furthermore promised to restore immediately all lands, castles and other property he had taken from anyone without proper judgement and to have similar acts by his father or brother investigated and rectified once he himself had returned from crusade (clause 52). He also pledged himself to return all hostages that he had taken 'as security for peace or faithful service' (clause 49) and to expel from his kingdom all mercenary troops and foreign knights and crossbowmen (clause 51). The most startling concession wrung from John by the barons was a written promise to clamp down on the activities of Gérard d'Athée and his kinsfolk, explicitly named in clause 50 as follows: 'Engelard de Cigogne, Peter and Guy and Andrew de Chanceaux, Guy de Cigogne, Geoffrey de Martigny with his brothers, Philip Mark with his brothers and his nephew Geoffrey, and all their followers.'

The legal reforms of Magna Carta were momentous. The barons did not attack those aspects of John's reforms which had benefited litigants, even though they were primarily designed to swell his coffers, but they did object to the king's manipulation of legal processes for his own advantage. In future he was not to deny a man justice, to take money from anyone for helping to get him a favourable verdict or for delaying a suit, to sell writs or to try to make a profit out of the sale of writs that initiated legal actions or to try to use writs to bring into the royal court matters that could be perfectly well dealt with in the barons' own feudal courts. It was stipulated that no action against an offender should deprive a man of his liberty, rights at law or property 'except by the lawful judgement of his peers or by the law of the land'. The limitation of the power of sheriffs was another prime aim of the

Charter (clauses 4, 24, 26, 30, 48). John's foreign henchmen were specifically targeted in the requirement that the king could not simply appoint anyone he wished as sheriff and that no one could be appointed sheriff or justice who did not know the law of the land (clause 45). Moreover, in a significant new development, common pleas could be held in a fixed place and those who entered them did not have to follow the king's court around the country to secure a hearing (clause 17). Clause 18 stated that judges were to hear the assizes of novel disseisin, mort d'ancestor and darrein presentment — exactly the sort of jargon that makes the past seem a foreign country to all but scholars. In plain English, it offered safeguards to anyone who felt he had been wrongly dispossessed of property, who claimed to be the lawful heir to a deceased person's property or who disputed patronage of churches. Whereas, previously, writs had to be prepared and presented by the plaintiff, with all the attendant expense and risk, under the new system the sheriff had the duty to prepare such writs and to convene a jury to hear the case when the king's judges next visited the county. As has been pointed out more than once, clause 18 was an anomaly in that it was the only clause in the Charter that asked for *more* government rather than less. The demand that royal judges should hold county court sessions four times a year proved beyond the administrative capability of the governments that succeeded John's.

Although most of the Charter was designed to satisfy the demands and aspirations of the barons, either explicitly or implicitly, the fact that they claimed to be campaigning for justice, not to mention the prudential requirements of simple politics, meant that they had to include some sops or inducements for their actual or potential allies. Wales and Scotland were placated in clauses 56–59, while London was specifically favoured by the provisions of clauses 12 and 13, which effectively gave the capital the status of 'most favoured city'. The barons realised the growing importance of the merchant classes, and sought protection for the privileges of towns, freedom of trade, liberty of movement for merchants, including the right to pass freely to and from national borders; foreign merchants were given the same rights except in wartime (clauses 41–43). There is something almost pettifogging about the barons' concern for commerce in clause 35: 'Let there be one measure of wine throughout our kingdom and one measure of ale and one measure of corn, namely the London quarter, and one width of cloth, whether dyed, russet or halberjet, namely two ells within the selvedges. Let it be the same with weights as with measures.' Even infrastructure got a mention, with clause

23 emphasising the importance of bridge-building. But for a modern reader perhaps the most interesting provisions of the Charter are the 'universal' ones, real or alleged. All classes, even the peasantry, benefited from the mitigation of 'amercements' – those notoriously draconian punishments ordained for misdemeanours – such as neglect of public duties, failing to bring a criminal to justice, mumbling or pleading falteringly in court or minor offences against public order. Clause 20 of Magna Carta tried to make the fine fit the crime and declared that no fine should make a peasant economically unviable; moreover, only local men, not royal officials, were to decide the amercement. Hitherto it had been a simple matter for the king's officials to declare almost anyone in default on this score and at the king's mercy – a plight only to be relieved on payment of a fine. Amercements rarely came to less than half a mark (six shillings and eight pence) in an era when the average wage of a day labourer was thirty shillings a year and the total value of a peasant's goods and chattels seldom exceeded ten shillings. On other aspects of the 'General Good', some critics have attempted to read clauses 12 and 14 as adumbrating an embryonic parliament. The one incontestable breakthrough came in clause 39 in the famous *nullus homo liber* provision: 'No free man shall be taken or imprisoned or disseised or outlawed or exiled or in any way ruined, nor will we go or send against him, except by the lawful judgement of his peers or by the law of the land.' The original wording was to have been 'any baron'; by changing it to 'any free man' the drafters of Magna Carta turned a medieval document into something that has often been hailed as a charter of freedom that belongs to the ages.[55]

Since many have asserted that the only significant thing about John's reign was Magna Carta, any student of John must pause to consider the Great Charter in slightly more depth. Sceptics have claimed that, far from being a beacon on the road to freedom, it is a reactionary document drawn up by a set of benighted barons concerned only for their own selfish interests.[56] The leaders of the 'Army of God' cared little for God and even less for liberty, but only for their own estates, wealth and aristocratic exemptions; in this regard it is often remarked that 'liberty' originally meant 'privilege' rather than 'freedom' and that any freedoms in the Charter were concerned with the freedom of the Church or freedom from taxation. As one historian with little time for the barons puts it: 'There is in it no high-sounding statement of principle and no clearly defined political theory. It is in fact a Charter of Liberties not a Charter of Liberty, concerned to secure practical reforms which would protect the upper classes against an overmighty ruler in current matters of grievance, not to enunciate abstract 'rights of man'.[57] Others argue that Magna Carta had little to do with the history of the freedom of the individual in England and was not even important in the development of modern law. Proponents of the 'myth of Magna Carta' claim that the document was moribund and neglected for three centuries and, when revived, was misinterpreted, possibly wilfully, by the jurist Sir Edward Coke in the seventeenth century and then taken up by the even more influential Sir Edward Blackstone in the eighteenth. From these misinterpretations come the notion of Magna Carta as a document legitimating the resistance of Parliament to Charles I in the English Civil War and of the American colonists to the mother country in the American War of Independence. The great academic battlefield, unsurprisingly, is clause 39, which sceptics deny gives any support to the modern notions of trial by jury.[58]

The defence of Magna Carta as a document for the ages rests on a twofold counter-attack: the denial that so-called offending clauses really are reactionary; and the assertion that the either/or dichotomy of reactionary medieval document versus epochal charter of freedom is methodologically unsound and depends on a secret and unjustifiable 'law of excluded middle' – as if a proposition in logic rather than a matter of historical interpretation was at stake. Clause 34, which appears to disallow the use of the writ in proprietary actions, is often cited as a manifestly reactionary provision, but compelling arguments have established that the barons were merely ensuring that they did not lose the right to hear certain cases in their feudal courts because of some legal technicality.[59] Most of the clauses, such as those on amercements, are clearly progressive on any reading of the evidence. Because the wording of Magna Carta is sometimes opaque, the phrasing loose, and the provisions without any precise meaning, a kind of biblical exegesis has grown up, with all the notorious orthodoxies and heresies connected with the Bible reappearing in the Charter. Some have therefore argued that there is no necessary collision between benighted reactionary document on the one hand and charter of modern freedom on the other, since the very act of interpreting Magna Carta in ways the men of 1215 did not intend is an intrinsic consequence of the document itself. On this point two modern authorities may be cited: 'There is no inherent reason why an assertion of law originally conceived in aristocratic interests should not be applied on a wider scale';[60] and: 'It is not at all anachronistic to see in Magna Carta the animating principles of consent to taxation, due process and the rule of law.'[61] Lovers of paradox will relish the fact that this written document is supposed to be the foundation of the British Constitution, yet the British have always made a fetish of having an unwritten constitution, governed by conventions that increasingly presidential prime ministers increasingly ignore. The real influence of Magna Carta is on the written constitution of the United States.

More relevant for a biographer of King John are the many criticisms that have been made about the wisdom and practicability of Magna Carta from the barons' own viewpoint. It would, however, be naive to take the old, discredited view that Magna Carta's detailed clauses were really the work of churchmen, with the barons relegated to the sidelines as intellectual boneheads; for one thing it was Saer de Quincy, earl of Winchester, the barons' best administrator, who conducted the final negotiations.[62] But whether barons or clerics made the greater contribution to a document that was the work of many hands and many different interests, homogenised and streamlined by Chancery clerks to give the appearance of unity and coherence, it is clear that in many ways the Charter was severely deficient. Stephen Langton and the more intelligent of the barons were determined to prevent any royal fudge or obfuscation; they knew what they were dealing with in John. They were determined to stop him using key matters of high politics and foreign policy as a smokescreen behind which he could meddle with routine and everyday issues of justice and lordship. But the result was that Magna Carta was a farrago, an olio, a gallimaufry: some clauses were just, reasonable and excellent; some were vindictive and designed to humiliate John; some were ill-thought-out, impracticable, quixotic and chimerical. Clauses 12 and 13 left it vague what the future basis for taxation should be; it was a classic case of all rights and no duties. Clause 14, it has been pointed out, for some an embryonic parliament, would have entailed an impossibly large and unwieldy assembly of more than 800 people. Clause 11 dealt with the Jews, and simply tapped antisemitism in an obvious or facile way; nothing was said about the acquisition of Jewish bonds at very high interests by the monasteries. Throughout the Charter it is unclear who are the 'peers' who are supposed to judge matters, particularly if an issue affecting all the barons arose: who, then, could conceivably be their peers?[63]

Yet the worst political miscalculations occurred over clauses 52 and 61. Clause 52 stated: 'If, without lawful judgement of his peers, we have deprived anyone of lands, castles, liberties or rights, we will restore them to him at once. And if any disagreement arises on this let it be settled by the judgement of the twenty-five barons.' Clause 61 declared: 'The barons shall choose any twenty-five barons of the realm they wish . . . so that if we or any of our servants offend in any way . . . then those twenty-five barons together with the community of the whole land shall distrain and distress us in every way they can, namely by seizing castles, lands and possessions . . . until in their judgement amends have been made.' Hitherto kings had kept their promises only through fear of God or rebellion, but the barons, rightly, knew that neither of these factors weighed much with John. It was entirely possible that the whole structure of Magna Carta would topple the second John was back in Winchester, that he would instantly try to wriggle out of his commitments, as was his habitual practice. In logic, they had therefore to put in place some kind of enforcement procedure, so that their labours on the Charter did not turn out in vain. They proposed a system whereby all the barons would take an oath to obey the instructions of their 25-strong executive committee, or a majority if they could not all agree. But the barons sharpened the edge of conflict by insisting that only 'northerners' or rebel barons could serve on the Committee of Twenty-Five; there was to be no place for the William Marshals or any of the moderate lords.[64] John was therefore faced by a committee of his sworn enemies. It did not take a genius to see that if all real decision-making was henceforth to be the prerogative of this committee, and that they could strip the monarch of castles and all the sinews of war without any possibility of appeal against their judgement, then the king had in effect been dethroned. Everyone who knew John also knew that he was negotiating in the first place only to buy time, that he would repudiate the Charter once he felt strong enough. But the formation of the Committee of Twenty-Five meant that the differences between him and the barons had now become irreconcilable, and that civil war would break out again sooner rather than later. The barons had created a kind of Frankenstein's Monster in Magna Carta, for its provisions placed the unfolding of events beyond their control.[65]

The month after Magna Carta was superficially peaceful. At first John seemed to have turned over a new leaf. Commencing 19 June, his Chancery issued a shoal of writs to correct the most notorious individual baronial grievances and began by implementing the provisions of clause 25. Saer de Quincy, who claimed that John had unjustly barred him from his inheritance in Leicestershire, was given possession of Mountsorrel Castle; Richard Fitzallan retrieved the keepership of Richmond Castle; Robert Fitzwalter was given Hertford Castle; the earl of Clare received the town of Buckingham to be held in wardship for his grandson, one of the hated (by John) Braose brood; the earl of Huntingdon got back Fotheringhay Castle, which had been wrested from him by John in 1212 in the most brutal manner.[66] Even the sacrosanct Forest Laws were bent to accommodate the barons. Sheriffs were instructed to choose twelve knights in each county, charged with the task of investigating all legal abuses, especially the evil customs of the Forest. Some changes in Forest provisions were immediate. Eustace de Vesci was conceded his ancient hunting rights – hitherto in conflict with the Forest Laws – and Richard Montfichet was allowed the office of forester in Essex, held by his forefathers but abruptly taken from him by John.[67] There were many similar concessions. All sheriffs were notified that the king was now at peace with his barons, that the Charter be publicly read and that all men should swear allegiance to the Committee of Twenty-Five. Orders were issued for the repatriation of all foreign troops stationed at Dover.[68] Feeling humiliated and plagued by gout, John nonetheless summoned up the energy to attend a council meeting at Oxford in July, where his favourite officials were due to be dismissed or demoted.[69] But although he was prepared to conciliate the barons in ad hoc ways, John had no intention of honouring the more radical and extreme clauses of the Charter that would reduce him to a cipher. His duplicity was manifest when, the day after granting the Charter, he wrote a one-sided and tendentious account of the events at Runnymede to Innocent III, asking the Pope to declare the concessions granted there illegal. Here was breathtaking hypocrisy and sidewinding double-dealing: on the one hand instructions to the sheriffs to accept the sovereignty of the Twenty-Five; on the other a plea to the Pope to declare the Twenty-Five outlaw.[70] It was pure John, the youngest of the Devil's Brood at his most diabolical.

John was pinning very great hopes on papal intervention and, pending receipt of the news from Rome, he stalled as much and as far as he dared. He accepted the proposal at Oxford in July that the Tower of London be handed over to Stephen Langton as honest broker, to be returned to the king provided a formal peace was signed by 15 August.[71] But signs of royal resistance can be discerned even at Oxford. He had Peter des Roches issue two letters that breathed an implicit defiance. One tried to clarify clause 28, to ensure that the royal prerogatives concerning the Forest in general were not outlawed, and the other registered the barons' refusal to acknowledge in writing their legal obligations to the Crown.[72] For those capable of reading the runes, this was obviously not a king who intended abdicating meekly to the Committee of Twenty-Five. Moreover, John dragged his feet over the aliens he was supposed to expel. He did remove four of the alien castellans mentioned in Magna Carta but he kept Philip Mark on in the crucial royal castle at Nottingham and did not expel his other foreign favourites but kept them on ice, ready to use if (he clearly expected it to be when) the civil war reopened.[73] On 9 August John tried to jump the gun by asking Stephen Langton to surrender Rochester Castle to des Roches. Langton correctly read this as the sign of a king who had no intention whatever of submitting peacefully to the Twenty-Five. Not only did he refuse John's request but he pointedly made no attempt whatsoever to return the Tower of London to him after 15 August.[74] Langton was finding the position of supposedly neutral arbiter difficult. Despite his contribution to the Charter and his drafting skills, and the formal nod of obeisance to the Church in clause 1, the more extreme barons were clearly in the ascendant by the time of the Runnymede meeting. Clause 61 – which in effect transferred sovereignty from the king to the Committee of Twenty-Five – virtually brushed the Church aside by forbidding any appeal to Rome against the decisions of the Twenty-Five.[75]

Maybe news of John's appeal to Rome had leaked out to the barons, for they certainly acted after Runnymede as if John could not be trusted and a renewal of hostilities was only a matter of time. There was clearly a hardline faction that wanted no settlement whatever with John and thought themselves secure only if he was dead, deposed or abdicated. Some members of this clique slipped away from Runnymede once it appeared that a peace deal was likely, intending to carry on the war against John on the grounds that they were not present at the signing of Magna Carta and therefore could not be bound by it.[76] Some spoke openly of electing a new king, and others began fortifying the castles they had just received from John, as if war was imminent. Still others sought ways to avoid disarming. The obvious pretext for remaining in arms was a tournament, so there was suddenly a spate of these, all held suspiciously close to London; one such, with the venue originally advertised as Stamford, was transferred to Hounslow, so that armed men would be at hand in case John tried to retake London.[77] That this was clearly in John's mind became apparent from the ill-tempered exchanges at the conference in Oxford in July, whose sullen tone was set by the barons' refusal to stand when the king entered. John demanded to know why the barons were strengthening the defences of London if it was really true that peace had broken out; the magnates replied that the preconditions in the Charter were far from having been met: castles had not yet been given up or privileges granted and, most importantly, not everyone had yet taken the oath to the Twenty-Five.[78] Even Stephen Langton, no particular friend to John, began to urge a more conciliatory attitude on the barons. But they were right to be suspicious, for John had not the slightest intention of surrendering a jot or tittle of his powers long-term.[79] Their suspicions seemed justified when John, raging at the insulting treatment he had received at the July conference in Oxford, refused to attend a second one in mid-August. He declared that since Runnymede he had received nothing but insults, and that he no longer felt safe venturing among the barons with their huge bristling-armed retinues.[80]

It was at this juncture that John received the news from Rome he had been waiting for. With no knowledge of Magna Carta Innocent III wrote the first in a long series of letters on 18 June, ordering the barons to come to terms with the king or face excommunication.[81] On 7 July, still ignorant of Magna Carta, the Pope wrote to Pandulph his legate and the justiciar des Roches (with the abbot of Reading as a third addressee), praising John's decision to take the Cross and opining that the lords who opposed him in England were worse than Saracens; at least the benighted heathens had no true appreciation of what they were doing, but the English lords were contradicting God's will by impeding the crusade. Innocent gave des Roches carte blanche to use the weapons of interdict and excommunication against 'those who disturbed the realm' and to suspend any clergy who refused to cooperate.[82] Innocent may have suspected that Stephen Langton was secretly abetting the rebels, for he added the following in the last paragraph of his letter: 'That our mandate may not be impeded by anyone's evasion, we entrust you with the execution of the above instructions and charge you to proceed as you see fit, disregarding all appeals. If you cannot all discharge the business, let two of you do so.' Stephen Langton justifiably refused to promulgate these letters, and their threats of interdict and excommunication, on the grounds that they were out of date, written with no knowledge of Magna Carta. On 5 September Pandulph and des Roches, who had become close collaborators and fellow ideologues, duly excommunicated the barons.[83] There remained Langton. Elated by the confirmation of papal support, John had outwitted the archbishop of Canterbury by appearing ultra-conciliatory: he even released a further 2,000 marks of the sum agreed

in 1214 for the settlement of the Interdict and made a point of letting
Innocent know that he was also settling Queen Berengaria's long-standing
claim for a dower as widow of Richard I.[84] Confident that he had secured
his position at all points, John gave the nod to des Roches and Pandulph.
They proceeded to suspend Langton and all clergy who supported the
rebels. John added a vindictive twist of his own by refusing to let any but
ultra-loyal English clerics attend Innocent's Fourth Lateran Council, which
was even then assembling in Rome.[85]

The disconsolate Stephen Langton nonetheless set out for Rome to
plead his case in person. Here was a clear case of the world turned upside
down, for it was John's refusal to accept his appointment and the Pope's
insistence that had precipitated the long conflict between England and
the Vatican. Now he, Langton, had been turned out by the Pope's express
mandate. It is no wonder that he thought bitterly of resigning his see
and becoming a Carthusian monk.[86] But the worst was yet to come.
Langton had clung to the belief that Innocent's letters so far related to
the situation before Magna Carta, that he might change his mind once
he had read the settlement contained in the Charter. Innocent's indignant repudiation of Magna Carta, in a letter dated 24 August,[87] was therefore the last straw. Innocent's argument was twofold: John had been
coerced into agreement; and as overlord of England, only he, Innocent,
could decide disputes about government and governance. The machiavellian brilliance of John's 'surrender' to the Pope was now clear.
Innocent wrote that Magna Carta was an insult to John who:

> was forced to accept an agreement which is not only shameful and
> base but illegal and unjust . . . We refuse to pass over such shameless
> presumption, for thereby the Apostolic See would be dishonoured,
> the king's right injured, the English nation shamed and (the Charter)
> a serious danger to the whole crusade, a danger that would be immi-
> nent if the concession thus wrested from a great king who had
> taken the Cross were not cancelled by our authority, even though he
> should prefer them to be upheld. On behalf of Almighty God,
> Father, Son and Holy Ghost, and by the authority of Saints Peter
> and Paul His apostles . . . we utterly reject and condemn this settle-
> ment, and under threat of excommunication we order that the king
> should not dare to observe it and the barons and their associates
> should not insist on it being observed. The charter, with all under-
> takings and guarantees, whether confirming it or resulting from it,
> we declare to be null and void of all validity forever.[88]

Magna Carta is both myth and historical document. To an extent the two interpenetrate, for the version so admired by English 'libertarians' in the seventeenth century was not the original of 1215 but a truncated and modified version published by Henry III in 1225.[89] The pure myth was best expressed by Rudyard Kipling:

> And still when Mob or Monarch lays
> Too rude a hand on English ways,
> The whisper wakes, the shudder plays,
> Across the reeds at Runnymede.
> And Thames that knows the mood of kings,
> And crowds and priests and suchlike things,
> Rolls deep and dreadful as he brings their warning down from Runnymede.

But the historical fact is that Magna Carta was a dead duck within ten weeks and thereafter both sides had recourse to civil war. Immediately the rebel barons faced a problem. They were presumably fighting to replace John, but by whom? Since 1066 there had been many civil wars in England, but in each case there was an obvious pretender to the throne for whom the rebels fought: the Young King against Henry II in 1173–74, the younger Angevins against old King Henry in the 1180s, even John against Richard in 1193–94. In 1215 there was neither an alternative royal dynasty nor a dissatisfied plotter from the present ruling family – John's murder of Arthur had seen to that. It was one thing to say that the barons opposed John on the basis of Liberty, the Ancient Constitution or the Charter. But would men fight for such abstract ideals? Besides, now that the Pope had weighed in with his influential opinion, the barons badly needed an ideological counterweight, someone who would add political legitimacy to their cause. And, the xenophobia exhibited in the Charter notwithstanding, for lack of any domestic candidates this would have to be a foreign prince. This was the context in which they began to look across the Channel at the headstrong French version of the Young King, a man moreover who had the vital attribute of being on the side God and the Fates seemed to favour: Louis, son of the successful Philip Augustus. It was time to call in the power of France to redress the imbalance caused by the Pope and to bring the victorious ethos of Bouvines to bear on the detested John.

5. John's Campaigns 1215–16

19

THE GLOVES WERE OFF, the veils ripped asunder and at last the two sides stood forth in all their nakedness. All pretence of peace and goodwill could be laid aside. For ten weeks John had scarcely been able to contain himself. While in public he maintained an equable statesmanlike demeanour, in private he seethed and raged with fury and frustration: he 'gnashed his teeth, rolled his eyes, caught up sticks and straws and gnawed them like a madman, or tore them into shreds with his fingers' – the circumstantial details inevitably recall Henry II in one of his tantrums.[1] The papal endorsement had been the necessary condition for his breakout into total war against the barons; the sufficient conditions would now be supplied by mercenaries from Europe. This was what Roger of Wendover meant when he commented: 'After much reflection, he (John) chose, like the Apostle Peter, to seek vengeance upon his enemies by means of two swords, that is, by a spiritual sword and a material one, so that if he could not triumph by the one, he might safely count upon doing so by the other.'[2] In Flanders his man Hugh de Boves was actively recruiting troops, while the chancellor, Richard Marsh, was doing the same in Aquitaine. John went so far as to try to draw Britanny once more into his web, writing on 12 August to Count Peter of Britanny with an offer of 'the honour of Richmond' if he would come with a goodly company of knights to levy war on the English rebels.[3] When one realises that John's sole official reason for not attending the Oxford conference three days later was that he was 'cast down' by the treatment he had received so far, the extent of the king's duplicity really needs no further comment.

After the first abortive conference at Oxford in mid-July, John withdrew into Wiltshire and from there made his way into his beloved Dorset. He placed his queen and eldest son in Corfe Castle for safety then proceeded to Wareham and then overland to Southampton, intending to proceed along the south coast by sea and land in the rear of the rebels at Dover, to which point he had summoned all his putative continental allies for a grand muster on Michaelmas Day. As was the custom in those sea-fearing days, he put in at as many ports as he could overnight and it was at Portsmouth on 24 August that the bishops acting as go-between met him, bringing a 'last chance' offer of peace from the barons.[4] John indignantly refused it but sent the bishops back to a meeting with the barons at Staines on 26 August, where the king's remonstrance was read out, declaring that 'it was not his fault if the peace was not carried out according to the Charter'. The barons had meanwhile got hold of the first papal letters (not the later one condemning Magna Carta) and claimed that the general condemnation of 'disturbers of the king and kingdom' applied to John. Although they did not use such terminology, they claimed in effect that a schizoid king could well be his own worst disturber, and therefore that the papal condemnation could as well apply to John as to themselves.[5] This was clearly disingenuous, but the rebels were in a quandary of their own making. By accepting the Pope as over-lord of England in 1214, and even claiming that this surprise outcome was their own doing, they had cut the ground from under their own feet. Their acceptance of the Pope meant that in feudal law clause 61 of Magna Carta, disallowing any appeal to the Vatican, was itself null and void. While the barons thus split hairs, John landed at Sandwich on 28 August, taking the enemy by surprise. With the taste for rationalisation that seemed to increase daily, the rebels then claimed that John had been trying to quit the kingdom and escape abroad but that foul weather had driven him ashore.[6] Yet by early September John was ensconced at Dover Castle and beginning to collect around him the nucleus of a foreign army. The rebel magnates had been overconfident, and John had success-fully used the element of surprise against them.[7]

The initiative soon switched back to the barons after John's hopes received a severe check from a disaster at sea. Hugh de Boves, a skilled organiser, was returning from Flanders with a picked force of mer-cenaries when his transports were overwhelmed by high seas in the Channel; among the hundreds of drowned was Hugh himself, and it was said that the coasts of Suffolk were littered with bleached bones for months thereafter as more and more dead bodies were washed ashore.[8] The rebels decided to take advantage of John's predicament by advancing on Rochester, to bar the king's route to London. Something of an *opéra bouffe* ensued, with John advancing to Canterbury, the rebels to Ospring, then both sides retreating, the king to Dover, the rebels to Rochester. Reginald of Cornhill, the castellan acting on Stephen Langton's behalf as official keeper of Rochester Castle, made no pretence of his master's official neutrality and at once opened the gates to the 'Army of God', triggering yet another paroxysm of rage and fury in John, who had long coveted this stronghold.[9] Such was his anger that he decided on instant retaliation, despite his small numbers. His routier captains remonstrated with him, but John brushed their objection aside. 'In truth, sire,' said one of the mercenary leaders, 'you hold your enemies of little account if you go to fight them with such a tiny force.' 'I know them well enough,' said John. 'They are not to be feared or made much of. We could safely fight them with fewer men than we have.'[10] John knew his opponents well enough. The boastful Robert Fitzwalter, who had proved his cowardly mettle in many a fray from which he had fled, ran true to type. After making a mess of intercepting the royal mercenaries when they broke down the bridge over the Medway, he thought better of facing John and retreated to London, leaving a garrison in Rochester Castle.[11] This inexplicable action can only be partially palliated by the argument that the barons were expecting massive reinforcements from France; it was an error of egregious proportions. With the Medway bridge destroyed, there was no obvious way the garrison at Rochester could be reinforced from London.

John's assault on Rochester town was something of a walkover. The Brabantines and Flemings routed the citizen levy with contemptuous ease, and the panic-stricken rabble raced for the Medway bridge only to find it gone; with undisguised relish the mercenaries described how they cut down men 'many of whom would gladly have fled to London if they could'.[12] The citadel, naturally, was a different proposition. In command in Rochester Castle was William of Aubigny, lord of Belvoir, by repute one of the ablest of the rebel commanders. He had at his side ninety-five knights and forty-five men-at-arms but they were desperately short of provisions. John saw the chance for a knockout victory that would demoralise the barons in London. He ordered all the blacksmiths in Canterbury to work day and night making pickaxes, and meanwhile staged a deliberate campaign of terror to weaken the resolve of the defenders, burning, looting and marauding in the town in full view of the garrison, deliberately showing contempt for the 'Army of God' by acts of overt blasphemy and sacrilege, such as stabling their horses in the cathedral.[13] The barons in London seemed paralysed by John's energy. Although Fitzwalter had promised William of Aubigny that they would return at once if the king was bold enough to besiege them, for two weeks they sat in London, biting their nails in indecision, dithering and prevaricating.

At last, on 26 October Fitzwalter set out with 700 knights but got only as far as Dartford before unaccountably turning back. Clearly Fitzwalter's cowardice was at the root of this: he was said to have panicked when he heard that John had been reinforced from the continent and now possessed a formidable host.[14] Roger of Wendover's contempt for the barons was palpable: he portrays them as staggering drunkenly from stews to gaming table while their comrades faced John's fury at Rochester. Once again they rationalised their folly, telling each other that huge re-inforcements were expected by the end of November, and the Rochester garrison could easily hold out until then.[15]

The Rochester garrison was actually in a desperate plight from the very first day of John's siege, and it says much for the calibre and valour of William of Aubigny that he held out so long. John threw everything at the citadel and exhausted his store of military knowledge. 'Living memory does not recall a siege so fiercely pressed or so staunchly resisted', said the most reliable annalist of the time.[16] John tried mining, sapping, direct assault and finally assault by siege engines; five trebuchets pounded the castle day and night. The defenders were convinced they could expect no mercy from John so fought like tigers. According to Roger of Wendover, John finally defeated Aubigny in a singular way: on 25 November he ordered his new justiciar to send him with all speed 'forty bacon pigs of the fattest, and of those which are least good for eating, to be put to set fire to the stuff that we have got together under the tower'.[17] A tunnel was dug, shored up by timbers and filled with all manner of combustibles; then the fat of the forty pigs was used as a kind of porcine Greek Fire. The resulting conflagration finally brought the corner towers of the keep crashing down. But even in the burning ruins of the gutted keep the defenders fought on like madmen, contesting every foot. At last, when human courage could do no more, they surren-dered, on 30 November, St Andrew's Day.[18] Their worst fears seemed about to be realised when John erected a gallows and announced he would hang every last man. But Savaric de Mauléon, no humanitarian, protested and pointed out to John that if men as brave as these were hanged, not only would the barons retaliate, involving both sides in a savage 'no prisoners' war (which the Pope would hardly sanction), but they would score a huge propaganda advantage, as John would seem to have proved that he was a vicious tyrant, just as his enemies alleged. John took the force of the argument, and contented himself with hanging a single crossbowman who had deserted from his household service. He imprisoned the wealthy knights until ransoms could be paid for their release, leaving the men-at-arms to languish in jail against the unlikely event of their raising a ransom.[19] John's success at Rochester caused a great éclat. The myth of the impregnable castle had taken a hammering, and from now on no rebel would feel safe in a keep or citadel.

The barons' performance so far had been remarkably lacklustre: they lacked energy, ideas or even a common strategy, with half-hearted sieges of Northampton and Oxford Castles going on when they should have been relieving Rochester.[20] Meanwhile they had virtually advertised their weakness by putting out equally half-hearted peace feelers to John throughout November and December.[21] They also concentrated on setting up administrations in the east and north of the country, controlled by their partisans, and seeking ways and means to implement clause 61 of Magna Carta, instead of making an all-out effort to defeat John. The consequence was that, by drawing in mercenaries from the continent, the king grew gradually stronger and the rebels weaker; in particular, he retained control of some 150 castles throughout the kingdom which, lacking siege artillery, the barons were unable even to put a dent in.[22] As Christmas 1215 approached, the one advantage they enjoyed was that the Celtic fringes, which John had thought definitively subdued, once more rose in rebellion. Preoccupied as he was with the Charter in summer 1215, John was also forced to spend a great deal of time on Irish affairs; from May to July the Close and Charter Rolls are full of letters and writs relating to Ireland.[23] Although William Marshal and the Irish barons gave John unstinting support, the native Irish became the first exponents of what would become a seven-hundred-year-old truism: England's danger is Ireland's opportunity. Seeing John caught up in civil war, the Gaelic chieftains struck hard. Aed Ua Neill defeated an English army in Ulster, destroyed Clones Castle and gutted the port of Carlingford in County Louth. Cormac Ua Mail Sechnail attacked the castles of Kinclare in Westmeath, Athboy in Meath and Birr in Offaly.[24] So concerned did John become about the state of affairs in Ireland that he persuaded his papal ally to enter the fray. In February 1216 Innocent III wrote to his legate in Ireland to tell him to put down all conspiracies against John in Ireland and to punish all clerics who communicated with the English barons and other excommunicated persons.[25] Meanwhile the whole of Wales blazed into rebellion: the unprecedented situation arose whereby not only were all the Welsh princes in alliance with each other but also with the English barons. Llewellyn was on the warpath again and captured the town and castle of Shrewsbury in May 1215 (the fall of this town to the Welsh was also unprecedented); all the evidence suggests this move was concerted with the barons' seizure of London.[26] Alexander II of Scotland was also in the field, threatening Carlisle and euphoric at the award to him by a baronial court of the long-coveted lands of Cumberland, Westmorland and Northumberland.[27]

Yet the Celtic fringes could act only as gadflies on John's flank. To overthrow him the barons needed intervention from France, and they hit on the idea of trying to substantiate a claim to the English throne from Louis, son of Philip Augustus. The lack of a pretender to John's crown was a perceived weakness in the barons' revolt and they had earlier tried to plug the gap by putting forward the claims of Simon de Montfort, titular earl of Leicester. Whether the notorious cruelties and atrocities visited by de Montfort on the Albigensians – as part of Innocent III's crusade against these harmless heretics – persuaded the barons that he would prove a more tyrannical king than John ever was, or whether it was simply that the extremists in the baronial party found him unacceptable, by late summer this idea was definitively abandoned. Geoffrey de Mandeville headed a faction that besought Prince Louis to cross the Channel and save them from 'this tyrant'.[28] What the basis for Louis's claim was supposed to be in terms of succession or feudal law is unclear. The pragmatic reason for the choice was to strip John of his foreign mercenaries, since most of the routiers were subjects of Louis (he had inherited the county of Artois from his mother), Philip Augustus or their allies.[29] The barons' ploy was utterly cynical: they had no intention of ceding the English crown to Louis's heirs, and simply wanted to have him as a temporary ruler to unseat John, after which they would make up their own minds on whether they wanted a permanent arrangement. John had spotted the likelihood of a baronial overture to France and, incredibly, tried to get in first. Not surprisingly, Philip Augustus treated his absurd overtures with contempt.[30] The barons began negotiating with France as early as September 1215, once it was clear Magna Carta was not going to hold. The only energetic response they made to the siege of Rochester was to send the earls of Winchester and Hereford to France with an explicit offer of the Crown to Louis.[31]

The mercurial Louis was keen, but his father was more cautious. The arrival of the earls in Paris was soured by a ludicrous scene when Philip Augustus presented them with a declaration, purporting to come from the barons' leaders, stating that French help was no longer needed since a lasting peace had been signed between king and magnates. The earls were able to convince the French king that this was a crude forgery put out by John to obfuscate and diminish the credibility of the barons,[32] but Philip remained suspicious on other fronts. Were the rebels serious in their offer or merely desperate because the fortunes of war had started to favour John? What guarantees were the barons offering his son and his heirs? How could the French be sure that this was not some cynical ad hoc offer, which would be withdrawn once John was defeated?[33] His own position was difficult. Having suffered under the papal lash because of his adulterous marriage, he had no wish to enter into conflict with Innocent III again, and it seemed as though Innocent was backing John to the hilt over this baronial rebellion. Philip Augustus therefore decided on a 'wait and see' policy. He handed the entire matter over to his son, saying that he must act as he thought fit. Louis at once earmarked a 'small' force of Frenchmen to embark for England, and promised that he himself would follow with a much larger force at Easter 1216. The immediate expedition was not quite so exiguous as Louis pretended: altogether it was 7,000 strong, including 140 knights. The Frenchmen landed in the Orwell estuary and proceeded to London, where they proved to be as lacking in energy as the barons. They did not venture out of the capital all winter and made free in the fleshpots, inconvenienced only by having to drink beer when their wine ran out, as one of John's mercenary captains scornfully reported.[34]

John was meanwhile as restless as his enemies were supine. Enormously elated by the news that the castles of Tonbridge and Bedford had surrendered to his mercenary captains – in both places it was Rochester all over again, with pleas for relief being sent out to the barons by the garrison but ignored[35] – he decided to emulate William the Conqueror's strategy after Hastings in 1066, marching all round London and trying to close the ring on it. He left Rochester on 6 December, marched through Essex and Surrey into Hampshire and completed the circle by proceeding to Windsor and then east to St Albans. It was in St Albans, at a council of war on 20 December, that he decided on his winter strategy. His army would be divided, and one detachment, under the troika of the earl of Salisbury, Fawkes de Bréauté and Savaric de Mauléon, would pen the rebels up in London; with the other detachment he himself would march north and reconquer the rebel-held territory there.[36] This was typical of John's tendency to go for the softer option. A Richard or even a Philip Augustus would have concentrated all their attention on London, for this was the principal head of the hydra-like rebellion. Admittedly, a siege of London would have been difficult, protracted and costly, and maybe that was the key to John's dilemma, for if he ran short of funds to pay his mercenaries, it would be his army, not the barons', that collapsed.

The chaos in England meant that he had been living largely on the stored wealth of past taxation, nothing more was coming in, and the reservoir was beginning to run dry. A 'harrying of the north' expedition like William the Conqueror's notorious expedition in 1067, a pure campaign of looting and plunder, in other words, would keep his routiers happy and allow him to replenish his war chest. On the best-case scenario, he would be able to restore royal administration everywhere except London, start the taxes flowing, and at the same time depress and demoralise the enemy.[37] All the same, he should have gone for the jugular and attacked London. John was neither the first nor the last to discover that in warfare peripheral strategies rarely work.

John's march north was a chapter of atrocities – rape, arson, murder, pillage – even worse than William the Conqueror's harrying of the north – 'scenes of atrocity such as events in the reign of Stephen alone in English history afford a parallel'.[38] John added war crimes and crimes against humanity to his tally of depravity as his army marched to Nottingham. The track of his army ran through Dunstable, Northampton and Rockingham and a trail of wanton destruction marked its path. Everything was killed, destroyed or put to the torch: humans, cattle, sheep, poultry, buildings. Such was John's lust for slaughter and mayhem that even when his men were exhausted by the day's burning, looting and raping, he sent out parties at night to fire all the hedges and villages within a ten-mile radius. Scorched-earth tactics hardly does justice to a mindless insistence that his army march along roads where every single thing should be uprooted, burnt and charred; he told his intimates that his heart leapt like a fawn when he saw the visible evidence of his revenge on enemies in the form of smoking stumps and gutted houses. All human beings his troops encountered were butchered or raped unless they were rich enough to pay massive ransoms.[39] The reign of terror paid off. Rebel castellans lost their nerve and bolted rather than face such a horde of ravening dervishes. He spent Christmas at Nottingham, in the understated words of one chronicler, 'not in the usual manner but as one on the warpath'.[40] Rather than spreading yuletide peace and goodwill, John seemed determined that his men should live out the meaning of Tacitus's description of the Romans: 'they created a wilderness and called it peace'. On the feast of St Stephen (26 December) John evinced the Christmas spirit by serving notice on the garrison of William of Aubigny's castle at Belvoir that if they did not surrender at once, their lord would be taken and starved to death. The garrison knew the king meant business and duly surrendered.[41]

The whirlwind of terror and destruction continued north, through Newark, Doncaster, Pontefract, York, Northallerton, Durham and Newcastle. Only occasionally did John rein in his brutal mercenaries, as when he cut off the hand of a man who had seized a cow in the churchyard – it was not the cow he was concerned with but possible ecclesiastical, and papal, repercussions.[42] The Church aside, only huge payments in the form of taxes or ransoms could ward off the Flemings and Brabantines posing as the wrath of God. The towns of York and Beverley bought John off for £1,000 and the holders of large houses had to pay anything between 80–150 marks for the privilege of not having their manors burned down around their ears. Minor knights could usually buy freedom from atrocity for anything between ten and a hundred marks, provided they threw in a couple of palfreys as a sweetener.[43] As he neared Newcastle, John focused on Alexander of Scotland, who had tried to set his seal on the baronial grant of Northumberland by a vain siege of Norham Castle. John determined to punish him and told his followers: 'By God's teeth we shall run the little sandy fox-cub to his earth.' An alternative, and perhaps more plausible version is that he vowed 'to run the red fox out of his lairs'.[44] January 1216 saw the first invasion of Scotland since 1072 and the first by an English army since 1097. On the 11th of the month John reached Alnwick, then took and burned Berwick on the 15th, making sure that his routiers tortured the inhabitants before butchering them. The madness of King John was surely proven by his insistence on personally setting a torch to the house in which he lodged overnight.[45] He then took and burned Roxburgh, Dunbar and Haddington, but he dared not stay more than ten days in Scotland because of the reports of fresh dangers in England, so turned back before reaching Edinburgh. The dauntless Alexander thereupon reinvaded England in February and laid siege (unsuccessfully) to Carlisle.[46]

At the end of January John turned south again, cutting a swathe of destruction through a different stretch of countryside. The journey south followed the same pattern of rapine, fire, atrocity, scorched earth, cruelty and barbarism. A rapid march took him through Newcastle and Durham to Barnard Castle by 30 January, after which he swung east to the North Sea and, passing through Skelton, paused to catch breath at Scarborough (12–14 February). He then swung west to York, south to Pontefract and east again in a loop to reach Lincoln, where there was an extended, four-day stopover (23–27 February). Having chastised the north, it was now his intention to ravage that other heartland of the rebels, in East Anglia and Essex. He was at Fotheringhay at the end of February, and from there launched his locusts on Norfolk and Suffolk.[47] A vanguard went ahead while John had another pause at Bedford (29 February – 3 March). After rampaging and ravishing through Bury St Edmunds, his hordes came to rest outside the castle of Roger of Bigod at Framlingham, which collapsed before him as all the other rebel strongholds had done.[48] Swinging down through Ipswich, he laid siege to Colchester on 4 March. Although the garrison here had been stiffened by some of the French troops who had finally levered themselves out of the stews and gambling dens of London, it proved no more capable than other defenders; surrender was immediately agreed on condition the French troops were allowed to march out free, leaving their English comrades to languish in prison until ransomed. When the French reached London, their alleged perfidy in agreeing to such self-satisfying terms caused a sensation. The barons called them traitor, arrested them and even contemplated a mass execution, until someone pointed out that that was a sure way to deter Louis and Philip Augustus from coming to England. It was decided to hold them to await Philip's pleasure.[49]

On 25 March John proceeded to Hedingham, seat of Robert de Vere, earl of Oxford. This too surrendered and de Vere, an important rebel leader, came to beg the king's mercy and renew his oath of fealty. His submission was a clear sign that the barons were losing heart. Soon other important magnates were joining the queue to make submission. The earl of Clare and his son were the next in a series of defections from the rebel ranks, and very shortly members of the inner circle like Robert de Ros, Peter de Bruis and the egregious Eustace de Vesci were trying to discover what terms they could make.[50] A string of safe-conducts signed by the king showed how clearly the rebels had been cowed by John's lightning campaign of terror. The Gadarene rush of one-time fire-eaters to compose their peace with John threatened to become a mass panic. John played his hand cleverly. Those who returned to their allegiance found that it was a simple matter to regain their confiscated lands. Indeed, by March the claims for recovery of expropriated manors were so numerous that the Chancery devised a common-form writ to deal with them.[51] The process was accelerated because John's southern detachment had not been idle while the king was harrying the north, but had overrun the whole of Essex, Cambridgeshire, Huntingdonshire, Hertfordshire and even Middlesex, confining the barons even more closely in London.[52] John had every reason to feel complacent about what he had achieved through war crimes. He was now amply supplied with money, more than enough to keep his brutal mercenaries happy, and, just to make sure there was no temptation to desert, he topped up their pay and perquisites with further lavish bonuses. Next John announced that his victorious army would march on London.[53] But he had tarried too long in the north. Facing mortal peril, the barons had at last secured the massive reinforcements from France they had been hoping for.

The previous arrival of 7,000 French troops ought to have been the fillip the barons needed to galvanise them into decisive action, but a weary defeatism and lassitude seems to have overcome them during the winter of 1215–16, to the point where they convinced themselves that only the appearance of Philip Augustus or his son in England would suffice to overthrow John. Around Christmas there was another embassy to France, this time headed by the two top-ranking magnates, Saer de Quincy and Robert Fitzwalter. The duo entreated Louis to come at once to England to be crowned but did not explain how that could be done when Stephen Langton was still in Rome – even if he could be persuaded openly to defy Innocent III in this matter. Philip Augustus cut through the nonsense by asking for further security – more particularly twenty-four hostages for the barons' good faith.[54] So desperate were the rebels for French help that they agreed, and the hostages were conveyed to Paris by two further baronial envoys, the earls of Hereford and Gloucester. Evidently Philip Augustus and Louis then asked for action from the barons before making the crossing, and to encourage them dispatched another large force of infantry and crossbowmen headed by three hundred knights. This second expedition sailed up the Thames and joined their compatriots in London on or around 7 January 1216; Louis meanwhile took an oath that he would follow with a third force in about two weeks' time.[55] He was, however, reliable only in his unreliability. Although a third body of troops reached London from France at the end of February, Louis was not with them, only a letter from him claiming that he would be ready 'with God's grace' to cross from Calais on Easter Sunday, 10 April.[56]

The unconscionable delays to Louis's crossing seem to have been caused mainly by Philip Augustus's apprehension about the Pope's likely reaction and the need to find an argument that would justify French intervention. Certainly Innocent's support for John seemed stronger than ever. On 4 November 1215 he had reiterated the suspension of Stephen Langton and on 16 December, fresh from his triumphs at the Fourth Lateran Council, returned to the ideological fray in England by confirming his excommunication of the barons, this time explicitly naming thirty-one ringleaders.[57] He also placed the city of London under interdict and sent two commissioners to execute the mandate; they arrived in England at the end of February 1216. They soon managed to promulgate Innocent's decrees everywhere in the realm except London. There the clergy, barons and people were at one in vehemently rejecting it, both on the grounds that Innocent had been gulled by mendacious disinformation and that the internal politics of England were no affair of his anyway.[58] Although the barons' stance was disingenuous – a year earlier they had boasted about how they had made John submit to the Pope and explicitly recognised the pontiff as the temporal ruler of England – there is no doubt that Innocent's intervention was counterproductive; paradoxically it raised morale in London and stiffened the resolve of the rebels. John soon had an unpleasant taste of the new spirit. Having emulated William the Conqueror in so many ways recently, he decided to ape Harold Godwinson also, by sleeping at Harold's beloved sanctuary at Waltham Abbey, little more than twenty miles from London. This was open provocation, and when Savaric de Mauléon ventured even closer to London with the intention of blockading the Thames, he and his comrades were badly mauled and made their escape only after heavy losses.[59] As so often after a reverse, John retired to the West Country to lick his wounds, swinging in a great arc through Enfield, Berkhamstead and Windsor before coming to rest in Hampshire (early April 1216).

Everything now hinged on French policy. John was very much alive to this dimension and sent a further embassy to Philip Augustus headed by William Marshal asking the king to forbid his son's proposed expedition, stressing his friendliness and the fact that he was still issuing safe-conducts to French merchants. There was something frenzied and desperate about John's diplomacy at this juncture, for he even sent a personal letter to Prince Louis, promising to put right any hurt, injury or insult he had inadvertently done him. He also rather foolishly tried to appeal above Philip Augustus's head to the guardians of the truce he had signed with Philip, asking for their good offices.[60] But it was all in vain, for Philip Augustus had by now decided to give his son the go-ahead, and all that remained was the task of ideological rationalisation. At a grand council of the French barons at Melun in April, Philip Augustus secured their approval for a descent on England; thereafter they bent their collective minds to a justification of the project. This was the very moment when the new papal legate to England, bearing important letters from Innocent, arrived at Melun on his way from Rome to the Channel.[61] On 25 April Cardinal Guala Bicchieri met Philip Augustus and presented him with Innocent's epistles, requiring him to forbid his son to invade England, to change his entire policy and to protect and assist John as a vassal of Holy Mother Church. The French king gave the request short shrift. In a published letter, he made the following trenchant points: the realm of England never was, was not now and never would be, St Peter's patrimony; John on the other hand was guilty of treason against his brother Richard and had been condemned for it by Richard's court, and for this reason, as much as by his foul murder of Arthur, the true heir to the throne, he had forfeited all his kingly claims. This declaration, when read out in the full conclave, was rousingly cheered by the French barons.[62]

Next day there was a second meeting. Philip Augustus swept in, ignoring Guala, and Louis then entered, openly scowling at the legate. The cardinal formally requested Louis not to go to England and begged his father to forbid him. Philip then invited Louis to speak. One of his knights, acting as his advocate, rose to his feet and presented the prince's case. This was simply that John was no true king, being both the murderer of Arthur and a ruler who had been repudiated by his barons. As for the Pope's alleged role as temporal ruler of England, this was a unilateral action by John, done without the consent of his barons and thus against all precedent and the norms of England's ancient constitution. John's unconstitutional actions amounted in law to de facto resignation, which meant the English throne was vacant; and now finally the English barons had invited Louis to be king, as was their right, his title being established by his wife Blanche, granddaughter of Henry II, whose mother, the queen of Castile, was the sole survivor of the English king's siblings.[63] Moreover, there was no point in Guala's asking Philip Augustus to forbid him to pursue this claim, for Philip was liege lord in France, but Louis's wife's rights in England were outside his jurisdiction. This ingenious and specious case was no more than casuistry, and one of John's defenders rightly calls it 'a barrage of fictions and half-truths'.[64] Nonetheless, the flustered cardinal, obviously no expert in the finer dialectics of feudal law, was unable to refute it on the spot. He evaded this issue by switching the argument to the other issue of crusade, pointing out that John should be left unmolested until he had fulfilled his crusader's vow. Louis's advocate replied that the war between John and Louis predated John's bogus 'taking of the Cross', so that consideration was irrelevant.

Guala's inability to rebut John's counsel convinced any wavering French barons that the Pope really had no case. Unable to make any headway, Guala finally lost patience and threatened excommunication to both Philip and Louis if they went ahead with the English expedition.[65] Louis then asked his father if he had any just cause for impeding the prosecution of his rightful claim. Philip made no answer, indicating that he had no objection. Guala, convinced that further argument was useless, simply bowed his head and asked the king for a safe-conduct to England. Philip replied contemptuously: 'I will gladly give you a safe-conduct through my realm, but if you fall into the hands of my soldiers who are guarding the coast, don't blame me if you come to harm.'[66] At this obvious threat Guala finally lost his temper and stormed out. Louis then sent envoys to Rome to prolong the farce, presenting a case to the Pope they knew would fail but thereby playing for time. Surprisingly, some scholars still believe that Philip and Louis were not colluding. One biographer of Philip Augustus says that when Louis told his father he had no jurisdiction over England, 'this sounds more like a petulant son than one in conspiracy with his father'.[67] Others think that, while Philip wanted to defeat John, he had genuine reservations both about Louis's venture and the wisdom of alienating the Pope.[68] Much controversy has centred on the actions of the countess of Champagne and her son who, when asked to contribute to the costs of the expedition, flatly refused to do so, on the grounds that they could not fight against a king recognised as a crusader by the Pope. The upshot was that a group of French knights then forced her to contribute. Philip Augustus's supporters say this kind of duress was not typical behaviour by the king and that the ruffianly Louis alone was responsible.[69] But surely it is obvious that Philip Augustus and his son were engaged in an elaborate charade, a 'dumb show'; Philip could claim, within the letter if not the spirit of things, that he had not explicitly authorised his son to invade England.

John must have been well informed by his spies of what was afoot, for on 14 April he ordered twenty-one coast towns to send all shipping to the Thames estuary to prevent a French landing. On 17 April he issued his 'last chance' proclamation, calling on all rebels to submit by 24 May (one month after Easter) or forfeit their lands and possessions forever.[70] Forced marches took him from Hampshire to Windsor and thence through Surrey to Rochester and Dover, where he arrived on 25 April. For three weeks he ranged up and down the coast of Kent, awaiting the arrival of the French and Guala. Dover was ordained as a grand mustering point for all shipping, to be fetched from as far away as Yarmouth and Lynn (King's Lynn). At this stage John entertained a grand design of setting sail with the assembled flotilla and blockading Louis in Calais, where he was assembling a mighty armada to be piloted across the Channel and into the Thames estuary by a notorious pirate called Eustace the Monk.[71] But from the evening of 18 May a ferocious gale howled in the Channel. Giant waves smashed into John's armada at Dover, engulfing, overwhelming, smashing and shattering his ships. It was a critical blip in the weather on which so much hinged, for at the first sign of calmer seas Louis cleared from Calais (on the evening of the 20th). Next morning the watchers on the shore at Thanet saw his ships in the distance and notified John. The king himself then looked on gloomily as the French passed the mouth of Pegwell Bay in safety. He gave the order to march, trumpets sounded, and his soldiers formed up ready but the final order never came.[72] As with so many of John's actions, this one remains mysterious. Perhaps he was, to use a modernism, 'in denial' – an inference strengthened by his initial pretence that the sighted ships were some of his own storm-tossed vessels. Perhaps he was distracted because a messenger had brought him word that Guala had just landed at Romney. Three more rational motives have been suggested: that William Marshal advised him against offering battle; that the mercenaries were unreliable both because their pay was in arrears and because many of them were Louis's subjects; and that a foreign invasion was certain to swing Englishmen over to his side long-term. But the most likely explanation is that, when faced with an imminent and decisive encounter, John as commander always ducked the issue. He had turned aside from London in December 1215 and he turned aside from a trial of strength with Louis now.[73] He performed his old trick of simply riding away in silence when he was deeply frustrated and was three miles down the road from Sandwich to Dover before most of his men knew he had gone. Leaving Dover under Hubert de Burgh, well fortified and provisioned, he sped through Sussex to Winchester where, at a safe distance, he awaited the drift of events.[74]

John derived what comfort he could from the presence of Cardinal Guala, who at the very first meeting with the English king at once pronounced Louis excommunicate and rode, resplendent in scarlet robes on a white palfrey, at the king's side to Canterbury. Guala explained his mission to John. Innocent had given him extraordinarily wide-ranging powers as legate, and he was specifically charged to fill the void at the highest level of the hierarchy left by Langton's suspension; as far as John was concerned, the legate was to give him every assistance so as to put down the rebellion and speed him on his way to the crusade.[75] On 29 May, at Winchester Guala passed formal sentence of excommunication against Louis and his followers, and in the months to come would extend the same anathema to the Scots and Welsh rebels.[76] But Guala's bell, book and candle methods were something in the nature of a papal bull against a comet, for Louis and the barons treated the papal interdict with the same contempt, openly expressed, that John felt for religion and all its works in his secret heart. In the context of the ferocious civil war in England in 1216, 'how many divisions has the Pope?' had a compelling resonance, especially since Louis's arrival electrified the waverers and won new converts to the barons' cause. Many who had only just beaten John's May deadline for surrender immediately apostasised at news of the latest development for, they reasoned, how could this deeply unpopular king prevail against the combined might of France and his own barons? Many others who had remained neutral and sat on the fence for fear of the consequences now thought they saw clearly which way the wind was blowing and jumped on Louis's bandwagon. Among the host of defections from John's camp were Hugh Neville and Warin Fitzgerald, hitherto considered solid king's men, and the earls of Arundel, Surrey and York. The most shattering blow to John's cause was the apostasy of his half-brother William of Salisbury, one of his most trusted commanders.[77]

At first Louis swept all before him. From the moment of his landing at Stonor, he seemed a veritable dynamo. He began by issuing a manifesto to the English Church expressing the utmost contempt for Guala, whom he described as a venal cleric bought by John's gold. He promised religious toleration and special consideration for the secular clergy, always provided they accepted the legitimacy of his claim to the throne, which he now reiterated without any of the frills and obfuscations used at Melun. He had the early satisfaction, on marching for Canterbury, of turning the detested Guala out of his lodgings helter-skelter; the legate hastened after John to Winchester.[78] Louis proceeded to Rochester, which capitulated within a week; observers were not slow to remark that this supposedly mighty fortress had taken John two months to crack but now it had fallen to a doughtier warrior. On 2 June Louis entered London, to the acclamation of the people, there to receive the homage of barons and citizens and the awed deference of the clergy. He took a solemn oath on the Gospels that he would restore the golden age of just laws and the ancient English constitution, and called on all magnates who had not yet paid homage to do so rapidly, or leave the country – or face the obvious consequences.[79] After just four days in the capital, Louis took his army on the hunt for John – the prince may have been reckless but he did not believe in shirking battles. But John had quit Winchester the day before, on 5 June, leaving Savaric de Mauléon to conduct the defence. Louis's rapid sweep through Surrey was something of a walkover: the castles of Reigate, Guildford and Farnham surrendered in quick succession so that the French were in sight of Winchester by the morning of 14 June. Savaric de Mauléon did not stay to try conclusions but withdrew, not before setting fire to the suburbs – whether on his own initiative or in obedience to John is unclear. The blaze quickly got out of hand and had gutted most of Winchester by the time the French marched in, but Savaric had left a strong garrison in the chief keep at the west end of the city, which held out for ten grim days in face of Louis's siege engines, until Savaric returned with permission from John for the defenders to surrender.[80]

John seemed to be in headlong retreat and the French unstoppable but now, once more, the weathercock of war in this ever-oscillating conflict turned round again to give the English king respite. Louis's problems were twofold: he proved inept at siegecraft and he had no real idea how to scotch the growing Anglo-French conflict within his own army. The siege of Odiham was a case in point. From Winchester Louis quickly 'ate up' the garrison at Porchester, but at Odiham a tiny garrison – no more than three knights and ten men-at-arms – held him at bay for a week. Although the gallant defenders were then allowed to march out with full honours, Louis's ineptitude at pressing the siege did not inspire confidence.[81] Meanwhile his army was riven with jealousies and rivalries as French and English notables vied with one another for the same places, positions and prizes. William Marshal junior, the apostate son of the earl of Pembroke, claimed the right to be marshal of Louis's army – a position that really should have gone to Adam de Beaumont, his chief French captain; so as not to alienate the English Louis was obliged to give Marshal what he wanted. Not satisfied with this signal honour, the greedy young William Marshal threw a sulk when he further claimed the castle of Marlborough but was turned down by Louis in favour of his own cousin Robert of Dreux. By not alienating the barons and giving them most of what they wanted, Louis managed to disillusion his own compatriots, who began to drift away back to the continent in dribs and drabs, convinced that the English campaign was a waste of French blood and treasure from which only the English barons would benefit.[82]

While Louis was thus engaged, the barons in London, now much more confident, sortied into Essex and East Anglia and visited on these areas some of the same rapine and destruction they had recently suffered at the hands of John.[83] Another party ventured into the East Midlands to pen John's men up more closely in the seemingly impregnable castles of Nottingham and Newark. Gilbert de Gant and Robert de Ropesley, leaders of this expedition, did not achieve as much as was expected from them, managing to sack Lincoln city but without taking the citadel.[84] A third detachment, under Robert de Ros, Peter de Brus and Richard de Percy, were more successful in Yorkshire, and meanwhile Alexander of Scotland opened the siege of Carlisle and sent marauding forces into Northumberland and Durham.[85] By mid-July Louis had a spotty control of England from the Channel to the Cheviots, but worryingly many major centres still held out for John. Most of the royal castles remained inviolate, and at least four of John's lieutenants had humiliated their besiegers in one way or another: Engelard de Cicogne in Windsor Castle, Hubert de Burgh in Dover, Philip Oldcoates in Durham and Hugh Balliol in Barnard Castle.[86] The burghers of the Cinque Ports had taken an oath to Louis but were in the field against him, causing particular damage by their harrying of French shipping. There was even a band of guerrillas operating in Sussex and Kent against the French under a leader code-named Willikin of the Weald (William of Kensham).[87] William Marshal senior and Ranulph of Chester had the West Midlands in a secure royalist grip. John, typically, for ever hankering after the near West Country, spent most of June and July roaming the hunting lodges of Wiltshire and Dorset. He seems to have settled in for a war of attrition, holding out olive branches to Louis while he tried to suborn his supporters and detach the rebel barons by lavish promises – usually total amnesty and full restoration of lost estates.[88]

Trying to second-guess Louis's strategy, John concluded that the French prince's next step must logically be an offensive against the West Midlands. He therefore began to advance northwards towards the end of July, moving from Sherborne (Dorset) to Bristol, Berkeley, Gloucester, Tewkesbury, Hereford and Leominster. Ever restless, ever the optimist, ever the pursuer of the chimera, he put out feelers for an alliance with the Welsh princes, but there were no takers. The peripatetic existence continued in August: Radnor (Wales), Clun, Shrewsbury, Whitchurch, Bridgnorth, Worcester, Gloucester.[89] But still the expected French attack did not come. Unknown to John, Louis had decided that he must take Dover to regain his credibility so had shifted the theatre of operations east, not west. There were strong rumours that Philip Augustus had sent over a message taunting his son with being a strategic ignoramus: he was trying to unlock England without using the key (Dover).[90] Louis decided on an all-out assault on John's two vital strongholds at Dover and Windsor, reasoning that the blow to the king's prestige if these two fell would have a multiplier effect. While he himself directed operations at Dover, he sent the counts of Dreux and Nevers, with some of the leading barons, to deal with Cigogne at Windsor. They proved spectacularly incompetent and still had nothing to show after two months of invest-ment.[91] Louis did not fare much better at Dover, to the point where desertion rates in his army reached critical levels.[92] Finally, on 8 August, there was a ray of sunlight on the horizon for him when Alexander of Scotland succeeded in reducing Carlisle. The euphoric Alexander sent word that he was marching south to meet Louis at Dover. But it took a month for the two armies to meet. Alexander wasted time on the way south by turning aside for an abortive siege of Barnard Castle, in the course of which Eustace de Vesci was killed. Other barons who were ineffectively besieging the citadel at Lincoln used the excuse of Alexander's advent to break off an investment they had no idea how to conclude successfully. It was a large host that arrived in Canterbury from the north in the second week of September, but even the reunited army had no clue how to reduce Dover Castle, still stubbornly held by Hubert de Burgh.[93]

By the beginning of September the see-saw civil war, already nearly two years old, once more seemed to be favouring John. Relations between the French and the rebel barons had not improved; many apostates were returning to their previous loyalty to John, including the earls of Salisbury and York, surely two of the most short-term trimmers in history, as well as William Marshal's son, despite the high honour Louis had done him. None of the royalist castles had fallen, and every day there were more reports of desertions in the French army. John had managed to win over the comte de Nevers, commanding the rebel forces at Windsor, as a double agent. Even the small things seemed to be going against the rebels, as when Geoffrey de Mandeville was killed in a pointless joust with a French knight.[94] John sensed the changing pulse of events and by now had a clearer picture of French strategy and Louis's military limi-tations. He decided to go over to the offensive and relieve Dover. Forced marches took him from Cirencester on 2 September via Burford, Oxford and Wallingford to Reading on the 6th. He feinted towards Windsor, causing momentary panic in the rebel besiegers there, then struck due east, having learned that the king of the Scots was returning homewards.[95] John was hoping for a brilliant stroke whereby he would rout the Scots in East Anglia and then turn south to deal with Louis at Dover. Having dallied at Reading – some said this was to get proper intelligence from Nevers at Windsor[96] – he made another of his lightning moves on 15 September, taking his armies at an incredible speed for a medieval host through Walton-on-Thames, Aylesbury and Bedford to Cambridge. Nevers and his confrères used this excuse to save face and raise the vain siege of Windsor; they pretended to be 'pursuing' John and did indeed come close to overhauling him; whether through luck, treachery or simple incompetence John ended up in Stamford while the pursuers bivouacked in Cambridge.[97]

At this point in the campaign something went wrong with John's thinking, and there is a mystery here which no historian has ever satisfactorily cleared up. John's strategy in making the lightning march east is clear enough, and seems eminently sound: had he caught Alexander of Scotland on the way home and crushed him, Louis at Dover might well have thrown in the towel. But suddenly we learn that the double agent Nevers is escorting Alexander north; that there is a rendezvous between the Scots and Gilbert de Gant's army at Lincoln; and that John is in the throes of some kind of brainstorm.[98] Matthew Paris tells a superficially wild story about John spending time gutting abbeys and monasteries in Oundle, Peterborough and Crowland, torching cornfields with his own hand, and berating Savaric de Mauléon for accepting money from monks instead of slaughtering them and burning their church.[99] There is much that is obscure here, and the only solid ground is that John reached Lincoln on 28 September to find that Alexander and the Scottish host had already slipped past him and were in Yorkshire. Whether in response to this bad news or simply as continuation of the king's madness, John set his troops to a mini-version of his scorched earth policy of the previous winter. His actions now were pure terrorism not linked to any strategic or tactical imperative. As wheat fields went up in smoke and the newly garnered harvests were wantonly destroyed, John seemed to be doing his best to match his legend as an evil king.[100] But when he appeared in Lynn (King's Lynn) on 9 October, he appeared to be once more a rational monarch. Relations between Lynn and John had always been good – he had sold the burghers privileges and made a lot of money from them over the years – and all attested that he was well satisfied with the lavish feasts the citizens laid on for him and their further contributions to his war chest.[101] The news from the south was good too. Despite throwing everything he had at Dover Castle, Louis had failed to make any impression. Hubert de Burgh's complement of

140 knights and more than a thousand men-at-arms were easily abreast of anything the French could bring against them. Louis swore that he would hang every last defender from the walls and even managed by a superhuman effort to capture one of the towers, but was as far away as ever from cracking the inner defences. Meanwhile there was more and more desertion from Louis's army, and resistance to the French in Kent stiffened daily.[102]

It was at Lynn that the pendulum then swung back against John once more. First came news that Innocent III, the king's most steadfast champion had died, opening the possibility that a successor might be elected who was more favourable to the barons. Then came word from Hubert de Burgh in Dover that the garrison could no longer hold out and asking John's permission to conclude a truce with the French. Wearily John gave his assent.[103] But then, even while he tucked into the sumptuous repasts provided by the burghers of Lynn, he fell violently ill with dysentery. Instead of trying to get over the illness by rest, John insisted on pressing on farther inland, and on 11 October he set off on the road to Wisbech 'like a swiftly advancing storm'.[104] His route then lay north-west and it was while his army was crossing the mouth of the River Wellstream (near the River Welland), which empties into the Wash, that probably the best-known incident in his reign (after Runnymede) occurred. Part of his baggage train was swallowed by quicksands on the morning of 12 October. That much is certain. Ralph, abbot of Coggleshall, relates: 'He lost his chapel and its relics and some of his packhorses with divers household effects at the Wellstream, and many members of his household were submerged in the waters of the sea, and sucked into the quicksand there, because they had set out incautiously and hastily before the tide had receded.'[105] But the exact circumstances of the disaster, its location and magnitude remain a subject of impassioned debate. One can readily see that the entire issue is problematical, for Coggleshall's account is by far the most reliable one extant and yet it is itself confused. If you are drowned by the sea, you cannot at the same time be sucked down by quicksands. Yet the other main chroniclers of this event – Roger of Wendover and Matthew Paris – simply compound the confusion. Wendover lurches into absurdity by a simultaneous assertion that not a single foot soldier got away to bring the news to the king *and* that John barely escaped with his life.[106] Some authorities try to make sense of the disaster in the Wash by claiming that what overwhelmed John's baggage train was not quicksands but a tidal bore, though this is a mere 'educated guess' with no sanction in the sources.[107]

Both Wendover and Matthew Paris portray a major disaster. The leading horses and pack animals get bogged down in the quicksands, but the vanguard cannot back up out of the danger for the rest of the train keep pressing them forward, so that more and more men and animals get sucked into the vortex.[108] The first question then is: was the 'disaster in the Wash' a major debacle, as depicted by Paris and Wendover, or a more limited affair, as narrated by Coggleshall? This in turn hinges on where the fiasco was supposed to have taken place and on this too there is no agreement, with some authorities opting for the route across the estuary from Cross Keys to Long Sutton, others plumping for a narrow 40-yard stretch between Walsokes and Wisbech, and a third version preferring the area between Walpole and Tydd Gote.[109] The change in the shape of the coastline in the last eight hundred years makes the location very hard to determine. And then there is another problem. Was John with the baggage train when the accident/disaster happened, or had he already split his forces? The fact that he reached Swineshead on the evening of 12 October argues powerfully against his presence with the stricken baggage train. It has therefore been hypothesised that the imbroglio with the baggage train happened very early in the day, possibly because John gave orders that he wanted the baggage with him in Lincolnshire that night, that the commanders of the train did not wait long enough for the tide to go out, but that they sustained only significant damage rather than outright disaster. Faced with a surplus of baggage over pack animals, John might then have decided to send the surplus baggage to Lincolnshire by sea, only to discover that the necessary seamen were all in Wisbech, to which place he hastened to expedite matters.[110] Admittedly, all is hypothesis piled on supposition. But the most likely course of events is that quicksands claimed some of the baggage train but not all, that the occurrence was more accident than disaster, and that John did indeed split his forces, even though this was risky in territory that was far from staunchly royalist. What, then, of the extent of losses? Did John really lose his crown and his treasure in the Wash? We know from royal inventories that the baggage train was carrying the coronation regalia and a huge collection of precious objects – gold and silver goblets, jewelled belts, candelabra, pendants, robes.[111] The fact that these objects were missing when sought for the coronation of Henry III in 1220 creates the inference that they did indeed vanish into the Wash. Some sceptics, however, say that only the royal regalia and some other artefacts were lost, and that most of the jewels were stolen in the confusion surrounding John's death.[112]

The loss of valuables would have had a peculiarly piercing impact on John, already suffering from dysentery as he was. He was reported as oscillating between rage and grief at Swineshead Abbey but the third of misfortune's legendary trios was lying in wait for him that night; whether to assuage his grief or simply through his habitual gluttony, he managed to overeat when supping on a collation of peaches and new cider – an incredible dietary choice for one suffering from dysentery.[113] On 14 October he could barely sit in the saddle, and the whole journey to Sleaford was agony. Urged to rest, he would have none of it, and insisted on pressing on to Newark. But on the 16th he finally had to admit defeat: having ridden just three miles, he dismounted from his horse panting and groaning, and ordered his followers to make a litter on which he could be carried. There were no decent artisans or carpenters to hand, so his household knights struggled to make a crude cradle of willows which they chopped down at the roadside; their inexpert weaving was topped off with the addition of a horse blanket. Moreover, the so-called litter had no cushions or straw to relieve its hardness. The unrelieved pressure on the king's back would have been painful enough but in addition, lacking carriage-horses, his men slung the cradle between some skittish destriers.[114] Soon the jolting and bumping was making John cry out in agony; to relieve him the foot soldiers took it in turns to carry him shoulder-high, like African bearers in the era of Victorian exploration. The king's cries of pain and rage made for very slow going. It may be that now for the first time was uttered the prophetic rhyme, said to have been composed by a French seer in the time of Henry II, which so appealed to Matthew Paris: 'Henry the fairest shall die at Martel; Richard the Poitevin shall die in the Limousin; John shall die a landless king, in a litter.'[115]

Alas for Paris's neat formulations, John avoided the fate thus portended; making a slight recovery, he was able to ride the last few miles to Newark on an 'ambling nag'. But there, in the bishop of Lincoln's castle, he collapsed and took to his bed. It is possible that he then suffered at least one heart attack, but the paucity of records and the crudity of medieval medical diagnosis makes certainty on the cause of death impossible. The abbot of Croxton, who had a reputation as a doctor and healer, was sent for but could do little except offer words of spiritual comfort and persuade John to confess and take the last sacraments.[116] He named his son Henry as his heir and extracted an oath of fealty to him from the assembled lords. Then he appointed William Marshal as regent and guardian of his two sons (the younger, Richard, was at Corfe Castle).

He also dictated a brief will, expressing ritual remorse for his sins but *not*, contrary to the legend, forgiving the barons. He also asked to be buried in the Church of the Blessed Virgin at St Wulfstan in Worcester.[117] Shortly after midnight, in the early hours of 19 October 1216, John died; perhaps appropriately a strong gale howled outside. The abbot of Croxton took away the king's heart and intestines and had the body hastily embalmed.[118] Little sorrow was in evidence around the deathbed. A monk named John of Savigny, who came to Newark at daybreak to mount vigil over the body and say Mass for the king's soul, testified that the sole interest of John's household seemed to be to make away with as much loot as they could before some official arrived to seal the royal chambers.[119] John's corpse was then richly caparisoned, and a company of his mercenaries in full armour escorted it on the long journey from Newark to Worcester. There they laid it before the altar of St Wulfstan.

The death of John 'stilled war's raging storm', as Wendover put it,[120] in the sense that the barons had no compelling reason to oppose the coronation of his nine-year-old son Henry. The real loser by the king's death was Prince Louis, as one by one the English rebels gradually drifted back into a grudging fealty to his son and the new regime headed by William Marshal. Louis found himself deserted on all sides, particularly by the clergy, and his claims to the throne widely regarded as nugatory.[121] The crucial turning point was a meeting of magnates at Bristol on 11 November, when Magna Carta was reissued in the young king's name. A few of the more radical clauses of the Charter were omitted or held in abeyance, but its essential spirit remained.[122] Louis's only chance now was to achieve some striking success that would win over the still large number of fence-sitting waverers. Any chance of this disappeared when William Marshal decided to take vigorous steps to expel the French invaders. Lincoln Castle still held out, and in May Marshal and a strong army burst through the French lines to relieve it; in a short but bloody battle Louis's knights were routed and his infantrymen cut down 'like pigs' in the streets of Lincoln.[123] The defeat at Lincoln on 20 May 1217 effectively ended Louis's hopes, and the *coup de grâce* came shortly afterwards when a second invasion fleet under the infamous Eustace the Monk was heavily defeated at sea by Hubert de Burgh and Richard of Chilham; Eustace was taken and beheaded and his corpse dragged through the streets of Canterbury.[124] Louis promptly ended the siege of Dover and entered peace talks with William Marshal. He managed to avoid humiliation in the Treaty of Lambeth and secretly received 10,000 marks compensation for abandoning his claim to the English throne. Louis returned to France, campaigned in the Cathar region of Toulouse,[125] and survived to be a shortlived king of France (1223–26) after the death of his father. But John, by his opportune death, ensured that *his* son, Henry III, would succeed to become one of the longest-reigning of all English monarchs (1216–72). Truly it could be said of John that nothing in his life became him like the leaving it.

20

◅◦▻

Richard and John, Conclusion

I T IS A STRANGE thing to be at once the victim of academic orthodoxies *and* political correctness, but such appears to be the fate of
Richard the Lionheart. No English (or later British) monarch ever
made the impact on his or her contemporaries that Richard I made on
his. His fame and reputation were known in lands from the Orkneys
to the Atlas Mountains and from Cork to Baghdad. He had a direct or
indirect impact on the politics of many different lands: Scotland, Ireland,
France, Flanders, Spain, Germany, Austria, Italy, Sicily, Cyprus,
Byzantium and the Middle East. At the same time he held together an
unwieldy Angevin empire that was beginning to come under severe threat
from the Capetian dynasty in France. His achievements as a warrior were
stupendous. And yet in the twentieth century his star dimmed even as
his brother John's rose. His very status as a military hero made him
suspect and out of line with the main currents in academic thought. The
'great man' theory of history was suspect to Marxists, who stressed
instead socio-economic structures and class struggle; his very machismo
was a standing affront to feminists; structuralists denied the importance
of the human subject anyway; while psychoanalysis often unduly stressed
the psychopathological element in heroes and rulers, to the point where
one recent writer can with a straight face refer to Richard as 'to modern
minds . . . a kind of maniac'.[1] At the same time Richard is indelibly associated with the Crusades, which to modern sensibilities are the high point
of western imperialism and racism – a naked attempt to apply supposedly
superior military technology for the purpose of loot, rapine and
economic exploitation. Moreover, from the 1960s on, the idea of heroism
itself became suspect, and the courage evinced by those who fought in
1939–45 for the very freedom to be sceptical about courage is often
dismissed with a quiet contempt. Liberals like the idea that between the
so-called hero and the so-called coward there is not the thickness of a
sheet of paper. Political correctness, and the feeling that we would all

do better if we remained quietly in our rooms, shades into Little Englanderism. Richard is condemned for his exotic foreign adventures and blamed for not being an effective king of England. It has become a cliché of commentary on the Lionheart to point out po-facedly that he spent no more than six months in England. Typical is this, from a widely-used and influential textbook: 'He used England as a bank on which to draw and overdraw in order to finance his ambitious exploits abroad.'[2]

Most general modern criticisms of Richard can be dismissed *a priori* as they depend for their supposed force on historical hindsight and anachronism. David Hume's critique of the crusades shows the problem. His *History of England*, far more famous in the eighteenth century than his philosophical output, worked itself into a lather about the crusades, which he described as 'the most signal and durable monument of human folly that has yet appeared in any age or nation'.[3] *Sub specie aeternitatis*, the judgement is incontestable, and no one in the modern age would wish to defend the crusades, particularly in an era when 'crusade' has been annexed to describe both Franco's excesses in the Spanish Civil War and the American assault on Iraq. Yet the point, surely, is that no one in the twelfth and thirteenth centuries regarded crusades as immoral, sinful or otherwise evil. On the contrary, successive Popes inculcated the notion that it was the sacred duty of rulers to go on crusade. In terms of medieval morality, Richard was a paladin who did his Christian duty; his father Henry and brother John, both of whom disingenuously took the Cross when they had not the slightest intention of campaigning in the Holy Land, evaded this clear imperative. Unless one derives satisfaction from gloating over both the real and imaginary superiority of twenty-first century modes of thought over those of previous centuries, no point whatever is served by fulminating about the medieval Christian campaigns to 'liberate' the land of Outremer. A recent book sums this up neatly: the authors remark that modern writers are no more capable of understanding the Crusades than medieval writers would understand landing a man on the Moon.[4] Anachronistic too is the perception that Richard was a 'bad king' because he neglected England. From a contemporary standpoint (Richard's own), England was only part of the Angevin empire, and there was no overarching reason why he should prioritise it above Normandy, Poitou, Anjou or Aquitaine. It was Aquitaine that he loved, Aquitaine where was born, educated and 'formed' and therefore Aquitaine that occupied the bulk of his attention. England in the late twelfth century was a fairly insignificant kingdom, not the great power it would later become. Modern critics of the Little England type seem to imagine that Richard should somehow have guessed at England's future significance – doubtless by gazing in a crystal ball – and behaved accordingly. Moreover, if it can be alleged on a superficial reading that Richard neglected England, it can be stated with even greater authority that John neglected those parts of the Angevin empire that were not England – with disastrous results.

By combining modern judgements – the condescension of posterity once again – with a selective reading of the disinformation churned out by Richard's political enemies in France, Germany and Austria, it is possible to provide a devastating portrait of the Angevin king, but it is one that depends on tacking in and out of propaganda and anachronism. It cannot be denied that Richard had a difficult personality, that he suffered from pride, and could be insensitive, high-handed and arrogant; indeed it was said that the city of Tyre would not let Richard and his English crusaders land there at the start of Richard's Palestine campaign because they feared his 'arrogance'.[5] But these are normal human faults and in no way mark him down as anything exceptional for his – or indeed any – era. To establish that Richard was wicked, evil or egregiously depraved, we would need far, far more than this. The final nail in the coffin for the idea that Richard can be judged as 'racist' or 'imperialistic' comes from the high regard entertained for him by his Muslim adversaries. There is no whiff of the 'Great Satan' or 'Little Satan' about Saladin's opinions or those of his courtiers and advisers. Ibn al-Athir called him 'the most remarkable man of the age'.[6] Another Muslim historian managed to achieve the empathy that has so often eluded later western historians with fewer cultural barriers to cross: 'With him to wage war in God's name was a veritable passion; his whole heart was filled with it, and he gave body and soul to the cause.'[7] The consensus of all who met Richard, from Saladin's envoy al-Adil to St Hugh of Lincoln, was that the English king had many striking human virtues: he was magnanimous, openhanded, capricious, impulsive but not vengeful, cruel or treacherous; the canard that he attacked Saracens while they were under Philip Augustus's flag of truce was simply black propaganda by the French.[8] Although he is sometimes accused of lack of self-control, it is striking that he did not lose friends or make enemies purely through the gratification of his passions, as John habitually did. And the historical record does not even show him to be arrogant in any normal sense, unless arrogance is defined as a healthy realisation of one's own abilities.

The worst sins alleged against Richard were that he was an unfilial,

ungrateful and treacherous son, that he was a man of blood who cared
nothing for human life and that, by his massacre of the Muslim prisoners at Acre, he proved himself a war criminal even in contemporary
medieval terms. The charge of treachery towards his father will not really
hold, for Henry had no idea how to manage sons and at various times
alienated all four of his male offspring.[9] It was not really surprising that
Richard had no real affection for his father, since Henry wronged him
four times over: he mistreated his mother, seduced his fiancée, set his
brothers against him and even threatened to disinherit him in favour of
John. Much of the later bad blood between Richard and Philip Augustus
can be traced to Henry, since his seduction of Alice placed Richard in
an impossible position: he had either to insult Philip by setting her aside
or take as wife a woman whom his detested father had 'defiled', as he
saw it. Quite apart from the issue of Alice and the imprisonment of
Eleanor of Aquitaine, Henry alienated Richard by his soft spot for John,
which led him to try to give his lastborn son a bigger share in the Angevin
inheritance than was justified by custom and precedent. Indeed, if Gerald
of Wales can be believed, Henry wanted to restrict Richard's inheritance
to the Anglo-Norman realm and give John all the fiefs held of the French
crown (except Normandy).[10] In a larger sense the charge that Richard
was heedless of human blood and suffering must be sustained, although
he always took care to see that his troops were well equipped and fed –
not something that can be said for every medieval ruler. Richard was
one of those rare men who seemed to live only for combat and martial
glory – this is a distinctive type that runs from Alexander the Great to
moderns like General Phil Sheridan and General Patton, but excludes
Caesar, Napoleon and Robert E. Lee who, despite their prowess on the
battlefield, had other concerns and other interests. He was not a man of
blood in the sense that he sanctioned murder for political ends: although
he was accused of compassing the death of Conrad of Montferrat,
the charge is totally false, and received the currency it did only because
the canard was assiduously milked by Philip Augustus and his spin
doctors. Conrad had made so many enemies in so many different spheres
that it is surprising he lasted as long as he did; among his myriad treacheries was a secret channel of negotiation with Saladin, by which he hoped
to double-cross the other crusaders.[11]

A creature of impulse and therefore neither treacherous nor cruel,
Richard erred rather on the side of naivety and over-trustingness, as he
showed in his relations with his brother John. A more ruthless or cynical
man would have insisted that John accompany him to the crusades, and

probably his half-brother Geoffrey as well. Richard was forever forgiving the treachery of the Lusignans, taking them back as allies and then being disappointed once again when they reratted. The one clear moral blemish on Richard's record and by any standards a war crime was his massacre of the Muslim prisoners at Acre on 20 August 1191. Richard's defenders say that he was within the strict letter of the law in so doing, that Saladin could have ransomed the prisoners if he chose, and that the killing was justified by Saladin's massacre of the Templars after the battle of Hattin. Richard's further justification was that he could not afford to stay in Acre indefinitely while Saladin stalled, using the prisoners as a bargaining counter, that Saladin was deliberately trying to wear down the English king, confident that western notions of chivalry and honour would prevent Richard from taking the obvious way out of his dilemma.[12] From Richard's point of view, he could not march away leaving the Acre garrison to play warder to 3,000 prisoners, and there was barely enough food to feed the garrison, never mind thousands of 'useless' mouths. Contemporary Christian opinion had no intellectual problem with the killings; after all, had not Bernard of Clairvaux declared that 'The Christian glories in the death of a pagan, because thereby Christ himself is glorified.' Ambroise thought the killing entirely justified as a reprisal for the sufferings of the Christians at Acre; he does not even bring Hattin into the equation.[13] The French chronicler Jacques de Vitry took the line that if the Muslims had not been butchered, they would have lived another day to kill and maim Christians, so that on a brutal utilitarian calculus Richard was vindicated.[14] The Cistercian monk Ralph of Coggleshall thought that Saladin's failure to help Acre effectively delivered the other coastal towns (Haifa, Caesarea, Arsuf, Ascalon and Jaffa) into Richard's hands, since they came to realise they could look for nothing from Saladin.[15] But modern historians tend to see Richard's action as a clear-cut war crime, engendered by his rage and frustration. It certainly gave another twist to the cycle of atrocity, and for a time (until mid-September 1191), all Christians taken prisoner were summarily executed in reprisal. One hundred years later, when Acre fell to the Muslims, Richard's actions were cited as the justification for Muslim massacre of the Christians. We should remember, however, that the entire cycle of butchery was begun by Saladin at Hattin.[16] Nonetheless, when all allowances have been made, probably the most judicious comment is that passed by Napoleon's chief of police Fouché, after Napoleon executed the duc d'Enghien: 'It was worse than a crime, it was a mistake.'

If most historians have conceded that Richard was a great warrior, this is usually balanced by the judgement that he was a poor king of England, a hopeless politician and a weak administrator. If one's merit as a king of England is to be judged merely by 'presentism', then clearly John wins hands down. But there must have been many, whether barons, merchants or clergy who suffered under John, who would have given much for the return of Richard's absentee kingship; never has the phrase 'less is more' looked so appealing as when applied to England without Richard. John, the so-called 'hands on' king of England, managed to incite a civil war, whereas the arrangements Richard made before departing on crusade and while battling Philip Augustus in the years 1194–99 were remarkably successful; the Angevin empire as a whole did better under Richard's cavalier kingship than under John's centralist authoritarianism.[17] Since Richard was not systematically manipulative, dishonest and duplicitous, there is a sense in which he must, by definition, have been a bad politician. But what will not work is the thesis that Richard was habitually governed by pride.[18] Despite his superlative military talent, he would always adopt the best plan for the occasion, even if he had not thought of it, and regardless of who suggested it. He often deferred to decisions he did not support, such as the advance to Beit Nuba, and always believed in consulting the opinions of men who knew the local terrain or who knew how the Arab mind worked.[19] Moreover, his choice of underlings, lieutenants and henchmen was shrewd. He chose the right men for the job, and did not value the company of flatterers, sycophants, toadies and hangers-on, as the Young King had done.[20] Recent research into how the Angevin empire was governed under Richard shows that he did a remarkably good job of holding together his polyglot dominions, evincing a remarkable sensitivity to local mores, customs, traditions and folkways, making no attempt to impose a common currency or to forge a coherent political identity on such disparate domains.[21] The legend of Richard as a poor administrator dies hard, but is not borne out by the best scholarship.

The ultimate assault on Richard's reputation comes with the assertion that his military reputation has been absurdly exaggerated, that he was indeed no more than a journeyman warrior who made many bad, and sometimes egregious, mistakes. The *reductio ad absurdum* of this tendency comes in recent works purporting to cast doubt on the very idea of a 'crusade' or in the assertion that Richard's fame was unjustified, since medieval battles were no more than a glamorised form of gangland warfare without strategy, with one pack of thugs attacking another.[22] A more nuanced criticism accepts Richard's talent, but then subjects his conduct of the crusades to a ferocious critique. Among the charges levelled at the Lionheart are that he unconscionably delayed the arrival of his forces in the Holy Land, that he directed campaigns for personal gain, alienated his allies by his arrogance, needlessly risked himself in personal combat, was an inadequate master of logistics and commissariat, and was conservative and circumspect in his strategy; the charge-sheet ends with the incontestable fact that he failed to take Jerusalem, the ostensible point of the crusade.[23] The issue of arrogance has already been dealt with, and it might be added in passing that no 'great man' in any walk of life, whether soldier, statesman, banker, writer, actor, director could ever achieve anything without an above-average share of ego, which to their opponents is always construed as arrogance. As to Richard's needlessly exposing himself to danger, the critics are on sounder ground. Certainly his captains thought the criticism valid and often reproached him with it – and Richard responded by boasting about how he had disregarded their advice.[24] Whether his Saracen opponents, who came close to capturing him on several occasions because of his excessive daring, thought him rash and foolish in insisting on being in the thick of action, is far less certain.[25] So, yes, Richard was reckless and heedless of his own safety but contingency pays no regard to actuarial probabilities; Frederick Barbarossa was not reckless, yet the German emperor perished before reaching the Holy Land and the English king did not.

The long period that elapsed between Richard's taking the Cross and his eventual arrival in Outremer does, however, merit further consideration. Richard took his vows as a crusader in 1187 but did not land near Acre until four years later. Why was this? We must remember first of all the money that had to be raised – the Saladin tithe – and the meticulous military preparations necessary before a credible force could sail from England. The death of Henry II in 1189 further complicated matters, for Richard had to attend to the succession, have himself crowned and settle England before he could depart. It is worth pointing out that the very same people who accuse Richard of being an absentee king of England also charge him with being dilatory in departing on crusade, yet in logic both charges cannot be sustained simultaneously. The transfer of power on Henry's death effectively meant that Richard departed a full year after Frederick Barbarossa. Thereafter the gap between the two could only widen, as the Germans proceeded overland while Richard went by sea. And at sea he proceeded slowly, both because he suffered from seasickness and because he was travelling with large numbers of troops; above all he did not want his transports scattered by the winds because he was crowding on sail.[26]

But here the critics have another string to their bow. Granted that Richard was making a difficult sea voyage, why did he have to pause so long in Sicily and Cyprus? Were not his conquests of those islands clearly self-serving actions?[27] Here one is tempted to taunt the critics with the same kind of ignorance of the realities of sea power that bedevilled Napoleon. Both Philip and Richard made attempts to clear from Sicily after the conquest of that kingdom but were driven back by storms and high seas; in the days of primitive sailing ships, no rational commander would take a large fleet across the Mediterranean in midwinter.[28] But what about Cyprus? Was this not a self-serving enterprise, as flagrant a diversion from the main purpose as Drake's diversion from Howard of Effingham's fleet during the battle with the Spanish Armada in order to loot the *Rosario*? The critics further allege that the conquest of Cyprus was contrary to the Pope's directives, a bad precedent and act of grotesque irresponsibility because it delayed Christian reinforcements and thus jeopardised operations at Acre.[29] Here the critics seem to forget that it was Isaac Comnenus who started the fighting. And so far from excessive delay, Richard wound up his business on the island in just six days after completing military operations. Moreover, Richard's conquest of Cyprus contained clear benefits for the Third Crusade. Richard sold the island shortly after his victory there, gained extra funds for the Crusade thereby, and later used Cyprus to placate and remove his troublesome ally King Guy of Jerusalem. Moreover, Cyprus turned out to be a vital forward supply post, a crucial logistical asset – as Saladin had already recognised by his negotiations with Byzantium, aimed at stopping the crusaders using it. Even some of Richard's most vociferous critics concede his strategic insights in the matter of Cyprus.[30]

It may seem almost preposterous, after the brilliant victories at Acre, Ascalon, Darum, Jaffa and, above all, Arsuf, that Richard's calibre once landed in the Holy Land should be questioned, but the critics allege that Richard was over-cautious, to the point where he can be suspected of having a secret agenda, possibly a plot with the Templars to invade Egypt instead of taking Jerusalem. After all, it is said, it is a matter of record that Richard did not besiege Jerusalem even though the Pope's instructions expressly directed him to that target.[31] But Richard did not advance to Jerusalem, as a lesser captain would have done, because his acute military mind never lost sight of supply and logistics. Richard was a great leader precisely in his restraint and absence of mindless glory-seeking. He anticipated the very greatest leaders like Ernest Shackleton by turning back when almost within sight of his goal, because he realised that the so-called final goal was actually a bridge too far. Critics of Richard's careful, systematic approach to the campaign in Palestine would presumably apply the same thinking to the cautious build-up for OVERLORD in 1944 and argue that the Second Front should have been opened in 1943. Richard may have been a Patton in tempera-ment and sensibility but he was an Eisenhower when it came to down-to-earth concern for practicalities and the art of the possible. He knew that lack of careful preparations and poor supply lines had doomed the Second Crusade and severely impeded the First (they were also to cause the failure of the Fifth and Sixth), and he was determined not to fall into that obvious trap. As for Jerusalem, Richard made it quite plain that there was no point in expending blood and treasure on a target which would have to be abandoned soon after capture, simply because there were not enough permanent settlers from Christendom to make its permanent occupation feasible. The Third Crusade, conceived purely as an expedition to reclaim Jerusalem for Christianity, was doomed to failure before a single crusader left Europe, precisely because the Western nations were not exporting large enough populations to make perma-nent retention of Outremer practicable. For all that, Richard's heroic endeavours in effect prolonged the life of Christian Palestine for another hundred years. He cannot be blamed for failing to solve a problem that was beyond any single person's capacity.

If we except the case of the prisoners at Acre, most of the charges in the indictment against Richard, whether on political, administrative or military grounds, fail to convince. Although he was not the greatest general in the medieval era – that title clearly belongs either to Tamerlane or Genghiz Khan's great commander, Subudei – he was almost certainly the greatest Western Christendom produced. Furthermore, it is worth remem-bering that he managed to avoid the head-on collisions with the papacy and the all-England primates that soured the reigns of both Henry II and John. If there is an equivalent of Henry's Becket or John's Stephen Langton in Richard's reign, the only possible candidate is Hugh of Lincoln. Twenty years Richard's senior, the only Carthusian monk who became a bishop in England, and famous for his pet swan, Hugh was notable for taking a Becket-like stance whenever he thought Richard was violating the Church's rights. In 1197 at the Council of Oxford Hugh (wrongly in the opinion of most experts on feudalism) refused to provide knights for overseas service at a critical juncture of Richard's struggle with Philip

Augustus, on the grounds that none of his predecessors had ever made such a concession and he could therefore not commit his church to such a damaging precedent; the bishop of Salisbury joined him in this protest.[32] In response Richard ordered the confiscation of the estates of the see of Lincoln. Hugh decided that the only solution was to go to Normandy to confront the king. He found Richard in his chapel at Château-Gaillard, hearing High Mass on the feast of St Augustine, with the two bishops of Durham and Ely at his side. According to his biographer, Hugh was encouraged to boldness by hearing the choir chant the words 'Hail, renowned bishop of Christ' when he reached the chapel steps. Adam of Eynsham takes up the story: 'When the bishop greeted the king he did not reply, but frowned at him and after a little while turned his face away. The bishop said to him "Lord king, kiss me." But Richard turned his head even further and looked the other way. Then the bishop firmly gripped the king's tunic round his chest and shook it violently, saying again, "You owe me a kiss because I have come a long way to see you." The king answered: "You deserve no kiss from me." Hugh shook him more vigorously by the cloak, and said boldly: "I have every right to one," adding, "kiss me." After a while Richard, overcome by his courage and determination, kissed him with a smile.'[33]

After Mass Hugh and Richard discussed the reasons for the king's anger. Hugh claimed he had never failed in duty to the king, and Richard rather weakly claimed that Hubert Walter had poisoned his mind against him (Hugh). Reiterating his stance, Hugh said: 'Except for the honour of God and the salvation of my soul and yours, I have never till now opposed anything trivial which was to your advantage.' Thoroughly won over, Richard sent Hugh presents and gave him a fine pike for his dinner. Pressing his advantage, Hugh next day moved into territory which a more cautious man would certainly have avoided. Describing Richard as 'his parishioner' he insisted on preaching to him about his sins. Richard blandly replied that his conscience was clear in everything except his hatred for his enemies. Hugh put it to him that he was not making a full confession, since it was widely known that Richard was unfaithful to Berengaria with other women (in view of the homosexual canard, it is most significant that Hugh does not accuse him of the sin of sodomy), and that he promoted men to high positions, and especially bishoprics because they were his personal favourites or because they gave him money. Richard listened attentively and respectfully, without any signs of the expected Angevin rage at such 'impertinence'. The two men parted on good terms. Richard remitted the fines and confiscations he had levied on Lincoln (those on Salisbury remained, as Hugh's colleague there had not had the wisdom to travel to Normandy).[34]

When Hugh had left, Richard told his courtiers: 'If the other bishops were like him, no king or ruler would dare to raise up his head against them.'[35] However, shortly afterwards Richard decided that he could not after all exempt the Lincoln canons from military service and that they should serve abroad in the 'diplomatic service' at their own expense and his own pleasure. This was a particular blow to Hugh, as he had hand-picked his canons for their intellectual, moral and administrative qualities and regarded them as the apple of his eye. There was nothing for it but another trip to Normandy to plead in person once more. Perhaps Hugh need not have bothered, for already men feared his curses as the malediction of a truly holy man. It was said that Richard contemplated sending his fearsome mercenary captain Mercadier to seize the assets of Lincoln this time but that his counsellors, doubtless abetted by Mercadier himself, who did not relish the assignment, argued him out of it.[36] There is no way of telling whether the second encounter between monarch and saint would have ended so happily, for Hugh was still on his way through France to see Richard when he heard of the king's death. In spite of the danger from travelling through countryside riven by bandits and anarchy, Hugh insisted on completing the journey to Fontevraud. It was thus that he assisted at the funeral instead, comforted Berengaria and later, at John's insistence, was one of the witnesses of the treaty of Le Goulet. Hugh explained to his followers that any other course of action would have been ungrateful, since, whenever they were together, Richard had always shown him the utmost kindness and respect.[37]

If Richard ultimately passes all the tests except that posed by the prisoners at Acre, John by contrast fails almost all those that can be legitimately set. As a ruler he lost Normandy through incompetence, became involved in a quite unnecessary conflict with the Pope, which ended in abject surrender, taxed his subjects to the point where they rebelled, bringing on a two-year civil war, and ended by losing his Crown jewels in the Wash. As a tyrant he murdered the young Arthur, by all laws of succession the true heir to the throne, murdered William de Braose's family, executed twenty-eight Welsh hostages, brutally dispatched an eccentric hermit and his son, and was frequently prevented from further atrocities by the advice of his counsellors and even, incredibly, by his bloodthirsty mercenary captains. In the light of all this, it is unbelievable that he has had such a good press from modern historians, some of whom seem determined to prove that black is white in their protestation that John was a decent monarch. Although John ducked every significant military encounter, especially pitched battles, and was a percentage player as commander where Richard had been inspirational, we are still told that he was a competent military planner and strategist.[38] He is often praised for his inspired military vision when attempting to relieve Château-Gaillard in 1203, but surely the crucial point is that John's grand conception turned out to be a disastrous failure. Military talent does not consist in merely having bright ideas on paper, but in being able to think through every last detail of the planning necessary to bring them to fruition. This was precisely the quality Richard had in abundance; the irony is that because he had it and therefore did not attempt quixotic schemes, he has been criticised for caution and conservatism. A little more caution and conservatism, as opposed to bipolar bouts of lethargy and extreme, goalless, energy would have done John a lot of good during the campaign for Normandy.

The litany of John's military failures is tedious: the failed strategy in Europe before Bouvines; the inability to prevent the French landing in 1216; the failure to march on London in 1215 during the civil war; the inability to pacify Ireland, where the best research establishes that John wholly failed, despite the efforts of his supporters to 'talk up' his achievements.[39] Modern historians dismiss Roger of Howden as unreliable, and it is true that all the most barbed criticism of John as commander occurs in Howden, though it is from Gervase of Canterbury that John derived his devastating nickname Softsword.[40] But it is not so easy to dismiss the far less sensational evidence in the monastic annals (Barnwell, Margam, etc) which tells essentially the same story: here John is actually accused of being frightened to face Philip Augustus in battle, and of having made no real effort to prevent the conquest of Normandy.[41] As a student of John has remarked: 'John's good military reputation is largely a modern interpretation.'[42] Some of the modern judgements seem truly astonishing. Professor Ralph Turner writes: 'many who tangled with John . . . underrated his capability and found themselves quickly defeated'.[43] One would like to know who exactly these 'many' were. Far more accurate, down-to-earth and trenchant is this assessment from John Gillingham, commenting on the unopposed French landings in 1215–16: 'This time it was on the beaches of England that John chose not to fight.'[44]

The more one examines John's good press among modern historians, the more bizarre it seems. One writer praises John's 'thoughtful kindness' to Arthur's sister Elinor, which was obvious compensation by a guilty murderer. The same writer blames Richard's taxes for all John's troubles, as if Richard had somehow come back to life and ordered a virtually annual scutage, and speaks of the barons' 'irresponsible behaviour' in opposing John's excesses.[45] Even more amazing is the defence of John mounted by the historian Maurice Ashley. Those who accuse John of being 'cruel, lascivious and superstitious' are accused of 'censuring ... with true Victorian moral approbation'.[46] It is unclear why cruelty and superstition should be disapproved of only by Victorians, but this author seems to have a 'Victorian complex'. Elsewhere he inveighs against those who are 'inclined to measure men long dead by Victorian ethical standards'. Again, it is unclear whether it is 'men long dead' or 'Victorian ethical standards' that constitute the problem. Ashley rounds of his tour-de-force of pro-John apologia by describing his catastrophic blundering in Ireland in 1185 as 'like a non-swimmer being tipped into a pool'.[47] Truly, granted enough extenuating circumstances, anyone can be exonerated of anything. John has never lacked his champions, who will blame all his woes on Henry II, Richard, Innocent III, the barons, Philip Augustus – the list is potentially endless. We must remember that not even Shakespeare was proof against propagandist nonsense when it came to John. The Bard absurdly makes John a defender of English liberty against the papacy – a worthy forerunner of Henry VIII and the Tudors, that dynasty to which Shakespeare was forced to truckle:

> *This England never did, nor never shall,*
> *Lie at the proud foot of a conqueror,*
> *But when it first did help to wound itself.*
> *Now these her princes are come home again,*
> *Come the three corners of the world in arms,*
> *And we shall shock them. Nought shall make us rue*
> *If England to itself do rest but true.*[48]

There are only four arguments for the rehabilitation of John that command any respect, but even they turn out in the end to be inadequate. The first is simply that John was extremely unlucky, that the roll of the dice consistently went against him. He was unfortunate in that his reign was a roll-call of failures, contrasting so strikingly with the glittering successes achieved by Henry II and the martial glory won by Richard. He left his kingdom in chaos after two years of civil war and, by his opposition to Magna Carta, which was absorbed into the political system by his son, came to seem no more than a mindless despot. Most of all, he fell foul of the Church. All the medieval chroniclers were monks or churchmen, and John's hostility to the Church was requited with a uniformly hostile portrayal in the medieval sources. Some historians think it enough merely to state the hostility of churchmen to John, as if that in itself constitutes a refutation of their opinions. But nothing substantial, except John's commitment to archives and record-keeping – in itself bound to commend him warmly to professional historians – has emerged to alter the picture. We should remember that it is not enough to establish a famous chronicler's parti pris, like that of Matthew Paris towards John. Tacitus and Suetonius were notoriously hostile to the Julio-Claudian emperors, yet historical research has not thrown up anything that substantially alters our perception of Tiberius, Caligula, Nero and Domitian. Part of the problem is that the kinds of materials professional historians relish are 'value-neutral'; just as modern research can establish that Nero debased the Roman currency, but this tells us nothing about his personality, so John's administrative reforms cannot establish that he was a 'good king'.

The second line of defence for John is to assert that, even if he was cruel and despotic, he was small beer alongside modern dictators or even the tyrants of the late Middle Ages and the Renaissance. Here is Professor Turner again: 'Compared to Hitler, Stalin or Pol Pot, he seems quite tame.'[49] Yes, and also alongside Henry VII, Henry VIII and Elizabeth I. The simple truth is that John lacked both the technology and the political culture to be a mass murderer. John's control over England was episodic and that over the greater Angevin empire practically non-existent. Modern dictators depend on electronic communications, mass media and advanced infrastructure in roads and railways to impose their bloody will; such things were simply not available to John. And in Western Europe c. 1000–1300 there was no political culture that would legitimate state violence on the grand scale. It has long been noted that in this period, unlike the later Middle Ages or the Renaissance, the penalties even for major rebellion were slight. Earl Waltheof (executed 1075) and William of Eu (blinded and castrated in 1095) are almost the only examples of the high-born losing life or limb as the result of rebellion.[50] Nor were there the post-battlefield slaughters that disgraced the Wars of the Roses. Although John, both in temperament and in his conflict with the Church, adumbrated Henry VIII, he was utterly unlike the Tudor ogre in not operating within a culture that sanctioned killing on whim; in Henry's reign, by contrast, he was able to murder or execute 150,000 people out of a total population of 2.7 million, though admittedly, even within the context of early sixteenth-century Europe, an era that produced Cortes, Pizarro, Aguirre and Cesare Borgia, Henry VIII was regarded by contemporaries as an egregious tyrant, a modern Nero.

The third option for John's supporters is to allege that he inherited from Henry and Richard most of the problems that dragged him down; he was thus like Charles I, who inherited a baneful legacy from the last Tudor monarch, Elizabeth I and ended up paying the penalty that should have been the Virgin Queen's. Or, to use another analogy, that he was like Lyndon Johnson inheriting the mess John F. Kennedy had made in Vietnam and taking all the blame for it; in light of the comparison some-times made, with Richard and John featuring as Kennedy and Nixon in 1960, it is more than just interesting to read Professor Turner's comment that John had personality flaws similar to those of Nixon and LBJ.[51] John, then, according to this argument, personally carried the can for problems that were endemic to the entire Angevin empire. Certainly it was true that when John demanded the surrender of castles, when he imposed financial penalties or exacted charters of fealty as guarantees of his vassals' good behaviour, he was doing only what his predecessors did and what Philip Augustus did on the continent. And it was also true that Magna Carta was aimed not just at John personally, but at the entire imperial Angevin system, as the monastic chroniclers acknowledged.[52] But, although a necessary explanation for the Great Charter, the pre-existing Great Charter is not a sufficient one. Abbot Coggleshall ex-plicitly made the point that, in addition to the grievances inherited from previous Angevin rulers, John had added abuses of his own.[53]

Richard's financial exactions, it is claimed, had drained England and left John without the financial resources to combat Philip Augustus in Normandy. But the thesis that John lagged behind Philip in wealth and resources is highly questionable (see above, pp.319) The defeat in Normandy was not a function of historical inevitability in the guise of economics, but was grounded simply in John's deficiencies as a commander and his failings as a man. He could not inspire the Normans, he alienated them with the free hand he gave his mercenary captains, at key moments he flinched from essential head-on encounters with the French. So far from having inherited an intractable problem from Richard, John squan-dered what his brother had built up. It is simply inconceivable that Normandy could have fallen to Philip Augustus had Richard lived; his energy, his charisma, his military genius would all have been enough to see the French off.[54] John's flight from La Roche-au-Moine was something that would never have occurred under Richard. This is something even John's most stalwart defenders concede. Here is Professor Warren:

> If Richard had lived for another five years . . . there would have been
> one notable difference in the course of the campaign. The king
> himself would have been in the heights above Les Andelys as dawn
> broke, to give the signal for the combined attack on the French camp;
> however ready the Normans were to surrender, Philip would not have
> been able to march up the valley of the Orne to Caen without fear of
> a sudden assault by Richard and his household cavalry; and even
> when all else had gone, Richard would have been urging the citizens
> of Rouen to arms, and parrying the first assault with blows from his
> great sword. John stayed in England biting his nails.[55]

The final entry in the dossier for John's defence is the most plausible. This states that the Angevin empire was an unwieldy, disparate hotchpotch of elements, in no sense a true empire, doomed to implode and, as such, one of the clearest of all victims of historical inevitability;[56] it was just John's bad fortune that the process of coming apart at the seams happened in his reign rather than that of Henry II. To use the jargon of contemporary sociologists, one might say that the Angevin 'empire' was hegemonic, not territorial; in other words, it was not centrally directed but was a domain of overlapping spheres in most of which indirect rule was practised. On this model, the centre was Anjou, based at Loches and Chinon, and the periphery was Aquitaine, Normandy and England; there was also a third zone where control was contested with others, as in the extreme south with the counts of Toulouse.[57] Given that 'hegemonic' or indirect rule, rather than centralisation (impossible in this era because of the lack of technology) was the norm, and the Angevins never tried to mould their diverse lands into a monolithic union, the whole system was peculiarly vulnerable to break-up. Starting in Henry II's reign, the entire ramshackle structure came under severe threat from Capetian France. Long-term, it is considered that the French held all the cards, but exactly why this was is disputed. Some say Louis's non-interventionism was considered more attractive in the francophone territories than Henry II's authoritarian and dirigiste approach, that Henry leaned more on Roman and Carolingian models of government instead of feudal realities.[58] This thesis, however, sits uneasily alongside the idea of the Angevin empire as a ramshackle entity and the known fact that Henry conceived his dominions as a federation, not an empire.[59]

Others say the Angevins had no unifying myth, ideology or common culture to bind their empire together, whereas France was always able to promote the attractive notion of a geographical and linguistic unity; the cult of King Arthur is sometimes interpreted as the Angevins attempt to plug this cultural gap, creating a myth to counter the French one.[60] It is surely significant that England and Gascony, the only two Angevin territories not formally subject to the French crown, were the only two to survive after 1204. Still others say that from about 1150 the Capetians started to become dissatisfied with a vague system of over-lordship and wanted a clear feudal pyramid, which in turn made them more aggressive and expansionist.[61] What is clear is that it was vital from about 1170 that Henry II and his sons should not fall out, given the scale of the threat from France. This of course is precisely what they proceeded to do. Historians who love 'dialectical' processes are fond, too, of pointing out the myriad 'contradictions' in the Angevin empire: between the Mediterranean culture of Aquitaine and the Frankish culture of the north; between Normandy and England as rivals in the Anglo-Norman realm, with Normans increasingly thinking that Angevin rule benefited England rather than them; and between the necessity for Henry to think coherently and imperially and his own preference for thinking of the separate parts of his domain as territories he could divide and give to his sons.[62] On a much smaller scale and to a lesser extent, Henry's 'solution' to the problem of empire – dividing it among his sons – was much like that adopted by Genghiz Khan with the Mongol empire fifty years later – and with similarly unhappy results.

Yet even if the Angevin empire was, long-term, doomed to destruction, none of the above arguments compel us to accept that the process had to occur in the reign of John. Again and again, one is forced back onto the sheer personal inadequacy of Henry II's lastborn. John, indeed, sometimes seems a kind of avatar of the seven deadly sins, a man who almost possessed all the moral blemishes at one time. As for sloth, we have had occasion enough to note his bipolar intervals of indolence and paralysis; even Warren talks of his 'biting his nails', and no one has explained his lethargy during the latter stages of the loss of Normandy in 1204–05 convincingly on any other basis. All the chronicles are full of stories about John's volcanic rage – often the product of frustration when a clever, cunning and ingenious man (like John) is not quite clever enough, fails to think through all the implications of a given policy, or overrates his own intellectual capacity. Rage and paranoia are often close cousins, so it is no surprise to find John almost pathologically suspicious of everyone: 'treacherous himself, he was always on the lookout for treachery in others' is one recent, and valid, judgement.[63] No one could ever be certain of retaining his favour, and even faithful and blameless royal servants such as Hubert de Burgh, Brian de Lisle, John Fitzhugh, William de Comhill and Peter de Paulay were in disgrace at various times during his reign.[64] He was forever demanding hostages and castles from his barons as pledges of good faith and loyal behaviour. The ultimate in absurdity occurred when he took hostages from his own mercenary captains, even though their livelihoods depended entirely on his whim.[65] Even the administrative innovation of the chancery rolls, that has evoked paeans from historians who see John as, albeit unwittingly, the historian's friend, was probably 'conceived by a suspicious minded monarch who wanted to keep close supervision of the operations of his government'.[66]

Pride was one of the defining characteristics of John: 'the central features of John's character were his pride, ambition and jealousy . . . the loss (of Normandy) was a cruel blow to John's pride'.[67] John's gluttony is also copiously attested to; it was his gourmandising at Lynn that brought on his final, fatal illness. His lechery is confirmed by his illegitimate children: Joan, Geoffrey, John, Henry, Oliver, Richard and Osbert Giffard. One of the most reliable of contemporary chronicles describes him as 'too covetous of pretty ladies'.[68] His lustfulness was one of the factors that alienated the barons, who objected to having their wives and daughters play the role of odalisques in John's informal harem. Both Eustace de Vesci and Robert Fitzwalter, two of the ringleaders in the 1215 revolt, had grievances on this score but John, typically, thought he was the wronged party because of their objections and is said to have hated de Vesci because of his trick in substituting a prostitute instead of his own wife in John's bed.[69] Another notorious incident, where John put his own sexual desires ahead of *raison d'etat*, came after Bouvines when John had William of Salisbury imprisoned because he lusted after his wife.[70] As for the deadly sin of covetousness, greed was the main motive for most of the actions he took during the long conflict with Rome, just as it was with Henry VIII in his similar dispute three hundred years later. Apart from depriving England of Christian worship for seven years, he pillaged Church wealth, expelled bishops, Cistercians and Cluniacs who opposed him, and even banned music in churches if the localities would not disgorge the required amount of loot quickly enough. The entire saga of opposition to Innocent III, originally triggered by John's false pride and egomania and falsely presented as a struggle against papal oppression, was simply an excuse for a gigantic looting session.[71]

As for envy, the entire story of John's relations with Richard breathes a spirit of envy for his more talented elder brother. It may even be that envy of Richard's international reputation, and the fact that he bestrode the known world like a colossus, was the reason John hankered inter-mittently after more exotic forays that might rival Richard in the Holy Land; might this explain, for example, John's little-known desire to estab-lish diplomatic relations with Muslim Spain and North Africa?[72] Envy's brother (or twin?) is jealousy, and of this John had a full measure: 'his almost frantic jealousy was a real weakness . . . while other motives than jealousy had a part in his quarrels with William Marshal and William de Braose, that emotion alone seems to have produced his dislike of Hubert Walter and Geoffrey Fitzpeter'.[73] John was not just jealous of some men with wealth and power; he hated them all. This pathological view of the world had the severe political disadvantage that John could never divide and rule, or play off one great baron against another; as with Nero and the Roman people, he wished the barons had just one head which he could chop off. In addition to the seven deadly sins, we can add an eighth: wanton cruelty. It has been impossible in a life of John to avoid the egregious cases of Arthur, the de Braose family, the Welsh hostages or Peter the Hermit and his son, but I have purposely not dwelt on the many other instances of John's vicious behaviour. He also murdered in prison Geoffrey de Norwich, the justiciar of the Jews and Honorius, archdeacon of Norwich, ostensibly because he owed the king money but probably really because he had failed in a mission to persuade Innocent III to accept John's choice as archbishop of Canterbury.[74] He took Evreux by pretending to be Philip Augustus, slew the garrison treacherously and then displayed their heads on poles. He starved to death forty knights captured at Mirebeau. John encouraged his armies to behave brutally and gave them a free hand to commit atrocities: hanging men by the thumbs, roasting them on tripods and gridirons, rubbing salt and vinegar in men's eyes.[75] Almost certainly he killed a large number of children and other hostages, though the chroniclers' accounts of these are countered by modern historians, absurdly demanding to see the evidence in the Rolls or other official archives.

John was also a pathological liar, systematically duplicitous, treach-erous, serpentine and unscrupulous 'beyond the limits allowed by the ethics of his day'.[76] He invented a system of countersigns to be attached to official orders, so that the recipients would know to disobey them.

This system was used particularly in connection with freeing prisoners or transferring the command of a castle. A double-crosser himself, John feared that he might be double-crossed, so devised his symbolism of secret signs and tokens to make sure there could be no identity fraud or other imposture. On one occasion he issued standing instructions that a certain prisoner was never to be freed unless the instructions for the release arrived in the hands of Thomas de Burgh. But never was the adage that you need a phenomenal memory to be a good liar better borne out than in John's case. Like squirrels who forget where they have buried their nuts, John often forgot what his secret signs and passwords were. When Guy de Lusignan was taken prisoner at Mirebeau, John left instructions that he was not to speak to anyone unless the person was accompanied by three named members of the royal house. Chaos then ensued when John himself forgot who the three named persons were. There were other similar cases, all illustrating the principle that John's level of duplicity approached genuine mental illness.[77] He solemnly approved Magna Carta even while he was writing to the Pope to get him to declare it invalid. He forged letters to confuse his enemies, wrong-foot his advisers and to give himself 'deniability'.[78] Even though in the feudal era a safe-conduct was supposed to be a sacred guarantee, nobody trusted those issued by John. When Stephen Langton and his fellow prelates prepared to return from exile, they did so only after the king's safe-conduct was confirmed by a large number of the leading magnates and prelates.

A final case study may perhaps be allowed, revealing that Richard really did have some of the lineaments of a good king, while John was incorrigible. One of the great disfiguring events of Richard's reign – though not one for which he personally can be blamed, as he had already left the country – was the great antisemitic pogrom of 1190, where the great defender of the Jews was the saintly St Hugh of Lincoln.[79] On his return to England in 1194 Richard reformed the system of moneylending in such a way as to protect the Jews, to make sure that no one could murder a Jewish creditor and destroy the evidence of debt, a favourite option before that date. Only six or seven places were permitted to exist as 'Jewish' banks, and the promissory notes were held not just by the moneylender but by a troika of Jews, Christians and royal officials, who kept copies in a triple-locked chest, to which each custodian had one of the three keys.[80] In 1200 John changed the system and appointed three men as custodians or justices of the Jews; all three were royal nominees, and they were the men who judged disputes arising from Jewish moneylending and debts. John had realised that the Jewish transactions were a lucrative business and wanted all the proceeds for himself. He bent his energies and his considerable ingenuity to squeezing the maximum possible revenue from the Jews. First he issued a royal charter on Jewish affairs; this cost the Jews 4,000 marks and it protected them from the ravages of unscrupulous Christians, but said nothing about the case when they might be victims of an unscrupulous king.[81] John did not want the Jews molested not because he had any affection or respect for them, but because he regarded them as a cash-cow; his essentially contemptuous attitude comes through in a reprimand issued to the mayor and magnates of London in 1203 when he heard that Jews were being harassed there: 'If we give our peace to a dog, it ought to be preserved inviolate.'[82]

That John had absolutely no regard for the Jews became clear in 1210 when he levied another of his 'tallages' against them; some scholars think he had already visited one of these crippling taxes on them in 1205, presumably to show what he thought of the 'dogs' to whom he had given the king's peace.[83] This time the sums he aimed to extract were enormous; the annalists all agree that he demanded 66,000 marks from them, or two-thirds the amount asked for the ransom of Richard in 1193–94.[84] Faced with ruin and catastrophe, the Jews at first tried to avoid payment, but John came down hard on them, imprisoning the non-payers and then torturing them. Some modern historians have affected to disbelieve the worst stories of torture, like the one that John ordered a tooth extracted daily from one recalcitrant usurer until he disgorged the tallage money but, as a judicious observer has put it: 'While the stories of the tortures used to persuade the Jews to contribute adequately to the tallage of 1211 may well be exaggerated, it is hard to believe that they are purely imaginative.'[85] Although the parentage of the Devil's Brood was particularly distinguished for a medieval dynasty, only one of them emerges with much credit from the historical record. The Young King was a posturing wastrel, in many ways a psychological inadequate, while Geoffrey seems pure cunning and malevolence, a totally negative personality. John was a more intellectual form of Geoffrey, with a good mind and some intellectual interests which he used almost entirely for selfish or depraved ends. For all his faults, Richard did at least try to live out the true meaning of a medieval knight. If we 'cash' the Devil's Brood in terms of the Arthurian knights, Geoffrey is the Mordred of the piece, John the Kay and the Young King the Lamorack. Richard, if not Lancelot, is certainly Sir Percival.

Notes

CHAPTER 1

1. Olivier de Laborderie, 'Du souvenir à la réincarnation: image de Richard Coeur de Lion dans la Vie et Mort du Roi Jean de William Shakespeare', in Janet L. Nelson, *Richard Coeur de Lion in History and Myth* (1992), pp.141–65.
2. John Gillingham, *Richard I* (1999), pp.1, 3.
3. See W.L. Warren, *Henry II* (1973).
4. See R.H.C. Davis, *King Stephen, 1135–1154* (1967).
5. Walter Map, *De Nugis Curialium*, ed. M.R. James (1914), pp.237–42.
6. Ibid.
7. Giraldus Cambrensis (Gerald of Wales), *Opera*, eds J.S. Brewer, J.F. Dimock & G.F. Warner, 8 vols (RS 1891) – hereinafter Gerald of Wales – v. pp.302–06; J.C. Robertson, ed., *Materials for the History of Thomas Becket, Archbishop of Canterbury*, 7 vols (RS 1885), vii. p.570.
8. Peter of Blois, *Petri Blesensis Archidiaconi Opera Omnia*, ed. J.A. Giles, 4 vols (Oxford, 1847), i. p.193.
9. Walter Map, op. cit. ibid.; cf. R. Anstruther, ed., *Radulphi Negri Chronica* (1851), p.169.
10. Peter of Blois to the Archbishop of Palermo, c. 1177 in J.P. Migne, ed., *Patrologia Latina* (1864), vol. 207, pp.48–49 (letter 14).
11. Gerald of Wales, *Opera*, op. cit. v. p.304; Robertson, ed., *Materials*, op. cit. vii. pp.124, 249, 251; Ralph of Diceto, *Radulfi de Diceto Decani Lundonienis Opera Historica*, ed. W. Stubbs, 2 vols (RS 1876), i. pp.406–07; William of Newburgh, *Historia Rerum Anglarum* in R. Howlett, ed., *Chronicles and Memorials of the Reigns of Stephen, Henry II and Richard I*, 4 vols (RS 1890), i. p.282.
12. Robertson, ed., *Materials*, iii. pp.18–25; vi. p.72.
13. Warren, *Henry II*, op. cit. pp.10, 219, 402, 432.
14. Walter Map, *Courtiers Trifles*, ed. and trans. M.R. James, C.N.L. Brookes & R.A.B. Mynors (Oxford, 1983), pp.478–79.
15. For background to the complex history and politics of France at this time see: J. Dunbabin, *France in the Making 843–1180* (Oxford, 1985); G. Duby, *France and the Middle Ages* (Oxford, 1991); E.M. Hallam, *Capetian France 987–1328* (1980); S. Reynolds, *Fiefs and Vassals* (Oxford, 1994); C.W. Hollister & T. Keefe, 'The Making of the Angevin Empire', *Journal of British Studies* 12 (1973), pp.1–25.
16. William of Malmesbury, *Historia Novella*, ed. H.R. Potter (1955), p.2.
17. Howlett, ed., *Chronicles*, op. cit. iv. p.123.
18. B. Bachrach, 'Henry II and the Angevin tradition of family hostility', *Albion*

16 (1984), pp.128–30; T. Keefe, 'Geoffrey Plantagenet's Will and the Angevin Succession', *Albion* 6 (1974), pp.266–74.

19. Gerald of Wales, op. cit. viii. p.301.

20. There is an enormous literature on Eleanor of Aquitaine. Representative titles include Régine Pernoud, *Aliénor d'Aquitaine* (Paris, 1965); W.W. Kibler, ed., *Eleanor of Aquitaine: Patron and Politician* (Austin, Texas, 1976); Alison Weir, *Eleanor of Aquitaine by the Wrath of God, Queen of England* (1999). There are also some first-rate essays: Jane Martindale, 'Eleanor of Aquitaine', in Janet Nelson, ed., *Richard Coeur de Lion in History and Myth*, op. cit. pp.17–50; E.R. Labande, 'Pour une image véridique d'Aliénor d'Aquitaine', *Bulletin de la Société des Antiquaires de l'Ouest*, 4th series 2 (1952), pp.174–234; H.G. Richardson, 'The letters and charters of Eleanor of Aquitaine', EHR 74 (1959), pp.191–213.

21. Dunbabin, *France in the Making*, op. cit. pp.56–63; Hallam, *Capetian France*, op. cit. pp. 52–63; E.A. Richard, *Histoire des comtes de Poitou*, 2 vols (Paris, 1903), ii. pp.60–457.

22. Labande. 'Pour une image', loc. cit.; R. Bartlett, *Gerald of Wales 1146–1223* (Oxford, 1982), pp.91–99.

23. John of Salisbury, *Historia Pontificalis* (Memoirs of the Papal Court), ed. Marjorie Chibnall (1956), pp.52–53; Richard of Devizes, *Chronicon Richardi Divisensis de tempore Regis Richard Primi*, ed. J.T. Appleby (1963), pp.25–26; Labande, 'Pour une image', loc. cit. pp.184–87; Martindale, 'Eleanor of Aquitaine', loc. cit. p.40; Pernoud, *Aliénor*, op. cit. pp. 86–93; G. Duby, *The Knight, the Lady and the Priest: The Making of Modern Marriage in Medieval France*, trans. B. Bray (1985), pp.192–96; Elberg Foster, ed., *Medieval Marriage: Two Models from Twelfth Century France* (Johns Hopkins, 1978) pp.54–62.

24. John Gillingham, 'Love, marriage and politics in the twelfth century', *Forum for Modern Language Studies* 25 (1989), pp.292–303; C. Brooke, *The Medieval Idea of Marriage* (Oxford, 1991), pp.123–24.

25. W. Stubbs, ed., *The Historical Works of Gervase of Canterbury*, 2 vols (RS 1880), i. p.49; Gerald of Wales, op. cit. viii. pp.300–01; Howlett, ed., *Chronicles*, op. cit. ii. p.165; Richard, *Histoire des comtes de Poitou*, op. cit. ii. p. 457; Labande, 'Pour une image', p.198.

26. John of Salisbury, *Memoirs of the Papal Court*, op. cit. pp.61–62.

27. Labande, 'Pour une image', p.197; Martindale, 'Eleanor of Aquitaine', loc. cit. p. 42; A. Molinier, ed., *Vie de Louis Le Gros par Suger, suivie de l'histoire du roi Louis VII* (Paris, 1887), pp.165–66.

28. Stubbs, ed., *Historical Works of Gervase of Canterbury*, op. cit. i. p.49.

29. Ralph of Diceto, op. cit. i. p.303; Martindale, 'Eleanor', loc. cit. pp.31–32.

30. Warren, *Henry II*, pp.45–47.

31. Pernoud, *Aliénor*, p.114.

32. Martindale, 'Eleanor', loc. cit. p.43.

33. Pernoud, *Aliénor*, p.186; Pauline Stafford, 'Sons and mothers: family politics in the early Middle Ages', in D. Baker, ed., *Medieval Women* (Oxford, 1978), pp.79–100; Alison Weir, *Eleanor of Aquitaine*, op. cit. pp.361–62.

34. B. Lyon, 'Henry II: A Non-Victorian Interpretation', in J.S. Hamilton & R.

Bradley, eds, *Essays in Medieval History presented to G.P. Cuttino* (Woodbridge, 1989).

35. R.V. Turner, 'Eleanor of Aquitaine and her children: an inquiry into medieval family attachment', JMH 14 (1988), pp.32–35; Martindale, 'Eleanor', loc. cit. p.37; cf. Kibler, ed., *Eleanor of Aquitaine*, op. cit.

36. Martindale, 'Eleanor', loc. cit. p.33.

37. Howlett, ed., *Chronicles*, op. cit. iv. pp.180, 186; W. Stubbs, ed., *Chronica Rogeri de Houdene*, 4 vols (RS 1871) – hereinafter Howden, *Chronica* – i. p.215; Z.N. & C.N.L. Brooke, 'Henry II, duke of Normandy and Aquitaine', EHR 61 (1946), pp.81–89 (at pp.86–88); J. Boussard, *Le gouvernment d'Henri II Plantagenêt* (Paris, 1956), pp.397–98; Warren, *Henry II*, pp.64–65.

38. Kate Norgate, *Richard the Lionheart* (1924), pp.2–3. For Nequam see R.W. Hunt, *The Schools and the Cloister. The Life and Writings of Alexander Nequam* (Oxford, 1984); see also review by John J. Contreni in AHR 90 (1985), pp.917–18.

39. Alison Weir, *Eleanor of Aquitaine*, p.153.

40. W.J. Miller, H.E. Butler & C.N.L. Brooke, eds, *Letters of John of Salisbury*, 2 vols (1979), i. pp.199–200.

41. The best synoptic work of research is Bonnie Wheeler & John Carmi Parsons, eds, *Eleanor of Aquitaine. Lord and Lady* (2002). Cf. also D.D.R. Owen, *Eleanor of Aquitaine* (1993) and Douglas Boyd, *Eleanor, April Queen of Aquitaine* (2004).

42. X. de Planhol, *A Historical Geography of France* (Cambridge, 1994).

43. Ralph of Diceto, i. pp.293–94.

44. R. Dion, *Histoire de la vigne et du vin en France des origines au XIXe siècle* (Paris, 1959); R. Faureau, 'Les debuts de la ville de La Rochelle', *Cahiers de civilisation médiévale* 30 (1987), pp.23–28; C. Page, *Voices and Instruments of the Middle Ages* (1987); L. Seidel, *Songs of Glory. The Romanesque Facades of Aquitaine* (Chicago, 1981).

45. J. Viellard, *Le guide du pèlerin de Saint-Jacques de Compostelle* (Mâcon, 1938), pp.16–32, 62–78.

46. John Frederick Rowbotham, *The Troubadours and the Courts of Love* (1895); Simon Gaunt & Sarah Keys, eds, *The Troubadours: An Introduction* (1999); Jack Lindsay, *The Troubadours and their World in the Twelfth and Thirteenth Centuries* (1976); F.X. Newman, *The Meaning of Courtly Love* (N.Y., 1968); Elizabeth Aubrey, *The Music of the Troubadours* (1996); Sarah Spence, *Rhetoric of Reason and Desire: Vergil, Augustine and the Troubadours* (1988).

47. Amy Kelly, *Eleanor of Aquitaine and the Four Kings* (Cambridge, Mass., 1950), pp.158–67; J. Chaban-Delmas, *La dame d'Aquitaine* (Monte Carlo, 1987), p.144; J. Markdale, *La vie, la légende, l'influence d'Aliénor comtesse de Poitou, duchesse d'Aquitaine, reine de France, puis Angleterre, dame des troubadours et des bardes bretons* (Paris, 1979); Régine Pernoud, *Aliénor*, op. cit. p.364.

48. P.G. Walsh, ed., *Andreas Capellanus on Love* (1982), pp.92–93, 252–57; Martindale, 'Eleanor', loc. cit. p.39; John Gillingham, 'Love, marriage and politics', loc. cit. pp.292–303; J. McCash, 'Marie de Champagne and Eleanor of Aquitaine: a relationship reexamined', *Speculum* 54 (1979), pp.698–711. The most recent research is in Marcus Bull & Catherine Leglu, *The World of Eleanor of Aquitaine* (Woodbridge, 2005).

49. F.K. Akeheurst & Judith M. Davis, eds, *A Handbook of the Troubadours* (Berkeley, 1995); Jean Boutière & Alexander H. Schutz, eds, *Biographies des Troubadours* (n.d.); Robert Briffault, *The Troubadours* (Bloomington, Indiana, 1961); Raymond Thompson Hill & T.G. Bergin, eds, *Anthology of the Provençal Troubadours* (1973).

50. William of Malmesbury, *Gesta Anglorum*, eds R.A.B. Mynors, R.M. Thomson & M. Winterbottom (Oxford, 1998), ii. pp.392–93; Jane Martindale, '*Cavalaria et Orgueil*. Duke William IX and the historian', in Christopher Harper-Bill & Ruth Harvey, eds, *The Ideals and Practice of Medieval Knighthood* (1988), pp.87–116; A. Jeanroy, ed., *Les chansons de Guillaume IX, duc d'Aquitaine* (Paris, 1972).

51. M. Lazar, ed., *Chansons d'Amour by Bernard de Ventadour* (Strasbourg, 1966); R. Lejeune, 'Role littéraire d'Aliénor d'Aquitaine et de sa famille', *Cultura Neo-Latina* 14 (1954), pp.6–57 (at pp.17–19); Amy Kelly, *Eleanor of Aquitaine*, op. cit. pp.158–67.

52. J.Weiss, *The Birth of Romance* (1992), pp.59, 66.

53. P. Bec, 'Troubadours, trouvères et espace Plantagenêt', *Cahiers de civilisation médiévale* 29 (1986), pp.10–11; J. Stevenson, ed., *Radulphi de Coggleshall Chronicon Anglicanum* (RS 1875) – hereinafter Coggleshall – p.97; George Henry Needler, *Richard Coeur de Lion in Literature* (Leipzig, 1890), pp.7–18.

54. Warren, *Henry II*, pp.82–92.

55. Howlett, *Chronicles*, op. cit. iv. p.211.

56. Ralph of Diceto, i. p.331; J.C. Robertson, ed., *Materials*, op. cit. v. p.197; L. Delisle & E. Berger, eds, *Recueil des Actes de Henri II roi d'Angleterre et duc de Normandie, concernant les provinces françaises et les affaires de France*, 4 vols, i. p.416; Boussard, *Le gouvernment d'Henri II*, op. cit. p.354; P. Boissonade, 'Administrateurs laïques et ecclésiastiques anglo-normands en Poitou à l'époque d'Henri II Plantagenêt 1152–1189', *Bulletin de la Société des Antiquaires de l'Ouest*, 3rd series 5 (1919), pp.159–60; Richard, *Histoire des comtes de Poitou 778–1204*, 2 vols (Paris, 1903), ii. pp.130–34.

57. Howlett, *Chronicles*, op. cit. iv. pp.235–36; S. Painter, 'The Houses of Lusignan and Châtellerault 1150–1250', *Speculum* 30 (1955), pp.374–84; Painter, 'The Lords of Lusignan in the eleventh and twelfth centuries', *Speculum* 32 (1957), pp.27–47.

58. Millor & Brooke, eds, *Letters of John of Salisbury*, op. cit. ii. pp.552–70; *History of William Marshal*, eds & trans., A.J. Holden, S. Gregory & D. Crouch (2002) – hereinafter WM – i. pp.85–91.

59. Howlett, *Chronicles*, iv. p.208; Gillingham, *Richard I*, pp.29–30.

60. Howlett, *Chronicles*, iv. p.240; *Letters of John of Salisbury*, op. cit. ii. pp.636–49.

61. Robertson, ed., *Materials*, iii. pp.418–39; Gervase of Canterbury, i. pp.207–11; Ralph of Diceto, i. pp.336–37.

62. Howlett, *Chronicles*, iv. pp.241–42; Richard, *Histoire des comtes de Poitou*, op. cit. ii. p.150.

63. Frank Barlow, *Thomas Becket* (1986), pp.225–50.

64. Richard, *Histoire des comtes de Poitou*, ii. pp.150–53.

65. Vigeois, 'Chronica', in P. Labbe, ed, *Novae Bibliothecae Manuscriptorum Librorum*, 2 vols (Paris, 1657), ii. pp.279–329.
66. W. Stubbs, ed., *Chronicles and Memorials of the Reign of Richard I*, RS38 (1864) I p.144.
67. Gerald of Wales, viii. p.309; Gillingham, *Richard I*, pp.255–56.
68. W.S. Davies, ed., *The De Inventionibus of Gerald* (1920), pp.100–101; Coggleshall, pp.59–60.
69. Gerald of Wales, iv. p.54; J.L. Thorpe, ed. & trans., *Journey through Wales by Gerald of Wales* (1978), pp.104–05.
70. Gillingham, *Richard I*, pp.256–57.
71. J. Vieillard, *Le Guide du pèlerin de Saint-Jacques de Compostelle* (Mâcon, 1938), pp.16–32, 62, 66, 78.

CHAPTER 2

1. Gerald of Wales, viii. pp.177–79; Roger of Howden, *Gesta Regis Henrici Secundi*, ed. W. Stubbs (RS 1867), 2 vols, i. p.297.
2. BN Latin MSS.5480; W.L. Warren, *King John* (1961), p.26.
3. Ralph of Diceto, i. p.382.
4. Andrew L. Lewis, 'The Birth and Childhood of King John: Some Revisions', in Bonnie Wheeler & John C. Parsons, *Eleanor of Aquitaine. Lord and Lady* (2002), pp.159–75. Cf. also Robert of Gloucester, *Chronicle*, in *Works of Thomas Hearne*, 2 vols (1810), ii. p.484, Howlett, *Chronicles*, op. cit. iv. pp.195, 207, 221, 233, 252.
5. Ralph of Diceto, ii. pp.16–17, 269–70; Howlett, *Chronicles*, iv. pp.176, 183, 195, 197, 211, 226; R.W. Eyton, *Court, Household and Itinerary of Henry II* (1878), ii. pp.54–55.
6. Georges Duby, *Dames au XIIe siècle* (Paris, 1996), p.32; Elizabeth A.R. Brown, 'Eleanor of Aquitaine: Parent, Queen and Duchess', in Kibler, ed., *Eleanor of Aquitaine*, op. cit. pp.9–23 (at p.16); Labande, 'Pour une image véridique', loc. cit. pp.202–03; Lewis, 'Birth and Childhood of King John', loc. cit. p.165.
7. Jacqueline Smith, 'Robert of Arbussel's relations with women', in Baker, ed., *Medieval Women*, op. cit. pp.175–84.
8. Lewis, 'Birth and Childhood of King John', loc. cit. pp.167–68, 175.
9. Ralph V. Turner, 'Eleanor of Aquitaine and her children: an inquiry into medieval family attachment', *Journal of Medieval History* 14 (1988), pp.325–26.
10. Elizabeth A.R. Brown, 'Eleanor of Aquitaine', loc. cit; Lois L. Huneycutt, 'Public Lives, Private Ties, Royal Mothers in England and Scotland c. 1070–1204', in John Parsons & Bonnie Wheeler, eds, *Medieval Mothering* (1996), pp.297–98, 306–08.
11. Lewis, 'Birth and Childhood of King John', loc. cit pp.168–69.
12. Op. cit. p.175.
13. Howlett, *Chronicles*, iii. p.408.
14. Coggleshall, pp.324–25; S. Painter, *The Reign of King John* (Baltimore, 1949), pp.48–54.

15. Gerald of Wales, viii. pp.292–93.

16. Walter Map, *Courtiers' Trifles* (Oxford, 1983), pp.450–51.

17. See Susan Reynolds, *Fiefs and Vassals. The Medieval Evidence Reinterpreted* (Oxford, 1994); Elizabeth A.R. Brown, 'The Tyranny of a Construct Feudalism and Historians of Medieval Europe', AHR 79 (1974), pp.1063–88; Paul R. Hyams, 'The End of Feudalism?', *Journal of Interdisciplinary History* (1997), pp.655–72.

18. Susan Mosher Stuard, *Women in Medieval Society* (Pennsylvania, 1993); David Herlihy, *Women, Family and Society in Medieval Europe. Historical Essays* (1995); Henrietta Leyser, *Medieval Women. A Social History of Women in England 450–1500* (1995).

19. William of Newburgh, i. p.114; Howlett, *Chronicles*, iv. p.197.

20. Warren, *Henry II*, op. cit. pp.108–09.

21. J.F. Le Marignier, *Recherches sur l'hommage en marche et les frontières féodales* (Lille, 1945), pp.38–45; Howlett, *Chronicles*, iv. pp.160–64.

22. F. Barlow, ed., *The Letters of Arnulf of Lisieux* (Camden Society, 1939), pp.32–33 (letter 24); Barlow, 'The English, Norman and French councils called to deal with the papal schism of 1159', EHR 51 (1936), pp.264–68.

23. Warren, *Henry II*, pp.88–90.

24. Robertson, ed., *Materials*, op. cit. vi. pp.206–07, 323; vii. p.217; Raymond Foreville, *L'Eglise et la royauté en Angleterre sous Henri II Plantagenêt 1154–1189* (Paris, 1943), pp.280–83; Anne Heslin, 'The Coronation of the Young King in 1170', in G.J. Cuming, ed., *Studies in Church History* 2 (1968), pp.165–78.

25. Howlett, *Chronicles*, iv. p.245; Robertson, ed., *Materials*, vii. pp.309, 316–17.

26. Howden, *Gesta*, i. pp.6–7; Howlett, *Chronicles*, pp.247–48.

27. Gervase of Canterbury, i. pp.207–08; Ralph of Diceto, i. pp.336–37; Richard, *Les comtes de Poitou*, ii. p.150.

28. Howden, *Gesta*, i. p.31.

29. Ibid., pp.35–41; Howden, *Chronica*, ii. pp.41–45; C. Devic & J. Vaissete, *Histoire générale de Languedoc*, 6 vols (Toulouse, 1905), v. pp.11–12; M. Pacaut, *Louis VII et son royaume* (Paris, 1964), p.191; Howlett, *Chronicles*, iv. p.255; *Recueil des Actes de Henri II roi d'Angleterre et duc de Normandie*, ed. Delisle & Berger, op. cit. ii. pp.1–4; Prévité-Orton, *The Early History of the House of Savoy 1000–1233* (Cambridge, 1912), pp.337–41.

30. Howlett, *Chronicles*, ii. p.146; Kate Norgate, *John Lackland* (1902), p.2.

31. Howden, *Gesta*, i. pp.34–35, 41; Howlett, *Chronicles*, iv. p.255.

32. WM, i. p.101.

33. Ibid., i. p.135.

34. See O.H. Moore, *The Young King Henry Plantagenet 1155–1183 in History, Literature and Tradition* (Columbus, Ohio, 1925), passim; cf. also R.J. Smith, 'Henry II's Heir: the Acta and Seal of Henry the Young King, 1170–83', EHR 116 (2001), pp.297–326.

35. A. Thomas, *Poésies complètes de Bertran de Born* (Toulouse, 1888), p.6.

36. Howden, *Gesta*, i. p34; Howden, *Chronica*, i. p.32.

37. Dante, *Divine Comedy*, Canto 28, lines 133–35.

38. Howlett, *Chronicles*, pp.255–56.

39. Howden, *Gesta*, i. p.41; Howden, *Chronica*, ii. pp.41–45; Gervase of Canterbury, i. p.242; Howlett, *Chronicles*, i. pp.169–70; P. Labbe, *Novae Bibliothecae Manuscriptorum Librorum* (Paris, 1657), ii. p.319.

40. Robertson, ed., *Materials*, iii. pp.116, 118–19, 478–83; v. pp.57, 270, 328–29; vi. pp.57–58; vii. pp.216, 330, 357–58, 382–95, 400.

41. Warren, *Henry II*, p.118.

42. Kate Norgate, *England under the Angevin Kings*, 2 vols (1887), ii. p.134.

43. Labbe, *Novae Bibliothecae*, op. cit. ii. p.319; Howlett, *Chronicles*, i. pp.170–72; iv. p.256; Gervase of Canterbury, i. pp.242–43; Howden, *Gesta*, i. pp.41–43; Howden, *Chronica*, ii. p.46; Ralph of Diceto, i. p.355.

44. Howden, ibid.

45. Ralph of Diceto, i. pp.355–66.

46. M. Bouquet et al, eds, *Recueil des historiens de Gaule et de la France*, 24 vols (Paris, 1904), xvi. pp.629–30.

47. Millor, Butler & Brooke, eds, *Letters of John of Salisbury*, op. cit. ii. pp.342–46; Gervase of Canterbury, i. p.242.

48. Alison Weir, *Eleanor of Aquitaine*, op. cit. pp.196–97.

49. Warren, *Henry II*, pp.519–49.

50. Ibid., pp.119–21.

51. D.D.R. Owen, *Eleanor of Aquitaine* (Oxford, 1993), pp.114–48.

52. Labande, 'Pour une image', loc. cit. pp.208–09; cf. J. Brundage, *Law, Sex and Christian Society in Medieval Europe* (Chicago, 1987).

53. Pernoud, *Aliénor d'Aquitaine*, op. cit. p.151.

54. Martindale, 'Eleanor of Aquitaine', loc. cit. p.44.

55. J.F. Benton, 'The Courts of Champagne as a Literary Center', *Speculum* 36 (1961), pp.551–91; J.M.H. McCash, 'Marie de Champagne and Eleanor of Aquitaine: A Relationship Reexamined', *Speculum* 54 (1979), pp.698–711.

56. Amy Kelly, 'Eleanor of Aquitaine and her courts of love', *Speculum* 12 (1937), pp.3–19; F.W. Chambers, 'Some legends regarding Eleanor of Aquitaine', *Speculum* 16 (1941), pp.459–68.

57. Gillingham, *Richard I*, pp.45–46.

58. Martindale, 'Eleanor', loc. cit. pp.24–25, 28–31.

59. Gillingham, *Richard I*, p.47.

60. Ralph of Diceto, i. p.371.

61. Boussard, *Le gouvernment d'Henri II*, op. cit. p.477; Warren, *Henry II*, pp.121–23; Norgate, *England under the Angevin Kings*, op. cit. ii. p.136.

62. Howden, *Chronica*, ii. p.47.

63. Howden, *Gesta*, i. pp.43–44.

64. W. Strickland, *War and Chivalry. The Conduct and Perception of War in England and Normandy 1066–1217* (Cambridge, 1966), pp.291–329; unfortunately the outstanding work of Kenneth Alan Fowler, *Medieval Mercenaries. The Great Companies* (2001), does not deal with this period.

65. Ralph of Diceto, i. pp.367–75; William of Newburgh, i. pp.173–75; Howden, *Gesta*, i. pp.47–57.

66. Howden, *Gesta*, i. pp.59–60.
67. Howden, *Gesta*, i. pp.60–63; Ralph of Diceto, i. pp.377–79; Howden, *Chronica*, ii. pp.54–55.
68. Pipe Rolls 22 Henry II, pp.119–20; Ralph of Diceto, i. pp.379–80; Howden, *Gesta*, pp.64–71; Howlett, *Chronicles*, i. pp.179–82.
69. Gervase of Canterbury, i. pp.247–49; Ralph of Diceto, i. pp.381–82.
70. Ralph of Diceto, i. pp.383–84; Gervase of Canterbury, i. p.249; Howden, *Gesta*, i. p.72; Howden, *Chronica*, ii. pp.61–63.
71. Gervase of Canterbury, i. p.250; Ralph of Diceto, i. pp.385–87; Howden, *Gesta*, i. pp.74–76; Howden, *Chronica*, ii. pp.65–66; Howlett, *Chronicles*, i. pp.190–96; iv. p.265.
72. C. Johnson, ed., *Dialogus de Scaccario* (1950), p.76.
73. Ralph of Diceto, i. p.380; Howden, *Gesta*, i. p.71.
74. Howden, *Gesta*, i. pp.76–79; Howden, *Chronica*, ii. pp.66–69.
75. Warren, *Henry II*, p.138.
76. Pipe Rolls 22 Henry II, pp.60, 179; GM, iii. p.33; Ralph of Diceto, i. pp.398, 404; Howden, *Gesta*, i. pp.126–27.
77. Ralph of Diceto, i. pp.395–98; Howden, *Gesta*, i. pp.134–35; Howden, *Chronica*, ii. p.118; T. Rymer, A. Clarke & F. Holbrook, eds, *Foedera, conventiones litterae*, Part One (1816), i. p.30.
78. Howden, *Gesta*, i. pp.92, 127, 160–61.
79. Ibid., pp.81–83.
80. Ibid., p.101.
81. Ibid., pp.115, 121.
82. Ralph of Diceto, i. p.407; Howden, *Gesta*, i. p.120.
83. Gillingham, *Richard I*, p.255.
84. Ralph of Diceto, i. p.414; Howden, *Gesta*, i. pp.120–21.
85. Johnson, *Dialogus de Scaccario*, op. cit. p.2.
86. Gervase of Canterbury, i. pp.260–61; Ralph of Diceto, i. pp.408, 415–16, 418–20; Howden, *Gesta*, i. pp.115–17, 128–30, 139–43; Howden, *Chronica*, ii. pp.94–95, 102–04; Howlett, *Chronicles*, iv. p.278.
87. Gerald of Wales, v. p.303.
88. Gerald of Wales, viii. p.247.

CHAPTER 3

1. Warren, *Henry II*, pp.560–61.
2. Howden, *Gesta*, i. pp.131–32.
3. Duplès-Agier, ed., *Chroniques de Saint-Martial de Limoges*, op. cit. p.189.
4. Ralph of Diceto, i. p.425; Howden, *Gesta*, i. pp.127, 132, 168–69; Howlett, *Chronicles*, iv. p.274.
5. Howden, *Gesta*, i. pp.180–81.
6. Ibid., pp.190–94.
7. Ibid., pp.194–96.
8. Ibid., pp.196–97; Ralph of Diceto, i. p.450; Howlett, *Chronicles*, iv. pp.274–76.

9. T.N. Bisson, *The Medieval Crown of Aragon* (Oxford, 1986), pp.35–37.

10. Howden, *Gesta*, pp.212–13.

11. P. Boissonade, 'Les comtes de l'Angoulême – les lignes féodales contre Richard Coeur de Lion et les poésies de Bertran de Born', *Annales de Midi* 7 (1895), pp.275–95.

12. Ralph of Diceto, i. p.431; Howden, *Gesta*, i. p.213.

13. Ralph of Diceto, i. pp.431–32; Howden, *Gesta*, i. p.213; Howlett, *Chronicles*, iv. pp.281–82.

14. Ralph of Diceto, i. p.401.

15. S. Rogers, *Latin Siege Warfare in the Twelfth Century* (Oxford, 1992); Strickland, *War and Chivalry*, op. cit.

16. Gillingham, *Richard I*, p.64.

17. Gervase of Canterbury, i. p.303; Ralph of Diceto, ii. p.19.

18. Geoffrey of Vigeois in P. Labbe, ed., *Novae Bibliothecae*, op. cit. ii. p.326,

19. Ibid., ii. pp.330–31; Ralph of Diceto, ii. p.19; Gervase of Canterbury, i. p.303; Howden, *Gesta*, i. pp.288–92.

20. L. Clédat, *Du rôle historique de Bertran de Born 1178–1200* (Paris, 1879); A. Stimming, ed., *Bertran de Born* (Halle, 1913); A. Thomas, ed., *Poésies complètes de Bertran de Born* (Toulouse, 1888).

21. M. Bloch, *Feudal Society* (1961), pp.293, 296.

22. Moore, *Young King Henry Plantagenet*, p.47.

23. Warren, *Henry II*, pp.578–79.

24. Dunbabin, *France in the Making*, op. cit. p.371.

25. Jim Bradbury, *Philip Augustus, King of France 1180–1223* (1998), p.43.

26. Gerald of Wales, vi. pp.293–94.

27. W.D. Paden, T. Sankovitch & P.H. Stablein, *The Poems of the Troubadour Bertran de Born* (Berkeley, 1986), pp.176–83.

28. D. Crouch, *William Marshal*, p.20.

29. Ibid., p.38.

30. Juliet Barker, *The Tournament in England 1100–1400* (Woodbridge, 1986); Juliet Barker & Richard Barber, *Jousts, Chivalry and Pageants in the Middle Ages* (Woodbridge, 1989).

31. WM, i. pp.361–69.

32. Ibid.

33. H. J. Schroeder, *Disciplinary Decrees of the General Council: Text, Translation and Commentary* (St Louis, 1937), pp.195–213.

34. Crouch, *William Marshal*, pp.48–50.

35. WM, i. pp.173–75.

36. Ralph of Diceto, i. p.428.

37. Howden, *Gesta*, i. p.207; Howden, *Chronica*, ii. pp.166–67.

38. WM, i. p.183.

39. Gerald of Wales, v. p.194.

40. Howden, *Gesta*, i. p.289; Crouch, *William Marshal*, pp.45–46.

41. Ralph of Diceto, ii. p.19; Howden, *Gesta*, i. p.291.

42. Raynouard, ed., *Bertran de Born*, op. cit p.47; Stimming, *Bertran de Born*, p.114.

43. Gerald of Wales, viii. pp.177–79; Howden, *Gesta*, i. p.29.

44. B.A. Pocquet du Haut-Jussé, 'Les Plantagenêts et la Bretagne', *Annales de Bretagne* 53 (1946), pp.1–27.

45. Ralph of Diceto, i. p.406; Howden, *Gesta*, i. p.239; Howden, *Chronica*, ii. p.192; Howlett, *Chronicles*, iv. p.275; Boussard, *Le gouvernment d'Henri II*, op. cit. p.548.

46. Pocquet du Haut-Jussé, 'Les Plantagenêts', loc. cit. pp.15–26.

47. Gerald of Wales, v. p.200.

48. S. Painter, 'The houses of Lusignan and Chatellerault 1150–1250, *Speculum* 30 (1955), pp.374–84; Painter, *Feudalism and Liberty*, ed. F.A. Cazel (Baltimore, 1961), pp.73–89; Gillingham, *Richard I*, p.69.

49. Howden, *Gesta*, i. pp.18, 294; Kate Norgate, *Richard the Lionheart*, op. cit. p.46.

50. Warren, *Henry II*, p.587.

51. WM, i. pp.315, 335.

52. Paden, Sankovitch & Stablein, eds, *Bertran de Born*, op.cit. pp.182–83.

53. Ibid., pp.160–73.

54. Gervase of Canterbury, i. p.304; Ralph of Diceto, i. pp.18–19; Howden, *Gesta*, i. p.292; Howlett, *Chronicles*, iv. p.240.

55. Gervase of Canterbury, i. p.304; Ralph of Diceto, ii. p.19; Howden, *Gesta*, i. pp.292, 296.

56. Howden, *Gesta*, i. pp.295; Kate Norgate, *Richard the Lionheart*, p.50.

57. Ralph of Diceto, ii. pp.18–19; Howden, *Gesta*, i. pp.291–96; Howden, *Chronica*, ii. p.274.

58. Geoffrey of Vigeois in Labbe, ed., *Novae Bibliothecae*, ii. p.331; Howden, *Gesta*, pp.296–97; Norgate, *Richard the Lionheart*, pp.50–56.

59. Vigeois, op. cit. ii. pp.332–38; Howden, *Gesta*, i. pp.297–300.

60. WM, i. pp.323–25.

61. Howden, *Gesta*, i. pp.302–04; Howlett, *Chronicles*, iv. pp.305–06.

62. Paden, Sankovitch & Stablein, *Bertran de Born*, pp.184–89.

63. Ibid., pp.280–81.

64. Ibid., pp.278–79.

65. Howden, *Gesta*, i. pp.302–04.

66. Paden, Sankovitch & Stablein, *Bertran de Born*, pp.204–13.

67. Op. cit. pp.286–87.

CHAPTER 4

1. Ralph of Diceto, i. p.415; Howden, *Gesta*, i. pp.124–25; ii. p.73.

2. Howlett, *Chronicles*, iv. p.268; Howden, *Gesta*, i. pp.77–79.

3. Gerald of Wales, viii. pp.177–79. On John's height see V. Green, *An Account of the Discovery of the Body of King John in the Cathedral Church of Winchester, July 17, 1797* (1797).

4. Howden, *Gesta*, i. pp.335–36.

5. Gerald of Wales, viii. pp.177–79.

6. J.T. Appleby, ed., *Chronicon Richardi Divisensis de tempore Regis Richardi Primi* – hereinafter Richard of Devizes – (1963), p.60; Matthew Paris, *Chronica Majora*, ed. H.R. Luard, 7 vols (RS 1883), ii. pp.560–63.

7. J.P. Appleby, *England without Richard 1189–99* (1965), p.8.

8. Warren, *Henry II*, pp.78, 119, 134, 559, 625.

9. Paden et al., *Bertran de Born*, op. cit. pp.186–87.

10. N. Vincent, 'King Henry II and the Poitevins', in M. Aurell, ed., *Actes du Colloque* (Poitiers, 2001), pp.103–35.

11. Howden, *Gesta*, i. pp.304–08.

12. Ibid., p.311; F.M. Powicke, *The Loss of Normandy* (1961), p.232.

13. Ralph of Diceto, ii. pp.28–29; Howden, *Gesta*, i. pp.311, 319–20.

14. Howden, *Gesta*, i. pp.313, 319–21; U. Kessler, *Richard I. Löwenherz, König, Kreuzritter, Abenteurer* (Graz, 1995), pp.34–35; Ferdinand, Opll, *Friedrich Barbarossa* (Darmstadt, 1990), pp.141, 144, 291.

15. Howden, *Gesta*, i. pp.334, 337.

16. Ibid., pp.337–38.

17. Ibid., pp.343–44, 350; Gerald of Wales, viii. pp.175–76.

18. Ralph of Diceto, ii. pp.33–34; Gervase of Canterbury, i. p.32; William of Newburgh, i. p.247; Gerald of Wales, viii. pp.208–09.

19. Howlett, *Chronicles*, iv. p.186.

20. Warren, *Henry II*, pp.197–98; M.T. Flanagan, *Irish Society, Anglo-Norman Settlers, Angevin Kingship* (Oxford, 1989), pp.7–55; Warren, 'The Interpretation of Twelfth Century Irish History', in J.C. Beckett, ed., *Historical Studies* 7 (1969), pp.1–19.

21. William of Newburgh, i. p.167.

22. Gerald of Wales, v. p.227; Flanagan, *Irish Society*, op. cit. pp.56–78.

23. Gerald of Wales, v. pp.228–30, 246–47.

24. Flanagan, *Irish Society*, pp.79–136.

25. Gervase of Canterbury, i. pp.234–35; G.H. Orpen, *Ireland under the Normans 1169–1333*, 4 vols (Oxford, 1920), i. pp.81–84; M.T. Flanagan, 'Strongbow, Henry II and Anglo-Norman Intervention in Ireland', in J. Gillingham & J.C. Holt, eds, *War and Government in the Middle Ages: Essays in Honour of J.O. Prestwich* (Woodbridge, 1984), pp.74–77.

26. Gerald of Wales, v. pp.227–28, 259; William of Newburgh, i. p.168.

27. William of Newburgh, i. pp.167–68; Flanagan, *Irish Society*, pp.167–228.

28. Gervase of Canterbury, i. p.235; Gerald of Wales, v. p.273.

29. Gerald of Wales, v. pp.277–79; Gervase of Canterbury, i. p.235.

30. Gerald of Wales, v. pp.355–56; Howden, *Gesta*, i. p.270.

31. Howden, *Gesta*, i. pp.102–03; Howden, *Chronica*, ii. pp.84–85.

32. A.B. Scott & F.X. Martin, *The Conquest of Ireland by Gerald of Wales* (Dublin, 1978), p.169; Howden, *Gesta*, i. pp.161–65; Howden, *Chronica*, ii. pp.100, 133; Flanagan, *Irish Society*, pp.229–272.

33. Howden, *Gesta*, i. p.336.

34. Ibid., p.339; Howden, *Chronica*, ii. pp.306–07; Flanagan, *Irish Society*, pp.273–304.

35. Scott & Martin, eds, *Conquest*, op. cit. pp.205, 229; Lewis Warren, 'King John

in Ireland, 1185', in J. Bosy & P. Jupp, eds, *Essays Presented to Michael Roberts* (Belfast, 1976), pp.11–23.

36. *Conquest*, op. cit. pp.237–39.

37. Sean Duffy, 'John and Ireland: the Origin of England's Irish Problem', in S.D. Church, ed., *King John: New Interpretations* (Woodbridge, 1999), pp.221–45 (at p.230).

38. *Conquest*, pp.235–39.

39. W.M. Hennessy, ed., *The Annals of Loch Cé*, 2 vols (RS 1871), i. pp.171–73.

40. W.L. Warren, 'The Historian as "Private Eye"', in J.G. Barry, ed. *Historical Studies* (Belfast, 1974), pp.1–18.

41. *Conquest*, p.235; Howden, *Gesta*, i. p.339.

42. William of Newburgh, i. p.237; J. T. Gilbert, ed., *Chartularies of St Mary's Abbey, Dublin*, 2 vols (RS 1886), ii. p.305; Gilbert, ed., *Historic and Municipal Documents of Ireland* (RS 1870), p.49; J. O'Donovan, ed., *Annals of the Kingdom of Ireland by the Four Masters*, 7 vols (Dublin, 1851), iii. pp.68–69.

43. W.L. Warren, 'John in Ireland 1185', loc. cit., convincingly rebutted by Sean Duffy, 'John in Ireland', in Church, ed., *King John. New Interpretations*, pp.221–245.

44. Gerald of Wales, v. pp.395–97.

45. Howden, *Gesta*, i. p.339, ii. pp.3–4; Howden, *Chronica*, ii. pp.306–07. Some historians claim there never was such a crown (Duffy, 'John in Ireland', p.229).

46. R.C. Christie, ed., *Annales Cestrienses: or the Chronicle of the Abbey of S. Werburg at Chester* (LCRS 14, 1886), pp.34–35.

47. Gerald of Wales, viii. p.176.

48. R. Benjamin, 'A Forty Year War. Toulouse and the Plantagenets, 1156–1196', *Historical Research* 61 (1988), pp.276–84.

49. Howden, *Gesta*, i. pp.345–47.

50. Ralph of Diceto, ii. pp.43–44; Howden, *Gesta*, i. pp.350–55.

51. Rigord, *Oeuvres*, i. p.77; Gervase of Canterbury, i. p.346; Jim Bradbury, *Philip Augustus. King of France 1180–1223* (1998), pp.64–65.

52. Rigord, *Oeuvres*, i. pp.77–78; Gervase of Canterbury, i. p.346.

53. R. Anstruther, ed., *Radulphi Nigri Chronica* (1852), p.168; Robertson, ed., *Materials*, iii. p.43; vi. p.456.

54. Rigord, *Oeuvres*, ii. pp.89, 101; Gerald of Wales, viii. p.232; Richard of Devizes, p.26; Andreas of Marchiennes, *Historia Regum Francorum* in *Monumenta Historica Germaniae. Scriptores* 26, p.211; U. Kessler, *Richard I Löwenherz*, op. cit. pp.38–44. For the son borne by Alice to Henry see E.A. Bond, ed., *Chronica monasterii de Melsa* – hereinafter Chronicle of Meaux – 3 vols (RS 1868), i. p.256.

55. Gervase of Canterbury, i. pp.370–72.

56. Ibid., pp.371–73; Howden, *Gesta*, ii. p.7.

57. J. Gillingham, 'Some legends of Richard the Lionheart: their development and their influence', in Janet L. Nelson, *Richard Coeur de Lion in History and Myth* (1992), pp.51–70 (at pp.60–64); C. Morris, *The Discovery of the Individual 1050–1200* (1972), pp.96–97.

58. Howden, *Gesta*, ii. pp.78–79; Geoffrey of Monmouth, *Historia Regum Britanniae*, ed. A. Griscom (1928), pp.456–57; James Brundage, *Richard the Lionheart* (N.Y. 1974), pp.255–58; Gillingham, 'Some legends', loc. cit. p.63.

59. Supporters include the historians W. Stubbs, *Memorials of Richard I* (RS 1864), i. pp.xx–xxi; also W.L. Warren, Steven Runciman and G.W.S. Barrow. Cf. also Emma Mason, 'William Rufus. Myth and Reality', *Journal of Medieval History* 3 (1977), pp.1–20; Richard, *Histoire des comtes de Poitou*, op. cit. ii. p.330.

60. Howden, *Chronica*, iii. pp.288–90; Gillingham, 'Some legends', pp.61–62.

61. R.F. Burton, *Arabian Nights* (1885); Laurence Echard, *The History of England* (1707), pp.211, 226; Paul de Papin-Thoyras, *The History of England* (1732), pp.241, 257; J.H. Harvey, *The Plantagenets* (1948), pp.33–34.

62. Richard, *Histoire des comtes de Poitou* op. cit. ii. p.272; P. Rassow, *Der Prinzgemahl. Ein Pactum matrimoniale aus dem Jahre 1188* (Weimar, 1950), p.79; H.G. Richardson, 'The Letters and Charters of Eleanor of Aquitaine', EHR 24 (1959), pp.191–213; E.R. Labande, 'Pour une image véridique d'Aliénor d'Aquitaine', loc. cit. pp.218–19; E.A.R. Brown, 'Eleanor of Aquitaine: parent, queen and duchess', in Kibler, ed., *Eleanor of Aquitaine*, op. cit. pp.20–21; Gillingham, *Richard I*, p.264.

63. Howden, *Gesta*, ii. p.292.

64. Howden, *Chronica*, iv. p.97; Olivier de Laborderie, 'L'image de Richard Coeur de Lion dans *La Vie et Mort du Roi Jean* de William Shakespeare', in Nelson, ed., *Richard Coeur de Lion*, pp.141–65.

65. A. Lecoy de la Marche, ed., *Anecdotes historiques . . . d'Etienne de Bourbon* (Paris 1877), pp.211, 431; Broughton, *The Legends of King Richard I*, op. cit. pp.132–36.

66. Adam of Eynsham, *Magna Vita Sancti Hugonis*, ed. D.L. Douie & H. Farmer, 2 vols (Edinburgh, 1962), ii. p.136.

67. Chronicle of Meaux, op. cit. i. p.403.

68. William of Newburgh, i. p.521.

69. R. V. Turner, *King John* (1994), p.216.

70. H.R. Luard, ed., *Annales Monastici*, 5 vols (RS 1869), i. p.101; C.T. Flower, ed., *Curia Regis Rolls*, 7 vols (1935), iii. p.321; T.D. Harvey, ed., *Rotuli Litterarum Patentium* (1835), i. p.117; Matthew Paris, *Chronica Majora*, op. cit. iii. p.41; S. Painter, *The Reign of King John*, op. cit. pp.232–35.

71. Charles Petit-Dutaillis, *L'essor des états d'Occident* (Paris, 1944), p.137.

72. F.S. Haydon, ed., *Eulogium historiarum* (RS 1863), iii. p.82.

73. Gerald of Wales, viii. pp.295–96.

74. Howden, *Gesta*, ii. p.9.

75. Ralph of Diceto, ii. p.50; *Conquest*, op. cit. pp.206–09; Richard of Devizes, p.5; Gerald of Wales, viii. pp.239–40; Howden, *Gesta*, ii. p.29; Anstruther, ed., *Radulphi Nigri Chronica*, op. cit. p.95; Andreas of Marchiennes, *Historia Regum Francorum*, op. cit., in MGH, Scriptores 26, p.211.

76. Paden et al., eds, *Bertran de Born*, op. cit. pp.386–87.

77. Gervase of Canterbury, i. p.389.

CHAPTER 5

1. J. Richard, *The Latin Kingdom of Jerusalem*, 2 vols (Amsterdam, 1979); J. Prawer, *Histoire du royaume latin de Jérusalem*, 2 vols (Paris, 1970); J. Prawer, *The Latin Kingdom of Jerusalem. European Colonialism in the Middle Ages* (1972).

2. J.H. Pryor, *Geography, Technology and War* (Cambridge, 1988), pp.112–116; J. Prawer, 'Crusader Security and the Red Sea', in Prawer, *Crusader Institutions* (Oxford, 1980), pp.472–73.

3. Introduction to N. Elisee, *Nur-al-Din* (Damascus, 1967).

4. T.E. Lawrence, *Crusader Castles* (1986).

5. Hugh Kennedy, *Crusader Castles* (1994); R.D. Pringle, *The Red Tower* (1986).

6. P. Deschamps, *Le Crac des Chevaliers* (Paris, 1934).

7. Malcolm C. Lyons & D.E.P. Jackson, *Saladin. The Politics of the Holy War* (Cambridge, 1982), p.286.

8. A.J. Forey, *The Military Orders from the Twelfth to the Early Fourteenth Centuries* (1992); M. Barber, *The New Knighthood. A History of the Order of the Temple* (Cambridge, 1993); Jonathan Riley-Smith, *The Knights of St John in Jerusalem and Cyprus c.1050–1310* (1967).

9. H.E. Mayer, 'Latins, Muslims and Greeks in the Latin Kingdom of Jerusalem', *History* 63 (1978), pp.175–92.

10. Lyons & Jackson, *Saladin*, op. cit. p.2.

11. Hamilton A.R. Gibb, 'The Career of Nur-al-din', in Marshal W. Baldwin, ed., *A History of the Crusades* (Philadelphia, 1958), i. pp.513–27.

12. Lyons & Jackson, op. cit. pp.7–27.

13. Andrew Ehrenkreuz, *Saladin* (N.Y., 1972), p.59.

14. H.A.R. Gibb, 'The Rise of Saladin', in Baldwin, *History of the Crusades*, op. cit. i. pp.563–89 (at pp.565–66).

15. Ehrenkreuz, *Saladin*, op. cit. pp.72–116.

16. Lyons & Jackson, *Saladin*, pp.68–69.

17. B. Hamilton, *The Leper King and his Heirs: Baldwin IV and the Crusader Kingdom of Jerusalem* (Cambridge, 2000).

18. Ehrenkreuz, *Saladin*, pp.128–32, 135–38, 143–47, 149–51, 169–81, 184–93; Lyons & Jackson, *Saladin*, op. cit. pp.196–200, 220–41.

19. Lyons & Jackson, op. cit. p.239.

20. Ehrenkreuz, op. cit. pp.185–88.

21. Ibid., p.171.

22. Bernard Lewis, 'Saladin and the Assassins', *Bulletin of the School of Oriental and African Studies* 15 (1953), pp.239–45; cf. also Bernard Lewis, *The Assassins: A Radical Sect in Islam* (N.Y., 1968), p.115.

23. Ehrenkreuz, p.161.

24. H.A.R. Gibb, 'The Achievements of Saladin', in Gibb, *Studies on the Civilisation of Islam* (Boston, 1962), pp.91–107 (at pp.99–100).

25. Ehrenkreuz, pp.158, 162–63, 182–83.

26. J. Phillipps, *Defenders of the Holy Land: Relations between the Latin East and West to 1187* (Oxford, 1996); R.C. Smail, 'The Predicaments of Guy of Lusignan',

in B.Z. Kedar, K.E. Mayer & R.C. Smail, eds. *Outremer. Studies in the History of the Crusading Kingdom of Jerusalem Presented to Joshua Prawer* (Jerusalem, 1982), pp.159–76; P.W. Edbury, 'Propaganda and Faction in the Kingdom of Jerusalem: the background to Hattin', in M. Shatzmuller, ed., *Crusaders and Muslims in Twelfth Century Syria* (Leiden, 1993), pp.173–89.

27. J.O. Prestwich, 'Richard Coeur de Lion: rex bellicosus', in Nelson, ed., *Richard Coeur de Lion in History and Myth*, op. cit. pp.6–7.

28. M.W. Baldwin, *Raymond III of Tripoli and the Fall of Jerusalem 1140–1187* (Princeton, 1936).

29. Lyons & Jackson, *Saladin*, op. cit. pp.157–58, 185–87, 218–19, 248.

30. Ibid., pp.247–48.

31. Ibid., pp.249–51; R.C. Smail, *Crusading Warfare 1097–1193*, 2nd ed. (Cambridge, 1995), pp.196–97.

32. Smail, *Crusading Warfare*, p.192.

33. 'L'estoire de Eracles empereur et la conquête de la terre d'outremer. La continuation de l'histoire . . .', in *Recueil des Historiens des croisades. Historiens occidentaux* (Paris, 1859), ii. p.52.

34. There is a huge literature on Hattin. There are good insights in Baldwin, *Raymond III*, op. cit. pp.96–135; R. Grousset, *Histoire des croisades et du royaume franc de Jérusalem* (Paris, 1936), ii. pp.788–799; Steven Runciman, *A History of the Crusades*, 3 vols (Cambridge, 1954), ii. pp.455–60, 486–91; Stanley Lane-Poole, *Saladin* (1906), pp.204–14. The most recent research is in B.Z. Kedar, 'The Battle of Hattin Revisited', in B.Z. Kedar, *The Horns of Hattin* (1992), pp.190–207.

35. Ehrenkreuz, *Saladin*, p.202.

36. Lyons & Jackson, *Saladin*, pp.266–72.

37. Ibid., pp.273–77.

38. P.W. Edbury, *The Conquest of Jerusalem and the Third Crusade. Sources in Translation* (Aldershot, 1996), p.73.

39. C. Tyerman, *England and the Crusades 1095–1588*, cf. Jonathan Phillips, *Defenders of the Holy Land* (Oxford, 1996).

40. H.E. Mayer, 'Henry II of England and the Holy Land', EHR 97 (1982), pp.721–739.

41. Howden, *Gesta*, ii. pp.30–32.

42. Ibid., p.34; Ralph of Diceto, ii. p.54; Gerald of Wales, viii. p.245.

43. Rigord, *Oeuvres*, i. p.90; Ralph of Diceto, ii. p.55; Howden, *Gesta*, ii. pp.34–36.

44. Gerald of Wales, viii. pp.244–45; Ralph of Diceto, ii. p.55; Howden, *Gesta*, ii. p.36.

45. Rigord, *Oeuvres*, i. pp.90–92; Gervase of Canterbury, i. p.432; Ralph of Diceto, ii. p.55.

46. Gervase of Canterbury, i. p.453; Howden, *Gesta*, ii. pp.39–40.

47. Gervase of Canterbury, i. p.434.

48. Rigord, *Oeuvres*, i. p.92; Howden, *Gesta*, ii. pp.45–49.

49. WM, i. pp.375–81.

50. Rigord, *Oeuvres*, i. pp.188–89; Howden, *Gesta*, ii. p.47; Ralph of Diceto, ii. p.55.

51. Howden, *Gesta*, ii. pp.46.

52. Gervase of Canterbury, i. p.435; Howden, *Gesta*, ii. pp.46, 49.

53. WM, i. pp.411–15; Ralph of Diceto, ii. p.56; Howden, *Gesta*, ii. pp.48–49.

54. Rigord, *Oeuvres*, i. pp.92–93; Gervase of Canterbury, i. pp.435–36; Ralph of Diceto, ii. p.58; Howden, *Gesta*, ii. p.50.

55. Gerald of Wales, viii. p.283

56. WM, i. pp.417–21.

57. Ibid., p.325; Gervase of Canterbury, i. p.436.

58. Warren, *Henry II*, pp.622–23.

59. Gervase of Canterbury, i. p.436; Howden, *Chronica*, ii. p.435; Rigord, *Oeuvres*, i. p.93; Kessler, *Richard Löwenherz*, pp.22, 45.

60. Anstruther, *Radulphi Nigri Chronica*, op. cit. p.95; Gerald of Wales, viii. p.232; Kate Norgate, *John Lackland*, p.70.

61. Warren, *Henry II*, pp.622–23.

62. Gerald of Wales, iv. pp.369–72; Howden, *Gesta*, ii. pp.67–71; Howden, *Chronica*, ii. pp.63–67.

63. Gervase of Canterbury, i. pp.438–39; William of Newburgh, i. p.277–78.

64. Gervase of Canterbury, i. pp.446–47; Howden, *Gesta*, ii. pp.66–67; Howden, *Chronica*, ii. p.363.

65. Gerald of Wales, viii. pp.282–83.

66. WM, i. p.449; Gerald of Wales, viii. pp.286–87.

67. Howden, *Gesta*, ii. pp.68–70.

68. Gerald of Wales, viii. pp.294–99.

69. Howden, *Chronica*, ii. p.366; Howden, *Gesta*, ii. p.72.

70. WM, i. p.473.

71. Gerald of Wales, viii. p.305; Howden, *Chronica*, ii. p.367; Howden, *Gesta*, ii. p.71.

72. WM, i. pp.473–75.

CHAPTER 6

1. Howden, *Gesta*, ii. pp.73–76.

2. Rigord, *Oeuvres*, i. p.97.

3. Gillingham, *Richard I*, pp.104–05.

4. Jane Martindale, 'Eleanor of Aquitaine: the Last Years', in Church, *King John*, op. cit. pp.137–64.

5. Gervase of Canterbury, i. p.451.

6. WM, i. p.483.

7. Ibid., p.477.

8. Ralph of Diceto, ii. p.67; Howden, *Gesta*, ii. pp.74–75; Howden, *Chronica*, ii. pp.4–5.

9. For Stephen of Tours, see J. Boussard, *Le comte d'Anjou sous Henri Plantagenêt et ses fils 1151–1204* (Paris, 1938), pp.114–17.

10. Coggleshall, p.91; Howden, *Gesta*, ii. pp.75–76.

11. Richard of Devizes, p.384.

12. Howden, *Gesta*, ii. pp.78–83.

13. Ralph of Diceto, ii. p.69; Howden, *Gesta*, ii. pp.83–84.

14. N. Golb, *The Jews in Medieval Normandy* (Cambridge, 1998), pp.356–59; H.G. Richardson, *The English Jewry under the Angevin Kings* (1960), pp.164–65; R.B. Dobson, *The Jews of Medieval York and the Massacre of March 1190* (York, 1974); H. Thomas, 'Portrait of a Medieval Anti-Semite: Richard Malebisse', *Haskins Society Journal* 5 (1993), pp.1–15.

15. Richard of Devizes, p.7; Coggleshall, p.97; Howden, *Gesta*, ii. p.85.

16. Gerald of Wales, iv. pp.373–79; D.L. Douie, *Geoffrey Plantagenet and the Chapter of York* (York, 1960).

17. Gervase of Canterbury, i. pp.372–439; Gillingham, *Richard I*, pp.110–12.

18. Warren, *Henry II*, pp.306–07.

19. H.G. Richardson, 'The Marriage and Coronation of Isabelle of Angoulême', EHR 61 (1946), pp.289–314 (at p.289).

20. Appleby, *England without Richard*, op. cit. pp.38–39.

21. Richard of Devizes, pp.382, 392; Gerald of Wales, i. p.186; Howden, *Gesta*, ii. p.206, iii. pp.217, 321; Lionel Landor, *Itinerary of Richard I* (RS 1935), p.198.

22. Warren, *Henry II*, pp.153–69.

23. Ralph of Diceto, ii. pp.8, 34.

24. Gerald of Wales, i. pp.80–84; vi. p.80; Gervase of Canterbury, i. p.457; J. Gillingham, 'Henry II, Richard I and the Lord Rhys', *Peritia* 10 (1996), pp.225–236.

25. Richard of Devizes, p.7.

26. Howden, *Gesta*, ii. p.97; J. Williams ap Ithel, ed., *Annales Cambriae* (RS 1860), p.57; Kate Norgate, *Richard the Lionheart*, pp.25–26.

27. Howden, *Gesta*, ii. pp.81, 97–98; Gerald of Wales, viii. p.156; *Foedera*, op. cit. i. p.50.

28. Howden, *Gesta*, ii. p.99.

29. Ibid., i. p.292.

30. Ibid., ii. p.77; Howden, *Chronica*, iii. p.8.

31. Gerald of Wales, viii. p.316.

32. Richard of Devizes, pp.7–9; Ralph of Diceto, ii. pp.12, 68.

33. Howden, *Gesta*, ii. p.91.

34. Richard Heiser, 'The Sheriffs of Richard I: Trends of Management as seen in the Shrieval Appointments from 1189 to 1194', *Haskins Society Journal* 4 (1992), pp.109–22; Heiser, 'Richard I and his Appointments to English Shrievalties', EHR 112 (1997), pp.1–19.

35. Jonathan Riley-Smith, ed., *The Crusades, Idea and Reality* (1981), pp.63–67; James A. Brundage, 'The Crusade of Richard I: Two Canonical Quaestiones', *Speculum* 38 (1963), pp.443–52.

36. Howden, *Gesta*, ii. p.90.

37. Howlett, *Chronicles*, iii. p.388.

38. William of Newburgh, i. pp.301–02, 408; A.L. Poole, *Domesday Book to Magna Carta* (Oxford, 1955), p.349.

39. Richard of Devizes, p.6.
40. Gillingham, *Richard I*, p.120.
41. Gerald of Wales, iv. p.380; Howden, *Gesta*, ii. p.101; *Chronica*, iii. p.28.
42. Paden, Sankovitch & Stablein, *Bertran de Born*, pp.380–81.
43. Bradbury, *Philip Augustus*, p.78; Kessler, *Richard Löwenherz*, pp.62–65.
44. Boussard, *Le comté d'Anjou*, op. cit. pp.114–17; Landon, *Itinerary*, op. cit. pp.25–26. On *teste me ipso*, see J.C. Holt, 'Ricardus rex Anglorum et dux Normannorum', in Holt, *Magna Carta and Medieval Government* (1985), pp.29–30.
45. W. Stubbs, ed., *Itinerarium* in *Chronicles and Memorials of the reign of Richard I* (RS 1864), i. p.146; Ralph of Diceto, ii. p.77; Rigord, *Oeuvres*, i. pp.97–98.
46. Howden, *Chronica*, iii. p.35.
47. J. Gillingham, 'Richard I and Berengaria of Navarre', BIHR 53 (1980), pp.157–72.
48. Gillingham, *Richard Coeur de Lion* (1994), pp.119–39.
49. Howden, *Gesta*, ii. pp.110–11; Howden, *Chronica*, iii. p.36.
50. Howden, *Gesta*, ii. pp.115–22.
51. Ibid., p.111; Howden, *Chronica*, iii. pp.36–37.
52. D. Matthew, *The Norman Kingdom of Sicily* (Cambridge, 1992), pp.74–75.
53. Marianne Ailes, ed. & trans., *The History of the Holy War or Ambroise's Estoire de la Guerre sainte* – hereinafter Ambroise – (Woodbridge, 2003), ii. p.35; Rigord, *Oeuvres*, i. pp.97–98.
54. For other implications of the Vézelay agreement, see C.R. Cheney & W.H. Semple, eds, *Selected Letters of Pope Innocent III Concerning England* (1953), p.6; M. Keen, 'Brotherhood in Arms', *History* 47 (1962), pp.1–17; M.J. Ailes, 'The Medieval Male Couple and the Language of Homosociality', in D.M. Hadley, ed., *Masculinity in Medieval Europe* (1999), pp.214–37 (at p.221).
55. Ambroise, p.36; *Itinerarium*, p.151.
56. *Itinerarium*, p.153.
57. Ralph of Diceto, ii. p.73; Coggleshall, p.26.
58. William of Newburgh, i. pp.303–305.
59. Coggleshall, pp.28–29.
60. Gerald of Wales, iv. pp.418–20; Howden, *Gesta*, ii. p.216; Howden, *Chronica*, iii. p.142.
61. Pipe Roll 2 Richard I, p.116; Pipe Roll 9 Richard I, p.xxvi.
62. Landon, *Itinerary*, pp.215–18.
63. William of Newburgh, i. p.333.
64. Pipe Roll 2 Richard I, p.21.
65. Howden, *Gesta*, ii. p.110.
66. Thomas, 'Portrait of a Medieval Antisemite', loc. cit. pp.1–15.
67. William of Newburgh, i. pp.337–38; Howlett, *Chronicles*, iii. p.406.
68. Howden, *Chronica*, iii., p.64.
69. Landon, *Itinerary*, p.196.
70. William of Newburgh, i. p.335.
71. Richard of Devizes, iii. p.392; Gerald of Wales, i. p.86.
72. *Recueil des Actes de Henri II*, op. cit. p.108.

73. Gerald of Wales, iv. p.200; Ralph of Diceto, ii. p.90.

74. *Itinerarium*, p.176; Howden, *Chronica*, iii. p.100; Landon, *Itinerary*, pp.192–94.

75. Richard of Devizes, pp.402–06; Howden, *Gesta*, ii. p.207; Howden, *Chronica*, iii. p.141; Appleby, *England without Richard*, pp.61–62; F.J. West, *The Justiciarship in England 1066–1232* (Cambridge, 1966), pp.69–77.

76. Gervase of Canterbury, i. p.497; Howden, *Chronica*, iii. p.135.

77. Ralph of Diceto, ii. p.96; Gerald of Wales, iv. p.389; Howden, *Gesta*, ii. p.106; Howden, *Chronica*, iii. p.135.

78. Pipe Roll 3 Richard I, p.141; Richard of Devizes, iii. p.392; Gervase of Canterbury, i. p.505; Ralph of Diceto, ii. pp.97–101; Howden, *Gesta*, ii. p.211; Howden, *Chronica*, iii. p.250.

79. Howden, *Chronica*, lxx–lxxxii.

80. Howden, *Gesta*, ii. pp.215–20.

81. Richard of Devizes, iii. pp.415–16; Ralph of Diceto, ii. p.99; Howden, *Chronica*, iii. p.140; J.H. Round, *The Commune of London* (1899), p.207.

82. Gerald of Wales, iv. p.213; Howden, *Gesta*, ii. pp.207, 221, 242; Landor, *Itinerary*, pp.215–18; H. Tillmann, *Die Päpstlichen Legaten in England* (1954), p.87.

83. Richard of Devizes, p.406.

84. Howden, *Gesta*, ii. p.236; Howden, *Chronica*, iii. p.204.

85. Richard of Devizes, pp.433–35; Howden, *Gesta*, ii. p.239.

86. Lyons & Jackson, *Saladin*, pp.280–81; Ehrenkreuz, *Saladin*, pp.209–10.

87. Ehrenkreuz, p.195.

88. Lyons & Jackson, p.290.

89. D. Jacoby, 'Conrad, Marquis of Montferrat and the kingdom of Jerusalem 1187–92', in *Atti del Congresso Internazionale 'Dai Feudi Monterrini e dai Piemonte Nuovi Mondi Oltre gli Oceani, Alessandria 2–6 Aprile 1990* (Alessandria, 1993), pp.187–238; Bourrienne, *Memoirs of Napoleon Bonaparte* (Paris, 1831), p.158.

90. Lyons & Jackson, pp.279–83.

91. S. Lane-Poole, *Saladin and the Fall of the Kingdom of Jerusalem* (1906), p.243.

92. Ehrenkreuz, p.211.

93. Charles N. Brand, 'The Byzantines and Saladin, 1185–1192: Opponents of the Third Crusade', *Speculum* 37 (1962), pp.167–81; cf. also C.N. Brand, *Byzantium Confronts the West, 1180–1204* (Cambridge, Mass, 1968).

94. Lyons & Jackson, pp.292–95.

95. Ibid., pp.297–98.

96. Ibid., pp.301–04.

97. Edgar N. Johnson, 'The Crusades of Frederick Barbarossa and Henry VI', in R.L. Wolf & Harry W. Hazard, *The Later Crusades 1189–1311* (Madison, 1989), pp.87–122; R. Hiestand, 'precipua tocius christianismi columna: Babarossa und der Kreuzzug', in A. Haverkamp, ed., *Friedrich Barbarossa: Handlungsspielräume und Wirkungsweisen des staufischen Kaisers* (Sigmaringen 1992), pp.51–108; *Historia de expeditione Friderici imperatoris* in A. Chroust, ed., *Quellen zur Geschichte des Kreuzzuges Kaiser Friedrichs I* (Berlin, 1928).

98. Lyons & Jackson, pp.313–16.

CHAPTER 7

1. W. Stubbs, ed., *Chronicles and Memorials of the Reign of Richard I* (R 1865), ii. pp.328–29; Howden, *Chronica*, iii. p.42; P.W. Edbury, *The Conquest of Jerusalem and the Third Crusade* (Aldershot, 1996), p.171.

2. C. Imperiale si Sant'Angelo, *Codice diplomatico della Repubblica di Genova*, 3 vols (Genoa, 1942), ii. pp.366–68.

3. Richard of Devizes, p.15; Tyerman, *England and the Crusades*, op. cit. p.81.

4. Howden, *Gesta*, ii. pp.112–13; Howden, *Chronica*, iii. p.39.

5. Ralph of Diceto, ii. p.84; Howden, *Gesta*, ii. pp.114–15; Howden, *Chronica*, iii. p.41.

6. Howden, *Gesta*, ii. p.124.

7. Ibid., pp.124–25; Howden, *Chronica*, iii. pp.41, 54.

8. R.H.F. Lindemann, 'The English *Esnecca* in Northern European Sources', *Mariner's Mirror* 74 (1988), pp.75–82; Pryor, *Geography, Technology and War*, op. cit. pp.57–60; J.H. Pryor, 'Transportation of Horses by Sea during the Era of the Crusades: 8th century to 1285', *Mariner's Mirror* 68 (1982), pp.9–27, 103–25; N.A.A. Rodger, *The Safeguard of the Sea: A Naval History of Great Britain* (1997), i. pp.46–47.

9. Ambroise, p.38; Howden, *Gesta*, ii. pp.125–26.

10. D.J.A. Matthew, *The Norman Kingdom of Sicily* (Cambridge, 1992), pp.286–91; John Julius Norwich, *The Kingdom in the Sun* (1970), pp.356–61.

11. E. Jamison, *Admiral Eugenius of Sicily* (1957), pp.80–85.

12. Roger of Devizes, p.17; Howden, *Gesta*, ii. pp.132–33.

13. Roger of Devizes, p.17.

14. Howden, *Gesta*, ii. p.126.

15. Ambroise, pp.39–40.

16. Ibid., p.40; Howden, *Gesta*, ii. pp.127–28, 138; cf. also H. Mohring, *Saladin und der dritte Kreuzzug* (Wiesbaden, 1980), pp.149–52.

17. Roger of Devizes, pp.19–22.

18. *Itinerarium*, p.162; Howden, *Gesta*, ii. pp.128–29.

19. Ambroise, p.41.

20. Ibid., p.42.

21. Howden, *Chronica*, iii. p.58.

22. Ambroise, pp.42–43; Nicolson, *Chronicle of the Third Crusade*, op. cit. p.164.

23. Ambroise, p.44; Howden, *Gesta*, ii. p.138.

24. Howden, *Gesta*, ii. pp.133–35; Howden, *Chronica*, iii. pp.61–64; Mohring, *Saladin*, op. cit. pp.190–207.

25. Rigord, *Oeuvres*, i. p.106; William of Newburgh, i. p.335; Howden, *Gesta*, ii. pp.101, 140.

26. Rigord, *Oeuvres*, i. p.106; Cheney & Semple, eds, *Selected Letters*, op. cit. p.6.

27. Richard of Devizes, pp.16–17; Ambroise, p.46.

28. Howden, *Gesta*, ii. pp.129–32; Howden, *Chronica*, iii. p.58.

29. Landon, *Itinerary*, p.44.

30. Howden, *Gesta*, ii. pp.142–43, 151–55; Howden, *Chronica*, iii. pp.71, 80–86; iv. pp.161–62; Marcus Bull & Norman Housley, *The Experience of Crusading*, 2 vols (Cambridge, 2003), i. p.128.

31. Gervase of Canterbury, i. p.488; Ambroise, p.46.

32. Boyd, *Eleanor, April Queen*, op. cit. p.269.

33. Howden, *Gesta*, ii. pp.155–57; *Chronica*, iii. p.95.

34. Howden, *Gesta*, ii. pp.157–60; M. Warren, 'Roger of Howden strikes back: investing Arthur of Britanny with the Anglo-Norman Future', ANS 21 (1998), pp.261–72.

35. Rigord, *Oeuvres*, iv. p.129; Howden, *Gesta*, ii. p.160; Kessler, *Richard I Löwenherz*, p.40.

36. Landon, *Itinerary*, pp.228–32; Kessler, *Richard I Löwenherz*, pp.72–73.

37. *Itinerarium*, p.175; Howden, *Gesta*, ii. p.161.

38. Rigord, *Oeuvres*, i. pp.107–08; Kessler, *Richard I Löwenherz*, p.75.

39. *Itinerarium*, p.176.

40. Ibid., p.175.

41. William of Newburgh, i. p.346; Richard of Devizes, p.25; Ambroise, p.47.

42. *Itinerarium*, p.179.

43. Richard of Devizes, pp.28, 35; Tyerman, *England and the Crusades*, p.66.

44. Howden, *Chronica*, ii. p.51; Pryor, *Geography, Technology and War*, pp.69–71.

45. *Itinerarium*, pp.179–84.

46. Ambroise, p.51; Howden, *Gesta*, ii. pp.162–63.

47. R.H. Rudt de Collenberg, 'L'empereur Isaac de Chypre et sa fille (1155–1207)', *Byzantion* 38 (1968), pp.123–53; P.W. Edbury, *The Kingdom of Cyprus and the Crusades 1191–1374* (Cambridge, 1991), pp.3–4.

48. Imad al-Din, *Conquête de la Syrie et de la Palestine par Saladin*, trans. H. Masse (Paris, 1972), p.291; Ambroise, p.50; Howden, *Gesta*, ii. pp.163–65; J.A. Brundage, 'Richard the Lionheart and Byzantium', *Studies in Medieval Culture* 6–7 (1976); Brundage, *Richard Lionheart* (N.Y., 1974), p.100; Prestwich, 'Rex bellicosus', loc. cit. pp.8–9; Kessler, *Richard I Löwenherz*, pp.127–50.

49. M.R. Morgan, ed., *La continuation de Guillaume de Tyr 1184–1197* (Paris, 1982), pp.115–19; Edbury, *Conquest of Jerusalem*, op. cit. pp.100–104, 176–78.

50. Ambroise, p.50; Mohring, *Saladin*, pp.186–87.

51. Ambroise, pp.51–52; Howden, *Gesta*, ii. pp.163–64; Howden, *Chronica*, iii. p.107.

52. Chronicle of Meaux, i. pp.257–58.

53. Ambroise, p.53; Howden, *Gesta*, ii. p.164.

54. *Itinerarium*, p.196; Howden, *Gesta*, ii. pp.166–67; Howden, *Chronica*, iii. p.110; iv. p.164.

55. B. Hamilton, *The Leper King and His Heirs. Baldwin IV and the Crusader Kingdom of Jerusalem* (Cambridge, 2000), pp.150–58; M.W. Baldwin, *Raymond III of Tripoli and the Fall of Jerusalem*, op. cit. pp.35–40, 76–78; P.W. Edbury, 'Propaganda and Faction in the Kingdom of Jerusalem. The Background to Hattin', in M. Shatzmiller, ed., *Crusaders and Muslims in Twelfth Century Syria* (Leiden, 1993), pp.173–89.

56. Ambroise, p.55; Howden, *Gesta*, ii. pp.163–65.

57. Ambroise, p.58; Edbury, *Conquest*, op. cit. p.96; J.W. Baldwin, *The Government*

of Philip Augustus: Foundations of French Royal Power in the Middle Ages (Berkeley, 1986), pp.104–06.

58. Ambroise, p.58.

59. Ibid., pp.56–57; Howden, *Gesta*, ii. p.165.

60. Ambroise, pp.58–59.

61. Ibid., p.59; Edbury, *Kingdom of Cyprus*, op. cit. p.13.

62. Chronicle of Meaux, i. pp.258–59.

63. *Itinerarium*, pp.196–203; Howden, *Gesta*, ii. p.167; Morgan, *La continuation*, op. cit. pp.119–20.

64. Stubbs, ed., *Chronicles*, RS 38 (1864), i. pp.182–205; Edbury, *Conquest*, p.179.

65. Howden, *Gesta*, ii. pp.167–68, 172–73.

66. Chronicle of Meaux, pp.258–60; Stubbs, ed., *Chronicles*, ii. p.347; Rigord, *Oeuvres*, i. p.118; Edbury, *Conquest*, p.112.

67. Ambroise, p.61; Coggleshall, pp.31–32; Edbury, *Kingdom of Cyprus*, pp.11–12.

68. Rudt de Collenberg, 'L'empereur Isaac', loc. cit. pp.23–79 and esp. pp.155–75.

69. Prawer, *Histoire du royaume latin*, op. cit. ii. pp.43–47; D. Jacoby, 'Crusader Acre in the 13th Century. Urban Layout and Topography', *Studia Medievali*, 2nd series 10 (1979), pp.1–45.

70. *Itinerarium*, p.62; Nicholson, *Chronicle*, op. cit. p.71; D. Jacoby, 'Montmusard, suburb of Crusader Acre: the first stage of its development', in B.Z. Kedar, H.E. Mayer & R.C. Smail, eds., *Outremer*, op. cit. pp.205–13.

71. R. Rogers, *Latin Siege Warfare in the Twelfth Century* (Oxford, 1992), p.215.

72. Lyons & Jackson, *Saladin*, p.299–308.

73. Ambroise, pp.82–84; F. Gabrieli, *Arab Historians of the Crusades* (1969), p.182.

74. *Itinerarium*, pp.342–43; Lyons & Jackson, pp.310–11.

75. Andreas Dandolo, *Chronica per extensum descripta*, ed. Pastorello (Bologna, 1938), pp.270–72; Rogers, *Latin Siege Warfare*, op. cit. p.214.

76. R. Rohricht, 'Die Belagerung von Akka (1189–91)', in *Forschungen zur Deutschen Geschichte* 16 (1876), pp.493–514.

77. Ehrenkreuz, *Saladin*, p.214.

78. Baha al-Din Ibn Shaddad, *The Rare and Excellent History of Saladin*, trans. D.S. Richards – hereinafter Baha al-Din – (Aldershot, 2001), pp.110–111; *Itinerarium*, p.325; Rohricht, 'Belagerung', loc. cit. pp.497–98; D.R. Hill & A.Y. al-Hassan, *Islamic Technology. An Illustrated History* (Cambridge, 1986), pp.109–12.

79. Lyons & Jackson, *Saladin*, op. cit. p.313.

80. Ambroise, p.81; Baldwin, *Government of Philip Augustus*, op. cit. pp.8–9.

81. Baha al-Din, pp.130–31; Ambroise, p.85.

82. E. Warhops, *The Flemish Nobility before 1300*, trans. J.B. Ross & H. Vandermoere (Hortrijk, 1975), pp.325–26; J. Falmagne, *Baudouin V Comte de Hainaut 1150–1195* (Montreal, 1966), pp.119–22; H. van Werwercke, 'La constitution de la Flandre et du Hainaut à la troisième croisade', *Le Moyen Age* 78 (1972), pp.55–90 (at pp.58, 67–68, 85); P. Riant, *Expéditions et pèlerinages des Scandinaves en Terre Sainte au temps des croisades* (Paris, 1865), pp.275–86.

83. Lyons & Jackson, pp.315–17.

84. Baha al-Din, pp.129–33.

85. Baha al-Din, p.127; Ambroise, pp.84–85; Rohricht, 'Belagerung', loc., cit. p.503.

86. Baha al-Din, p.127; Lyons & Jackson, p.317.

87. Ambroise, p.88; Lyons & Jackson, pp.317–21.

88. Lyons & Jackson, pp.317–18.

89. Howden, *Chronica*, iii. p.21 (also Appendix to Preface pp.cv–cxxvi, esp. cxi–cxii).

90. Ambroise, pp.88–92.

91. Baha al-Din passim; Ambroise, pp.74, 76, 81; Rohricht, 'Belagerung', loc. cit. p.520; Tyerman, *England and the Crusades*, pp.156–58.

92. Haymar's *Expugnatio* in Howden, *Chronica*, ibid., pp.cxxv–cxxvi; Lyons & Jackson, pp.322–23.

93. Lyons & Jackson, p.325.

94. Baha al-Din, pp.147–48; Ambroise, p.94; F. Gabrieli, *Arab Historians of the Crusades* (1969), p.212; Lyons & Jackson, p.326; T.A. Archer, *The Crusade of Richard I, 1189–92* (1888), p.55.

CHAPTER 8

1. Howden, *Gesta*, ii. p.168.

2. Sicard of Cremona in G. Scalia, ed., *Salimbene de Adam Cronica* (Bari, 1966), p.22; Ambroise, p.63; J.R. Partington, *A History of Greek Fire and Gunpowder* (Cambridge, 1960), p.18.

3. Baha al-Din, p.151.

4. *Itinerarium*, pp.206–09; Ambroise, p.64.

5. Rigord, *Oeuvres*, i. pp.108–09; Archer, *Crusade of Richard I*, op. cit. p.55; Bradbury, *Philip Augustus*, p.90.

6. Howden, *Gesta*, ii. p.169; R. Rohricht, *Geschichte des Königsreich Jerusalem 1100–1291* (Innsbruck, 1898), pp.547–49.

7. Gabrieli, *Arab Historians*, op. cit. p.213; Pryor, *Geography, Technology and War*, pp.43–54.

8. Ambroise, pp.65–66.

9. Ibid., pp.95–96.

10. Rohricht, *Geschichte*, op. cit. pp.551–52; Rogers, *Latin Siege Warfare*, pp.226–28; Lyons & Jackson, *Saladin*, p.327.

11. Ambroise, p.95; for the chronic illness, see William of Newburgh, i. p.306.

12. Gabrieli, *Arab Historians*, pp.205–06; Lyons & Jackson, pp.327–28.

13. *Itinerarium*, p.225; Baha al-Din, pp.153–56.

14. Ambroise, p.100; Howden, *Gesta*, ii. pp.172–74; Howden, *Chronica*, iii. pp.117–20.

15. Lyons & Jackson, p.329; Rogers, *Latin Siege Warfare*, pp.228–29.

16. Baha al-Din, p.160; Gabrieli, p.220; Howden, *Gesta*, ii. pp.174–76.

17. Baha al-Din, pp.161–62; Gabrieli, p.222.

18. Baha al-Din, p.161; Ambroise, p.104.

19. Howden, *Gesta*, ii. pp.178–79.

20. Imad al-Din, op. cit. pp.317–18; Sicard of Cremona, op. cit. p.22; cf. also Pryor, *Geography, Technology and War*, pp.125–30.
21. Baha al-Din, p.161; Howden, *Gesta*, ii. pp.173–74.
22. Howden, *Chronica*, iii. p.72; Prawer, *Histoire du royaume latin*, op. cit. ii. p.46.
23. Ambroise, pp.95–96; Rigord, *Oeuvres*, i. p.106; Howden, *Gesta*, ii. pp.170, 176; Howden, *Chronica*, iii. p.113.
24. Ambroise, pp.100–01; Howden, *Chronica*, iii. pp.116–18.
25. Rogers, *Latin Siege Warfare*, pp.232–35.
26. Imad al-Din, *Conquête*, op. cit. pp.304–05; lbn al-Athir, *el-Kamil* in *Recueil des historiens: historiens orientaux*, ii. Pt. 1 (Paris, 1887), p.51.
27. Howden, *Gesta*, ii. pp.171, 179–82; Howden, *Chronica*, iii. p.123; Cheney & Semple, *Selected Letters*, pp.6–7.
28. Coggleshall, p.31; Prestwich, 'Rex bellicosus', in Nelson, ed., *Richard Coeur de Lion*, op. cit. p.8.
29. *Itinerarium*, p.236; Howden, *Gesta*, ii. pp.181–83.
30. *Itinerarium*, p.235; Howden, *Gesta*, ii. pp.183–84.
31. *Itinerarium*, p.239; Howden, *Gesta*, ii. p.184.
32. William of Newburgh, i. pp.350, 354; *Itinerarium*, p.200.
33. Ambroise p.105; Richard of Devizes, p.78; Sicard of Cremona, op. cit. p.23; Andreas of Marchiennes, *Historia regum Francorum*, MGH, Scriptores xxvi. p.212; Howden, *Gesta* ii. pp.183–85.
34. Rigord, *Oeuvres*, i. pp.108–10, 115–17, 193; Richard of Devizes, p.80; Ambroise, p.152; A. Maalouf, *The Crusades through Arab Eyes* (1984), p.213.
35. Andreas of Marchiennes, *Sigeberti Continuatio Aquicincta*, MGH, Scriptores pp.427–28; A. Chroust, ed. *Historia de Expeditione Friderici de Ansbert*, MGH, Scriptores (1929), p.100; G. Duby, *France in the Middle Ages 987–1460*, trans. J. Vale (Oxford, 1991), p.212; Baldwin, *Government of Philip Augustus*, op. cit. p.22; C. Petit-Dutaillis, *Feudal Monarchy in France and England from the Tenth to the Thirteenth Centuries* (1936), p.181.
36. *Itinerarium*, p.239; Howden, *Gesta*, ii. pp.192–98, 203–06, 227–30; Bradbury, *Philip Augustus*, p.96.
37. Chroust, ed. *Historia de Expeditione*, op. cit. p.98.
38. Rigord, *Oeuvres*, i. p.118; Richard of Devizes, pp.146–47; Gervase of Canterbury, i. p.514; ii. p.88; Coggleshall, p.59; A. Hofmeister, ed., *Chronica of Otto of St Blasien*, MGH SRG (1912), p.54; A. Cartellieri, *Philip II August, König von Frankreich*, 4 vols (Leipzig, 1922), ii. pp.240–44.
39. Chroust, ed., *Historia de Expeditione* p.98; Hofmeister, *Chronica of Otto*, op. cit. pp.53–54; H. Bloch, ed., *Annales Marbacenses*, MGH SRG (1907), p.165.
40. Richard of Devizes, p.46; Gillingham, *Richard I*, pp.224–26.
41. Richard of Devizes, p.80; Rigord, *Oeuvres*, i. pp.120–21; *Itinerarium*, p.238.
42. Ambroise, p.152.
43. Howden, *Gesta*, ii. p.209.
44. Chroust, ed., *Historia de Expeditione*, p.100; Hofmeister, *Chronica of Otto*, p.56; Howden, *Gesta*, ii. p.228; Howden, *Chronica*, iii. p.67; Csendes, *Heinrich VI*, op. cit. p.104.

45. Howden, *Gesta*, ii. pp.186–87.

46. *Itinerarium*, p.241.

47. Ambroise, p.107.

48. *Itinerarium*, pp.242–43.

49. Howden, *Gesta* ii. pp.186–89.

50. *Itinerarium*, p.246; Gabrieli, *Arab Historians*, pp.223–24.

51. Rigord, *Oeuvres*, i. pp.117–18; ii. pp.218–24; S.D. White, 'The Politics of Anger', in B.H. Rosenwein, *Anger's Past* (Ithaca, 1998), pp.127–52.

52. Imad al-Din, *Conquête*, op. cit. pp.328–30.

53. Howden, *Gesta*, ii. pp.189–90; Howden, *Chronica*, ii. p.131.

54. Baha al-Din, pp.164–65.

55. R. Grousset, *Histoire des croisades* (Paris, 1936), iii. pp.61–62.

56. Ambroise, p.108; Gabrieli, pp.108–09.

57. Baha al-Din, p.165; Sicard of Cremona, op. cit. p.23.

58. Coggleshall, pp.33–34.

59. Lyons & Jackson, p.333.

60. C. Marshall, *Warfare in the Latin East 1192–1291*, (Cambridge, 1992), p.210.

61. D. Hill, *Islamic Science and Engineering* (Edinburgh, 1993), p.120; Kennedy, *Crusader Castles*, op. cit. p.109; Carole Hillenbrand, *The Crusades. Islamic Perspectives* (Edinburgh, 1999), p.525.

62. Andrew Ehrenkreuz, 'The Place of Saladin in the naval history of the Mediterranean in the Middle Ages', *Journal of Arabic and Oriental Studies* 75 (1955), pp.100–16.

63. David Miller, *Richard the Lionheart* (2003), pp.80–82.

64. J.R. Sweeney, 'Hungary and the Crusades, 1169–1218', *The International History Review* 3 (1981), pp.467–81; H. van Werwercke, 'La contribution de la Flandre et de Hainaut à la troisième croisade', *Le Moyen Age* 78 (1972), pp.55–90.

65. Y. Lev, *War and Society in the Eastern Mediterranean 7th–15th Centuries* (Leiden, 1997), pp.115–22; V.J. Parry & M.E. Yapp, *War, Technology and Society in the Middle East* (1975), pp.100–101; R.C. Smail, *Crusading Warfare*, op. cit. p.83.

66. J. Richard, 'Les Turcopoles au service des royaumes de Jérusalem et de Chypre: Musulmans convertis ou Chrétiens orientaux?', *Revue des études islamiques* 54 (1986), pp.259–70; Parry & Yapp, *War, Technology and Society*, op. cit. p.116.

67. G.T. Scanlon, trans. *The Muslim Manual of War of al-Ansari* (Cairo, 1961), p.29; John Keegan, *A History of Warfare* (1993), p.294; Hillenbrand, *The Crusades. Islamic Perspectives*, op. cit. pp.513–19.

68. Ambroise, p.110.

69. J.F. Verbruggen, *The Art of Warfare in Western Europe during the Middle Ages* (Woodbridge, 1997), pp.232–39; J. France, *Victory in the East: A Military History of the First Crusade* (Cambridge, 1994), pp.147–49; R.C. Smail, *Crusading Warfare*, op. cit. pp.75–83, 112–15.

70. David Miller, *Richard the Lionheart*, op. cit. pp.166–76, 180–81.

71. Ambroise, p.110.

72. *Itinerarium*, pp.248–52.

73. Baha al-Din, p.166; Ibn al-Athir, *el-Kamil*, op. cit. p.249.
74. Ambroise, pp.96, 102, 108; Prestwich, 'Rex bellicosus', loc. cit. pp.9–10.
75. Baha al-Din, p.170.
76. Ambroise, p.113.
77. *Itinerarium*, p.256.
78. Ambroise, p.114.
79. Ibid.
80. Baha al-Din, p.171, Nicholson, *Chronicle*, op. cit. p.242.
81. *Itinerarium*, pp.257–58.
82. Ambroise, p.115.
83. Baha al-Din, pp.172–73.
84. Miller, *Richard the Lionheart*, p.91.
85. Ambroise, p.116.
86. Baha al-Din, p.174; *Itinerarium*, p.265.
87. Ambroise, p.119; *Itinerarium*, p.265.
88. Jonathan Riley-Smith, *The Knights of St John in Jerusalem and Cyprus c.1050–1310* (1967), pp.107–08, 112–13, 118–19; van Werwercke, 'La contribution de la Flandre', loc. cit. p.86.
89. Ibn al-Athir, *el-Kamil*, p.49; *Itinerarium*, p.269.
90. Ambroise, p.120.
91. Baha al-Din, pp.175–76.
92. Ambroise, pp.121–22; *Itinerarium*, p.272.
93. Ambroise, pp.123–25.
94. Lyons & Jackson, pp.338–39; R.C. Smail, *Crusading Warfare*, p.165.
95. *Itinerarium*, pp.261, 277.
96. J. France, *Western Warfare in the Age of the Crusades 1000–1300* (1999), p.142.

CHAPTER 9

1. Imad al-Din, *Conquête de la Syrie*, op. cit. pp.345–46.
2. *Itinerarium*, p.283.
3. Ambroise, pp.126–27; Ibn al-Athir, *el-Kamil*, op. cit. pp.51–52.
4. Lyons & Jackson, pp.340–41, 343.
5. Ambroise, pp.128–29; *Itinerarium*, p.286.
6. Ambroise, pp.128–29; Imad al-Din, *Conquête*, p.347; *Itinerarium*, p.286.
7. Howden, *Chronica*, iii. pp.130–33; Edbury, *Conquest of Jerusalem*, op. cit. pp.179–81.
8. C. Imperiale di Sant'Angelo, *Codice diplomatico della Repubblica di Genova*, 3 vols (Genoa, 1942), iii. pp.19–21, M.L. Favreau-Lilie, *Die Italiener im Heiligen Land* (Amsterdam, 1989), pp.288–93.
9. Prestwich, 'Rex bellicosus', loc. cit. p.9; Gillingham, *Richard I*, pp.182–83.
10. Baha al-Din, p.184.
11. Ibid., pp.185–86.
12. Gabrieli, *Arab Historians*, op. cit. pp.225–26.

13. Baha al-Din, pp.187–88.
14. Imad al-Din, *Conquête*, pp.349–51; Gabrieli, op. cit. pp.226–28.
15. Baha al-Din, pp.192–93; Imad al-Din, *Conquête*, pp.352–53; *Itinerarium*, p.292.
16. Ambroise, p.131.
17. Ibid.
18. Baha al-Din, pp.185–88, 193–96.
19. Lyons & Jackson, p.341.
20. Imad al-Din, *Conquête*, p.354; Ambroise, p.132; Gabrieli, op. cit. pp.229–30; *Itinerarium*, pp.297–98.
21. Gabrieli, pp.230–31.
22. Gillingham, *Richard I*, pp.188–89.
23. Imad al-Din, *Conquête*, pp.354–55; Ambroise, p.135.
24. *Itinerarium*, pp.298–303.
25. Ambroise, p.136; Imad al-Din, *Conquête*, p.356; *Itinerarium*, p.307.
26. Ibn al-Athir, *el Kamil*, pp.55–56; *Itinerarium*, p.308.
27. Ambroise, pp.136–37.
28. *Itinerarium*, pp.310–12.
29. Imad al-Din, *Conquête*, pp.356, 367–68, 371.
30. Ibid., pp.373–75; Ambroise, pp.141, 143; D. Pringle, 'Richard I and the Walls of Ascalon', *Palestine Exploration Quarterly* 116 (1984), pp.133–47.
31. *Itinerarium*, pp.319–20; Ambroise, pp.106, 139, 141.
32. *Itinerarium*, pp.321–23; Ambroise, pp.142–43; Favreau-Lilie, *Die Italiener in Heiligen Land*, op. cit. pp.294–95.
33. Ambroise, pp.143–45.
34. Baha al-Din, p.186.
35. Lyons & Jackson, p.347.
36. Imad al-Din, *Conquête*, p.378; *Itinerarium*, pp.324–33.
37. Ambroise, pp.146–48.
38. Sicard of Cremona, *Salimbene de Adam Cronica*, op. cit. p.25.
39. Baha al-Din, pp.195–96, 199–200.
40. Ambroise, p.154; Edbury, *Conquest*, pp.112–13; Edbury, 'The Templars in Cyprus', in M. Barber, ed., *The Military Orders: Fighting for Faith and Caring for the Sick* (Aldershot, 1994), pp.189–91.
41. Sicard of Cremona, op. cit. p.25; Rigord, *Oeuvres*, i. p.118; Howden, *Chronica*, iii. p.181.
42. Ambroise, pp.149–50; *Itinerarium*, p.338.
43. Lyons & Jackson, p.348.
44. Baha al-Din, pp.200–1.
45. B. Lewis, *The Assassins: A Radical Sect in Islam* (N.Y., 1967), pp.110–18
46. Ibid., passim, but esp. pp.4–5.
47. Lyons & Jackson, pp.87–88, 105–06.
48. Ambroise, p.151.
49. Baha al-Din, pp.200–1; Imad al-Din, *Conquête*, p.376; Ibn al-Athir, *el-Kamil*, p.58.
50. Gabrieli, pp.239–41; Kessler, *Richard I Löwenherz*, p.230.
51. Ambroise, p.152; Kessler, op. cit. p.214.

52. P.A. Williams, 'The Assassination of Conrad of Montferrat: Another Suspect?', *Traditio* 6 (1970), pp.381–88.

53. Ralph of Diceto, ii. pp.127–28; William of Newburgh, i. pp.363–65, ii. p.457; Rigord, *Oeuvres*, i. pp.120–21; Edbury, *Conquest*, pp.114–15; M.R. Morgan, ed., *La Continuation*, op. cit. p.141.

54. Ambroise, p.152.

55. *Itinerarium*, p.347; Edbury, *Conquest*, pp.115–16; Favreau-Lilie, *Die Italiener*, pp.304–10; Mohring, *Saladin*, op. cit. p.187.

56. Ralph of Diceto, ii. p.104; Sicard of Cremona, op. cit. p.25; Ambroise, pp.153–54; Edbury, *Conquest*, pp.115–16.

57. Gillingham, *Richard I*, pp.201–03.

58. *Itinerarium*, pp.345–47.

59. Imad al-Din, *Conquête*, p.378.

60. Baha al-Din, p.203; Ambroise, pp.155–58; Howden, *Chronica*, iii. p.180; *Itinerarium*, pp.352–56.

61. Imad al-Din, *Conquête*, p.379; Lyons & Jackson, p.349.

62. Ambroise, p.159; *Itinerarium*, pp.358–59.

63. Ambroise, pp.160–62; *Itinerarium*, pp.360–65.

64. Ambroise, pp.159, 162.

65. Imad al-Din, *Conquête*, pp.379–80.

66. Ambroise, pp.164–65; *Itinerarium*, p.370.

67. M.R.B. Shaw, ed. & trans., *Chronicles of the Crusades* (1963) – translation of Jean de Joinville, *Histoire de Saint Louis* – pp.304–05.

68. *Itinerarium*, p.373. For the personalities present see M. Parisse, *Noblesse et chevalerie en Lorraine médiévale: les familles nobles du XIe au XIIIe siècle* (Nancy, 1982), pp.400–01; H. d'Arbois de Jubainville, *Histoire des ducs et comtes de Champagne* (Paris, 1860), iv. p.48; A. Longnon, ed., *Documents relatifs au comté de Champagne en Brie 1172–1361* (Paris, 1901), p.29; L. Longnon, *Les compagnons de Villehardouin: Recherches sur les croisés de la quatrième croisade* (Geneva, 1978), pp.42–45.

69. Ambroise, pp.166–67; Baha al-Din, p.203.

70. Ambroise, pp.167–68.

71. Ibid., p.168; *Itinerarium*, p.379.

72. Ambroise, p.169.

73. Ibid.; Lyons & Jackson, p.350.

74. *Itinerarium*, pp.380–83.

75. Ambroise, p.170.

76. Lyons & Jackson, p.351.

77. *Itinerarium*, pp.384–89; Ambroise, pp.171–72.

78. Baha al-Din, pp.206–08.

79. Ibid., pp.208–09.

80. Ibid., p.210; Lyons & Jackson, p.353.

81. Ambroise, p.173.

82. *Itinerarium*, pp.392–93; Ambroise, pp.173–74.

83. L. de Mas-Latrie, ed., *Chronique d'Ernoul* (Paris, 1871), pp.278–79; Coggleshall,

pp.52, 91; Howden, *Chronica*, iii. pp.175, 183; Shaw, *Chronicles of the Crusades*, op. cit. p.304.

84. Baha al-Din, p.213.
85. *Itinerarium*, pp.397–98.
86. Baha al-Din, pp.214–16; Ambroise, p.175.
87. *Itinerarium*, p.399.
88. Imad al-Din, *Conquête*, p.384.
89. Ambroise, p.176; *Itinerarium*, p.401.
90. Baha al-Din, pp.217–20; *Itinerarium*, pp.402–03.
91. *Itinerarium*, p.405.
92. Ambroise, p.178.
93. Baha al-Din, pp.221–23.
94. Ambroise, pp.179–80; *Itinerarium*, p.408.
95. Baha al-Din, pp.216–20; Ambroise, p.181; *Itinerarium*, pp.412–13.
96. *Itinerarium*, pp.413–15.
97. Coggleshall, pp.49–50.
98. Ambroise, pp.182–83; *Itinerarium*, pp.416–24.
99. Baha al-Din, pp.225–26; Ambroise, p.184.
100. Miller, *Richard the Lionheart*, op. cit. p.146.
101. Lyons & Jackson, p.358.
102. Baha al-Din, pp.224–26.
103. *Itinerarium*, p.425; Howden, *Chronica*, iii. p.184.
104. Ambroise, pp.185–86; Lyons & Jackson, p.359.
105. Imad al-Din, *Conquête*, pp.389–91; *Itinerarium*, pp.428–29.
106. Gabrieli, pp.234–37.
107. *Sigeberti Continuatio Aquicincta*, op. cit. MGH, Scriptores vi. p.429; Rigord, *Oeuvres*, iv. pp.382–86; A. Chroust, ed., *Historia de Expeditione Friderici* (1929), p.99.
108. Richard of Devizes, pp.78–79; Coggleshall, pp.78–79.
109. Ambroise, pp.188–91; Joinville, *History of the Crusades*, op. cit. p.304.
110. Imad al-Din, *Conquête*, p.394; Baha al-Din, pp.197–98.
111. Ambroise, p.192; *Itinerarium*, p.440.
112. *Itinerarium*, p.192; Ambroise, pp.192–93.
113. H.E. Mayer, 'Henry II and the Holy Land', loc. cit. p.739.

CHAPTER 10

1. David Boyle, *Blondel's Song* (2005), p.99.
2. J.H. Pryor, *Geography, Technology and War* (Cambridge, 1988), pp.13, 92, 196.
3. *Itinerarium*, p.441.
4. Boyle, *Blondel's Song*, op. cit. pp.118–20.
5. Roger of Howden, iii. pp.193–94; G. Waitz, ed., *Chronica Regia Coloniensis Monumenta Germaniae Historica. Scriptorum rerum Germanicarum in usum scholarum* (1880), p.154; A. Hofmeister, ed., *Chronica of Otto of St Blasien* in ibid. (1912), pp.54–56; A. Chroust, ed., *Historia de Expeditione Friderici de Ansbert* (1929), op. cit. p.100.

6. Richard of Devizes, p.80; Ambroise, p.152; Rigord, *Oeuvres*, i. pp.120–21.

7. Ralph of Diceto, ii. p.106; Howden, iii. p.194.

8. F. Michel, ed., *Histoire des ducs*, op. cit. p.87; Andreas of Marchiennes, *Sigeberti Continuatio Aquicincta*, op. cit. p.430; *Continuatio Admuntensis*, MGH SS, ix. p.87; H. Bloch, ed., *Annales Marbacenses*, MGH SRG (1907), p.164; P. Csendes, *Heinrich VI* (Darmstadt, 1993), p.113.

9. Ralph of Diceto, ii. p.106.

10. Howden, *Chronica*, iii. pp.185, 194; Coggleshall, pp.53–54.

11. Boyle, *Blondel's Song*, op. cit. p.131.

12. P. Csendes, *Heinrich VI*, op. cit. p.113.

13. Howden, *Chronica*, iii. p.194; Coggleshall, pp.54–55.

14. Kate Norgate, *Richard the Lionheart* (1924), p.267; Boyle, op. cit. p.132.

15. Lander, *Itinerary*, p.70.

16. Coggleshall, p.54.

17. Peter Spufford, *Power and Profit: The Merchant in Medieval Europe* (2002), pp.176–87.

18. Gillingham, *Richard I*, p.232; Csendes, *Heinrich VI*, p.113; Boyle, op. cit. p.147.

19. Coggleshall, pp.54–55; Howden, *Chronica*, iii. pp.185–86.

20. Coggleshall, p.55.

21. Howden, *Chronica*, iii. pp.185–86; Boyle, op. cit. pp.146–50.

22. Howden, *Chronica*, iii. pp.195–96; Rigord, *Oeuvres*, i. pp.121–22; *Annales Marbacenses*, op. cit. p.165.

23. *Annals of Zwettl*, MGH, Scriptores, ix. p.679; xiii. p.240; Ralph of Diceto ii. p.106; Coggleshall pp.54–56.

24. Ralph of Diceto, ii. p.107; Coggleshall, pp.56–57; L. Halphen, ed., *Recueil d'Annales angevines* (Paris, 1903), p.26; H. Duplès-Agier, *Chroniques de Saint-Martial de Limoges* (Paris, 1874) p.192.

25. Ansbert, op. cit. p.102; *Annals of Zwettl*, op. cit. MGH, Scriptores, ix. p.679.

26. N. de Wailly, *Récits d'un ménestrel de Reims* (Paris, 1876), pp.41–44; E. N. Stone, *Three Old French Chronicles of the Crusades* (Seattle, 1939); B.B. Broughton, *The Legends of King Richard* (The Hague, 1966), pp.126–28.

27. Howden, *Chronica*, iii. pp.195–96; Ansbert, op. cit. p.105.

28. John Gillingham, 'Some Legends of Richard the Lionheart: their development and their influence', in Janet Nelson, ed., *Richard Coeur de Lion in History and Myth* (1992), pp.51–69 (at pp.55–57); Norah Lofts, *The Lute Player* (1951); A. L. Rowse, *Homosexuals in History* (1977), p.3; Broughton, *The Legends of King Richard*, op. cit.

29. Yvan G. Lepage, ed., *L'Oeuvre lyrique de Blondel de Nesle* (Paris, 1994); Avner Bahat & Gérard de Vot, eds, *L'oeuvre lyrique de Blondel de Nesle: mélodies* (Paris, 1996); Samuel N. Rosenberg, ed. *Songs of the Troubadours and Trouveres* (N.Y., 1998).

30. Boyle, *Blondel's Song*, op. cit. pp.166–79 (esp. p.176).

31. P. Csendes, *Heinrich VI*, op. cit. pp.106–14.

32. R.H. Schmandt, 'The Election and Assassination of Albert of Louvain, Bishop of Liège 1191–92', *Speculum* (1967), pp.653–60.

33. Theodor Toeche, *Kaiser Heinrich VI* (n.d.), p.647.

34. H.F. Delaborde, ed., *Recueil des Actes de Philippe Auguste* (Paris, 1916), p.528.

35. William of Newburgh, i. p.389.
36. Ansbert, pp.103–05.
37. Richard of Devizes, pp.433–35.
38. Gervase of Canterbury, i. pp.514–15.
39. Howden, *Chronica*, iii. pp.196–97, 204–05.
40. Ibid., pp.196–98.
41. Coggleshall, pp.59–60; Ralph of Diceto, ii. p.106; Rigord; *Oeuvres*, iv. pp.393–96.
42. William of Newburgh, i. p.388.
43. W. Stubbs, *Chronicles* (RS 1865), ii. pp.362–63.
44. Howden, *Chronica*, iii. pp.205–11; Ralph of Diceto, ii. pp.106–07; Gervase of Canterbury, i. p.516.
45. Nick Barratt, 'English Revenues', loc. cit.; Boyle, *Blondel's Song*, p.213.
46. A.L. Poole, *Domesday Book to Magna Carta*, op. cit. pp.365–66.
47. James A. Ramsay, *A History of the Revenues of the King of England 1066–1399* (Oxford, 1925), i. pp.211–218; Frank Barlow, *The Feudal Kingdom of England 1042–1216* (1961), p.389.
48. Stubbs, *Chronicles*, op. cit. ii. p.362; Howden, *Chronica*, iii. p.290; Pipe Roll 6 Richard I, p.118; Pipe Roll 7 Richard I, p.259; cf. Pipe Roll Society N.S., vol. 6, pp.261–62; vol. 14, pp.xxiii–xxiv.
49. David Sinclair, *The Pound. A Biography* (2001), pp.100–04.
50. Powicke, *Loss of Normandy*, p.345.
51. Gervase of Canterbury, i. p.516; Howden, *Chronica*, iii. pp.206–07.
52. Howden, *Chronica*, iii. p.218.
53. William of Newburgh, i. pp.396–97; Howden, *Chronica*, iii. pp.212–14.
54. Howden, *Chronica*, iii. p.207; J. Laporte, ed., *Annales de Jumièges* (Rouen, 1954), p.75; Gervase of Canterbury, i. pp.515–16; J. Green, 'The Lords of the Norman Vexin', in Gillingham & Holt, eds, *War and Government in the Middle Ages* (Woodbridge, 1984), pp.58–59.
55. Howden, *Chronica*, iii. pp.224–25; Rigord, *Oeuvres*, i. p.124; Jim Bradbury; *Philip Augustus*, pp.177–85.
56. Howden, *Chronica*, iii. pp.212–15.
57. Add, MSS. 39,758 f.72; Howden, *Chronica*, iii. pp.216–17; J. Ahlers, *Die Welfen un die englischen Könige 1156–1235* (Hildesheim, 1987), pp.162–63.
58. Howden, *Chronica*, iii. p.217.
59. Ralph of Diceto, ii. p.111; Howden, *Chronica*, iii. pp.217–20; Halphen, ed., *Annales Angevines* (Paris, 1903), p.26.
60. HMC Belvoir, iv. p.23; Sir John Gilbert, ed., *'Crede Mihi.' The Most Ancient Register Book of the Archbishops of Dublin* (1897), p.34.
61. Howden, *Chronica*, iii. pp.227–28.
62. T. Rymer, A. Clarke, F. Holbrooke & J. Caley, eds, *Foedera* (1816), p.57; Powicke, *Loss of Normandy*, pp.97–99.
63. Rigord, *Oeuvres*, i. p.126, 170; A. Castellieri, *Philippe II August*, 4 vols (Leipzig, 1821), iii. p.73.
64. Howden, *Chronica*, iii. pp.225–27.

65. Ibid., p.229.

66. *Annales Stedbergenses*, MGH, Scriptores, xvi. p.227; Ahlers, *Die Welfen*, op. cit. pp.164–65; A.L. Poole, 'England and Burgundy in the last decade of the Twelfth Century', in *Essays Presented to Reginald Lane Poole* (Oxford, 1927) pp.261–73.

67. Ralph of Diceto, ii. p.111; Howden, *Chronica*, iii. p.228.

68. Ralph of Diceto, ii. p.112.

69. H.J. Freytag, 'Der Nordosten des Reich nach dem Sturz Heinrichs des Löwen', *Deutsches Archiv* 25 (1954), pp.517–20; K. Jordan, *Henry the Lion* (Oxford, 1986), p.197; P. Csendes, *Heinrich VI*, op. cit. p.142.

70. Ralph of Diceto, ii. pp.113–18; Howden, *Chronica*, iii. pp.232–33.

71. *Annales Marbacenses*, MGH, Scriptores, xiii. p.240; xvii. p.165; xxi. p.478; *Annales Stederburgenses*, MGH, xvi. p.229; Howden, *Chronica*, pp.231–33.

72. Howden, *Chronica*, iii. pp.202–03.

73. Ibid., iii. p.233.

74. H. Duplès-Agier, *Chroniques de Saint-Martial*, op. cit; V. Moss, 'The Norman Fiscal Revolution 1193–98', in R. Bonney & M. Ormrod, *Crises, Revolutions and Self-Sustained Fiscal Growth* (Stamford, 1999) p.48.

75. Gillingham, *Richard I*, p.248; Poole, *Domesday Book*, op. cit. p.366.

76. MGH, xviii. p.522; Landor, *Itinerary*, pp.78, 100–01.

77. Howden, *Chronica*, iii. pp.233–34.

78. MGH, xvii. pp.521–23; U. Kessler, *Richard I Löwenherz* (Graz, 1995), pp.260–61, 301–02; C.R. Cheney & W.H. Semple, *Selected Letters of Pope Innocent III concerning England* (1953), pp.4–5.

79. Howden, *Chronica*, iii. pp.276–78.

80. Ibid., p.301.

81. L. Vanderkinde, ed., *Chronicon Hanoniense of Giselbert of Mons* (n.d.), pp.284–85; Howden, *Chronica*, iii. p.234.

82. A.L. Poole, 'Richard I's Alliances with the German Princes in 1194', in R.W. Hunt, W.A. Pantin & R.W. Southern, eds, *Studies in Medieval History Presented to F.M. Powicke* (Oxford, 1948), pp.90–99.

83. Ralph of Diceto, ii. p.214; Howden, *Chronica*, iii. p.235; J. Falmaque, *Baudouin Vicomte de Hainault 1150–95* (Montreal, 1966), pp.278–79.

84. Coggleshall, pp.61–62; Gillingham, *Richard I*, p.250.

85. Gervase of Canterbury, i. p.524.

86. William of Newburgh, i. p.406.

87. WM, ii. p.5–7; Crouch, *William Marshal*, pp.72–74.

88. Coggleshall, p.62; Rigord, *Oeuvres*, iv. p.428; *Annales angevines*, op. cit. p.28.

89. Howden, *Chronica*, iii. pp.236–38.

90. WM, ii. pp.9–11; Howden, *Chronica*, iii. pp.238–40.

91. Howden, *Chronica*, iii. p.239; iv. pp.14–15; M. Strickland, *War and Chivalry* (Cambridge, 1996), pp.180–81, 202, 223.

92. Coggleshall, p.63; Howden, *Chronica*, iii. pp.232–33, 287; Andreas of Marchiennes, *Sigeberti Continuatio Aquicincta*, MGH, vi. p.431.

93. Pipe Roll 6 Richard I, pp.68, 102, 132, 145.

94. Howden, *Chronica*, iii. pp.241–42, 246–50; D.A. Carpenter, 'The Decline of the Curial Sheriff in England 1194–1258', EHR 91 (1976), pp.3–7.
95. Pipe Roll 7 Richard I, p.191; Howden, *Chronica*, iii. pp.286–87.
96. Coggleshall, p.64; Gervase of Canterbury, i. pp.524–27.
97. Roderick Hunt, *Robin Hood* (2000); Stephen Knight, *A Complete Study of the English Outlaw* (Oxford, 1994); Stephen Knight, ed., *Robin Hood: an Anthology* (Cambridge, 1999).
98. John Maddicott, 'The Birth and Setting of the Ballads of Robin Hood', EHR 93 (1978), pp.276–99; David Crook, 'Robin Hood. Some Further Evidence concerning the dating of the origins of the legend of Robin Hood', EHR 99 (1984), pp.53–54; R.H. Hilton, 'The Origins of Robin Hood', PP 16 (1958), pp.30–44; J.C. Holt, 'The Origins and Audience of the Ballads of Robin Hood', PP 19 (1961), pp.89–109; M. Keen, 'Robin Hood. Peasant or Gentleman', PP 19 (1961), pp.7–15; Peter Coss, 'Aspects of Cultural Diffusion in Medieval England: Early Romances, Local Society and Robin Hood', PP 108 (1985), pp.35–79.
99. Walter Bower, *The Continuation of Fordun's Scotichronicon*, ed. T. Keane (Oxford, 1722); G.P.R. James, *Forest Days* (1843).
100. Valentine P. Harris, *The Truth about Robin Hood* (1973).
101. J.C. Holt, *Robin Hood* (1982).
102. J.C. Holt, 'The Ballads of Robin Hood', PP 18 (1960), pp.89–110.
103. John Major, trans. A. Constable, *A History of Greater Britain* (Scottish History Society 10, 1892), pp.156–57; *Oeuvres d'Augustin Thierry* (Brussels, 1939), i. pp.299–300; John G. Bellamy, *Robin Hood. An Historical Enquiry* (Indiana, 1985), p.20.
104. Maurice Keen, *The Outlaws of Medieval England* (2000), p.176.
105. See Robert Graves, *Homer's Daughter* (1948).
106. Howden, *Chronica*, iii. pp.243–46.
107. Ibid., pp.247–48.
108. Roger of Wendover (RS 84), i. p.236.
109. Howden, *Chronica*, iii. pp.249–50.
110. A.A.M. Duncan, *Scotland. The Making of the Kingdom* (Edinburgh, 1975), pp.239–40; D.D.R. Owen, *William the Lion* (East Linton, 1997), pp.83–85.
111. Howden, *Chronica*, iii. pp.250–51.
112. J. Gillingham, 'Richard I, Galley-Warfare and Portsmouth: the beginnings of a Royal Navy', in M. Prestwich, R.H. Britnell & R. Frame, eds, *Thirteenth-Century England* 6 (1995), pp.1–15.
113. Howden, *Chronica*, iv. pp.12–13.
114. M.T. Flanagan, *Irish Society*, op. cit. pp.282–83; J.E. Lloyd, *History of Wales* (1939), ii. pp.579–80; J.J. Crump, 'The Mortimer Family and the Making of the March', *Thirteenth Century England* 6 (1997), pp.119–20.
115. WM, ii. pp.53–55; J. Barker, *The Tournament in England 1100–1400* (Woodbridge, 1986), pp. 10–11; R. Barber, *The Knight and Chivalry* (Woodbridge, 1995), pp.141–42; Barber & Barker, *Tournaments, Jousts, Chivalry and Pageants in the Middle Ages* (Woodbridge, 1989), pp.160–61.

116. Appleby, *England without Richard*, op. cit. p.223; H.G. Richardson & G.O. Sayles, *The Governance of Medieval England* (Edinburgh, 1963), pp.328–29.

117. Howden, *Chronica*, iv. pp.62, 172; N. Barrett, 'The English Revenues of Richard I', loc. cit.; T.H. Lloyd, *The English Wool Trade in the Middle Ages* (Cambridge, 1977), p.8.

118. J.C. Holt, *Magna Carta and Medieval Government* (1985), pp.74–77; A.L. Poole, *Domesday Book*, op. cit. pp.442–43.

CHAPTER 11

1. WM, ii. p.23.

2. Gillingham, *Richard I*, pp.283–84.

3. Howden, *Chronica*, iii. pp.252–53.

4. Powicke, *Loss of Normandy*, pp.290, 333.

5. Pipe Roll 20 Henry 2, pp.88, 135; Howden, *Chronica*, iii. p.251.

6. Pipe Roll 6 Richard 1, p.175; T. Stapleton, ed., *Magni Rotuli Scaccarii Normanniae*, 2 vols (1844), i. p.221; ii. p.350.

7. Andreas of Marchiennes, *Sigeberti Continuatio Aquicincta*, MGH, v. p.431.

8. Rigord, *Oeuvres*, i. p.127.

9. Rigord, *Oeuvres*, iv. pp.481–85.

10. Ralph of Diceto, ii. pp.114–18; Rigord, *Oeuvres*, i. p.127; Howden, *Chronica*, iii. pp.252–53.

11. Vincent Moss, 'The Norman Fiscal Revolution 1193–98', in R. Bonnery & M. Ormrod, eds, *Crises, Revolutions and Self-Sustained Financial Growth* (Stamford, 1999), pp.38–59 (at p.48).

12. WM, ii. pp.19–21.

13. Ralph of Diceto, ii. p.114; Howden, *Chronica*, iii. p.252.

14. Rigord, *Oeuvres*, ii. p.143.

15. Rigord, *Oeuvres*, ii. p.115.

16. Rigord, *Oeuvres*, i. p.127; ii. p.117 Andreas of Marchiennes, MGH, vi. pp.431–32; *Annales angevines*, op. cit. p.26.

17. Ralph of Diceto, ii. p.116; Howden, *Chronica*, iii. p.253.

18. Rigord, *Oeuvres*, i. p.127; Howden, *Chronica*, pp.254–55.

19. Ralph of Diceto, ii. p.117; Howden, *Chronica*, iii. p.252; André Salmon, *Chroniques de Touraine* (Paris, 1847), p.144.

20. Ralph of Diceto, ii. pp.116–17; Howden, *Chronica*, iii. p.252; *Annales angevines*, p.27; Rigord, *Oeuvres*, ii. p.118 WM, ii. p.27.

21. Chronicle of Melrose, i. p.180; *Annales angevines*, p.27; Ralph of Diceto, ii. p.117; Howden, *Chronica*, iii. p.253.

22. Ralph of Diceto, ii. p.118; *Annales angevines*, pp.26–27; Rigord, *Oeuvres*, i. p.129; iv. pp.530–42; Howden, *Chronica*, iii. pp.255–56; WM, ii. pp.29–35.

23. Ralph of Diceto, ii. pp.118–19; Howden, *Chronica*, iii. p.257.

24. WM, ii. p.29.

25. Rigord, *Oeuvres*, i. p.130; ii. pp.124–25.

26. William of Newburgh, ii. p.420; Howden, *Chronica*, iii. pp.257–60.

27. Howden, *Chronica*, iii. p.267.

28. Ralph of Diceto, ii. pp.124–25; Howden, *Chronica*, iii. p.268.

29. Landon, *Itinerary*, op. cit. pp.98–103.

30. Howden, *Chronica*, iii. pp.286.

31. Ibid., pp.273, 287.

32. Ibid., p.289; J. Delaville le Roux, *Cartulaire Générale des Hospitaliers*, 4 vols (Paris, 1906), ii. p.179.

33. Gillingham, *Richard Coeur de Lion*, p.119–139.

34. Ralph of Diceto, ii. p.121; Howden, *Chronica*, iii. p.206. For the context see M. Strickland, 'Provoking or avoiding battle? Challenge, Judicial Duel and Single Combat in Eleventh and Twelfth-Century Warfare', in Strickland, ed., *Armies, Chivalry and Warfare in Medieval Britain and France* (Stamford, 1998), pp.317–43.

35. William of Newburgh, ii. p.434; T. Toeche, 'Kaiser Heinrich V', in *Jahrbücher der deutschen Geschichte* (1867), p.676; MGH, xxiii. p.870; Leon Vanderkinde, ed., *La chronique de Giselbert de Mons* (1904), p.330.

36. Howden, *Chronica*, iii. p.300.

37. William of Newburgh, ii. p.456; Rigord, *Oeuvres*, i. p.130; Howden, *Chronica*, iii. p.301; WM, ii. p.23.

38. William of Newburgh, ii. p.456.

39. Rigord, *Oeuvres*, i. p.131; Howden, *Chronica*, iii. p.302; G. Lacroix de Marles, *Histoire de la domination des Arabes en Espagne et en Portugal* (Paris, 1825), p.435.

40. Howden, *Chronica*, iii. pp.302–03.

41. William of Newburgh, ii. pp.457–59.

42. Rigord, *Oeuvres*, i. p.130; Leopold Victor Delisle, *Catalogues des Actes de Philippe-Auguste* (Paris, 1856), p.108.

43. Gervase of Canterbury, i. p.530; Howden, *Chronica*, iii. p.303.

44. D.M. Stenton, *English Justice between the Norman Conquest and the Great Charter* (1964); R. Bartlett, 'The Hagiography of Angevin England', *Thirteenth Century England* 5 (1995), pp.49–51.

45. Howden, *Chronica*, iii. p.304.

46. Rigord, *Oeuvres*, i. pp.131–32.

47. Howden, *Chronica*, iii. pp.304–05.

48. William of Newburgh, ii. pp.460–62; Rigord, *Oeuvres*, i. pp.132–33; Powicke, *Loss of Normandy*, p.107.

49. Gervase of Canterbury, i. p.531; Howden, *Chronica*, iii. pp.282, 308.

50. H.F. Delaborde, ed., *Recueil des actes de Philippe-Auguste*; Landon, *Itinerary*, pp.107–09; Alexander Teulet, *Layettes du Trésor de Charts* (Paris, 1863), p.182; Rymer, *Foedera*, i. p.66.

51. Rigord, *Oeuvres*, i. p.133; Gervase of Canterbury, i. p.532.

52. Ralph of Diceto, ii. pp.138–40; *Layettes du Trésor*, op. cit. p.184.

53. Ralph of Diceto, ii. pp.138–40; *Layettes du Trésor*, pp.184–85.

54. Howden, *Chronica*, iv. p.7.

55. Rigord, *Oeuvres*, ii. p.130.

56. Landon, *Itinerary*, p.112.

57. Rigord, *Oeuvres*, i. p.135; *Layettes du Trésor*, pp.188–89.

58. Rigord, *Oeuvres*, i. p.135; ii. pp.168–257; Andreas of Marchiennes, *Sigeberti Continuatio Aquicincta*, MGH, vi. p.433.

59. Rigord, *Oeuvres*, i. pp.135–36; Howden, *Chronica*, iv. p.5.

60. J. Laporte, ed., *Annales de l'abbaye royale de Saint-Pierre de Jumièges* (Rouen, 1954), p.177.

61. Rigord, *Oeuvres*, i. p.136; Howden, *Chronica*, iv. p.5.

62. Rigord, *Oeuvres*, ii. p.137; Dominique Pitte, *Château-Gaillard* (Vernon, France, 1996); Powicke, *Loss of Normandy*, pp.190–95; Kate Norgate, *England under the Angevin Kings*, op. cit. ii. pp.375–80, 411–23.

63. Gerald of Wales, viii. p.290.

64. William of Newburgh, ii. p.500.

65. T. Stapleton, ed., *Magni Rotuli Scaccarii Normanniae* op. cit. ii. pp.309–10, 386; Powicke, *Loss of Normandy*, pp.204–06; R.A. Brown, 'Royal Castle Building in England 1154–1216', EHR 70 (1955), pp.353–98; Brown, *English Castles* (1954), pp.160–61.

66. Rigord, *Oeuvres*, ii. pp.177–78, 193; Ralph of Diceto, ii. p.154.

67. Rigord, *Oeuvres*, ii. p.183; N.A.M. Rodger, *The Safeguard of the Sea* (1997), pp.64–67.

68. Stapleton, ed., *Magni Rotuli*, op. cit. i. p.xl; ii. p.307; J. Gillingham, 'Galley, Warfare and Portsmouth. The Beginnings of a Royal Navy', in *Thirteenth Century England* 6 (1995), pp.1–15.

69. Howden, *Chronica*, iv. pp.3–4, 17–18.

70. Ralph of Diceto, ii. pp.148–50; Howden, *Chronica*, iv. p.4; Martin Bouquet, *Recueil des historiens des Gaules et de la France*, xviii. p.358.

71. Howden, *Chronica*, iv. pp.14, 16–17.

72. Ibid., p.18; Powicke, *Loss of Normandy*, p.174.

73. J.A. Brutails, *Documents des archives de la Chambre de Comptes de Navarre 1196–1384* (Paris, 1890), pp.1–3.

74. Howden, *Chronica*, iv. pp.13, 124–25; R. Benjamin, 'A Forty Years War: Toulouse and the Plantagenets 1156–96', *Historical Research* 61 (1988).

75. J. Vaisette, *Histoire de Languedoc* (Paris, 1879), v. p.21.

76. William of Newburgh, i. p.459; Rigord, *Oeuvres*, i. p.135; Howden, *Chronica*, iv. pp.147–48; G. Bordonove, *Philippe Auguste le conquérant* (Paris, 1986), p.134.

77. T.H. Lloyd, *The English Wool Trade* pp.8–9; G.G. Dept, *Les influences anglaise et française dans le Comté de Flandre* (Ghent, 1928), pp.24–32.

78. Pipe Roll 9 Richard 1, pp.62, 164; Coggleshall, p.77; Ralph of Diceto, ii. pp.152–53; Howden, *Chronica*, iv. pp.19–20; Rigord, *Oeuvres*, i. p.138; Rymer, *Foedera*, i. pp.67–68; Stapleton, ed., *Magni Rotuli*, op. cit. ii. pp.307, 369.

79. Ralph of Diceto, ii. p.152; Howden, *Chronica*, iv. p.19.

80. WM, ii. pp.55–57.

81. William of Newburgh, ii. p.493; Gervase of Canterbury, i. p.544; *Annales Monastici*, op. cit. ii. p.152; Rigord, *Oeuvres*, i. pp.141–43.

82. WM, ii. p.65.

83. Ralph of Diceto, ii. p.158.
84. WM, ii. pp.57-61; Howden, *Chronica*, iv. pp.20–24.
85. Coggleshall, p.77; Howden, *Chronica*, iv. p.20.
86. William of Newburgh, ii. p.495.
87. Coggleshall, pp.77–79; Howden, *Chronica*, iv. pp.20–21; Andreas of Marchiennes, *Sigeberti Continuatio Aquicincta*, MGH, vi. p.434.
88. William of Newburgh, ii. p.496; Gervase of Canterbury, i. p.544.
89. Howden, *Chronica*, iv. p.24; Martene et Durand, *Thesauraus Novus Anecdotorum* (1717), i. pp.1158–59.
90. Landon, *Itinerary*, p.122.
91. Howden, *Chronica*, iv. pp.30–31; Bouquet, ed., *Recueil des Historiens*, op. cit. xviii. p.710.
92. Gervase of Canterbury, i. p.545; Coggleshall, p.88; Howden, *Chronica*, iv. pp.37–39; Michel, ed., *Histoire des ducs de Normandie*, op. cit. p.90.
93. J. Strange, ed., *Dialogus Miraculorum*, 2 vols (Cologne, 1851), i. p.102; J.M. Lappenberg, ed., *Chronica Slavorum of Arnold of Lübeck*, MGH (1868), SRG, p.50; J. Ahlers, *Die Welfen und die englischen Könige 1165–1235*, op. cit. pp.169–84; B.U. Hucker, *Kaiser Otto IV* (Hanover, 1990), pp.4–15, 22–35.
94. Ralph of Diceto, ii. p.163; Gervase of Canterbury, p.545; Howden, *Chronica*, iv. p.39; Bouquet, *Recueil*, op. cit. xviii. p.615.
95. A.V. Murray, 'Richard the Lionheart, Otto of Brunswick and the Earldom of York: Northern England Angevin Succession 1109–91', *Medieval Yorkshire* 23 (1994), pp.5–12; B.U. Hucker, *Kaiser Otto IV*, op. cit. pp.17–19.
96. Ahlers, *Die Welfen*, op. cit. pp.190–96; Rigord, *Oeuvres*, i. pp.138, 143.
97. Bouquet, *Recueil*, op. cit. xix. p.360; Rymer, *Foedera*, i. p.69.
98. Cheney & Semple, eds, *Selected Letters*, op. cit. pp.4–5; Csendes, *Heinrich VI*, p.193.
99. R.H. Bautier, *La France de Philippe Auguste. Le temps des mutations* (Paris, 1982), p.40.
100. Cheney & Semple, op. cit. p.5.
101. Gillingham, 'Richard I and Berengaria of Navarre', BIHS 53 (1980), pp.155–72.
102. Coggleshall, p.136; Rigord, *Oeuvres*, i. p.138; iii. pp.90–95; WM, ii. pp.35–37; Howden, *Chronica*, iv. pp.19–20, 54.
103. Bouquet, *Recueil*, xxiv. p.758; J. Strange, ed., *Dialogus Miraculorum of Caesarius of Heisterbach* (Cologne, 1851), i. p.102; M. de Godefroy, *Chronique de Guînes et d'Ardres by Lambert of Ardres* (Paris, 1855), p.371.
104. Andreas of Marchiennes, *Sigeberti Continuatio*, op. cit. p.435; Gervase of Canterbury, i. p.573; Bouquet, *Recueil*, xviii. p.572.
105. Howden, *Chronica*, iv. pp.55–56.
106. WM, ii. pp.47–49.
107. Rigord, *Oeuvres*, i. pp.141–42.
108. WM, ii. pp.47–81; Rigord, *Oeuvres*, v. pp.428, 437; Ralph of Diceto, ii. p.164; Gervase of Canterbury, i. p.574, Andreas of Marchiennes, op. cit. p.435; Howden, *Chronica*, iv. pp.59–60; Matthew Paris, *Chronica Majora*, op. cit. ii. p.448.
109. Rigord, *Oeuvres*, i. pp.141–42; ii. pp.138–42.

110. Ibid., ii. pp.136–37; Howden, *Chronica*, iv. p.60.
111. Howden, *Chronica*, iv. pp.61, 68.
112. Rigord, *Oeuvres*, i. pp.143–44; WM, ii. pp.67–69; Howden, *Chronica*, iv. pp.70–75.
113. WM, ii. p.77.
114. Ibid., p.81.
115. Ibid., p.87.
116. Gillingham, *Richard I*, p.320.

CHAPTER 12

1. Howden, *Chronica*, iv. pp.79–81; Léopold Victor Delisle, *Catalogue des Actes de Philippe-Auguste* (Paris, 1856), p.130.
2. Coggleshall, p.99; Adam of Eynsham, *Magna Vita Sancti Hugonis*, ed. D.L. Douie & H. Farmer, 2 vols (Edinburgh, 1962), ii. p.137; Howden, *Chronica*, iv. p.81.
3. Coggleshall, pp.94–96; *Rogeri de Wendover Chronica sive Flores Historiarum* – hereinafter Roger of Wendover – (RS 1886), i. p.282.
4. Gervase of Canterbury, i. p.593; *Annales Monastici*, ii. p.71; Adam of Eynsham, *Magna Vita*, op. cit. ii. pp.134–37, 147.
5. D.A. Carpenter, *The Reign of Henry III* (1996), p.436; E.M. Hallam, 'Royal Burial and the Cult of Kingship in France and England, 1060–1330', JMH 8 (1982), pp.359–80; Jane Martindale, 'The Sword on the Stone: Some Resonances of a Medieval Symbol of Power', ANS 15 (1993), pp.219–30.
6. Landon, *Itinerary*, p.145; J.H. Round, *Calendar of Documents Preserved in France* (1899), p.389.
7. Kathleen Nolan, 'The Queen's Choice: Eleanor of Aquitaine and the Tombs at Fontevraud', in Wheeler & Parsons, eds, *Eleanor of Aquitaine*, op. cit. pp.376–405; Charles T. Wood, 'Fontevraud, Dynasticism of Eleanor of Aquitaine', in ibid., pp.407–22.
8. Jane Martindale, 'Eleanor of Aquitaine: the Last Years', in Church, ed., *King John*, op. cit. pp.137–64 (at p.142).
9. Rigord, *Oeuvres*, i. pp.144–45, ii. pp.142–49; *Annales Monastici*, i. pp.23–24; Howden, *Chronica*, iv. p.86.
10. Keith Thomas, *Religion and the Rise of Magic* (1971), pp.279–82.
11. Howden, *Chronica*, iv. pp.82–86.
12. Coggleshall, pp.51–52, 56–57, 74–77, 91–98.
13. Rigord, *Oeuvres*, i. pp.147, 204.
14. J. Gillingham, 'The Unromantic Death of Richard I', *Speculum* 54 (1979), pp.18–41; F. Arbellot, *La vérité sur la mort de Richard Coeur de Lion* (Paris, 1878).
15. Arbellot, op. cit. pp.61–64; Duplès-Agier, *Chronique de St-Martial de Limoges*, op. cit. p.66.
16. Gillingham, *Richard I*, op. cit. pp.326–27.
17. WM, ii. pp.89–93; Adam of Eynsham, *Magna Vita*, op. cit. ii. pp.130–31; Matthew Paris, *Chronica Majora*, ii. pp.451–52.
18. Coggleshall p.96; Rigord, *Oeuvres*, p.148; H.G. Rothwell, ed., *Chronicles of Walter*

of Guiseborough (1957), pp.142–44; N. de Wailly, *Récits d'un ménestrel de Reims* (Paris, 1876), pp.69–70; C. Kohler, 'Notices et extraits de manuscrits', *Revue de l'Orient latin* 5 (1897), pp.22–26.

19. Coggleshall, p.96.

20. Wailly, *Récits*, op. cit. p.69; A. Perrier, 'De nouvelles précisions sur la mort de Richard Coeur de Lion', *Bulletin de la Société Archáéologique et Historique du Limousin* 87 (1958), pp.38–44; Rothwell, ed., *Chronicle of Walter of Guiseborough*, op. cit. p.142; K. Brunner, ed., *Der mittelenglische versroman über Richard Löwenherz* (Vienna, 1913), p.450.

21. Arbellot, *La vérité sur la mort*, op. cit. pp.61–64; Rigord, *Oeuvres*, ii. section v. lines 440–620; Howden, *Chronica*, iv. pp.82–84.

22. Gervase of Canterbury, i. pp.592–93; *Annales monastici*, ii. p.71; Howden, *Chronica*, iv. pp.82–84.

23. Brunner, ed., *Der mittelenglische versroman*, op. cit. pp.9–14; H. Barckhausen, ed., *Archives municipales de Bordeaux* (Bordeaux, 1890), v. p.396; C. Babington & J.L. Lumby, *Polychronicon Ranulphi Higden*, 9 vols (RS 1886), v. p.336.

24. B.B. Broughton, *The Legends of King Richard*, op. cit.

25. Gillingham, 'Legends of Richard', in Nelson, ed., *Richard Coeur de Lion*, op. cit. pp.53–55; M. Bloch, *Les rois thaumaturges* (Strasbourg, 1924), pp.256–58.

26. Shakespeare, *King John*; Chaucer, *The Nun's Priest's Tale*, in N. Coghill, trans. *Canterbury Tales* (1951), p.244; O. de Laborderie, 'Du souvenir à la réincarnation: l'image de Richard Coeur de Lion dans la Vie et Mort du roi Jean de William Shakespeare', in Nelson, ed., *Richard*, op. cit. pp.141–65; E.M.W. Tillyard, *Shakespeare's History Plays* (1944), pp.221–24.

27. Martin H. Jones, 'Richard in German Literature', in Nelson, ed., *Richard*, op. cit. pp.70–116.

28. Ibn al-Athir, *el-Kamil*, op. cit. p.43.

29. Howden, *Chronica*, iv. p.85; Jane Martindale, 'Eleanor of Aquitaine: the Last Years', in Church, ed., *King John*, op. cit. pp.137–64 (at pp.153–56); Ralph V. Turner, 'Eleanor of Aquitaine in the government of her sons Richard and John', in Wheeler & Parsons, eds, *Eleanor of Aquitaine. Lord and Lady*, op. cit. pp.77–95 (at pp.86–89).

30. Adam of Eynsham, *Magna Vita*, op. cit. ii. p.137; Coggleshall, p.99.

31. Ralph of Diceto, ii. pp.85–86; *Annales monastici*, i. p.24; iv. p.51; Howden, *Chronica*, iii. pp.63–65; Martindale, 'Eleanor of Aquitaine: the Last Years', loc. cit. p.147.

32. Howden, *Chronica*, iv. p.83; Glanville, *De legibus et consuetudinibus Angliae*, ed. Woodbine, pp.101–04; Powicke, *Loss of Normandy*, p.130.

33. Rymer, *Foedera*, i. p.77.

34. Nicholas Vincent, *Peter des Roches* (Cambridge, 1996), pp.23–26.

35. WM, ii. p.95.

36. Howden, *Chronica*, iv. pp.86–87.

37. Adam of Eynsham, *Magna Vita*, ii. pp.136–38.

38. Tardif, ed., *Le très ancien contumier de Normandie*, pp.12–13.

39. Howden, *Chronica*, iv. pp.87–88.

40. Coggleshall, pp.98–99; WM, ii. p.97; Howden, *Chronica*, iv. pp.88–90.

41. Rigord, *Oeuvres*, i. pp.145–46; Richard, *Comtes de Poitou*, op. cit. ii. pp.332–53; Delaborde, ed., *Recueil des Actes de Philippe*, ii. Nos 607–08.

42. Howden, *Chronica*, iv. p.95.

43. Powicke, *Loss of Normandy*, p.133.

44. J. Laporte, ed., *Annales de l'Abbaye Royale de Saint-Pierre de Jumièges* (Rouen, 1954), p.77; T.D. Hardy, ed., *Rotuli Chartarum 1199–1216* (1837), 30–31; Howden, *Chronica*, iv. pp.93–95.

45. Rigord, *Oeuvres*, i. p.146; Howden, *Chronica*, iv. p.95; Richard, *Comtes*, op. cit. ii. pp.352–54; J.C. Holt, 'Aliénor d'Aquitaine. Jean sans terre et la succession de 1199', *Cahiers de civilisation médiévale* 29 (1986), pp.95–100.

46. WM, ii. p.105; Hardy, ed., *Rotuli Chartarum*, op. cit. p.30; Howden, *Chronica*, iv. pp.94, 96.

47. Howden, *Chronica*, iv. pp.96–97; Norgate, *John Lackland*, pp.70–71; Gillingham, *Richard I*, pp.337–38.

48. Ralph of Diceto, ii. pp.166–67.

49. Rigord, *Oeuvres*, i. p.153; D.E. Queller, *The Fourth Crusade* (Leicester, 1978), pp.1–3.

50. Gervase of Canterbury, ii. p.92.

51. Delaborde, ed., *Recueil des Actes de Philippe*, ii. pp.178–85; E. M. Hallam, *Capetian France 987–1328* (Harlow, 1980), p.183.

52. Coggleshall, p.101; Rigord, *Oeuvres*, i. p.148; Hardy, ed., *Rotuli Chartarum*, 96; Howden, *Chronica*, iv. p.115.

53. Howden, *Chronica*, iv. pp.106–07; J.Boussard, 'Philippe Auguste et les Plantagenêts', in R.H. Bautier, *La France de Philippe Auguste: Le temps de mutations* (Paris, 1982), pp.263–89 (at p.279).

54. Coggleshall, p.101; *Annales monastici*, i. p.25; iii. p.27; Howden, *Chronica*, iv. p.157; E. Lavisse, *Histoire de la France depuis les origines jusqu'à la Révolution*, (Paris, 1911), iii. Pt 1 pp.124–26.

55. F. Lot, *Fidèles ou vassaux* (Paris, 1904), pp.23–25; Warren, *King John*, p.56.

56. Howden, *Chronica*, iv. p.148.

57. Delaborde, ed., *Recueil des Actes de Philippe*, ii. pp.180, 186, 205–08.

58. Gervase of Canterbury, ii. pp.92–93.

59. Smail, *Crusading Warfare*, op. cit. pp.60–62.

60. William of Newburgh, i. pp.484–85; Pipe Roll 9 Richard I, pp.xix–xxii; H.E. Butler, ed., *The Chronicle of Jocelin of Brakeland* (1949), pp.85–86; Howden, *Chronica*, iv. p.40.

61. C. Johnson, ed., *Dialogus de Scaccario*, op. cit. p.1; William of Newburgh, i. p.406; Hardy, ed., *Rotuli Normanniae* (1835), p.79; Howden, *Chronica*, iv. pp.62–63; J.H. Round, *Feudal England*, op. cit. pp.539–51; J.O. Prestwich, 'War and Finance in the Anglo-Norman State', TRHS 5th Series iv (1954), pp.19–43.

62. J.C. Holt, 'The Loss of Normandy and Royal Finance', in Gillingham & Holt, eds, *War and Government in the Middle Ages*, op. cit. Nick Barratt, 'The Revenues of John and Philip Augustus Revisited', in Church, ed., *King John*, pp.75–99; V. Moss, 'The Norman Fiscal Revolution 1193–98', in R. Bonney & M. Ormrod, eds, *Crises, Revolutions and Self-Sustained Fiscal Growth* (Stamford, 1999), pp.38–57; V. Moss, 'Normandy and England in 1180: the Pipe Roll

Evidence', in D. Bates & A. Curry, eds, *England and Normandy in the Middle Ages* (1994).

63. Warren, *King John*, p.63.

64. Gervase of Canterbury, ii. pp.92–93; Ralph of Diceto, ii. p.168; Andreas of Marchiennes, *Sigeberti Continuatio Aquicincta*, op. cit. vi. pp.435–36; Howden, *Chronica*, iv. pp.106–07, 148–51; J. Gillingham, 'Historians without Hindsight', in Church, ed., *King John*, pp.1–26.

65. Ralph of Diceto, ii. pp.116–18, 167–70.

66. Howden, *Chronica*, iv. pp.92, 139–40.

67. William of Newburgh, i. pp.335–36.

68. Ralph of Diceto, ii. p.166; Howden, *Chronica*, iv. pp.88–92.

69. Hardy, ed., *Rotuli Chartarum*, 85, 100; Howden, *Chronica*, iv. pp.107, 140; A.A.M. Duncan, 'John King of England and the King of Scots', in Church, ed., *King John*, pp.247–71 (at pp.251–54).

70. Rigord, *Oeuvres*, i. p.141.

71. Adam of Eynsham, *Magna Vita*, pp.135, 146–47, 147–48.

72. Rigord, *Oeuvres*, ii. pp.147–48; Howden, *Chronica*, iv. pp.19–20.

73. Baldwin, *The Government of Philip Augustus*, op. cit. p.91; Gillingham, *Richard I*, pp.337–40.

74. Gerald of Wales, viii. pp.173–75; V. Green, *An Account of the Discovery of the Body of King John in the Cathedral Church of Worcester, July 17 1797* (1797); A.L. Poole, *Domesday Book to Magna Carta*, op. cit. p.486.

75. Jim Bradbury, 'Philip Augustus and King John: Personality and History', in Church, ed., *King John*, pp.347–61 (at pp.348–50).

76. Roger of Wendover, ii. pp.42–43, 48–49, 62–63, 76–77; iii. p.229; S. Painter, 'Norwich's Three Geoffreys', *Speculum* 28 (1953), pp.808–13.

77. Rymer, *Foedera*, i. pp.107–08; Michel, *Histoire des ducs de Normandie*, op. cit. pp.111–15; Coggleshall, p.164; Roger of Wendover, iii. p.235; Norgate, *John Lackland*, pp.287–88.

78. Painter, *King John*, pp.247–50; N. Vincent, 'Isabella of Angoulême: John's Jezabel', in Church, ed., *King John*, pp.165–219 (at p.196).

79. Warren, *King John*, pp.257, 291; Turner, *King John*, p.262; Bradbury, 'Philip Augustus and King John', loc. cit. p.351.

80. F. Palgrave, ed., *Rotuli Curiae Regis* (1835), i. pp.278–79; Poole, *Domesday Book*, op. cit. p.427.

81. *Rotuli Curiae Regis*, vii. p.170.

82. Powicke, *Loss of Normandy*, pp.152, 192.

83. Warren, *King John*, p.191; Turner, *King John*, pp.20–21; Norgate, *John Lackland*, p.286.

84. Coggleshall, p.167; Roger of Wendover, iii. pp.240, 248, 255–56; Michel, *Histoire des ducs*, pp.122–26.

85. Roger of Wendover, ii. p.67; Bradbury, 'Philip Augustus and King John', loc. cit. p.350.

86. T.D. Hardy, ed., *Rotuli Litterarum Clausarum in Turri Londinensi Asservati* (1835), i. 75; Pipe Roll 9 John, p.139.

87. Hardy, ed., *Rotuli Chartarum*, op. cit. 134; Palgrave, ed., *Rotuli Curiae Regis*, op. cit. vii. p.272; Pipe Roll 9 John, p.72; Pipe Roll 10 John, p.59.

88. *Annales monastici*, i. p.101; H. Cole, ed., *Documents Illustrative of English History in the Thirteenth and Fourteenth Centuries* (1844), p.267.

89. *Rotuli Curiae Regis*, iii. 321; Hardy, ed., *Rotuli Litterarum*, op. cit. i. 117; Roger of Wendover, iv. p.29; Matthew Paris, *Chronica Majora*, iii. p.41; S. Painter, *Feudalism and Liberty* (Baltimore, 1961), pp.240–43; Painter, *King John*, pp.231–35; G. Given-Wilson & A. Curtis, *The Royal Bastards of Medieval England* (1984), pp.127–31.

90. William of Newburgh, i. p.521; Warren, *King John*, p.189; Bradbury, 'Philip Augustus and King John', loc. cit. p.352.

91. Vincent, 'Isabella', loc. cit. p.193.

92. Adam of Eynsham, *Magna Vita*, ii. p.143.

93. Warren, *King John*, pp.64–65; Norgate, *John Lackland*, p.76.

94. Roger of Wendover, iii. p.171.

95. Poole, *Domesday Book*, op. cit. p.427.

96. C. Petit-Dutaillis & P. Guinard, *L'Essor des états d'Occident* (Paris, 1944), p.137.

97. Pipe Roll 5 John, p.139; Hardy, ed. *Rotuli Litterarum Clausarum* (1833), i. 108.

98. T.D. Hardy, ed., *Rotuli de liberati ac de Misis et Praestitis regnante Johanne* (1844), 115, 137, 151.

99. Matthew Paris, *Chronica Majora*, ii. pp.560–63.

100. Bradbury, 'Philip Augustus and King John', loc. cit. p.350.

101. C.N.L. Brooke, *The Medieval Idea of Marriage* (Oxford, 1989), pp.138–39.

102. Howden, *Gesta*, ii. p.236.

103. H.G. Richardson, 'The Marriage and Coronation of Isabelle of Angoulême', EHR 61 (1946), pp.289–314 (at pp.289–95).

104. Ralph of Diceto, ii. p.167; Howden, *Chronica*, iv. p.119.

105. Coggleshall, p.103; Vincent, 'Isabella', loc. cit. p.196.

106. *Rotuli Chartarum*, op. cit. p.97.

107. S. Painter, 'The Lords of Lusignan in the Eleventh and Twelfth Centuries', *Speculum* 32 (1957), pp.27–47; Boussard, *Le gouvernment d'Henri II*, op. cit. p.133.

108. R. Hadju, 'Castles, castellans and the structure of politics in Poitou 1152–1271', JMH 4 (1978), pp.27–54; A. Debord, *La société laïque dans les pays de la Charente X – XIIe siècles* (Angoulême, 1984), pp.375–402.

109. *Rotuli Chartarum*, 586–89; S. Painter, ed., *Feudalism and Liberty*, op. cit. p.66; Ralph V. Turner, 'The role of Eleanor of Aquitaine in the government of her sons', in Wheeler & Parsons, ed., *Eleanor of Aquitaine*, op. cit. pp.77–95 (at p.88).

110. Boussard, *Le gouvernment d'Henri II*, op. cit. p.119; Powicke, *Loss of Normandy*, p.44; Vincent, 'Isabella of Angoulême', loc. cit. p.170.

111. Coggleshall, p.103; Howden, *Chronica*, iv. p.119.

112. F.A. Cazel & S. Painter, 'The Marriage of Isabelle of Angoulême', EHR 63 (1948), pp.85–86; Vincent, 'Isabella', loc. cit. p.172; Warren, *King John*, p.67.

113. Norgate, *John Lackland*, pp.76–77.

114. *Rotuli Chartarum*, i. pp.57, 58, 97.

115. Ralph of Diceto, ii. p.170.

116. Norgate, *John Lackland*, p.77.

117. *Rotuli Chartarum*, i. p.75; Duplès-Agier, *Chroniques de Saint-Martial*, op. cit. p.67; T. Arnold, ed., *Memorials of St Edmund's Abbey* (RS 1896), ii. p.8; Howden, *Chronica*, iv. p.120.

118. Ralph of Diceto, ii. p.170; Coggleshall, p.103; Howden, *Chronica*, iv. pp.139–43, 156, 160; Richard, *Histoire des comtes de Poitou*, op. cit. ii. p.379.

119. H.G. Richardson, 'The Marriage and Coronation of Isabelle of Angoulême', EHR 61 (1946), pp.289–314; Richardson, 'King John and Isabelle of Angoulême', EHR 65 (1950), pp.360–71; Fred A. Cazel & Sidney Painter, 'The Marriage of Isabelle of Angoulême', EHR 67 (1952), pp.233–35; cf. also Cazel & Painter, 'The Marriage of Isabelle of Angoulême', EHR 63 (1948), pp.83–89.

120. Ralph of Diceto, ii. p.54; S. Painter, *William Marshal*, p.27.

121. Vincent, 'Isabella of Angoulême', loc. cit. pp.175–81.

122. F. Marvaud, 'Isabella d'Angoulême ou la comtesse reine', *Bulletin de la Société Archéologique et Historique de la Charente*, 2nd series i. (1856) pp.116–252; H.S. Snelgrove, *The Lusignans in England 1247–1258* (Albuquerque, 1950), passim.

123. Richardson, 'The Marriage and Coronation', loc. cit. pp.298–307; Vincent, 'Isabella of Angoulême', loc. cit. p.185.

124. Brooke, *The Medieval Idea of Marriage*, op. cit. pp.138–40.

125. Vincent, 'Isabella', loc. cit. pp.174–75; J.C. Parsons, *Medieval Queenship* (Stroud, 1986).

126. Howden, *Chronica*, iv. p.199.

127. Vincent, 'Isabella', loc. cit. pp.174–75.

128. Matthew Paris, *Chronica Majora*, ii. pp.481–82.

129. Ibid., p.563; iv. p.253.

130. Painter, *King John*, p.236; Vincent, 'Isabella', loc. cit. pp.201–04.

131. Gervase of Canterbury, ii. pp.102, 107.

132. Arnold, ed., *Memorials of St Edmund's Abbey*, op. cit. ii. p.23.

133. T. Hardy, ed., *Rotuli de Oblatis et Finibus in Turri Londinensi Asservati* (1835), 275; Painter, *King John*, pp.231–32.

134. Vincent, 'Isabella', loc. cit. pp.196–97.

135. Ibid.

136. Ibid., pp.185–87.

137. *Dialogus de Scaccario*, op. cit. pp.122–23.

138. H.G. Richardson, 'The Letters and Charters of Eleanor of Aquitaine', EHR 74 (1959), pp.209–11.

139. Vincent, 'Isabella', loc. cit. pp.190–93, 199–200.

140. Michel, *Histoire des ducs*, op. cit. pp.64–65.

CHAPTER 13

1. Howden, *Chronica*, iv. pp.97, 114.

2. Rymer, *Foedera*, i. pp.81–82; *Rotuli Chartarum*, op. cit. 102b – 103; Ralph V. Turner, 'The Role of Eleanor of Aquitaine in the government of her sons', in Wheeler & Parsons, ed. *Eleanor of Aquitaine. Lord and Lady*, op. cit. pp.77–95 (at p.90).

3. Warren, *King John*, p.71.

4. Coggleshall, pp.128–29, 135.

5. Howden, *Chronica*, iv. pp.160–63.

6. Ibid., pp.163–64.

7. Ibid. pp.164, 172; T.D. Hardy, *Rotuli Litterarum Patentium in Turri Londinensi Asservati* (1835), i. 3, 5.

8. Howden, *Chronica*, iv. p.176.

9. Rigord, *Oeuvres*, ii. pp.155–58.

10. Gervase of Canterbury, ii. p.93; Ralph of Diceto, ii. p.173.

11. Rigord, *Oeuvres*, i. pp.151–53; Gervase of Canterbury, ii. p.93; Coggleshall, pp.135–36.

12. Cheney & Semple, *Selected Letters*, op. cit. pp.56–58; C. Petit-Dutaillis, *Le déshéritement de Jean Sans Terre et le meurtre de Arthur de Bretagne* (Paris, 1925), pp.4–18; Kate Norgate, 'The Alleged Condemnation of King John by the Court of France in 1202', TRHS, NS 14 (1900), pp.53–68.

13. *Catalogue des Actes de Philippe Auguste*, op. cit. ii. Nos 723, 726; Rigord, *Oeuvres*, i. p.152; Coggleshall, p.137.

14. *Rotuli Litterarum Patentium*, 14, 106, 116.

15. Natalie Fryde, 'King John and the Empire', in Church, ed., *King John*, pp.335–46.

16. Bradbury, 'Philip Augustus and King John', in Church, ed., *King John*, pp.347–61.

17. R.H. Bautier, 'La personnalité du roi', in Bautier, ed., *La France de Philippe Auguste: le temps des mutations* (Paris, 1982), pp.33–57; cf. R. Foreille, 'L'image de Philippe Auguste dans les sources contemporains', in ibid., pp.115–32.

18. Martin Bouquet, ed., *Recueil des Historiens des Gaules et de la France*, op. cit. xviii. p.263; Petit-Dutaillis & Guinard, *L'Essor des états d'Occident*, op. cit. p.138.

19. Roger of Wendover, iii. p.168; *Rotuli Litterarum Patentium*, i. 10–12.

20. Coggleshall, pp.137–38; Michel, *Histoire des ducs*, op. cit. pp.93–96.

21. WM, ii. pp.101, 127.

22. Rigord, *Oeuvres*, i. p.152; Roger of Wendover, iii. pp.169–70; WM, ii. p.103; *Rotuli Litterarum Patentium*, i. 17–18; Richard, *Comtes de Poitou*, op. cit. ii. p.407.

23. Michel, *Histoire des ducs*, p.94.

24. André Salmon, *Recherches sur les chroniques de Touraine* (Paris, 1847), i. p.147.

25. Coggleshall, p.138; Rigord, *Oeuvres*, i. p.152; *Rotuli Litterarum Patentium*, i. 20, 23.

26. WM, ii. p.106; Coggleshall, p.138; *Annales Monastici*, i. p.26.

27. Petit-Dutaillis, *Le déshéritement de Jean sans Terre*, op. cit.; Powicke, *Loss of Normandy*, pp.309–26.

28. Matthew Paris, *Historia Anglorum*, ed. F. Madden, 3 vols (RS 1869), ii. p.95; iii. p.21.

29. Coggleshall, pp.139–45.

30. William of Newburgh, i. pp.235, 463–64; W. Stubbs, ed., *Memoriale Fratris Walteri de Coventria*, 2 vols (RS 1873) – hereinafter Walter of Coventry – ii. p.196; V. H. Galbraith, 'Nationality and Language in Medieval England', TRHS 4th Series, 23 (1941), pp.113–28.

31. *Annales monastici*, i. p.27.

32. Matthew Paris, *Chronica Majora*, ii. p.659.

33. Powicke, *Loss of Normandy*, pp.174–77, 285, 314.

34. Roger of Wendover, ii. pp.48–49.

35. Delisle, *Catalogue des Actes de Philippe-Auguste*, op. cit. p.177.

36. Rigord, *Oeuvres*, ii. p.173.

37. WM, ii. pp.111–23; *Rotuli Litterarum Patentium*, 236.

38. Rigord, *Oeuvres*, i. pp.157–58.

39. *Rotuli Litterarum Patentium*, 28, 28B, 35; Salmon, *Chroniques de Touraine*, op. cit. i. pp.149–50.

40. Coggleshall, p.144; Michel, *Histoire des ducs*, p.97; *Rotuli Litterarum Patentium*, i. 31.

41. Roger of Wendover, i. pp.316–17.

42. Cheney & Semple, *Selected Letters*, pp.56–59; Powicke, *Loss of Normandy*, pp.163–64.

43. Rigord, *Oeuvres*, ii. p.178.

44. A. Cartellieri, *Philip II*, op. cit. iv. p.167; Bradbury, *Philip Augustus*, p.148.

45. Rigord, *Oeuvres*, ii. p.184.

46. Ibid., p.191.

47. Ibid., i. p.212.

48. WM, ii. pp.125–27.

49. Ibid., pp.137–39.

50. Ibid., p.147.

51. Roger of Wendover, iii. pp.175, 318–20.

52. Baldwin, *The Scutage and Knight Service in England* (Chicago, 1897); F. Pollock & F. W. Maitland, *A History of English Law*, 2 vols (Cambridge, 1898), i. p.256; A.L. Poole, *Obligations of Society in the Twelfth and Thirteenth Centuries* (1946), pp.40–52; Maurice Powicke, 'Distraint of Knighthood and Military Obligation under Henry III', *Speculum* 25 (1950), pp.457–70.

53. Powicke, *Loss of Normandy*, p.235.

54. Hardy, ed., *Rotuli de liberate ac de Misis et Praestitis regnante Johanne*, op. cit. pp.82–83.

55. Rigord, *Oeuvres*, ii. pp.202–04; Norgate, *England under the Angevin Kings*, ii. pp.411–23.

56. Rigord, *Oeuvres*, i. p.160; ii. p.216; Chéruel, *Histoire de Rouen pendant l'époque communale* (Rouen, 1843), i. p.86; *Recueil des Actes de Philippe Auguste*, op. cit. ii. Nos 790–792, 803, 809; C.H. Haskins, *Norman Institutions* (Cambridge, Mass., 1925), p.144.

57. *Rotuli Litterarum Patentium*, i. 39; *Rotuli de Liberate*, op. cit. pp.85, 87, 96; Coggleshall, pp.144–45; Gervase of Canterbury, ii. p.95.

58. Coggleshall, p.147; Martindale, 'Eleanor of Aquitaine: the last years', loc. cit. pp.137–64.

59. Rigord, *Oeuvres*, i. pp.160, 220; ii. pp.211–12.

60. Powicke, *Loss of Normandy*, pp.257–58; A. de la Borderie, *Histoire de Bretagne*, op. cit. iii. p.293.

61. Rigord, *Oeuvres*, i. pp.160, 220–21; Roger of Wendover, i. p.320.

62. Rigord, *Oeuvres*, i. p.151; ii. p.216; *Recueil*, ii. p.381; Michel, *Histoire des ducs*, op. cit. p.98; Powicke, *Loss*, pp.261–63.

63. *Recueil des Actes*, op. cit. ii. pp.403–11, 418–21, 460–61, 470–72, 475, 483–85, 493–503.

64. Powicke, *Loss*, pp.174–77.

65. Coggleshall, p.144; Gervase of Canterbury, ii. p.95; Walter of Coventry, ii. p.197; Semple & Cheney, *Selected Letters*, op. cit. p.40.

66. WM, ii. p.131–37.

67. Gerald of Wales, viii. pp.257–59.

68. Powicke, *Loss*, pp.301–02.

69. Ibid., pp.233–39.

70. R.V. Turner, 'Good or Bad Kingship? The Case of Richard Lionheart', *Haskins Society Journal* 8 (1999), pp.73–78 (at p.78); J.C. Holt, 'The Loss of Normandy and Royal Finance', in Gillingham & Holt, eds, *War and Government in the Middle Ages*, op. cit. pp.92–105 (at p.98); N. Barratt, 'The Revenues of John and Philip Augustus Revisited', in Church, ed., *King John*, pp.75–79.

71. S.D. Church, *The Household Knights of King John* (Cambridge, 1999).

72. *Rotuli Litterarum Patentium*, op. cit. i. 30, 326; T.D. Hardy, ed., *Rotuli Normanniae in Turri Londinensi Asservati* (1835), 103, 105; Richard, *Comtes de Poitou*, op. cit. ii. p.321.

73. *Rotuli Litterarum Patentium*, i. 20b.

74. WM, ii. p.131; Pipe Roll John 6, p.150.

75. WM, ii. p.131.

76. *Rotuli Litterarum Patentium*, i. 356.

77. P. Chaplais, ed., *Diplomatic Documents Preserved in the Public Record Office 1101–1272* (1964), No.206; Daniel Power, 'King John and the Norman Aristocracy', in Church, ed., *King John*, pp.117–36 (at pp.133–34).

78. Howden, *Chronica*, iv. p.114; Richard, *Comtes de Poitou*, op. cit. ii. pp.370–71.

79. Powicke, *Loss*, p.232.

80. *Rotuli Litterarum Patentium*, i. 15, 21b, 24a.

81. Powicke, *Loss*, pp.231–32.

82. Walter of Coventry, ii. p.197; J.C. Holt, 'The End of the Anglo-Norman Realm', in *Proceedings of the British Academy* 61 (1975), pp.223–65; J.B. Baldwin, 'La décennie décisive: les années 1190–1203 dans le règne de Philippe Auguste', *Revue Historique* 266 (1981), pp.311–37.

83. R.V. Turner, 'Good or Bad Kingship', loc. cit. p.73.

84. Baldwin, *Government*, pp.141–52; V.D. Moss, 'The Norman Exchequer Rolls of King John', in Church, *King John*, pp.101–16 (at p.116).

85. J.C. Holt, 'The Loss of Normandy and Royal Finance', in Holt & Gillingham, eds, *War and Government*, op. cit. pp.92–105.

86. Powicke, *Loss*, p.239.

87. Gillingham, *Richard I*, pp.338–40.

88. *Recueil des historiens de France*, op. cit. xxiv. Pt.2 p.758: MGH, Scriptores, ix. p.330.

89. Gillingham, in Church, *King John*, loc. cit.

90. Daniel Power, 'King John and the Norman Aristocracy', in Church, *King John*, pp.117–36 (at pp.122–23).

91. Rigord, *Oeuvres*, i. pp.129, 141.

92. William of Newburgh, i. pp.306, 406.

93. D.A. Carpenter, 'The Abbot Ralph of Coggleshall's account of the last years of King Richard and the first years of King John', EHR 113 (1998).

94. V.D. Moss, 'Norman Exchequer Rolls', loc. cit. p.116.

95. Roger of Wendover, i. pp.316–17; *Annales monastici*, i. pp.26–27; Gerald of Wales, viii. pp.258–59.

96. L. Halphen, ed., *Recueil d'annales angevines et vendômoises* (Paris, 1903), pp.21–22; Coggleshall, pp.143–46; Michel, *Histoire des ducs*, p.97.

97. Gillingham, *Richard I*, pp.347–48.

98. Pollock & Maitland, *History of English Law*, op. cit. ii. pp.500–508.

99. Delaborde, *Recueil des Actes de Philippe*, op. cit. No.933A; T.D. Hardy, ed., *Rotuli de Oblatis et Finibus in Turri Londinensi Asservati* (1835), pp.334–35.

100. Powicke, *Loss*, pp.288–90.

101. WM, ii. p.151.

102. Michel, *Histoire des ducs*, pp.99–100.

103. Powicke, *Loss*, pp.281, 290–91.

104. A.L. Poole, *Domesday Book*, pp.433–41.

105. N. Barratt, 'The Revenue of King John', EHR 111 (1996), pp.835–55.

106. Powicke, *Loss*, p.305.

107. Sean Duffy, 'John and Ireland'; A.A.M. Duncan, 'John King of England and the King of Scots'; Ifor W. Rowlands, 'King John and Wales', in Church, *King John*, pp.221–87.

108. Powicke, *Loss*, pp.303–06.

CHAPTER 14

1. Rigord, *Oeuvres*, i. p.223; ii. p.227.

2. *Recueil des Actes de Philippe-Auguste*, ii. pp.403–11, 418–21, 460–62, 470–72, 483–85, 493–503.

3. Coggleshall, p.103.

4. *Curia Regis Rolls of the Reigns of Richard I, John and Henry III preserved in the Public Record Office*, 7–8 John, pp.101–02.

5. WM, ii. p.151.

6. Ibid., ii. p.155.

7. Coggleshall, p.151.

8. Gervase of Canterbury, ii. pp.96–97.

9. *Rotuli Litterarum Patentium*, i. 55.

10. Coggleshall, pp.148–49.

11. Gervase of Canterbury, ii. pp.97–98.

12. Painter, *King John*, pp.25–29.

13. Ifor W. Rowlands, 'King John and Wales', in Church, *King John*, pp.273–87 (at pp.275–76).

14. Norgate, *John Lackland*, p.105.

15. WM, ii. p.149.

16. Gervase of Canterbury, ii. p.96.

17. WM, ii. pp.151–53.

18. Ibid.

19. Warren, *King John*, p.113.

20. WM, i.

21. Painter, *William Marshal*, pp.138–44.

22. Pipe Roll 7 John, pp.xviii–xx.

23. *Rotuli Litterarum Clausarum*, i. 25–42; Pipe Roll 7 John, pp.xiii–xxv.

24. Gervase of Canterbury, ii. p.98; Coggleshall, pp.152–53.

25. Coggleshall, p.154.

26. Miller, *Richard the Lionheart*, op. cit. p.156.

27. F.W. Brooks, *The English Naval Forces 1199–1272* (1933), p.136; N.A.M. Rodger, *The Safeguard of the Sea*, pp.45–47.

28. Pipe Roll 7 John, p.10; 14 John, p.xix; *Rotuli Litterarum Clausarum*, i. 55, 117.

29. *Rotuli Litterarum Clausarum*, i. 62–63.

30. F.W. Brooks, 'William de Wrotham and the Office of Keeper of the King's Ports and Galleys', EHR 40 (1925), pp.570–79; W.R. Powell, 'The Administration of the Navy and the Stannaries', EHR 71 (1956), pp.177–88.

31. Hardy, ed., *Rotuli de liberate ac de misis et praestitis*, op. cit. 139–40; Painter, *King John*, p.40.

32. WM, ii. p.159.

33. Coggleshall, pp.152–53.

34. Roger of Wendover, ii. p.10.

35. Gervase of Canterbury, ii. p.98.

36. Coggleshall, pp.154–55.

37. *Rotuli Litterarum Patentium*, i. 61; *Rotuli Litterarum Clausarum*, i. 55.

38. Pipe Roll 8 John, p.xviii.

39. Roger of Wendover, iii. p.182; *Rotuli Litterarum Patentium*, i. 62–64.

40. Coggleshall, p.146; Michel, *Histoire des ducs*, pp.100–104.

41. *Annales monastici*, v. p.394; Roger of Wendover, ii. pp.13–14; Walter of Coventry, ii. p.198.

42. Roger of Wendover, iii. p.183; Coggleshall, p.156; Gervase of Canterbury, ii. p.98.

43. Rigord, *Oeuvres*, i. pp.164, 223–224.

44. Bradbury, *Philip Augustus*, p.156.

45. Rymer, *Foedera*, i. p.95.

46. Warren, *King John*, p.120.

47. W.F. Skene, ed., *Johannes de Fordun Chronica Gentis Scotorum*, 2 vols (Edinburgh, 1872) – hereinafter Fordun – i. p.279.

48. D.E.R. Watt, ed., *Scotichronicon of Walter Bower* (Edinburgh, 1994) – hereinafter Bower – iv. p.449; A.O. Anderson, ed., *Chronicle of Melrose* (1936), p.54.

49. Gervase of Canterbury, ii. pp.102–03; Bower, op. cit. pp.449–51.

50. Roger of Wendover, ii. p.50; Fordun, i. p.297; *Annales Monastici*, i. p.29; ii. p.262; F.X. Martin, *A New History of Ireland* (Oxford, 1987), ii. p.139; A.A.M. Duncan, 'John King of England and the King of Scots', in Church, ed., *King John*, pp.244–71 (at p.257).

51. Baldwin, *Government of Philip Augustus*, op. cit. p.207; Castellieri, *Philip II*, op. cit. iv. pp.277–81, 296–97.

52. Rymer, *Foedera*, i. p.103; Gervase of Canterbury, ii. pp.102–03; Bower, iv. pp.451–53; Anderson, ed., *Chronicle of Melrose*, op. cit. p.54.

53. A. Lawrie, *Annals of the Reigns of Malcolm and William, 1153–1214* (Glasgow, 1910), p.358.

54. Fordun, i. p.278; Bower, iv. pp.466–69.

55. Duncan, 'John, King of England and the King of the Scots', loc. cit. pp.262–67.

56. *Rotuli Chartarum*, i. 23, 44, 63, 100b, 103, 103b, 104; *Rotuli Litterarum Patentium*, i. 39, 40, 44b, 51b, 88, 89b, 91; *Rotuli Litterarum Clausarum*, i. 236, 240.

57. *Rotuli Litterarum Patentium*, i. 86; *Rotuli Litterarum Clausarum*, p.12.

58. *Rotuli Litterarum Patentium*, i. p.86; *Rotuli Litterarum Clausarum*, i. p.12; Rymer, *Foedera*, i. p.101; J.E. Lloyd, *A History of Wales from the Earliest Times to the Edwardian Conquest*, 2 vols (1939), ii. pp.631–36; C.W. Lewis, 'The Treaty of Woodstock: its Background and Significance', *Welsh History Review* 2 (1965), pp.37–65.

59. *Annales Monastici*, i. p.60; for W. Rowlands, 'King John and Wales', in Church, *King John*, pp.273–87 (at pp.279–81).

60. Walter of Coventry, ii. p.203.

61. R.F. Treharne, 'The Franco-Welsh treaty of alliance in 1212', *Bulletin of the Board of Celtic Studies* 18 (1958–60), pp.60–75.

62. *Rotuli Litterarum Clausarum*, 121b–122; Rolands, 'King John and Wales', loc. cit. p.281.

63. H. Cole, ed., *Documents Illustrative*, op. cit. p.231.

64. T. Jones, ed., *Brut y Tywysogyon* (Cardiff, 1952), pp.89–92.

65. Poole, *Domesday Book*, p.313.

66. Martin, *New History of Ireland*, op. cit.

67. *Rotuli Chartarum*, 98.

68. *Rotuli Litterarum Patentium*, i. 54.

69. Rowlands, 'King John and Wales', loc. cit. p.275.

70. Warren, *King John*, pp.107–08.

71. *Rotuli Litterarum Patentium*, i. 4, 7, 16b, 18b, 19b, 24b.

72. H.S. Sweetman, ed., *Calendar of Documents Relating to Ireland*, 4 vols (1875), i. Nos.145–148; S. MacAirt, ed., *The Annals of Inisfallen* (Dublin, 1951), p.329.

73. *Rotuli Chartarum*, 107b.

74. Duffy, 'John and Ireland', in Church, ed., *King John*, pp.221–45 (at p.240).

75. Ibid.

76. Helen Perros, 'Crossing the Shannon Frontier: Connacht and the Anglo-Normans 1170–1224', in T.B. Barry, R. France, H. Simms, eds, *Colony and Frontier in Medieval Ireland* (1995), pp.117–38.

77. J.O. O'Donovan, ed., *Annals of the Kingdom of Ireland by the Four Masters*, 7 vols (Dublin, 1851), iii. p.125.

78. Perros, 'Crossing the Shannon Frontier', loc. cit.

79. *Rotuli Litterarum Clausarum*, i. 476; *Rotuli Litterarum Patentium*, 69b, 70b.

80. WM, ii. pp.167–69.

81. *Rotuli Litterarum Patentium*, i. 72.

82. *Rotuli Litterarum Clausarum*, i. 77b.

83. WM, ii. pp.181–91.

84. Ibid., pp.191–99.

85. Painter, *William Marshal*, pp.149–69.

86. *Rotuli Litterarum Clausarum*, i. 105, 105b; *Rotuli Chartarum*, 17b.

87. Rymer, *Foedera*, i. p.107.

88. ibid., i. p.108; *Rotuli Litterarum Patentium*, 86b.

89. WM ii. pp.209–11.

90. Ibid., pp.211–13.

91. Sean Duffy, 'King John's Expedition to Ireland in 1210: the Evidence Reconsidered', *Irish Historical Studies* 30 (1997), pp.1–24.

92. WM, ii. p.215.

93. Rymer, *Foedera*, i. p.108; G.H. Orpen, *Ireland under the Normans*, 4 vols (Oxford, 1920), ii. pp.242–77.

94. WM, ii. p.215.

95. *Annals of Inisfallen*, op. cit. p.339.

96. Michel, *Histoire des ducs*, pp.112–114; W.M. Hennessy, ed, *The Annals of Loch Cé*, 2 vols (RS 1871), i. p.243.

97. WM, ii. pp.211–17.

98. Lewis Warren, 'The Historian as Private Eye', *Historical Studies*, ed. J.G. Barry (Belfast, 1974), ix. pp.1–18; A.J. Otway-Ruthven, *A History of Medieval Ireland* (1968), p.81; J. Lydon, *The Lordship of Ireland in the Middle Ages* (Dublin, 1972), p.65; Painter, *King John*, p.227; Warren, *King John*, p.196.

99. Michel, *Histoire des ducs*, pp.114–15.

100. Coggleshall, p.164; Norgate, *John Lackland*, pp.287–88.

101. Poole, *Domesday Book*, p.315.

102. *Annals of Loch Ce*, op.cit. i. p.245.

103. Duffy, 'King John's Expedition to Ireland, 1210', loc. cit. p.17.

104. Duffy, 'John and Ireland', in Church, *King John*, pp.242–43.

CHAPTER 15

1. Warren, *King John*, p.135.

2. Pipe Roll 9 John, p.xiv.

3. VCH, Dorset (1908), ii. pp.135–36.

4. Danny Danziger & John Gillingham, *1215. The Year of Magna Carta* (2002), pp.170–71.

5. Robert Bartlett, *England under the Norman and Angevin Kings 1075–1225* (Oxford, 2000), pp.135–36.

6. Nicholas Vincent, *Peter des Roches*, op. cit. p.55.

7. S.D. Church, *The Household Knights of King John* (Cambridge, 1999), pp.14, 68–69.

8. J.E.A. Jolliffe, *Angevin Kingship* (1955), pp.189–209.

9. J.E.A. Jolliffe, 'The Chamber and the Castle Treasuries under John', in R.W. Hunt, W.A. Pantin, R.W. Southern, eds, *Studies in Medieval History Presented to F.M. Powicke* (Oxford, 1948), pp.117–42.

10. Brian Hindle, *Medieval Roads* (Princes Risborough, 1989) pp.5–28.

11. Pipe Roll 12 Henry II, pp.49, 89; Pipe Roll 31 Henry II, p.191.

12. Cole, ed., *Documents Illustrative*, op. cit. pp.232, 240.

13. See below, Chapter 18.

14. Pipe Roll 6 John, pp.xxiv–xxxvi, 213; Pipe Roll 4 John, p.280; Pipe Roll 3 John, pp.139, 154–55; Pipe Roll 7 John, pp.12, 121.

15. *Rotuli de liberate ac de misis et praestitis*, 151.

16. Pipe Roll 10 John, p.59; Pipe Roll 9 John, p.72; *Curia Regis Rolls*, op. cit. vi. p.189; *Rotuli Litterarum Patentium*, 13; Rymer; *Foedera*, i. p.93; *Rotuli Chartarum*, i. 34; Pipe Roll 2 John, p.150; 13 John, p.109; 4 John, p.276; *Rotuli Litterarum Patentium*, i. 145–50.

17. Pipe Roll 8 John, p.xxvi; 7 John, p.160; 13 John, pp.xxii, 109.

18. Rymer, *Foedera*, i. p.67.

19. Danziger & Gillingham, *The Year 1215*, op. cit. p.27.

20. N.S.B. Gras, *The Early English Customs System* (Harvard, 1918), pp.37–41; A.L. Simon, *The History of the Wine Trade in England*, 3 vols (1906).

21. Howden, *Chronica*, iv. pp.99–100.

22. Poole, *Domesday Book*, pp.241–42.

23. Bartlett, *England under the Norman and Angevin Kings*, op. cit. p.577.

24. Richard Eales, 'The Game of Chess: An Aspect of Medieval Knightly Culture', in C. Harper-Bill & Ruth Harvey, eds, *The Ideals and Practice of Medieval Knighthood* (Woodbridge, 1986), pp.12–34.

25. *Rotuli Litterarum Clausurum*, i. 108, 296; F.M. Powicke, *Stephen Langton* (Oxford, 1928), p.99.

26. Bartlett, *England under*, op. cit. pp.482–86.

27. Michel, *Histoire des ducs*, p.109.

28. Pipe Roll 3 John, p.xviii; Pipe Roll 6 John, pp.xlv, 99; Pipe Roll 7 John, p.9.

29. Bartlett, *England under*, pp.668–69.

30. H. Cole, *Documents Illustrative*, op. cit. pp.250, 253; *Rotuli de liberate ac de misis et praestitis*, p.124.

31. M. L. Bazeley, 'The Extent of the English Forest in the Thirteenth Century', TRHistS, 4th series, iv (1921), pp.140–72.

32. Raymond Grant, *The Royal Forests of England* (1991), p.155; Howden, *Chronica*, iv. p.63.

33. Charles R. Young, *The Royal Forests of Medieval England* (Pennsylvania, 1979), pp.29–30.

34. *Dialogus de Scaccario*, op. cit. p.60.

35. C.C.J. Webb, ed., *Policraticus by John of Salisbury*, 2 vols (Oxford, 1909), i. pp.30–31.

36. Bartlett, *England under*, p.674.

37. J.G. Turner, *Select Pleas of the Forest* (1899), pp.3–4, 9; Raymond Grant, *The Royal Forests*, op. cit. pp.49–50.

38. H.E. Salter, ed., *Vision of the Monk of Eynsham* (Oxford, 1908), p.348.

39. John H. Mozley & Robert R. Raymo, *Speculum Stultorum of Nigel Longchamp aka Wireker* (L.A., 1960), p.88.

40. Grant, *The Royal Forests*, pp.104–05.

41. Young, *The Royal Forests of Medieval England*, op. cit. p.21.

42. Turner, *Select Pleas*, op. cit. p.9.

43. Howden, *Chronica*, iv. pp.144–45.
44. Douie & Farmer, *Magna Vita of Adam of Eynsham*, op. cit. i. p.114; Gervase of Canterbury, i. p.257; Howden, *Gesta*, i. p.105.
45. Walter Map, *De Nugis Curialium*, op. cit. pp.5–6; *Dialogus de Scaccario*, pp.58–59.
46. Warren, *Henry II*, p.390.
47. Pipe Roll 11 John, p.72; Grant, *The Royal Forests*, pp.90–91.
48. Pipe Roll 22 Henry II, p.193.
49. Grant, *The Royal Forests*, pp.136–37.
50. Pipe Roll 3 John, p.256; Pipe Roll 5 John, pp.143–44; *Rotuli Chartarum*, 132.
51. Young, *The Royal Forests*, op. cit. pp.136–37.
52. Oliver Rackham, *Trees and Woodland in the British Landscape* (1976), pp.66–96.
53. Vincent, *Peter des Roches*, op. cit. pp.185–90.
54. *Dialogus de Scaccario*, op. cit. pp.59–60.
55. Pipe Roll 13 Henry II, p.77.
56. Bartlett, *England under*, p.671.
57. Urban T. Holmes, *Daily Living in the Twelfth Century* (Madison, 1952), p.41.
58. *Rotuli de liberate ac de misis et praestitis*, 144; Cole, ed., *Documents Illustrative*, pp.233, 256.
59. *Rotuli de liberate*, op. cit. 144, 233, 246–47.
60. Bartlett, *England under*, pp.672–73.
61. *Chronicle of Melrose*, op. cit. i. p.233.
62. Gervase of Canterbury, i. p.246.
63. T.H. Lloyd, *The English Wool Trade in the Middle Ages* (Cambridge, 1977), pp.11–14; P. Chorley, 'The Cloth Exports of Flanders and Northern France during the Thirteenth Century: A Luxury Trade?', *Economic History Review*, 2nd Series, 40 (1987), pp.349–79; H. Pirenne, 'The Place of the Netherlands in the Economic History of Medieval Europe', *Economic History Review* 2 (1929), pp.20–40; G. Dept, *Les influences anglaises et françaises dans le comté de Flandre* (Paris, 1928).
64. H.S.A. Fox, 'The Alleged Transformation from the Two-Field to the Three-Field systems in Medieval England', *Economic History Review*, 2nd series, 39 (1986), pp.526–48.
65. P.D.A. Harvey, 'The English Inflation of 1180–1220', PP 61 (1973), pp.3–30; Harvey, 'The Pipe Rolls and the Adoption of Demesne Farming in England', *Economic History Review*, 2nd series, 27 (1974), pp.345–59.
66. P.H. Britnell, *The Commercialisation of English Society 1000–1500* (Cambridge, 1993), ii. pp.79–151.
67. E. Miller, 'England in the Twelfth and Thirteenth Centuries: An Economic Contrast?' *Economic History Review*, 2nd series, 24 (1971), pp.1–14; J.L. Bolton, 'The English Economy in the early Thirteenth Century', in Church, *King John*, pp.27–40.
68. Christopher Dyer, *Making a Living in the Middle Ages. The People of Britain 850–1520* (Yale, 2002), pp.95–96; Bartlett, *England under*, pp.290–97; J.C. Russell, *British Medieval Population* (N.M., 1948).

69. N. Barratt, 'The Revenues of King John', EHR 111 (1996), pp.835–55.

70. Bolton, 'The English Economy', loc. cit. p.40.

71. Maurice Beresford, *New Towns of the Middle Ages* (1967), p.328.

72. Ibid., pp.88, 336–37.

73. Pamela Nightingale, *A Medieval Mercantile Community: The Grocers' Company and the Politics of Trade of London 1000–1465* (Yale, 1995), pp.54–55.

74. N.S.B. Gras, *The Early English Customs System* (Harvard, 1918), pp.221–22; Beresford, *New Towns*, op. cit. p.89.

75. Beresford, op. cit. p.336.

76. Nightingale, op. cit. p.35.

77. Peter Spufford, *Money and its Use in Medieval Europe* (Cambridge, 1988), pp.382–83.

78. Bartlett, *England under*, pp.339–40.

79. Ibid., p.216.

80. Ibid., pp.316–30.

81. David Knowles, *The Monastic Order in England* (1963), pp.363–70.

82. Alice M. Cooke, 'The Settlement of the Cistercians in England', EHR 8 (1893), pp.625–76.

83. J.C. Dickinson, *The Origin of the Augustinian Canons* (1950); H.M. Colvin, *The White Canons in England* (Oxford, 1951).

84. M.D. Knowles & R.N. Hadcock, *Religious Houses of Medieval England* (1953), pp.59–72, 73–78, 80–95, 104–112, 115–116.

85. H.E. Butler, *The Chronicle of Jocelin of Brakeland* (1949), pp.12–17.

86. Gervase of Canterbury, i. pp.372–481.

87. Joan Wardrop, *Fountains Abbey and its Benefactors 1132–1300* (Kalamazoo, Michigan, 1987).

88. *Rotuli Litterarum Patentium*, i. 14.

89. Bartlett, *England under*, pp.199–201.

90. Vincent, *Peter des Roches*, op. cit. pp.89–90.

91. Warren, *King John*, p.126.

92. F. West, *The Justiciarship in England 1066–1232* (Cambridge, 1966), passim.

93. Painter, *King John*, p.92.

94. Gervase of Canterbury, i. pp.216–19; Howden, *Gesta*, ii. pp.4–5.

95. Bartlett, *England under*, p.151.

96. Gillingham, *Richard I*, p.121.

97. Poole, *Domesday Book*, pp.403–05.

98. Vincent, *Peter des Roches*, pp.100–06.

99. Bartlett, *England under*, p.191.

100. Poole, *Domesday Book*, pp.406–08.

101. Ralph Turner, 'John and Justice', in Church, *King John*, pp.317–33 (at p.323).

102. Ibid., p.325.

103. Ralph Turner, 'King John's Concept of Royal Authority', *History of Political Thought* 17 (1996), pp.157–78.

104. Robert Bartlett, *Trial by Fire and Water. The Medieval Judicial Ordeal* (Oxford, 1986).

105. Pocock & Maitland, *The History of English Law*, op. cit. ii. p.599; Bartlett, *Trial*, op. cit. pp.66, 69.

106. See J. Sayers, *Innocent III, Leader of Europe, 1198–1216* (1994); C.R. Cheney, *Pope Innocent III and England* (1976); Norman P. Tanner, ed., *Decrees of the Ecumenical Councils* (Washington D.C., 1990).

107. Hugh Thomas, *Vassals, Heiresses, Crusaders and Thugs: the Gentry of Angevin Yorkshire 1154–1216* (Philadelphia, 1993), pp.73–85.

108. Warren, *King John*, pp.143–44.

109. Turner, 'John and Justice', loc. cit. pp.321–22.

110. Bartlett, *Trial*, p.53, 98, 100.

CHAPTER 16

1. Z.N. Brooke, *The English Church and the Papacy from the Conquest to the Reign of John* (Cambridge, 1931); C.R. Cheney, *From Beckett to Langton; English Church Government 1170–1213* (Manchester, 1956); C.R. Cheney, *Hubert Walter* (1967); C.R. Cheney, *Pope Innocent III and England* (Stuttgart, 1976).

2. F. Pollock & F.W. Maitland, *History of English Law before the Time of Edward I*, 2 vols (Cambridge, 1898), ii. pp.197 et seq.

3. L. Delisle & E. Berger, eds, *Recueil des Actes de Henri II* (Paris, 1927), i. p.587.

4. J.C. Holt, *King John* (1963), pp.13–14; R.V. Turner, *King John* (1994), p.263.

5. A. Biggs, trans. & ed., *Handbook of Church History 4: From the High Middle Ages to the Reformation* (1970), p.152.

6. C.R. Cheney, *Innocent III and England* (Stuttgart, 1976), pp.99–100.

7. C.R. Cheney et al., ed, *The Letters of Innocent III (1198–1216) Concerning England and Wales* (Oxford, 1967), pp.32, 65, 76, 78, 94–95 (Nos. 184, 398, 465, 476–77, 578–79).

8. Roger of Wendover, ii. p.10; Cheney, *Hubert Walter*, pp.105–106.

9. V.H. Galbraith, *An Introduction to the Use of Public Records* (Oxford, 1934), p.20; Galbraith, *Studies in the Public Records* (1948), pp.71–80.

10. Rymer, *Foedera*, i. pp.75–76; Pipe Roll 7 Richard I, pp.179, 225.

11. Cheney, *Hubert Walter*, pp.93–94.

12. Curia Regis Rolls, vi. p.271; Pipe Rolls 7 John, p.116.

13. M.D. Knowles, *The Monastic Order in England. A History of its Development from the times of St Dunstan to the Fourth Lateran Council 943–1216* (Cambridge, 1940), pp.208–226.

14. Walter of Coventry, pp.xlix–liii; M.D. Knowles, 'The Canterbury Election of 1204–05', EHR 53 (1938), pp.211–20; cf. Knowles, *Monastic Order*, op. cit. pp.319–22, 325–27.

15. Painter, *King John*, p.155.

16. C. Harper-Bill, 'John and the Church of Rome', in Church, ed., *King John*, pp.289–315 (at p.294).

17. Cole, *Documents Illustrative*, op. cit. p.274; Pipe Roll 7 John, p.10.

18. Gervase of Canterbury, ii. p.99.

19. C.R. Cheney, 'A Neglected Record of the Canterbury Election of 1205–06',

Bulletin of the Institute of Historical Research 21 (1918).

20. F.M. Powicke, *Stephen Langton* (1929), pp.3-4, 75.

21. *Rotuli Litterarum Patentium*, i. 74; Walter of Coventry, ii. p.199; R.A.L. Smith, 'The Central Financial System of Christchurch Canterbury, 1186–1512', EHR 55 (1940), pp.353–369.

22. B. Bolton, 'Philip Augustus and John. Two Sons in Innocent III's Vineyard', in D. Wood, ed., *The Church and Sovereignty c.590–1918* (Oxford, 1991), pp.113–34; Warren, *King John*, pp.171–72.

23. Adam of Eynsham, *Magna Vita*, eds Douie & Farmer, ii. pp.137–44.

24. Ibid., pp.142–44.

25. H.E. Butler, ed., *The Chronicle of Jocelin of Brakeland* (1949), pp.116–17.

26. Jim Bradbury, 'Philip Augustus and King John', in Church, *King John*, p.350.

27. Gervase of Canterbury, ii. pp.xcii–iii; T.M. Parker, 'The Interdict of Innocent III', *Speculum* 11 (1936), pp.258–60.

28. Cheney, *From Becket to Langton*, op. cit. p.94.

29. Cheney, ed., *Letters of Innocent III*, p.126.

30. Cheney & Semple, *Selected Letters*, op. cit. pp.91–96; E.B. Krehbiel, *The Interdict, its History and Operation* (Washington, 1909).

31. C.R. Cheney, 'King John and the Papal Interdict', *Bulletin of the John Rylands Library* 31 (1948), pp.295–317.

32. *Annales monastici*, i. p.28.

33. Warren, *King John*, p.166.

34. *Rotuli Litterarum Patentium*, i. 80.

35. *Annales monastici*, i. p.28.

36. Cheney & Semple, *Selected Letters*, pp.97–98.

37. Bradbury, *Philip Augustus*, pp.184–87.

38. C.R. Cheney, 'King John's Reaction to the Interdict in England', *Transactions of the Royal Historical Society*, 4th series, 31 (1949), pp.129–50.

39. Adam of Eynsham, *Magna Vita*, op. cit. ii. p.143.

40. Cheney, 'King John's Reaction', loc. cit. p.131.

41. H.T. Riley, ed., *Gesta Abbatum S. Albani* (RS 1869), i. pp.241–43; Pipe Roll 12 John, pp.215–16; Pipe Roll 13 John, p.65.

42. *Letters of Innocent III*, p.157 (No.947); Harper-Bill, 'John and the Church of Rome', loc. cit. pp.306–07.

43. Gerald of Wales, iv. p.313.

44. Poole, *Domesday Book*, op. cit. p.183.

45. *Annales monastici*, ii. p.261.

46. Cheney & Semple, *Selected Letters*, pp.117–20.

47. *Annales monastici*, iii. p.32.

48. Roger of Wendover, iii. pp.228–237; Warren, *King John*, p.169.

49. J. Sayers, *Innocent III, Leader of Europe, 1198–1216* (1994), p.80.

50. Gervase of Canterbury, ii. pp.102–03.

51. Pipe Roll 10 John, p.110.

52. S.K. Mitchell, *Studies in Taxation under Henry II* (Yale, 1914) pp.105–109.

53. Cheney, 'King John and the Papal Interdict', loc. cit. pp.310–11.

54. Cheney, 'King John's Reaction', loc. cit. p.129.

55. Cheney, 'King John and the Papal Interdict', loc. cit. pp.304–05; Cheney, 'King John's Reaction', loc. cit. pp.147–48.

56. Harper-Bill, 'John and the Church of Rome', loc. cit. pp.306–07.

57. *Annales monastici*, iv. p.397.

58. Gervase of Canterbury, ii. pp.103–04; *Rotuli Litterarum Patentium*, i. 89–90.

59. Nicholas Vincent, *Peter des Roches* (Cambridge, 1999), pp.47–55.

60. Gervase of Canterbury, ii. pp.cviii–cx; Walter of Coventry, ii. p.199; Coggleshall, p.165.

61. Harper-Bill, 'John and the Church of Rome', loc. cit. p.306.

62. *Annales monastici*, ii. p.173; Cheney, 'King John and the Papal Interdict', pp.279–300.

63. Norgate, *John Lackland*, p.136.

64. *Rotuli litterarum clausarum*, i. 111.

65. Walter of Coventry, ii. p.203; Michel, *Histoire des ducs*, p.109.

66. *Rotuli de liberate ac de misis*, 112, 141, 149, 151, 153, 158, 165.

67. Cheney & Semple, *Selected Letters*, pp.125–27; Powicke, *Stephen Langton*, op. cit. pp.86–87; Painter, *King John*, pp.186–87.

68. Cheney & Semple, *Selected Letters*, pp.130–36.

69. Cheney, 'The Alleged Deposition of King John', in *Studies Presented to F.M. Powicke* (Oxford, 1948), pp.100–16.

70. Cheney & Semple, *Selected Letters*, p.164.

71. Ibid., pp.141–42.

72. Cole, *Documents Illustrative*, pp.260, 263.

73. Walter of Coventry, ii. p.210.

74. Rymer, *Foedera*, i. pp.111–12; *Rotuli Chartarum*, i. p.195.

75. *Rotuli Chartarum*, i. 191–92; *Rotuli Litterarum Patentium*, i. 140–41; Rymer, *Foedera*, i. p.122; *Annales monastici*, ii. p.268; Coggleshall, p.165.

76. Semple & Cheney, *Selected Letters*, pp.149–51.

77. Ibid., p.150.

78. *Letters of Innocent*, p.157 (No.947); *Rotuli Chartarum*, i. 208–09; Roger of Wendover, ii. pp.100–03; Cheney, 'King John's Reaction to the Interdict', loc. cit. p.129.

79. Matthew Paris, *Historia Anglorum*, op. cit. ii. pp.135, 146–48.

80. Powicke, *Stephen Langton*, pp.98, 104, 130, 134.

81. Roger of Wendover, ii. p.81.

82. Walter of Coventry, ii. p.210; Roger of Wendover, ii. pp.97–98.

83. Walter of Coventry, ii. pp.213–14; Coggleshall, p.170; Harper-Bill, 'John and the Church of Rome', loc. cit. pp.309–10.

84. *Letters of Innocent*, pp.162, 167. (Nos 976, 1004)

85. Natalie Fryde, 'King John and the Empire', in Church, *King John*, pp.335–46.

86. Ralph of Diceto, i. p.371.

87. H. Hall, ed., *Red Book of the Exchequer*, 3 vols (1896), i. pp.11–12.

88. *Dialogus de Scaccario*, p.96.

89. Warren, *King John*, p.183.

90. Pipe Roll 6 John, p.30; *Rotuli Chartarum*, i. 201.

91. S. Painter, *Studies in the History of the English Feudal Barony* (Baltimore, 1943), pp.185–87; J.E.A. Jolliffe, *Angevin Kingship* (1955), pp.79–84.

92. H.G. Richardson, *The English Jewry under the Angevin Kings*, op. cit.; Norgate, *John Lackland*, p.137.

93. *Rotuli Clausarum*, i. 84; Pipe Roll 12 John, p.139.

94. Pipe Roll 5 John, p.197; *Rotuli de Oblatis et Finibus*, 102, 520, 530.

95. *Rotuli Clausarum*, i. 87.

96. Curia Regis Rolls, iii. pp.27–28, 57, 215.

97. Ralph V. Turner, 'John and Justice', in Church, *King John*, pp.317–33 (esp. pp.320–25).

98. S.D. Church, *The Household Knights of King John* (Cambridge, 1999), pp.74–99.

99. Walter of Coventry, ii. p.232.

100. F.W. Maitland, *Pleas of the Crown for the County of Gloucester in 1221* (1884), p.xiii.

101. Roger of Wendover, iii. p.241.

102. Ibid., pp.238–40; Coggleshall, p.165; Walter of Coventry, ii. p.207; *Annales monastici*, ii. p.268; iii. pp.33–34.

103. Cheney & Semple, *Selected Letters*, iii. p.213.

104. Cheney, 'King John's Reaction', loc. cit. pp.142–45.

105. Norgate, *John Lackland*, pp.287–88.

106. Cheney & Semple, *Selected Letters*, p.213.

CHAPTER 17

1. Ralph of Diceto, ii. p.163; Howden, *Chronica*, iv. pp.37–39.

2. Fritz Tautz, *Die Koenige von England und das Reich*, (Heidelberg, 1961) pp.81–101.

3. Georges Duby, *The Legend of Bouvines*, trans. C. Tihanyi (1990), p.27; Jane Sayers, *Innocent III* (Harlow, 1994), p.52; W. Ullmann, *A Short History of the Papacy in the Middle Ages* (1972), p.212.

4. *Annales monastici*, i. p.201; ii. p.73; Howden, *Chronica*, iv. pp.83, 116; Alexander Cartellieri, *Philip II August König von Frankreich*, 4 vols (Leipzig, 1922), iv. p.38.

5. Natalie Fryde, 'King John and the Empire', in Church, *King John*, pp.335–46.

6. *Rotuli Chartarum*, 133; *Rotuli Litterarum Patentium*, i. 11b, 40, 44, 48.

7. *Rotuli Chartarum*, 133b.

8. Cartellieri, *Philip II*, p.103.

9. Walter Kienast, *Die deutschen Fürsten im Dienste der Westmächte bis zum Tode Philipps des Schönen von Frankreich* (Utrecht, 1924), i. p.173.

10. *Rotuli Litterarum Clausarum*, i. 826; Rymer, *Foedera*, i. p.99; Luard, ed., *Flores Historiarum*, RS 95 (1890), ii. pp.133–34.

11. *Rotuli Litterarum Patentium*, 89; Walter of Coventry, ii. p.200.

12. *Annales monastici*, ii. p.261; Rymer, *Foedera*, op. cit. p.103; Cole, ed., *Documents*, p.238.

13. Rymer, *Foedera*, i. pp.103–08; *Rotuli Litterarum Patentium*, 91–92.

14. Roger of Wendover, iii. p.227; *Rotuli de liberate ac de misis*, 138–42.

15. Walter of Coventry, ii. p.202; Roger of Wendover, iii. pp.232–33.

16. Malcolm Barber, *The Cathars: Dualist Heretics in Languedoc in the High Middle Ages* (2000).

17. H. Malo, *Un grand feudataire, Renaud de Dammartin et la coalition de Bouvines* (Paris, 1937).

18. Rymer, *Foedera*, i. p.104; *Rotuli Litterarum Clausarum*, i. 116–17; *Rotuli Chartarum*, 18b; *Rotuli Litterarum Patentium*, 93.

19. E. Lavisse, ed., *Histoire de France depuis les origines jusqu'à la Révolution* (Paris, 1911), iii. Pt. 1 pp.170–71; Georges Duby, *France in the Middle Ages 987–1460*, (Oxford, 1991), p.32.

20. *Rotuli Litterarum Patentium*, 92; Rymer, *Foedera*, i. p.106.

21. Rymer, *Foedera*, i. p.104.

22. *Rotuli Litterarum Patentium*, 506; *Rotuli Litterarum Clausarum*, i. 109b.

23. G.G. Dept, *Les influences anglaise et française dans le Comté de Flandre*, op. cit. pp.83–87; D. Nicholas, *Medieval Flanders* (Harlow, 1992), p.151.

24. Lavisse, *Histoire de France*, op. cit. p.172.

25. Roger of Wendover, iii. p.257.

26. Rymer, *Foedera*, i. pp.106–07; *Rotuli Litterarum Clausarum*, 130b; *Liber Feodorum. The Book of Fees commonly called Testa de Neville*, 3 vols (1931), i. pp.55–228; Painter, *King John*, pp.208–211.

27. Pipe Roll 14 John, pp.xv–xvi, xxiii–xxiv; *Rotuli Litterarum Clausarum*, i. 117, 131.

28. *Annales monastici*, ii. p.267; iii. pp.33–34; Coggleshall, p.165; Roger of Wendover, ii. p.61.

29. *Rotuli Litterarum Clausarum*, i. 121; Roger of Wendover, ii. p.62; Walter of Coventry, ii. p.207; *Annales monastici*, ii. p.268; iii. pp.33–34; Painter, *King John*, pp.267–72.

30. Walter of Coventry, ii. p.207.

31. Walter of Coventry, ii. p.208; Roger of Wendover, iii. pp.240, 248.

32. Michel, *Histoire des ducs*, pp.122–23.

33. Roger of Wendover, iii. pp.255–56.

34. *Annales monastici*, iii. p.34; Coggleshall, p.167; Michel, *Histoire des ducs*, pp.125–26.

35. Roger of Wendover, iii. p.256; *Rotuli Litterarum Clausarum*, i. 132.

36. C. Harper-Bill, 'John and the Church of Rome', in Church, ed., *King John*, p.307.

37. Warren, *King John*, p.203.

38. WM, ii. p.225.

39. Roger of Wendover, iii. pp.245–46.

40. Ibid., ii. pp.66–68.

41. Rymer, *Foedera*, i. p.104; Delisle, *Catalogue des Actes de Philippe Auguste*, No. 1437.

42. E. Lavisse, ed., *Histoire de France*, op. cit. iii. Pt 1. p.164.

43. Bradbury, *Philip Augustus*, p.289.

44. Stephen O'Shea, *The Perfect Heresy: The Life and Death of the Cathars* (2000).

45. W. Stuerner, *Friedrich II. Teil 1. Die Königsherrschaft in Sizilien und Deutschland 1194–1220* (Darmstadt, 1992).

46. Cartellieri, *Philip II*, op. cit. iv. pp.289–90, 294–95, 298, 311.

47. Rigord, *Oeuvres*, ii. pp.305–08.

48. Roger of Wendover, ii. pp.66–68.

49. *Annales monastici*, iii. p.35; *Rotuli Litterarum Clausarum*, i. 34–35.

50. Rymer, *Foedera*, i. p.113.
51. Roger of Wendover, iii. p.257.
52. Cartellieri, *Philip II*, iv. p.363.
53. Roger of Wendover, iii. p.258; Walter of Coventry, ii. p.211.
54. Rigord, *Oeuvres*, i. p.251; Michel, *Histoire des ducs*, pp.130–33.
55. WM, ii. p.233.
56. Ibid., pp.233–39.
57. Coggleshall, p.167.
58. Roger of Wendover, iii. pp.261–62.
59. Matthew Paris, *Historia Anglorum*, 3 vols, ed. F. Madden, RS 44 (1869), ii. p.141.
60. Roger of Wendover, iii. pp.262–63.
61. *Annales monastici*, iii. p.40; Coggleshall, p.167.
62. Powicke, *Stephen Langton*, pp.113–16.
63. Rymer, *Foedera*, i. p.177; A.E. Levett, 'The Summons to a Great Council, 1213', EHR 31 (1916), pp.85–90.
64. Roger of Wendover, iii. p.278.
65. Michel, *Histoire des ducs*, pp.139–41.
66. Coggleshall, p.168; *Annales monastici*, iii. p.39; *Rotuli Litterarum Patentium*, 106b, 108b.
67. *Annales monastici*, ii. p.281.
68. Ibid., i. p.110.
69. *Rotuli Litterarum Patentium*, i. 109b, 110, 110b.
70. Coggleshall, p.168.
71. Duby, *The Legend of Bouvines*, op. cit. p.28.
72. *Rotuli de liberate ac de misis*, 157.
73. Rigord, *Oeuvres*, ii. p.227.
74. *Rotuli Litterarum Patentium*, 111.
75. Ibid., 112b.
76. Rymer, *Foedera*, i. p.118.
77. *Rotuli Litterarum Patentium*, 115a.
78. *Rotuli Chartarum*, 197b; Rymer, *Foedera*, i. pp.123–25; Roger of Wendover, iii, pp.280–81.
79. Bradbury, *Philip Augustus*, p.280.
80. Roger of Wendover, iii. pp.285–86.
81. Coggleshall, p.169; Michel, *Histoire des ducs*, p.143.
82. Rigord, *Oeuvres*, ii. p.289.
83. Roger of Wendover, ii. pp.104–05; Rigord, *Oeuvres*, i. pp.263–64.
84. Coggleshall, pp.169–70.
85. *Rotuli Litterarum Patentium*, i. p.118.
86. C. W. C. Oman, *A History of the Art of War in the Middle Ages*, 2 vols (1924), i. p.471.
87. Susan Reynolds, *Fiefs and Vassals* (Oxford, 1994), p.320; Baldwin, *Government of Philip Augustus*, op. cit. pp.280–81.
88. J.F. Verbruggen, *The Art of Warfare in Western Europe during the Middle Ages* (Woodbridge, 1997), pp.239–60.
89. Baldwin, *Government*, p.198; G. Bordonove, *Philip Augustus* (Paris, 1986); A.

Luchaire, *Social France at the Time of Philip Augustus* (N.Y. 1912), p.160; Bradbury, *Philip Augustus*, pp.281–82, 299, 310–11.

90. John France, *Western Warfare in the Age of the Crusades, 1000–1300* (1999), p.235.

91. Rigord, *Oeuvres*, ii. pp.308–09.

92. Ibid., p.311.

93. Ibid., p.315.

94. Ibid., p.313.

95. Duby, *Legend of Bouvines*, op. cit. pp.38–39, 194, 197–99.

96. Ibid., p.200.

97. Roger of Wendover, iii. p.287.

98. Ibid., pp.288–90.

99. France, *Western Warfare*, op. cit. p.239.

100. Duby, *Legend*, p.200.

101. Baldwin, *Government*, op. cit. pp.269, 276; Verbruggen, *The Art of Warfare*, op. cit. p.246.

102. France, *Western Warfare*, pp.239–40.

103. Rigord, *Oeuvres*, i. p.283.

104. Duby, *Legend*, p.211.

105. Ibid., p.201; France, *Western Warfare*, p.240.

106. Matthew Paris, *Historia Anglorum*, op. cit. p.191.

107. Rigord, *Oeuvres*, i. p.285, ii. p.332.

108. Baldwin, *Government*, p.217.

109. Coggleshall, p.169; Walter of Coventry, ii. p.216.

110. H. Delbruck, *The History of the Art of War* (Westport, Conn., 1982), p.417.

111. Rigord, *Oeuvres*, ii. p.353.

112. Duby, *Legend*, p.216.

113. Ibid., pp.195, 216; F. Lot, *L'Art militaire et les armées au Moyen Age*, 2 vols (Paris, 1946), i. pp.223–25; Oman, *Art of War*, op. cit. pp.445–57.

114. Rigord, *Oeuvres*, i. p.297.

115. *Rotuli Litterarum Clausarum*, i. 210b.

116. *Rotuli Litterarum Patentium*, i. 139.

117. Coggleshall, pp.167–70.

118. Rymer, *Foedera*, i. p.124; *Rotuli Litterarum Patentium*, 140b.

119. Coggleshall, p.170.

120. Rymer, *Foedera*, i. p.215.

121. Roger of Wendover, iii. p.293.

CHAPTER 18

1. A.F. Teulet, *Layettes du Trésor de Chartes* (Paris, 1909), i. p.423; W.S. McKechnie, ed., *Magna Carta* (Glasgow, 1915), pp.485–86; J.H. Round, 'An Unknown Charter of Liberties', EHR 8 (1893), pp.288 et seq. J.C. Holt, *Magna Carta* (Cambridge, 1992), pp.418–28.

2. Howlett, *Chronicles*, op. cit. ii. pp.517–18; T. Arnold, ed., *Memorials of St Edmund's Abbey*, RS (1896), ii. p.24.

3. *Rotuli Litterarum Clausarum*, i. 166b.

4. Walter of Coventry, ii. pp.217–18.

5. Roger of Wendover, iii. pp.263–66.

6. Ibid., pp.293–94; Coggleshall, p.170; Holt, *Magna Carta*, pp.406–11.

7. Walter of Coventry, ii. pp.217–18.

8. Warren, *King John*, pp.226–27.

9. Rymer, *Foedera*, i. p.160.

10. Walter of Coventry, ii. p.207; Coggleshall, p.165; Roger of Wendover, iii. p.240.

11. Cheney & Semple, *Selected Letters*, pp.132–33; Kate Norgate, *John Lackland*, p.293.

12. Howlett, *Chronicles*, ii. p.521.

13. Michel, *Histoire des ducs*, pp.97, 115–25; Coggleshall, pp.143–44; Roger of Wendover, iii. p.172; J.H. Round, 'King John and Robert Fitzwalter', EHR 19 (1904), pp.707–11.

14. Coggleshall, pp.143–44; GM, iii. pp.172–73; Painter, *King John*, p.295.

15. Painter, *King John*, pp.29–30.

16. Ibid., p.286; Powicke, *Stephen Langton*, pp.207–13.

17. Michel, *Histoire des ducs*, pp.147–49.

18. Roger of Wendover, iii. pp.300–01.

19. Coggleshall, pp.167–70.

20. Walter of Coventry, ii. pp.217–20.

21. *Annales monastici*, iii. p.240; *Letters of Innocent III*, p.163 (No.981); Rymer, *Foedera*, i. p.126.

22. Walter of Coventry, ii. p.218.

23. *Rotuli Litterarum Patentium*, i. pp.128–30; *Rotuli Litterarum Clausarum*, i. 187b.

24. C.R. Cheney, 'The Eve of Magna Carta', *Bulletin of John Rylands Library* 38 (1956), pp.311–41.

25. Rymer, *Foedera*, i. p.120.

26. *Letters of Innocent III*, p.169 (No. 1017).

27. Ibid., p.167 (No. 1001); Rymer, *Foedera*, i. p.127.

28. *Letters of Innocent III*, p.167 (No. 1002).

29. Ibid., pp. 167–68 (No. 1005); Rymer, *Foedera*, i. p.128.

30. *Letters of Innocent III*, pp.169–70 (No. 1016).

31. *Rotuli Litterarum Patentium*, i. p.130.

32. Roger of Wendover, iii. p.299.

33. Coggleshall, p.171; Walter of Coventry, ii. p.219; Rymer, *Foedera*, i. p.133.

34. Roger of Wendover, iii. p.299.

35. *Rotuli Litterarum Patentium*, 134b, 135, 135b; *Rotuli Literarum Clausarum*, i. 141, 198, 198b; *Rotuli Chartarum*, p.207.

36. Walter of Coventry, ii. p.220; *Rotuli Litterarum Patentium*, 136b.

37. Roger of Wendover, iii. pp.300–01.

38. Holt, *Magna Carta*, op. cit. p.242.

39. *Rotuli Chartarum*, i. p.209.

40. *Rotuli Litterarum Patentium*, i. p.141.

41. Cheney, 'Eve of Magna Carta', loc. cit. p.231; Painter, *King John*, p.307.

42. Michel, *Histoire des ducs*, pp.147–48.

43. Ibid., pp.148–49.

44. *Rotuli Litterarum Patentium*, 138.

45. Ibid., 138b, 141b.

46. Rymer, *Foedera*, i. p.129.

47. Coggleshall, pp.171–72; Walter of Coventry, ii. pp.220–21.

48. Roger of Wendover, iii. p.301.

49. *Rotuli Litterarum Patentium*, 42b, 143.

50. W. Stubbs, ed., *Selected Charters* (Oxford, 1921), pp.284–91; McKechnie, *Magna Carta*, op. cit. pp.487–93.

51. Roger of Wendover, iii. p.301.

52. Coggleshall, p.172.

53. Roger of Wendover, iii. p.302.

54. J.C. Holt, 'The Making of Magna Carta', EHR 72 (1957), pp.401–22.

55. The literature of Magna Carta is enormous and would take a lifetime to digest in its totality. I have used the following: W.S. McKechnie, *Magna Carta*, op. cit.; J.C. Holt, *Magna Carta* (Cambridge, 1992); Ralph Turner, *Magna Carta* (2003); John Hudson, *The Formation of the English Common Law* (1996); William F. Swindler, *Magna Carta: Legend and Legacy* (Indianapolis, 1965); J.A.P. Jones, *King John and Magna Carta* (Bristol, 1971).

56. L. Petit-Dutaillis, *Etude sur la vie et règne de Louis VII* (Paris, 1894), pp.57–58; Petit-Dutaillis, *Studies Supplementary to Stubb's Constitutional History of England*, 3 vols (Manchester, 1908), i. p.129; E. Jenks, 'The Myth of Magna Carta', *Independent Review* 4 (1904), pp.260–73.

57. Warren, *King John*, pp.236–37.

58. Harry Street, *Freedom, the Individual and the Law* (1963), p.271; Jenks, 'Myth', loc. cit.; J.G.A. Pocock, *The Ancient Constitution and the Feudal Law* (Cambridge, 1957), pp.45–47; J.C. Holt, 'The Barons and the Great Charter', EHR 70 (1955), pp.1–24.

59. N.D. Hurnard, 'Magna Carta, Clause 34', in R.W. Hunt, W.A. Pantin & R.W. Southern, *Studies in Medieval History Presented to Maurice Powicke* (Oxford, 1948), pp.157–79.

60. J.C. Holt, *Magna Carta* (Cambridge, 1992), p.18.

61. Bartlett, *England under the Angevin Kings*, op. cit. p.65.

62. Holt, *Magna Carta*, pp.281–91.

63. Ibid., pp.196–97, 321–24, 329, 335.

64. Matthew Paris, *Chronica Majora*, ii. pp.604–05.

65. Danziger & Gillingham, *The Year 1215*, op. cit. p.262.

66. *Rotuli Litterarum Patentium*, i. pp.143–45; *Rotuli Litterarum Clausarum*, i. pp.215–16; Painter, *King John*, pp.330–33.

67. Walter of Coventry, ii. p.221.

68. Rymer, *Foedera*, i. pp.133–34.

69. Michel, *Histoire des ducs*, p.151; Painter, *King John*, pp.337–38.

70. *Rotuli Litterarum Patentium*, i. 140; H.G. Richardson, 'The Morrow of the Great Charter', *Bulletin of the John Rylands Library* 28 (1944), pp.442–43; 29 (1945), pp.184–200.

71. C.R. Cheney, 'The Twenty-Five Barons of Magna Carta', *Bulletin of the John Rylands Library* 50 (1968), pp.280–307.

72. Vincent, *Peter des Roches*, op. cit. p.122.

73. Michel, *Histoire des ducs*, p.181; J.C. Holt, *The Northerners* (Cambridge, 1992), pp.123–24.

74. *Rotuli Litterarum Patentium*, 179b, 181b; Rymer, *Foedera* i. p.121; Coggleshall, pp. 173–74; I. Rowlands, 'King John, Stephen Langton and Rochester Castle, 1213–15', in C. Harper-Bill et al., eds, *Studies in Medieval History Presented to R. Allen Brown* (Woodbridge, 1989), pp.267–79.

75. C. R. Cheney, 'The Church and Magna Carta', *Theology* 68 (1965), pp.266–72; A. J. Collins, 'The Documents of the Great Charter of 1215', *Proceedings of the British Academy* 34 (1948), pp.233–79.

76. Walter of Coventry, ii. p.222.

77. H.G. Richardson, 'The Morrow of the Great Charter', loc. cit.

78. Roger of Wendover, ii. p.137; Michel, *Histoire des ducs*, p.151.

79. Holt, *Magna Carta*, p.228.

80. Walter of Coventry, ii. p.223.

81. *Letters of Innocent III*, p.169 (No. 1013).

82. ibid., p.169–70 (no. 1016); Roger of Wendover, iii. pp.336–38; Cheney, *Pope Innocent and England* (Stuttgart, 1976), pp.374–79; F.M. Powicke, 'The Bull Miramur Plurimum and a letter to Archbishop Stephen Langton', EHR 44 (1929), pp.87–93.

83. Vincent, *Peter des Roches*, pp.123–25; Richardson, 'The Morrow of the Great Charter', loc. cit. p.193; Cheney, *Innocent III*, op. cit. pp.379–80.

84. *Rotuli Litterarum Patentium*, 153b, 154b, 181b, 182; *Rotuli Chartarum*, 219b; Rymer, *Foedera*, p.137.

85. Coggleshall, pp.173–74; Walter of Coventry, ii. p.225; Roger of Wendover, iii. p.340.

86. Gerald of Wales, i. p.401; Powicke, *Stephen Langton*, pp.132–34.

87. *Letters of Innocent III*, p.170 (Nos 1018–1019).

88. Cheney & Semple, *Selected Letters*, pp.212–16.

89. Herbert Butterfield, *The Englishman and his History*, (Cambridge, 1945).

CHAPTER 19

1. Matthew Paris, *Chronica Majora*, ii. p.611.

2. Roger of Wendover, iii. p.319.

3. *Rotuli Litterarum Patentium*, 152b.

4. Walter of Coventry, ii. p.224; Michel, *Histoire des ducs*, pp.152–53.

5. Roger of Wendover, iii. p.341; Walter of Coventry, ii. p.224.

6. Roger of Wendover, iii. pp.220–21.

7. Michel, *Histoire des ducs*, p.153.

8. Walter of Coventry, ii. p.224; Roger of Wendover, ii. pp.147–48.

9. *Rotuli Litterarum Patentium*, i. p.181.

10. Michel, *Histoire des ducs*, pp.158–59.

11. Coggleshall, p.176; Walter of Coventry, ii. p.226.

12. Michel, *Histoire des ducs*, p.159.

13. *Rotuli Litterarum Clausarum*, i. 231b; Coggleshall, p.176.

14. Walter of Coventry, ii. p.226; Roger of Wendover, iii. p.331; Coggleshall, pp.174–75; Michel, *Hisoire des ducs*, pp.155–56, 160; Matthew Paris, *Historia Anglorum*, op. cit. ii. p.165.

15. Roger of Wendover, iii. p.333.

16. Walter of Coventry, ii. p.227.

17. *Rotuli Litterarum Clausarum*, i. pp.231, 238; Roger of Wendover, iii. pp.334–35.

18. Michel, *Histoire des ducs*, p.163.

19. Roger of Wendover, iii. p.336; Walter of Coventry, ii. p.227.

20. Walter of Coventry, ii. p.226.

21. *Rotuli Litterarum Patentium*, 157, 157b, 158.

22. Richardson, 'Morrow of the Great Charter', loc. cit.

23. *Rotuli Litterarum Clausarum*, i. 218, 218b, 219, 219b; *Rotuli Chartarum*, 210–13.

24. *Annals of the Four Masters*, op. cit. iii. pp.179–81; *Annals of Ulster*, op. cit. ii. p.257; *Annals of Loch Cé*, i. pp.249–51.

25. P.J. Dunning, 'The Letters of Innocent III to Ireland', *Traditio*, 18 (1962), pp.246–47.

26. Ifor W. Rowlands, 'King John and Wales', in Church, *King John*, p.285.

27. A.A.M. Duncan, 'John King of England and the Kingdom of the Scots', in Church, ed., *King John*, p.267.

28. *Annales monastici*, iii. p.303; Walter of Coventry, ii. pp.207, 225.

29. Roger of Wendover, iii. p.359.

30. Walter of Coventry, ii. p.222.

31. Ibid., pp.225–26; Michel, *Histoire des ducs*, p.160.

32. Coggleshall, p.176.

33. Walter of Coventry, ii. p.224; Roger of Wendover, ii. pp.147–48.

34. Coggleshall, pp.176–77; Michel, *Histoire des ducs*, p.161.

35. Roger of Wendover, iii. pp.349–50; Michel, *Histoire des ducs*, pp.161–62.

36. Roger of Wendover, iii. pp.344–47.

37. Warren, *King John*, pp.248–49.

38. Poole, *Domesday Book*, p.480.

39. Roger of Wendover, iii. pp.347–48.

40. Walter of Coventry, ii. p.228.

41. Roger of Wendover, iii. p.350.

42. Warren, *King John*, p.249.

43. Poole, *Domesday Book*, p.481.

44. Michel, *Histoire des ducs*, pp.163–64; Matthew Paris, *Chronica Majora*, ii. pp.641–42.

45. *Chronicle of Melrose*, op. cit. p.62.

46. A.A.M. Duncan, 'John King of England and the Kingdom of the Scots', loc. cit. p.267.
47. Roger of Wendover, iii. p.352.
48. Michel, *Histoire des ducs*, p.165.
49. Coggleshall, pp.179–80.
50. *Rotuli Litterarum Patentium*, i. 172b, 176.
51. Poole, *Domesday Book*, p.482.
52. Roger of Wendover, iii. pp.349–50, 352, 358; Walter of Coventry, ii. p.229; Coggleshall, pp.177–78.
53. Coggleshall, p.180.
54. Roger of Wendover, iii. pp.359–60.
55. Michel, *Histoire des ducs*, p.162.
56. Coggleshall, p.178.
57. *Letters of Innocent III*, p.172 (Nos.1026–27, 1029)
58. Roger of Wendover, iii. pp.354–57; Coggleshall, p.179.
59. Coggleshall, p.180; Michel, *Histoire des ducs*, p.165.
60. Coggleshall, pp.180–81; *Rotuli Litterarum Patentium*, 170, 170b, 171, 172b, 175b, 176, 179.
61. N. Vincent, ed., *The Acta of the Legate Guala* (Woodbridge, 1996), pp.xxxix–xxxx.
62. Roger of Wendover, iii. pp.364–67; W.H. Hudson, *Philip Augustus* (1896), p.200.
63. Lavisse, op. cit. iii. Pt 1 pp.255–57.
64. Warren, *King John*, p.251.
65. Vincent, *Acta*, pp.xl–xli.
66. Matthew Paris, *Historia Anglorum*, ii. pp.176–77.
67. Bradbury, *Philip Augustus*, p.319.
68. Rigord, *Oeuvres*, i. p.359; Hallam, *Capetian France*, op. cit. p.133.
69. Bradbury, *Philip Augustus*, p.320.
70. *Rotuli Litterarum Clausarum*, i. 270, 270b.
71. *Rotuli Litterarum Patentium*, 178b; Coggleshall, p.181; Matthew Paris, *Chronica Majora*, iii. p.29.
72. Michel, *Histoire des ducs*, pp.167–69.
73. Roger of Wendover, iii. p.368; Walter of Coventry, ii. pp.229–30.
74. *Rotuli Litterarum Patentium*, 184; Michel, *Histoire des ducs*, p.170.
75. Vincent, *Acta*, p.lxvi.
76. Ibid. (No.56).
77. Coggleshall, p.182; Walter of Coventry, ii. p.232; *Rotuli Litterarum Patentium*, 190; Michel, *Histoire des ducs*, pp.174–77.
78. Coggleshall, p.181; Michel, *Histoire des ducs*, pp.170–71.
79. Walter of Coventry, ii. p.230; Roger of Wendover, iii. pp.368–69; Michel, *Histoire des ducs*, p.171.
80. Coggleshall, p.182; *Rotuli Litterarum Patentium*, 188b; Michel, *Histoire des ducs*, pp.173–74.
81. Roger of Wendover, iii. p.371; Michel, *Histoire des ducs*, p.174.
82. Michel, *Histoire des ducs*, pp.175–77.
83. Matthew Paris, *Historia Anglorum*, ii. p.182.

84. Roger of Wendover, iii. pp.378–81.

85. *Chronicle of Melrose*, pp.62–64.

86. Roger of Wendover, iii. p.379.

87. Rymer, *Foedera*, i. p.142; *Rotuli Litterarum Patentium*, i. 196; G.R. Stephens, 'A Note on William of Cassingham', *Speculum* 16 (1941), pp.216–33.

88. *Rotuli Litterarum Patentium*, 184, 184b, 185, 185b, 186, 186b, 187, 187b, 188, 189b, 192, 193–95.

89. Ibid., 191b, 194.

90. Matthew Paris, *Chronica Majora*, ii. p.664.

91. Michel, *Histoire des ducs*, pp.177–79.

92. *Annales monastici*, iii. p.49.

93. Coggleshall, pp.179, 182; Roger of Wendover, iii. pp.380–83; Walter of Coventry, ii. p.230.

94. Roger of Wendover, iii. pp.380–81; Coggleshall, p.179.

95. Roger of Wendover, iii. pp.381–82; Coggleshall, p.182.

96. Matthew Paris, *Historia Anglorum*, ii. p.185.

97. Coggleshall, p.183; Walter of Coventry, ii. p.231; *Rotuli Litterarum Patentium*, 197b.

98. Michel, *Histoire des ducs*, p.179.

99. Matthew Paris, *Chronica Majora*, ii. p.667; Paris, *Historia Anglorum*, ii. pp.189–90.

100. Roger of Wendover, iii. pp.381–82; Walter of Coventry, ii. p.231; *Rotuli Litterarum Clausarum*, i. 289.

101. Coggleshall, p.183; Roger of Wendover, iii. p.384; Walter of Coventry, ii. p.232; *Rotuli Litterarum Patentium*, 199; *Rotuli Litterarum Clausarum*, i. 291.

102. Roger of Wendover, iii. p.380; Michel, *Histoire des ducs*, pp.179–81; Matthew Paris, *Chronica Majora*, ii. p.655; *Rotuli Litterarum Patentium*, 185, 186, 196.

103. Coggleshall, p.182; Walter of Coventry, ii. p.232; Michel, *Histoire des ducs*, p.180.

104. Coggleshall, p.183; Walter of Coventry, ii. p.231.

105. Coggleshall, pp.183–84.

106. Roger of Wendover, iii. p.384.

107. G. Fowler, 'King John's Treasure', *Proceedings of the Cambridge Antiquarian Society* 46 (1953), pp.4–20.

108. Roger of Wendover, iii. p.384; Matthew Paris, *Historia Anglorum*, ii. p.190.

109. Fowler, 'King John's Treasure', loc. cit.; W. St John Hope, 'The Loss of King John's Treasure in the Wellstream in October 1216', *Archaeologia* 60 (1906), pp.93–110; J.C. Holt, 'King John's Disaster in the Wash', *Nottingham Medieval Studies* 5 (1961), pp.75–86.

110. Warren, *King John*, pp.280–84.

111. A.V. Jenkinson, 'The Jewels Lost in the Wash', *History* 8 (1924), pp.163–66.

112. Coggleshall, p.184.

113. Roger of Wendover, iii. p.385; Coggleshall, p.183.

114. Norgate, *John Lackland*, pp.282–83.

115. Matthew Paris, *Historia Anglorum*, ii. pp.191–92.

116. *Annales monastici*, iii. p.48; Roger of Wendover, iii, p.385; Coggleshall, p.184; Walter of Coventry, ii. p.231.

117. Rymer, *Foedera*, i. p.144.

118. *Chronicle of Melrose*, p.124; Bartlett, *England under the Angevin Kings*, pp.595–97.
119. Roger of Wendover, iii. pp.385–86; Walter of Coventry, ii. p.232.
120. Roger of Wendover, iii. p.386.
121. D. A. Carpenter, *The Minority of Henry III* (1990), pp.51, 109, 154.
122. Holt, *Magna Carta*, pp.378–84.
123. Rigord, *Oeuvres*, i. p. 314; Roger of Wendover, iv. p.22.
124. Rigord, *Oeuvres*, i. p.314.
125. Ibid., i. p.319.

CHAPTER 20

1. Jim Bradbury, *Philip Augustus*, p.333.
2. Poole, *Domesday Book*, p.350.
3. David Hume, *History of England* (1871), i. p.162.
4. Ralph V. Turner & Richard R. Keiser, *The Reign of Richard Lionheart, Ruler of the Angevin Empire, 1189–1199* (2000), p.4.
5. William of Newburgh, ii. p.31; J.A. Brundage, *Richard Lionheart* (N.Y., 1974), p.116.
6. Ibn al-Athir, *el-Kamal*, op. cit. p.43.
7. Baha al-Din, *Rare and Excellent History*, op. cit.
8. P.W. Edbury, *The Conquest of Jerusalem and the Third Crusade*, pp.97–113, 115–24.
9. William of Newburgh, i. p.281; Gerald of Wales, v. pp.130–33; viii. pp.172–73.
10. Gerald of Wales, iv. p.369; viii. p.232.
11. Geoffrey Hindley, *Saladin* (N.Y., 1976), pp.168–69.
12. Gillingham, *Richard I*, pp.167–71.
13. Ambroise, p.108.
14. Jacques de Vitry, *History of Jerusalem* (1896), pp.112–13.
15. Coggleshall, pp.33–34.
16. Gabrieli, *Arab Historians of the Crusade*, op. cit. pp.138–39, 223–24, 349.
17. Turner & Heiser, *The Reign of Richard Lionheart*, op. cit. p.86.
18. William of Newburgh, ii. p.31.
19. Ambroise, pp.159–63.
20. Gerald of Wales, v. pp.106–07; J. Gillingham, 'Richard I and the Science of War in the Middle Ages', in J. Gillingham & J.C. Holt, eds., *War and Government in the Middle Ages: Essays in Honour of J.O. Prestwich* (1984), p.87.
21. Turner & Heiser, *The Reign of Richard Lionheart*, passim.
22. H. G. Richardson & G.O. Sayles, *The Governance of Medieval England* (Edinburgh, 1963), p.366; Christopher Tyerman, *The Invention of the Crusades* (1988).
23. M. Markowski, 'Richard Lionheart: Bad King, Poor Crusader', *Journal of Medieval History* 23 (1997), pp.351–65.
24. Ambroise, p.191; Howden, *Chronica*, iv. pp.59–60.
25. Gillingham, *Richard I*, p.17.
26. Nicholson, *Chronicle*, op. cit. pp.144–48.
27. Markowski, loc. cit. p.353.

28. Edbury, *Conquest*, p.93.
29. Markowksi, loc. cit. pp.358, 361.
30. S. Runciman, *A History of the Crusades*, op. cit. iii. pp.43–45; Hinley, *Saladin*, op. cit. pp.168–69.
31. Markowksi, loc. cit. p.361.
32. Adam of Eynsham, *Magna Vita*, ii. pp.98–100.
33. Ibid., p.101.
34. Ibid., pp.103–05.
35. Ibid., p.105; xli.
36. Ibid., p.114.
37. Ibid., p.xlvii.
38. Ralph V. Turner, *King John*, op. cit. p.15.
39. Sean Duffy, 'John and Ireland', in Church, *King John*, pp.221–45.
40. Howden, *Chronica*, iii. pp.198, 253; Gervase of Canterbury, ii. pp.92–93.
41. *Annales monastici*, i. p.27; Walter of Coventry, ii. p.197.
42. J. Bradbury, 'Philip Augustus and King John', in Church, *King John*, p.349.
43. Turner, *King John*, pp.14–15.
44. Gillingham, *Angevin Empire*, p.80.
45. J. T. Appleby, *John King of England* (1958), p.85.
46. Maurice Ashley, *King John* (1972), p.143.
47. Ibid., p.145.
48. *King John*, Act Five, Scene Seven.
49. Turner, *King John*, p.262.
50. Pollock and Maitland, *The History of English Law*, op. cit. ii. p.506; Bartlett, *England under the Angevin Kings*, pp.58–62.
51. Turner, *King John*, pp.13–19.
52. *Annales monastici*, ii. p.282.
53. Coggleshall, p.170.
54. Warren, *King John*, p.99.
55. Hallam, *Capetian France*, op. cit. p.182.
56. Robert Henri Bautier, *Etudes sur la France capétienne* (Paris, 1992), p.33.
57. Gillingham, *Angevin Empire*, op. cit.; John le Patourel, *The Norman Empire* (Oxford, 1976); C. Warren Hollister, *Monarchy, Magnates and Institutions in the Anglo-Norman World* (1986), pp.17–58.
58. Charles Coulson, 'Fortress Policy in the Capetian tradition and Angevin practice: Aspects of the conquest of Normandy by Philip II', ANS 6 (1984), pp.12–38.
59. Warren, *Henry II*, pp.561–62.
60. Ralph V. Turner, 'The Problem of Survival for the Angevin Empire', AHR 100 (1995), pp.78–96 (at pp.93, 96).
61. Hallam, *Capetian France*, pp.168–73.
62. Turner, 'The Problem', loc. cit. p.95.
63. J. Gillingham, *Richard Coeur de Lion* (1994), p.199.
64. Painter, *King John*, p.229.

65. *Rotuli Litterarum Clausarum*, i. 162.

66. Painter, *King John*, p.104.

67. Ibid., p.226.

68. Michel, *Histoire des ducs*, p.105.

69. William of Newburgh, i. p.521.

70. Carpenter, *The Minority of Henry III*, op. cit.

71. Bradbury, 'Philip Augustus and King John', loc. cit. p.350.

72. N. Barbour, 'The Embassy sent by John of England to Miramolin, King of Morocco', *Al-Andalus* 25 (1960), pp.373–81; N. Vincent, 'Simon of Atherfield: A Martyr to his Wife', *Analecta Bollandiana* 113 (1995), pp.349–61 (at pp.355–56).

73. Painter, *King John*, p.228.

74. *Annales monastici*, iii. pp.31, 33–34, 62–63; Coggleshall, p.165.

75. Roger of Wendover, ii. pp.42–43, 48–49, 62–63, 76–77, 94; Warren, *King John*, pp.12–13.

76. Painter, *King John*, p.230.

77. Ibid., pp.107–08.

78. Coggleshall, pp.176–77; Matthew Paris, *Chronica Majora*, ii. p.588.

79. Adam of Eynsham, *Magna Vita*, i. p.xl.

80. Howden, *Chronica*, iii. pp.266–67.

81. Painter, *King John*, pp.142–43.

82. *Rotuli Litterarum Patentium*, p.133.

83. Painter, *King John*, p.144.

84. *Annales monastici*, i. p.29; ii. p.264; Roger of Wendover, ii. pp.54–55.

85. Painter, *King John*, p.237.

Guide to Most Frequently
Cited Primary Sources

<o>

Acta of the Legate Guala, ed. N. Vincent (1996)

Ambroise's Estoire de la Guerre Sainte, ed. Marianne Ailes (Woodbridge, 2003)

Annales monastici, ed. H.R. Luard, 5 vols, RS 36 (1869)

Baha, al-Din Ibn Shaddad, *The Rare and Excellent History of Saladin*, trans. D.S. Richards (Aldershot, 2001)

Catalogue des Actes de Philippe-Auguste, ed. L. Delisle (Paris, 1856)

Chronicles of the Reigns of Stephen, Henry II and Richard I, ed. R. Howlett, 4 vols, RS 1890

The Chronicle of Meaux (Chronica de Monasterii de Melsa), ed. E.A. Bond, 3 vols, RS 1868

The Chronicle of Melrose, ed. A.O. Anderson (1936)

Chronique de Saint-Martial de Limoges, ed. H. Duplès-Agier (Paris, 1874)

Coggleshall, Radulphi de, Chronicon Anglicanum, ed. J. Stevenson, RS 46 (1875)

Devizes, Richard of, *Chronicle of the Time of Richard the First*, ed. J.T. Appleby (1963)

Dialogus de Scaccario, ed. C. Johnson (1950)

Diceto, Ralph, *The Historical Works of*, ed. W. Stubbs, 2 vols, RS 68 (1876)

Documents Illustrative of English History in the Thirteenth and Fourteenth Centuries, ed. H. Cole (1844)

Foedera, Conventiones, Litterae et cuiuscunque Generis Acta Publica, ed. T. Rymer (1816)

Gerald of Wales, Giraldi Cambrensis Opera, ed. J.S. Brewer et al., 8 vols (1918)

Gervase of Canterbury, *The Historical Works of*, ed. W. Stubbs, 2 vols, RS 73 (1880)

Histoire des ducs de Normandie et des rois d'Angleterre, ed. F. Michel (Paris, 1840)

Histoire de Guillaume le Maréchal, ed. P. Meyer, 3 vols (Paris, 1901)

Howden, Roger, *Chronica*, ed. W. Stubbs, RS 51 (1871)

Howden, Roger, *Gesta Regis Henrici*, ed. W. Stubbs, 2 vols, RS 49 (1867)

Itinerarium, ed. W. Stubbs in *Chronicles and Memorials of the Reign of Richard I*, RS (1864)

Johannis de Fordun Chronica Gentis Scotorum, ed. W.F. Skene, 2 vols (Edinburgh, 1872)

Layettes du Trésor des Chartes, ed. A. Teulet et al, 5 vols (Paris, 1909)

The Letters of Pope Innocent III (1198–1216) concerning England and Wales, ed. C.R. Cheney et al. (Oxford, 1967)

Magna Vita Sancti Hugonis, ed. D.C. Douie & D.H.Farmer, 2 vols (Oxford, 1985)

Matthew Paris, *Chronica Majora*, ed. H.R. Luard, 7 vols, RS 57 (1883)

Matthew Paris, *Historia Anglorum*, ed. F. Madden, RS (1869)

Oeuvres de Rigord et Guillaume le Breton, ed. H.F. Delaborde, 2 vols (Paris, 1885)

Recueil des actes de Philippe Auguste, roi de France, ed. H.F. Delaborde et al., 4 vols (Paris, 1979)

Recueil des historiens de la Gaule et de la France, ed. M. Bouguet et al., 24 vols (Paris, 1904)

Red Book of the Exchequer, ed. H. Hall, 3 vols (1896)

Rotuli Chartarum in Turri Londinensi Asservati, ed. T.D. Hardy (1837)

Rotuli de Liberate ac de Misis et Praestitis, ed. T. Hardy (1844)

Rotull de Oblatis et Finibus in Turri Londinensi Asservati, ed. T.D. Hardy (1835)

Rotuli Litterarum Clausarum in Turri Londinensi Asservati, ed. T.D. Hardy, 2 vols (1844)

Rotuli Litterarum Patentium in Turri Londinensi Asservati, ed. T.D. Hardy (1835)

Selected Letters of Pope Innocent III concerning England (1198–1216), ed. C.R. Cheney et al. (1953)

Select Pleas of the Forest, ed. G.J. Turner (1899)

Torigny, Robert de, Chronique, ed. L. Delisle, 2 vols (1972)

Walter of Coventry, Memoriale Fratris Walteri Coventriae, ed. W. Stubbs, 2 vols, RS 58 (1873)

Wendover, Roger of, Flores Historiarum, ed. H.R. Luard, 3 vols (RS 95) (1890)

William Marshal, History of, ed. A.J. Holden, S. Gregory, D. Crouch, 2 vols (2002)

William of Newburgh, Historia Rerum Anglicarum in Chronicles, ed. Howlett (see above), i. pp.1–408; ii. pp.409–53

Bibliography

◄○►

For ease of reference I append a list of secondary sources. Details of primary
    sources and scholarly articles in learned journals will be found in the notes.

Abulafia, D., *The Two Italies* (Cambridge, 1977)

Abulafia, D., *Frederick II, A Medieval Emperor* (1988)

Ahlers, J., *Die Welfen und die englischen Könige 1165–1235* (Hildesheim, 1987)

Akehurst, F.R.P. & Davis, Judith M., *A Handbook of the Troubadours* (Berkeley,
    1995)

Appel, C., *Bertran de Born* (Halle, 1931)

Appleby, J.T., *England without Richard* (1965)

Appleby, J.T., *John, King of England* (1958)

Arbellot, F., *La vérité sur la mort de Richard Coeur-de-Lion* (Paris, 1987)

Archer, T.A., *The Crusade of Richard I, 1189–92* (1888)

Arnold, Benjamin, *Medieval Germany 500–1300: A Political Interpretation* (Basingstoke,
    1997)

Ashley, Maurice, *King John* (1972)

Astill, Grenville & Grant, A., eds, *The Countryside of Medieval England* (Oxford, 1988)

Bahat, Anver & de Vot, Gerard, *L'Oeuvre lyrique de Blondel de Nesle: melodies* (Paris,
    1996)

Baker, D., ed. *Medieval Women* (Oxford, 1978)

Baldwin, J.W. *The Government of Philip Augustus. Foundations of French Royal Power in
    the Middle Ages* (Berkeley, 1986)

Baldwin, M.W., *Raymond III of Tripolis and the Fall of Jerusalem 1140–87* (Amsterdam,
    1969)

Baldwin, M.W., ed., *A History of the Crusades* (Philadelphia, 1958)

Barber, M., *The Military Orders. Fighting for the Faith and Caring for the Sick* (Aldershot,
    1994)

Barber, M., *The New Knighthood: A History of the Order of the Temple* (Cambridge,
    1994)

Barber, Richard, *Henry Plantagenet* (Woodbridge, 2001)

Barber, Richard, *The Knight and Chivalry* (Woodbridge, 1995)

Barber, Richard & Barker, Juliet, *Tournaments, Jousts, Chivalry and Pageants in the Middle
    Ages* (Woodbridge, 1989)

Barker, Juliet, *The Tournament in England 1100–1400* (Woodbridge, 1986)

Barlow, Frank, *Thomas Beckett* (1986)

Barry, T.B., France, R. & Simms, K., *Colony and Frontier in Medieval Ireland* (1995)

Bartlett, Robert, *England under the Norman and Angevin Kings 1075–1225* (Oxford, 2000)

Bartlett, Robert, *Gerald of Wales 1146–1225* (Oxford, 1982)

Bartlett, Robert, *Trial by Fire and Water: The Medieval Judicial Ordeal* (Oxford, 1986)

Bates, D. & Curry, A., eds, *England and Normandy in the Middle Ages* (1994)

Bautier, R.H. ed., *La France de Philippe Auguste: Le temps de mutations* (Paris, 1982)

Bautier, R.H., *Etudes sur la France capétienne* (Paris, 1992)

Beech, G.T., *A Rural Society in Medieval France: The Gatine of Poitou in the Eleventh and Twelfth Centuries* (Baltimore, 1964)

Bellamy, John G., *Robin Hood: An Historical Enquiry* (Indiana, 1985)

Beresford, Maurice, *New Towns of the Middle Ages* (1967)

Bisson, T.N., *The Medieval Crown of Aragon* (Oxford, 1986)

Bloch, M., *Les rois thaumaturges* (Strasbourg, 1924)

Bloch, M., *Feudal Society* (1961)

Bolton, J.L., *The Medieval English Economy 1150–1500* (1980)

Bonney, R. & Ormrod, M., *Crises, Revolutions and Self-Sustained Fiscal Growth* (Stamford, 1999)

Bordonove, G., *Philip Augustus* (Paris, 1986)

Bosy, J. & Jupp, P., eds, *Essays Presented to Michael Roberts* (Belfast, 1976)

Boswell, J., *Christianity, Social Tolerance and Homosexuality* (Chicago, 1980)

Boussard, J., *Le comté d'Anjou sous Henri Plantagenêt et ses fils 1151–1204* (Paris, 1938)

Boussard, J., *Le gouvernement d'Henri II Plantagenêt* (Paris, 1956)

Boutière, Jean & Schutz, Alexander, eds, *Biographies des troubadours* (n.d.)

Boyd, Douglas, *Eleanor, April Queen of Aquitaine* (Stroud, 2004)

Boyle, David, *Blondel's Song: The Capture, Imprisonment and Ransom of Richard the Lionheart* (2005)

Bradbury, Jim, *Philip Augustus, King of France, 1180–1223* (1998)

Bradbury, Jim, *The Medieval Archer* (Woodbridge, 1985)

Bradbury, Jim, *The Medieval Siege* (Woodbridge, 1992)

Brand, C.N., *Byzantium Confronts the West, 1180–1204* (Cambridge, Mass., 1968)

Bridge, A., *Richard the Lionheart* (1989)

Briffault, Robert, *The Troubadours* (Bloomington, Indiana, 1961)

Britnell, R.H., *The Commercialisation of English Society* (Cambridge, 1993)

Britnell, R.H. & Hatcher, J., eds, *Progress and Problems in Medieval England* (Cambridge, 1996)

Brooke, C., *The Medieval Idea of Marriage* (Oxford, 1991)

Brooke, Christopher & Keir, Gillian, *London 800–1216: The Shaping of a City* (1975)

Brooke, Z.N., *The English Church and the Papacy from the Conquest to the Reign of John* (Cambridge, 1931)

Brooks, F.W., *The English Naval Forces 1199–1272* (1933)

Broughton, Bradford B., *The Legends of Richard Coeur de Lion: A Study of Sources and Variations to the Year 1600* (The Hague, 1966)

Brundage, J.A., *Richard Lionheart* (N.Y., 1974)

Brundage, J.A., *Law, Sex and Christian Society in Medieval Europe* (Chicago, 1987)

Brunner, K., *Der Mittelenglische Versroman über Richard Löwenherz* (Vienna, 1913)

Bull, Marcus & Housley, Norman, *The Experience of Crusading*, 2 vols (Cambridge, 2003)

Bullough, Vern I. & Brundage, James A., eds, *Handbook of Medieval Sexuality* (N.Y., 1996)

Burton, J., *Monastic and Religious Orders in Britain 1000–1300* (Cambridge, 1994)

Byrne, Eugene H., *Genoese Shipping in the 12th and 13th centuries* (Cambridge, Mass., 1930)

Carpenter, D.A., *The Minority of Henry III* (1990)

Carpenter, D.A., *The Reign of Henry III* (1996)

Cartellieri, A., *Phillip II August, König von Frankreich*, 4 vols (Leipzig, 1922)

Chaban-Delmas, J., *La Dame d'Aquitaine* (Monaco, 1987)

Cheney, C.R., *From Becket to Langton: English Church Government, 1170–1213* (Manchester, 1956)

Cheney, C.R., *Pope Innocent III and England* (Stuttgart, 1976)

Cheney, C.R., *Hubert Walter* (1967)

Cheney, C.R. et al, eds, *The Letters of Innocent III (1198–1216) concerning England and Wales* (Oxford, 1967)

Church, S.D., *King John: New Interpretations* (Woodbridge, 1999)

Church, S.D., *The Household Knights of King John* (Cambridge, 1999)

Cledat, P., *Du rôle historique de Bertran de Born 1178–1200* (Paris, 1879)

Colvin, H.M., *The White Canons in England* (Oxford, 1951)

Consitt, F., *The London Weavers' Company* (Oxford, 1993)

Crosland, J., *William the Marshal* (1962)

Crouch, D., *William Marshal: Court, Career and Chivalry in the Norman Empire, 1147–1219* (1990)

Csendes, P., *Heinrich VI* (Darmstadt, 1993)

Danziger, Danny & Gillingham, John, *1215: The Year of Magna Carta* (2003)

Davies, R.R., *The First English Empire: Power and Identities in the British Isles 1093–1343* (Oxford, 2000)

Davies, R.R., *The Age of Conquest: Wales 1063–1415* (Oxford, 1987)

Debord, A., *La société laïque dans les pays de la Charente X–XIIe siècles* (Angoulême, 1984)

Delbruck, H., *The History of the Art of War* (Westport, Conn., 1982)

Dept, G.G., *Les Influences anglaises et françaises dans le comté de Flandres* (Ghent, 1928)

Deschamps, P., *Le Crac des Chevaliers* (Paris, 1934)

Devic, C. & Vaissete, J., *Histoire générale de Languedoc*, 6 vols (Toulouse, 1905)

Dickinson, J.C., *The Origins of the Austin Canons* (1950)

Dion, R., *Histoire de la vigne et du vin en France des origines au XIXe siècle* (Paris, 1959)

Dobson, R.B., *The Jews of Medieval York and the Massacre of March 1190* (York, 1974)

Douie, D.L., *Archbishop Geoffrey Plantagenet and the Chapter of York* (York, 1960)

Duby, Georges, *William Marshal: The Flower of Chivalry* (1986)

Duby, Georges, *Dames au XIIe siècle* (Paris, 1996)

Duby, Georges, *The Legend of Bouvines* (Cambridge, 1990)

Duby, Georges, *France in the Middle Ages 987–1460* (Oxford, 1991)

Duby, Georges, *The Making of Modern Marriage in Medieval France* (1985)

Dunbabin, J., *France in the Making 843–1180* (Oxford, 1985)

Duncan, A.A.M., *Scotland: The Making of the Kingdom* (Edinburgh, 1975)

Dyer, Christopher, *Making a Living in the Middle Ages: The People of Britain 850–1250* (Yale, 2002)

Edbury, Peter W., *The Kingdom of Cyprus and the Crusades: 1191–1374* (Cambridge, 1991)

Edbury, Peter W., *The Conquest of Jerusalem and the Second Crusade: Sources in Translation* (Aldershot, 1996)

Falmagne, J., *Baudouin V, Comte de Hainaut 1150–1195* (Montreal, 1966)

Ferrante, Joan M. & Economou, Georges D., *In Pursuit of Perfection: Courtly Love in Medieval Literature* (Port Washington, 1975)

Flanagan, M.T., *Irish Society, Anglo-Norman Settlers, Angevin Kingship* (Oxford, 1989)

Forey, A.J., *The Military Orders: From the Twelfth to the Early Fourteenth Centuries* (Basingstoke, 1992)

Foster, Elberg, ed., *Medieval Marriage: Two Models from Twelfth-Century France* (Johns Hopkins, 1978)

Fowler, Kenneth Allan, *Medieval Mercenaries: The Great Companies* (2001)

France, John, *Western Warfare in the Age of the Crusades 1000–1300* (1999)

Frappier, Jean, *Chrétien de Troyes: The Man and his Work*, trans. Cormier (Athens, Ohio, 1982)

Gardiner, Robert, ed., *The Age of the Galley: Mediterrranean Oared Vessels since Pre-classical times* (1975)

Garrett, George & Hudson, John, eds, *Law and Government in Medieval England and Normandy* (Cambridge, 1994)

Gaunt, Simon & Kay, Sarah, eds., *The Troubadours: An Introduction* (Cambridge, 1999)

Gibb, Hamilton, *The Life of Saladin* (Oxford, 1973)

Gibb, Hamilton, *Studies on the Civilisation of Islam* (Boston, 1962)

Gillingham, J.B., *The Kingdom of Germany in the High Middle Ages 900–1200* (1971)

Gillingham, John, *Richard I* (Yale, 1999)

Gillingham, John, *Richard Coeur de Lion: Kingship, Chivalry and War in the Twelfth Century* (1994)

Gillingham, John, *Richard the Lionheart* (1978)

Gillingham, John, *The Angevin Empire* (1984)

Gillingham, John, *The English in the Twelfth Century: Imperialism, National Identity and Political Values* (Woodbridge, 2000)

Gillingham, John & Holt, J.C. eds, *War and Government in the Middle Ages: Essays in Honour of J.O. Prestwich* (Woodbridge, 1984)

Givern-Wilson, G. & Curtis, A., *The Royal Bastards of England* (1984)

Golb, N., *The Jews in Medieval Normandy* (Cambridge, 1998)

Gras, N.S.B., *The Early English Customs System* (Harvard, 1918)

Grousset, R., *Histoire des croisades et du royaume franc de Jerusalem* (Paris, 1936)

Hadley, D.M., ed, *Masculinity in Medieval Europe* (1999)

Hallam, E.M., *Capetian France 987–1328* (1980)

Hamilton, B., *The Leper King and his Heirs: Baldwin IV and the Crusader Kingdom of Jerusalem* (Cambridge, 2000)

Hamilton, J.S. & Bradley, P., eds, *Essays in Medieval History Presented to G.P. Cuttino* (Woodbridge, 1989)

Harper-Bill, Christopher, et al., eds, *Studies in Medieval History Presented to Allen Brown* (Woodbridge, 1989)

Harper-Bill, Christopher & Harvey, Ruth, eds, *The Ideals and Practice of Medieval Knighthood* (Woodbridge, 1999)

Harris, Valentine, *The Truth about Robin Hood* (1973)

Haverkamp, Alfred, *Medieval Germany 1056–1273* (1962)

Haverkamp, Alfred, *Friedrich Barbarossa: Handlungsspielräume und Wirkungsweisen des staufischen Kaisers* (Sigmaringen, 1992)

Herlihy, David, *Women, Family and Society in Medieval Europe: Historical Essays* (1995)

Hill, D.R. & al-Hassan, A.Y., *Islamic Technology: An Illustrated History* (Cambridge, 1986)

Hindle, Brian Paul, *Medieval Roads* (Princes Risborough, 1982)

Hollister, C. Warren, *Monarchy, Magnates and Institutions in the Anglo-Norman World* (1986)

Holmes, Urban T., *Daily Living in the Twelfth Century* (Madison, Wisconsin, 1952)

Holt, J.C., *King John* (1963)

Holt, J.C., *Robin Hood* (1989)

Holt, J.C., *Magna Carta* (Oxford, 1992)

Holt, J.C., *Magna Carta and Medieval Government* (1985)

Holt, J.C., *The Northerners: A Study in the Reign of King John* (Oxford, 1961)

Hucker, B.U., *Kaiser Otto IV* (Hanover, 1990)

Hudson, John, *The Foundations of the English Common Law* (1996)

Hunt, R.W. et al, *Studies in Medieval History Presented to F.M. Powicke* (Oxford, 1948)

Hunt, R.W., *The Schools and the Cloister: The Life and Writings of Alexander Nequam* (Oxford, 1984)

Hunt, Roderick, *Robin Hood* (2000)

Hutchinson, Gillian, *Medieval Ships and Shipping* (1994)

Jacoby, David, ed., *Trade, Commodities and Shipping in the Medieval Mediterranean* (Aldershot, 1997)

Jamison, E., *Admiral Eugenius of Sicily* (1957)

Jeep, John M., *Medieval Germany: An Encyclopedia* (N.Y., 2001)

Jolliffe, J.E.A., *Angevin Kingship* (1963)

Jones, J.A.P., *King John and Magna Carta* (Bristol, 1971)

Jones, Terry & Ereira, Alan, *Medieval Lives* (2004)

Jordan, K., *Henry the Lion* (Oxford, 1986)

Kedar, B.Z., ed., *The Horns of Hattin* (1992)

Kedar, B.Z., Mayer, H.E. & Smail, R.C., eds, *Outremer – Studies in the History of the Crusading Kingdom of Jerusalem Presented to J. Prawer* (Jerusalem, 1982)

Keefe, Thomas K., *Feudal Assessments and Political Community under Henry II and his Sons* (Berkeley, 1983)

Keen, Maurice, *Chivalry* (1984)

Keen, Maurice, *Outlaws of Medieval England* (2000)

Keen, Maurice, ed., *Medieval Warfare: A History* (Oxford, 1999)

Kelly, Amy, *Eleanor of Aquitaine and the Four Kings* (1950)

Kennedy, Hugh, *Crusader Castles* (Cambridge, 1994)

Kessler, U., *Richard I. Löwenherz. König, Kreuzritter, Abenteurer* (Graz, 1995)

Kibler, W.W., *Eleanor of Aquitaine: Patron and Politician* (Austin, Texas, 1976)

Knight, Stephen, *Robin Hood: A Complete Study of the English Outlaw* (Oxford, 1994)

Knight, Stephen, ed., *Robin Hood: An Anthology* (Cambridge, 1999)

Knowles, M.D., *The Monastic Order in England: A History of its Development from the Times of St Dunstan to the Fourth Lateran Council 943–1216* (Cambridge, 1963)

Knowles, M.D. & Hadcock, R.N., *Religious Houses of Medieval England* (1953)

Lacroix de Marles, G., *Histoire de la domination des Arabes en Espagne et en Portugal* (Paris, 1825)

Landon, Lionel, *Itinerary of King Richard I* (1935)

Lane-Poole, Stanley, *Saladin and the Fall of the Kingdom of Jerusalem* (1906)

Lavisse, E., *Histoire de France depuis les origines jusqu'à la Revolution* (Paris, 1911)

Lawrence, T.E., *Crusader Castles* (1986)

Lepage, Yvan G., *L'Oeuvre lyrique de Blondel de Nesle* (Paris, 1994)

Le Patourel, John, *The Norman Empire* (Oxford, 1976)

Lewis, B., *The Assassins* (1967)

Leyser, Henrietta, *Medieval Women: A Social History of Women in England 450–1500* (1995)

Leyser, K.J., *Medieval Germany and its Neighbours 900–1250* (1982)

Liddiard, Robert, ed., *Anglo-Norman Castles* (Woodbridge, 2003)

Lindsay, Jack, *The Troubadours and their World of the Twelfth and Thirteenth Centuries* (1976)

Lloyd, J.E., *History of Wales* (1939)

Lloyd, T.H., *The English Wool Trade in the Middle Ages* (Cambridge, 1977)

Longnon, L., *Les compagnons de Villehardouin: Recherches sur les croisés de la quatrième croisade* (Geneva, 1978)

Lot, F., *Fidèles ou Vassaux* (Paris, 1904)

Lot, F., *L'Art Militaire et les Armées du Moyen Age*, 2 vols (Paris, 1946)

Luchaire, A., *Social France at the Time of Philip Augustus* (N.Y., 1912)

Lydon, J., *The Lordship of Ireland in the Middle Ages* (Dublin, 1972)

Lydon, J., ed., *England and Ireland in the Later Middle Ages; Essays in Honour of Jocelyn Otway-Ruthven* (Dublin, 1987)

Lyons, M.C. & Jackson, D.E.P., *Saladin: The Politics of the Holy War* (Cambridge, 1982)

Maalouf, A., *The Crusades through Arab Eyes* (1984)

McGrail, Sean, *The Ship: Rafts, Boats and Ships from Prehistoric Times to the Medieval Era* (1981)

McKechnie, W.S., *Magna Carta: A Commentary on the Great Charter of King John* (Glasgow, 1914)

Markale, J., *La vie, la légende, l'influence d'Aliénor comtesse de Poitou duchesse d'Aquitaine, reine de France, puis Angleterre, dame des troubadours et des bardes bretons* (Paris, 1979)

Marshall, Christopher, *Warfare in the Latin East 1192–1291* (Cambridge, 1992)

Martin, F.X., *A New History of Ireland* (Oxford, 1987)

Martindale, Jane, *Status, Authority and Regional Power: Aquitaine and France, 9th to 12th Centuries* (Aldershot, 1997)

Matthew, D., *The Norman Kingdom of Sicily* (Cambridge, 1992)

Mayer, H.E., *The Crusades* (Oxford, 1988)

Mayr-Harting, H., ed., *St Hugh of Lincoln* (Oxford, 1987)

Miller, David, *Richard the Lionheart: The Mighty Crusader* (2003)

Mitchell, S.K., *Studies in Taxation under John and Henry III* (New Haven, 1914)

Mohring, H., *Saladin und der dritte Kreuzzug* (Wiesbaden, 1980)

Moore, O.H., *The Young King Henry Plantagenet* (Columbus, Ohio, 1925)

Morris, C., *The Discovery of the Individual 1050–1200* (1972)

Mortimer, Richard, *Angevin England 1154–1258* (Oxford, 1994)

Munz, P., *Frederick Barbarossa: A Study in Medieval Politics* (1969)

Needler, George Henry, *Richard Coeur de Lion in Literature* (Leipzig, 1890)

Nelson, Janet L., ed., *Richard Coeur de Lion in History and Myth* (1992)

Newman, F.X., *The Meaning of Courtly Love* (N.Y., 1968)

Newman, William, *Les Seigneurs de Nesle en Picardie: Leurs chartes et leur histoire* (Paris, 1971)

Nicholas D., *Medieval Flanders* (Harlow, 1992)

Nightingale, Pamela, *A Medieval Mercantile Community. The Grocers' Company in the Politics and Trade of London 1000–1465* (Yale, 1995)

Norgate, Kate, *John Lackland* (1902)

Norgate, Kate, *Richard the Lionheart* (1924)

Norwich, John Julius, *The Kingdom in the Sun* (1970)

Ohler, Norbert, *The Medieval Traveller* (Suffolk, 1989)

Oman, C.W.C., *A History of the Art of War in the Middle Ages*, 2 vols (1924)

Orme, N., *From Childhood to Chivalry: The Education of the English Kings and Aristocracy 1066–1530* (1984)

Orpen, G.H., *Ireland under the Normans, 1169–1216* (Oxford, 1911)

O'Shea, Stephen, *The Perfect Heresy: The Revolutionary Life and Death of the Medieval Cathars* (2000)

Otway-Ruthven, A.J., *A History of Medieval Ireland* (1968)

Owen, D.D.R., *Eleanor of Aquitaine: Queen and Legend* (Oxford, 1993)

Owen, D.D.R., *William the Lion* (East Lothian, 1997)

Pacaut, J., *Louis VII et son royaume* (Paris, 1964)

Paden, W.D., Sankovitch T. & Stablein, P.H., *The Poems of the Troubadour Bertran de Born* (Berkeley, 1986)

Page, C., *Voices and Instruments of the Middle Ages* (1987)

Painter, Sidney, *Studies in the History of the English Feudal Barony* (Baltimore, 1943)

Painter, Sidney, *The Reign of King John* (Baltimore, 1949)

Painter, Sidney, *William Marshal: Knight Errant, Baron and Regent of England* (Baltimore, 1933)

Painter, Sidney, *Feudalism and Liberty,* ed. F.A. Cazel (Baltimore, 1961)

Parisse, M., *Noblesse et chevalerie en Louvaine médiévale: les familles nobles du XIe au XIIIe siècle* (Nancy, 1982)

Parsons, John & Wheeler, Bonnie, eds, *Medieval Mothering* (1996)

Pernoud, Régine, *Aliénor d'Aquitaine* (Paris, 1965)

Petit-Dutaillis, *Le déshéritement de Jean sans Terre* (Paris, 1925)

Phillips, Jonathan, *Defenders of the Holy Land: Relations between the Latin East and West 1119–1187* (Oxford, 1996)

Pitte, D., *Château-Gaillard* (Vernon, France, 1996)

Planhol, X. De, *A Historical Geography of France* (Cambridge, 1994)

Pollock, Frederick & Maitland, F.W., *The History of English Law before the Time of Edward*, 2 vols (Cambridge, 1968)

Poole, A.L., *From Domesday Book to Magna Carta* (Oxford, 1955)

Poole, A.L., *Henry the Lion* (Oxford, 1912)

Poole, A.L., *Obligations of Society in the Twelfth and Thirteenth Centuries* (1946)

Powicke, F.M., *The Loss of Normandy 1189–1204* (Manchester, 1961)

Powicke, F.M., *Stephen Langton* (1929)

Prawer, Joshua, *Histoire du royaume latin de Jérusalem*, 2 vols (Paris, 1970)

Prawer, Joshua, *The Latin Kingdom of Jerusalem: European Colonials in the Middle Ages* (1972)

Prawer, Joshua, *The World of the Crusaders* (1972)

Prawer, Joshua, *Crusader Institutions* (Oxford, 1980)

Pringle, R.D., *The Red Tower* (1986)

Pryor, J.H., *Geography, Technology and War: Studies in the Maritime History of the Mediterranean 649–1571* (Cambridge, 1988)

Queller, D.E., *The Fourth Crusade* (Leicester, 1978)

Rackham, Oliver, *Trees and Woodland in the British Landscape* (1996)

Ralls, Karen, *The Templars and the Grail: Knights of the Quest* (Wheaton, 2003)

Regan, G., *Lionhearts: Saladin and Richard I* (1998)

Reston, James, *Warriors of God: Richard the Lionheart and Saladin in the Third Crusade* (2001)

Reynolds, Susan, *Fiefs and Vassals* (Oxford, 1994)

Riant, P., *Expéditions et pèlerinages des Scandinaves en Terre Sainte au temps des croisades* (Paris, 1865)

Richard, A., *Histoire des comtes de Poitou, 778–1204*, 2 vols (Paris, 1903)

Richard, J., *The Latin Kingdom of Jerusalem*, 2 vols (Amsterdam, 1979)

Richards, Jeffrey, *Sex, Dissidence and Damnation: Minority Groups in the Middle Ages* (1990)

Richardson, H.J., *The English Jewry under Angevin Kings* (1960)

Richardson, H.G. & Sayles, G.O., *The Governance of Medieval England from the Conquest to the Magna Carta* (Edinburgh, 1963)

Riley-Smith, Jonathan, *The Feudal Nobility and the Kingdom of Jerusalem 1174–1277* (1973)

Riley-Smith, Jonathan, *The Knights of St John in Jerusalem and Cyprus c. 1050–1310* (1967)

Robinson, I.S., *The Papacy 1073–1198: Continuity and Innovation* (Cambridge, 1990)

Rodger, N.A.M., *The Safeguard of the Sea: A Naval History of Great Britain 660–1649*, Vol.1 (1997)

Rogers, S., *Latin Siege Warfare in the Twelfth Century* (Oxford, 1992)

Rosenberg, Samuel N., ed., *Songs of the Troubadours and Trouveres* (N.Y., 1998)

Rosenwein, B., ed., *Anger's Past* (Ithaca, N.Y., 1998)

Roth, Cecil, *A History of the Jews in England* (Oxford, 1964)

Round, J.H., *The Commune of London* (1899)

Rowbotham, John Frederick, *The Troubadours and the Courts of Love* (1895)

Runciman, Stephen, *A History of the Crusades*, Vol.3 (Cambridge, 1954)

Salmon, André, *Recherches sur les chroniques de Touraine* (Paris, 1847)

Sayers, Jane, *Innocent III, Leader of Europe, 1198–1216* (Harlow, 1994)

Seidel, L, *Songs of Glory, the Romanesque Facades of Aquitaine* (Chicago, 1981)

Shatzmiller, M., ed., *Crusaders and Muslims in Twelfth Century Syria* (Leiden, 1993)

Siberry, E., *Criticism of Crusading 1095–1274* (Oxford, 1985)

Sinclair, David, *The Pound: A Biography* (2001)

Smail, R., *Crusading Warfare 1097–1196* (Cambridge, 1956)

Snelgrove, H.S., *The Lusignans in England 1247–1258* (Albuquerque, 1950)

Spence, Sarah, *Rhetoric of Reason and Desire: Vergil, Augustine and the Troubadours* (1988)

Spufford, Peter, *Money and its Use in Medieval Europe* (Cambridge, 1988)

Spufford, Peter, *Power and Profit: The Merchant in Medieval Europe* (2002)

Stenton, D.M., *English Justice between the Norman Conquest and the Great Charter* (1964)

Stimming A., ed., *Bertran de Born* (Halle, 1913)

Strickland, Matthew, *War and Chivalry: The Conduct and Perception of War in England and Normandy, 1066–1217* (Cambridge, 1996)

Strickland, Matthew, ed., *Anglo-Norman Warfare* (Woodbridge, 1992)

Strickland, Matthew, ed., *Armies, Chivalry and Warfare in Medieval England and France* (Stamford, 1998)

Stuard, Susan Mosher, *Women in Medieval Society* (Pennsylvania, 1993)

Stuerner, W., *Friedrich II. Teil 1. Die Königsherrschaft in Sizilien und Deutschland 1194–1220* (Darmstadt, 1992)

Sumption, Jonathan, *Pilgrimage: An Image of Medieval Religion* (1975)

Sumption, Jonathan, *The Albigensian Crusade* (1978)

Swanson, R.N., *The Twelfth Century Renaissance* (Manchester, 1999)

Swindler, William F., *Magna Carta: Legend and Legacy* (Indianapolis, 1965)

Tautz, Fritz, *Die Koenigen von England und das Reich* (Heidelberg, 1961)

Thomas, A., ed., *Poésies complètes de Bertran de Born* (Toulouse, 1888)

Thomas, Hugh, *Vassals, Heiresses, Crusaders and Thugs: The Gentry of Angevin Yorkshire 1154–1216* (Philadelphia, 1993)

Thomson, Janice E., *Mercenaries, Pirates and Sovereigns: State-building and Extraterritorial Violence in Early Modern Europe* (Princeton, 1994)

Tillyard, E.M.W., *Shakespeare's History Plays* (1944)

Toeche, Theodor, *Kaiser Heinrich VI* (n.d.)

Trindade, Ann, *Berengaria: In Search of Richard the Lionheart's Queen* (Dublin, 1999)

Turner, Ralph V., *King John* (1994)

Turner, Ralph V. *The King and his Courts: The Role of John and Henry III in the Administration of Justice 1199–1240* (N.Y., 1968)

Turner, Ralph V., *Magna Carta* (2003)

Turner, Ralph V. & Heuser, R.R., *The Reign of Richard Lionheart* (Harlow, 2000)

Tyerman, Christopher, *England and the Crusades 1095–1588* (Chicago, 1988)

Ullmann, W., *A Short History of the Papacy in the Middle Ages* (1972)

Unger, Richard W., *The Ship in the Medieval Economy 600–1600* (1980)

Vaisette, J., *Histoire de Languedoc* (Paris, 1879)

Verbruggen, J.F., *The Art of Warfare in Western Europe during the Middle Ages* (Woodbridge, 1997)

Vincent, Nicholas, *Peter des Roches, Bishop of Winchester 1205–38: An Alien in English Politics* (Cambridge, 1996)

Vincent, Nicholas, ed., *The Letters and Charters of Cardinal Guala Bicchieri Papal Legate in England 1216–1218* (1996)

Wardrop, Joan, *Fountains Abbey and its Benefactors 1132–1300* (Kalamazoo, Michigan, 1987)

Warlop, E., *The Flemish Nobility before 1300*, trans. J.B. Ross & H. Vandermoere (Hortrijk, 1975)

Warren, W.L., *Henry II* (1973)

Warren, W.L., *King John* (1978)

Weir, Alison, *Eleanor of Aquitaine, by the Wrath of God, Queen of England* (1999)

Weiss, J., *The Birth of Romance* (1992)

West, F.J., *The Justiciarship in England, 1066–1232* (Cambridge, 1966)

Wheatcroft, Andrew, *Infidel: the Conflict between Christendom and Islam 683–2002* (2003)

Wolf, R.L. & Hazard, H.W., eds, *The Later Crusades 1189–1311* (Madison, 1989)

Young, C.R., *The Royal Forests of Medieval England* (Leicester, 1979)

Index

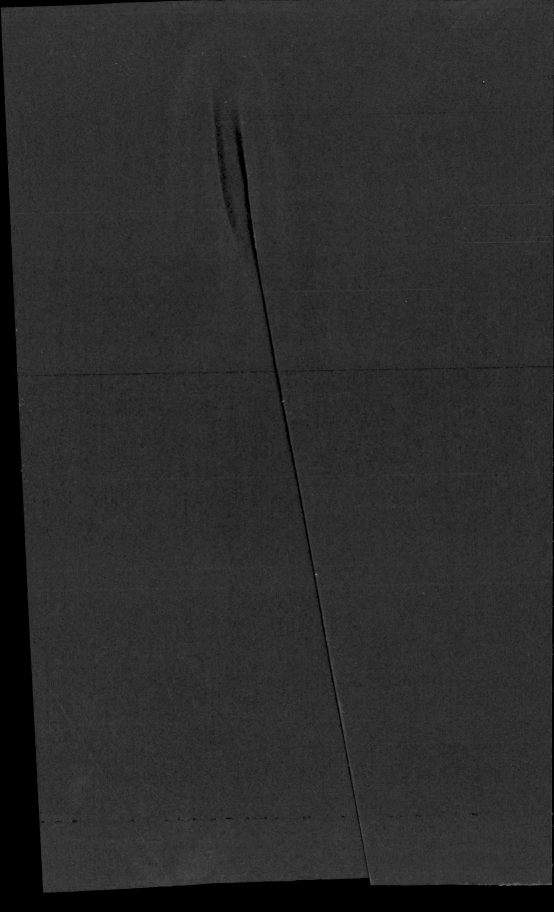